american|GOVERNMENT

bju press®

Greenville, South Carolina

american GOVERNMENT
for Christian Schools™

Tim Keesee

Second Edition

Note:

The fact that materials produced by other publishers may be referred to in this volume does not constitute an endorsement of the content or theological position of materials produced by such publishers. Any references and ancillary materials are listed as an aid to the student or the teacher and in an attempt to maintain the accepted academic standards of the publishing industry.

American Government
Second Edition

Tim Keesee, EdD

Contributing Authors
 Carl Abrams, PhD
 Michael Cole
 Lynn Garland
 Thomas Luttmann
 John Matzko, PhD
 Bryan Smith, PhD
Editor
 Manda Kalagayan

Project Manager
 Dan Woodhull
Compositor
 Carol Ingalls
Design
 John Bjerk (cover)
 Duane Nichols
 Wendy Searles

Permissions
 Joyce Landis
 Susan Perry
 Holly Nelson

Photograph credits are listed on pages 468–70.

Produced in cooperation with the Bob Jones University Departments of History and Social Studies of the College of Arts and Science, the School of Education, and Bob Jones Academy.

© 2004, 2010 BJU Press
Greenville, South Carolina 29614
First Edition © 1989 BJU Press

Printed in the United States of America
All rights reserved

ISBN 978-1-60682-036-0

15   14   13   12   11   10   9   8   7   6   5   4   3

CONTENTS

The American's Creed

Many people will be surprised to learn that the United States has an official national creed. William Tyler Page—a descendant of both a signer of the Declaration of Independence and John Tyler, tenth president of the United States—wrote it in 1917 and submitted it in a national contest. His entry won over more than three thousand other entries. On April 3, 1918, the U.S. House of Representatives adopted it as the official creed of the nation. It captures and summarizes the basic philosophy of American patriotism and is sometimes used in the naturalization ceremony for new Americans.

As you study America's history this year, look for reasons why Tyler might have included each phrase of his statement of Americanism. How has America lived up to (or failed to live up to) this statement of ideals? How can you fulfill *your* responsibilities as an American?

I believe in the United States of America as a Government of the people, by the people, for the people; whose just powers are derived from the consent of the governed; a democracy in a republic, a sovereign Nation of many sovereign States; a perfect Union one and inseparable; established upon those principles of freedom, equality, justice, and humanity for which American patriots sacrificed their lives and fortunes. I therefore believe it is my duty to my country to love it, to support its Constitution, to obey its laws, to respect its flag, and to defend it against all enemies.

Blessed is the nation whose God is the Lord

—Psalm 33:12

UNIT I

FOUNDATIONS

THE ONLY SURE FOUNDATION

Quotation in the Chamber of the House of Representatives

Now these be the last words of David . . . , "He that ruleth over men must be just, ruling in the fear of God. And he shall be as the light of the morning, when the sun riseth, even a morning without clouds; as the tender grass springing out of the earth by clear shining after rain." (II Sam. 23:1, 3–4)

King David Playing the Harp; *Simon Vouet; from the Bob Jones University Collection*

The end was near for David, and he knew it. Soon the reins of his government would be handed over to his son. But Solomon was young, inexperienced, and therefore vulnerable to the wiles of several influential men whom even David had struggled to control. "Shew thyself a man," he exhorted his successor, "and keep the charge of the Lord thy God, to walk in his ways, to keep his statutes, and his commandments" (I Kings 2:2–3). The dying king's advice was not without specifics. "Thou knowest also what Joab the son of Zeruiah did to me, and what he did to the two captains of the hosts of Israel" (v. 5). Those familiar with the Books of Samuel will remember what David was referring to. Stubborn and proud Joab, the captain of Israel's armies, had killed Abner and Amasa in cold blood. David's charge regarding Joab was unmistakable: "Let not his hoar [gray] head go down to the grave in peace" (v. 6).

Soon after David's death, Solomon proved himself to be a skilled monarch. Through a number of shrewd decisions, he established his authority and brought stability to the empire his father had built. One of those shrewd decisions concerned Joab. When the former military chief learned that he had fallen out of favor with the crown, he fled to the tabernacle and seized the horns of the altar. It was there that one of Solomon's emissaries, Benaiah, found him. "Thus saith the king, Come forth," Benaiah demanded (v. 30). But Joab was not about to abandon the protection that this holy site was affording him: "Nay; but I will die here." Not knowing what to do, Benaiah returned to Solomon for further orders. The new king's reply was simple, and it demonstrated that he was the worthy successor to the throne of David: "Do as he hath said" (v. 31). And Benaiah did.

This slice of biblical history, taken from the early years of Solomon's reign, provides the Christian with an important reminder: the work of governing—even in the best of governments—is often an ugly business. It involves handling great

The Visit of the Queen of Sheba to Solomon; *Jacopo Robusti, called Il Tintoretto; from the Bob Jones University Collection*

authority and constantly deciding what is right and what is wrong. And based on those decisions, governments must determine who will live behind bars and, in some cases, who will not live at all. History is filled with examples of those who have abused that authority and made wrong decisions—David and Solomon included. Such a negative track record has caused many believers to conclude that government is no place for the Christian. "Power corrupts," many warn, "and no Christian can wield that kind of power without becoming corrupt himself." Out of concern to protect their souls, such Christians leave their society unprotected. By directing the would-be Solomons away from government, they leave the public square to be dominated by the Joabs.

Is it God's will that Christians abandon governmental involvement to unbelievers? Not if the God of the New Testament is the same God as the God of the Old Testament. Is it not true that the Christians' God gave His law through Moses, raised up David to rule over Israel, and led David to choose Solomon as his successor? If so, then the "charge of the Lord, thy God," which Solomon was to keep, was the charge of the Christians' God. And the work of establishing Solomon's authority over Israel, though a bloody task, was the work of our God.

But what God wished to do in Israel is quite different from what He wished and wishes to do among the Gentile nations, right? Certainly this statement is in part true. God's purpose, plan, and expectations for Israel are and will always be unique. But that fact does not imply that God has no expectations for the other nations of the earth. Long ago the psalmists expressed their wish that all peoples acknowledge Jehovah alone as God: "All the gods of the nations are idols: but the Lord made the heavens. . . . Give unto the Lord, O ye kindreds of the people, give unto the Lord glory and strength" (Ps. 96:5, 7). "The Lord reigneth; let the earth rejoice; let the multitude of isles be glad thereof" (Ps. 97:1). These statements from ancient Israelites are not vain expressions of nationalistic fancy. Psalm 2 states that God Himself holds all governments responsible to submit themselves to the rule of His Son: "Be wise now therefore, O ye kings: be instructed, ye judges of the earth. Serve the Lord with fear, and rejoice with trembling. Kiss the Son, lest he be angry, and ye perish from the way" (vv. 10–12).

This concern for the rulers of the earth to recognize the greater rule of God and His Son can be seen in the New Testament as well. One of the most memorable confrontations that Jesus had with the Pharisees concerned a question of human government: "Is it lawful to give tribute to Caesar?" (Mark 12:14). After asking to see a Roman coin, Jesus held it up and asked, "Whose is this image?" (v. 16). "Caesar's," they answered, of course. Jesus' reply was as simple as it was profound: "Render to Caesar the things that are Caesar's, and to God the things that are God's" (v. 17). That which bears a person's image belongs to that person and may therefore be called for by that person at any time. For the Pharisees that meant surrendering their Roman coins whenever Rome asked for them. But what does this command mean for the Caesars of the world? Just as the coin in Jesus' hand bore Caesar's image, so Caesar bore God's image—as we all do (cf. Gen. 1:26; 9:6; James 3:9). Whether a slave or a king, all people are obligated to do what the Pharisees in Mark 12 were refusing to do—render to God total devotion by recognizing His Son for who He is.

This was an obligation that Jesus later pressed on one of Caesar's own governors. Only hours before the crucifixion, He told Pilate that to be a follower of truth, he must accept His teaching as true (John 18:37–38). It was a lesson that Pilate learned too late.

During the early years of the church, God's people repeatedly appealed to Gentile rulers to recognize the Lordship of Jesus Christ. Under the direction of the Holy Spirit, Philip persuaded the Ethiopian eunuch—a man "of great authority" (Acts 8:27)—to accept Jesus as the Son of God. After receiving a vision from God, Peter preached to Cornelius, a high-ranking official in the Roman army, that Jesus was Lord of all and that He "was ordained of God to be the Judge of quick [living] and dead" (Acts 10:42). And Paul exhorted the Roman governors Sergius Paulus, Felix, and Festus to receive Jesus as their Savior and Lord (Acts 13:6–12; 24:24–25; 26:1–30).

Why does the New Testament give such emphasis to confronting governmental officials in this way? Rulers, like all men, are people in need of a Savior (cf. I Tim. 2:1–6). And since that Savior is also the King of kings, all human lords who wish to embrace this Savior must also acknowledge Him as their greater Lord (cf. I Tim. 6:14–15; Rev. 1:5). As Paul stated, the gospel is to be "made known to all nations for the obedience of faith" (Rom. 16:26). Thus, the last words of David must not be viewed as the outmoded advice of a king long-since dead. Those words remain God's mandate for all rulers everywhere. If a government desires to be blessed of its Maker, it "must be just." And the only way for a government to be truly just is for it to commit itself to "ruling in the fear of God."

Of course, "ruling in the fear of God" means different things to different people. Can anyone know what God expects of the governments of the earth? Indeed, anyone can because God has revealed Himself in Scripture. In the pages of the Old and New Testaments, one finds the only sure foundation for the task that stands before us in this book—a useful analysis and critique of human government in general and of United States government in particular. This opening chapter will begin the task by examining what the Bible reveals regarding *why* government exists, *what* government's duties should be, and *how* believers should respond to their government.

I. The Necessity of Government

Simply stated, **government** is any system of public rule or authority. This definition is as broad as the vast array of types and levels of government that exist throughout the world. There are literally thousands of governments in operation, from simple county or town meeting organizations to the complex machinery of national governments. In examining these various forms of government and the history of their operation, one can easily become discouraged, even despondent. Repeatedly, we see human government moving too slowly to correct certain social injustices but at other times moving too swiftly to correct that which needs no correction. "If human government can do no better than it has," the cynic in us all has wondered, "perhaps our race would be better without it." This view is cynicism indeed, and it fails to reckon with the Bible's teaching about the nature of God and His world and the problem of human depravity.

First self-governing assembly, House of Burgesses, Colonial Williamsburg

The Nature of God and His World

The Trinity—The fundamental principles of government are woven into the fabric of the universe. In the beginning, when there was nothing but God, there was a hierarchy of authority. God is a single being, but He exists in three distinct persons: the Father, the Son, and the Holy Spirit. Within the Trinity there is no dissension and no sin, and each person is equally divine. Nevertheless, the Father (as His title suggests) is the leader and the "policymaker." He has authored the plan for the creation and redemption of the world, and He has appointed the other two persons specific tasks to fulfill. The Son recognized the leadership role of the Father when He said, "The Son can do nothing of himself, but what he seeth the Father do. . . . I seek not mine own will, but the will of the Father which hath sent me" (John 5:19, 30). Just as the Son is submitted to the authority and plan of the Father, so the Holy Spirit follows the leadership of the Son. The night before He was crucified, Jesus told His disciples, "When he, the Spirit of truth, is come, he will guide you into all truth: for he shall not speak of himself; but whatsoever he shall hear, that shall he speak. . . . He shall glorify me: for he shall receive of mine, and shall shew it unto you" (John 16:13–14).

Mankind Before the Fall—The Bible presents our race as God's unique creation. We are unique, first of all, because God made us in His own image (Gen. 1:26–27). When we say that mankind was made in the **image of God,** we mean that God invested humans with certain qualities that reflect His own character: reason, moral capacity, spiritual nature, sociability, and emotion. Each of the creatures in God's world exists to declare His glory (Rom. 11:33–36), but the nature of our existence is different from that of all the others. We declare the greatness and goodness of God's being not simply as demonstrations of His beauty, His power, or His creativity. We declare God's glory by being like Him.

We are unique, second, because God has called us to the work of exercising wise and responsible dominion over His world (Gen. 1:28). By managing God's world under Him as the only beings made in His own image, we reflect the glories of our Maker out across the broader stage of creation, back to one another, and back to God Himself. Many have called this first command of God to man the **creation mandate.**

It is instructive to note that although God made mankind in His image and gave him the high calling of managing His world under Him, God from the beginning intended that there be an authority structure in the race. When there were only two members of the human race, there was a hierarchy of authority similar

Grand Canyon

to the one already noted between the persons of the Trinity. God appointed Adam to be in charge of maintaining the Garden of Eden, and He appointed Eve to be his helper in the task (Gen. 2:15, 18). Thus, God never intended that every human fulfill the creation mandate in the same capacity. Some are to be leaders in this endeavor, and some are to be followers or helpers.

These observations regarding the nature of our God and the original nature of our race do not demonstrate that the Trinity or human marriage is government. They do, however, show that the need for a system of public rule is anticipated in the Bible's most fundamental teachings. Once we consider that God established an authority structure within our race even when only two humans existed, we are not surprised to find that city and national governments began to arise when humans became very numerous (cf. Gen. 4:17; 10:5, 20, 31). Also, by observing that an authority structure exists even within the being of God, we learn that a system of rule is necessary whenever there is a task or mission to be accomplished. If we as a race are to be effective and efficient in our task of fulfilling the creation mandate, we will need a government of some sort. Some of us must lead by establishing a vision and formulating a plan, and some of us must follow by fleshing out that vision and that plan with our obedience.

The Problem of Human Depravity

Government is a necessary part of this world, not only because of the fundamental nature of the world and its Maker but also because of sin. God made man in His own image, and therefore man was originally good (Gen. 1:26–27, 31). But when Adam and Eve chose to disobey God, the image of God in them—and in all of their descendants—was severely marred, though not destroyed (cf. Gen.

9:6; James 3:9). The result of this marring of God's image is called **human depravity.** When we say that humans are depraved, we do not mean that we all are as wicked as we can be. Rather, we mean that every part of our being (the mind, will, emotions, etc.) has been twisted by our fall into sin.

Whereas before the Fall, our race delighted in fulfilling God's basic expectations of loving God supremely and loving others as much as self, after the Fall, each member of the race naturally has delighted in loving self supremely. This fundamental, tragic change in the race evidenced itself only moments after the first sin. When God confronted Adam with his disobedience, Adam showed that he had already begun to love himself more than God and more than his fellow human. Instead of accepting responsibility for his deed, he tried to put the blame on Eve in a way that implied God Himself was partly at fault: "The woman whom thou gavest to be with me, she gave me of the tree, and I did eat" (Gen. 3:12). In the Bible's next chapter, man's sad situation gets much worse. Stung in his conscience by the upright testimony of his brother, Cain murdered Abel and then attempted to hide the deed from God.

The Dead Abel; *Peter Paul Rubens; from the Bob Jones University Collection*

One of the most condemning truths concerning the human race is that we cannot thrive on this planet (or even survive) unless a system of public rule is in place to protect us from ourselves. Recognizing the severity of human depravity, God long ago instituted the punishment that has traditionally served as the defining right of government, the death penalty (Gen. 9:6; cf. Rom. 13:4). To right the wrongful deeds of certain humans and to restrain the evil intentions of others, the human race has the authority, under certain circumstances, to take human life.

Those who sincerely believe that humanity would be better without government do not have a proper appreciation for human depravity. Left unrestrained, the human race will destroy itself. Despite the fact that **anarchy** (the absence of any government) is the goal of many people's political philosophy, it is always frightfully tragic and mercifully short-lived whenever it appears on the stage of history. In each generation our race learns the painful lesson that any government is better than no government.

Today belief in human depravity is scorned by many Americans. Such people would do well to consider what John Adams told the framers of our government: "Whoever would found a state, and make proper laws for the government of it, must presume that all men are bad by nature." In a similar vein, James Madison observed in *Federalist No. 51,* "If men were angels, no government would be necessary."

The allegorical figure of Justice located on the West Frieze in the courtroom of the Supreme Court Building

Section Review

1. Why is it not wrong for a Christian to be involved in even the "ugly business" of government?
2. How can government be truly just?
3. What is the only sure foundation for understanding government?
4. How is the Trinity a prototype for human government?
5. How does man declare God's glory uniquely?
6. What is the creation mandate?
7. Why does human depravity demand government?

II. The Obligations of Government

The Bible reveals not only why human government exists but also what it is supposed to do. Ultimately, as with all human institutions, government exists to glorify God by assisting mankind in the work of fulfilling the most basic command of God to man, the creation mandate (Gen. 1:26–28). By examining various passages—especially Romans 13:1–7 and I Peter 2:13–14—we learn that government is called by God, more specifically, to reward righteousness and punish unrighteousness.

Reward Righteousness

In exhorting Christians to live in submission to governmental officials, the apostle Peter tells his readers that government exists by God's appointment. Men and women in positions of authority are "sent by him [God] . . . for the praise of them that do well" (I Pet. 2:14). Solomon repeatedly emphasizes the importance of fulfilling this obligation in the Book of Proverbs—a book written, in part, to prepare the next generation of governmental leaders. Some of the clearest statements of warning come from Proverbs 17: "Whoso rewardeth evil for good, evil shall not depart from his house" (v. 13); "He that justifieth the wicked, and he that condemneth the just, even they both are abomination to the Lord" (v. 15); "Also to punish the just is not good, nor to strike princes for equity" (v. 26). Examples in Scripture of the government rewarding good include David's honoring of Barzillai's faithfulness during Absalom's revolt (II Sam. 19:31–38) and Publius's gifts to the apostle Paul for his many good deeds done in Melita (Acts 28:7–10).

Despite the Bible's many admonitions about government's obligation to reward the righteous, rulers have on many different occasions punished the righteous. This failure is another manifestation of human depravity. Like Cain, governmental officials are often offended by the righteousness of the righteous rather than encouraged by it. More concerned to preserve their sinful and selfish ways than to be changed by such righteous examples, rulers sometimes seek to have the testimony of good men silenced.

When governments choose this course of action, they choose their own undoing. As the Bible shows in Acts 12, rulers are themselves ruled by a far greater King. This King sees the deeds of all men, and as "the Judge of all the earth" (Gen. 18:25), He will judge governments if they fail to deal with the Christian church as they ought to. When a ruler stretches out his hand to interfere with God's working in the world through the church, he may for a time seem to thwart the good of the church. But in the end God will see to it that His people prosper while that ruler is overturned: "And immediately the angel of the Lord smote [King Herod], because he gave not God the glory: and he was eaten of worms, and gave up the ghost. But the word of God grew and multiplied" (Acts 12:23–24).

A Lesson from Literature

Percy Shelley's "Ozymandias" gives a poignant commentary on the rise and fall of nations. Poems such as these remind the believer of what the apostle John said long ago: *"The world passeth away, and the lust thereof: but he that doeth the will of God abideth for ever" (I John 2:17).*

I met a traveler from an antique land
Who said: "Two vast and trunkless legs of stone
Stand in the desert. Near them, on the sand,
Half sunk, a shattered visage lies, whose frown,
And wrinkled lip, and sneer of cold command,
Tell that its sculptor well those passions read
Which yet survive, stamped on these lifeless things,
The hand that mocked them, and the heart that fed;
And on the pedestal these words appear:
'My name is Ozymandias, king of kings:
Look on my works, ye mighty, and despair!'
Nothing beside remains. Round the decay
Of that colossal wreck, boundless and bare
The lone and level sands stretch far away."

Punish Unrighteousness

Governmental officials must also punish the unrighteous. Paul states that government "is the minister of God, a revenger to execute wrath upon him that doeth evil" (Rom. 13:4). Again, the Book of Proverbs has much to say concerning government's responsibility in this regard. Consider these two verses: "A wise king scattereth the wicked, and bringeth the wheel over them" (Prov. 20:26). "He that saith unto the wicked, Thou art righteous; him shall the people curse, nations shall abhor him" (Prov. 24:24). In carrying out this obligation, government has been given the authority to take property away from individuals (Prov. 6:30–31), to inflict physical harm (Prov. 20:30), and even to take life (Gen. 9:6; Rom. 13:4).

We usually view the punishing of evildoers as a matter of domestic policy only. However, not all evildoers come from within. In punishing the unrighteous, government also has the obligation to protect its citizens from the evil designs of those who would seek to trouble its people from without. Historically, the threat of foreign invasion has been one of the primary reasons for governments to form. As James Madison once observed, "Security against foreign danger is one of the primitive objects of civil society." The Bible recognizes the legitimacy of this function of government, but it cautions rulers not to be hasty in carrying out this function: "Every purpose is established by counsel: and with good advice make war" (Prov. 20:18). "By wise counsel thou shalt make thy war: and in multitude of counsellors there is safety" (Prov. 24:6).

Revolutionary War reenactment

At this point in this brief survey of the obligations of government, we must ask a fundamental question that will give meaning and significance to our discussion: *what is righteousness?* To state it very generally, **righteousness** is conformity to a standard. What that standard is depends on the context in which the word is used. When speaking of law and morality, the ultimate standard is the character of the God of the Bible. As the Son of God revealed during His earthly ministry, "There is none good but one, that is, God" (Matt. 19:17). Since God is the only supremely good Being in the universe, only His character qualifies as the criterion by which good and evil are to be distinguished. That which is like God in His justice, truth, and love is righteous. Whatever is unlike Him is unrighteous. Can we as humans know what God's character is like? We can if we will take the Bible as our authority. The Bible, through its explicit teaching and through its historical record of God's interaction with mankind, reveals to us what God loves, what He hates, what He expects from His creatures, and therefore what is righteous and what is unrighteous.

Good government, therefore, proves itself to be good by upholding that which is good and right in *God's* sight. That means the moral code established by the state should reflect God's character and its resulting expectations for man. It is important to remember that governments established today are not like Israel in the Old Testament. They do not exist as a **theocracy** (a government ruled directly by God or the clergy), and God never commands them to be. However, their moral code should reflect the character of God.

It is not enough for men and women to depend on their "innate sense of goodness" as they seek to govern well. All humans are depraved, and therefore that "innate sense" is not as "good" as it must be to function as an adequate standard for determining right and wrong. Because we as fallen beings are fundamentally selfish, we tend to prefer definitions of justice that justify the things we desire and that make us look good and noble. Such standards may make us feel good about ourselves, but as Solomon observed long ago, they are not themselves good. They may, in fact, prove to be quite dangerous: "There is a way which seemeth right unto a man, but the end thereof are the ways of death" (Prov. 14:12). Man must judge himself by the objective standard established by the Judge of all the earth: "All the ways of a man are clean in his own eyes; but the Lord weigheth the spirits" (Prov. 16:2). Here again we find that the last words of David prove to be God's message for rulers even today. The only way for a government to be truly just is for it to define justice by the standard of God's character. To be truly just, in other words, requires that rulers choose to rule "in the fear of God" (II Sam. 23:3).

Section Review

1. What is the ultimate obligation of government?
2. Can God use human rulers for His purposes even when they make wrong decisions?
3. What criterion is the basis for distinguishing good from evil?
4. Why should those in government not simply rely on an innate sense of goodness?

III. The Obligations of the Governed

So far in this chapter we have focused on the obligations of government. But our investigation of what the Bible teaches about government will not be complete until we consider what God says about the obligations of the governed. Since this textbook is designed to be used by Christians, this section will focus on the obligations that Christians have to their government.

Submission

Whenever the New Testament deals with the issue of the Christian's relationship to civil government, it emphasizes the believer's obligation to obey and submit. Obedience simply means doing what authority commands. Paying taxes, keeping speed limits, and serving jury duty are all examples of obedience. However, God is interested not only in *what* the Christian does but also in *how* he does it. The type of obedience God requires comes from an attitude of submission.

Submission is more than the recognition of government's sphere of authority; it is an attitude of the heart. Christian citizens are to have an attitude of reverence and respect for government and those who exercise it. It is important to note that Scripture does not limit submission only to good governments. In many cases, God's servants have submitted to and even served under unjust or pagan governments. For the Christian, submission and obedience to the state are not options; they are commands.

> Submit yourselves to every ordinance of man for the Lord's sake: whether it be to the king, as supreme; or unto governors, as unto them that are sent by him for the punishment of evildoers, and for the praise of them that do well. For so is the will of God, that with well doing ye may put to silence the ignorance of foolish men: as free, and not using your liberty for a cloak of maliciousness, but as the servants of God. Honour all men. Love the brotherhood. Fear God. Honour the king. (I Pet. 2:13–17)

In this passage the apostle Peter urges that Christians live in submission to their government in order to have a good testimony. The Christian's submission sets an example for the unsaved world of what proper citizenship should be, and thus enables him to "put to silence the ignorance of foolish men" regarding the Christian religion.

The reasoning that the apostle Paul employs in Romans 13 forms a complement to Peter's, and it may surprise you: "[A ruler] is the minister of God, a revenger to execute wrath upon him that doeth evil. Wherefore ye must needs be subject, not only for wrath, but also for conscience sake" (Rom. 13:4–5). The believer should fear to disobey government not simply because he needs to be a good

testimony but also because God is on government's side. Rulers are God's ministers, or servants. God has established government to do certain things such as to bring order and justice to a society. To fulfill these tasks, government needs citizens who respect its authority and obey its commands. Even a corrupt government may fulfill much of God's calling for it. Therefore, to disobey government is to violate one's conscience and to rebel against God.

Ungodly Governments

God's servants have often found themselves in difficult situations facing ungodliness. In some cases the source of that ungodliness has been the government they were under. Although America has a much different system of government than those in Old and New Testament times, we can learn much from biblical examples about the proper attitude towards an ungodly government.

David—Before becoming king, David faced an ungodly government in the form of King Saul's personal vendetta against him. Despite almost being run through with a spear and then being hounded across the land, David remained respectful of Saul. On two occasions when presented with the opportunity to kill the king, David refused. He even expressed genuine sorrow for cutting off part of Saul's robe (I Sam. 24:4–6), as this could be interpreted as a sign of rebellion. Furthermore, he commanded those under him to show Saul respect and refrain from hurting him. Later, when David received word of Saul and Jonathan's deaths, he lamented over both of them. As for the Amalekite who claimed to have put Saul out of his misery, instead of being rewarded he was put to death on the spot. Before the execution, David rebuked the Amalekite, "How wast thou not afraid to stretch forth thine hand to destroy the Lord's anointed?" (II Sam. 1:14)

David's attitude of respect for civil authority came from a deep understanding of divine authority. Like Daniel, he knew that God "changeth the times and the seasons: he removeth kings, and setteth up kings" (Dan. 2:21). David reminded Abishai of God's sovereignty while they stood in Saul's camp over the slumbering king. "As the Lord liveth, the Lord shall smite him; or his day shall come to die; or he shall descend into battle, and perish" (I Sam. 26:10).

Paul—The apostle Paul faced ungodly government on two fronts—civil (Roman) and religious (the Sanhedrin). Even Paul, bold and blunt Paul, remained respectful of their authority. In fact, he was willing to stand trial and use their legal systems to his advantage. Just before Paul was to be whipped by Roman authorities, he appealed to them on the basis of his citizenship: "Is it lawful for you to scourge a man that is a Roman, and uncondemned?" (Acts 22:25) Paul regarded his citizenship highly and politely reminded the authorities of civil laws relating to it. Later, when Paul stood before Felix the governor, he acted courteously and recognized Felix's many years of experience (Acts 24:10). That was perhaps the only nice thing that could be said of Felix, who was known for his brutality and cruelty.

Even in Rome, imprisoned for his faith, Paul did not spend his time bewailing his situation or inciting a rebellion. Rather, he used his time to encourage and instruct fellow believers. In fact, he later wrote to young Timothy that "prayers" and "giving of thanks" should be made "for kings, and for all that are in authority" (I Tim. 2:1–2).

Through their responses, both men remind us that an attitude of respect for authority is important whether the government is godly or not. They also are a reminder of God's blessing in providing an American government in which there are legal means to express opinions and even bring reform.

The scriptural commands regarding submission and obedience to government are always set in the context of God's authority structure; that is, God maintains sovereignty over His creation, and the state is simply His instrument. If the government attempts to force a Christian to do something that violates a *clear biblical command* and the believer has exhausted every avenue of appeal, then he or she must obey the higher authority—which is God.

The Christian's response in such a situation is not so much a matter of disobedience as a principle of obeying the highest authority. For example, the Lord Jesus gave His apostles a clear parting command before His ascension: "Ye shall be witnesses unto me both in Jerusalem, and in all Judea, and in Samaria, and unto the uttermost part of the earth" (Acts 1:8). When the hostile Jewish leadership in Jerusalem said, "Did not we straitly command you that ye should not teach in this name? and, behold, ye have filled Jerusalem with your doctrine" (Acts 5:28), the apostles had clear and conflicting commands from Christ and the council. The apostles then plainly declared their allegiance: "We ought to obey God rather than men" (v. 29). They then continued to obey the highest authority, "and daily in the temple, and in every house, they ceased not to teach and preach Jesus Christ" (Acts 5:42).

Even in cases such as this, where higher obedience to God is called for, the response is to be tempered with respect for government. The apostles continued to preach but did not go on to foment a rebellion. Daniel and his friends maintained this same attitude of submission even when disobeying the king's command to eat meat and drink wine that would defile them (Dan. 1). God blessed and used them to His glory as they served under Nebuchadnezzar.

Interaction

The Bible's many commands regarding our duty to submit to government do not require that we abandon attempts to change our government. Indeed, if we fail to confront rulers with their obligation to rule in the fear of God, we have failed to fulfill the Great Commission (Matt. 28:18–20), for then there is a segment of society to which we have not declared that God "now commandeth all men every where to repent" (Acts 17:30). The believer's obligation to press for governmental change involves basically two activities.

Evangelism—We should seek to see government change, first of all, by evangelizing our governmental officials. Paul speaks of his concern to see rulers transformed by the gospel in I Timothy 2:1–4.

> I exhort therefore, that, first of all, supplications, prayers, intercessions, and giving of thanks, be made for all men; for kings, and for all that are in authority; that we may lead a quiet and peaceable life in all godliness and honesty. For this is good and acceptable in the sight of God our Saviour; who will have all men to be saved, and to come unto the knowledge of the truth.

Here Paul calls on believers to intercede on behalf of all who exercise authority. Often we feel powerless to pray for the salvation of men and women in government because we do not think of rulers as being open to the gospel. Paul anticipates such doubtful responses, and he therefore reminds his readers that our God is a God of great love. He is not the God of the lowly and oppressed only. He commands that "prayers . . . be made for all men" because He desires for "all men to be saved"—even the men and women in our government.

In the Book of Acts, we see that Paul lived out this passion for the souls of his rulers. On several

Attorney General John Ashcroft, 2003

different occasions we find him pleading with governmental officials to allow their lives to be changed by the gospel. Most memorable is his emotional appeal before Agrippa, a Jewish monarch: "I continue unto this day, witnessing both to small and great, saying none other things than those which the prophets and Moses did say should come. . . . King Agrippa, believest thou the prophets? I know that thou believest" (Acts 26:22, 27). Agrippa did not submit to the gospel that day, but many people in government did convert to Christianity during Paul's life. In encouraging the saints at Philippi, Paul wrote to them that his imprisonment at Rome, though unpleasant, had advanced the spread of the gospel: "My bonds in Christ are manifest in all the palace" (Phil. 1:13). At the end of the same letter, Paul indicates that the gospel was not only made known in the palace but also embraced by many: "All the saints salute you, chiefly they that are of Caesar's household" (Phil. 4:22).

As our rulers are converted, one after another, government changes because the hearts and minds of those who lead the government are transformed. This is the best way to ensure that we are able to "lead a quiet and peaceable life in all godliness and honesty" (I Tim. 2:2). Such conversions also delight our Lord and Savior, "who gave himself a ransom for all, to be testified in due time" (I Tim. 2:6).

Participation—It has never been God's will for Christians to avoid participating in government, as though political involvement is somehow a sin. We must remember that the person who governs is "the minister of God . . . for good" (Rom. 13:4). Being involved in government, then, is just as legitimate as teaching in school or working for a manufacturer. But such involvement is not simply something *permissible*. God *desires* for Christians to govern. This desire is seen in His concern that rulers repent and believe the gospel. By leading the members of the early church to persuade rulers to become Christians, God reveals that the work of governing can and should be a Christian work. But, some may counter, Christ and the apostles also appealed to sorcerers and fortunetellers to repent without any suggestion that these should be Christian occupations. The difference, of course, is that leaving a life of sorcery or demon possession is presented in the New Testament as a necessary result of true Christian conversion. Such is never the case, however, when rulers come to Christ (cf. Mark 5:1–20; Acts 13:1–12).

The reason that God wishes to see His people in government should not be hard to discern. So long as a government has no believers involved in its operations, it is incapable of fulfilling its obligations well. Only those who are right with God are able to define righteousness and unrighteousness as those ideas must be defined. Therefore, any government that is void of Christian participation is a government that rests on a cracked foundation.

The results of trying to build government on a cracked foundation are always disastrous. Incapable of formulating a stable and accurate way to distinguish right from wrong, governmental officials are forced to rule by expediency. Good then tends to be treated as evil, and evil is often praised as good. As the condition worsens, God's people are often denied the liberty they need to fulfill God's commands—they lose their ability to enjoy "a quiet and peaceable life in all godliness and honesty." But something far greater than religious liberty is lost. Under such governments the glories of our matchless God are not declared. He who made man to reflect His unique greatness and goodness is rejected and denied His central place in society. The end of all such governments is certain and sad: "The wicked shall be turned into hell, and all the nations that forget God" (Ps. 9:17).

In the United States, citizens enjoy the opportunity to participate freely in their government—indeed, they *are* the government. This is a blessing that millions living under the heel of dictatorial regimes are deprived of. Citizens in America may participate in their government by voting, voicing their opinion, supporting a candidate, or even becoming one. Getting involved in the work of seeing government change for the glory of God is far easier for us today than it was during the days of the Roman Empire.

But this kind of involvement demands that believers be willing to learn about government. Understanding the structure, mechanics, and operation of government is a necessary first step toward more effective participation in it. Thomas Jefferson summed up this fact well when he pointed out, "If a nation expects to be ignorant and free . . . it expects what never was and never will be."

Understanding how the government of the United States functions is an ongoing process. Naturally, becoming informed on the basics such as constitutional provisions or how laws are made is essential, but staying informed is also necessary. Being knowledgeable about the forces of change—men, movements, and events in our government—helps produce contributing citizens rather than careless critics.

True Patriotism

THIS EMBATTLED SHORE, PORTAL
    OF FREEDOM,
IS FOREVER HALLOWED BY THE
    IDEALS,
THE VALOR AND THE SACRIFICES
OF OUR FELLOW COUNTRYMEN

The limestone memorial on which these words are etched faces out toward the graves of 9,386 soldiers buried at the Normandy American Cemetery above Omaha Beach. Words and images like these stir some of the strongest feelings of patriotism in us as American citizens.

But what is **patriotism**? Simply defined, it is love and devotion to one's country. However, it has also been defined as "the hatred of other countries disguised as the love of our own" or as "the last refuge of a scoundrel." Calvin Coolidge defined it as "looking out for yourself by looking out for your country." These negative definitions reflect the atrocities that have been committed in the name of "patriotism." During the golden age of the sail, there was little difference between a pirate and a privateer except that the latter flew a nation's flag. In Nazi Germany patriotism was taken to an extreme form in which the state was not only honored but deified. Unquestioning support for the state characterizes this corruption

Normandy American Cemetery and Memorial, Colleville-Sur-Mer/St. Laurent-Sur-Mer (Calvados), France

of patriotism, known as **jingoism.** Themistocles summed it up as the belief that "whatever is advantageous to one's country is just."

Consequently, it is vitally important that Christians have a proper perspective on patriotism. Some degree of patriotism arises naturally from man's social nature. A shared language, location, or ideology can bind a people together in a powerful way. Shared experiences, such as war, can do the same. Following the September 11 terrorist attacks in 2001, America experienced an immediate outpouring of patriotism.

At the heart of true patriotism is a spirit of thankfulness for the blessings of good government. But good government does not arise from the dust. It comes about through particular circumstances—often the toils and prayers of our ancestors and ultimately by God's grace. As Americans we can look back to many individuals and events that helped shape our government, but we must remember that God, not the state, should be the main object of our gratitude.

Today, America has sadly drifted from its godly heritage, but rather than simply lamenting this decline, our nation *needs* Christian patriots who passionately pray for our nation and fervently desire to reestablish those principles that honor God. While Christian patriotism includes such overt acts as voting, singing the national anthem, saluting the flag, and honoring patriots past and present, it has an even deeper meaning for the Christian. A Christian patriot is not interested in the social and political welfare of his country to the exclusion of its spiritual well-being. He recognizes that the latter is the chief cause of the former. Therefore, he knows that patriotism must involve sharing the Word of God and being a Christlike example to a needy nation.

As we embark on our study of United States government, we are exploring a subject interwoven into the very fabric of American society, past and present. We do so with the guiding lamp of Scripture to provide discernment, and the realization that as believers our dual citizenship in heaven and earth doubles rather than diminishes our responsibility as Christian citizens and leaders in our day. Because we have been enlightened by the truth of the gospel of Jesus Christ, we are responsible to declare to our rulers that the Christ who saves is also the Christ who is the "prince of the kings of the earth" (Rev. 1:5) and who therefore expects the submission of those rulers (Ps. 2:10–12). Through this declaration God will be glorified, our leaders will be blessed, and we may come to enjoy the blessing of good government. If they listen to God's Word, they will be to us as "the light of the morning, when the sun riseth, even a morning without clouds" (II Sam. 23:4).

Section Review

1. Why is God interested in how we respond to government?
2. What is the result of living in submission to government?
3. Why should the Christian fear to disobey government?
4. How should a Christian determine whether to obey his government or not?
5. Why does failure to confront rulers with their obligations violate the Great Commission?
6. How do we know that God desires for Christians to be involved in government?
7. Why is it vital for the Christian to understand his government?
8. What motivates Christians to participate in their government?

Chapter Review

Terms

government
image of God
creation mandate

human depravity
anarchy
righteousness

theocracy
patriotism
jingoism

Content Questions

1. What is the Christian's main concern for his rulers?

2. How can we tell that government is part of God's plan for mankind?

3. What happens when humans are left ungoverned?

4. What are the obligations of government?

5. Why should the Christian submit to imperfect human government?

6. How does the Great Commission affect our relationship to government?

4. If Christ didn't condemn those who put Him to death, why should Christian judges condemn those who break the law?

5. What would an ideal government look like, according to the Bible? Is this kind of government possible in the United States?

6. What is the role of government in God's plan for His creation?

7. What is the primary means God provided for man to glorify Himself?

8. What are the consequences of human depravity for government?

9. Can laws be good and still not earn favor with God?

10. Why should submission to government be easy for the Christian?

Application Questions

1. Was Solomon a godly ruler? Defend your answer.

2. If the Bible is our guide for human government, why do we not support a monarchy such as the kind Israel had?

3. If you were involved in government, how could you ensure that you ruled justly?

CHRISTIAN BEGINNINGS IN AMERICA

As we continue to lay the foundation for our study of United States government, we must examine the impact of Christianity on the development of our nation and the devising of its Constitution.

The study of Christian influence on American society and government generally suffers from two extremes: it is either overlooked or overdone. Many historians and political scientists ignore the pervasive role of religion in the settling of this continent. Other writers tend to view American history and government through stained glass. They place halos over our founders and often confuse Christian symbols and slogans (such as the motto "In God We Trust") with national salvation. We need a balanced approach that views the past with understanding and gratitude for God's gracious dealings, while not glossing over our history with the varnish of selective and sentimental thinking.

The United States is not now, nor has it ever been, a Christian nation. That is, it is not Christian in the biblical sense that all of its citizens and leaders have been saved through faith in Christ and lead their lives reflecting their conversion. However, Christianity has been a powerful shaping force in the governing of America. Theodore Roosevelt understood this fact well when he said,

> Every thinking man, when he thinks, realizes that the teachings of the Bible are so interwoven and entwined with our whole civic and social life that it would be literally—I do not mean figuratively, but literally—impossible for us to figure what that loss would be if these teachings were removed. We would lose almost all the standards by which we now judge both public and private morals.

The value of this chapter in our study of United States government is twofold. First, it provides background for an understanding of how Christianity shaped our social, political, and judicial systems. Thus it will help answer key questions raised later in this text such as *What are "unalienable rights"? What is separation of church and state? Where do laws originate?* Second, it provides an example of Christian influence and involvement in government. Christians, from the Pilgrims and Puritans to those believers who helped frame the Constitution, realized that good government is not an accident. They became involved and left a profound mark for Christ on their society.

I. Settlement

Reformation Influences

For over a century beginning in the 1520s, Europe had suffered the ravages of the religious wars and persecution that grew out of the Reformation. Today, looking back over nearly half a millennium, we find it remarkable that an obscure monk in a backwater town in sixteenth-century Germany could cause such a stir.

Martin Luther's rediscovery of the simple gospel truth that the "righteousness of God" is by faith, not works, transformed not only his life but the course of history as well. When the knowledge of saving faith broke over his soul, Luther declared, "I felt that I was altogether born again and had entered paradise itself through open gates." The grip of Roman Catholicism's hold loosened—but not without a struggle. Bloody wars between

Catholics and Protestants engulfed the continent. Thousands of believers lost their lands, and many lost their lives as Catholic armies sought to crush the Protestant movement. Yet just as spiritual, political, and economic forces were merging to produce the Reformation, a new world was discovered beyond the ocean. God, in timely fashion, provided a refuge for His people.

Bloodied, hounded, and oppressed, many Protestants came to America. They chose the hardships of the wilderness to have the privilege of worshiping and preaching freely. Of course, other things attracted settlers from Europe. Fortune seekers, farmers, and political misfits all found America to be a land of refuge from creditors and constables. Yet the important role that Christianity had in motivating settlement is clear and foundational and was demonstrated early in the colonization of New England.

Martin Luther Discovering Justification by Faith, *by Edward Matthew Ward, Bob Jones University Museum and Gallery*

Pilgrims and Puritans

On the day after Christmas, 1620, shivering, huddled families rowed through the icy waters of Plymouth Bay. William Bradford, their chronicler and later governor, recorded, "Being thus arrived in a good harbor, and brought safe to land, they fell upon their knees and blessed the God of Heaven who had brought them over the vast and furious ocean, and delivered them from all the perils and miseries thereof, again to set their feet on the firm and stable earth, their proper element."

The Pilgrims were Separatists who opposed worldliness and weakness in the state church of England. Consequently, they faced persecution, which brought them to America. The little congregation disembarking from the *Mayflower* numbered 101; however, in the winter months to follow, disease and starvation reduced their number by half.

The Pilgrims, in spite of their dismal beginnings, left America an important legacy. Many people think of the Pilgrims only when they are enjoying turkey and dressing on Thanksgiving Day; the Pilgrims, though, left us far more than a holiday. First, they showed that the freedom to worship and serve God was a driving force in the settling of this continent. Second, the Pilgrims practiced an important governmental principle, embodied in their **Mayflower Compact.**

The Mayflower Compact, signed by forty-one of the men onboard the *Mayflower,* established a temporary government for their pioneer community. This government was based on the idea of a covenant, that is, that God had a covenant or agreement with His people and they in turn had a covenant with one another to pursue common goals. This principle of **social contract,** that government is formed by the consent of the governed, has long lain at the heart of American political thought and practice.

This principle would play an important part in the future American War for Independence. The belief that rulers must meet requirements or fulfill responsibilities to remain rulers provided a justification to resist an "illegitimate" authority. It also provided an answer to the contrary belief in the **divine right of kings,** which had long supported Europe's monarchies. According to this theory, kings received their authority directly from God. They could not be removed from authority no matter how tyrannical or contrary to God's laws they acted because they were accountable only to God. Although the Pilgrims were the first major group to bring covenant thinking to America, they were soon followed by others.

A decade after the Pilgrims landed at Plymouth, large numbers of Puritans came to Massachusetts to establish a Christian community. Despite today's depiction, the Puritans were not mean and gloomy witch-hunters. Rather, most were dedicated believers who were committed to building a society where God was honored. John Winthrop, their first governor, expressed his expansive vision for the colony's future and concern for its godly testimony when he wrote in 1630,

> Wee shall be as a Citty upon a Hill, the eies of all people are uppon us; soe that if wee shall deale falsely with our god in this worke wee have undertaken and soe cause him to withdrawe his present help from us, wee shall be made a story and a by-word through the world.

The government of the Puritans, like that of their Pilgrim neighbors, was influenced by their congregational form of church government. In **congregationalism,** church members elect their leaders, such as elders and the pastor. Similarly, church members in early Massachusetts elected their governor, and each town chose its representatives and leaders, known as magistrates. Although the state was shaped by the church, the Puritans did make a distinction between religious and civil authority. However, today's separation of church and state, designed to cut off all Christian influence on civil government, was unthinkable.

A biblical foundation of government was also laid in Connecticut. The constitution there, the **Fundamental Orders of Connecticut (1639),** was the first written constitution in the New World. The

Fundamental Orders outlined a more democratic government than the one in Massachusetts by not making church membership a prerequisite for government participation. However, this important constitution did continue to affirm biblical purposes for civil government—liberty and order—beginning with its preamble, which states that government is "to mayntayn and presearve the liberty and purity of the gospell of our Lord Jesus which we now professe, as also the disciplyne of the Churches, which according to the truth of the said gospell is practised amongst us."

Educational Practices

After God had carried us safe to New England, and wee had builded our houses, provided necessaries for our livli-hood, rear'd convenient places for Gods worship, and setled the Civill Government: One of the next things we longed for, and looked after was to advance Learning and perpetuate it to Posterity; dreading to leave an illiterate Ministery to the Churches, when our present Ministers shall lie in the Dust.

DOCUMENTS OF DEMOCRACY

Mayflower Compact, 1620

This agreement, signed aboard the Mayflower, established the first government in the New World based on a social contract. The signatories agreed to "covenant and combine" themselves into "a civill body politick." The text of the compact below is taken from Gov. William Bradford's Historie of Plimoth Plantation.

In the name of God, Amen. We, whose names are underwritten, the loyal subjects of our dread sovereigne Lord, King James, by the grace of God, of Great Britaine, France, and Ireland king, defender of the faith, etc., having undertaken, for the glory of God, and advancement of the Christian faith, and honour of our king and country, a voyage to plant the first colony in the Northerne parts of Virginia, doe, by these presents solemnly and mutually in the presence of God, and one of another, covenant and combine ourselves together into a civill body politick, for our better ordering and preservation and furtherance of the ends aforesaid; and by virtue hereof to enacte, constitute, and frame such just and equall laws, ordinances, acts, constitutions, and offices, from time to time, as shall be thought most meete and convenient for the generall good of the Colonie unto which we promise all due submission and obedience. In witness whereof we have hereunder subscribed our names at Cap-Codd the 11 of November, in the year of the raigne of our sovereigne lord, King James, of England, France, and Ireland, the eighteenth, and of Scotland the fifte-fourth. Anno. Dom. 1620.

The Mayflower Compact, 1620; by Allyn Cox

These words, penned in 1643, provide an interesting commentary on Puritan values. In building their "city upon a hill," the Puritans first raised houses and churches. Then they organized a government, after which they provided for the education of their children.

These schools had a tremendous influence on the formative generations of nation-builders. Many received their training in an educational atmosphere in which Scripture pervaded the curriculum. This in no way implies that everyone trained in colonial schools graduated as a Christian. It does mean, however, that biblical principles and morals shaped community values because they had already shaped community leaders in the classroom.

The Massachusetts government encouraged education and its biblical emphasis. The landmark **Act of 1642** issued by the Massachusetts General Court required parents to provide for the education of their children that they might "read and understand the principles of religion and the capital laws of the country." Christianity and good citizenship were viewed as complementary, not conflicting.

That initial legislation was followed with the **"Old Deluder Satan" Act (1647),** which required every town of fifty families or more to provide a primary school for its children. Larger towns of at least one hundred households were required to provide both a primary school and a grammar school (the forerunner of the high school). The wording of the 1647 legislation makes it clear what the state hoped to see accomplished through the school:

> It being one chief project of the old deluder, Satan, to keep men from the knowledge of the Scriptures . . . [and] that learning may not be buried in the graves of our fathers . . . [i]t is therefore ordered that every township in this jurisdiction, after the Lord has increased their number to 50 householders, shall then forthwith appoint one within their town to teach all such children as shall resort to him to write and read.

The colonial primary school, especially in New England, provided reading skills to both boys and

New England Primer

girls. Reading was taught to enable the student to read the Bible on his own. In the *New England Primer,* the standard reading text for a century and a half, scriptural lessons were reinforced even in the learning of the ABCs.

For most girls and many boys of the period, the primary school was the extent of their formal training, but it did provide them with a basic education, along with the tools for coming to know God, the Author of the Book.

Higher education during the colonial period was also shaped by Christianity. Many of today's Ivy League schools were established to fill the pulpits of America with trained, fervent ministers and to prepare missionaries to take the gospel to the Indians in the wilderness.

The first college in America, Harvard, was started in 1636, and despite its humble beginnings, it eventually exercised great influence on New England and the nation. The driving force behind

Harvard's founding was not to build an institution of academic excellence, which it did, nor to provide the churches of New England with articulate preachers, which it also did; rather, its purpose was summed up in Harvard's 1646 *Rules and Precepts.*

> Every one shall consider the main end of his life and studies to know God and Jesus Christ which is eternal life.
>
> Seeing the Lord giveth wisdom, every one shall seriously by prayer in secret seek wisdom of Him.

In other early colleges the story was much the same. Virginia's William and Mary College, chartered in 1693, sought to improve the quality of the clergy and the spiritual life of the colony. Similarly, in Connecticut, Yale College opened its doors in 1701 to provide an orthodox alternative to Harvard, whose Christian fervor had begun to cool.

Today these colleges enjoy a wealth of tradition and prestige but an even greater poverty of spirit and faith. Having rejected their founders' God, they have become monuments of apostasy. However, in the years before the War for Independence, these schools trained our nation's leaders in an atmosphere where the Word of God was taught and honored, which in turn left a biblical mark on American society and government.

Section Review

1. Why did the Pilgrims come to America?
2. What legacy did the Pilgrims leave future generations of Americans?
3. What important governmental principle is embodied in the Mayflower Compact? in the Fundamental Orders of Connecticut?
4. What was the original purpose of education in America, according to the Act of 1642 and the Act of 1647?
5. Why was Harvard founded? Why was Yale founded?

II. Revolution

Many of our leaders during the War for Independence and the founding of the Republic were influenced by Christianity, as evidenced by their laws, letters, and political thought. But their work alone was not enough to steer the entire nation in the right course. Biblical influence had to be pervasive in American society as well. How did the Bible pervade the society of that day? The way it always does—through the preaching and teaching of the Word.

The Great Awakening

Beginning in the last quarter of the seventeenth century, the colonies experienced a spiritual decline. Materialism and rationalism began to replace the faith possessed by the founding generation. Unconverted colonists started to fill pews and even pulpits. Yet in the midst of this general state, God sent a revival known as the **Great Awakening** that rekindled the spiritual life of the colonies.

One of the earliest flickerings of revival was on the Massachusetts frontier in 1734. Under the preaching of Jonathan Edwards, the town of Northampton experienced conviction, conversion, and renewed spiritual life. Edwards wrote at the time,

> This town never was so full of Love, nor so full of Joy, nor so full of distress as it has lately been. . . . I never saw the Christian spirit in Love to Enemies so exemplified, in all my Life as I have seen it within this half-year.

From Northampton and other centers, the revival spread throughout Massachusetts and Connecticut and prepared the region for the arrival of an evangelist whose powerful voice for Christ would shake America to its very foundation—George Whitefield.

Whitefield, a British evangelist, preached from Georgia to New England, drawing large crowds everywhere. His open-air preaching and clear gospel appeal reached thousands from every rank of an increasingly unchurched society. Whitefield laid much of the blame for the general spiritual decline in the colonies on unconcerned and even unconverted ministers. He wrote, "I am verily persuaded, the Generality of Preachers talk of an unknown, unfelt Christ. And the Reason why Congregations have been so dead, is because dead Men preach to them."

As a result of Whitefield's efforts, others were motivated to spread out and reach the lost. For instance, evangelist Gilbert Tennent preached from Massachusetts to Pennsylvania in pulpits, at street corners, and on hillsides. As for Whitefield, he made a total of seven evangelistic tours of America and continued his ministry until his death in Massachusetts on the eve of the Revolution.

The Awakening brought notable changes to American society in such areas as church growth, missions, and education. First, there were significant increases in church membership. During the peak of the revival in 1739, as many as fifty thousand new members were added to the church rolls in New England out of a population of about three hundred thousand.

Increased missionary activity was another result of the Great Awakening. Missionaries challenged by the Great Commission evangelized both the Indians and the white man on the frontier. Two factors encouraged this effort. First, Dartmouth College was opened in 1754 as a Christian school for Indians, but it was soon expanded to train missionaries in general to take the gospel into the wilderness. Second, the publication of David Brainerd's diary also promoted the cause of Indian missions. Brainerd had devoted his brief life to taking the gospel to Indians living in New York, New Jersey, and Pennsylvania. Although he died of tuberculosis at twenty-nine, his life story inspired others to go into America's wilderness and take his place.

George Whitefield (1714–1770), *by John Russell (1745–1806)*

The effect of the revival on higher education also ensured that the Awakening would continue as a pervasive force in America. Colleges were founded that supplied ministers and other leaders for the growing nation. Unlike today, a college education was uncommon and a diploma prized and respected. In the eighteenth century, the minister was usually the best-educated man in his community and, consequently, an influential leader in local affairs and standards.

Another institution that resulted from the Great Awakening was Princeton College. Chartered in 1746, Princeton (originally known as the College of New Jersey) became a school of distinguished spiritual character and leadership—a position it maintained until the beginning of the twentieth century. Many of its early leaders were important revival figures, and their love for Christ shone in their school and in many of its graduates.

Whitefield's portable pulpit

Blair Hall, Princeton University

The Great Awakening was a spiritual force with social and political consequences. The revival brought different religious and ethnic groups together in a spirit of cooperation and fellowship. These groups found common ground in the new birth and in their sense of Christian mission and heritage. The revival fostered a growing sense that God was blessing *America,* not merely Massachusetts, or Pennsylvania, or Virginia, and that *America* had a destiny of her own.

The belief was a renewal of Governor Winthrop's "city upon a hill" vision for America; only now the city had grown into a nation. John Adams put it this way:

What do we mean by the American Revolution? Do we mean the American war? The Revolution was effected before the war commenced. The Revolution was in the minds and hearts of the people; a change in their religious sentiments of their duties and obligations.

The Great Awakening therefore transformed lives, influenced society, and shaped the generation whose ideas and arms gave birth to our Republic.

Parsons and Patriots

The church was an important source of support during the War for Independence. It not only lent its voice to the cause of liberty but also provided leadership.

The decade from 1765 to 1775 was a crisis time for the American colonies. Actions taken by the

British Parliament, aimed at controlling the colonies, met with increasing resistance. Through laws such as the Stamp Act and the Townshend Acts, Parliament levied taxes on the colonists without providing them a voice in the decision. Furthermore, these acts undermined the authority of the colonial governments. In most cases the opposition to British policies was not over how much the taxes cost in terms of money but rather how much they cost in terms of freedom and self-government.

A popular cry of the time, "No taxation without representation!" asserted that the traditional rights of Englishmen were being denied the American colonists. The real grievance was not over parliamentary representation, however. Both sides rejected that idea; the British rejected it because it seemed unnecessary, and the Americans rejected it because it seemed ineffective, since a few colonial representatives could simply be outvoted and ignored. What the Americans sought was to preserve the freedom of self-government that they had enjoyed for well over a century.

The church viewed with apprehension these attempts at increased control by the mother country. Many church leaders believed that a loss of political liberty would lead to a loss of religious liberty. Their concern was heightened in 1774, when Parliament passed the Quebec Act on behalf of the French settlers living in the recently acquired territory of Canada. Colonists believed that act gave privileged status to Roman Catholicism and that it potentially extended that religion's sphere westward to encompass the Great Lakes region and southward to the Ohio River.

"Now Put Watts in 'Em, Boys."

James Caldwell was one of many ministers who gallantly supported the cause of independence during the Revolutionary War. He was a graduate of Princeton and pastored in Elizabethtown, New Jersey, beginning in 1761. When war came, he eagerly served, variously as chaplain, spy, supply officer, and ever-present aid for the patriot troops in New Jersey. At the same time, he

also maintained his pastoral duties (sometimes removing his pistols from his belt as he stepped into the pulpit).

Caldwell's efforts gained wide recognition among both the patriots and the British. His honest reputation and wide popularity helped him rally discouraged troops for continued service and collect provisions more easily than other officers could. The British and their loyalist supporters, however, saw Rev. Caldwell as a major threat to be eliminated. They eventually killed his wife as she stood in her home in 1780.

The death of his wife only strengthened Caldwell's resolve to fight. At Springfield, New Jersey, he found himself engaged along with American troops in a hot battle, and he noticed that one of the regiments was running out of wadding for their guns. Caldwell quickly rode to a nearby Presbyterian church and filled his arms with hymnbooks from the pews. Racing back to the troops, he pitched the hymnals to the men, saying, "Now put Watts in 'em, boys." The troops cheered as they tore the pages, rammed them into their muskets, and fired with the aid of the hymns of Isaac Watts.

About a year after the Battle of Springfield, a sentinel at a wharf inexplicably shot the great patriot through the heart. Caldwell was buried with his wife in the church cemetery in Elizabethtown, and a monument was erected there with this inscription:

> This monument is erected to the memory of Rev. James Caldwell, the pious and fervent Christian, the zealous and faithful minister, the eloquent preacher, and a prominent leader among the worthies who secured the independence of his country. His name will be cherished in the Church and in the State so long as virtue is esteemed, and patriotism honored.

Though this act was not a direct attack on the colonies, it came at the worst possible time. Parliament had just passed a series of acts known in the colonies as the Intolerable Acts. These acts closed Boston Harbor, nullified the Massachusetts charter of government, and permitted peacetime quartering of British soldiers in private homes. With these and the presence of Catholicism in the west, warnings about the growing threats to liberty began to sound from pulpits throughout the colonies.

Naturally there were divided loyalties in the church, particularly among Anglicans, just as there were loyalist sentiments throughout the colonies. For the most part, however, the church sided with the patriot cause and even supplied manpower. Some ministers served as chaplains, while others shouldered muskets and went off to war. One such patriot-parson was Reverend Peter Muhlenberg. Muhlenberg, a Virginia pastor, stood before his congregation in January 1776 and after completing his sermon declared, "There is a time to preach and a time to pray; but there is also a time to fight, and that time has come." With that he removed his clerical robe to reveal a soldier's uniform; he then marched out of his church, joined by several men in his congregation. Muhlenberg attained the rank of major general and served under George Washington with gallantry and distinction throughout the war.

Other church leaders offered their services to the fledgling government. General Muhlenberg's brother Frederick, a Lutheran minister, served in the Continental Congress and later in the United States Congress as the nation's first Speaker of the House. The Reverend John Witherspoon, the president of the College of New Jersey at Princeton (now Princeton University), was an influential Christian leader in the Continental Congress and the only minister to sign the Declaration of Independence. When a New York delegate objected that the Congress was not "ripe" for adoption of the Declaration of Independence, Witherspoon fired back, "We are more than ripe for it, and some of us are in danger of rotting for want of it!"

Witherspoon brought his Christian perspective and convictions to bear on his political career. Sought out for his spiritual insight and broad knowledge of government, history, and current issues, Witherspoon served on more than a hundred twenty committees in the Continental Congress, providing valuable service in setting the new nation on a steady course. Probably Witherspoon's most important contribution to our government was made not at Philadelphia but at Princeton. As a Christian educator, Witherspoon greatly shaped the political thought of his most famous student—James Madison, the father of our Constitution.

Christianity and the Constitution

To understand how Christianity influenced the writing of the Constitution, we must take a closer look at how John Witherspoon influenced its chief architect, James Madison.

John Witherspoon (1723-1794) *by Rembrandt Peale (1778-1860)*

Witherspoon assumed his duties as president of the College of New Jersey in 1768, and in the following year, eighteen-year-old James Madison arrived at Princeton from the Virginia piedmont. For the next three years, Madison sat under the tutelage of Witherspoon, whom he fondly called the "old doctor."

Witherspoon was a gifted pastor-teacher. He emphasized the demands of the gospel while also introducing his students to the most important political thinkers of his age, such as Locke and Montesquieu. Witherspoon taught that God was sovereign and the source of all law. Just as God had created the universe with physical laws to maintain the cosmic order, so He had created man under the natural law to maintain the moral order.

Madison's study with Witherspoon climaxed a Christian education that began in his earliest youth. While Madison and many others of the founders were not believers, they developed their intellects within a Christian context, and this biblical worldview dictated their understanding of man and government. These Christian insights were incorporated in the Constitution, a document that recognized, in Madison's words, "a degree of depravity in mankind which requires a certain degree of circumspection and distrust."

Section Review

1. List four benefits the Great Awakening had on American society.
2. Why was Dartmouth founded?
3. Why were the colonists outraged by the Quebec Act?
4. What did the American Revolution owe to the Christians Peter Muhlenberg and John Witherspoon?
5. What important framer of the Constitution developed many of his biblical convictions from John Witherspoon, his teacher at Princeton?

Wittenberg, October 31, 1517; *by Eyre Crowe, A.R.A.; from the Bob Jones University Collection*

III. Conclusion

What does the record of Christian influence in the building of our nation and government mean to us today? Obviously a great deal has changed since that time. Denominations that once preached Christ with power and stood firm on the authority and infallibility of Scripture have drifted into doctrinal weakness and spiritual decline. American society in the past, though not thoroughly Christian, was yet largely God-fearing. Biblical standards provided a basis for public morals, judicial decisions, and social values. That society has now been replaced by one that is often antagonistic to what the Bible has to say. Secular humanistic thought, which puts man at the center of all things, now provides a basis for public morals, judicial decisions, and social values. Schools that once echoed with prayers and Bible reading now have expelled God from the classroom and relegated His Book to literature that is not on the recommended reading list. In light of this spiritual and moral shift, what remains of our Christian heritage? How should this heritage affect believers in the America of today?

The answers to these questions lie in an understanding of the three major contributions of Christianity to American government. These contributions are the Reformation idea of personal liberty, the tradition of dissent, and the pervasive influence of Scripture.

Personal Liberty

When Martin Luther stood before the Council of Worms in 1521 to defend his view that salvation was by grace through faith alone, he carefully presented his position to the unfriendly assembly and concluded by saying, "Here I stand; I can do no other." That simple declaration of faith and freedom would shake the kingdom of God and the kingdom of man for centuries to follow.

The Protestant Reformation was a spiritual awakening that produced potent political forces, central among these being the idea of personal liberty. Luther rediscovered the truth that every believer is a priest before God, and thus a person does not need an earthly priest to pray for him or to interpret the Scripture for him. The spiritual monopoly of Rome and the political monopoly of the state church was therefore broken by the conviction that every person could know God personally and must honor the voice of his or her own conscience before God. This personal liberty was, in Jefferson's words, an **"unalienable right"**—that is, a right that cannot be given by government because it is not government's to give; it is a gift of God. The Reformation fathered much of the political and social thinking behind American independence.

Presidential Views of the Bible

I speak as a man of the world to men of the world, and I say to you: Search the Scriptures. The Bible is the Book of all others to read at all ages and in all conditions of human life; not to be read once or twice through, and then laid aside; but to be read in small portions of one or two chapters a day and never to be intermitted unless by some overwhelming necessity.

—**John Quincy Adams**

There are some old things we cannot dispense with, and among these are God's Word and truth, and those religious influences by which He brings the heart of man into subjection to moral law. Do not be ashamed to confess yourselves Christians.

—**Benjamin Harrison**

The more profoundly we study this wonderful book, and the more closely we observe its divine precepts, the better citizens we will become and the higher will be our destiny as a nation.

—**William McKinley**

I plead for a closer and wider and deeper study of the Bible, so that our people may be in fact as well as in theory "doers of the word and not hearers only."

If a man is not familiar with the Bible, he has suffered a loss which he had better make all possible haste to correct.

—**Theodore Roosevelt**

The Bible . . . is the one supreme source of revelation of the meaning of life, the nature of God and spiritual nature and need of men. It is the only guide of life which really leads the spirit in the way of peace and salvation.

—**Woodrow Wilson**

If American democracy is to remain the greatest hope of humanity, it must continue abundantly in the faith of the Bible.

—**Calvin Coolidge**

Within the covers of the Bible are all the answers for all the problems men face. The Bible can touch hearts, order minds, and refresh souls.

—**Ronald Reagan**

In Comparison

Religion in America, Europe, and Japan

In 1831–32 Alexis de Tocqueville, a French aristocrat, visited America and wrote about it in what is now a classic, *Democracy in America.* One major characteristic of America that he noted was the powerful role religion played in American society: "It must never be forgotten that religion gave birth to Anglo-American society. In the United States, religion is therefore mingled with all the habits of the nation and all the feeling of patriotism, whence it derives a peculiar force. . . . Christianity has therefore retained a strong hold on the public mind in America. . . . Christianity itself is an established and irresistible fact."

Tocqueville was correct for that time period, the early part of the Second Great Awakening, but in a comparative sense he is still correct today. While the modern, developed nations of the world, notably Japan and various nations of Europe, grew increasingly secular after the urbanizing influence of the Industrial Revolution in the late nineteenth century and continuing to the present, the United States has remained, relatively speaking, a religious nation. Despite the separation of church and state, a public school system with no prayer or Bible reading, a liberal media, and the immorality promoted by the entertainment industry, a large majority of Americans regularly indicate in public opinion polls that they believe in God and pray. A large number attend church regularly. The influence of the "religious right" in politics shows the influence of religion in public life. Evangelical churches are among the fastest growing ones in the country.

The religious heritage of the colonial era, maintained somewhat by revivals (two Great Awakenings, Finney, Moody, and Sunday), has continued until today. Although America is not what it was spiritually in the seventeenth century, by God's grace it is not as secular as Europe or Japan. Our country breaks the pattern: we are both modern and religious.

The First Prayer in Congress; the lower portion of The Liberty Window at Christ Church, Philadelphia

Tradition of Dissent

A second major Christian influence on American government and history was the tradition of dissent. A variety of religious groups came to the New World because of their opposition to religious tyranny in the Old World. Pilgrims, Puritans, Quakers, Baptists, Presbyterians, and Huguenots all brought their opposition to ecclesiastical and political authoritarianism with them—an import that would later add an influential voice to the arguments favoring independence from Britain. The Presbyterian John Witherspoon, for example, said in 1776,

> There is not a single instance in history, in which civil liberty was lost, and religious liberty preserved entire. If, therefore, we yield up our temporal property, we at the same time deliver the conscience into bondage.

The right of dissent was therefore closely associated with personal liberty and freedom of conscience, matters important for the practice and propagation of the Christian faith. It must be emphasized that the tradition of dissent provided by our founding fathers was **moral dissent.** It was, in the Protestant tradition, a protest against concentrated power in both the church and the state. It was not dissent against government authority as such but against the abuse of that authority.

Gospel Salt

The third contribution that Christianity made to American governance was a pervasive biblical influence upon society. As we have seen earlier, many of our founding fathers established schools, courts, and local systems of government on biblical standards. In addition, the Great Awakening swept through the country and left revitalized, growing churches and transformed lives in its wake. This revival reached every level of colonial society with the gospel and prompted Christians to establish colleges that helped reach the frontier and the next generation with the gospel.

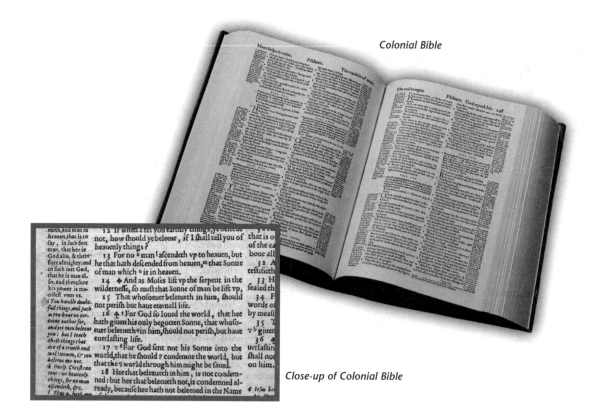

Colonial Bible

Close-up of Colonial Bible

Not all of our leaders during the War for Independence and the framing of our Constitution were Christians. Many plainly were not, but their thinking and their work were shaped by a society that was greatly influenced by the Scripture.

Just as Christ described believers as the "salt of the earth," so among the generation of nation-builders were believers—whether in the home, in the classroom, or in the statehouses and courts of America. These godly men and women seasoned society with the salt of the gospel. Their influence provides us with an example of how Christians may shape their government and their generation. The morality of the nation or the salvation of an individual can never result from an act of Congress, but rather through the power of the Word of God and the testimony of changed lives.

Christian citizens today must realize that the rich spiritual legacy from America's past is not simply history—it is inheritance. Inheritance implies present possession, and it is by our generation that the liberties dearest to Christians must be valued, protected, and used for the glory of Christ.

Section Review

1. What religious movement in Europe rekindled man's desire for personal liberty?
2. What religious tradition is closely associated with freedom of conscience and was influential in the colonists' decision to break away from Great Britain?
3. How did the preaching of the gospel and the widespread teaching of the Bible benefit America during its early stages?

Chapter Review

Terms

Mayflower Compact (1620)
social contract
divine right of kings
congregationalism

Fundamental Orders of
Connecticut (1639)
Act of 1642
"Old Deluder Satan" Act
(1647)

Great Awakening
unalienable right
moral dissent

Content Questions

1. Did this country begin as a "Christian nation"? Defend your answer.

2. What motivated the Pilgrims to colonize America?

3. How is American government indebted to the following documents and concepts: Mayflower Compact, Fundamental Orders of Connecticut, the unifying influence of the gospel, the depravity of mankind, the priesthood of believers, and the tradition of dissent?

4. What place did the Bible have in the education of early America?

5. What were the long-term benefits of the Great Awakening?

6. What are some specific examples of the influence of Christians in the course of the American Revolution?

7. Why did Christians in America think that rebellion against their mother country was proper and acceptable?

8. In what qualified sense is the United States Constitution a "Christian" document?

Application Questions

1. Why do you think God blessed the young American nation and allowed it to grow? What has changed since then, and what effect do you think those changes will have upon God's continued blessing?

2. What are some of the major differences between education today and education in the early years of this country?

3. How can a Christian best be the "salt" in American society?

FORMS OF GOVERNMENT

3

Canadian Parliament Building

A study of the world's governments reveals a wide variety of practices. Some operate without the people's consent; some operate with limited involvement by the people; and some receive power from the people. How does the government's workings in China differ from those of Thailand's government? How does the prime minister of Canada differ from the president of the United States of America? What is the difference between governments in Cuba and Australia? All of these questions can be answered by a survey of the different forms of governments.

I. Types of Government

It is evident from the questions above that there are great differences between the governments of nations. In order to clarify the differences, this section will look at (1) the systems of government that are used, (2) the relationship between the levels of those governments, and (3) the methods of electing the executive. Scholars use these three broad categories to classify governments.

Systems of Government

Voting, town meetings, and the freedom to write to members of Congress without fear of reprisal are all privileges dear to most Americans. One major difference between systems of government is the level of participation that citizens have in the decision-making process. A system in which the people participate is called a **popular government,** while a system that denies participation is called a dictatorship.

Popular Governments—Popular governments exist when political power resides with the people, not with a monarch or an elite group. Two types of popular governments exist: democracy and republic.

Democracies are usually divided into two types: direct (pure) or indirect (representative). The **direct democracy,** also called pure democracy, is a government in which the people *directly* affect a government's policies and actions. The people practice direct influence through gatherings resembling those of the ancient city-state Athens as well as New England town meetings. Each citizen hears the proposals and arguments and then participates directly by vote. Today direct democracy is rare because of geographic and population limitations.

In **indirect democracy,** or representative democracy, the people elect their peers to operate the government on their behalf. This form of democracy allows voters to participate in the government through representatives. These representatives are held accountable by means of frequent elections. Modern examples of indirect democracy exist in the United States of America, Japan, Canada, and France.

Not every country that claims to be democratic is. Many countries have claimed to be democratic while limiting or denying the people's participation in governmental affairs. The former Soviet and East German governments are historical examples of governments that claimed the attribute of personal freedom without the principles of personal freedom.

"I pledge allegiance to the flag . . . and to the republic for which it stands." The United States of America was from the outset attached to the idea of a republic. In Article IV, Section 4, the Constitution requires the United States to guarantee a republican form of government for each state of the Union. The question "What is a republic?" is therefore very important to understanding American government. The Oxford English Dictionary defines a **republic** as a "state in which the supreme power rests in the people and their elected representatives or officers." James Madison, in *Federalist No. 10,* distinguished a republic from a democracy as "a government in which the scheme of representation takes place." In America, then, the government can be called a "democratic republic" because it is republican in structure and democratic in principle. The people are sovereign, but they elect representatives to exercise the government's powers according to written laws.

Think About It

Could the Internet make representative government unnecessary by circumventing the problems inherent to a geographically large direct democracy? The increased use and accessibility of the Internet make direct involvement in the government feasible, but not without difficulties. One potential benefit is that all citizens could participate in discussions and vote from their homes or cities, avoiding travel and lodging costs and boosting voter participation. The Internet could make direct democracy possible on a scale never before seen; however, any system of direct democracy via the Internet would face certain difficulties. Arizona authorized the United States' first vote via Internet in its 2000 Democratic presidential primary. Over thirty-five thousand voters cast their votes online, but whether the trial was a success is debated. The issues of computer

Dictatorship—Another system of government is dictatorship. In a **dictatorship** the government acts without the people's consent or input. Absolute power lies within the ruling class, which often seeks to exercise control over every aspect of the people's lives (**totalitarianism**).

Dictatorial governments are categorized as either autocratic or oligarchic. Rule by one person with supreme authority is an **autocracy.** In an **oligarchy,** an elite group rules. Often this elite group is self-appointed, dividing the governmental departments among themselves.

Dictatorships often rely upon fear imposed by military might to obtain and maintain control within the country and respect on the world stage. A recent example would be Iraq under the control of Saddam Hussein. For years he maintained order and support for his regime through terror-induced fear. On the world stage, Hussein's desire for power led Iraq into wars with Iran, Kuwait, and finally the United States and Britain, culminating in a wrecked Iraqi economy, the loss of thousands of lives, and the end of Hussein's reign.

Dictatorships are not inherently evil; sin has produced the oppression and vice associated with dictatorships throughout history. Murders, unlawful imprisonment, confiscated property, and poverty exist because sinful rulers use their power for personal gain. Human depravity ensures, as the historian Lord Acton wrote, "that absolute power corrupts absolutely." But corruption does not necessarily follow absolute power. For instance, we know that God reigns with all power today yet without corruption. "God is light, and in him is no darkness at all" (I John 1:5).

Anarchy—Although anarchy is technically a lack of government, it needs to be discussed under this section. **Anarchy,** according to the Oxford English Dictionary, is an "absence of government; a state of lawlessness due to the absence or inefficiency of the supreme power." To the anarchist, complete freedom (total lack of restraint) is ideal; therefore, any government, including a democratic government, is an imposition and an unnecessary evil. Anarchy's underlying theory is that people do not need a superior force to ensure that they live together peacefully. In fact, April Carter wrote in her book *The Political Theory of Anarchism,* "Society may create the kind of individuals who have strongly internalized values and can live co-operatively and freely without the threat of force." In contrast, Thomas Hobbes, a seventeenth-century philosopher, asserted that without government men would continually fight one another and that their lives would be "nasty, brutish, and short."

Although the idea of men living together peacefully in complete freedom sounds great, the Bible teaches that this will never be the case because man is inherently sinful. Jeremiah 17:9 says, "The heart is deceitful above all things, and desperately wicked: who can know it?" Paul wrote in Ephesians 2:3 that we are all "the children of wrath." Also, since God ordained human government (Rom. 13:1–4), the anarchists belief that government is evil attacks God's wisdom and goodness. No matter how good the theory sounds, the Christian must reject it because its bases are contrary to Scripture.

Somali gunmen in Mogadishu, 1992

A modern example of anarchy is Somalia. War and strife in the past few decades have decimated the country politically and economically. Because of bitter fighting between tribal factions, the country has no functioning government. Bands of heavily armed citizens are free to engage in bloody conflicts.

Relationship Between Government Levels

Another way to understand government is to examine how the different levels of government relate to one another. Are the different levels of government closely or loosely related? A variety of answers to this question can be found in the following systems: unitary, federal, and confederate governments.

Unitary Governments—In the **unitary system,** governmental power resides in the central government, but unlike a dictatorship, it receives all of its power from the people. Once the central  government has been established, it creates local units to help administer government. Since these units exist by the central government's authority, they can theoretically be disbanded if the central government considers them no longer necessary. The unitary system is the most commonly used form of government today and is found in Great Britain, France, Japan, and Israel.

Federal Governments—**Federalism** divides a nation's power among national, regional, and local governments. (Different governments simultaneously asserting authority on the people is also called federalism.) In one situation, local government might exert more influence, while in another the national government might be more influential. A constitution rules the nation's levels of government, delegating to each the powers it is to exercise. A benefit of the federal system is that it guards against tyranny by separating the powers of the government, but this separation also impedes the efficient working of the national government. Federalism works well in large countries consisting of people with differing goals and needs. The national government meets the nation's needs as a whole, but the regional governments meet the needs of specific groups. The United States, Brazil, and India are modern examples of governments that divide power between national and regional governments.

Confederate Governments—The final category is the confederate form of government. A **confederate government** is one in which the regional governments retain supremacy and delegate few tasks to the national government. The national government has few or no powers, and the powers it has are exercised only by permission of the states. The Articles of Confederation established a confederate government in early American history. Another example is the Confederate States of America, which was established in 1861. The twenty-five countries that have joined the European Union (EU) provide a good example of a modern confederacy. Each member country retains its individual sovereignty while loosely combining to promote integration in European economics and politics. For example, the EU issued a new currency called the euro to be used by its members. However, each country was free to participate or not. The United Kingdom, Sweden, and Denmark chose not to use the new currency.

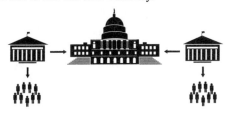

Electing the Executive

The third means of categorizing governments is analyzing the relationship between the legislative (law-making) and executive (law-enforcing) branches. Is the executive branch an independent branch of the government, or is it an extension of the legislative branch? Is the executive head elected by the people or by the legislature? These questions distinguish two categories concerning the legislative and executive branches.

Presidential System—In the **presidential system,** the people directly elect the president, the head of the executive branch, independently of the legislative branch. This practice is normal to American citizens but is in the minority worldwide. One

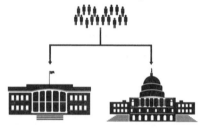

benefit of this system is the president's accountability to the people. Another is the executive branch's ability to operate independently from the legislative branch. There are drawbacks as well. One drawback is inefficiency. Differences in policy between the branches can create stalemates that slow down or even stop the governing process.

Parliamentary System—The **parliamentary system** is more widely practiced worldwide than the presidential. In this system the legislative and executive branches are inseparably linked.

The parliamentary system differs from the presidential system in that the people elect their representatives (called members of Parliament, or MPs) by voting. The candidate in each district whose party wins the most votes becomes the representative for that district. The major-ity party in the legislature then appoints the executive head, the prime minister, who establishes a cabinet to run the affairs of the country. While this system enables the executive and legislative branches to work together efficiently, some dangers exist. Without independence, the executive branch is susceptible to domination by the legislative branch. The possibilities for tyranny also increase with the close relationship between the branches that both make and enforce the nation's laws. Great Britain, France, Japan, and Indonesia are examples of this type of government.

Section Review

1. What three broad categories do scholars use to classify governments?
2. How do a pure democracy and a republic differ?
3. On what do dictatorships rely for power?
4. Which types of government described in this section best describe the United States?
5. Who chooses the executive head in the parliamentary system?

Euros

IN COMPARISON

Parliamentary vs. Congressional Systems in Canada and the United States

In democracies around the world parliamentary systems are common. Because the majority party or a coalition of parties chooses the prime minister, Parliament is the focal point for the organization and function of the government. The American congressional system is quite different. Members of Congress are elected separately from the president, and the members of the majority party in the House and Senate simply choose leaders for those bodies. Often in recent decades, the party of the president and the majority parties in Congress have been different.

In Canada, and in other nations with a parliamentary system, the Parliament's power has declined recently and the prime minister's power has increased. For example, Parliament does not create legislation but reacts to what the prime minister proposes. Often it merely ratifies what the prime minister wants. Since he is the head of the majority party and that party controls Parliament, proceedings are more efficient. Nonetheless, Parliament does have important functions. Parliament can reflect the public's views when it debates various issues. It also can address the concerns of the constituents. It can monitor the actions of the prime minister and investigate any wrongdoing. Parliament's ultimate show of power would be a "no confidence" vote.

Because of the weakness of Parliament, some in Canada want to adopt the American congressional system. Many see the individual American member of Congress or senator as more powerful because he or she can go against the president or party if the party's ideology is in conflict with the congressman's own or with that of the constituents. American party discipline is weak. The downside for the American congressional model is that members of Congress can be so powerful that "gridlock," or a stalemate, may occur.

Fixed terms in office, some Canadians feel, is another advantage of the congressional system. Legislators know when they will face the voters in their state or district, and they are elected independently from the president. Ultimately they must please their voters, not the president. In the parliamentary system the majority party usually schedules elections at a time advantageous to it, although there is a limit to the number of years they can wait.

Some Americans envy the Canadian parliamentary system because its "no-confidence" provision is a more practical method for ousting an executive. Impeachment in the American model is such an extreme measure that the two presidents who have been impeached for offenses less than "treason, bribery, or other high crimes and misdemeanors" have survived the process, though severely damaged. Take, for example, the 1999 impeachment of Bill Clinton.

Which system is better? The congressional system may spread power more evenly in the national government while the parliamentary one is more efficient. On the other hand, congressional government parties are weak and may suffer gridlock; while Parliament, the prime minister, and the majority party dominate the parliamentary system. The two systems are fundamentally different, and one envying the other is just a case of the "grass being greener on the other side of the fence."

II. American Government

The remainder of this chapter will introduce the different levels of American government: the national, state, and local levels.

National Government

The heart of American government is the Constitution. It limits the national government's authority by assigning it specific **delegated powers** (discussed in Chapter 7). To the national government the founders wisely gave those powers that would allow it to effectively serve the country.

Montesquieu

When Madison defended separation of powers between the legislative and executive branches of government, his ultimate source was *The Spirit of Laws* (1748), written by Charles-Louis de Secondat, Baron de Montesquieu (1689–1755), a French aristocrat. Wealthy enough to devote himself to intellectual pursuits, Montesquieu traveled around Europe (and in the highest political circles) investigating the nature of men and their governments. Learning was his passion. Montesquieu once said that study was a "sovereign remedy against the worries of life. I have never had a care that an hour's reading could not dispel."

Montesquieu was no advocate of democracy or revolution, but he was a powerful critic of absolute monarchy. He believed that a legislature composed of educated aristocrats with a genuine interest in serving the people—men like himself—could establish honest and efficient government. Montesquieu's ideas were well received in his own day and became even more influential during the late eighteenth century. The framers of the American Constitution were enthusiastic readers of *The Spirit of Laws*.

Although Montesquieu had little interest in religion, he was not an aggressive opponent of Christianity or the Catholic Church as were many of his intellectual contemporaries such as Voltaire and Diderot. He once wrote, "What a wonderful thing is the Christian religion! It seems to aim only at happiness in a future life, and yet it secures our happiness in this life also."

The national government is divided into three branches: the legislative, executive, and judicial. This separation serves to limit the government's power and protect the freedom of the people. Each branch exercises specific powers and contributes to the government's overall operation.

Legislative Branch—The legislative branch makes the nation's laws. Of the three branches, it has the closest ties to the people because it is elected directly by the people. The legislative branch is divided into two houses, collectively called **Congress.** The lower house is called the **House of Representatives,** and the higher house is called the **Senate.**

Executive Branch—The executive branch enforces the nation's laws. The **president** is the chief executive officer and is therefore the head of the executive branch. The president chooses people to head the various government departments. These officials (known collectively as the cabinet) along with the vice president, the Executive Office of the President, and different agencies help the president execute the laws passed by the legislative branch.

Judicial Branch—The judicial branch interprets the nation's laws. It judges whether the acts and laws of the other two branches are constitutional. It also interprets how the laws should be applied. The Constitution provides for a **Supreme Court** to be the highest court of the land, the final judge for all questions concerning American laws. The national government has also created inferior courts to lighten the caseload for the Supreme Court.

Following chapters will discuss each branch in greater detail. Although this book as a whole focuses on the national government, the remainder of this chapter will introduce the state and local levels of government to give a proper understanding of America's federal government system.

State Government

State governments make up the second part of American federalism. The American government consists of fifty states joined together for the common good of all.

Becoming a State

Since its beginning, the United States has added thirty-seven states to the original thirteen colonies. How did those states enter the Union? What would a territory need to do if it wanted to be admitted into the Union as a state?

The Northwest Ordinance of 1787 required that a prospective state have a minimum population of sixty thousand people and that its government and constitution be republican in nature. If the area desired statehood, its lawmakers had to petition the United States Congress for admission into the Union. If Congress approved, it would issue an order, called an enabling act, directing the petitioning group's lawmakers to write a constitution for the proposed state, which would be put before the people for a popular vote. If the people approved the proposed constitution, the lawmakers then presented it to Congress for consideration. If Congress approved the constitution, it would pass an act of admission organizing the area into a state. All that remained was the president's signature, and a new state would be added to the Union.

Is there a possibility for any new states to be added to the United States now? At the moment, the United States possesses five territories with sufficient population: Puerto Rico, the Northern Mariana Islands, Guam, American Samoa, and the Virgin Islands. Puerto Rico made the most recent bid for statehood in 1993, but the move was rejected in a popular vote. The debate for Puerto Rico's statehood still rages, making a fifty-first state very possible.

State Powers—According to the Constitution, the states retain powers not delegated to the national government or prohibited to the states. States are also limited by their own constitutions as to what powers they might exercise. The fifty states that make up the United States of America exist of their own right and practice powers that are sometimes distinct from and sometimes shared by the national government.

Reserved Powers   The Constitution protects the states' powers from federal domination in the Tenth Amendment. There the Constitution declares that

Paris Mountain State Park, Greenville, S.C.

all powers not granted to the national government nor prohibited to the states are reserved to the states or the people. The powers granted to the states by this amendment are extensive; however, these powers are necessary since it is the state and local governments that provide the majority of services to the people. The Constitution leaves to the states the responsibility and power to police, to educate, to make land-use laws, and to require licensing for professionals. These are just a few of the powers that states possess.

Prohibited Powers   The Constitution limits the states' powers in order to preserve the national government's powers. The Constitution lists these restrictions in Article I, Section 10, and in the

Amendments Restricting State Powers	
The Fourteenth Amendment	Citizenship; every citizen of the United States enjoys the rights and privileges of citizenship.
The Fifteenth Amendment	African American voting rights
The Nineteenth Amendment	Women's suffrage
The Twenty-fourth Amendment	No poll tax
The Twenty-sixth Amendment	Voting age lowered to eighteen

Fourteenth, Fifteenth, Nineteenth, Twenty-fourth, and Twenty-sixth Amendments. States may not coin money or enter into any binding agreements with other states or nations. States may not raise and sustain an army or navy during times of peace; nor may they lay duties or levies on imports or exports. The amendments prohibit states from passing laws that would violate the privileges of United States citizens.

Separation of Powers—The states' systems of governments are separated, having the same branches as the national government: legislative, executive, and judicial.

Norris Chamber, Nebraska legislative building

Legislative Branch   Every state has a legislative branch responsible for passing that state's laws. State laws are different from national laws passed by Congress. In every state except Nebraska, the legislature is **bicameral;** that is, the legislature has two separate houses. Nebraska's legislature is **unicameral,** made up of one house. The names of the different houses differ from state to state, but the distinction of higher and lower houses remains the same. Generally, the state legislatures possess all powers not specifically delegated to the executive and judicial branches or prohibited by the state or national constitutions. More specifically, the state legislatures exercise the powers to tax, maintain public schools, regulate business, and provide police protection as well as many more services necessary for the well-being of the state. State legislatures can also approve gubernatorial appointments, impeach state officials, and propose amendments to the state constitution.

Executive Branch   The chief officer of the executive branch is the **governor.** He is directly elected by the people of the state and is responsible for administering the state government and enforcing state laws. The governor is usually assisted by a lieutenant governor, who functions somewhat like the vice president of the United States.

The governor can appoint and fire his assistants in the executive branch, make budgets, and supervise the executive branch's staff, and he is the commander in chief of the state militia. He has the power to veto, call special sessions of the state legislature, and suggest legislation. The governor's judicial powers are the ability to pardon, commute sentences, issue reprieves, and parole. The governor also must receive official visitors, dedicate new buildings and parks, and deliver speeches to different state organizations.

Judicial Branch   The judicial branch of the state is responsible for interpreting the law and judging criminal cases. The highest state court is a supreme court, which is assisted by lower courts. Judges are chosen by popular election or appointed by the legislature or the governor. Legislative appointment

Florida State Supreme Court building

is the least often used method, while popular election and appointment by the governor are used evenly throughout the states. There have been many arguments about which method is better, but generally appointment by the governor is considered better since the most popular person might not be the best qualified.

Local Governments

Local government is the most familiar and observable level of government for most people since the actions of local government overtly affect citizens each day. Contrary to popular conception, local governments are not prescribed in the Constitution as the basic building blocks of American government. The Constitution provides for a federal government consisting of national and state governments, leaving states responsible for establishing local governments. Local governments usually exist as counties and municipalities.

Counties—States create county governments to assist in administering the state laws and policies. (These local divisions are called boroughs in Alaska and parishes in Louisiana.)

Citizens of the county elect, by popular vote, a governing board to administer the county's business. The governing board exercises both executive and legislative powers and is called either a board

of commissioners or a board of supervisors. The board of commissioners is more common and usually consists of three to five members, while the board of supervisors normally consists of between fifteen and eighty members. These members are elected from the different divisions of the county called **townships.** (Note that townships in the Midwest are geographic units of thirty-five or thirty-six square miles. They may or may not be political units.)

Although both the state and national constitutions restrict the powers of the county governments, counties are still responsible for a wide variety of services. They can tax, pass health and zoning ordinances, manage welfare, oversee county roads, maintain county prison systems, and appoint certain county officers. The county government is also responsible for education. County governments include various boards and commissions to accomplish the various responsibilities, and elected officers with countywide jurisdiction. The workers on these boards perform the day-to-day business of the county.

Special Districts

The past few decades have seen a proliferation of **special districts** that provide specific government functions on the local level. These are entities independent of both the county and the city that meet policing, sewage, transportation, or educational needs not met or unable to be met by the local governments. For the most part, special districts meet the needs of rural areas and suburbs. An elected board provides the government necessary for proper execution of a special district's responsibilities. Either taxes or fees pay for the services rendered by the special district.

Municipality—Municipalities are urban, local systems of government that include cities, villages, and towns. Cities are the largest of these and will be discussed as representative of the others. Villages and towns operate on a smaller scale and with less power than do the city governments, but they are very similar.

States have control over the creation and existence of cities. For a city government to legally exist, the state must establish it as a legal body through a process called **incorporation.** When the population of an area reaches a certain level, the citizens of that area are eligible to begin the process. The state requires that the citizens gather signatures, submit the petition, and then hold a vote so that all the citizens in the proposed city can have a voice in the decision. After this process is completed, the state issues the new city's charter. The **charter** gives the city a name and serves as its constitution. States do not, however, create the administrative aspects of city governments. Citizens of the city form various administrative bodies based on their needs and wants.

The city government provides many services for its citizens, such as a police force, fire department, public welfare, public transportation, and public utilities. Modern cities have a council, a mayor, or a city manager as the executive head of the government.

Section Review

1. List the three levels of American government.
2. List the three branches of the national government.
3. What powers are reserved to the states?
4. Explain the responsibilities of each branch of a state's government.
5. What are the different levels of local government?

Chapter Review

Terms

popular government
direct democracy
indirect democracy
republic
dictatorship
totalitarianism
autocracy
oligarchy
anarchy

unitary system
federalism
confederate government
presidential system
parliamentary system
delegated powers
Congress
House of Representatives
Senate

president
Supreme Court
bicameral
unicameral
governor
townships
special districts
incorporation
charter

Content Questions

1. List the benefits and drawbacks of the presidential system.

2. Why did America's founders choose the federal system of government?

3. Why would a direct democracy not be appropriate for the United States?

4. What are the two forms of dictatorship?

5. What are the two types of boards most commonly used for county governments?

6. Which local government systems are considered municipalities?

Application Questions

1. Consider the statement "Power corrupts, and absolute power corrupts absolutely." What does this statement reveal about human nature? Do you agree or disagree with the statement? Defend your answer.

2. Contrast the presidential and parliamentary systems of government. If you were establishing a government, which would you choose? Why?

3. Could the Internet make direct democracy in the United States possible? Defend your answer. Assess the dangers and benefits of Internet voting.

THE MEANING OF DEMOCRACY

Ruins of the Parthenon in Athens, Greece

Democracy is a product of the past and the present, a melding of people and politics, of promise as well as problems. The ancient Greeks, who first practiced democracy, also coined the term. The Athenian statesman Pericles declared, "Our constitution is named a *democracy* because it is in the hands not of the few, but of the many." He added, "Our government is not copied from those of our neighbors: we are an example to them rather than they to us." Today, after nearly twenty-five centuries, democracy remains an example to its neighbors. It is an example, not of perfect government but of participatory government. And to those living under repressive regimes, democracy is an example of a government in which citizens have a voice in how they shall be ruled. As we shall see, the word *democracy* has come to mean many things, and the system is certainly not without its critics. Being a government of imperfect humans, democracy has its share of difficulties. Yet with all its shortcomings, democracy under the rule of law remains the form of government in which liberty, equality, and individualism find their best blend. Democracy's spread in the twentieth century, coupled with communism's decline, has vindicated those who supported democratic principles against communism and tyranny.

Ruins of the Parthenon

I. History of Democracy

Democratic Developments

Although the Bible does not mandate popular government, popular government incorporates many biblical truths, such as the individual worth of man (Gen. 1:27) and his equality before God (Rom. 2:11). Moses told the Israelites that if they would select wise and understanding men, he would appoint them as rulers (Deut. 1:13). Likewise, before David and Jehoiada were anointed kings, each made a covenant with his people (II Sam. 5:3, II Kings 11:17).

The word "democracy," often used to describe popular government, comes from two Greek words, *demos* (the people) and *kratos* (authority or government). Therefore, **democracy** means "government by the people."

Greeks who lived in the city-state of Athens during the fifth and fourth centuries B.C. created the first society that claimed to be a "government by the people." Even so, Athenian democracy excluded most of its population, including females, slaves, and foreign residents. Furthermore, Athens was usually directed by a small group of aristocrats—and was usually *mis*directed when it was not. Modern Americans would not consider the Athenian government democratic, but then Athenians would not consider the American government democratic either. In Athens, citizens were proud to exert their rule directly, not through elected representatives; and they probably worked harder at governing themselves than any group of people before or since. (A quorum of six thousand was customary. Athenians didn't count heads, but they would not vote unless the assembly area was obviously full.) A serious weakness of Athenian democracy was that the assembly's final say was often unchecked by established law. Another problem was that popular leaders called *demagogues* could manipulate the assembly with emotional speeches in order to achieve their own ends.

The Roman Republic also incorporated democratic principles into its system of government, which functioned remarkably well between the fifth and first centuries B.C. Although aristocratic families supervised the Roman Republic, popular assemblies elected the leaders and ratified important governmental decisions. Magistrates called *tribunes* were even charged to protect the rights of individuals against abuses by the powerful. Nevertheless, once Rome had conquered most of the lands that bordered the Mediterranean, the republic disappeared into an empire governed by autocrats and their armies. The framers of America's Constitution were well aware of popular governments in Greece and Rome, including their shortcomings, and *The Federalist Papers* are full of lessons drawn from classical history *(Federalist Nos. 6, 9, 18, 38, 63, 70)*.

Roman Forum

Greek and Roman Influence on the Lincoln Memorial

United States history indicates that Greece and Rome influenced American democracy, but their influence extends into aspects other than government. Greek and Roman culture made its mark in American symbolism and architecture as well. The Lincoln Memorial is a familiar example that well shows the influence both cultures have had in the United States.

Henry Bacon, the Lincoln Memorial's architect, deliberately designed the memorial to resemble the Parthenon, a Greek temple. He did so because he thought a memorial to the man who had saved democracy in the United States should take its design from a monument in democracy's birthplace. The memorial is 188 feet long, 118 feet wide, and 99 feet tall. The memorial has a colonnade of 36 Doric columns representing the 36 states existing during Lincoln's presidency. Each of the columns is 44 feet tall with a diameter of 7 feet 5 inches at the base. Bacon divided the memorial into three chambers, also patterned after the Parthenon. These features ably honor the man who did so much to preserve the Union.

Lincoln's statue rests in the central chamber and shows the Roman influence on American symbolism. The statue is nineteen feet tall and was made of twenty-eight separate pieces of marble. Daniel Chester French, the sculptor, desired to present Lincoln as a powerful war president. He used Roman symbols for power and authority to convey those characteristics. French patterned the chair Lincoln sits in after the Roman curule chair, which signified one holding a powerful position. The chair's arms are decorated with fasces, bundles of rods used to symbolize authority in ancient Rome.

The Lincoln Memorial provides a clear example of how Greek and Roman cultures have influenced the United States, not only in government, but in architecture and symbolism.

During the Middle Ages, aspects of popular government could still be found in the *communes,* or independent towns where the inhabitants found themselves outside the feudal system of lords and manors. Some of these communes survived (or were reestablished) in Italy during the Renaissance. The city-state of Florence even developed an ideology of republicanism based on the ideas from republican Rome. Nevertheless, Florence's theory

DOCUMENTS OF DEMOCRACY

Magna Carta: A.D. 1215

King John of England had squeezed the last shilling out of his subjects, yet he always seemed to be short of cash. The English king's foreign wars, castle construction projects, and mercenaries were expensive, and if trampling the feudal rights of his barons was what it took to pay for his pastimes, then so be it. John's barons thought otherwise, however. After the king's reputation was further diminished by his defeat in France in 1214, his barons met at Runnymede and forced him to set his seal to a list of demands that became known as the Magna Carta (the Great Charter). The Charter was primarily a document restoring the feudal rights of English barons, but it contained principles that caused it to later be heralded as a foundational document of constitutional government.

*First of all, it established the "law of the land" as superior to the demands of the king. In addition, it provided the basis for **due process,** that is, that certain legal procedures must be enforced to protect the rights of the accused.*

King John's consent to the Magna Carta lasted only two months. Pope Innocent III was only too happy to nullify the agreement after John appealed to him. In fact, John did not live long after that, for in the autumn of the next year (1216), following a meal of peaches and cider, he died suddenly. The Magna Carta's impact, though, continues to leave an enduring mark, especially through its constitutional descendants. The excerpts from the Magna Carta on these two pages represent the most pertinent sections.

John, by the grace of God King of England, Lord of Ireland, Duke of Normandy and Aquitaine, and Count of Anjou, to his archbishops, bishops, abbots, earls, barons, justices, foresters, sheriffs, stewards, servants, and to all his officials and loyal subjects, greeting.

(1) FIRST, THAT WE HAVE GRANTED TO GOD, and by this present charter have confirmed for us and our heirs in perpetuity, that the English Church shall be free, and shall have its rights undiminished, and its liberties unimpaired. That we wish this so to be observed, appears from the fact that of our own free will, before the outbreak of the present dispute between us and our barons, we granted and confirmed by charter the freedom of the Church's elections—a right reckoned to be of the greatest necessity and importance to it—and caused this to be confirmed by Pope Innocent III. This freedom we shall observe ourselves, and desire to be observed in good faith by our heirs in perpetuity.

TO ALL FREE MEN OF OUR KINGDOM we have also granted, for us and our heirs for ever, all the liberties written out below, to have and to keep for them and their heirs, of us and our heirs:

(17) Ordinary lawsuits shall not follow the royal court around, but shall be held in a fixed place.

(30) No sheriff, royal official, or other person shall take horses or carts for transport from any free man, without his consent.

(38) In future no official shall place a man on trial upon his own unsupported statement, without producing credible witnesses to the truth of it.

(39) No free man shall be seized or imprisoned, or stripped of his rights or possessions, or outlawed or exiled, or deprived of his standing in any other way, nor will we proceed with force against him, or send others to do so, except by the lawful judgement of his equals or by the law of the land.

(40) To no one will we sell, to no one deny or delay right or justice.

(45) We will appoint as justices, constables, sheriffs, or other officials, only men that know the law of the realm and are minded to keep it well.

(63) IT IS ACCORDINGLY OUR WISH AND COMMAND that the English Church shall be free, and that men in our kingdom shall have and keep all these liberties, rights, and concessions, well and peaceably in their fulness and entirety for them and their heirs, of us and our heirs, in all things and all places for ever.

of popular government was more impressive than its reality because the city was actually dominated by the Medici, a family of merchant princes.

Of much more importance for American democracy was the gradual development of popular government in England. Just why England had such an advantage over other European states is not completely clear. But England was an island, separated from almost constant warring on the European continent, and it was far from Rome, the seat of Catholicism. In their conflicts with the Church and other European states, English kings needed at least the appearance of popular approval more than other monarchs. However small its opportunity at first, the English Parliament clearly dominated its kings by the eighteenth century.

Because England has had such an important influence on the development of democracy in America, it is important to examine some foundational documents, including the Magna Carta (1215) and the English Bill of Rights (1689), which demonstrate the gradual rise of popular government.

The Magna Carta originally protected only the English nobility from the king's encroachments, but its principles laid the foundation for freedoms that would eventually extend to all Englishmen. The English Bill of Rights marks the beginning of a democratic government in England. After a taxing civil war, a failed commonwealth, and a heavy-handed King James II, the English invited William and Mary to become their monarchs. However, before William and Mary could ascend the throne,

DOCUMENTS OF DEMOCRACY

English Bill of Rights: A.D. 1689

The English Bill of Rights was the most important development in constitutional government since the thirteenth-century Magna Carta. The Bill of Rights reflected much of the thinking of John Locke, who held that government—in this case a monarchy—was responsible for protecting the lives and property of its citizens. If the king failed to meet his obligations, the people were justified in overthrowing him. During the next century, the English Bill of Rights, with its advocacy of limited government and personal liberty, would have an enormous impact on America's Declaration of Independence and Constitution.

Whereas the Lords Spiritual and Temporal, and Commons, assembled at Westminster, lawfully, fully, and freely representing all the estates of the people of this realm, did . . . present unto their Majesties . . . a certain declaration in writing . . . in the words following. . . .

Whereas the late King James II . . . did endeavor to subvert and extirpate the Protestant religion, and the laws and liberties of this kingdom . . .

[The king's actions] are utterly and directly contrary to the known laws and statutes, and freedom of this realm. . . .

And thereupon the said Lords Spiritual and Temporal, and Commons . . . being now assembled in a full and free representation of this nation . . . do in the first place (as their ancestors in like case have usually done), for the vindicating and asserting their ancient rights and liberties, declare:

1. That the pretended power of suspending of laws or the execution of laws by regal authority without consent of Parliament is illegal.
2. That the pretended power of dispensing with laws . . . as it hath been assumed . . . of late, is illegal.
3. That the commission for electing the late court . . . for ecclesiastical causes, and all other commissions and courts of like nature, are illegal and pernicious.
4. That levying money for or to the use of the Crown . . . without grant of Parliament . . . is illegal.
5. That it is the right of the subject to petition the king. . . .
6. That the raising or keeping a standing army within the kingdom in time of peace, unless it be with consent of Parliament, is against the law.
7. That the subjects which are Protestants may have arms for their defence suitable to their condition, and as allowed by law.
8. That elections of members of Parliament ought to be free.
9. That the freedom of speech, and debates or proceedings in Parliament, ought not to be impeached or questioned in any court or place out of Parliament.
10. That excessive bail ought not be required, nor excessive fines imposed; nor cruel and unusual punishment inflicted.
11. That jurors ought to be duly impanelled and returned, and jurors which pass upon men in trials for high treason ought to be freeholders.
12. That all grants and promises of fines and forfeitures of particular persons before conviction are illegal and void.
13. And that for redress of all grievances, and for the amending, strengthening, and preserving of the laws, Parliaments ought to be held frequently.

they had to agree to the English Bill of Rights, which limited the monarchy's power and asserted the people's rights. This event is known as England's Glorious Revolution of 1688 because it marked a major shift in political power.

The Founders' Contributions

The democratic developments discussed so far in this chapter influenced America's founding fathers greatly. They, in turn, made valuable contributions and innovations to democratic-republican government. Clearly, they were breaking new ground among the community of nations, many of which had been ruled for centuries by a succession of kings.

Modern Americans, perhaps, fail to appreciate the problems with which the founders grappled. The founders faced a situation that was, like a rose, both delicate and thorny. Striking a successful balance between rule by monarch and rule by mob was a daunting task, particularly since it was a pioneering effort. In addition, the founders had to struggle with difficult political questions, many of which had never before been answered or even asked.

Jefferson's View of Kings

The contempt that many of our founding fathers felt toward monarchy only strengthened their commitment to democratic ideals. In the following excerpt, Thomas Jefferson, who had

The practice of kings marrying only in the families of kings has been that of Europe for some centuries. Now, take any race of animals, confine them in idleness and inaction, whether in a sty, a stable or a state room, pamper them with high diet, . . . immerse them in sensualities, nourish their passions, let everything bend before them, and banish whatever might lead them to think, and in a few generations they become all body and no mind. . . . Such is the regimen in raising kings, and in this way they have gone on for centuries.

While in Europe, I often amused myself with contemplating the characters of the then reigning sovereigns of Europe. Louis the XVI was a fool, of my own knowledge, and in despite of the answers made for him at his trial. The King of Spain was a fool, and of Naples the same. They passed their lives in hunting, and dispatched two couriers a week, one thousand miles, to let each other know what game they had killed the preceding days. The King of Sardinia was a fool. All these were Bourbons. The Queen of Portugal, a Braganza, was an idiot by nature. And so was the King of Denmark. Their sons, as regents, exercised the powers of government. The King of Prussia, successor to the great Frederick, was a mere hog in body as well as in mind. Gustavus of Sweden and Joseph of Austria were really crazy, and George of England, you know, was in a strait waistcoat. . . . These animals become without mind and powerless; so will every hereditary monarch be after a few generations. And so endeth the book of kings, from all of whom the Lord deliver us.

The two major issues that the Constitutional framers confronted were, first, how to incorporate democratic ideas into the new American government, and second, how to make a democratic republic work over a vast territory.

Democratic Ideas—As we have seen already, many of America's early leaders feared direct democracy. They feared the instability of a government in which a majority could become little better than a mob—an easy prey for a tyrant. In addition, they distrusted the general public's ability to govern themselves directly, believing them to be too fickle and too prone to making snap decisions that could lead the government and the nation into disaster. This distrust grew out of concern that the masses might not possess wealth and property enough to provide incentive for stable government. In short, the great fault of democracy was that it could potentially degenerate into tyranny, the rule of many becoming the rule of one.

Direct Democracy	Majority rules through direct participation
Indirect Democracy	Majority rules through elected officials
Republic	Government of elected officials ruled by law.

Despite their opposition to democracy as a system, many of the founders were democratic in their thinking. Such democratic ideals as liberty and equality were eloquently set forth in the Declaration of Independence:

We hold these truths to be self-evident, that all Men are created equal, that they are endowed by their Creator with certain unalienable Rights, that among these are Life, Liberty and the pursuit of Happiness. That to secure these rights, Governments are instituted among Men, deriving their just powers from the consent of the governed.

The challenge that the founders undertook, then, was how to preserve these ideals in a working, stable government while avoiding the pitfalls of the past.

First of all, the founders recognized the source of the problem—man's sinful nature. The mob-rule tendency of direct democracy is the result of man's inclination to do wrong when he is not restrained—a problem that is only multiplied when individuals get together to form a majority.

In order to protect individual liberty and equality from the power of an unruly majority, the founders made the Constitution the key. Thomas Jefferson described the need for constitutional limits this way:

> Free government is founded on jealousy, not in confidence; it is jealousy and not confidence which prescribes limited constitutions, to bind those we are obligated to trust with power. In questions of power, let no more be heard of confidence in man but bind him down from mischief by the chains of the constitution.

The Declaration of Independence *by John Trumbull*

The Constitution limited both the government and the governed in their access to power. The government was limited by its division into three branches: the legislative, executive, and judicial. In addition, each branch was checked by the other branches so that no department took more than its share of power. The government was also limited in its power over its citizens by the **Bill of Rights.** The Bill of Rights, or the first ten amendments to the Constitution, embodied the democratic ideals of liberty and equality by protecting the freedom of all citizens to speak, assemble, and worship without government intrusion.

Although the Constitution limited the power of government, it also limited the power of the governed by restricting their influence on the national level. Reflecting the founders' belief that it was unwise to entrust the general public with too much direct control over government, the Constitution made the House of Representatives the only body elected directly by the people. Other top officials, including the president, were elected indirectly by the people. Senators, for example, were initially elected by their respective state legislatures rather than by a straight vote from their constituents. Likewise the president was elected through the indirect means of the **electoral college.** Under this constitutional provision (Article II, Section 1), each state has a number of electors equal to the state's representation in Congress. For example, Virginia currently has eleven representatives in the

House of Representatives and two senators, giving it a total of thirteen electoral votes. In general, all the electoral votes from a state go to the candidate who receives the majority of popular votes from that state.

Geography—Neither a republic nor a direct democracy had ever been successful over a large geographic area. Eighteenth-century Enlightenment thinkers, such as Rousseau and Voltaire, correctly observed that direct democracy was practiced only on a very small scale. Republics also, such as those in Renaissance Italy, had survived only in small settings. It was widely believed that successful self-government required a population of similar self-interests. Participatory government, therefore, seemed unlikely in a country as diverse and as large as the United States. The founders, however, had other ideas about how to unite thirteen states into a national republic while preserving democratic ideals.

First, self-government by representation was established. This republican practice was not a new thing, but in the United States it was established for the first time on a large, national scale based on state population.

Representation provides a degree of self-governing by allowing citizens to choose their leaders. At the same time it solves the problems of time and space that come with direct democracy on a large scale. Imagine what it would be like if all the citizens of the United States had to leave their jobs and families to go to Washington, D.C., to vote on laws—factories would shut down, crops would be left untended, and society in general (as well as the traffic in and around the capital) would come to a standstill. Although the very idea sounds ludicrous, it emphasizes the importance of representation in our system of government.

Second, the founders instituted **federalism,** the division and distribution of governmental power into national and state levels. The federal system forged at the Constitutional Convention permitted democratic practices of local government and protected democratic principles of liberty and equality—all under the umbrella of a republican national government.

Democracy or Republic?

Was the United States founded as a democracy or a republic? That question still lingers over two hundred years after this country's establishment. Part of the difficulty lies in the way the founders used the terms. As seen before, the founders did not think highly of democracy. They also held different views of what a democracy or a republic was. James Madison, for example, defined a republic as "a government in which the scheme of representation takes place." In *Federalist No.10,* he compared the two forms and defined democracy as "a society consisting of a small number of citizens, who assemble and administer the government in person." To Madison, a democracy was limited to a direct democracy while a republic was a representative democracy. Jefferson, however, defined a republic as a "government by its citizens in mass, acting directly and personally according to rules established

by the majority." That definition seems to be the same as direct democracy. Yet another definition is offered by John Adams: "There is no good government but what is Republican . . . because the very definition of a Republic, is 'an Empire of Laws, and not of men.'"

What then did the founders mean when they wrote that the "United States shall guarantee to every state in this union a republican form of government" (Article IV, Section 4)? The answer seems to lie in what the founders attempted to avoid. As noted before, the founders distrusted pure democracy because it had so often degenerated into tyranny. They feared that pure democracy would lead to a tyranny of an even worse nature than in England: tyranny of the majority. Jefferson expressed this fear when he wrote, "One hundred and seventy-three despots would surely be as oppressive as one." The founders established a republican form of government to circumvent the danger of mob rule. So, the difference between a democracy and a republic could not have been merely the representative scheme as defined by Madison. The difference was that the founders restrained mob rule through a written constitution and by removing government operations from the direct control of the majority. The founders' very purpose to protect against oppression by the majority proves that the initial government was not a democracy but a representative republic ruled by a constitution and based on democratic principles.

The Constitutional framers gave us a representative self-government that bridged distances and shared power with citizens on the local level. However, constitutional provisions and unfolding events over the next two centuries would actually increase the democratization of the republic.

Section Review

1. Where was the first significant example of pure democracy practiced?

2. Is the United States a democracy or a republic? Explain your answer.

3. What two major questions confronted the framers of the U.S. Constitution?

4. What characteristic of mankind eventually destroys direct democracy?

5. What key policies did the founders include in the Constitution to ensure that the majority would not tyrannize the minority?

6. What two innovations were adopted in the Constitution in order to overcome the geographic limitations of a democracy?

II. Characteristics of Democracy

Ask almost anyone on the street what *democracy* means, and you are likely to hear a variety of positive, patriotic, but vague descriptors, "full of sound and fury" but signifying little in the way of a clear definition. *Democracy* is a word that is much in vogue in the world. Even communist leaders in states such as China and North Korea refer to their countries as democracies, but any citizen bold enough to criticize their "government by the people" is sentenced to hard labor in prison.

Communist states refer to themselves as *economic* democracies because citizens supposedly enjoy economic equality, at least by the state's definition of equality. However, democracy has, since the days of Pericles, been understood as a *political* system, not an economic one. Every democracy will have its own distinctive features given the particular influences in the country where it develops. Democracy in the United States differs on specific practices from democracy in Canada, which in turn differs on specifics from democracy in Japan. Yet all of these are political systems that share certain essential characteristics, making them democracies in the traditional sense.

Majority Rule

It has been said that "democracy is the recurrent suspicion that more than half of the people are right more than half the time." This tongue-in-cheek definition underscores an important characteristic of democracy: the principle of **majority rule,** that is, a numerical majority of the electorate makes decisions that are binding upon the entire electorate. There are in a democratic republic two kinds of majorities: a **popular majority** and a **representative majority.** A popular majority consists of the majority of all citizens, or at least of all the voters that participate in their government through free elections. A representative majority is a majority of elected officials, such as members of Congress. There may in fact be a great gulf between the will of the popular majority and that of the representative majority. For example, a July 1999 Gallup/CNN/*USA Today* poll found that 70 percent of those surveyed favored prayer in public schools, yet a prayer amendment has consistently been thwarted by a majority in Congress.

The representative majority is, therefore, not necessarily representative. Because representatives may not know what the popular will is on every given issue, they must make decisions based on the best information available. Furthermore, there are times when representatives must make decisions that are in the best interest of the nation even though a popular majority may not agree. Yet if a representative is perceived as having consistently thwarted the will of his constituents, the voters can register their complaint at the ballot box and that congressman may be looking for another job.

The principle of majority rule has been criticized for being potentially repressive to the rights and opinions of the minority. One question understandably arises concerning majority rule: Why should 51 percent of the people be able to impose their will on 49 percent of the people? We will answer this question by making several observations.

Electing A Representative Majority

Why do the processes for electing a representative government differ in the United States and Denmark (both being democratic countries)? If both are seeking the majority's will, then should not the process for finding it be the same? The fact is that there are several systems used by democratic societies to elect representation, and each has its advantages as well as its disadvantages. These several systems can be reduced to two general categories: Majority-Plurality Representation and Proportional Representation.

Electoral Systems

Majority-Plurality Representation—This electoral system awards the position to the candidate that wins the highest percentage of votes even if he lacks the majority. This system is also called the first-past-the-post system (FPTP) because it is often likened to a horse race since the candidate with the highest percentage wins. For example, if candidate A wins 42 percent of the votes, candidate B 36 percent, and candidate C 12, then candidate A wins the seat even though he did not obtain the majority of the votes. FPTP is often criticized because it does not fairly represent the people's will. For example, in a vote to fill one hundred seats in legislature, party A wins 59 percent and party B wins 41 percent of the votes. In this system, it is possible for party A to win 100 percent of the legislative seats if the percentage of voters is equally distributed throughout the districts. If in every district 59 percent of the people supported party A while only 41 percent supported party B, then party A

would gain every seat even though it only had 59 percent of the vote.

Majority-Plurality Representation
Advantages
1. Condenses the voter's choices to two, making the voting process easier
2. Handicaps third parties, thus providing a more efficient and stable government
Disadvantages
1. Makes it possible for a party to gain a higher percentage of seats in legislature than the percentage of votes it received
2. Limits the minority voters' opportunities to influence the government

Proportional Representation
Advantages
1. Gives minority parties a greater voice in the legislature
2. More accurately represents the citizens' will
Disadvantages
1. Promotes multiple parties, thus leading to less efficient and less stable government
2. Provides a potentially confusing list of slightly differing candidates for the citizenry to choose from

Proportional Representation—In this system, the number of seats won by a party equals the percentage of voters who supported it. So in a legislature of one hundred seats, 53 percent of the votes would give a party 53 seats. This system works well in countries with multiple parties because each segment of society would earn places in the legislature reflective of their constituency.

First of all, majority rule provides a better approach to governance than its alternative—unanimity, which requires total agreement before action can be taken. Unanimity creates a much greater problem than the majority principle since

Party A won 59% of the votes and all 9 congressional seats.
Party B won 41% of the votes and zero congressional seats.

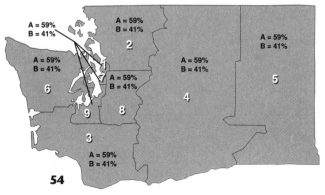

one negative vote is enough to stop a proposal regardless of how widely it is supported. Unanimity in effect makes a "majority" of one. This was one of the chief flaws of the United States government under the Articles of Confederation (1776–1789). Amending the articles required the unanimous consent of the states, which meant that one state could thwart the demands of all the rest.

Second, the majority is not a fixed, well-defined group. A citizen may vote with the majority on one issue and find himself in the minority on the next. This means that in a **pluralistic society,** where differing opinions and parties exist freely, the strength of a majority is limited because of the fluid nature of pluralism.

Third, in a successful democracy, majority rule must take into account minority rights. The rule of law must limit the power of the majority so that, to cite an extreme example, the majority is not permitted to enslave the minority as in the case of the Jews in Nazi Germany. James Madison pointed out in *Federalist No. 10,*

> Complaints are everywhere heard from our most considerate and virtuous citizens, equally the friends of public and private faith, and of public and personal liberty, that our governments are too unstable, that the public good is disregarded in the conflicts of rival parties, and that measures are too often decided, not according to the rules of justice and the rights of the minor party, but by the superior force of an interested and overbearing majority.

In the United States, the rights of the minority are protected by the Constitution. The Constitution offers control and stability in dealing with the issue of rival factions. It is also important that the minority as well as the majority respect the law. If a minority faction loses at the polls or its representatives fail to get their interests translated into laws, they must not try to overthrow the government by unlawful means.

Presidential inaugurations provide perhaps the best positive example of this principle. In 2000, Vice President Al Gore and George W. Bush squared off for the Oval Office. The election was highly controversial. Mr. Bush was not declared president until December because of contested ballot counts in Florida, but in January 2001 Bush took the oath of office. Standing near his predecessor, President Clinton (of the opposing party), he recited the oath, and with the concluding petition "so help me God," all the power of the presidency was transferred to him. Americans generally take the peacefulness of their inaugurations for granted, yet in many countries bitter and bloody power

President Bush being sworn in as the forty-third president of the United States

feuds between majority and minority factions surround leadership transitions.

Finally, the majority principle must be accompanied by other democratic principles. Democracy does not consist only of majority rule—that would more nearly define *mobocracy.* There must also be present both the principle of individual equality under the law and the freedom of political action by which the minority may legitimately confront and even become the majority.

Equality

The second democratic principle is equality. In one of the most potent political statements ever penned, Jefferson declared, "We hold these truths to be self-evident: That all men are created equal."

The equality of men was chief among Jefferson's self-evident truths. Yet what is equally self-evident is that Jefferson was not referring to absolute equality. All people differ from each other in various physical, social, financial, educational, and cultural ways. God has created each of us with unique characteristics of ability, personality, and background. Christians have a special place of service since God has molded their lives for His glory. The Scripture teaches that this is true concerning even our physical limitations (John 9:1–3). Clearly, absolute equality is absolutely impossible. The democratic principle of **equality** means *political* equality, or legal equality, its chief characteristics being equality of justice and equality of the franchise (vote).

Equality under the law was what the framers of the Declaration of Independence and the Constitution had in mind. Every citizen, regardless of his station in life, would enjoy constitutional guarantees of his liberty. Jefferson defined this chief characteristic of political equality in his first inaugural address:

> It is proper that you should understand what I deem the essential principles of our Government . . . equal and exact justice to all men, of whatever state or persuasion, religious or political; . . . freedom of religion, freedom of the press; freedom of person under the protection of the habeas corpus.

In fact, justice cannot exist apart from equality. The law must be blind to a person's name, income, and social status and must provide all—whether presidents or paupers—with equal protection and enforcement of the law.

Voting has also become an important aspect of political equality. Although the matter was not as important to the Constitutional framers as guarantees of justice, their pioneering effort provided an essential foundation for the franchise. Our founders forged a democratic republic in a world of nations headed by royalty and structured by birth and rank. Equality was a driving force for our forefathers; it broke down barriers of social caste and gave Americans a standing before kings and princes that did not require so much as a curtsy. Yet, as we have seen, political equality in voting was a *growing* reality in America. Restrictions of race, sex, and income were gradually lifted, so that today all adult citizens enjoy the equality of the ballot.

Finally, equality of opportunity is important to democracy. Equal opportunity ensures that no one is restricted from educational, occupational, or political opportunities based on race, religion, or sex.

Liberty

Liberty is a popular word that enjoys a wide circulation. America has the Liberty Bell, the Statue of Liberty, and over thirty towns and counties named Liberty. During World War I, when Americans tried to remove everything German from their vocabulary, they naturally reached for one of their favorite words to fill the gap: hamburgers became Liberty burgers, German Shepherds became Liberty dogs, and German measles was referred to as Liberty measles (also known as patriotic spots). Liberty, though, is much more than a popular word; it is a key term in our political vocabulary and a fundamental characteristic of our democratic system.

Liberty involves personal and political freedom, both of which are embodied in the Declaration of Independence, the Constitution, and the Bill of Rights. Personal liberties such as freedom of conscience, freedom of association, and freedom of expression provide not only the cherished right to worship and serve God openly, but also the opportunity for political associations and the expressing of opinions. Political liberty involves the right to vote, campaign, and hold elective office. In short, it is the freedom to influence the government through any legitimate means available.

56

Both liberty and equality are closely linked in our democratic system. However, current trends in America have shifted the meaning of equality from equality before the law to mean equality in wealth and talent at the expense of personal liberty. While equality provides an open society in which personal liberty may flourish, an overemphasis on equality can actually infringe upon personal freedom. An example of this imbalance is Affirmative Action (a program seeking to rectify past discrimination by increasing opportunities for minorities in areas such as education and occupation). Although Affirmative Action seeks to accomplish worthy goals, its racial quotas limit the employer's liberty to hire whoever he thinks best fills the available position and the educational administrator's liberty to accept those who are best qualified regardless of race or sex. Equality and liberty must co-exist on the same level in order for political, social, and economic opportunity to be possible. Implementation of that truth has contributed much to the growth and success of our republic.

Necessity of Compromise

The fourth democratic principle is the necessity of compromise. This principle most likely causes uneasiness in Christians' minds because of the negative connotation associated with it, but in a popular government compromise is permissible if not necessary because there will be as many opinions as there are voters. Some opinions will agree, some will differ slightly, and some will completely oppose other opinions. Without compromise, opposing opinions could hamper and even stop a democracy's legislative processes. Compromise on methods and amoral issues provides a way for each differing opinion to accomplish its most important objectives without causing a deadlock in legislation. This is the genius of majority rule—it is the best way for every citizen to take part equally in the government, even if his cause loses. For a democracy to operate smoothly, differing factions must be willing to compromise on the nonessentials.

As beneficial as compromises are to democracy, they should never compromise the truth or God's law. While seeking to find a balance that best represents the majority's wishes, the Christian politician cannot overlook God's thoughts concerning murder, abortion, homosexuality, and economics even if popular opinion demands so. The Christian, like Peter, must say that he will obey God rather than compromise to accommodate men's desires (Acts 5:29). Christians involved in government need special wisdom to discern what can be compromised and what cannot. Understanding that compromising God's laws is not an option, the Christian should not shrink from compromising on issues that do not contradict God's Word. It is that type of compromise that allows democracies to function and to represent the majority's wishes.

Individual Worth

The fifth principle of democratic government is the fundamental worth of every individual. For true democracy to exist, each individual must be recognized and respected as a distinct being created in God's image (Gen. 1:27; 9:6) and loved by God (John 3:16). If not, the result will be a majority or an elite who oppress those they deem to be less worthy.

Individual worth does not entitle one to ignore or reject the majority's will. The majority is not a faceless mob but a group of individuals united in a common goal. Individual worth does, however, protect the minority of individuals from majority coercion. In a democracy, individual worth protects the minority from oppression but does not allow them to do whatever they please.

Section Review
1. What is the difference between a popular majority and a representative majority?
2. Give four observations concerning majority rule in America that show why it has been effective.
3. In what two ways are all American citizens "equal"?
4. What is the difference between personal and political liberty?

III. Conditions for Democracy

Democracy has met with varying degrees of success throughout the world. Many of the new democracies formed since World War II have struggled against enormous odds in their bid for political liberty. A number of these nations were carved out of Europe's colonial holdings and had little experience in self-government. Consequently, some have succumbed to civil war or communist subversion. What then are the conditions that contribute to the success of a democratic system?

Opportunity

A democratic system must be one that provides a person with the opportunity to improve himself economically, to expand himself educationally, and to involve himself politically. Such opportunity boosts prosperity and provides channels for productive energies. Such opportunity also provides preventive medicine for social unrest.

Economic opportunity is particularly important in our democratic republic because it provides a sense of hope. Economic opportunity also enhances economic prosperity, which in turn results in a larger middle class. If a country's middle class is largely absent and there are instead great extremes of economic conditions (a small wealthy class and a poor majority), democracy will struggle. This kind of economic division poses the real threat of political division. Madison emphasized this problem in *Federalist No. 10:*

> The most common and durable source of factions has been the various and unequal distribution of property. Those who hold and those who are without property have ever formed distinct interests in society. . . . A landed interest, a manufacturing interest, a mercantile interest, a moneyed interest, with many lesser interests, grow up of necessity in civilized nations, and divide them into different classes, actuated by different sentiments and views.

The question naturally arises: To what extent should the government lessen economic inequities by ensuring the basic welfare of its citizens? Franklin Roosevelt said, "True individual freedom cannot exist without economic security and independence." Here Roosevelt redefined personal freedom in economic terms rather than in its traditional political sense.

The United States government has established a "safety net" to provide its citizens a measure of economic security. For example, Social Security provides a basic pension for retired or disabled persons, Medicare provides old-age health care assistance, and unemployment compensation provides financial aid to those who lose their jobs for reasons beyond their control, such as a layoff.

Who is responsible for taking care of the destitute—the government or Christians? Some Christians believe that welfare is not the responsibility of the government. They quote II Thessalonians 3:10, in which Paul says, "If any would not work, neither should he eat." Paul was referring to those who were capable of working, but who were lazy "busybodies" (3:11). It is obvious he was not referring to those who were incapable of working. David, for example, offered food and shelter to the feeble: to the lame Mephibosheth (II Sam. 9:13) as well as the aged Barzillai (II Sam. 19:32–33).

David's generosity reflects the compassion that God commands of His people.

> And when ye reap the harvest of your land, thou shalt not wholly reap the corners of thy field, neither shalt thou gather the gleanings of thy harvest. And thou shalt not glean thy vineyard, neither shalt thou gather every grape of thy vineyard; thou shalt leave them for the poor and stranger: I am the Lord your God. (Lev. 19:9–10)

> For the poor shall never cease out of the land: therefore I command thee, saying, Thou shalt open thine hand wide unto thy brother, to thy poor, and to thy needy, in thy land. (Deut. 15:11)

In the New Testament, James points out that part of our relationship with the Lord involves helping the needy:

> Pure religion and undefiled before God and the Father is this, To visit the fatherless and widows in their affliction, and to keep himself unspotted from the world. (James 1:27)

Clearly the church has a responsibility to help the disadvantaged and the downtrodden. In addition, meeting physical needs may provide an effective opportunity to meet the direst of human needs—regeneration—even as Christ fed the multitude and then taught them about the Bread of Life.

What if the church fails to meet the needs of those in poverty, and what about those who are outside of the church's influence? Though there are differing viewpoints on the subject, some Christians believe that the state must then assume a role in helping the poor. Their position is based on such passages as Daniel 4:27 where God, through His prophet Daniel, commanded the Chaldean king Nebuchadnezzar to "break off . . . thine iniquities by shewing mercy to the poor." If God could demand this of a pagan king, it might well indicate a purpose He holds for the state: protecting the weak from abuse.

Good News Ministries, Indianapolis, Indiana

The welfare programs of the United States provide help to many needy individuals. However, they also have features that fly in the face of some important democratic principles. For example, when individuals choose to stay on welfare because it is more profitable than working, this stifles individual initiative and closes doors of opportunity. Also, many welfare programs have become bloated with federal monies and managing bureaucracies, saddling the future with burdensome debts. Such debt, if not responsibly met, promises to deprive the next generation of its economic freedom and security.

Educated Society

An educated society is also an important condition for a successful democratic system. Of course, citizens must be literate in order to read newspapers, shape informed opinions, and cast intelligent votes, but they must also be educated for *civic thinking*. Civic thinking involves an understanding of the political ideas and institutions that shape our government, a valuing of our heritage, and an ability to evaluate current issues and national direction. An important purpose of this textbook is to encourage civic thinking.

Horace Mann, a nineteenth-century proponent of public education, asserted that "the establishment of a republican government, without well-appointed and efficient means for the universal education of the people, is the most rash and foolhardy experiment ever tried by man." Mann's assertion is only a half-truth. Although education is important to the success of a democracy, it is by no means its guarantor. There was certainly no "means for the universal education of the people" in 1787; yet the founders' efforts both survived and thrived. Today, despite our widespread systems of public and private education, the ignorance of our heritage and political ideals does not provide an encouraging picture for the future of our participatory government. A 1999 survey by the University of Connecticut gave a high school–level American history test to seniors at fifty-five of America's leading liberal arts colleges. Eighty-one percent earned a grade of D or F on the test. Only 23 percent of those surveyed were able to identify James Madison as the "Father of the Constitution," while only 22 percent knew that the phrase "government of the people, by the people, and for the people" is from the Gettysburg Address.

Education: Liberty's Building Block

Men have understood since centuries past that a free society could not exist without education. The following are quotations from well-known men concerning education's importance in a popular government.

> A popular Government, without popular information, or the means of acquiring it, is but a Prologue to a Farce or a Tragedy; or, perhaps both. Knowledge will forever govern ignorance: And a people who mean to be their own Governors, must arm themselves with the power which knowledge gives.
>
> — *James Madison*

> Liberty cannot be preserved without a general knowledge among the people.
>
> — *John Adams*

> The cultivated mind is the guardian genius of democracy and, while guided and controlled by virtue, is the noblest attribute of man. It is the only dictator that freemen acknowledge, and the only security which freemen desire.
>
> — *Mirabeau B. Lamar*

> Education makes people easy to lead, but difficult to drive, easy to govern, but impossible to enslave.
>
> — *Henry Peter Brougham*

> Education is a better safeguard of liberty than a standing army.
>
> — *Edward Everett*

> Next in importance to Freedom and Justice is popular education, without which neither Freedom nor Justice can be permanently maintained.
>
> — *James A. Garfield*

> If a nation expects to be ignorant and free, in a state of civilization, it expects what never was and never will be.
>
> — *Thomas Jefferson*

Successful democratic government requires intelligent participation, and such participation is grounded in civic thinking. The importance of this

kind of education is underscored by the fact that if a system of beliefs is not valued, there will be little motivation for defending it.

Education, though, is by no means a cure-all for democracy. Prewar Germany was one of the best-educated countries in Europe, yet this did not prevent their fledgling democracy from being crushed by Hitler's Nazism. There is a further condition that is necessary for the strength and survival of our democratic republic.

Moral Responsibility

Moral responsibility strengthens democracy in a number of ways. First of all, moral responsibility among citizens implies submission to the rule of law. Apart from the rule of law, democracy would rapidly degenerate into tyranny or worse. For Christians, submission to the rule of law does not stem simply from concern for social order; it stems from a concern for obeying God, who commands,

> Submit yourselves to every ordinance of man for the Lord's sake: whether it be to the king, as supreme; or unto governors, as unto them that are sent by him for the punishment of evildoers, and for the praise of them that do well. For so is the will of God. (I Pet. 2:13–15)

Moral responsibility also provides a standard for judging the actions of the majority. Tocqueville observed that one of the greatest dangers in a democracy was the coercive power of public opinion. In his insightful work *The Closing of the American Mind,* Allan Bloom explained that

> unless there is some strong ground for opposition to majority opinion, it inevitably prevails. This is the really dangerous form of the tyranny of the majority, not the kind that actively persecutes minorities but the kind that breaks the inner will to resist because there is no qualified source of nonconforming principles and no sense of superior right.

Moral responsibility counteracts the force of public opinion by asking, "What is right?" rather than "What is popular?"

In this respect, moral responsibility also determines the limits of compromise. Christians must not compromise biblical principles, but what should Christians do in a democracy where *political* compromise is a necessity? Moral responsibility helps the Christian judge whether a compromise is moral or immoral. Current popular thought in American society tends toward pragmatism, doing what works regardless of morality. Moral responsibility guards against pragmatism by judging solutions to be right or wrong according to the standard of the Bible. For instance, debate concerning the use of embryonic stem cells has pitted two ideologically opposed camps in Congress against one another. Those opposing embryonic stem cell research argue that it is unethical, while those supporting it argue that the potential medical benefits merit support. Both sides argue forcefully. The decision, however, must not rest on an argument's forcefulness but on its faithfulness to the Bible. Stem cell research involves the destruction of a new, unique combination of genetic codes contained in a group of cells created at conception. Debate about this procedure focuses on the question "Do these cells constitute human life?" The Bible teaches that life begins with conception. In Psalm 51:5, David states, "Behold, I was shapen in iniquity; and in sin did my mother conceive me."

Whether created in the womb or in a "test tube," life begins at conception. Therefore, moral responsibility prevents a Christian from supporting embryonic stem cell research because human life is sacrificed in the process of harvesting those stem cells.

Democracy is a word that has become hackneyed by widespread use and abuse—everyone from capitalists to communists talks of democracy. And yet its common use is indicative of its common appeal, even where it is only preached and not practiced. H. L. Mencken, an outspoken critic of democracy, once said that "it provides the only really amusing form of government ever endured by mankind." This smug observation, however, sees only democracy's defects—its factional tendencies and slavish regard for public opinion. Yet democracy in its best sense embodies the ideals of liberty and equality within a system that promises opportunity. It is a government of people under the law, providing the freedom that men desire and tyrants fear.

Section Review

1. What are the three main conditions necessary for a successful democracy?
2. What dangers arise when people lack economic opportunity?
3. What is potentially undemocratic about the welfare system in America today?
4. What is the difference between universal education and civic thinking?
5. How does moral responsibility help to moderate the power of the majority?

For Richer or for Poorer: Democracy in the United States and India

Democracy for America is assumed. Widespread land-ownership and the English political tradition have produced a climate of respect for economic and political liberty, which is guaranteed by representative government. With a desire to protect property and with a high rate of literacy, Americans are willing and able to secure their democracy from threats. Compared to most of the world, America's citizens are wealthier and better educated; therefore, democracy should, and does, work well.

But what about democracy in a poor nation with about one billion people? Prospects for democracy are not as good in such a case. Nonetheless, India is one of a few third-world countries since World War II and the advent of independence to maintain its democracy and respect for liberties. India is divided by language, religion (mostly Hindu and Muslim), race, and caste. With its economy eroded by dramatic population growth, India remains a poor country. Religious and racial violence and border wars with Pakistan and China threaten its stability.

Surprisingly, India's democracy endures. The British left a strong civil service in India, which provides basic services and unites Indians from various backgrounds. The Congress Party, which has dominated most of the time since 1947, enjoyed wide acceptance because it was the party of the independence movement. Although the family of Nehru (first Indian prime minister) has been important, no one charismatic leader has dominated as in other developing nations.

Also, opposition to the Congress Party was severely divided, and that ensured Congress Party power even though it garnered less than a majority in elections. Furthermore, the Indian military has been loyal to the democratic system. Ironically, India's continuing poverty has contributed to democracy, since the society is traditionally passive in India and unlikely to challenge the government, especially when local life is not threatened.

Only once was democracy challenged. In 1975 Prime Minister Indira Gandhi declared Emergency Rule, limiting the press and the activities of opposition groups. Fortunately, these conditions lasted only twenty-one months, and elections were held in 1977. Increasingly in recent years, India has become a two-party nation. The Congress Party has lost some national elections, and lower-caste Indians are playing an increasingly important role.

Chapter Review

Terms

democracy
due process
Bill of Rights
electoral college

federalism
majority rule
popular majority

representative majority
pluralistic society
equality

Content Questions

1. What four systems of government helped shape the United States government? Defend your answer.

2. What are some of the problems inherent in a pure democracy? What solutions did the founders adopt when introducing democratic elements into the new government?

3. What are the benefits and the dangers of majority rule?

4. What does the Declaration of Independence mean when it says "All men are created equal"?

5. What conditions made the American colonies ideally suited for democracy?

Application Questions

1. Why has democracy thrived in the United States as in no other country before or since?

2. What do third-world countries need before democracy can spread and flourish there?

3. Is welfare a responsibility of the state? Defend your answer.

4. How has the United States been hurt by a growing lack of civic knowledge and moral responsibility among its citizens?

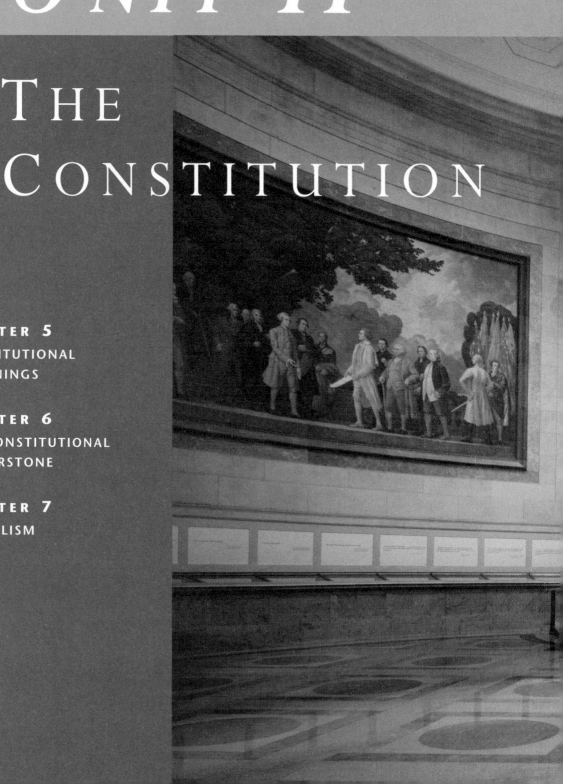

UNIT II

THE CONSTITUTION

Constitutional Beginnings

5

Scene at the Signing of the Constitution *by Howard C. Christy*

1619	Virginia House of Burgesses established
1688	Glorious Revolution in England
1760	French and Indian War ends
	George III becomes king
1765	Stamp Act passed
1770	Boston Massacre
1773	Boston Tea Party
1774	First Continental Congress
1775–89	Second Continental Congress
1775–83	Revolutionary War
1776	America declares independence
1777	Articles of Confederation proposed
1781	Articles of Confederation ratified
1785	Mount Vernon meeting
1786	Annapolis Convention
1786–87	Shays's Rebellion
1787	Constitutional Convention
1789	Constitution ratified

The Constitution is a powerful, eloquent, yet immensely practical legal instrument. It was written as the result of real men grappling with real problems. The men who gathered in Philadelphia to draft the Constitution were an impressive lot; they had distinguished themselves on the battlefields and in the statehouses of the youthful nation. Two future presidents, Washington and Madison, were numbered among them, as well as twenty-eight future congressmen. Jefferson, who was in France at the time of the Convention, called these Constitution makers "an assembly of demi-gods." Yet, even though their work was elevated, they walked on the same plane as their fellow-citizens. They argued among themselves, hammered out compromises, fretted over how history would remember them, and prayed for God's direction and blessing on their efforts. This chapter examines the historical context of the Constitution—the men at Philadelphia who wrote it, the national problems they struggled to solve, and the way their solutions gave birth to a republic that has been a model of successful self-government for over two centuries.

I. Confederation Crises

Political Influence and Innovation

America was largely an English export. The men and women who crossed the Atlantic to settle the American wilderness generally built their societies along English lines. These pioneers transported the political, social, and religious patterns and values from the Old World into the New. Anne Bradstreet, America's first poet, provides interesting insight into the extent of English culture in America. Her poems were first published in 1650 under the title *The Tenth Muse Lately Sprung Up in America.* Historian Perry Miller has noted that the title is the only thing about the volume that shows any sense of America, and that little merely in order to prove that the plantations had something in the way of European wit and learning, that they had not receded into barbarism. Anne's flowers are English flowers, the birds, English birds, and the landscape, Lincolnshire.

During its early development, American colonial government was also an English export. The mother country's three major influences were in the areas of **local government, legislative government,** and **limited government.** As we have seen earlier, local governments were organized quickly in the New World, providing order and leadership in the pioneer communities. The English influence on local government is still evident in our vocabulary with such terms as *grand jury, sheriff, bailiff, township,* and *county,* all of which are rooted in old English governance.

The legislatures that were established in the various seaboard colonies were influenced by the English Parliament. As early as **1619,** for example, the Virginia colony organized the **House of Burgesses**—the first representative assembly in the New World. Other legislatures were established in each of the colonies. These colonial assemblies reinforced the principle of representation, encouraged political participation, and provided leadership training in the difficult art of self-government.

Limited government was already a centuries-old principle in England when the first colonists waded ashore. Since the thirteenth-century Magna Carta, Englishmen had believed that there were certain rights of which the government could not rightfully deprive them. Government was limited in its reach by laws that all men, including the king, were bound to obey.

While the English influence in colonial government was understandably extensive, Americans also placed their own stamp on their politics. For one, the representative assemblies throughout the colonies exercised increasing authority over the royal governors. It is no accident that this power shift came after the 1688 Glorious Revolution, in which Parliament firmly established its authority over the king. In retrospect, this English example contributed to American independence in ways no one could have foreseen. Bolstered by the unparalleled strength that Parliament now commanded, the colonial legislatures assumed the right to levy taxes, alter colonial constitutions, and in some cases appoint or approve royal officers.

Britain's attitude toward these aggressive colonial governments was quite lenient, especially during the first half of the eighteenth century. The growth in colonial political power and experience was gradual and was nurtured by official neglect and geographic remoteness. Three thousand miles of ocean did much to assist the progress of self-government in America. In addition, within the colonies, poor roads, swollen rivers, and slow transportation meant that distances between people were greater and government was less centralized than in the old country. However, the growing confidence of the colonial legislatures, born out of their political gains, was soon to meet its most formidable challenge as the winds of change blew from the distant shores of England.

Tension and War in America

Years after the Revolution, John Adams concluded that the Revolution began not on the battlefields of Lexington and Concord in 1775 but rather in **1760.** Two catalytic events occurred then that over a period of time would shake an America ripe for independence.

In that year the French and Indian War ended after Montreal, the last French stronghold in North America, surrendered to the British. The French defeat removed a major obstacle from the path of American expansion, and at the same time the war left Britain strapped with a huge debt that Parliament would soon demand that the colonies help shoulder. Also in 1760, a twenty-two-year-old prince named George III acceded to the throne. For his part the young king fully intended to act on his mother's advice to "be a king" by reasserting the political strength of the crown, which had been on the decline for over a century. His brash efforts, however, combined with an inept group of advisors and parliamentary supporters, would strain and eventually snap the British hold on the American colonies.

Beginning with the **Stamp Act** in **1765,** Parliament passed a series of taxes and trade restrictions on the colonies that produced more resentment than revenue from America. In addition, the British government provided an unrequested peacetime

Boston Massacre

army for the colonies and passed a law forcing the colonials to provision these Redcoats. This law was in direct violation of the **Petition of Right,** a document guaranteeing basic civil liberties to all British subjects.

Over the next ten years, Britain continued to tighten its economic and military controls over the colonies. As for the colonies, which had enjoyed years of self-government largely free of parliamentary interference, the taxes and troops imposed without their consent were alarming. Naturally, tempers and violence flared on both sides. British customs officials were often tarred and feathered or burned in effigy by the more radical elements of the independence movement. Redcoats harassed and brawled with Bostonians and on March 5, 1770, opened fire on a group that was hurling snowballs and insults at them. When the smoke cleared, five killed and seven wounded citizens lay in the snow. The Boston Massacre strengthened American protests and fueled the growing patriot movement.

Organized colonial resistance, both military and political, came to a head, surprisingly enough, over tea. The British attempt to monopolize the tea trade was greeted with outrage and calls throughout the colonies for a **boycott**—an act of protest in which business is withheld or refused. Many homes and taverns banned the drink from their tables, and coffee became the patriot's favored brew. A week before Christmas in 1773, a group of Bostonians shouting "Boston Harbor a teapot tonight" effectively ended the governor's attempt to distribute three shiploads of English tea. The dumping of the chests of tea overboard infuriated royal officials and prompted punitive action from Parliament, known as the Intolerable or Coercive Acts.

The American colonists, however, refused to be coerced. In response to calls from the Virginia and Massachusetts assemblies, the **First Continental Congress (1774)** gathered in Philadelphia in September with representatives from every colony

John Adams *(1735–1826) by Gilbert Stuart (1755–1828)*

except Georgia. Numbered among this assembly were such distinguished leaders as Samuel and John Adams, Patrick Henry, and George Washington. The Congress met for two months, issued a Declaration of Grievances to George III, and, more importantly, defined their political rights as Americans, not simply as British subjects. John Adams wrote at the time that "the foundation . . . of all free government is a right in the people to participate in their legislative council." Adams added that Americans were "entitled to a free and exclusive power of legislation in their several provincial legislatures."

By the time the assembly reconvened as the **Second Continental Congress (1775–89)** during the late spring of the following year, the shots fired on Lexington green had shattered the uneasy calm—the call for complete independence was inevitable.

American Independence—1776

Two major tasks lay before the Congress: to deal with the military emergency around Boston and to present a formal declaration of independence. Congress dispatched George Washington to forge the ragtag volunteer militias around Boston into a Continental army. The task of creating the **Declaration of Independence** was left to a committee of five appointed by Congress. Although it included such notables as Benjamin Franklin, John Adams, Robert Livingston, and Roger Sherman, the committee unanimously agreed that its youngest member, thirty-three-year-old **Thomas Jefferson,** would do the actual writing.

Jefferson wrote up a draft of the Declaration and submitted it to Congress on June 28, 1776, after Franklin and Adams had made minor changes. On July 2, Congress began debating the proposed Declaration and continued until July 4. Late in the afternoon of that day, Congress approved the document. It would take several days, even weeks, for news to spread throughout all the colonies. Although the document had been approved, the official copy was not prepared and signed until August 2. As president of the Continental Congress, **John Hancock** signed first with a large,

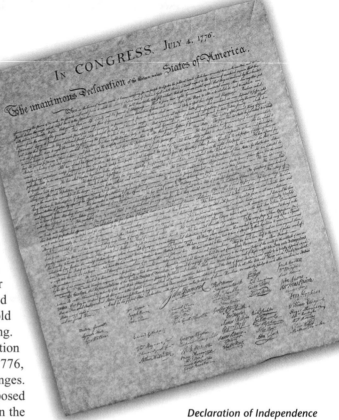

Declaration of Independence

Interior of the Graff House, Philadelphia, Parlor Room (where Jefferson penned the Declaration)

bold signature and was reported to have said, "There, King George will be able to read that without his spectacles."

What Jefferson penned in elegant fashion was not something new. Rather, he brought together established "self-evident" principles of government that he thought justified the colonies' break with England. Indeed, without such a clear statement the colonies would appear to be in lawless rebellion—something other European governments would certainly not stand for. The result was a document that reflected both the **Age of Enlightenment** in which it was written as well as Christian political thought tracing back to the Puritans and Scottish dissenters.

Consistent with the Enlightenment, the Declaration stressed the importance of natural laws that govern the universe—and in this case, government. In the introduction Jefferson presented four major laws or truths. (1) "All men are created equal"; (2) "they are endowed by their creator with certain unalienable rights," which include "life, liberty, and the pursuit of happiness"; (3) governments are instituted to secure these rights; and (4) if governments become "destructive of these ends," they may rightfully be abolished. What followed was a list of grievances that showed how King George had not only neglected the colonists' rights but also actively sought to destroy them.

While natural law was emphasized in the Enlightenment, the idea was by no means new. Rather, Jefferson, and even John Locke before him, was influenced by earlier Christian political thinking, which held that "nature law" and "God's law" were synonymous. God had revealed His laws in His Word (specific revelation), which was reflected in creation (general revelation). Paul spoke of this truth in Romans 1:20—"For the invisible things of him from the creation of the world are clearly seen, being understood by the things that are made, even his eternal power and Godhead; so that they are without excuse." But the twofold error of many Enlightenment thinkers was to rely solely on human reason to decipher God's will through creation while ignoring God's Word. God makes clear that without the Holy Spirit, man's mind and reason are corrupted (Rom. 8:5–6; Eph. 4:17–18). While one can see God's hand in nature, he cannot understand what he is seeing unless he views it through the lens of Scripture. It is God's Word that humans must rely on for truth in all things, including government.

Locke and the Declaration

One of the most significant philosophers of the Enlightenment was Englishman John Locke (1632–1704). His writings on the **social contract** theory of government influenced America's founding fathers, including Thomas Jefferson. In Locke's *Second Treatise on Civil Government,* he explained a natural law basis for government and justified political revolution. However, Locke's views were by no means revolutionary in themselves. Scottish Presbyterians, English Pilgrims and Puritans, and Dutch Protestants had all come before Locke and held somewhat similar views. While these groups had held that government was established by compact among God, subjects, and ruler(s), Locke focused more on a government contract between the last two. For the most part, his social contract theory seems to be a secularization of seventeenth-century Christian political thinking.

A comparison between the ideas and wording of Locke's *Second Treatise* and Jefferson's Declaration gives some indication of Locke's influence.

Jefferson might be more accurately labeled a deist. **Deism**—a religious outgrowth of the Enlightenment—regarded God as something of a heavenly clockmaker who had started the world in motion, established natural law, and then had little else to do with the affairs of man. However, despite Jefferson's personal beliefs, he was by no means surrounded by other deists. Many founding fathers testified to the personal and active nature of God, including Roger Sherman, who reviewed the Declaration. While by no means a perfect document, the Declaration of Independence, by God's grace, helped establish the nation upon Christian principles.

Revolutionary War reenactment

Second Treatise on Civil Government	Declaration of Independence
Ch. II, Sec. 6. The state of nature has a law of nature to govern it, which obliges every one: and reason, which is that law, teaches all mankind, who will but consult it, that being all equal and independent, no one ought to harm another in his life, health, liberty, or possessions: for men being all the workmanship of one omnipotent, and infinitely wise maker.	We hold these truths to be self-evident, that all men are created equal, that they are endowed by their Creator with certain unalienable Rights, that among these are Life, Liberty and the pursuit of Happiness.
Ch. XIX, Sec. 225. Great mistakes in the ruling part, many wrong and inconvenient laws, and all the slips of human frailty, will be born by the people without mutiny or murmur. But if a long train of abuses, prevarications and artifices, all tending the same way, make the design visible to the people, and they cannot but feel what they lie under, and see whither they are going; it is not to be wondered, that they should then rouze themselves.	Prudence, indeed, will dictate that Governments long established should not be changed for light and transient causes; and accordingly all experience hath shewn, that mankind are more disposed to suffer, while evils are sufferable, than to right themselves by abolishing the forms to which they are accustomed. But when a long train of abuses and usurpations, pursuing invariably the same Object evinces a design to reduce them under absolute Despotism, it is their right, it is their duty, to throw off such Government, and to provide new Guards for their future security.
Ch. XIII, Sec. 155. It may be demanded here, What if the executive power, being possessed of the force of the common-wealth, shall make use of that force to hinder the meeting and acting of the legislative, when the original constitution, or the public exigencies require it? I say, using force upon the people without authority, and contrary to the trust put in him that does so, is a state of war with the people. . . . [W]hen they are hindered by any force from what is so necessary to the society, and wherein the safety and preservation of the people consists, the people have a right to remove it by force.	He has refused to pass other Laws for the accommodation of large districts of people, unless those people would relinquish the right of Representation in the Legislature, a right inestimable to them and formidable to tyrants only. He has called together legislative bodies at places unusual, uncomfortable, and distant from the depository of their public Records, for the sole purpose of fatiguing them into compliance with his measures. He has dissolved Representative Houses repeatedly, for opposing with manly firmness his invasions on the rights of the people.
Ch. XI, Sec. 140. For if any one shall claim a power to lay and levy taxes on the people, by his own authority, and without such consent of the people, he thereby invades the fundamental law of property, and subverts the end of government: for what property have I in that, which another may by right take, when he pleases, to himself?	He has combined with others to subject us to a jurisdiction foreign to our constitution, and unacknowledged by our laws; giving his Assent to their Acts of pretended Legislation . . . For imposing Taxes on us without our Consent.
Ch. XIV, Sec. 168. And where the body of the people, or any single man, is deprived of their right, or is under the exercise of a power without right, and have no appeal on earth, then they have a liberty to appeal to heaven, whenever they judge the cause of sufficient moment.	We, therefore, the Representatives of the united States of America, in General Congress, Assembled, appealing to the Supreme Judge of the world for the rectitude of our intentions, do, in the Name, and by Authority of the good People of these Colonies, solemnly publish and declare, That these United Colonies are, and of Right ought to be Free and Independent States.

For the next five years the War for Independence raged, during which time two developments shaped America's emerging politics. First of all, the Second Continental Congress, which was born out of necessity and shaped by emergency, functioned as the national government. The various roles of government, such as finance and foreign relations, were largely managed by committees. Second, by 1777 new state governments were formed that superseded the colonial administrations. Since local representative government was viewed as a check against tyranny, the power of the state legislatures was enhanced, and executive power was weakened. Also, the states resisted yielding their power to tax to the Continental Congress. Having removed the interference of Parliament in their local affairs, they were not eager to submit to another "outside" government, though they would cooperate when it was in their best interests to do so. These two factors—a weak legislative central government and strongly independent state governments—molded the nature of United States government during the formative years following the American victory at Yorktown.

DOCUMENTS OF DEMOCRACY

Declaration of Independence—1776

The Declaration of Independence truly embodies the "Spirit of '76." There is a plucky streak that runs throughout the document. Like the grit of gunpowder, each sentence draws a determined battle line around which patriots would rally.

The Declaration, largely the work of Thomas Jefferson, opens with one of the most powerful and eloquent statements of personal liberty, proceeds to enumerate the "repeated injuries and usurpations" that George III had committed against his American subjects, and concludes that separation from Britain is necessary. Serious men debated, wrote, and signed this Declaration, for they were men who pledged to each other and to future generations their "lives, [their] fortunes, and [their] sacred honor." The actual document has had a fascinating history all its own. During the early years of the Republic, the Declaration, though valued, was not viewed as a national treasure. The youthful country, with its lack of a sense of history as well as the demands of war and peace, gave little thought to the parchment. When the British burned Washington during the War of 1812, the document was spirited away in a linen sack and stored overnight in a barn in northern Virginia.

Following the War of 1812, America's growing appreciation for her heritage brought the Declaration into the national spotlight—a position it has retained ever since. However, as historian Dumas Malone noted about the Declaration, "While immortal in spirit, it was by no means imperishable in form." Handling, temperature changes, and the fading effects of light did much harm to the old parchment. Even restoration attempts sometimes did damage. In 1940 a detached corner of the document was crudely repaired with tape that turned a "molasses color" within a few years. However, new technology has increased the long-term survival chances for the Declaration. In 1952, shortly before being moved to the National Archives in Washington, the document was placed in a helium-filled case with sensors to monitor humidity and other atmospheric conditions. Nearly fifty years later the Declaration was moved again to an even more sophisticated case, as were the Constitution and Bill of Rights. Perhaps the most interesting evidence of the value Americans place upon their Declaration of Independence came after the Japanese attacked Pearl Harbor in 1941. The Declaration was transferred from Washington and stored with the gold in a vault at Fort Knox, Kentucky, for three years.

A Declaration by the Representatives of the United States of America, in General Congress Assembled

When in the Course of human events, it becomes necessary for one people to dissolve the political bands which have connected them with another, and to assume among the powers of the earth, the separate and equal station to which the Laws of Nature and of Nature's God entitle them, a decent respect to the opinions of mankind requires that they should declare the causes which impel them to the separation.

We hold these truths to be self-evident, that all men are created equal, that they are endowed by their Creator with certain unalienable Rights, that among these are Life, Liberty and the pursuit of Happiness.—That to secure these rights, Governments are instituted among Men, deriving their just powers from the consent of the governed,—That whenever any Form of Government becomes destructive of these ends, it is the Right of the People to alter or to abolish it, and to institute new Government, laying its foundation on such principles and organizing its powers in such form, as to them shall seem most likely to effect their Safety and Happiness. Prudence, indeed, will dictate that Governments long established should not be changed for light and transient causes; and accordingly all experience hath shewn, that mankind are more disposed to suffer, while evils are sufferable, than to right themselves by abolishing the forms to which they are accustomed. But when a long train of abuses and usurpations, pursuing invariably the same Object evinces a design to reduce them under absolute Despotism, it is their right, it is their duty, to throw off such Government, and to provide new Guards for their future security.—Such has been the patient sufferance of these Colonies; and such is now the necessity which constrains them to alter their former Systems of Government. The history of the present King of Great Britain is a history of repeated injuries and usurpations, all having in direct object the establishment of an absolute Tyranny over these States. To prove this, let Facts be submitted to a candid world.

He has refused his Assent to Laws, the most wholesome and necessary for the public good.

He has forbidden his Governors to pass Laws of immediate and pressing importance, unless suspended in their operation till his Assent should be obtained; and when so suspended, he has utterly neglected to attend to them.

He has refused to pass other Laws for the accommodation of large districts of people, unless those people would relinquish the right of Representation in the Legislature, a right inestimable to them and formidable to tyrants only.

He has called together legislative bodies at places unusual, uncomfortable, and distant from the depository of their public Records, for the sole purpose of fatiguing them into compliance with his measures.

He has dissolved Representative Houses repeatedly, for opposing with manly firmness his invasions on the rights of the people.

He has refused for a long time, after such dissolutions, to cause others to be elected; whereby the Legislative powers, incapable of Annihilation, have returned to the People at large for their exercise; the State remaining in the mean time exposed to all the dangers of invasion from without, and convulsions within.

He has endeavoured to prevent the population of these States; for that purpose obstructing the Laws for Naturalization of Foreigners; refusing to pass others to encourage their migrations hither, and raising the conditions of new Appropriations of Lands.

He has obstructed the Administration of Justice, by refusing his Assent to Laws for establishing Judiciary powers.

He has made Judges dependent on his Will alone, for the tenure of their offices, and the amount and payment of their salaries.

He has erected a multitude of New Offices, and sent hither swarms of Officers to harrass our people, and eat out their substance.

He has kept among us, in times of peace, Standing Armies without the Consent of our legislatures.

He has affected to render the Military independent of and superior to the Civil power.

He has combined with others to subject us to a jurisdiction foreign to our constitution, and unacknowledged by our laws; giving his Assent to their Acts of pretended Legislation; For Quartering large bodies of armed troops among us; For protecting them, by a mock Trial, from punishment for any Murders which they should commit on the Inhabitants of these States; For cutting off our Trade with all parts of the world; For imposing Taxes on us without our Consent; For depriving us in many cases, of the benefits of Trial by Jury; For transporting us beyond Seas to be tried for pretended offences; For abolishing the free System of English Laws in a neighbouring Province, establishing therein an Arbitrary government, and enlarging its Boundaries so as to render it at once an example and fit instrument for introducing the same absolute rule into these Colonies; For taking away our Charters, abolishing our most valuable Laws, and altering fundamentally the Forms of our Governments; For suspending our own Legislatures, and declaring themselves invested with power to legislate for us in all cases whatsoever.

He has abdicated Government here, by declaring us out of his Protection and waging War against us.

He has plundered our seas, ravaged our Coasts, burnt our towns, and destroyed the lives of our people.

He is at this time transporting large Armies of foreign Mercenaries to complete the works of death, desolation and tyranny, already begun with circumstances of Cruelty & perfidy scarcely paralleled in the most barbarous ages, and totally unworthy the Head of a civilized nation.

He has constrained our fellow Citizens taken Captive on the high Seas to bear Arms against their Country, to become the executioners of their friends and Brethren, or to fall themselves by their Hands.

He has excited domestic insurrections amongst us, and has endeavoured to bring on the inhabitants of our frontiers, the merciless Indian Savages, whose known rule of warfare, is an undistinguished destruction of all ages, sexes and conditions.

In every stage of these Oppressions We have Petitioned for Redress in the most humble terms: Our repeated Petitions have been answered only by repeated injury. A Prince whose character is thus marked by every act which may define a Tyrant, is unfit to be the ruler of a free people.

Nor have We been wanting in attentions to our British brethren. We have warned them from time to time of attempts by their legislature to extend an unwarrantable jurisdiction over us. We have reminded them of the circumstances of our emigration and settlement here. We have appealed to their native justice and magnanimity, and we have conjured them by the ties of our common kindred to disavow these usurpations, which, would inevitably interrupt our connections and correspondence. They too have been deaf to the voice of justice and of consanguinity. We must, therefore, acquiesce in the necessity, which denounces our Separation, and hold them, as we hold the rest of mankind, Enemies in War, in Peace Friends.

We, therefore, the Representatives of the united States of America, in General Congress, Assembled, appealing to the Supreme Judge of the world for the rectitude of our intentions, do, in the Name, and by Authority of the good People of these Colonies, solemnly publish and declare, That these United Colonies are, and of Right ought to be Free and Independent States; that they are Absolved from all Allegiance to the British Crown, and that all political connection between them and the State of Great Britain, is and ought to be totally dissolved; and that as Free and Independent States, they have full Power to levy War, conclude Peace, contract Alliances, establish Commerce, and to do all other Acts and Things which Independent States may of right do. And for the support of this Declaration, with a firm reliance on the protection of divine Providence, we mutually pledge to each other our Lives, our Fortunes and our sacred Honor.

The Articles of Confederation

After independence was declared in 1776, the Second Continental Congress set about to establish a central government based on the consent of the newly formed state governments; the result was the **Articles of Confederation.** (See the Appendix for the text of the Articles.) Supported by states' rights advocates such as Patrick Henry and Thomas Jefferson, the Articles formalized the status quo by proposing a central government with characteristics very similar to the provisional Second Continental Congress. At the same time the Articles bound the various states into a "firm league of friendship." By November **1777** the Articles of Confederation were sent to the thirteen states for approval. This approval process, called **ratification,** required the unanimous consent of the states and was therefore difficult to complete. Eleven of the states ratified the Articles quickly, and New Jersey followed by 1779, but Maryland held out until **1781** because of a squabble with Virginia over western land claims. The ability of one state to impede the others under the provisions of the Articles was a sure indication of problems to come.

The Articles provided broad powers to the states, declaring in Article II,

Each state retains its sovereignty, freedom, and independence, and every Power, Jurisdiction, and right, which is not by this confederation expressly delegated to the United States, in Congress assembled.

The national government consisted of a **unicameral,** or one-house, legislature without a national executive or judiciary. Members of the Confederation Congress were chosen for one-year terms at the discretion of their respective state legislatures. States could send from two to seven

Articles of Confederation

Weaknesses	Federalist Papers Debate	Constitution Solution
Congress unable to act directly on individuals	#15	Article VI, Clause 2
Congress lacks power to enforce federal law	#21	Article I, Sec. 8, Clause 15
Congress lacks power to raise revenue through taxes	#21	Article I, Sec. 8, Clause 1
Congress lacks power to regulate commerce	#22	Article I, Sec. 8, Clause 3
Congress lacks power to raise military forces	#22	Article I, Sec. 8, Clause 12
Regardless of size, each state has one vote in Congress	#22	Article I, Sec. 2, Clause 3
Unanimous assent of states is needed to amend the articles	#22	Article V
No provision for a judiciary	#22	Article III, Sec. 1
Congress is made up of only one branch (unicameral)	#22	Article I, Sec. 1
Articles were not ratified by the people (through conventions)	#22	Article VII
Congress lacks sole power to coin money	#44	Article I, Sec. 8, Clause 5
Government lacks separation of powers	#84	Article I, Sec. 1; Article II, Sec. 2; Article III, Sec. 3

representatives, but each state had only one vote in the national assembly regardless of the size of the state's population or delegation.

The crucial weakness of the Articles of Confederation was the inability of the national government to enforce its policies. For example, Congress was authorized to build a navy and set up a banking system, but it could only request funds from the states; it could not levy taxes.

Strapped for cash, the Confederation Congress once proposed to levy a modest import duty, only to be thwarted by little Rhode Island. During the entire period of its existence, the Confederation government barely had enough funds for basic operating expenses.

Congress was also authorized to raise an army and declare war if necessary, yet the national government could do no more than request the cooperation of the states in such an effort and make paper protests against foreign encroachments. In fact, when the Barbary pirates seized American ships and crews in the Mediterranean, the Confederation Congress could not afford to pay the ransom demands, much less raise a navy to crush the pirates.

The weakness and ineptitude of this Congress did not encourage men of action and vision to participate. For only three days during the period from October 1785 to May 1786 was there a quorum of states present to conduct business. Obviously, state legislatures had little regard for the Confederation Congress. Most were occupied with commercial disputes and petty jealousies with their neighbors. George Washington expressed his fears for the nation in a letter to James Madison in 1786: "No morn ever dawned more favourable than ours did, and no day was ever more clouded than the present! Wisdom and good examples are necessary at this time to rescue the political machine from the impending storm."

Calls for Change

The deteriorating condition of the Confederation government was viewed with disappointment and alarm by those men who had worked so hard to secure American independence. John Hancock wrote, "How to strengthen and improve the Union so as to render it completely adequate demands the immediate attention of these states. Our very existence as a free nation is suspended upon it." John Jay voiced his concern about the weak Confederation: "I am uneasy and apprehensive; more so than during the war." George Washington concurred with Jay's fears: "We are fast verging to anarchy and confusion. Thirteen sovereignties pulling against each other, and all tugging at the Federal head, will soon bring ruin on the whole."

Two events focused the attention of the states on the woes of the national government and triggered changes that would result in a redefinition of national union. First, a commercial dispute between Virginia and Maryland over navigation rights on the Potomac brought representatives from both states to Alexandria, Virginia, in **1785** to negotiate a settlement. The hospitable George

A portrait of George Washington (1732–1799) by Rembrandt Peale, ca. 1853

Washington invited the men to meet at his **Mount Vernon** home just a few miles away. The meetings were friendly and quite productive, settling in just three days matters of navigation, fishing rights, and uniform currency. Hoping to apply the success of the Mount Vernon meetings on a national scale, where commercial disputes were nagging problems, the Virginia legislature called on all the states to send representatives to Annapolis in September **1786** in order to "recommend a federal plan for regulating commerce."

The **Annapolis Convention** was poorly attended. Only five states sent representatives, amounting to only a dozen delegates, but it provided the setting for a momentous invitation. Alexander Hamilton drafted a proposal that was quickly accepted by his fellow Annapolis delegates, namely that the states send delegates to Philadelphia in May of 1787 to "devise such further provisions as shall appear to them necessary to render the constitution of the Federal Government adequate to the exigencies of the Union." In the meantime, the call to convene received an added sense of urgency because of some disgruntled farmers in western Massachusetts.

Economic depression plagued the nation during the postwar period. The depression was fueled by wartime disruptions as well as the Confederation Congress's inability to deal with interstate commerce disputes and to restrict the circulation of inflationary paper money. These hard times resulted in a popular uprising in Massachusetts in 1786 and 1787 when Daniel Shays led a small army of debtor farmers to shut down county courthouses in order to prevent farm foreclosures and prison sentences for indebtedness. The Massachusetts state government, which had resisted the debtors' repeated calls for reform and assistance, dispatched a large force that easily routed the farmers.

Shays's Rebellion resulted in little bloodshed, and all of its leaders, including Shays, were quickly pardoned. However, its real impact lay in the fear of anarchy that it generated throughout the state legislatures. This fear convinced many to support a revision of the Articles that had been proposed at

Annapolis. In fact, just one month after the battle between the farmers and the militia, the Confederation Congress gave its reluctant endorsement to the proposed meeting in Philadelphia.

As early as 1781, Alexander Hamilton had written, "The republic is sick, and wants powerful remedies." The Confederation's symptoms of weakness only grew worse as the pressures of governing revealed its chronic defects. Those "powerful remedies" that Hamilton prescribed would be devised in Philadelphia throughout the long, hot summer of 1787.

Section Review

1. In what three major areas did England influence American colonial government?
2. What factors nurtured the growth of colonial political power during the first half of the eighteenth century?
3. What two events in 1760 brought about changes in British colonial rule that would eventually lead to American independence?
4. What influence did Christian thought have on the Declaration of Independence?
5. What two significant factors during the American Revolution profoundly molded the nature of the United States government following the war?
6. What was the crucial weakness of the Articles of Confederation?
7. What two major events focused attention upon the shortcomings of the American Confederation?

II. Constitutional Convention
Toward a New Government

Rain fell steadily, offering a cool change from the oppressive heat that had settled on the city. The wet weather had halted the sewer construction that was underway as the rain filled the trenches and washed mud down the untidy streets. As the delegates entered the door of the State House in their

Interior of Independence Hall, Assembly Room

dripping cloaks and tricorns, they bore little resemblance to the "demi-gods" that Jefferson declared them to be. Yet as they gathered in the Assembly Room where eleven years earlier the Declaration of Independence had been signed, there was a sense of anticipation about them—they knew that they were about to make history. Madison boasted that their work would "settle forever the fate of republican government."

On that rainy morning of May 25, **1787,** the **Constitutional Convention** got under way. Ahead of the delegates lay four months of difficult debates and tough questions. They were, however, leaders equal to the task. At the start they moved rapidly; the first item of business was to choose a president of the convention. **George Washington,** whose very presence helped ensure the success of their work in the eyes of the people, was unanimously elected to head the convention.

Next, two important procedural rules were adopted. First, a rule of secrecy was passed. No discussion of the activities of the Convention was to take place outside the hall. This rule was designed to keep speculation low in the newspapers and to protect the delegates from unnecessary public pressure. Although it is difficult to imagine such a rule working today over a four-month period without a single leak to the press, it did work in 1787. Fortunately, records of the Convention's activities do exist. Several delegates kept notes, and Secretary of the Convention, William Jackson, kept an official journal that recorded the resolutions and votes of the delegates. The most detailed notes, however, were made by the man whose political knowledge and immense influence earned him the title Father of the Constitution—**James Madison.** Like many other delegates, Madison chose not to publish his notes immediately. In fact, his notes were not published until 1840, four years after his death.

James Madison

The second procedural rule adopted by the convention was the decision to organize as a committee of the whole. This meant that the entire assembly could function like a committee, permitting informal discussions and flexibility in voting. The committee-of-the-whole rule greatly facilitated the essential compromises that were to come.

After setting the ground rules, the delegates turned to the question of whether the Articles of Confederation should be scrapped altogether or simply revised. On May 30, acting on a resolution by Gouverneur Morris, the delegates agreed overwhelmingly that "a national government ought to be established consisting of a supreme Legislative, Executive and Judiciary." Remarkably, just five days after the assembly convened, the most fundamental question of all was settled. A new national government—restructured and redefined—would provide the leadership to make the United States *united*, both in name and in fact.

Conflicts and Compromises

Not everything was to continue as smoothly as it had during the opening sessions of the convention. The delegates represented various states and regional interests, and as such there were some thorny issues ahead of them which would require patience, wisdom, and flexibility in order to hold the convention together. Three major areas required a compromise: representation, slavery, and commerce.

Representation—How the states were to be represented was surely the most difficult question that the delegates had to grapple with. The battle lines were drawn between the large states (such as Virginia, Pennsylvania, and Massachusetts) and the smaller states (such as New Jersey, Delaware, and Maryland).

James Madison had given a great deal of thought to the composition and structure of the new Congress. His thorough study and careful planning resulted in a proposal known as the **Virginia Plan,** which became the basis for much of the Constitution.

Madison's Virginia Plan, which was introduced to the convention by Edmund Randolph, advocated a bicameral Congress, with the number of representatives based on state population or on the amount of revenue that a state provided the national government. Election to the House of Representatives would be by popular vote. This lower house in turn would elect members of the Senate from nominees submitted by the state legislatures.

In contrast to the Confederation Congress, the legislature under the Virginia Plan was given greatly expanded powers. For example, the new Congress would be able to enforce its laws over the states and would also be empowered to elect both the chief executive and the national judiciary. These two branches, the executive and the judicial, could join together to veto congressional acts, although their veto could be overridden by a vote in both houses of Congress.

Since representation under the Virginia Plan was based on state population, it naturally favored the larger states. The smaller states were quick to react to this proposal, setting forth a scheme of their own known as the **New Jersey Plan.** This small-state plan, presented by William Paterson of New Jersey, advocated a unicameral Congress, maintaining the one-state one-vote principle of the Confederation. Congress, under the New Jersey

Plan, would also elect a weak plural executive with members who could be removed by a majority vote of the state governors. The Convention nearly reached an impasse over the issue of how representation would be determined. John Dickinson, representing Delaware, conceded that "some of the members from the small States wish for two branches in the General Legislature and are friends to a good National Government." But he added, "We would sooner submit to a foreign power than submit to be deprived of an equality of suffrage in both branches of the Legislature, and thereby be thrown under the domination of the large states." While the small states feared disenfranchisement through domination, the large states feared disenfranchisement through lack of representation, arguing that basic democratic principles favored proportional representation.

For weeks, long debates and short tempers, aggravated by the hot weather, threatened to break up the Convention and with it hopes for a strong, stable government. Roger Sherman of Connecticut offered the embroiled assembly a solution to their dead-end debating. Sherman, a believer with an unwavering testimony for Christ, whom John Adams referred to as "that old Puritan, honest as an angel," put together a skillful compromise that salvaged both the Convention and the Constitution. The **Connecticut Compromise,** or **Great Compromise,** proposed making representation in the lower house based on state population, whereas representation in the Senate would be equal for all states regardless of size. Sherman's proposal offers a classic example of political compromise: both sides got something and both sides were denied something.

Virginia and New Jersey Plans		
	Virginia	**New Jersey**
Written by	James Madison	Collaboration
Presented by	Edmund Randolph	William Paterson
Balance of power	• Strong national powers	• Strong state powers
Executive branch	• Chief executive consists of single person • Chosen by legislative branch • Ability to veto acts of Congress	• Chief executive consists of several men • Chosen by legislative branch • No veto power
Judicial branch	• One (or more) supreme courts, plus lower courts • Appointed by legislative branch • Ability to veto acts of Congress	• One supreme court • Appointed by executive office • Appointed for life • No veto power
Legislative branch	• Bicameral Congress • Ability to override executive and judicial branch vetos	• Unicameral Congress • Power to tax and to regulate trade
Representation in Congress (See illust. on p. 82)	• Both chambers based on population or wealth (one elected by people/one appointed by state legislatures)	• Equal representation of states in Congress

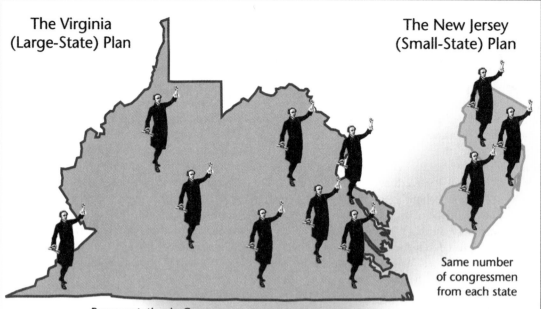

The Virginia (Large-State) Plan

The New Jersey (Small-State) Plan

Same number of congressmen from each state

Representation in Congress based on population

The Great Compromise

CONGRESS

SENATE

Virginia   New Jersey

Same number from each state

HOUSE OF REPRESENTATIVES

Virginia   New Jersey

Based on population

Roger Sherman: Uncompromising Compromiser

He was a man of approved integrity;
A cool, discerning Judge;
A prudent, sagacious Politician;
A true, faithful, and firm Patriot.
He ever adorned
The profession of Christianity
Which he made in youth;
And distinguished through life
For public usefulness,
Died in the prospect of a blessed immortality.

These words from the tomb of Roger Sherman testify of the personal and public faith of one of America's founding fathers. Sherman became a member of Congress in 1774 at age 53 and served there until 1793, the year of his death. During that period he placed his signature on the Articles of Association of 1774, the Articles of Confederation, the Declaration of Independence, and the Constitution—the only member to sign all four. He also served on the five-member committee responsible for drafting the Declaration of Independence. In the midst of the Constitutional representation debate, Sherman contributed his most notable accomplishment through the Connecticut Compromise. However, he maintained a much more subtle and steady influence over the federal government throughout his long tenure. A fellow representative once said, "If I am absent during the discussion of a subject, and consequently know not on which side to vote, I always look at Roger Sherman, for I am sure if I vote with him I shall vote right." Among his peers, Sherman maintained a reputation for wisdom, honesty, and integrity. Thomas Jefferson labeled him as "a man who never said a foolish thing in his life," and Nathaniel Macon said, "Roger Sherman had more common sense than any man I ever knew."

Statue of Roger Sherman by Chauncey B. Ives

What made Sherman's "common sense" so uncommon was that it was rooted in his faith and public walk for God. From his youth, Sherman had professed Christ and made his faith foremost in whatever he endeavored to do—and he did pretty much everything. In his early years he was a shoemaker, a merchant, and a surveyor. His skills as an astronomer were great enough for him to supply calculations for a New York almanac. Besides serving in national government, he held the position of mayor of New Haven and had a distinguished law career that culminated in a judicial appointment to the Connecticut Supreme Court. At home he was a father who brought up his fifteen children in prayer and daily Bible reading. He was a devoted son who took care of his aged mother within his household. He was also noted as a theologian by the likes of John Witherspoon, Jonathan Dickenson, and Jonathan Edwards, with whom he corresponded. His church in New Haven, Connecticut, even asked him to help revise their creed. Statements from it, such as the following, testify of his firm belief in the biblical truth he lived by. "I believe that God . . . did send his own son to

become man, die in the room and stead of sinners, and thus to lay a foundation for the offer of pardon and salvation to all mankind, so as all may be saved who are willing to accept the gospel offer." Few politicians, past or present, exemplify as clearly as Sherman obedience to God's command for a government leader to be a "minister . . . for good" within society.

Slavery—The next divisive issue that confronted the delegates of the Constitutional Convention was whether slaves should be counted in determining representation for slave-holding states. Delegates from those states, of course, said yes, whereas those from states that did not have slaves said no. Though slavery was predominantly in the agrarian South, it was not confined to that region. (Pennsylvania, for example, had several thousand slaves at the time.) The issue of how slaves should be counted caused heated debates among the delegates. Finally, a numerical compromise known as the **Three-Fifths Compromise** was reached. Under this unusual settlement, slaves would count as three-fifths of a person for purposes of representation in the House, but slave states would also have to pay taxes on them at the same rate. It is important to note that the compromise did not resolve the issue of slavery but merely postponed it. Ultimately, the issue would be resolved with the Civil War.

Commerce—Part of the original motivation behind calling the Philadelphia Convention was the inability of the Confederation to deal with interstate and international trade. While most delegates agreed that Congress needed to have a role in commerce, they were at odds over the extent of that role. The South, in particular, was concerned that the new Congress would halt the slave trade and raise revenue through export duties that would hurt their economy, which was dependent on the export of raw goods such as cotton, timber, and indigo.

A compromise, however, settled the issue. By the terms of the agreement, Congress was given power over foreign and interstate commerce. In exchange, the legislature was forbidden to impose any export duties on the states or to interfere with the slave trade for at least twenty years.

Besides the three major compromises, many other agreements helped fashion the language of the Constitution and shape the nature of our national government. For instance, a dispute over the election of the president was resolved through the creation of the electoral college, which gave direct power neither to the people or Congress but to intermediate electors. The issue of power over treaties was resolved by giving the president power to make them but then requiring Senate approval of the treaties. That the Constitution has been referred to as a "bundle of compromises" is no surprise.

Much of the Constitution, however, did not require compromise. There were broad, basic principles, such as limited government, that our constitution-makers readily agreed upon. The constitutional compromises dealt more with procedure than with principle.

Compromise is an important part of our political process. Differences of opinion are only natural in a free society. Therefore, when legislators representing various regions and interests meet to make laws, compromise and flexibility may be necessary in order to get a majority to agree. In spiritual matters, the Christian must determine in the light of Scripture what areas he may be flexible with and what matters he may not compromise. Simply put, we may compromise on nonessentials and matters of opinion and interpretation, but we may *not* yield on matters of principle and absolute truth. For example, Christ did not compromise with the moneychangers in the temple. He did not get them together to negotiate equal access laws; instead, He overturned their tables and drove them out because they were acting in plain violation of the Word of God by perverting the purpose of the temple. By contrast, when John reprimanded a man who was casting out demons because the man did not belong to their band of disciples, Christ rebuked John, saying, "Forbid him not: for he that is not against us is for us" (Luke 9:50).

Madison and Morris: Substance and Style

Of the fifty-five delegates who participated in the Philadelphia Convention, two left notable imprints on the final document of that meeting. The governmental ideas of James Madison laid the foundation of much of the content or substance of the Constitution, and the writing style of the great governmental charter was largely due to the literary eloquence of Gouverneur Morris.

James Madison of Virginia, who would later become the nation's fourth president, has often been called the Father of the Constitution. Though only thirty-six years old at the time of the convention, he had acquired a wealth of knowledge about governmental forms and constitutional law through his own intense studies. He put his abilities to work, formulating major points for the new government and frequently offering his thoughts in convention debates. His ideas formed the Virginia Plan, even though he did not take personal credit for it, and he spoke more times during the meetings at Philadelphia than did any other delegate apart from Gouverneur Morris. Madison's substantial participation helped shape the decisions of the convention as the delegates formulated our Constitution. Even though he stayed active in the debates of the meetings, he also managed to take the copious notes that have preserved for us the historic event in best detail.

After the delegates had reached agreement on most points of their governmental plan, they selected Madison to serve with Gouverneur Morris and three other men on the "Committee of Style and Arrangement." As these men worked to write down the plan in an acceptable form, Morris took the lead. Morris had already gained a reputation at the convention as a persuasive debater and colorful personality. The thirty-five-year-old Philadelphia lawyer had a wooden leg, which he had used to stomp the floor for emphasis during some of his many speeches before the delegates. It was his literary ability, however, which left the greatest impact on the Constitution, turning a mass of ideas into an organized document with clarity and a pleasing style. "The finish given to the style and arrangement of the Constitution fairly belongs to the pen of Mr. Morris," Madison later wrote. "A better choice could not have been made, as the performance of the task proved."

John thought he was taking an uncompromising stand, when in reality he was hindering the Lord's work. Much of the infighting among Bible

Chronology of the Constitutional Convention, 1787	
May 14–24	Preliminary meetings
May 25–28	Organization
May 29	Proposal of Randolph (Virginia) Plan and Pinckney Plan
June 15	The Paterson (New Jersey) Plan; revolt of the "small state" delegations
June 15–30	Two weeks of debate over the two plans
June 30	The Compromise Committee is appointed
July 5	Report of the Compromise Committee proposing proportional representation in the lower house, equal presentation in the upper, origin of all money bills in the lower house
July 16	Compromise adopted
August 15–23	Debate on the powers of Congress (Article I, Sections 8 and 9)
August 24–25	Debate on the powers of the president
August 29	The "three-fifths" clause; the slave trade; and the commerce clause
September 12	Report of the Committee of Style and Arrangement
September 17	Signing of the Constitution and adjournment

believers today is over personalities or procedures, not over clear biblical principles. We must have the wisdom to know the difference between inviolable matters of conscience and appropriate matters of compromise.

Although the constitutional compromises created mixed emotions among the delegates and the states, they also provided the benefit of drawing the states together into a *working* union, despite sectional differences. On **September 17, 1787,** after four months of exhausting work, the delegates gathered to sign the official engrossed copy of the Constitution. It was not a perfect document, but, as Madison correctly observed, no human government is perfect, therefore "that which is least imperfect is . . . the best government."

Some delegates viewed the Constitution as considerably less nearly perfect than their colleagues did, and thus refused to sign it. Prominent leaders such as George Mason of Virginia took issue with the absence of a Bill of Rights as a safeguard of individual liberty. Madison reported in his journal Mason's blunt statement that "he would sooner chop off his right hand than put it to the Constitution." Such opposition mirrored the difficult months ahead as the Constitution underwent the scrutiny of the ratification process throughout the states.

Section Review

1. What two key procedural rules, established at the very beginning of the Constitutional Convention, greatly facilitated the progress of the convention?

2. What major agreement did the Constitutional Convention reach after only five days of meetings?

3. Who is known as the Father of the Constitution?

4. In what three major areas did the Constitutional Convention need to make compromises?

III. Ratification Controversy

The public speculation that had been brewing for weeks about the closed-door convention was quelled with the publication of the Constitution in Philadelphia's daily, the *Pennsylvania Packet,* just two days after the delegates adjourned. The months ahead, though, held perhaps the most difficult and crucial political struggle that our Republic has ever known—the fight for ratification. Madison summed up the issue this way:

> The question on which the proposed Constitution must turn is the simple one whether the Union shall or shall not be continued. There is, in my opinion, no middle ground to be taken.

As the signers of the Constitution traveled back home to the tough job of selling the new government, nagging "what-ifs" plagued their minds. Article VII required that the Constitution be approved by nine of the thirteen states. But it could not be just any nine; the disapproval of any one of a half-dozen powerful states, such as Virginia or Massachusetts, would be enough to scuttle the Union because of the political and geographic divisions it would create.

In special ratification conventions that were held in each state (except the recalcitrant Rhode Island), the **Federalists,** as advocates of the Constitution were called, were pitted against the **Anti-Federalists,** who opposed the new plan of government. Their debates were fierce, their pens tireless, and their votes often close. Historian Clinton Rossiter noted that no national organization directed either the pro- or anti-ratification forces, and the states often debated the merits of the Constitution in the light of petty local issues.

The Federalist Papers

The Anti-Federalist forces did not waste time in their attacks on the Constitution. Just one week after the text was first published, a New York newspaper began a series of Anti-Federalist articles written under the pseudonym "Cato." Cato was in fact the governor of New York, George Clinton, and he was soon joined by "Brutus" and "Sydney" in denouncing the work of the Philadelphia convention.

Chronology of the Ratification of the Constitution	
Delaware	Thirty members ratified unanimously December 7, 1787
Pennsylvania	Ratified by a vote of 46 to 23, December 12, 1787
New Jersey	Thirty-nine delegates ratified unanimously December 18, 1787
Georgia	Twenty-six delegates ratified unanimously January 2, 1788
Connecticut	Ratified by a vote of 128 to 40, January 9, 1788
Massachusetts	Ratified by a vote of 187 to 168, February 16, 1788
Maryland	Ratified by a vote of 63 to 11, April 26, 1788
South Carolina	Ratified by a vote of 149 to 73, May 23, 1788
New Hampshire	Ratified by a vote of 57 to 47, June 21, 1788
Virginia	Ratified by a vote of 89 to 79, June 25, 1788
New York	Ratified by a vote of 30 to 27, July 26, 1788
North Carolina	Rejected, 193 to 75, August 4, 1788; finally ratified November 21, 1789
Rhode Island	Ratified by a vote of 34 to 32, May 29, 1790

Adapted from *The Convention and the Constitution* by David G. Smith

Alexander Hamilton, returning from the convention, responded to the Anti-Federalist charges with newspaper articles of his own under the pen name "Publius." Hamilton enlisted in this war of words the help of James Madison and John Jay, who were his neighbors at the time on Wall Street in New York City. From October 1787 through the following spring, the trio wrote eighty-five essays that were well reasoned and widely read, not only in New York but also in other states where ratification lay in the balance.

The essays, most of which were written by Hamilton, were compiled and published in two volumes in May 1788 under the title *The Federalist.* This work, also known as ***The Federalist Papers,*** answered the objections of the Anti-Federalists by carefully explaining and forcefully defending constitutional provisions of power and predicting dire consequences if the Constitution were rejected. Hamilton warned in *Federalist No. 1* that the "fate of an empire" hung upon the question of ratification and that the states could expect danger and dismemberment if the Anti-Federalists got their way.

Considering the circumstances under which *The Federalist* was written, it is a remarkable work. Despite the heat of political debate and the pressure of newspaper deadlines in which it was forged, it is a comprehensive commentary on republican government. In fact, Jefferson called it "the best commentary on the principles of government which has ever been written."

The Federalist Papers Today

Although *The Federalist Papers* were written over two hundred years ago, many of the topics they cover are still current issues. Whether it be defense spending, term limits, tax policies, or presidential nominations, *The Federalist Papers* give us important insight from those who helped establish the workings of government. Not that *The Federalist Papers* are always relevant. For instance, Hamilton predicted the Senate would rarely reject nominees to office chosen by the president. Hamilton could not have predicted that the rise of political parties would make such nominations contentious. Still, *The Federalist Papers* often reveal how our government works and, even more importantly, what traditions or values the founding fathers called upon in making their decisions.

Presidential pardons offer a good example. It is a recurrent issue because each president has

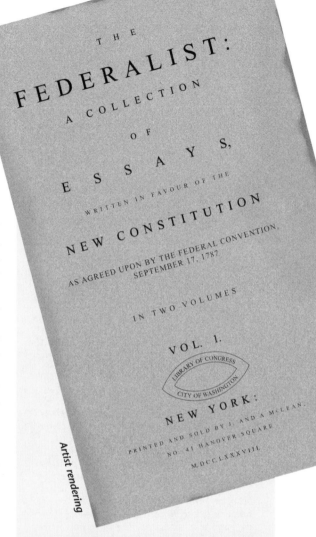

THE
FEDERALIST:
A COLLECTION
OF
ESSAYS,
WRITTEN IN FAVOUR OF THE
NEW CONSTITUTION
AS AGREED UPON BY THE FEDERAL CONVENTION,
SEPTEMBER 17, 1787

IN TWO VOLUMES

VOL. I.

LIBRARY OF CONGRESS
CITY OF WASHINGTON

NEW YORK:
PRINTED AND SOLD BY J. AND A. McLEAN,
NO. 41 HANOVER SQUARE
M.DCC.LXXXVIII.

Artist rendering

the opportunity to offer pardons—usually done at the end of his term of office. In essay 74, Hamilton explains why such a power was given to one man.

> (The president) is also to be authorized to grant "reprieves and pardons for offenses against the United States, EXCEPT IN CASES OF IMPEACHMENT."

> Humanity and good policy conspire to dictate, that the benign prerogative of pardoning should be as little as possible fettered or embarrassed. The criminal code of every country partakes so much of necessary severity, that without an easy access to exceptions in favor of unfortunate guilt, justice would wear a countenance too sanguinary and cruel.

As the sense of responsibility is always strongest, in proportion as it is undivided, it may be inferred that a single man would be most ready to attend to the force of those motives which might plead for a mitigation of the rigor of the law, and least apt to yield to considerations which were calculated to shelter a fit object of its vengeance. The reflection that the fate of a fellow-creature depended on his sole fiat, would naturally inspire scrupulousness and caution; the dread of being accused of weakness or connivance, would beget equal circumspection, though of a different kind.

On the other hand, as men generally derive confidence from their numbers, they might often encourage each other in an act of obduracy, and might be less sensible to the apprehension of suspicion or censure for an injudicious or affected clemency. On these accounts, one man appears to be a more eligible dispenser of the mercy of government, than a body of men.

In regards to pardons of treason, Hamilton continues,

But the principal argument for reposing the power of pardoning in this case to the Chief Magistrate is this: in seasons of insurrection or rebellion, there are often critical moments, when a well-timed offer of pardon to the insurgents or rebels may restore the tranquillity of the commonwealth; and which, if suffered to pass unimproved, it may never be possible afterwards to recall. The dilatory process of convening the legislature, or one of its branches, for the purpose of obtaining its sanction to the measure, would frequently be the occasion of letting slip the golden opportunity. The loss of a week, a day, an hour, may sometimes be fatal.

If it should be observed, that a discretionary power, with a view to such contingencies, might be occasionally conferred upon the President, it may be answered in the first place, that it is questionable, whether, in a limited Constitution, that power could be delegated by law; and in the second place, that it would generally be impolitic beforehand to take any step which might hold out the prospect of impunity. A proceeding of this kind, out of the usual course, would be likely to be construed into an argument of timidity

or of weakness, and would have a tendency to embolden guilt.

These reasons—the ability to show mercy and provide necessary peace—help to explain Ford's pardon of Nixon back in 1974. They also help us see how a president might abuse his power by using the presidential pardon for purposes not intended by the founding fathers. Like the Constitution, *The Federalist Papers* are more than just historical documents. They continue to give us insight into today's issues through the wisdom of yesterday's leaders.

Battles in Virginia and New York

Delaware led the way in a convincing manner by unanimously ratifying the Constitution on December 7, 1787. Within two months five more states added their consent to the Constitution. However, the toughest fights lay ahead in Virginia and New York, where the Anti-Federalists were better led and organized. In addition, the stakes were quite high, for the consent of both was crucial to the success of the new government despite the fact that the required nine states had ratified by June, 1788. In a very practical sense, nine were not enough. If New York had failed to ratify, New England would have been cut off from the rest of the nation; and if Virginia had voted nay, she would have severed the South.

In Virginia the Federalist forces were led by James Madison, while the Anti-Federalists had the fiery orator Patrick Henry as their spokesman. Henry was joined by two nonsigning Constitutional delegates—Governor Edmund Randolph (though he eventually changed his mind and voted with the Federalists) and George Mason—as well as three signers of the Declaration of Independence. However, the Anti-Federalists' boast that they were the true heirs of 1776 rang rather hollow since George Washington and Jefferson (after some persuasion from Madison) supported the Constitution.

New York Quarter

It would be unfair to portray the Anti-Federalists simply as cantankerous troublemakers. It is true that some merely used the ratification issue in hopes of furthering their political ambitions. Others opposed the Constitution because they opposed the national government's power to tax. There were, however, Anti-Federalists who were motivated by reasons far more elevated. The objections of the Virginia Anti-Federalists illustrate this point well.

Patrick Henry opposed the Constitution because of the way in which it curbed state power. Henry, a strong advocate of states' rights, even challenged the wording of the Preamble: "Who authorized them to speak of 'We the People,' instead of 'We the states'? States are the characteristics and the soul of a confederation. If the states be not the agents of this compact, it must be one great consolidated national government of the people of all the states." Henry's argument was not an empty one, considering the fact that the Constitution was approved by state conventions rather than popular vote.

Henry and his colleagues viewed the consolidation of power into the hands of a strong national government as a step toward tyranny. Henry had an almost prophetic sense of where the consolidation of political power would lead. He foresaw an irreversible growth in national government that would strangle the authority of the states and would be characterized by a burgeoning bureaucracy whose "salaries and fees of the swarm of officers and dependents on the government will cost this continent immense sums."

The force of Henry's arguments over states' rights and the expansion of national power is bolstered by their durability—they would long outlast the Richmond convention. The grandchildren of the Constitutional debaters would fight a bloody civil war in an effort to define the nature of the Union, and their descendants today still grapple with the problem of harnessing the tide of national power.

Another concern of the Anti-Federalists was the absence of a Bill of Rights protecting individual liberty. As was noted earlier, George Mason refused to sign the Constitution for this reason. Federalists were by no means opposed to personal freedom; many did not believe that a list of specified rights was necessary. Hamilton held that a Bill of Rights would in fact be dangerous since specified rights might more easily invite the government to assume power in *unspecified* areas.

On this point, however, the Federalists eventually conceded to a compromise by agreeing to send recommendations for amendments in conjunction

Virginia Quarter

with ratification. Madison pledged that following ratification he would do everything in his power to see that a Bill of Rights became law. With that compromise a few of the undecided were swayed, and the Constitution was approved in Virginia by a vote of 89 to 79.

At the same time as the Richmond ratification fight, a similar battle raged in Poughkeepsie, New York. New York was the last major obstacle to constitutional government, and Governor Clinton and his Anti-Federalist forces held a commanding majority in the ratifying convention against the pro-Constitution delegates led by Hamilton. However, with the news of the Federalist victory in Virginia, the New York Anti-Federalists suffered a fatal setback. A number of Clinton's delegates, with thoughts of their own political future, defected to the Constitution camp when they realized that the collapse of the Virginia Anti-Federalists meant theirs was a lost cause. By a slim three-vote margin, New York approved the Constitution on July 26, 1788, becoming the eleventh state to ratify.

The words of the Constitution now became the reality of working government. Elections for Congress were set, and a date fixed—March 4, 1789—for the inauguration of the new government in its temporary capital of New York City.

FEDERALISTS

James Madison

Alexander Hamilton

Patrick Henry

George Mason

Elbridge Gerry

John Jay

ANTI-FEDERALISTS

Federalist and Anti-Federalist Differences

The Federalists and Anti-Federalists differed in their approach to the correct government to establish for this new nation. The Federalists supported a strong central government while the Anti-Federalists centered on states' rights. The following issues were some of those debated during the ratification process, and they illustrate the differing viewpoints. The Federalists' viewpoints on these issues were taken from essays 10 and 14 of *The Federalist Papers,* in which Madison defended the Constitution.

Issue 1: The Proposed Constitution and Convention Legitimacy.

Federalists: Because they were appointed to the Constitutional Convention by legitimate means, they believed they had the right to construct a new document.

Anti-Federalists: Thought the Convention should have only amended the Articles of Confederation and that delegates went beyond their power when writing the Constitution.

Issue 2: The Fate of the Union and the States under the Proposed Constitution.

Federalists: Believed that the strength of the government outlined in the proposed Constitution would be sufficient to protect the liberties and general good of the people. Less strength would encourage the Union to split apart into possible separate confederacies. States would not be consumed by a strong central government but would eventually encroach upon the government's just powers.

Anti-Federalists: Opposed breaking up the Union but said the proposed Constitution was not the answer. Thought it would demote the states to administrative districts and take away the people's liberties and self-government rights.

Issue 3: The Lack of a Bill of Rights.

Federalists: Thought a bill of rights was not necessary since the Constitution did not give the federal government power to interfere or infringe on individual rights. Some Federalists

Interior of Independence Hall, Assembly Room, Rising Sun Chair and Syng Ink Stand

(e.g., John Adams and Thomas Jefferson) wanted to include a bill of rights.

Anti-Federalists: The lack of a bill of rights was their strongest argument against the proposed Constitution, because there were no means to defend individual civil liberties.

Issue 4: Amending the Constitution.

Federalists: Believed that the amending process under the Articles of Confederation was too difficult since all states had to agree on a single issue. Majority rule was supported.

Anti-Federalists: Said the proposed Constitution's amending process was too easy and that unanimous consent of all the states was the more appropriate method.

The ratification process was not limited to these issues. Other matters debated were the presidency, powers and representation of Congress, the judiciary, a permanent national capital, slavery, and religious tests for voting and holding office. These debates over the Constitution's ratification proved to be the most important in American history.

A Nation Arises

During the spring of **1789,** the world's first constitutional democracy was instituted. The obvious and unanimous choice for the first president was George Washington, who took the oath of office on April 30, 1789, from the balcony of Federal Hall on Wall Street in New York. The great Virginian placed his hand on the Bible and promised to preserve, protect, and defend the Constitution, adding, "So help me God." With that, President Washington kissed the Bible as the streets filled with the sound of cheering crowds, ringing bells, and booming cannon salutes. The experiment in liberty was launched.

The Constitution is not a perfect document, but it has demonstrated remarkable durability and adaptability over the past two centuries. It has also provided a model of successful self-government for other nations, confirming the observation of British prime minister William Gladstone that it was "the most wonderful work ever struck off at a given time by the brain and purpose of man."

Washington's inauguration was both an end and a beginning. It marked an end to the struggle for liberty and self-government that began in 1776, and it heralded a *national* beginning. Benjamin Franklin put it best in 1787, while observing the delegates signing the Constitution. Madison recorded that

> Dr. Franklin, looking towards the president's chair, at the back of which a rising sun happened to be painted, observed to a few members near him, that painters had found it difficult to distinguish in their art a rising from a setting sun. I have, said he, often and often during the course of the session, and the vicissitudes of my hopes and fears as to its issue, looked at that behind the president without being able to tell whether it was rising or setting: But now at length I have the happiness to know that it is a rising and not a setting sun.

George Washington, *Landsdowne portrait, by Gilbert Stuart*

Section Review

1. Who were the main leaders among the Anti-Federalists? the Federalists?
2. What were the two major arguments presented against adoption of the Constitution?
3. What were the two most crucial state conventions in the ratification of the Constitution? What factors led to the final approval of the Constitution in these states?

Chapter Review

Terms

local government
legislative government
limited government
House of Burgesses (1619)
1760
Stamp Act (1765)
Petition of Right
boycott
First Continental Congress (1774)
Second Continental Congress (1775–89)
Declaration of Independence

Thomas Jefferson
John Hancock
Age of Enlightenment
social contract
deism
Articles of Confederation
1777
ratification
1781
unicameral
Mount Vernon (1785)
Annapolis Convention (1786)

Constitutional Convention (1787)
George Washington
James Madison
Virginia Plan
New Jersey Plan
Connecticut (Great) Compromise
Three-Fifths Compromise
September 17, 1787
Federalists
Anti-Federalists
The Federalist Papers
1789

Content Questions

1. In what three major ways were colonial governments influenced by English government?

2. What actions by England threatened colonial governments and aroused revolution?

3. How did Jefferson justify the colonies' break with England in the Declaration?

4. Why did the Second Continental Congress create a weak confederation? What was the primary weakness of the Articles?

5. On what major issues did the Constitutional Convention agree?

6. Describe the major issues that required compromise at the Constitutional Convention. Name the compromises.

7. Summarize the positions of the Federalists and the Anti-Federalists.

8. In what states did the greatest threat to the ratification of the Constitution exist? What compromise was the deciding factor in the success of ratification?

Application Questions

1. What experiences prepared the "demi-gods" at the Constitutional Congress for the huge task of creating the first workable, large-scale republican government in history?

2. What were the political benefits that resulted from the piracy, rampant inflation, rebellion, and trade disputes that immediately followed the American Revolution?

3. What are the main benefits of compromise? When is compromise detrimental?

4. What compromises in the Constitution have endured to this day, and what compromises proved to be temporary?

5. What are some of the obvious benefits of the compromises made at the Constitutional Convention concerning commerce?

6. What Anti-Federalist warnings are still worth heeding today?

The Constitutional Cornerstone

6

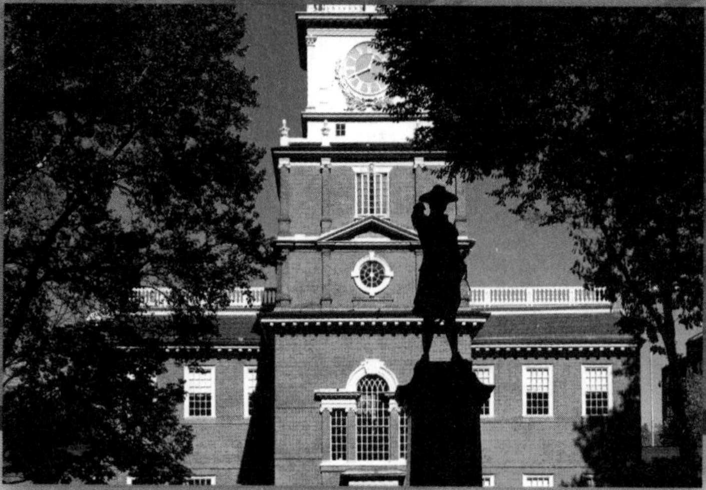

Independence Hall

- I. Practical Characteristics
  - A. Realistic View of Human Nature
  - B. Constitutional Interpretation
  - C. The Amendment Process
- II. Basic Principles
  - A. Limited Government
  - B. Separation of Powers
  - C. Checks and Balances
  - D. Judicial Review
  - E. Federalism
  - F. Popular Sovereignty
  - G. Conclusion
- III. The United States Constitution
  - A. Preamble and Articles I–VII
  - B. Bill of Rights: Amendments I–X
  - C. Amendments XI–XXVII

Dwarfed amid the glass and steel towers of today's Philadelphia, the old State House stands, stubbornly resisting the sprawl of the modern metropolis. Two centuries have altered the skyline dramatically, and the building where the Constitution delegates argued—and eventually agreed—seems locked in a distant past. These delegates have passed off the scene; their debates have been silenced by time, and the pages of their writings have yellowed with age. Though a few of these delegates became household names, most have been largely forgotten. Yet the Constitution they forged more than two hundred years ago has outlived its creators. The Constitution, now in its third century of governance, immortalizes principles that transcend its eighteenth-century setting.

The Constitution was not written simply to resolve the economic and political turmoil of the 1780s. Chief Justice John Marshall observed that the Constitution was designed "to endure for ages to come, and consequently, to be adapted to the various crises of human affairs." During the past two centuries the United States has grown from a rural seaboard country of four million to a large, industrial superpower. Our Constitution has shown remarkable resilience during that time, shaping and yet being shaped by the nation's character.

Ours was the earliest written constitution, and it remains the oldest one in continuous use; its effect, though, has not been confined to this country. Of the approximately one hundred sixty national constitutions in use today, most have been written or revised since 1970. (Only fourteen were penned before World War II.) Our Constitution has served as a model for many of these new constitutions and has been described as "this nation's most important export."

This chapter will take a closer look at the Constitution, beginning with its practical character and general principles, followed by the actual text of this remarkable cornerstone of our government.

I. Practical Characteristics

The Constitution is not a static, dusty document; it is a practical tool for governing. The success of the Constitution is due to the founders' fundamental understanding of man and the document's inherent adaptability.

Realistic View of Human Nature

The Constitutional framers wrote with a realistic view of human nature. They recognized man's desire for freedom and his capacity to govern, but they also had a clearheaded view of man's tendency to sin.

The Constitution is not a Christian document: in fact, God is not mentioned once in the entire work. But the Constitutional framers lived in a society where Scripture was pervasive, and their own thinking was often influenced by basic biblical principles. Madison wrote in *Federalist No. 51,*

> What is government itself, but the greatest of all reflections on human nature? *If men were angels, no government would be necessary. If angels were to govern men, neither external nor internal controls on government would be necessary.* In framing a government which is to be administered by men over men, the great diffi-

culty lies in this: you must first enable the government to control the governed; and in the next place oblige it to control itself. (emphasis added)

This attitude of distrust toward human nature—that man tends to use power corruptly and to be corrupted by power—led our founders to divide authority within the national government and to build in certain safety checks to prevent the concentration and abuse of power.

The French constitution of 1792 demonstrates what happens when men plan their government around a false view of the governed and of their governors. This constitution, written amid the turmoil of the French Revolution, held an idealistic and unbiblical view of man. The French leadership hoped to banish Christianity from public life, and their constitution rejected the biblical doctrine of human depravity. In this atmosphere the French wrote their new constitution with dreams of its serving generations to come—but they were only dreams. In a land where the guillotine, not the constitution, was the chief governing instrument, the republic lasted for just three years.

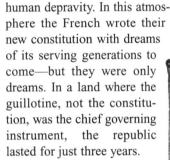

Our Constitution has provided a stable, practical guide for governing because it was written by men who understood both their capacity to rule and their need for restraint.

Guillotine

Constitutional Interpretation

Our Constitution has been a success because of its ability to adapt and change as American society has changed. This flexibility comes from the document's inherent need for a degree of interpretation. The founders understood that they were not prophets who could predict the future problems of America and write a document to solve those problems. Rather they wrote a brief and general charter—the original document is only about four thousand words long, and even its twenty-seven amendments extend its length to a total of only about seven thousand words. Unlike some state constitutions, which are more than ten times longer, the Constitution is not overladen with detail. Instead it provides a framework, with minimal structure and guiding principles, that has the flexibility to meet the demands of change.

Since the Constitution is a guide rather than a detailed manual on governing, it has been open to various interpretations over the years. As far back as Washington's administration men differed over how far such interpretations should go. Those who believe that the text of the Constitution is important, and that any interpretation should be kept to a minimum, are known as **strict constructionists.** Those who take a broader and sometimes more creative approach to constitutional interpretation are known as **broad constructionists.**

Constitutional interpretation has contributed to both the durability of and the controversy surrounding our national charter. Some of the interpretation arises naturally from the text. For example, the vast federal bureaucracy, which numbers over two million civilian employees, is not mentioned once in the Constitution. Yet Article II, Section 3 states that the president "shall take care that the laws be faithfully executed." The bureaucracy has grown out of the president's responsibility to see that constitutional laws are implemented and programs administered.

Other interpretations are not so readily tied to the text. In recent years the courts have "discerned" a constitutional right of privacy, for example. The

founders certainly favored the right of privacy, by which they meant that a law-abiding citizen should be protected from unnecessary government intrusion into his life and home. However, in *Griswold v. Connecticut* (1965) the Supreme Court interpreted such amendments as the Third (prohibiting the forced quartering of soldiers) and the Fourth (protecting citizens from unlawful searches and seizures) to imply a constitutional right of privacy. The *Griswold* decision overturned a Connecticut law which forbade the sale of contraceptives; but *Griswold* did more than that—the decision set a precedent for the courts by which the right to privacy provided an umbrella for a variety of liberal social causes, such as abortion and homosexual rights.

Supreme Court Justice Charles Evans Hughes correctly observed, "We are under a Constitution,

The Supreme Court's power to "say what the Constitution is" remains the Court's chief and most controversial prerogative. United States Supreme Court Building, Washington, D.C.

but the Constitution is what the judges say it is." Given the flexibility and general character of the Constitution, interpretations and new applications are to be expected. However, as we shall see in greater detail in Chapter 17, when judges leave the moorings of the Constitution's text and the original intent of its writers, they subject the country to a seesaw of shifting opinions that depend on the Court's composition.

In addition to the judicial interpretation of the Supreme Court, the Congress too has a role in adapting the Constitution to the needs of the nation. Article I, Section 8, Clause 18 authorizes Congress "to make all laws which shall be necessary and proper for carrying into execution the foregoing powers, and all other powers vested by this Constitution in the Government of the United States." The **"necessary and proper clause"** was added by the Constitutional framers so that future Congresses might have the authority to meet future needs.

Congressional legislation often defines the extent of constitutional power. For example, the Constitution grants Congress the right to establish lower courts, which it has done over the years, providing additional courts and judges as the nation and the backlog of cases have grown. In short, Congress puts the Constitution into practice by writing laws, establishing programs, and appropriating funds to meet national demands within constitutional guidelines.

Presidential actions also apply, expand, and adapt the Constitution. Longstanding executive precedents may carry the weight of law even though they are not specifically spelled out in the Constitution. For example, the founders established no limits on the number of terms a president could serve; however, Washington's two terms set a precedent that would last until Franklin Roosevelt sought and won a third and fourth term in 1940 and 1944. In response to Roosevelt's precedent-breaking terms, the Twenty-second Amendment was passed, making the two-term tradition into law.

A president may also *assume* powers that are not specifically given and thus expand the meaning of the Constitution and the power of his office.

FDR and his wife Eleanor riding to his inauguration in 1941 to begin an unprecedented third term

Prior to the Twenty-fifth Amendment in 1967, on the death of the president the vice president was authorized to assume the *responsibilities* of the office, but not necessarily the office itself. When this succession question was first raised in 1841 on the death of William Henry Harrison, John Tyler refused the title "Acting President" and assumed full control of the executive branch. Less than ten years later, Vice President Millard Fillmore took charge of the White House after the sudden death of President Zachary Taylor. Taylor's cabinet went through the routine formality of offering their resignations to Fillmore, of course not expecting him to accept them, but they were all wrong. Fillmore chose a new cabinet, demonstrating his firm grip on the presidential helm, despite the absence of a specific constitutional grant of full power.

The Amendment Process

In addition to interpreting and applying the Constitution through the various branches of government, there is a more formal means of adapting the Constitution to change—the **amendment process.**

The Constitution makes provision for its own amending in Article V. There are two major phases of the amendment process: proposal and ratification. **Proposal,** the formal introduction of an amendment, may be made through two means: either by a two-thirds vote in both houses of Congress or by a special national convention called at the request of two-thirds of the states. In practice only the first method has been used, making the proposal process largely a federal responsibility.

Failed Amendments

Only thirty-three amendments have ever been proposed for ratification—meaning they received the necessary two-third votes in Congress. Of these, twenty-seven have actually been ratified. However, many more amendments have been submitted for consideration. Over ten thousand have been offered during the past two centuries. These failed amendments come from all parts of America's political and social landscape, and range from the absurd to the profound. On the more serious side, generally, are those amendments that passed the proposal stage yet went unratified. These six are listed first, followed by a sampling of those amendments that were simply submitted.

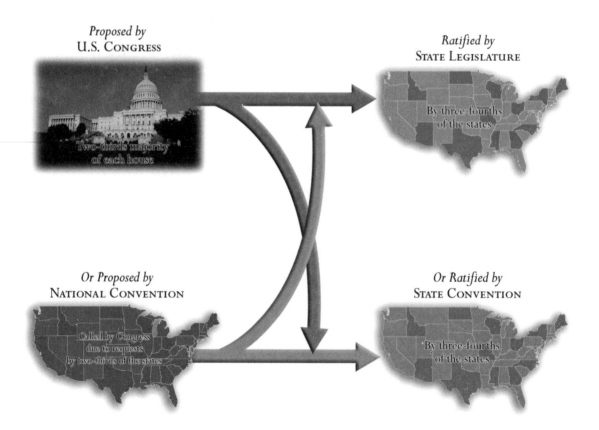

Proposed by
U.S. CONGRESS

Two-thirds majority
of each house

Ratified by
STATE LEGISLATURE

By three-fourths
of the states

Or Proposed by
NATIONAL CONVENTION

Called by Congress
due to requests
by two-thirds of the states

Or Ratified by
STATE CONVENTION

By three-fourths
of the states

PROPOSED BUT UNRATIFIED:

1789—Article I of the Bill of Rights

Based representation in the House of Representatives on a system that called for one representative for every 30,000 citizens until the number reached 100. Then, one representative for every 40,000 until the number reached 200, and finally one representative for every 50,000 people. Based on this final representative scale, there would be approximately 5,500 members of the House of Representatives today.

Ratified by ten states.

1810—Anti-Title Amendment

Forbade citizens of the United States from accepting any title of nobility from any king, prince, or foreign state. Citizens doing so would have their citizenship revoked and be incapable of holding any office of honor or profit under the United States.

Ratified by twelve states.

1861—Slavery Amendment

Forbade Congress from making any amendment to the Constitution that would give them the power "to abolish or interfere" with state domestic institutions, specifically slavery.

Ratified by two states.

1926—Child Labor Amendment

Gave Congress power to "limit, regulate, and prohibit" labor of children under the age of eighteen.

Ratified by twenty-seven states.

1972—Equal Rights Amendment

Provided equality under the law for men and women.

Ratified by thirty states.

1978—Voting Rights for Washington, D.C.

Provided citizens of Washington, D.C., with the same representation in Congress as the states.

Ratified by sixteen states.

SUBMITTED, BUT NEVER FORMALLY PROPOSED:

1876: The Senate shall be abolished.

1876: Religious leaders shall not hold political offices or receive federal funding.

1878: An executive council of three shall replace the office of president.

1893: The nation shall hereafter be known as the United States of the Earth.

1893: The army and navy shall be abolished.

1894: God and Jesus Christ shall be recognized in the Constitution as the supreme authorities in human affairs.

1914: Divorce shall be illegal.

1916: All acts of war shall be put to a national vote. All those affirming shall be registered as a volunteer for service in the United States Armed Forces.

1933: The personal wealth of any citizen may not exceed $1 million.

1938: Drunkenness shall be forbidden in the United States and all of its territories.

1948: Citizens shall have the right to segregate themselves from others.

1971: Citizens shall have the unalienable right to an environment free of pollution.

1989: Representatives shall be apportioned among the states based only on the total number of legal citizens of the United States.

1989: Naturalized citizens who have been citizens eleven years shall be eligible for the office of president.

1990: The flag shall be protected by the Constitution from physical desecration.

1991: English shall be the official language of the United States.

1997: Citizens shall have the right to a home.

1999: Life is declared to begin at conception, and thus the Fifth and Fourteenth Amendments apply to the unborn.

Once an amendment is proposed, it must go through the formal approval process called **ratification**—a state-level responsibility. Like the proposal process, ratification may also be made by two means: either by the approval of three-fourths of the states' legislatures or by the approval of three-fourths of special state ratification conventions. This last method is basically the way in which the Constitution was originally approved. The choice of ratification method, though, is left up to Congress, and only the Twenty-first Amendment (repeal of Prohibition) has been ratified by state conventions.

Generally, Congress places a seven-year time limit in which an amendment must be ratified or it expires. Amendments Twenty-one and Twenty-two actually spell this out as one of their provisions. One notable exception is the Twenty-seventh Amendment, which was proposed in 1789 as part of the Bill of Rights, but was not ratified until 1992—more than 202 years later. During the ratification period, even if a state fails to approve an amendment once, the proposal can be put up for approval again and again. If a state ratifies an amendment, its decision is considered final.

Of the twenty-seven amendments that have passed ratification, the first ten amendments, known as the **Bill of Rights,** were added in 1791 and were closely tied to the original ratification effort. Therefore, only seventeen amendments have been approved since the first session of Congress.

The small number of passed amendments reflects the stability of the Constitution. Interest groups or regions of the country cannot easily bend the Constitution to suit their particular desires. Generally, only amendments with broad appeal are ratified.

Not only are amendments difficult to ratify, they also are often not necessary. Congress may simply pass laws to deal with most problems. However, the amendment process remains an important aspect of the success of the Constitution. Amendments provide a means of fixing a law that has widespread popular support on a more or less permanent basis, such as giving eighteen-year-olds the vote, or correcting major deficiencies in the opera-

tion of the national government, such as clarifying presidential succession.

Section Review

1. How did their knowledge of human nature help the framers of the Constitution?
2. What characteristics of the United States Constitution give it flexibility in adapting to change?
3. What is the difference between a strict constructionist and a broad constructionist?
4. What are the two major phases in the amendment process? What are the various ways an amendment may pass through these phases?

II. Basic Principles

While the Constitution's basic principles are not stated word-for-word in its text, all are defined, embedded, or assumed within the document. These underlying principles of the Constitution were not invented in Philadelphia; they were gathered by the delegates from years of careful study of governments and political thinkers, and also from the painful lessons learned from the failed Confederation. All of these basic principles deal in some way with the issue of power—how to divide, balance, limit, and allot governmental power. The Constitutional framers forged a working balance with these principles that has provided our country with liberty, order, and an enduring charter.

Limited Government

Limited government is a theme of themes in the Constitution, underlying many of its other themes. It means that government does not have absolute power, but rather is limited to only those powers given it by the people through law. Therefore, this principle of limited government is inherent in the Constitution's form—being a *written* constitution. The Constitution is designed to establish boundaries of power for the state and therefore limits of liberty for the people. Since the law is written, the bounds of authority are not subject to the whims of rulers.

Written declarations of rights or demands were nothing new, but a written constitution that was distinct and superior to regular legislation was a novel idea in 1787.

The American colonists had lived under the unwritten British constitution, which Viscount Bolingbroke described as an "assemblage of laws, institutions, and customs derived from certain fixed principles of reason . . . that comprise the general system, according to which the community hath agreed to be governed." However, this collection of laws and traditions was not superior to Parliament, a fact which the colonists came to believe permitted Parliament to act capriciously with American rights.

All of this being a recent memory, the Philadelphia delegates charted a new course of action by establishing the Constitution as the "supreme law of the land," providing stability and a better safeguard for personal liberty. This is in fact the central purpose of limiting government—to protect individual freedom. As stated in Article VII, the supremacy of the Constitution

places not only the *governed* under its authority, but all who *govern* as well.

Since the founders understood that unchecked, concentrated power was simply another form of *tyranny,* they built certain obstacles into the system that would hinder the expansion of state power without harming its effectiveness to govern. These limitations involve the principles of separation of powers and checks and balances.

Separation of Powers

To prevent any group or individual from gaining too much control, national power is divided into three separate branches: the legislative branch, dealt with in Article I of the Constitution; the executive branch, the topic of Article II; and the judicial branch, explained in Article III. This **separation of powers** is more than just theoretical. Since 1935 all three branches have been housed in different buildings in Washington, D.C.—Congress at the Capitol building, the President at the White House, and the Supreme Court at the Supreme Court Building.

Influenced by the writings of Aristotle and Montesquieu, the founders differed with the British parliamentary system and the Confederation government, which lumped executive functions with the legislature. Under the

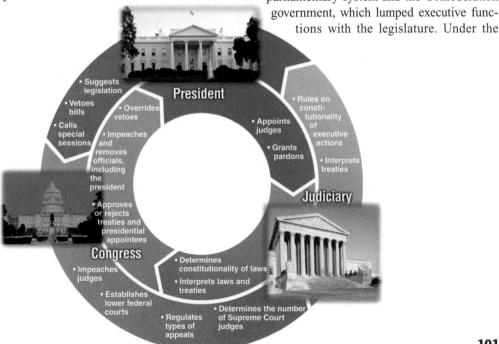

new Constitution, in broad terms, Congress makes the laws, the president executes and enforces the laws, and the courts interpret the laws.

Though these branches are separate, they are not independent. In many areas their responsibilities intersect, and a certain amount of cooperation is necessary for the national government to function properly.

Checks and Balances

Although separation of powers is often thought to be synonymous with **checks and balances,** there

Checks and Balances in the United States and South Africa

The Constitution of the United States provided numerous ways that the three branches of the national government would prevent each other from becoming too powerful. Compromises among different interests also are reflected in the Constitution. The two divisions of Congress represent a balance between the interests of large states and small ones. The House is based on population (therefore, the big states would have more representatives); and the Senate is composed of two per state, so small ones would have the same power in that chamber. Furthermore, in order to determine population for purposes of representation and taxes, the Constitution stated that three-fifths of slaves would be counted, a compromise between southern slaves states and northern nonslave states.

The Republic of South Africa, after the end of white-minority rule and apartheid, negotiated a new constitution that took effect in 1997. Balancing different parts of the new government and different racial and political interests was a painstaking process, and it produced one of the most complex constitutions in the world. South Africa's "rainbow" of races and cultures presented a challenge: black majority (the dominant African National Congress and the Zulus); white minority (Dutch, English, French, and German ancestry); Asian minority (Indians); and Coloured minority (mixed race).

The constitution borrows, appropriately, from several sources: German, American, Swiss, British, Indian, and South African history. South Africa was divided into nine provinces, comparable to American states. Parliament was divided into two bodies. The National Assembly has 400 members, 200 elected nationally and 200 provincially, based on proportional representation (each party's number of representatives corresponding to its percentage of the vote, not "winner-take-all" as in the U.S.). The National Council of Provinces, with 90 members, is also based on proportional representation. Ten are chosen by the individual provincial legislatures, a provision to give more power to the provinces. Throughout, there are some rough parallels to the American system.

Compromises are also evident in South Africa's executive branch. Unlike the U.S. system, the National Assembly elects the president. If a party has 80 seats in the National Assembly, even though it is a minority, it can name an executive deputy president. Both proportional representation in the election of members of Parliament and power sharing in the executive branch, on the national and provincial levels, protect minorities in South Africa. A "winner-take-all" system in South Africa would give virtually all power to the African National Congress in Parliament and in the executive branch; Zulus, whites, Asians, and Coloureds would have little voice in the government. If national and provincial legislation conflict, the national law prevails; therefore, South Africa does not have pure federalism. Similar to the U.S., the South African constitution has a bill of rights, one of the most liberal in the world.

is an important difference. If there were only a division of power in the national government, then one branch could expand its powers within its rightful sphere and come to dominate the other branches.

The principle of checks and balances thwarts such an accumulation of power. For example, Congress passes a bill to become law, but the president may reject or **veto** the bill if he opposes it. However, his veto may in turn be overridden by a two-thirds vote in both houses of Congress. Some other examples are the president's power to appoint justices and other top-level officials and his authority to make treaties. The Senate must approve his choices and treaties. The Supreme Court may nullify acts of both Congress and the president if a majority of justices interpret an act as unconstitutional. One particularly high-profile example is Congress's power of **impeachment:** the ability to charge the president and federal judges with misconduct in office. Most recently in 1998, the House of Representatives impeached President Bill Clinton. However, even within this process accumulation of power is avoided. Once impeached, Clinton faced an impeachment trial, not in the House but in the Senate, where he was acquitted.

Checks and balances hinder the concentration of power and thus protect personal liberty. There is an obvious disadvantage, however; the system is inefficient. In fact, the checks and balances system may actually prevent a branch from functioning properly. One branch may purposely bring the political process to a halt, creating **gridlock,** as in 1987 when it took President Reagan three attempts to get a Supreme Court nominee past a Democratic-controlled Senate. In the meantime, important high court cases had to be postponed while awaiting a full bench.

Part of the reason for this inefficiency comes from the development of political parties. When different parties control different branches of government, there is more incentive to use constitutional checks and balances for political purposes. For instance, in December of 1995 a Republican-controlled Congress and President Clinton deadlocked on budget issues. Congress refused to pass the president's budget proposal, while the president defeated congressional bills by exercising his veto. The result was a twenty-one-day government shutdown that left some 280,000 government workers temporarily unemployed. Each side attempted to convince voters that the other was to blame for the crisis.

Given the choice between tyranny and inefficiency, however, the advantages of checks and balances outweigh the disadvantages. This very inefficiency serves to further limit governmental power.

Judicial Review

Closely tied to the principle of check and balances is that of **judicial review**—the power of the judicial branch of government to review the constitutionality of laws passed by the legislative branch. Those laws found to be in contradiction to the judicial interpretation of the Constitution can be struck down.

Although the principle of judicial review is assumed today, it is not spelled out in the Constitution. In fact Thomas Jefferson, an opponent of judicial review, argued, "Certainly there is not a word in the Constitution which has given that power to them [the Judiciary] more than to the Executive or Legislative branches."

However, another founding father, Alexander Hamilton, explained the basis of the principle in *Federalist No. 78,*

> The complete independence of the courts of justice is peculiarly essential in a limited Constitution. By a limited Constitution, I understand one which contains certain specified exceptions to the legislative authority; such, for instance, as that it shall pass no bills of attainder, no ex-post-facto laws, and the like. Limitations of this kind can be preserved in practice no other way than through the medium of courts of justice, whose duty it must be to declare all acts contrary to the manifest tenor of the Constitution void.

The principle was not asserted until 1803 when Chief Justice John Marshall used it in the landmark Supreme Court case *Marbury v. Madison.* A more recent judicial review case involved the Line Item Veto Act (1996), which allowed the president to veto specific parts of a bill rather than the whole thing. The Supreme Court in 1998 declared the act unconstitutional on the basis that it would change the way a bill became law according to the Constitution.

Federalism

Federalism is the division of power between national and state levels of government. The federal system was a unique contribution in its day and grew out of the political realities of the colonial and confederation periods.

Thirteen separate colonies had grown up along the eastern coast. Begun at different times, for different reasons, with differing economies, climates, populations, and political systems, they nonetheless forged a loose-knit team to defeat the British and form a new government. The government was a confederation of thirteen fiercely independent states, an arrangement that soon began to fray at the seams.

The Constitutional framers represented these sovereign states, but most of the delegates also recognized the need for the strength and order of unity. Out of the need to balance state and national interests came federalism. This federal system not only further divides power, but, as we shall see in greater detail in Chapter 7, it also accommodates differences in various regions by giving people a greater voice in their affairs on the state and local level.

The Tenth Amendment contains the clearest definition of federalism:

> The powers not delegated to the United States by the Constitution, nor prohibited by it to the states, are reserved to the states respectively, or to the people.

Nevertheless, with the rise of the United States to world power and the growing economic interdependence of its people, the original authority of the states has necessarily waned. This decline in state power is an example of how modifications of the Constitution, shaped by circumstance, can be ratified by Supreme Court decisions over time. As writer James Kilpatrick has observed,

> John Marshall, the great chief justice, set about undermining state sovereignty in 1819. The Civil War accelerated the process. In 1941 the high court described the 10th as no more than a "truism." Now and then the justices have said a kind word for federalism, much as one pats an old dog, but it has been pretty much downhill all the way.

Popular Sovereignty

The Enlightenment emphasized the idea of **popular sovereignty**—that the people are the ultimate source of their government's authority. The Christian obviously has a problem with this theory since the ultimate authority over government is God, not man. However, there is a certain degree of truth in this idea if not taken to the extreme. In the United States, God establishes rulers through the vote of the people. Consequently, our rulers are accountable not only to God but to the people as well.

As important as popular sovereignty is, it is not explicitly expressed in the Constitution. Rather, it is a general theme. Much has been made of the opening phrase of the Preamble—"We the People"—as evidence of the strength of the popular sovereignty theme in the Constitution. This emphasis on popular sovereignty, however, is a later one. The original draft of the Preamble listed each of the thirteen states:

> We the People of the States of New-Hampshire, Massachusetts, Rhode-Island and Providence Plantations, Connecticut, New-York, New-Jersey, Pennsylvania, Delaware, Maryland, Virginia, North-Carolina, South-Carolina, and Georgia, do ordain, declare and establish the following Constitution for the Government of Ourselves and our Posterity.

When the Committee of Style, headed by Gouverneur Morris, put the final touches on the Constitution's text, they foresaw the difficulties that could arise by listing all of the states as consenting when some were positively hostile to the Constitution and ratification there promised to be an uphill battle. Morris, a skilled editor, solved the problem with a flourish—"We the People of the United States."

> We the People of the United States, in order to form a more perfect Union, establish Justice, ensure domestic tranquillity, provide for the common defense, promote the general welfare, and secure the blessings of liberty to ourselves and our posterity, do ordain and establish this Constitution for the United States of America.

Therefore, when it was first penned, "We the People" was more a triumph of editorial eloquence than a keynote for popular sovereignty.

The principle of popular sovereignty is more accurately expressed in the Constitution through representation and amendment provisions. Representation allows the people to have a voice in their government through their elected officials. The Constitutional framers, fearing the fickleness of public opinion, sought to limit the directness of the people's voice on the national level by providing direct election only for the House of Representatives. Over the years as democratic participation expanded, this limitation came to be viewed as too restrictive. The result was the Seventeenth Amendment (1913), which provided for the direct election of senators. This example in fact demonstrates popular sovereignty in another way—the amendment process.

Amendments are an expression of the people's sovereignty because those amendments that survive the arduous ratification process often reflect widespread popular support and are superior to the laws of Congress, the actions of the president, and the decisions of the courts. Chief Justice Marshall stated this point powerfully: "The people made the Constitution and the people can unmake it. It is the creature of their own will, and lives only by their will."

"We the People" is an enduring declaration not only of the people's power to rule themselves but also of the people's responsibility for that rule. Self-government is no easy task. It does not occur by accident; neither is it a well-oiled, self-propelled machine. The people of each generation must grapple with their government—use its principles, build on its process in order to make it work for their day. They must also be careful to guard the privilege of self-government from those who would twist its power to their own advantage.

Conclusion

While some constitutions are simply parchments of promises, our Constitution is rather a cornerstone for ordered liberty, true self-government, and personal liberties that have made America a "city set upon a hill" for millions living under repressive regimes around the world. Christians can see much in the Constitution and in the vision of its writers for which they should be thankful. While the believer's chief source of authority is the Scripture, he has an obligation to respect and obey the Constitution because it is the fundamental law of the land.

The Constitution and its first ten amendments have been the guarantor of our liberties: freedom of worship, freedom of speech and press, and freedom of association. However, these constitutional guarantees are empowered not by custom, but by commitment—a commitment that each generation must make to defend its law and cherish its liberties.

Section Review

1. What six basic principles of government guided the creation and interpretation of the Constitution?

2. What is the difference between separation of powers and checks and balances?

3. What is the obvious disadvantage of checks and balances? What benefit overshadows this disadvantage?

4. What is judicial review? Why did Hamilton believe it was necessary?

5. What unusual situation in America led to the unique federal system that developed?

6. What is popular sovereignty? Where is this principle applied in the Constitution? How has this principle expanded over the years?

Preamble

The **Preamble** introduces the Constitution by explaining its nature and purpose. First it states the source of the government's power: "We the people." Second, the Preamble establishes the purposes of government:

1. to form a more perfect union,
2. to establish justice,
3. to ensure domestic tranquility,
4. to provide for the common defense,
5. to promote the general welfare, and
6. to secure the blessings of liberty to our posterity.

Much of its text comes from Article Three of the Articles of Confederation, which stated,

> The said States hereby severally enter into a firm league of friendship with each other, for their common defense, the security of their liberties, and their mutual and general welfare, binding themselves to assist each other, against all force offered to, or attacks made upon them, or any of them, on account of religion, sovereignty, trade or any other pretense whatsoever.

Article I: The Legislative Branch

Section 1—Authority

Article I deals with the **legislative branch** of government, whose primary function is to make laws. This power belongs to Congress, which has two houses, an upper house called the Senate and a lower house called the House of Representatives. A two-house legislative system is called a **bicameral** system.

Section 2—The House of Representatives

(1) Members of the House serve two-year terms, with all House seats being up for election at the same time. House members have always been elected directly by the people.

(2) In order to qualify for office in the House of Representatives, members must be

a. at least twenty-five years old,
b. citizens for at least seven years, and
c. residents of the state they represent.

(3) The number of representatives each state receives is determined by its population, according to the agreement of the Great Compromise. Also, any direct federal taxation of the states must be distributed according to population. Amendment XVI, however, makes the income tax an exception to this rule. Special arrangements were made by the three-fifths compromise for counting slaves, indentured servants, and Indians in the population, but these rules no longer apply since the end of slavery and the beginning of Indian citizenship. Today the House membership has been set at 435. There are also five nonvoting members from

III. The United States Constitution

[Note: Sections in *light italic type* are sections of the Constitution which are no longer in force.]

Preamble

We the people of the United States, in order to form a more perfect union, establish justice, ensure domestic tranquillity, provide for the common defense, promote the general welfare, and secure the blessings of liberty to ourselves and our posterity, do ordain and establish this Constitution for the United States of America.

Article I: The Legislative Branch

Section I

All legislative powers herein granted shall be vested in a Congress of the United States, which shall consist of a Senate and House of Representatives.

Section 2

1. The House of Representatives shall be composed of members chosen every second year by the people of the several states, and the electors in each state shall have the qualifications requisite for electors of the most numerous branch of the state legislature.

2. No person shall be a representative who shall not have attained to the age of twenty-five years, and been seven years a citizen of the United States, and who shall not, when elected, be an inhabitant of that state in which he shall be chosen.

3. Representatives *and direct taxes* shall be apportioned among the several states which may be included within this Union, according to their respective numbers, *which shall be determined by adding to the whole number of free persons, including those bound to service for a term of years, and excluding Indians not taxed, three-fifths of all other persons.* The actual enumeration shall be made within three years after the first meeting of the Congress of the United States, and within every subsequent term of ten years, in such manners as they shall by law direct. The number of representatives shall not exceed one for every thirty thousand, but each state shall have at least one representative; *and until such*

enumeration shall be made, the state of New Hampshire shall be entitled to choose three, Massachusetts eight, Rhode Island and Providence Plantations one, Connecticut five, New York six, New Jersey four, Pennsylvania eight, Delaware one, Maryland six, Virginia ten, North Carolina five, South Carolina five, and Georgia three.

4. When vacancies happen in the representation from any state, the executive authority thereof shall issue writs of election to fill such vacancies.

5. The House of Representatives shall choose their speaker and other officers; and shall have the sole power of impeachment.

Section 3

1. The Senate of the United States shall be composed of two senators from each state, *chosen by the legislature thereof,* for six years; and each senator shall have one vote.

2. Immediately after they shall be assembled in consequence of the first election, they shall be divided as equally as may be into three classes. *The seats of the senators of the first class shall be vacated at the expiration of the second year, of the second class at the expiration of the fourth year, and of the third class at the expiration of the sixth year, so that one-third may be chosen every second year; and if vacancies happen by resignation, or otherwise, during the recess of the legislature of any state, the executive thereof may make temporary appointments until the next meeting of the legislature, which shall then fill such vacancies.*

3. No person shall be a senator who shall not have attained to the age of thirty years, and been nine years a citizen of the United States, and who shall not, when elected, be an inhabitant of that state for which he shall be chosen.

4. The Vice President of the United States shall be President of the Senate, but shall have no vote, unless they be equally divided.

5. The Senate shall choose their other officers, and also a president pro tempore, in the absence of the Vice President, or when he shall exercise the office of President of the United States.

Washington, D.C., Puerto Rico, Guam, American Samoa, and the Virgin Islands. A counting of the population, called a **census,** is taken every ten years to determine how many of these representatives each state receives.

(4) Vacancies in the House of Representatives are filled by special elections called by the state governors.

(5) The head of the House is called the Speaker of the House; he is elected by the House members. The House has the sole power of impeachment, the filing of charges against a major federal official.

Section 3—The Senate

(1) Each state has two senators according to the terms of the Great Compromise, with each serving six-year terms. Senators were first elected by state legislatures. Since the passage of Amendment XVII in 1913, the senators have been elected directly by the people.

(2) The Constitution made arrangements for one-third of the senators to stand for election every two years. By this method the Senate can act with continuity from one session of Congress to another because no more than one-third of the senators will be new to the body following an election. The experienced senators who did not stand for election at that time will be able to help keep order through the transition.

The process for filling Senate vacancies was changed by Amendment XVII, which allows state governors to appoint replacements or call for special elections to select one.

(3) In order to be able to serve as a U.S. senator, members must be

   a. at least thirty years old,
   b. citizens for at least nine years, and
   c. residents of the state they represent.

(4) The head (president) of the Senate is the vice president of the United States. He votes in case of a tie. In the case of a 50-50 split in party affiliation, the party of the vice president becomes the majority in the Senate.

(5) The Senate also elects its own **president pro tempore,** who serves as leader of the Senate when the vice president is absent. (*Pro tempore* simply means "for the time being.") The president pro tempore is third in line in the presidential succession following the vice president and the Speaker of the House.

(6) The Senate acts as a trial court for impeachment cases. Two-thirds of the senators must vote for conviction in order to remove the official from office. If the president is impeached, the Chief Justice of the Supreme Court presides over the trial rather than the vice president.

(7) When the House impeaches an official and the Senate tries and confirms the charges, Congress may punish him only by removing him from office and barring him from holding any government offices in the future. Even so, the person can be tried in a regular civil or criminal court afterwards and sentenced to further punishment if found guilty.

Section 4—Election and Assembly

(1) State legislatures have the right to administer congressional elections in their states, but they must follow any regulations established by Congress. For instance, national law requires that secret ballots be used in these elections. Congressional elections are held on the Tuesday following the first Monday in November in even-numbered years.

(2) Congress is to meet at least once a year. Originally it began its meeting on the first Monday in December. Now it first meets at noon on January 3 because the date was changed by Amendment XX.

Section 5—Procedures

(1) Each house judges its own elections. A **quorum** is the minimum number needed to transact business. In this case, a simple majority (just over one-half the members) constitutes a quorum. A **sergeant-at-arms** for both houses is responsible to bring in members who are absent and are needed to make up a quorum.

(2) The House and the Senate make their own rules for establishing committees, presenting bills, and other needed procedures. A disorderly member can be expelled by a two-thirds vote of the body in which he has served.

(3) Each house keeps a journal or record of what it does each day. Today this is called *The Congressional Record.* Some congressional proceedings may be kept secret, but a written record of any vote is kept if one-fifth of those present request it.

6. The Senate shall have the sole power to try all impeachments. When sitting for that purpose, they shall be on oath or affirmation. When the President of the United States is tried the chief justice shall preside: And no person shall be convicted without the concurrence of two-thirds of the members present.

7. Judgment in cases of impeachment shall not extend further than to removal from office, and disqualification to hold and enjoy any office of honor, trust or profit under the United States; but the party convicted shall nevertheless be liable and subject to indictment, trial, judgment and punishment, according to law.

Section 4

1. The times, places and manner of holding elections, for senators and representatives, shall be prescribed in each state by the legislature thereof; but the Congress may at any time by law make or alter such regulations, except as to the places of choosing senators.

2. The Congress shall assemble at least once in every year, *and such meeting shall be on the first Monday in December, unless they shall by law appoint a different day.*

Section 5

1. Each house shall be the judge of the elections, returns and qualifications of its own members, and a majority of each shall constitute a quorum to do business; but a smaller number may adjourn from day to day, and may be authorized to compel the attendance of absent members, in such manner, and under such penalties as each house may provide.

2. Each house may determine the rules of its proceedings, punish its members for disorderly behavior, and, with the concurrence of two-thirds, expel a member.

3. Each house shall keep a journal of its proceedings, and from time to time publish the same, excepting such parts as may, in their judgment require secrecy; and the yeas and nays of the members of either house on any question, shall at the desire of one-fifth of those present, be entered on the journal.

4. Neither house, during the session of Congress, shall, without the consent of the other,

adjourn for more than three days, nor to any other place than that in which the two houses shall be sitting.

Section 6

1. The senators and representatives shall receive a compensation for their services, to be ascertained by law, and paid out of the treasury of the United States. They shall in all cases, except treason, felony and breach of the peace, be privileged from arrest during their attendance at the session of their respective houses, and in going to and returning from the same; and for any speech or debate in either house, they shall not be questioned in any other place.

2. No senator or representative shall, during the time for which he was elected, be appointed to any civil office under the authority of the United States, which shall have been created, or the emoluments whereof shall have been increased during such time; and no person holding any office under the United States, shall be a member of either house during his continuance in office.

Section 7

1. All bills for raising revenue shall originate in the House of Representatives; but the Senate may propose or concur with amendments as on other bills.

2. Every bill which shall have passed the House of Representatives and the Senate, shall, before it becomes a law, be presented to the President of the United States; if he approves, he shall sign it, but if not, he shall return it, with his objections, to that house in which it shall have originated, who shall enter the objections at large on their journal, and proceed to reconsider it. If after such reconsideration, two-thirds of that house shall agree to pass the bill, it shall be sent, together with the objections, to the other house, by which it shall likewise be reconsidered, and if approved by two-thirds of that house, it shall become a law. But in all such cases the votes of both houses shall be determined by yeas and nays, and the names of the persons voting for and against the bill shall be entered on the journal of each house respectively. If any bill shall not be returned by the President within ten days (Sundays excepted) after it shall have been pre-

(4) Since the houses work together to pass legislation, one cannot adjourn (go out of official session) for more than three days, nor can it move its meeting to another location without the permission of the other.

Section 6—Benefits and Restrictions

(1) Senators and representatives are public employees paid salaries by the U.S. Treasury. Both senators and representatives receive an annual salary of around $150,000. They also receive allowances for travel, office expenses, and the **franking privilege** (the right to send official mail free of charge). They cannot be arrested going to or from the House or Senate (except for treason or serious crimes), nor can they be arrested for what they say on the floor of the House or Senate. This precaution gives members of Congress the freedom to voice even unpopular ideas without fear of being arrested to prohibit their participation in Congress.

(2) A member of Congress must give up any other federal offices he holds to become a member of Congress. He cannot take any federal office created by his house of Congress until his term is ended, and he cannot take an office for which Congress has increased the pay during his term until his term is expired. This prevents Congress from giving themselves offices with increased salaries.

Section 7—Law Making

(1) Bills dealing with taxation must start in the House, but the Senate may make changes if it desires. The Senate is not totally without power to initiate money legislation. Appropriations bills, which allocate funds, can be initiated by the Senate, as can revenue bills not dealing with taxation.

(2) In order for a bill to become a law, it must be passed by both houses and signed by the president. This is a part of the system of checks and balances. If the president opposes the bill, he may return it to the body where it started, stating his objections. This is a veto. Congress may override the president's veto with a two-thirds vote of both houses, and the bill becomes law. If the president does not sign a bill that comes to him and does not veto it, it becomes law in ten days as long as Congress remains in session. If he does not sign a bill and Congress adjourns within ten days, it is vetoed automatically. This is called a **"pocket veto."**

(3) All other acts requiring approval of both houses of Congress (except the decision to adjourn Congress) require the signature of the president or overriding his veto by a two-thirds vote of both houses.

Section 8—The Enumerated (numbered and listed) Powers of Congress

(1) *It has the power to tax.* Congress can lay (impose the amounts or system) and collect taxes, duties (taxes on imports), and excises (internal taxes on the production, sale, or consumption of certain items such as telephones).

(2) *It has the power to borrow money.* The government usually borrows money by selling bonds or certificates, which it pledges to repay later with interest.

(3) *It has the power to regulate trade with foreign nations, within the country, and with the Indians.* The power to regulate interstate commerce has been stretched greatly, beginning in the late nineteenth century, to allow government intervention in many business matters by federal laws and regulatory agencies.

(4) *It has the power to regulate naturalization and bankruptcy laws.* **Naturalization** is the process by which a foreign-born person gains citizenship. *Bankruptcy* is the way a debtor is declared unable to pay his creditors; all assets are first divided among any creditors. The laws are uniform throughout the United States so that it is not easier or harder to gain citizenship or declare bankruptcy in one state than another.

(5) *It has the power to control the currency system and the standard weights and measurements used in the country.* Congress has declared the metric system to be the preferred system of the United States although conformity is mostly voluntary.

(6) *It has the power to punish those who illegally interfere in the currency system. Counterfeiting* means forging or making copies of something (money in particular) and using it illegally.

(7) *It has the power to provide needed offices and roads for postal service.* Post roads are roads for delivering the mail. They became the basic roads of the U.S. highway system. This clause was also used as the legal basis for the creation of the interstate highway system.

(8) *It has the power to issue copyrights and patents.* Copyrights are issued by the Library of Congress and protect authors and their heirs from having their works copied by another person. (Today the length of the copyright is the lifetime of the author plus fifty years). Patents are granted by the Patent Office in the Department of Commerce, and they protect inventors from having their inventions or ideas taken by another person for use or profit. The Patent Office also registers trademarks.

sented to him, the same shall be a law, in like manner as if he had signed it, unless the Congress by their adjournment prevent its return, in which case it shall not be a law.

3. Every order, resolution, or vote to which the concurrence of the Senate and House of Representatives may be necessary (except on a question of adjournment) shall be presented to the President of the United States; and before the same shall take effect, shall be approved by him, or, being disapproved by him, shall be passed by two-thirds of the Senate and House of Representatives, according to the rules and limitations prescribed in the case of a bill.

Section 8
The Congress shall have power

1. To lay and collect taxes, duties, imposts and excises, to pay the debts and provide for the common defense and general welfare of the United States; but all duties, imposts, and excises shall be uniform throughout the United States;

2. To borrow money on the credit of the United States;

3. To regulate commerce with foreign nations, and among the several states, and with the Indian tribes;

4. To establish a uniform rule of naturalization, and uniform laws on the subject of bankruptcies throughout the United States;

5. To coin money, regulate the value thereof, and of foreign coin, and fix the standard of weights and measures;

6. To provide for the punishment of counterfeiting the securities and current coin of the United States;

7. To establish post-offices and post-roads;

8. To promote the progress of science and useful arts, by securing for limited times to authors and inventors the exclusive right to their respective writings and discoveries;

9. To constitute tribunals inferior to the Supreme Court;

10. To define and punish piracies and felonies committed on the high seas, and offenses against the law of nations;

11. To declare war, grant letters of marque and reprisal, and make rules concerning captures on land and water;

12. To raise and support armies, but no appropriation of money to that use shall be for a longer term than two years;

13. To provide and maintain a navy;

14. To make rules for the government and regulation of the land and naval forces;

15. To provide for calling forth the militia to execute the laws of the union, suppress insurrections and repel invasions;

16. To provide for organizing, arming and disciplining the militia, and for governing such part of them as may be employed in the service of the United States, reserving to the states respectively, the appointment of the officers, and the authority of training the militia according to the discipline prescribed by Congress;

17. To exercise exclusive legislation in all cases whatsoever, over such district (not exceeding ten miles square) as may, by cession of particular states, and the acceptance of Congress, become the seat of the government of the United States, and to exercise like authority over all places purchased by the consent of the legislature of the state in which the same shall be, for the erection of forts, magazines, arsenals, dockyards, and other needful buildings; and

(9) *It has the power to establish federal courts other than the Supreme Court.* The federal court system is like a pyramid with the Supreme Court on top. Beneath that are the thirteen circuit courts and the Court of Appeals for the Armed Forces. Next, are the ninety-four district courts throughout the states, courts with special jurisdiction (e.g., taxes, trade, veterans), and courts of review for specific branches of the military.

(10) *It has power to determine what acts committed at sea are crimes and to commit offenders along with pirates operating in U.S. waters or attacking U.S. ships to federal courts for trial.* Piracy is the robbing of ships at sea. Other offenses against international law, such as terrorism and hijacking, are included under Congress's jurisdiction.

(11) *Congress alone has the power to declare war.* Although the president is commander in chief of the armed forces, Congress holds many powers that keep the president's military powers in check and ensure civilian control of the military. Nevertheless, presidents have been permitted to commit troops to limited military engagements. The 1973 War Powers Act somewhat curtailed presidential power in this area. However, smaller military engagements continue to occur without congressional authorization.

Letters of marque and reprisal, discussed in this clause, were once used to permit private vessels to be outfitted to fight in wartime and to capture enemy goods and people. Such permissions are no longer used.

(12) *Congress may create an army, but it cannot vote to use money to support the army more than two years ahead of time.* Army appropriations (monies set aside for armies) are limited to two years to prevent a takeover or misuse of power by the military.

(13) *It has the power to create a navy and vote for money to support it.* America's first navy was actually created prior to the Constitution by the Continental Congress in 1775. However, it disbanded after the war. Congress, acting under this provision, created a new navy in 1794 to protect U.S. merchant ships in the Mediterranean.

(14) *It has the power to make the rules for the armed services.* Active-duty military personnel are bound by military law rather than civil law. This fact is reflected in the establishment of separate courts to deal with military cases. Military judges hear the cases and prosecution and defense attorneys are provided by Judge Advocates—officers in each military branch under the Judge Advocate General (JAG) who supply legal advice and services.

(15) *It may call the state militias into service for the national government under certain conditions.* The modern militia, known as the **National Guard,** is actually under the control of the army and air force. This change has allowed National Guard forces to support regular forces abroad since the conditions of this clause limited it to domestic situations only.

(16) *It has the power to organize, arm, and discipline the militias, while the states appoint the officers and train these troops.* When called into national service, the militia is under federal control as a part of the armed forces. However, by its nature the militia is also a check against the power of a standing army.

(17) *It has the power to make laws for the District of Columbia and for all other federal properties such as forts, military installations, or bases.* Today this also includes post offices, national historic sites, cemeteries, forests, parks, and fisheries.

(18) *It has power to do what it believes is necessary and proper to carry out any listed power.* This "necessary and proper clause" of the Constitution is sometimes also called the **elastic clause.** To borrow money, for example, Congress can sell bonds and even create a bank. The Supreme Court can check this power by deciding whether the laws Congress passes by this authority are really necessary and proper.

Section 9—Powers Forbidden to the Federal Government

(1) *Congress could not interfere with the slave trade until 1808, and it could not tax slavery out of existence by levying heavy taxes on slaves.* Congress did indeed abolish the importation of slaves on January 1, 1808, the earliest possible date. However, an illegal slave trade continued to flourish as well as the interstate trade.

(2) *Congress may not take away a person's right to the* **writ of habeas corpus** *except in times of extreme danger.* A writ of *habeas corpus* (Latin for "you should have the body," the first words in the writ) forces authorities who have arrested a person to quickly bring him before a judge and charge him with a crime or else release him. Because of this right, a person cannot be held prisoner unless a credible charge of a crime is made against him. People in dictatorships and other repressive regimes do not have this important right, and they may be held as prisoners indefinitely at the whim of government officials.

(3) *Congress cannot pass a* **bill of attainder,** *which permits punishment without a trial, or an* **ex post facto law,** *which makes the law retroactive.* Acts that were legal when they were done cannot be made illegal afterwards.

(4) *Congress cannot levy a direct tax that is not equal for all citizens.* For example, it could not make Californians pay a special tax of one hundred dollars when people from Ohio have to pay only fifty dollars. Amendment XVI made the income tax an exception. (People who make more money than others are supposed to pay more income tax than others.)

18. To make all laws which shall be necessary and proper for carrying into execution the foregoing powers, and all other powers vested by this Constitution in the government of the United States, or in any department or officer thereof.

Section 9

1. *The migration or importation of such persons as any of the states now existing shall think proper to admit, shall not be prohibited by the Congress prior to the year 1808, but a tax or duty may be imposed on such importations, not exceeding ten dollars for each person.*

2. The privilege of the writ of habeas corpus shall not be suspended, unless when in cases of rebellion or invasion the public safety may require it.

3. No bill of attainder or ex post facto law shall be passed.

4. No capitation, or other direct tax shall be laid *unless in proportion to the census or enumeration herein before directed to be taken.*

5. No tax or duty shall be laid on articles exported from any state.

6. No preference shall be given by any regulation of commerce or revenue to the ports of one state over those of another: nor shall vessels bound to, or from one state, be obliged to enter, clear, or pay duties in another.

7. No money shall be drawn from the treasury but in consequence of appropriations made by law; and a regular statement and account of the receipts and expenditures of all public money shall be published from time to time.

8. No title of nobility shall be granted by the United States: and no person holding any office of profit or trust under them, shall, without the consent of the Congress, accept of any present, emolument, office, or title, of any kind whatever: from any king, prince or foreign state.

Section 10

1. No state shall enter into any treaty, alliance, or confederation; grant letters of marque and reprisal; coin money; emit bills of credit; make any thing but gold and silver coin a tender in payment of debts; pass any bill of attainder, ex post facto law, or law impairing the obligation of contracts, or grant any title of nobility.

2. No state shall, without the consent of the Congress, lay any imposts or duties on imports or exports, except what may be absolutely necessary for executing its inspection laws; and the net produce of all duties and imposts, laid by any state on imports or exports, shall be for the use of the treasury of the United States; and all such laws shall be subject to the revision and control of the Congress.

3. No state shall, without the consent of Congress, lay any duty of tonnage, keep troops, or ships of war in time of peace, enter into any agreement or compact with another state, or with a foreign power, or engage in war, unless actually invaded, or in such imminent danger as will not admit of delay.

(5) *Congress cannot tax the exports of the states.* This means that neither those goods exported to other nations nor those exported to other states may be taxed.

(6) *Congress cannot give preference to any port or state through its laws, and it cannot tax trade between the states, even if that trade is carried on by sea or other water passage.*

(7) *Money from the treasury can be spent only if Congress approves, and a record of income and expenditures must be published.* An **appropriation** is a certain amount of money set apart for a certain purpose. This clause gives Congress the "power of the purse."

The Secretary of the Treasury is in charge of the government's financial report.

(8) *The United States cannot grant titles of nobility (duke, earl, baron, etc.) nor can its citizens accept titles or honors from foreign countries without the permission of Congress.*

Section 10—Powers Denied to the States

(1–3) With this section the federal government retains exclusive power to enter into treaties, coin money, and control various other governmental functions. The section also ensures certain rights and ideas by adding some federal restrictions to the states, including prohibitions against passing bills of attainder and ex post facto laws and granting titles of nobility. Congress also receives authority to approve or disapprove certain state actions such as charging import taxes and keeping military ships in peacetime. However, states may respond to attacks if they are invaded. By limiting state powers, the Constitution makes the central government stronger and produces a more united government.

Questions on Article I

1. What are the purposes of government as outlined by the Constitution's Preamble?
2. What is the primary function of Congress?
3. What is the difference between the House and the Senate in the following areas: frequency of elections, term of office, qualifications of members, and representation per state?
4. What are the respective roles of the House and Senate when a major federal official has committed a crime?
5. Why do members of Congress have special protection against arrest?
6. What is a veto? How can Congress override a veto?
7. Which of the enumerated powers deal with money?
8. Which of the enumerated powers deal with the military?
9. What legal powers is Congress forbidden to use?
10. What powers over commerce has Congress been restricted from using?
11. What powers over money and commerce have the states been denied?

Article II: The Executive Branch

Section 1—Authority and Office of President

Article II deals with the **executive branch** of government, whose primary function is to carry out the nation's laws.

(1) Both the president and vice president serve four-year terms. The four-year term strikes a balance by allowing enough time for the president to act with firmness and a level of independence in office, while hindering any officeholder from accumulating too much power.

(2) The **electoral college,** composed of electors from each state, elects the president. Currently the college is made up of 538 electors, which equals the total number of senators (100) and representatives (435) each state has in Congress, plus three electors from the District of Columbia, which gained representation by the terms of Amendment XXIII. The electors who participate in this process are usually prominent party members, and usually pledge their vote to the candidate popularly elected by their state. However, there is no federal provision requiring them to vote this way, and. barring state regulations, they are free to vote as they choose.

The Senate and House of Representatives oversee the counting of the electoral votes. If no candidate receives a majority of the votes, the House of Representatives votes by state to choose the new president, and the Senate must choose a vice president under such circumstances. The House had to make the presidential choice in two elections—1800 and 1824. The Senate had to choose the vice president for the 1836 election. Other details of this procedure were replaced by Amendment XII in 1804 because of the difficulties that arose after the formation of political parties.

Article II: The Executive Branch

Section I

1. The executive power shall be vested in a President of the United States of America. He shall hold his office during the term of four years, and, together with the Vice President, chosen for the same term, be elected as follows.

2. Each state shall appoint, in such manner as the legislature thereof may direct, a number of electors, equal to the whole number of senators and representatives to which the state may be entitled in the Congress; but no senator or representative, or person holding an office of trust or profit under the United States, shall be appointed an elector.

The electors shall meet in their respective states, and vote by ballot for two persons, of whom one at least shall not be an inhabitant of the same state with themselves. And they shall make a list of all the persons voted for, and of the number of votes for each; which list they shall sign and certify, and transmit sealed to the seat of the government of the United States, directed to the President of the Senate. The President of the Senate shall, in the presence of the Senate and House of Representatives, open all the certificates and the votes shall then be counted. The person having the greatest number of votes shall be the President, if such number be a majority of the whole number of electors appointed; and if there be more than one who have such majority, and have an equal number of votes, then the House of Representatives shall immediately choose by ballot one of them for President; and if no person have a majority, then from the five highest on the list, the said House shall, in like manner, choose the President. But in choosing the President, the votes shall be taken by states, the representation from each state having one vote; a quorum for this purpose shall consist of a member or members from two-thirds of the states, and a majority of all the states shall be necessary to a choice. In every case, after the choice of the President, the person having the greatest number of votes of the electors shall be the Vice President. But if there should remain two or more who have equal votes, the Senate shall choose from them by ballot the Vice President.

3. The Congress may determine the time of choosing the electors, and the day on which they shall give their votes; which day shall be the same throughout the United States.

4. No person except a natural-born citizen, *or a citizen of the United States, at the time of the adoption of this Constitution,* shall be eligible to the office, who shall not have attained to the age of thirty-five years, and been fourteen years a resident within the United States.

5. In case of the removal of the President from office, or of his death, resignation, or inability to discharge the powers and duties of the said office, the same shall devolve on the Vice President, and the Congress may by law provide for the case of removal, death, resignation, or inability, both of the President and Vice President, declaring what officer shall then act as President, and such officer shall act accordingly, until the disability be removed, or a President shall be elected.

6. The President shall, at stated times, receive for his services, a compensation, which shall neither be increased nor diminished during the period for which he shall have been elected, and he shall not receive within that period any other emolument from the United States, or any of them.

7. Before he enter on the execution of his office, he shall take the following oath or affirmation:—"I do solemnly swear (or affirm) that I will faithfully execute the office of President of the United States, and will to the best of my ability, preserve, protect and defend the Constitution of the United States."

Section 2

1. The President shall be commander in chief of the army and navy of the United States, and of the militia of the several states, when called into the actual service of the United States; he may require the opinion, in writing, of the principal officer in each of the executive departments, upon any subject relating to the duties of their respective offices, and he shall have power to grant reprieves and pardons for offenses against the United States, except in cases of impeachment.

(3) Congress determines the time for the president's election. Election day is the first Tuesday after the first Monday in November, and the electors meet in December at their respective capitals to cast their votes.

(4) Qualifications: The president must be

    a. a natural-born citizen,
    b. at least thirty-five years of age, and
    c. a resident of the U.S. for at least fourteen years.

(5) Presidential Succession: In 1948 Congress established the present line of succession:

    a. vice president, as stated in the Constitution;
    b. the Speaker of the House of Representatives;
    c. the president pro tempore of the Senate; and
    d. the members of the president's cabinet in order of the creation of their departments (secretary of state, secretary of the treasury, secretary of defense, attorney general, etc).

Amendment XXV, however, made provision for appointment of a new vice president when that office is vacant so that it is unlikely that succession would fall on anyone other than a vice president.

(6) The president's salary stays the same throughout his term. In 1999 it was increased from $200,000 to $400,000 per year, plus $50,000 to cover office expenses.

(7) The president's oath of office is dictated by the Constitution. The word "affirm" is offered because some religions object to the use of the word "swear." (See Matt. 5:34.) George Washington added the words "so help me God" to the end of the oath, and that addition has become tradition.

Section 2—Powers and Duties of the President

(1) Though Congress has some authority to check the president's military powers, his resources as commander in chief are many. Without a declaration of war the president may approve covert operations, send out military patrols, and take other military actions. After Congress has declared war, he has wide powers to direct military operations. It was the president who ordered the atomic bombs to be dropped on Japan in World War II, and it was the president who ordered American troops into the undeclared war in Vietnam.

The phrase "in each of the executive departments" became the basis for the establishment of the president's cabinet. George Washington's cabinet included only four departments (state, treasury, war, and attorney general). Currently, there are fifteen departments, although several other officials may be included in the cabinet.

Included among the president's powers is the power to grant **reprieves,** the temporary postponement of punishment, and **pardons,** the complete forgiveness of a crime and its consequent punishment. The president also has the power to offer amnesty, which is a general pardon to a group.

(2) This clause contains some of the checks and balances given to Congress over the president. The president or his diplomats may make treaties, but the Senate must approve them by a two-thirds majority. The president appoints ambassadors, ministers, consuls, judges, and other officials as allowed by Congress with approval of the Senate. Other positions are filled through the Civil Service Commission, an organization used since 1883 to distribute government jobs according to merit rather than as awards to political friends under the "spoils system" or patronage system.

(3) The president can fill vacancies in offices without Senate approval if the Senate is out of session. This clause was originally added to avoid long delays in government action when poor roads or weather kept senators from meeting. Today, presidents often avoid confirmation hearings this way, although they must be careful not to alienate the Senate or public by over-using this power.

Section 3—Duties of the President

a. The president gives Congress the required information in a written message or in a speech, called the State of the Union address. It is usually given near the end of January of each year.

b. The president can suggest that Congress pass certain legislation.

c. He can convene (call into official session) both houses. This has been done to deal with national emergencies, such as when President Wilson convened Congress to declare war on Germany in 1917.

d. If the House and Senate cannot agree on adjournment, the president can intervene.

e. He receives ambassadors and public ministers. This function is important to the presidential power in foreign affairs.

f. The president grants military officers their commissions.

2. He shall have power, by and with the advice and consent of the Senate, to make treaties, provided two-thirds of the senators present concur; and he shall nominate, and by and with the advice and consent of the Senate, shall appoint ambassadors, other public ministers and consuls, judges of the Supreme Court, and all other officers of the United States, whose appointments are not herein otherwise provided for, and which shall be established by law. But the Congress may by law vest the appointment of such inferior officers, as they think proper in the President alone, in the courts of law, or in the heads of departments.

3. The President shall have power to fill up all vacancies that may happen during the recess of the Senate, by granting commissions, which shall expire at the end of their next session.

Section 3

He shall, from time to time, give to the Congress information of the state of the union, and recommend to their consideration, such measures as he shall judge necessary and expedient; he may, on extraordinary occasions, convene both houses, or either of them, and in case of disagreement between them, with respect to the time of adjournment, he may adjourn them to such time as he shall think proper; he shall receive ambassadors and other public ministers; he shall take care that the laws be faithfully executed, and shall commission all the officers of the United States.

Section 4

The President, Vice President, and all civil officers of the United States shall be removed from office on impeachment for, and conviction of, treason, bribery, or other high crimes and misdemeanors.

Article III: The Judicial Branch

Section I

The judicial power of the United States, shall be vested in one Supreme Court, and in such court, and in such inferior courts as the Congress may, from time to time, ordain and establish. The judges, both of the Supreme and inferior courts, shall hold their offices during good behavior, and shall, at stated times, receive for their services a compensation, which shall not be diminished during their continuance in office.

Section 4—The Process of Impeachment

The president and other high officials can be impeached (have charges filed against them with the intention of removing them from office) for treason, bribery, high crimes (felonies such as murder and arson), and misdemeanors (lesser misdeeds). If the House of Representatives files such charges and the Senate convicts them of the charges, they will be removed from office. If the Senate does not convict them, however, they may remain in office after impeachment.

Questions on Article II

1. What is the primary function of the executive branch?
2. What are the president's qualifications and his term of office?
3. How is the president elected when no candidate receives a majority of electoral votes?
4. What is the current line of presidential succession if the president is removed from office?
5. What powers does the president possess with which he can influence judicial decisions?
6. What check does the Senate have on the president's power to make treaties and appointments?

Article III: The Judicial Branch

Section 1—Authority

The function of the **judicial branch** is usually defined as "to interpret the law." This function is not listed in the Constitution; it was established through court cases, especially the case of *Marbury* v. *Madison,* which established the principle of *judicial review,* allowing the court to rule on the constitutionality of federal laws. The nation's highest court is the Supreme Court, but inferior or lower courts may be and have been created by Congress. They include Circuit Courts of Appeal and Federal District Courts as well as tax, claims, and military courts. Federal judges are appointed by the president with Senate approval, and they do not have specific terms of office. They may serve as long as they behave well—usually for the rest of their lives unless they retire, resign, or are impeached.

Section 2—Jurisdiction and Procedure

(1) This section lists the cases that the federal courts must decide. No other courts can have jurisdiction in those cases. Amendment XI, however, returned the jurisdiction of cases between a state and citizens of another state to the state courts.

(2) **Original jurisdiction** means that the case can start in this court and that it has first opportunity to hear and decide the case. With **appellate jurisdiction** the case must have already been brought to trial at least once before it is sent up from a lower court and the court hears the case on appeal.

(3) Criminal trials are generally held in the same judicial district where the crime was committed, unless the person cannot get a fair trial there. The common method for trial is by jury.

Section 3—Treason

(1) Treason is defined specifically so that no one can be accused unjustly. To be convicted of treason, either the accused must confess to it or two people who saw it must testify in an open court.

(2) The punishment for treason is set by Congress and may extend only to the life of the person himself, not his family or descendants. Few people have actually been charged with treason. More often they are charged with espionage, a lesser crime easier to prosecute.

Questions on Article III

1. What is the traditional definition of the judicial branch's function?
2. What are the qualifications and the term of office for federal judges?
3. What is the only court specifically established by the Constitution?
4. Who has the power to create federal courts?
5. What is the usual method of criminal trials? Where are they held?
6. What constitutional requirements limit the abuse of accusations of treason?

Section 2

1. The judicial powers shall extend to all cases, in law and equity, arising under this Constitution, the laws of the United States, and treaties made, or which shall be made under their authority; to all cases affecting ambassadors, other public ministers and consuls; to all cases of admiralty and maritime jurisdiction; to controversies to which the United States shall be a party: to controversies between two or more states, *between a state and citizens of another state,* between citizens of different states, between citizens of the same state, claiming lands under grants of different states, *and between a state, or the citizens thereof, and foreign states, citizens or subjects.*

2. In all cases affecting ambassadors, other public ministers and consuls, and those in which a state shall be party, the Supreme Court shall have original jurisdiction. In all the other cases before-mentioned, the Supreme Court shall have appellate jurisdiction, both as to law and fact, with such exceptions, and under such regulations as the Congress shall make.

3. The trial of all crimes, except in cases of impeachment, shall be by jury; and such trial shall be held in the state where the said crimes shall have been committed; but when not committed within any state, the trial shall be at such place or places as the Congress may by law have directed.

Section 3

1. Treason against the United States shall consist only in levying war against them, or in adhering to their enemies, giving them aid and comfort. No person shall be convicted of treason unless on the testimony of two witnesses to the same overt act, or on confession in open court.

2. The Congress shall have power to declare the punishment of treason, but no attainder of treason shall work corruption of blood, or forfeiture, except during the life of the person attained.

Article IV: Interstate Relations

Section I

Full faith and credit shall be given each state to the public acts, records and judicial proceedings of every other state. And the Congress may by general laws prescribe the manner in which such acts, records and proceedings shall be proved, and the effect thereof.

Section 2

1. The citizens of each state shall be entitled to all privileges and immunities of citizens in the several states.

2. A person charged in any state with treason, felony, or other crime, who, shall flee from justice, and be found in another state, shall, on demand of the executive authority of the state from which he fled, be delivered up, to be removed to the state having jurisdiction of the crime.

3. *No person held to service or labor in one state, under the laws thereof, escaping into another, shall, in consequence of any law or regulation therein, be discharged from such service or labor, but shall be delivered up on claim of the party to whom such service or labor may be due.*

Section 3

1. New states may be admitted by the Congress into this union; but no new state shall be formed or erected within the jurisdiction of any other state, nor any state be formed by the junction of two or more states, or parts of states, without the consent of the legislatures of the states concerned as well as of the Congress.

2. The Congress shall have power to dispose of and make all needful rules and regulations respecting the territory or other property belonging to the United States; and nothing in this Constitution shall be so construed as to prejudice any claims of the United States, or any particular state.

Article IV: Interstate Relations

Section 1—Full Faith and Credit

This "Full Faith and Credit" clause requires each state to respect the public records and court decisions of other states. Thus items like marriage licenses, wills, and contracts are honored among the states.

Section 2—Rights and Responsibilities

(1) If a person passes through another state or moves there, he still has all his rights as an American citizen.

(2) A governor can request that a criminal who flees to another state be returned to the state where the crime was committed to stand trial. The process of returning the criminal is called **extradition.** However, the request for extradition may be denied by the governor of the state to which the criminal fled.

(3) Runaway slaves were to be returned to their owners on demand. This clause explains the necessity of the Underground Railroad in northern states. To avoid extradition, fugitive slaves escaped with the help of abolitionists to Canada through a series of safe houses and secret routes. Once outside the country they could avoid being returned to their former owners. Amendment XIII abolished slavery and with it the purpose for this clause.

Section 3—Powers of Congress

(1) Congress admits new states to the Union, but if a state is formed out of another state or by the combination of two states, the legislatures of those states involved must approve.

(2) Congress is in charge of regulating the territories. Today this applies to Puerto Rico, Guam, American Samoa, and the U.S. Virgin Islands, but these possessions are usually given a large measure of self-government. For instance, Puerto Rico has many of the powers the fifty states enjoy, but is exempt from certain federal tax measures and language laws. However, Puerto Rico lacks voting representation in Congress.

Section 4—Requirements and Guarantees

When it submits its constitution, each state is to have a republican form of government. The federal government guarantees the survival of that republican government by protecting the states from invasion or handling riots or domestic violence when a state legislature or a state's governor requests it.

Questions on Article IV

1. What duties do the states share?
2. What state act does not have to be respected by other states?
3. What branch of government admits new states and regulates territories?
4. What kind of government are new states required and privileged to have?

Article V: Amending the Constitution

Two-thirds of both houses of Congress or two-thirds of the states may call a convention to propose amendments to the Constitution. Ratification or approval to put an amendment into effect requires approval by three-fourths of the state legislatures or three-quarters of the states in their own conventions. When amendments are ratified they become part of the Constitution, but no amendment may ever be made to take away equal representation in the Senate.

The two other clauses protected temporarily from amendment dealt indirectly with importation and taxation of slaves. While this article protected the institution of slavery for twenty years, not all of the founding fathers necessarily supported it. James Madison hoped that this time would allow the institution to fall away on its own.

Questions on Article V

1. What groups have the power to propose amendments?
2. How much support is required to propose an amendment?
3. How much approval is needed to ratify an amendment?
4. What provision(s) of the Constitution can never be changed without the states' consent?

Section 4

The United States shall guarantee to every state in this union a republican form of government and shall protect each of them against invasion; and on application of the legislature, or of the executive (when the legislature cannot be convened), against domestic violence.

Article V: Amending the Constitution

The Congress, whenever two-thirds of both houses shall deem it necessary, shall propose amendments to this Constitution, or on the application of the legislatures of two-thirds of the several states, shall call a convention for proposing amendments, which, in either case, shall be valid to all intents and purposes, as part of this Constitution, which ratified by the legislatures of three-fourths of the several states, or by conventions in three-fourths thereof, as the one or the other mode of ratification may be proposed by the Congress; Provided that *no amendment which may be made prior to the year 1808 shall in any manner affect the first and fourth clauses in the ninth section of the first article; and that* **no state, without its consent, shall be deprived of its equal suffrage in the Senate.**

Article VI: Constitutional and National Supremacy

1. All debts contracted and engagements entered into, before the adoption of this Constitution, shall be as valid against the United States under this Constitution, as under the confederation.

2. This Constitution, and the laws of the United States which shall be made in pursuance thereof; and all treaties made, or which shall be made, under the authority of the United States, shall be the supreme law of the land; and the judges in every state shall be bound thereby, anything in the constitution or laws of any state to the contrary notwithstanding.

3. The senators and representatives before mentioned, and the members of the several state legislatures, and all executive and judicial officers, both of the United States and of the several states, shall be bound by oath or affirmation, to support this Constitution; but no religious test shall ever be required as a qualification to any office or public trust under the United States.

Article VI: Constitutional and National Supremacy

(1) The new government under the Constitution would accept all debts and agreements made previously by the Confederation government. This clause ensured foreign creditors that the new government would not somehow erase the debts made under the Articles of Confederation. A moral obligation to repay them remained.

(2) Known as the **"supremacy clause,"** this clause upholds the United States Constitution as the supreme (highest) law of the nation. The order of authority in the United States is

  a. the United States Constitution,
  b. laws of the U.S. government,
  c. treaties,
  d. constitutions of the states,
  e. state laws, and
  f. local laws.

State and local laws must always abide within the limits placed by the Constitution and federal legislation.

(3) All national and state officers must affirm their support for the Constitution. However, holding specific religious beliefs is not a qualification for holding public office.

Questions on Article VI

1. What provision did the Constitution make for debts that had been contracted before its ratification?

2. What is the second clause known as? What does it establish as the constitutional order of authority in the United States?

3. How does the Constitution ensure that members of the state legislatures will support it?

4. What can never be required as a qualification for seeking public office?

Article VII: Ratifying the Constitution

Nine of the thirteen states had to ratify the Constitution to begin the operation of the new form of government.

No one from Rhode Island signed the Constitution because no delegates from the state were sent to the Constitutional Convention. However, Rhode Island did ratify the Constitution in 1790—the last of the original thirteen states to do so.

Article VII: Ratifying the Constitution

The ratification of the conventions of nine states shall be sufficient for the establishment of this Constitution between the states so ratifying the same.

Done in convention by the unanimous consent of the states present, the seventeenth day of September, in the year of our Lord 1787, and of the independence of the United States of America the twelfth. In witness whereof we have hereunto subscribed our names.

George Washington, President and Deputy from Virginia

New Hampshire
John Langdon
Nicholas Gilman

Massachusetts
Nathaniel Gorham
Rufus King

Connecticut
William Samuel Johnson
Roger Sherman

New York
Alexander Hamilton

New Jersey
William Livingston
David Brearley
William Paterson
Jonathan Dayton

Pennsylvania
Benjamin Franklin
Thomas Mifflin
Robert Morris
George Clymer
Thomas Fitzsimons
Jared Ingersoll
James Wilson
Gouverneur Morris

Delaware
George Read
Gunning Bedford, Jr.
John Dickinson
Richard Bassett
Jacob Broom

Maryland
James McHenry
Daniel of St. Thomas Jenifer
Daniel Carroll

Virginia
John Blair
James Madison, Jr.

North Carolina
William Blount
Richard Dobbs Spaight
Hugh Williamson

South Carolina
John Rutledge
Charles Cotesworth Pinckney
Charles Pinckney
Pierce Butler

Georgia
William Few
Abraham Baldwin

Questions on Article VII

1. How many states had to ratify the Constitution before it became the law of the land?
2. On what day was the Constitution signed?
3. Which of the original thirteen states did not sign the Constitution? Why?

First Federal Congress, 1789 *by Allyn Cox*

Amendment I

Congress shall make no law respecting an establishment of religion, or prohibiting the free exercise thereof; or abridging the freedom of speech or of the press or the right of people peaceably to assemble, and to petition the government for a redress of grievances.

The Bill of Rights: Amendments I–X

James Madison introduced twelve amendments on July 21, 1789. Of these, one failed the process, and one lingered unratified for over two hundred years until 1992, when it became the Twenty-seventh Amendment. The other ten were ratified within a few years and are now known as the Bill of Rights. Although the Bill of Rights went into effect on December 15, 1791, the freedoms it listed were already in existence. However, the Bill of Rights protected them from national encroachment. The Constitution and Bill of Rights made the people's liberties secure. The amendments illustrate the principles of limited government. At first the limitations in the Bill of Rights were not all applied directly to the states but just to the central government. For example, state taxes were levied to support state churches in Connecticut until 1818 and until 1833 in Massachusetts. Supreme Court decisions have since bound the states to abide by the Bill of Rights.

Amendment I: Freedom of Expression

The First Amendment ensures five freedoms:

1. religion,
2. speech,
3. press,
4. assembly, and
5. petition.

Under freedom of religion, Congress cannot establish any church or denomination as a state-sponsored church. People are also free to worship as they choose. In recent times, these provisions have been interpreted as protecting government from religion, rather than vice versa.

Freedom of speech is important to our political system because it permits criticism of misdeeds of those in power. Freedom of speech is not, however, unlimited. **Slander** (defaming a person verbally) or **libel** (defaming a person in writing) are not included, and neither is any speech advocating the violent overthrow of the American government.

Without the right of assembly, there could be no clubs, parties, churches, or political meetings except those approved by the government. Assemblies must be peaceable, however; violent mobs are not protected by this amendment.

Amendment II: The Right to Bear Arms

This amendment forbids Congress from infringing on the rights of citizens to keep weapons. It protects this right as a necessity for the states to have militias that are orderly maintained, well trained, and able to check the power of a standing army.

Amendment III: No Quartering of Troops

This amendment protects the people from military intrusion into their homes. It was needed because of colonial resentment against Britain for forcing people to take soldiers into their homes during times of war.

Amendment IV: No Unreasonable Searches and Seizures

This amendment guarantees the privacy of homes from illegal searches. It does not keep authorities from conducting legal searches or seizures, but it does require them to get search warrants first, thereby protecting citizens from indiscriminate intrusions.

Amendment II

A well-regulated militia being necessary to the security of a free state, the right of the people to keep and bear arms shall not be infringed.

Amendment III

No soldier shall, in time of peace, be quartered in any house without the consent of the owner, nor in time of war but in a manner to be prescribed by law.

Amendment IV

The right of the people to be secure in their persons, houses, papers, and effects, against unreasonable searches and seizures, shall not be violated, and no warrants shall issue but upon probable cause, supported by oath or affirmation, and particularly describing the place to be searched, and the persons or things to be seized.

The Constitutional Convention, 1787 *by Allyn Cox*

Amendment V

No person shall be held for a capital or other infamous crime unless on a presentment or indictment of a grand jury, except in cases arising in the land or naval forces, or in the militia, when in actual service, in time of war or public danger; nor shall any person be subject for the same offense to be twice put in jeopardy of life or limb; nor shall be compelled in any criminal case to be a witness against himself, nor be deprived of life, liberty, or property, without due process of law; nor shall private property be taken for public use without just compensation.

Amendment VI

In all criminal prosecutions, the accused shall enjoy the right to a speedy and public trial, by an impartial jury of the state and district wherin the crime shall have been committed, which district shall have been previously ascertained by law, and to be informed of the nature and cause of the accusation; to be confronted with the witnesses against him; to have compulsory process for obtaining witnesses in his favor, and to have the assistance of counsel for this defense.

Amendment VII

In suits at common law, where the value in controversy shall exceed twenty dollars, the right of trial by jury shall be preserved, and no fact tried by a jury shall be otherwise re-examined in any court of the United States than according to the rules of the common law.

Amendment VIII

Excessive bail shall not be required, nor excessive fines imposed, nor cruel and unusual punishment inflicted.

Amendment V: Rights of the Accused

A **grand jury,** made up of a panel of citizens, considers the prosecution's case against the accused. Its finding is used to determine whether there is enough evidence against a person to warrant a jury trial for guilt or innocence.

This amendment ensures that no citizen can be forced to give evidence against himself. It protects citizens from being tortured, brainwashed, or otherwise forced to give information during interrogation. No person can be tried twice for the same crime if a legal judgment was reached in the first trial. A person cannot be imprisoned, have his property taken away, or be sentenced to death without a fair and proper trial (**due process**). Private property can be "condemned [taken] for the public good," but it has to be paid for. (For instance, government can take land needed for the building of a highway, but it must pay the owner a fair price for that land.)

Amendment VI: Rights of the Accused in Criminal Trials

Because some political trials in England had been held in secret and lasted for years (and the accused remained in jail for that time), the right to a speedy public trial was important to the framers. An accused person has the right to see and face his accuser and his witnesses. The court will call witnesses to appear by serving a **subpoena,** a document requiring a person to appear in court as a witness. A lawyer for the defense is provided at public expense if necessary.

Amendment VII: Rights of Citizens in Civil Trials

A litigant in any court case involving money or property of twenty dollars value or more can demand a trial by jury. Juries are made up of randomly selected members of society who meet certain qualifications. Thomas Jefferson regarded juries as a further way to involve the public in government (popular sovereignty) and check government power.

Amendment VIII: No Cruel, Unusual, and Unjust Punishment

Bail, money held by the court to ensure an accused person's appearance at court of trial, may be required, but it is not to be excessive. Unusual punishments had included whipping, hanging by the heels, branding, and stocks. Such abuses were here outlawed for federal offenses. It is the right of the courts to decide when bail and fines are excessive and punishments cruel or unusual.

Amendment IX: Unspecified Rights of the People

The fact that the Constitution does not list a specific right does not mean the right does not exist. For example, the rights to move and settle somewhere and to choose an occupation are unlisted, yet we still have them. This amendment actually helped calm fears that the Bill of Rights might endanger rights more than safeguard them. Some feared that because certain rights were specified, those things left out would be assumed *not* to be rights.

Amendment X: Reserved Rights of the States

The states or people have any rights that the Constitution does not forbid them to have. The federal government cannot take such rights away from them. Not all of the federal government's powers are expressly stated in the Constitution, though. Certain powers are implied by the very fact that a government must govern. These implied powers are further discussed in Chapter 7.

Amendment IX

The enumeration in the Constitution of certain rights shall not be construed to deny or disparage others retained by the people.

Amendment X

The powers not delegated to the United States by the Constitution, nor prohibited by it to the states, are reserved to the states respectively, or to the people.

Questions on Amendments I–X

1. What are the first ten amendments usually called?
2. What five freedoms are included in the first amendment?
3. What forms of speech are not protected by the First Amendment?
4. What are the four rights of the accused, according to the Fifth Amendment?
5. What restriction does the Constitution place on bails, fines, and punishments?
6. Why did some fear the Bill of Rights might endanger rights more than protect them? How did the Bill of Rights deal with this point?

Amendments XI–XXVII

Seventeen amendments have been passed since 1791. Some amendments corrected problems or more fully explained subjects touched upon by the Constitution. Some of them are related to each other, such as those passed during Reconstruction, and they deal with problems or ideas from a given time. Others deal with single issues.

Amendment XI

The judicial power of the United States shall not be construed to extend to any suit in law or equity, commenced or prosecuted against one of the United States, by citizens of another state, or by citizens or subjects of any foreign state.

Amendment XI: Suing States
(Proposed March 4, 1794; ratified January 8, 1798)

Amendment XI states that a citizen of another state or foreign country may not sue a state in a federal court without that state's consent. Suits must be in the state's own courts.

Amendment XII

The electors shall meet in their respective states, and vote by ballot for President and Vice President, one of whom at least shall not be an inhabitant of the same state with themselves; they shall name in their ballots the person voted for as President, and in distinct ballots the person voted for as Vice President; and they shall make distinct list of all persons voted for as President, and of all persons voted for as Vice President, and of the number of votes for each, which lists they shall sign and certify, and transmit, sealed, to the seat of government of the United States directed to the President of the Senate; the President of the Senate shall, in the presence of the Senate and House of Representatives, open all the certificates, and the votes shall then be counted; the person having the greatest number of votes for President shall be President, if such number be a majority of the whole number of electors appointed; and if no person have such majority, then from the persons having the highest numbers not exceeding three, on the list of those voted for as President, the House of Representatives shall choose immediately, by ballot, the President. But in choosing the President, the votes shall be taken by states, the representation from each state having one vote; a quorum for this purpose shall consist of a member or members from two-thirds of these states, and a majority of all the states shall be necessary to a choice. And if the House of Representatives shall not choose a President, whenever the right

Amendment XII: Separate Ballots for President and Vice President
(Proposed December 9, 1803; ratified September 25, 1804)

The provisions of this amendment replaced those outlined in Article II, Section 1, Clause 3, which had created some awkward political situations. Instead of electors voting for two persons, electors are to vote separately for the president and vice president. Thus the possibility of a tie between the president and vice president, such as had occurred in 1800, was eliminated. It also prevented the selection of a president and vice president from opposing parties who would have difficulty working together for the nation's good. Inauguration day was changed to January 20 by Amendment XX; thus the date necessary for the House to hold such a special presidential vote was moved up.

This amendment also provided resolution of deadlock in the electoral college. The House breaks the deadlock in the case of the president and the Senate does the same for the vice president. Because the vice president may have to act as president under certain circumstances, he or she must meet the same qualifications for office as those established for the president.

of choice shall devolve upon them, *before the fourth day of March next following,* then the Vice President shall act as President, and in case of the death or other constitutional disability of the President. The person having the greatest number of votes as Vice President shall be the Vice President, if such number be a majority of the whole number of electors appointed, and if no person have a majority, then from the two highest numbers on the list the Senate shall choose the Vice President; a quorum for the purpose shall consist of two-thirds of the whole number of senators, and a majority of the whole number shall be necessary to a choice. But no person constitutionally ineligible to the office of President shall be eligible to that of Vice President of the United States.

Reconstruction Amendment

Amendment XIII: Slavery Abolished

(Proposed January 31, 1865; ratified December 18, 1865)

Reconstruction Amendments (XIII–XV): Amendments XIII–XV were all ratified just after the Civil War and deal with problems of that era.

Although Lincoln's Emancipation Proclamation had declared an end to slavery, a constitutional amendment was still needed for two main reasons. For one, the president, not Congress, had made the Proclamation. His authority to abolish slavery was questionable. And if he did have authority during wartime, the Proclamation might be seen as valid only then and not after the war ended. Second, the Emancipation Proclamation abolished slavery only in the southern states that had seceded from the Union. Provision had to be made for the rest of the nation.

Amendment XIII also established greater guidelines for abolishing slavery.

Section 1—It included "involuntary servitude" as well as slavery. This kept sharecroppers (many of whom were black) from becoming virtual slaves due to unreasonable debts set by landowners. It also restricted the states as well as the national government on the issue of slavery.

Amendment XIII

Section I

Neither slavery nor involuntary servitude, except as a punishment for crime whereof the party shall have been duly convicted, shall exist within the United States, or any place subject to their jurisdiction.

Section 2

Congress shall have power to enforce this article by appropriate legislation.

Reconstruction Amendment

Amendment XIV

Section I

All persons born or naturalized in the United States, and subject to the jurisdiction thereof, are citizens of the United States and of the state wherein they reside. No state shall make or enforce any law which shall abridge the privileges or immunities of citizens of the United States; nor shall any state deprive any person of life, liberty, or property without due process of law; nor deny to any person within its jurisdiction the equal protection of the law.

Section 2

Representatives shall be apportioned among the several states according to their respective numbers, counting the whole number of persons in each state, *excluding Indians not taxed.* But when the right to vote at any election for the choice of electors for President and Vice President of the United States, representatives in Congress, the executive and judicial officers of a state, or the members of the legislature thereof, is denied to any of the male inhabitants of such state being of twenty-one years of age, and citizens of the United States, or in any way abridged, except for participation in rebellion or other crime, the basis of representation therein shall be reduced in the proportion which the number of such male citizens shall bear to the whole number of male citizens twenty-one years of age in such state.

Section 3

No person shall be a senator or representative in Congress, or elector of President and Vice President, or hold any office, civil or military, under the United States, or under any state, who having previously taken an oath, as a member of Congress, or as an officer of the United States, or as a member of any state legislature, or as an executive or judicial officer of any state, to support the Constitution of the United States, shall have engaged in insurrection or rebellion against the same, or given aid and comfort to the enemies thereof. But Congress may, by a vote of two-thirds of each House, remove such disability.

Amendment XIV: Citizenship Defined
(Proposed June 13, 1866; ratified July 28, 1868)

Section 1—By this amendment all persons, white or black, slave or free, born in the United States or naturalized, are both American citizens and citizens of the state they live in. A state cannot deprive any person of life, liberty, or property without due process (a fair trial based on just laws and carried out with proper procedures). This amendment extended the entire Bill of Rights to all citizens equally and decreed that all future laws should be the same for every citizen.

Section 2—This section prevented southern states from counting blacks for representation in Congress while preventing them from voting. The Fifteenth Amendment made this section unnecessary.

Section 3—Former Confederates could be banned from public office. Four years after the amendment was ratified, the ban was lifted from most former Confederates except certain government officials and military officers. In 1898 Congress lifted the ban entirely.

Section 4—Neither the federal or state governments were required to pay certain debts related to the Civil War and abolition of slavery.

Amendment XV: Black Voting Rights
(Proposed February 26, 1869; ratified March 30, 1870)

Section 1—Race, color, or former slave status cannot prevent any citizen from voting. Over time this amendment has been interpreted by the courts as a protection against numerous instruments used to keep racial minorities from voting or to lessen their vote:

1. **Grandfather clauses**—Allowed previous voters and their relatives to vote without facing a literacy test or other requirements.
2. **White primaries**—Restricted party primaries and candidate selection to whites only.
3. **Literacy tests**—Required voters to pass a literacy test in order to vote.
4. **Gerrymandering**—Drew district lines so that black districts' votes had less impact.

Section 2—In the aftermath of the Civil War, states' rights were diminished with amendments such as this, and the power of Congress increased.

Questions on Amendments XI–XV

1. What was the primary cause for a distinct ballot in the election of the vice president?
2. What was the primary cause for Amendments XIII–XV? How did each amendment increase individual rights?
3. Why was Amendment XIII necessary despite Lincoln's Emancipation Proclamation?
4. What instruments of discrimination have the courts interpreted as violations of Amendment XV?

Section 4

The validity of the public debt of the United States, authorized by law, including debts incurred for payment of pensions and bounties for services in suppressing insurrection or rebellion, shall not be questioned. But neither the United States nor any state shall assume or pay any debt or obligation incurred in aid of insurrection or rebellion against the United States, or any claim for the loss or emancipation of any slave; but all such debts, obligations, and claims shall be held illegal and void.

Section 5

The Congress shall have power to enforce, by appropriate legislation, the provisions of this article.

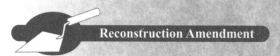
Reconstruction Amendment

Amendment XV

Section I

The right of the citizens of the United States to vote shall not be denied or abridged by the United States or by any state, on account of race, color, or previous condition of servitude.

Section 2

The Congress shall have power to enforce this article by appropriate legislation.

Lincoln's Second Inaugural *by Allyn Cox*

Progressive Amendment

Amendment XVI

The Congress shall have power to lay and collect taxes on incomes, from whatever source derived, without apportionment among the several states, and without regard to any census or enumeration.

Amendment XVI: Income Tax
(Proposed July 12, 1909; ratified February 25, 1913)

Progressive Amendments (XVI–XIX): Amendments XVI–XIX are sometimes called the Progressive Amendments because they were passed at the height of the Progressive Era (1900–1917).

Rather than using state apportionment to set a tax base so that each state paid a tax equal to the percentage of its population, Congress was given the power to tax incomes by standard rates according to the amount of the citizen's income.

Progressive Amendment

Amendment XVII

The Senate of the United States shall be composed of two senators from each state, elected by the people thereof for six years; and each senator shall have one vote. The electors in each state shall have the qualifications requisite for electors of the most numerous branch of the state legislatures.

When vacancies happen in the representation of any state in the senate, the executive authority of such state shall issue writs of election to fill such vacancies; provided, that the legislature of any state may empower the executive thereof to make temporary appointments until the people fill the vacancies by election as the legislature may direct.

This amendment shall not be so construed as to affect the election or term of any senator chosen before it becomes valid as part of the Constitution.

Amendment XVII: Direct Election of Senators
(Proposed May 13, 1912; ratified May 31, 1913)

The people rather than the state legislatures gained the right to elect their two senators. Anyone who is qualified to vote in a state congressional election is also qualified to vote in a United States Congress election. Senate vacancies may be filled by special election or by a state governor, who may appoint a senator if state law allows it.

Amendment XVIII: National Prohibition

(Proposed December 18, 1917; ratified January 29, 1919)

Prohibition refers to forbidding the manufacture, sale, or transportation of liquor. Congress passed the Volstead Act in 1919 to define "intoxicating liquor" and to enforce the amendment. This amendment was repealed by Amendment XXI in 1933.

Section 1—The consumption of alcohol was not actually prohibited by the federal government. Instead, Congress focused on the production and distribution of alcohol with a goal of affecting consumption.

Section 2—Initially, under the Volstead Act, the Internal Revenue Service assumed primary responsibility for enforcing the act. After eleven years the Department of Justice took over. Enforcement proved to be very difficult given the sheer size of the nation and the number of people willing to disobey the law.

Section 3—This was the first amendment to have a ratification deadline attached. Several others have had similar provisions added since then.

Prohibition officers raiding the lunchroom of 922 Pennsylvania Avenue, Washington, D.C., April 25, 1923

Progressive Amendment

Amendment XVIII
Section I

After one year from the ratification of this article the manufacture, sale, or transportation of intoxicating liquors within, the importation thereof into, or exportation thereof from the United States and all territory subject to the jurisdiction thereof, for beverage purposes is hereby prohibited.

Section 2

The Congress and the several states shall have concurrent power to enforce this article by appropriate legislation.

Section 3

This article shall be inoperative unless it shall have been ratified as an amendment to the Constitution by the legislatures of the several states, as provided in the Constitution, within seven years from the date of submission hereof to the states by the Congress.

Progressive Amendment

Amendment XIX

Section 1
The right of the citizens of the United States to vote shall not be denied or abridged by the United States or by any state on account of sex.

Section 2
The Congress shall have power to enforce this article by appropriate legislation.

Amendment XIX: Women's Suffrage
(Proposed June 4, 1919; ratified August 26, 1920)

Section 1—Women were hereby given the right to vote. The right to vote is also called **suffrage** or the **franchise.** A women's suffrage amendment had actually been introduced in Congress as early as 1878. By 1919 continued pressure by women's suffrage groups, the growth of women in the work force, and their support for World War I as well as military service contributed to ratification success. The final state needed for ratification, Tennessee, accepted the amendment with a narrow vote of 49 to 47.

Women's suffrage parade, 1913, New York City

Questions on Amendments XVI–XIX

1. What are Amendments XVI–XIX known as? Why?
2. Who elected senators prior to Amendment XVII?
3. Which amendment was later repealed?
4. What factors contributed to the passage of Amendment XIX?

Amendment XX: Lame Duck Amendment

(Proposed March 2, 1932; ratified February 6, 1933)

This amendment shortened the period in which a sitting president, senator, or representative might be a **"lame duck"**—an official who is still in office but has not been reelected. Lame-duck presidents especially have less political power, and their administration is usually least effective during that period. The amendment also addressed the issue of presidential succession in case of the president's death, incapacitation, or disqualification for office.

Section 1—The dates for starting terms for the president, senators, and representatives changed from March 4 to January 20 for the president and January 3 for senators and representatives. Improvements in transportation and communication technology made such a lengthy delay obsolete because election results could easily be sent out and elected officials could gather quickly to assume their offices.

Section 2—Congress must convene at least once a year. Following a November election, Congress shall convene the following year on January 3. Prior to this amendment the new Congress did not convene until December of the following year after election resulting in an interim period of thirteen months. The new Congress meets seventeen days prior to the president's inauguration to ensure that the old Congress does not oversee his election if there is a deadlock among the electors.

Section 3—If the president-elect dies before taking office, the vice president-elect takes his place until another president qualifies. If both the president and vice president die or are disqualified for office, Congress is responsible for succession. Under this authority, Congress passed the Presidential Succession Act of 1947, which places the Speaker of the House, the Senate president pro tempore, and cabinet officials successively after the vice president.

Section 4—Congress must decide what to do if a candidate dies before an election is to be decided by the House or Senate (following a tie or lack of a majority vote in the electoral college).

Section 5—The amendment was ratified in 1933 and took effect on October 15 of that year. Consequently, the president, senators, and representatives already in office had their terms shortened.

Amendment XX
Section 1

The terms of the President and the Vice President shall end at noon on the 20th day of January, and the terms of senators and representatives at noon on the 3rd day of January, of the years in which such terms would have ended if this article had not been ratified; and the terms of their successors shall then begin.

Section 2

The Congress shall assemble at least once in every year, and such meeting shall begin at noon on the 3rd day of January, unless they shall by law appoint a different day.

Section 3

If, at the time fixed for the beginning of the term of President, the President-elect shall have died, the Vice President-elect shall become President. If a President shall not have been chosen before the time fixed for the beginning of his term, or if the President-elect shall have failed to qualify, then the Vice President-elect shall act as President until a President shall have qualified; and the Congress may by law provide for the case wherein neither a President-elect nor a Vice President-elect shall have qualified, declaring who shall then act as President, or the manner in which one who is to act shall be selected, and such person shall act accordingly until a President or Vice President shall have qualified.

Section 4

The Congress may by law provide for the case of the death of any of the persons from whom the House of Representatives may choose a President, whenever the right of choice shall have devolved upon them, and for the case of the death of any of the persons from whom the Senate may choose a Vice President, whenever the right of choice shall have devolved upon them.

Section 5

Sections 1 and 2 shall take effect on the 15th day of October following the ratification of this article.

Section 6

This article shall be inoperative unless it shall have been ratified as an amendment to the Constitution by the legislatures of three-fourths of the several states within seven years from the date of its submission.

Amendment XXI
Section 1

The eighteenth article of amendment to the Constitution of the United States is hereby repealed.

Section 2

The transportation or importation into any state, territory, or possession of the United States, for delivery or use therein of intoxicating liquors, in violation of the laws thereof, is hereby prohibited.

Section 3

This article shall be inoperative unless it shall have been ratified as an amendment to the Constitution by conventions in the several states, as provided in the Constitution, within seven years from the date of the submission thereof to the states by the Congress.

Amendment XXII
Section 1

No person shall be elected to the office of the President more than twice, and no person who has held the office of President, or acted as President, for more than two years of a term to which some other person who was elected President shall be elected to the office of the President more than once. But this article shall not apply to any person holding the office of President when this article was proposed by the Congress, and shall not prevent any person who may be holding the office of President, or acting as President, during the term within which this article becomes operative from holding the office of President, or acting as President during the remainder of such term.

Section 2

This article shall be inoperative unless it shall have been ratified as an amendment to the Constitution by the legislatures of three-fourths of the several states within seven years from the date of its submission to the states by the Congress.

Amendment XXI: Repeal of Prohibition
(Proposed February 20, 1933; ratified December 5, 1933)

The Democrats included the repeal of Prohibition as part of their platform in the 1932 election. This amendment was made shortly after Roosevelt took office.

Section 1—This amendment repealed Prohibition as outlined in the Eighteenth Amendment.

Section 2—However, states and territories were allowed to regulate the sale of alcohol within their borders.

Section 3—Unlike the other amendments, Amendment XXI was ratified by state conventions rather than state legislatures. Lawyers for the anti-Prohibition groups promoted this form of ratification because they feared state legislatures were controlled by rural prohibitionist legislators.

Amendment XXII: Presidential Terms Limited
(Proposed March 24, 1947; ratified February 27, 1951)

In 1940 and 1944 Franklin D. Roosevelt broke with a tradition established by George Washington and ran for a third and fourth presidential term. Although World War II might have justified his unprecedented actions, many feared this gave too much power to one man. After the war this amendment was proposed to ensure that the "two-term" limit became law.

Section 1—Presidents can be elected for only two terms in their own right. If elevated from the vice-presidency during the second half of a previous president's term, a vice president who becomes president could serve a maximum of ten years. Harry Truman, who had become president shortly after Roosevelt's death in office, was exempted from this provision, but he declined to run for a third term in 1952.

135

Amendment XXIII: Voting for Washington, D.C.

(Proposed June 16, 1960; ratified April 3, 1961)

By 1960 Washington, D.C., had a population of over 750,000—more than that of several individual states. However, it still lacked voting rights in presidential elections until this amendment was made.

Section 1—By this provision, residents of the District of Columbia can vote in presidential elections. The district has three electoral votes, and its electors follow the procedures outlined in Amendment XII.

Amendment XXIV: Poll Tax Abolished

(Proposed August 27, 1962; ratified February 4, 1964)

Following the Civil War, **poll taxes** had been enacted by several southern states as a means of keeping poor blacks from voting. Poll taxes required each voter to pay a tax in order to vote. Other voting discrimination methods had been outlawed by Amendment XIV, but the poll tax had survived. It seemed a constitutional amendment would be necessary to eliminate it.

Ironically, shortly after the amendment was ratified, poll taxes were ruled to be unconstitutional not by this amendment, but by the Fourteenth.

Section 1—The payment of a poll tax to a state in any federal election was forbidden. Poll taxes were still allowed at the state election level until they were declared unconstitutional in the Supreme Court case *Harper* v. *Virginia Board of Elections.*

Amendment XXIII
Section I

The District constituting the seat of Government of the United States shall appoint in such manner as Congress may direct:

A number of electors of President and Vice President equal to the whole number of Senators and Representatives in Congress to which the District would be entitled if it were a state, but in no event more than the least populous state; they shall be in addition to those appointed by the states, but they shall be considered, for the purposes of the election of President and Vice President, to be electors appointed by a state; and they shall meet in the District and perform such duties as provided by the twelfth article of amendment.

Section 2

The Congress shall have power to enforce this article by appropriate legislation.

Amendment XXIV
Section I

The right of citizens of the United States to vote in any primary or other election for President or Vice President, for electors for President or Vice President, or for Senator or Representative in Congress, shall not be denied or abridged by the United States or any state by reasons of failure to pay any poll tax or other tax.

Section 2

The Congress shall have the power to enforce this article by appropriate legislation.

Amendment XXV
Section 1

In case of the removal of the President from office or of his death or resignation, the Vice President shall become President.

Section 2

Whenever there is a vacancy in the office of the Vice President, the President shall nominate a Vice President who shall take office upon confirmation by a majority vote of both Houses of Congress.

Section 3

Whenever the President transmits to the President pro tempore of the Senate and the Speaker of the House of Representatives his written declaration that he is unable to discharge the powers and duties of his office, and until he transmits to them a written declaration to the contrary, such powers and duties shall be discharged by the Vice President as Acting President.

Section 4

Whenever the Vice President and a majority of either the principal officers of the executive departments or of such other body as Congress may by law provide, transmit to the President pro tempore of the Senate and the Speaker of the House of Representatives their written declaration that the President is unable to discharge the powers and duties of his office, the Vice President shall immediately assume the powers and duties of the office as Acting President.

Thereafter, when the President transmits to the President pro tempore of the Senate and the Speaker of the House of Representatives his written declaration that no inability exists, he shall resume the powers and duties of his office unless the Vice President and a majority of either the principal officers of the executive department or of such other body as Congress may by law provide, transmit within four days to the President pro tempore of the Senate and the Speaker of the House of Representatives their written declaration that the President is unable to discharge the powers and duties of his office. Thereupon Congress shall decide the issue, assembling within forty-eight hours for that purpose, if not in

Amendment XXV: Presidential Succession and Disability

(Proposed July 6, 1965; ratified February 23, 1967)

Amendment XXV clarified a number of issues relating to presidential succession should the president die, resign, or be dismissed or incapacitated. These issues were on the minds of Americans following the assassination of President Kennedy in 1963.

Section 1—The vice president becomes president if the president dies, resigns, or is removed from office. This cleared up some ambiguity created by the Constitution in Article II, which stated that the "powers and duties" of the presidency would "devolve on the Vice President," but did not say if the vice president actually became president or not.

Section 2—If the vice-presidency becomes vacant, the president can appoint a new vice president with the approval of both the House and the Senate.

Section 3—The president can transfer his duties to the vice president when he is unable to perform them.

Section 4—If an executive or congressional panel declares to Congress that the president is unable to fulfill his duties, the vice president assumes them until the president again declares himself capable. If there is disagreement between the president and the panel as to his competency, Congress resolves the issue with a two-thirds vote in both houses.

This provision solved the problem of an unforeseen and possibly long-term incapacitation of the president. Such occasions had occurred with Presidents Garfield and Wilson, and nearly with Kennedy as well.

Amendment XXVI:
Eighteen-Year-Old Vote
(Proposed March 23, 1971; ratified July 5, 1971)

Pressure for voting age reform grew through the youth rebellion of the 1960s and the course of the Vietnam War—an unpopular war that eighteen- to twenty-year-olds bore the brunt of. Initially Congress attempted to bring reform by enacting the Voting Rights Act of 1970. Although this stated that eighteen-year-olds could vote, its jurisdiction was limited to federal elections in *Oregon* v. *Mitchell.* Congress then proposed Amendment XXVI, which was ratified by the states in record time.

Section 1—The national voting age was lowered to eighteen years of age for both federal and state elections.

Amendment XXVII: Restriction on
Congressional Pay Raises
**(Proposed September 25, 1789; ratified
May 7, 1992)**

In contrast to Amendment XXVI, which was ratified in record time, Amendment XXVII took over two hundred years to ratify. Madison originally proposed it as part of the Bill of Rights, but only six states ratified it. Since no time limit was placed on the amendment's ratification, it remained active though largely forgotten. Ohio added its ratification in 1873 to protest a congressional pay raise, but no other state ratified it for more than one hundred years.

Finally, the amendment took on new life in the 1980s when members of Congress voted for pay raises for themselves. Enough states had ratified the amendment by 1992 for it to become part of the Constitution. The amendment ensured that Congress would have greater accountability to the people. Through an intervening election, the public could express their approval or disapproval of members of Congress who supported a raise.

session. If the Congress, within twenty-one days after receipt of the latter written declaration, or, if Congress is not in session, within twenty-one days after Congress is required to assemble, determines by two-thirds vote of both Houses that the President is unable to discharge the powers and duties of his office, the Vice President shall continue to discharge the same as Acting President; otherwise, the President shall resume the powers and duties of his office.

Amendment XXVI
Section I
The right of citizens of the United States, who are eighteen years of age or older, to vote shall not be denied or abridged by the United States or by any state on account of age.

Section 2
The Congress shall have power to enforce this article by appropriate legislation.

Amendment XXVII
No law, varying the compensation for the services of the Senators and Representatives, shall take effect, until an election of Representatives shall have intervened.

Questions on Amendments XX–XXVII

1. What procedural changes were made by Amendments XX and XXII?

2. What is the only amendment ever to repeal another amendment?

3. What section of the country received the right to vote for president in 1961?

4. What is a poll tax? Why was it prohibited in Amendment XXIV?

5. What potential problems does Amendment XXV address?

6. What is the most recent group of people added to the electorate?

7. Which amendment took the longest amount of time to ratify?

Chapter Review

Terms

strict constructionists
broad constructionists
"necessary and proper
  clause"
amendment process
proposal
ratification
Bill of Rights
limited government
separation of powers
checks and balances
veto
impeachment
gridlock
judicial review
Marbury v. *Madison*
federalism
popular sovereignty
Preamble
legislative branch

bicameral
census
president pro tempore
quorum
sergeant-at-arms
The Congressional Record
franking privilege
"pocket veto"
naturalization
National Guard
elastic clause
writ of habeas corpus
bill of attainder
ex post facto law
appropriation
executive branch
electoral college
reprieves
pardons
judicial branch

original jurisdiction
appellate jurisdiction
extradition
"supremacy clause"
slander
libel
grand jury
due process
subpoena
bail
grandfather clauses
white primaries
literacy tests
gerrymandering
Prohibition
suffrage
franchise
lame duck
poll taxes

Content Questions

1. What characteristics of the Constitution permit it to "change with the times"?

2. Name the two major phases in the amendment process and describe each.

3. What basic principles of government guided the creation and interpretation of the Constitution? Give one example of each of these principles found in the Constitution or subsequent interpretation.

4. How many articles does the Constitution contain? What are the main topics of each article?

5. What is the primary function of each branch of government?

6. What are the first ten amendments called? Why?

7. Which amendments have changed or clarified constitutional procedures? What were the changes?

8. Which amendments have increased the size of the electorate? Name the group covered in each amendment.

Application Questions

1. Why should Christians study and understand the United States Constitution?

2. Why is the amendment process difficult?

3. What factors have rendered the Tenth Amendment ineffective?

FEDERALISM

7

The Morrill Act of 1862 provided states with land for universities. Clemson University in South Carolina is a land-grant university.

In the United States, the Constitution gives both the national and state governments authority to govern. When thinking of the United States government, most think first of the national government. But in addition to the national government, there are fifty state governments and over eighty thousand local governments that govern the United States. Federalism treats the relationships of these governments.

Federalism is a system in which governmental power is divided into two or more levels, usually a central government and component state governments. In the United States, government is divided between the national government in Washington, D.C., and fifty state governments. Although distinct, the two levels of government often overlap in responsibilities. As we saw in Chapter 6, this federal system is a basic constitutional principle and one of the outstanding achievements of the Philadelphia Convention in 1787. Federalism is based on the belief that limited government is a restraint to tyranny and that one way to limit government is to divide and to distribute power among several entities.

Inevitably, conflicts arise between the levels of government, even though both draw their power from "the people." Are the paper barriers of the Constitution enough to restrict the central government from infringing on the integrity of the states while fulfilling its own legitimate duties? It is not a question easily answered. Officially at least, the South went to war in 1861 to defend states' rights. Nor was the problem of nation-state balance totally resolved after 1865. Some recent presidents have tried to reduce the national role in the federal system—generally with little success. For instance, Ronald Reagan campaigned for a "new federalism" that would return power to the states. In 1976 he pledged to work for "an end to giantism, for a return to the human scale . . . the scale of the local fraternal lodge, the church organization, the block club, the farm bureau. . . . Activity on a small human scale creates the fabric of community."

The idea of community had already become an American tradition by the time of the nation's founding. This idea had an important influence in shaping the federal principle incorporated into the Constitution and the Bill of Rights. Ideally, the national government operates to meet national needs, whereas state and local governments serve community needs. At its best, federalism is cooperative coexistence within constitutional restraints that connect thousands of government units nationwide and permit regional diversity within a national union.

I. The Partitions of Power

The Constitution outlines the "division of labor" between national and state governments. Both levels have power acquired through constitutional provision, assumed through constitutional silence, or denied through constitutional safeguards.

National Power

The national government has **delegated powers** that define the limits of its authority, powers that are delegated (or given) to it by the Constitution. Delegated power is not only a grant of authority but also a limitation in the sense that the power is to be ultimately bound "with the chain of the Constitution," as Jefferson stated. This delegated authority of the national government takes two forms, enumerated and implied powers.

Enumerated powers, or expressed powers, are ones specifically granted. The Constitution authorizes particular powers to the three branches of government, such as the congressional powers in Article I, Section 8 to collect taxes, regulate commerce, and declare war; and the president's powers in Article II to appoint officials and negotiate treaties.

FDR signing war declaration against Japan, December, 1941

Implied powers are not spelled out in the Constitution's text but are *derived* from enumerated powers. Certain actions may not be specifically permitted in the Constitution, but those actions may be necessary or convenient in exercising the

Federalism in the U.S. and Germany

The United States and the Federal Republic of Germany are two excellent examples of federalism. Early in their histories, both nations revealed a natural federalism. The state legislatures in America elected delegates to the Constitutional Convention in Philadelphia. When the Constitutional Convention produced America's constitution, it had to be ratified by nine state conventions before it could become effective.

The German (or Holy Roman) Empire, dating back to the Middle Ages, rested on the power of regions and cities. Even after Germany became a nation in 1871, the kaiser (emperor) granted regional governments some important powers.

After World War II Germany was divided into democratic West Germany and communist East Germany. Elected leaders from the regions of West Germany chose the members of the constitutional assembly, which wrote the constitution, called the Basic Law, for the Federal Republic of Germany. The voters of West Germany did not elect the body that produced their constitution. Furthermore, their Basic Law was ratified by regional legislatures, not by a national referendum or vote.

Power for the regions was not the only consideration. West Germans hoping for an eventual reunification wanted East Germany to ratify it as well.

Germany's Basic Law provides for sixteen states (three are cities), or Laender, just as the U.S. has fifty states. Each German state has a legislature, just as every American one does. The majority party in a German state legislature elects a chief, called a minister-president, just as the voters in American states elect a governor. Unlike in the U.S., a German minister-president can hold that office and serve at the same time in the national legislature.

U.S. states have powers over education, transportation, marriage and divorce, welfare, courts, and police. In Germany the states control education, courts, police, and the mass media. In addition, German states have the authority to enforce federal laws, which makes them more powerful than American states. In recent years German states have won veto power over actions by the European Union that might interfere with their local authority. When the Cold War ended and Germany was reunited, the five states from the former East Germany joined the Federal Republic in a way similar to the addition of new states to the American union as the United States expanded westward.

The Bundesrat, Germany's upper house in Parliament, greatly reflects the power of the states in the federal government. Members of the Bundesrat are chosen by the state legislature. In the United States the people of a state elect its U.S. senators. Originally, before the Seventeenth Amendment, state legislatures selected senators in a way similar to Germany's present practice. Unlike the U.S., the size of a German state's delegation is dependent on the population, with larger states having more votes. In the U.S. Senate each state has two senators, regardless of population. In the Bundesrat, each representative must vote as the state government tells him, while U.S. senators may vote as they wish.

The Bundestag, Germany's lower house, deviates from the federal system in the sense that it, and not the people of the whole nation, elects the chancellor. In that sense Germany resembles the British parliamentary system. Similarly, in the U.S., elected officials in the electoral college determine the presidential election. In theory, the American people choose electors who in turn vote for president.

Members of the Bundestag are chosen through a complicated system that allows for two votes by the public—one by district and one by party. In the district vote, one member is elected from each district, just as a House member is elected from a congressional district in America. In the party vote, a party is entitled to a percentage of the seats in the Bundestag equal to its share of the vote nationwide.

powers that are enumerated. Minimum wage laws are an example of implied powers. The national government passed laws forcing states to set a minimum wage based on its power to regulate commerce "among the several states." This line of reasoning is supported by the **necessary and proper clause** (Article I, Section 8, Clause 18), which states that Congress is permitted

to make all laws which shall be necessary and proper for carrying into execution the foregoing powers, and all other powers vested by this Constitution in the government of the United States, or in any department or officer thereof.

Because this clause greatly enlarges the scope of national power and has at times been stretched to cover congressional acts, it is often referred to as the **elastic clause.**

State Power

According to the Tenth Amendment, the powers not delegated to the national government nor denied the states are reserved for the various states and their citizens. **Reserved powers** provide states with considerable freedom to exercise authority as they choose. States may, for example, establish systems of public education for their residents, set up speed limits and seat belt laws on their roads, and ban or permit liquor sales to eighteen-year-olds—since authority for these areas is not given to the national government nor denied to the states. States may even determine their

own structure of government, such as the extent of the governor's veto power or whether their legislative branch will consist of one or two houses. (Nebraska, for example, has a unicameral system, whereas the other forty-nine states have bicameral systems.)

When fifty separate governments make laws in many areas, the result is considerable diversity. Businesses may locate in a particular state because its laws are more favorable to that particular industry. Or the laws in one state may be circumvented by its residents when they travel to a neighboring state, where laws may be more relaxed, to obtain such things as firearms or marriage licenses. Sales tax provides a good example of how differing laws can produce friction between adjoining states. In states that have no sales tax, residents from a neighboring state frequently cross the border to take advantage of the savings, and in so doing reduce the revenue of their own states.

Although each state has considerable power over its own affairs, there are limits to its jurisdiction. The Constitution places specific restrictions on the states, many of which are outlined in Article I, Section 10. For example, a state may not make treaties, declare war, or coin its own money. In addition, the supremacy clause and subsequent Supreme Court decisions such as *McCulloch* v. *Maryland* prohibit states from taxing national institutions within their borders.

The Bill of Rights places restrictions on both the states and the national government. The last phrase of the final amendment of

In downtown Manhattan, President Bush meets with Governor Pataki at the site of the World Trade Center after the September 11, 2001, attacks.

the Bill of Rights is far more than a means of rounding out the sentence:

> The powers not delegated to the United States by the Constitution, nor prohibited by it to the states, are reserved to the states respectively, *or to the people.*

No government within the federal system may deny a citizen such constitutional rights as freedom of worship and the right of due process.

In addition, power not given to the national government, nor assumed by state governments, is reserved for the people. That is, where no law prohibits a certain action, responsible citizens are free to act. New laws are necessary to answer new demands, but whenever someone storms, "There ought to be a law against that," he should remember that in a free society, each new law reduces at least a bit of personal liberty.

Within each state are a variety of local governmental units, such as counties, cities, and townships. Unlike the national and state governments, which are mentioned in the Constitution, local governments have no constitutional identity. Traditionally, local units of government have served primarily to implement state laws. City government may not ignore state government, since local authority is derived from state authority. Nevertheless, recent

trends have enhanced the role of local government. The growth of suburbs and the complex expansion of government services have resulted in a more flexible relationship between the state house and the city halls and county councils within its jurisdiction.

This interdependence of state and local governments reflects a similar interrelationship within the entire federal system. During the past two centuries, various forces have blurred the lines of distinction and have strengthened the national role at the expense of the states.

Section Review

1. What is federalism?
2. What is the popular nickname for the "necessary and proper" clause? Why is it called this?
3. Which constitutional amendment guarantees the reserved powers of the states and of the people?
4. From what source do local, state, and national governments derive their respective powers?

II. Interstate Relationships

Because the Constitution gives the states sovereignty (supreme authority) over certain aspects of government, states can differ from one another. Some state constitutions create a strong governor's office, while others create a weak one; some have an income tax while others do not. How do states with different laws interact with one another? History shows that differing interests have led to cooperation as well as conflicts between the states. The Constitution addresses this issue in Articles IV and VI by listing responsibilities that the states owe to one another and to the national government.

State Relations

Although each state retains power to govern itself, no state can exist as a completely independent entity. States are required by Article IV of the

Constitution to maintain a certain level of cooperation between themselves.

Full Faith and Credit—Article IV, Section 1 requires that each state respect the laws, official records, and judicial rulings of the other states.

> Full faith and credit shall be given each state to the public acts, records and judicial proceedings of every other state.

According to this section of the Constitution, each state must recognize the validity of the other states' sovereignty. The **full faith and credit clause** ensures that driver's licenses issued in Montana will be recognized in Florida. A vacationing family from Massachusetts does not need to obtain a license from each state it will travel through. Each state is required by the Constitution to recognize other states' licenses. Most often the full faith and credit clause relates to judicial matters. For instance, a man ordered by a North Dakota court to pay for damages in an accident cannot flee to South Dakota to escape the responsibility of payment. South Dakota must give "full faith and credit" to North Dakota's ruling.

What About Homosexual 'Unions'?

In 2000 Vermont passed legislation making "civil unions" available to homosexuals. But what if two homosexuals were to acquire a civil union certificate in Vermont and then move to a different state? Would the "full faith and credit" clause require other states to acknowledge their union? As of 2008, forty-one states have passed "Defense of Marriage Acts" (DOMAs) that refuse to recognize homosexual marriage under the "full faith and credit" clause. But DOMAs have not been tested in federal court. Furthermore, state courts might rule that "civil unions" are not marriages and thus are not covered by the DOMAs.

Two exceptions to this clause exist. First, this section deals only with civil law, not criminal; second, states are not required to give full faith and credit in every case of divorce. The first exception limits a state to enforcing only its own laws. Georgia cannot enforce an Oregon law requiring all passengers (including back seat passengers) to wear seat belts unless the law is also on Georgia's law books. The second exception prevents people from moving to a state with lenient divorce laws just long enough to obtain a divorce and then moving back to their home state. The United States Supreme Court set the precedent for this exception in its ruling in *Williams* v. *North Carolina* (1945). This case involved a man and woman from North Carolina who left their spouses in order to obtain divorces in Nevada. (Nevada required the shortest amount of time, six weeks, before a state resident could legally file for a divorce.) After waiting six weeks, the two obtained divorces, married one another, and returned to live in North Carolina. North Carolina refused to accept the divorces and prosecuted the couple for bigamy. North Carolina argued that the two had never intended to live in Nevada and, therefore, they were not under Nevada's jurisdiction but North Carolina's. The ruling in favor of North Carolina established that a state can refuse to honor a divorce granted by a state if the divorcees never proved their intent to become permanent residents of that state.

Privileges and Immunities—According to Article IV, Section 2—the **privileges and immunities clause**—privileges enjoyed by United States citizens must be respected in every state.

> The citizens of each state shall be entitled to all privileges and immunities of citizens in the several states.

No state can lawfully restrict a nonresident's activities. Nonresidents of a state can work, purchase merchandise, travel, and buy a house with the full privileges and immunities granted to residents of that state. This also ensures that nonresidents are guaranteed all legal rights as well. A state government may not set aside a person's rights because he is a nonresident. This does not, however, restrict the states from making reasonable distinctions between residents and nonresidents concerning activities

supported by state taxes. One example especially relevant to high school students is the states' right to charge out-of-state students more for attending a state university. A student from Georgia will pay more to attend Colorado State University than a Colorado resident. States may also charge nonresidents more for hunting and fishing licenses since state taxes stock and maintain state parks.

Extradition—Article IV, Section 2, Clause 2 of the Constitution requires that

> A person charged in any state with treason, felony, or other crime, who, shall flee from justice, and be found in another state, shall, on demand of the executive authority of the state from which he fled, be delivered up, to be removed to the state having jurisdiction of the crime.

Extradition is the legal process of returning an alleged criminal to the state in which he is charged. This clause ensures that criminals cannot escape justice by fleeing to a different state. Almost from the beginning, states understood that the "shall on demand" was not an imperative but suggestive only. In other words, the states retained their right to not return a fugitive to the requesting state. This interpretation enabled states to protect escaped slaves from recapture once they left slave state soil. However, the Supreme Court in *Puerto Rico* v. *Branstad* (1987) asserted the national government's right to force a state to extradite a fugitive.

So how do states work together according to the Constitution to ensure that justice is served? Consider the following example. In 2001 Christian Longo fled Oregon after killing his wife and three children. Oregon authorities quickly mounted a search for him but found that he had fled to Mexico.

Mexican officers and FBI agents arrested Longo in January 2002 and, after he waived his right to fight extradition, escorted him to Houston, Texas. Oregon initiated the extradition process by asking Texas to release Longo into its authority. Longo again waived his right to fight extradition and was transported to Oregon to await trial.

Extradition Procedure

Alleged criminals often flee to other states to avoid prosecution. The following is the procedure a state must follow to obtain an extradition. (The list will use New Mexico as the state in which the crime was committed and Utah as the state to which the accused fled.)

1. New Mexico's executive officer, the governor, must ask Utah's executive officer to return the accused.
2. New Mexico's governor must present Utah's governor with a copy of an indictment or an affidavit made before a magistrate charging the accused with a crime.
3. New Mexico's governor or chief magistrate must certify the indictment or affidavit.
4. Utah's governor can then have the accused arrested and secured.
5. After the arrest, Utah's governor must inform New Mexico's governor of the arrest and request an agent from New Mexico to pick up the accused.
6. The fugitive has the right to contest the extradition in court, but he can waive that right.
7. New Mexico has thirty days after the arrest to pick up the fugitive. Otherwise, Utah's authorities can release him.

Constitutional and National Supremacy

Understanding the potential for conflict between the state and national governments, the founders included Article VI, Clause 2 in the Constitution to establish the proper relationship between the two:

> This Constitution, and the laws of the United States which shall be made in pursuance

thereof; and all treaties made, or which shall be made, under the authority of the United States, shall be the supreme law of the land; and the judges in every state shall be bound thereby, anything in the constitution or laws of any state to the contrary notwithstanding.

Under the United States federal system, the states have the constitutional right to pass their own legislation and judge their own cases, but their laws and judicial rulings cannot contradict national law or Supreme Court rulings.

Section Review

1. What factor makes it possible for states to differ from one another?
2. What matters does the full faith and credit clause most often relate to?
3. What are the two exceptions to the "full faith and credit" clause?
4. How does the "privileges and immunities" clause protect American citizens?
5. In what cases may states make a distinction between residents and nonresidents?
6. Define extradition. How did states historically interpret "shall on demand"?
7. What Court decision established the national government's right to force a state to extradite a fugitive?
8. What clause establishes the proper relationship between state and national governments? Why did the founders include that article in the Constitution?

III. Developments in Federalism
Sovereign and Separate

A single window glowed in the night adding its faint glimmer to the moonlit mansion. Across the Potomac lay the sleepy capital. Inside the mansion the stillness of night was scarcely broken by the steady pacing in an upstairs bedroom—the pacing of a soldier struggling over loyalties. To a man to whom duty and honor meant much, it was a strug-

gle indeed. He had been offered the opportunity of a lifetime, a chance to command the armies of the United States. Finally the pacing stopped, and Robert E. Lee penned these words:

I have felt that I ought no longer to retain my commission in the army. I therefore tender my resignation, which I request you will recommend for acceptance. It would have been presented at once, but for the struggle it has cost me to separate from a service to which I have devoted the best years of my life and all the ability I possessed. . . . Save in the defense of my native State, I never desire again to draw my sword.

In a second letter written the same day, Lee explained,

With all my devotion to the Union, and the feeling of loyalty and duty of an American citizen, I have not been able to . . . raise my hand against my relatives, my children, my home.

Lee's fateful struggle in April 1861 over loyalty between the national government and his beloved Virginia well illustrates how nation-state relations have changed. For many people today, identification with a state consists of little more than a mailing address and knowing which football team to support—hardly the sort of things to pace the floor over.

In the early years of the Republic, though, states played a much more important role in the lives of their citizens. When travel across states at times took weeks rather than hours, when there were no interstate highways connecting people and few bridges spanning swollen rivers, the country was in a very real sense much larger than it is today. States were more isolated, more independent, and more important in the social and political structure. In 1831 Tocqueville observed, that in America, "the legislature of each state is supreme; nothing can impede its authority."

The fact that states were a potent political force did much to shape federalism. The states stood alongside the national government, two pillars supporting a federal structure. State political strength was bolstered by constitutional provisions, such as the reserved powers and the ability of the state legislatures (before the Seventeenth Amendment) to select United States senators, and also by the relative weakness of the national government. Powerful voices defended **states' rights** and decentralization, such as those of Thomas Jefferson and James Madison of Virginia and John C. Calhoun of South Carolina.

Of course, the national government did hold supreme power. Its role was well established, both in the Constitution and by rulings of Chief Justice Marshall's "nationalist" Supreme Court. But during the early nineteenth century, the national government practiced more restraint in the exercise of its implied powers. For example, the father of the Constitution, James Madison, vetoed public works legislation from Congress with this message:

> I am not unaware of the great importance of roads and canals and the improved navigation of water courses, and that a power in the National Legislature to provide them might be exercised with signal advantage to the general prosperity. But seeing that such a power is not expressly given by the Constitution, and believing that it cannot be deduced from any part of it without an inadmissible latitude of

construction and a reliance on insufficient precedents; believing also that the permanent success of the Constitution depends on a *definite* partition of powers between the Federal and state Governments I have no option but to [veto the bill].

In this system of **dual federalism,** national and state governments were sovereign within their own spheres. Of course clashes occurred between national and state policies—clashes in Congress, in the courts, and, in the case of the Civil War, even on the battlefield. Nevertheless, dual federalism, or dual sovereignty, continued to dominate certain aspects of the political system well into the twentieth century even though new factors—economic, political, and social—would gradually redefine the nature of federalism in America.

At one time, a three-layer cake (left) could have illustrated the relationship between local, state, and national governments. Modern American federalism, however, is better illustrated by a marble cake (above).

The Growth of Interdependence

Northern victory in the Civil War proved to be the beginning of the end for the federalism imagined by the founders. The constitutional unity of the states was decided beyond further argument. Before the war, Americans tended to say, "the United States are," but afterward, "the United States is." The doctrine of states' rights did not disappear, but never again would the state legislatures be "supreme" as Tocqueville had claimed they were; nor

The New Deal begins: Franklin Roosevelt delivers his inaugural address in 1933.

would a soldier like Robert E. Lee put loyalty to his state above loyalty to his country.

Even during the war, the national government weakened federalism by imposing the first income tax, establishing a central bank, and printing a national paper currency. Abraham Lincoln used presidential powers in a manner unimagined during the early nineteenth century. By abolishing slavery the national government suggested just how great its power over "private property" had grown.

After the war America continued to industrialize. Ex-farmers and immigrants from Europe flocked to the cities, transforming the United States from an agrarian to an industrial nation. Railroads with thousands of employees now crossed state lines as if the borders did not exist. Instead of buying basic necessities from a local general store, Americans began to order unseen goods from strangers halfway across the country. The interdependence of producers and consumers far distant from one another further reduced the importance of state lines and increased the need for national legal uniformity.

Governments at all levels also grew larger as increased productivity and a higher standard of living allowed more money to be taken in taxes

with less detriment to the taxpayers. When the United States emerged as a world power at the end of the nineteenth century, the federal government was virtually forced to expand its revenue base to maintain its international position. The passage of the Income Tax Amendment (**Sixteenth Amendment**) in 1913 eventually created a spectacular source of federal dollars.

During World War I, the federal government expanded its regulatory powers over major corporations, and during World War II, it nearly co-opted the entire economy. A major shift in American perception of the federal government came during the Great Depression when economic collapse exhausted state welfare funds, and the American public clamored for federal relief. In 1933, the newly inaugurated Franklin D. Roosevelt began to implement a series of social and economic programs to address the poverty and unemployment of the depression. These programs spanned the 1930s and were known collectively as the **New Deal.** Although New Deal programs were often organized through the states, there was no question as to which level of government was footing the bill. Significantly, the funds to support New Deal

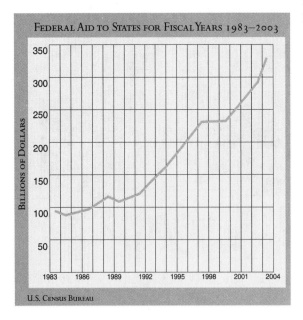

FEDERAL AID TO STATES FOR FISCAL YEARS 1983–2003

Billions of Dollars

U.S. CENSUS BUREAU

transportation, national television, and national fast food, it could hardly have been any other way.

Section Review

1. How does today's state loyalty differ from the loyalty felt in the early days of the American Republic?
2. List four defenders of states' rights and the states they represented.
3. Describe and illustrate the concept of dual federalism.
4. What event was the beginning of the end for federalism as the founders envisioned it?
5. What event in America's history significantly changed Americans' perceptions of the federal government?
6. Did the federal bureaucracy continue to grow during Ronald Reagan's presidency? Why or why not?

programs were generated by the bounty of the American capitalist system—national welfare programs were grounded on America's high standard of living. Contemporary humorist Will Rogers quipped that the United States would be the first country to go to the poorhouse in an automobile.

Of course, once settled in power, federal bureaucracies proved nearly impossible to eliminate, and, like all organizations, they had a tendency to grow bigger and stronger. New ones appeared during the 1950s and 1960s, especially when "Great Society" legislation ensured national supervision of voting rights, urban renewal, and environmental protection and increased involvement in education, health care, and a "war on poverty."

During the 1980s, Ronald Reagan spoke of a "new federalism" that would reduce government involvement and spending at the state level, and he did curb federal regulation to a certain extent. Nevertheless, the long growth of the federal bureaucracy and the comparative decline in state power continued under Reagan as under his predecessors. Given the interdependence of a nation bound by national

IV. Financing Federalism

Federalism today is much more complicated than the simple model outlined in the Constitution. It has been transformed in part because of the tremendous amount of federal resources available. Hundreds of programs have been created to assist the states with everything from education and social services to public transportation and law enforcement.

Federal **grants-in-aid** represent a major portion of the federal budget as well as a key force in implementing national policies on the local level. Federal grants are nothing new, although in the nineteenth century they came primarily in the form of land grants. As we have seen, cash grants did not become a significant form of state aid until the New Deal era, though the grants remained modest until the 1960s. Today federal grants-in-aid amount to over $300 billion annually, distributed to state and local governments primarily through categorical grants, block grants, and revenue sharing.

Categorical Grants

Categorical grants are those given to state and local governments for a specific purpose and with certain guidelines for their use. For example, a categorical grant given to Chicago for low-income daycare may not be used to refurbish city parks. Other restrictions may also accompany federal aid, such as minority hiring quotas or environmental protection guidelines. In addition, categorical grants generally require that the recipient provide matching funds for the project as well as an agency for managing the money.

Formula grants, as the name implies, are governed by demographic formulas in a given area. For example, unemployment figures may be used to compose a formula to determine the proportion of federal aid to be supplied for a job-training program. By contrast, **project grants** permit greater discretion in how much aid is given to a project.

With over five hundred programs available today, categorical grants are the most common form of federal aid and the most controversial. The controversy centers on "strings" attached to federal money. These accompanying regulations often involve the federal government in areas of state authority such as public education and urban policy, an association that tends to break down the national-state distinctions of federalism.

The states are under no obligation to accept federal aid, but states actively lobby in Washington for more aid. The millions of dollars available to them are irresistible, despite the accompanying loss of control over their own affairs. Road construction, for example, has long been a responsibility of the states. However, the interstate highway system, begun under Eisenhower, was a national project promoted for the purpose of national defense. Although the national government could not force the states to participate in building the interstate system, Washington made them an offer that none could refuse. The national government set up categorical grants with generous terms: for every dollar the state put into the superhighway fund, Washington would provide nine dollars. Of course, there were strings attached to the money in the form of continuing regulations and bureaucratic controls over highway construction, safety, maintenance, and administration. But because state jobs and budgets are built around federal aid, little effective resistance is offered to the creeping intervention of federal grant programs.

Block Grants

A second method of federal aid distribution is the block grant. Begun in 1966, this type of grant is designed to streamline federal aid to states and localities. Block grants make it simpler for a state or city to administer federal funds because they provide more flexibility in their use than the more closely monitored categorical grant. **Block grants** combine several categorical grants under a general umbrella, such as law enforcement or education,

Renovating public areas is just one of many purposes for which a state might request a grant.

but with fewer federal regulations and less red tape. For example, if Indianapolis wants to revitalize its inner city, it need not apply for a dozen categorical grants in areas such as housing, recreational facilities, and minority business loans. Instead the city may simply apply for a block grant for urban development.

Revenue Sharing

Federal aid may also be distributed through **revenue sharing.** The most recent program, begun in 1972, was eventually dismantled during the Reagan budget cuts in 1987 in the face of a trillion-dollar national debt. Revenue sharing, however, is nothing new; it can be traced back as far as the Jefferson and Jackson administrations.

In revenue sharing the national government allocates some of its tax revenues to the states. Revenue sharing reflected an attempt to return policy control to the states and reduce the level of federal intervention. In addition, revenue sharing required no matching funds from recipients. Obviously, this form of aid enjoyed great popularity with governors, state legislators, and mayors.

The difference between revenue sharing during the Nixon-to-Reagan period and earlier examples was that in the past, revenue was shared when there was a surplus in the national treasury. During the 1970s and 1980s, though, federal revenue was shared when there was really none to share; its billions merely added to the rising tide of red ink that engulfed the federal budget.

Section Review

1. What are the basic differences among the three forms of federal grants-in-aid?
2. What is the difference between a formula grant and a project grant?

V. The Problems of Federalism

Maintaining Federal Distinctions

Federalism is the division of political power between two or more governmental levels. This division is maintained through constitutional provisions as well as through political pressures. Potent political pressures often threaten rather than maintain this division.

The Constitution actually has little to say about what the national government can or cannot do in its relationship to the states. One requirement placed on the national government is that it must honor the territorial rights of the states (Article IV, Section 3). For example, Congress may not create a new state out of part of Alaska without the consent of the Alaskan legislature—which is not likely to be forthcoming. In addition, the national government is constitutionally pledged to guarantee that each state has a republican form of government.

The national government is also obligated, according to Article IV, Section 4, to protect the states from foreign invasion and to intervene if necessary to suppress domestic violence in a state. If the violence becomes too great for state law enforcement officers to handle, the president may send in troops to assist. For example, in 1967 and 1968, President Johnson ordered army units to help quell violent race riots that had erupted in Detroit, Chicago, and Baltimore.

There are also important political forces that help preserve the national-state levels of federalism. First, in our republican system, national office-holders are elected from the state and local levels. That is, members of Congress who pass national laws in the national legislature represent 435 districts and fifty states. These are states and districts to whom the members of Congress must answer. This accountability helps maintain a degree of independence for states and localities that might otherwise be overwhelmed by national power. Second, political parties are built on the state level and are to some degree independent from their

Riots in the Watts area of Los Angeles in 1965 caused much damage to local businesses.

national organizations. This independence strengthens their hold over their national representatives and enhances the political identity of the state and district.

Maintaining this identity is no easy task. As we have already seen, the fantastic change in the American law, society, and economy during the past century and a half has helped to alter the balance of federalism in favor of the national government.

National controls are reflected in state and municipal budgets, which are planned around the federal grants available. Localities may boost their revenues by millions if they provide matching funds for projects that support particular national policies. This forces local planners to think "federally" as they draw up a budget.

Give-and-Take

Federal aid provides both services and controls. Billions of dollars in grants permit states to provide a variety of services to their citizens. In addition, from Washington's perspective, federal aid permits national policies to be carried out on the local level. The biblical principle that the "borrower is servant to the lender" (Prov. 22:7) is certainly borne out in the present federal system. Federal grants give the national government a greater voice in state and local policymaking. This shifting direction has resulted in fundamental changes in the system and has created several problems in the process.

Areas that were previously matters of state prerogative now are entangled in a web of federal regulations. Public education, for example, had long been under state and local control; the neighborhood school was an important community center and symbol. Parents saw their children educated in an institution in which the community's voice was respected and its values instilled. Federal funds and regulations changed this traditional system.

At times federal judges have also intervened in local school systems to hasten the process of conformity, sometimes with unintended consequences. For instance, in 1975 a federal judge tried to improve racial integration in the Boston school system in order to satisfy federal standards. Ten years and over four hundred court orders later, the schools' enrollment had plummeted from 93,000 to 57,000. The integration ratio, which in 1975 stood at 65% white to 35% minority shifted to 28% white and 72% minority after the federal intervention. Federal watchdogs have reduced the power of local communities and institutions. Pornographers have been able to keep their doors open as local obscenity laws were struck down. Because of mandatory bussing, schoolchildren have risen early and arrived home late in order to satisfy some bureaucrat's sense of justice. And in the classroom, public prayer and Bible reading were forbidden.

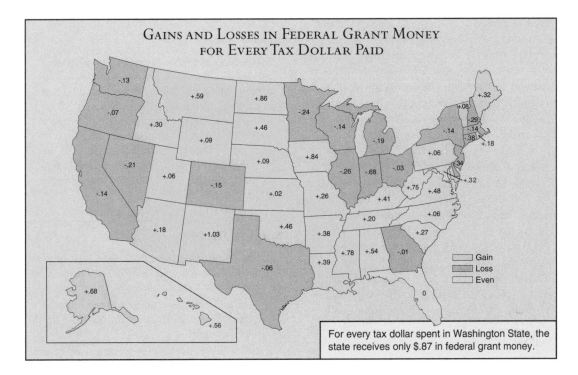

GAINS AND LOSSES IN FEDERAL GRANT MONEY
FOR EVERY TAX DOLLAR PAID

For every tax dollar spent in Washington State, the state receives only $.87 in federal grant money.

Growing National Debt

Federal aid to the states also contributes to the national debt, which in 2002 stood at over six trillion dollars. In 1970 the total amount of federal grants stood at an annual $24 billion; a decade later the figure was over $90 billion. By 2000 the total aid to state and local government had surpassed $300 billion. Special-interest groups and financially strapped states and cities have lobbied hard to retain the financial and political benefits gained from continued aid. States have become so accustomed to aid from the national government that reductions damage state budgets. This kind of "me-first" attitude merely expresses man's selfish nature on an institutional level and does nothing to correct irresponsible spending and crippling debt.

Competition for Funding

Another problem of federalism is in the relationship and competition among the states. Friction between the states is nothing new; the Constitution was written, at least in part, to lessen dissension among the states under the Articles of Confederation. Federalism today, as well as demographics, has produced problems of a different sort.

When it comes to receiving federal aid, not all states are created equal. As the map above indicates, some states receive more federal funds than their residents pay in federal taxes, whereas others receive less. States that pay more than they receive are in effect subsidizing mass transit, welfare, and education programs in those states that pay less than they receive. This inequity produces clamor and competition for federal tax dollars. Thus states and cities that lobby aggressively stand to receive a larger share of the federal pie.

The inequity is also fueled by a growing regionalism—namely the Frostbelt versus the Sunbelt. The Sunbelt, consisting of the old Confederate states and the Southwest, has become an economic rival of the Frostbelt, the Northeast and upper Midwest. More areas of the Frostbelt struggle with older industry, decaying cities, and a declining population. The Sunbelt, by contrast, enjoys a growing population, newer industry, and cheaper energy. One illustration of the rapid growth in this region is baseball. Before 1955 there were no professional baseball teams either south or west of St. Louis; today there are fourteen. The population shifts from the Frostbelt to the Sunbelt have also been a political bonus for the South. Florida, for example, has gained six new congressional seats since the 1980s, whereas New York has lost five.

Sectional debate is fueled by the fact that formula grants may be designed by Congress to favor one region over the other. Overall the Sunbelt tends to edge out the Frostbelt in the struggle for federal funds. As the map on page 155 indicates, many of the Sunbelt states get a better return on their tax dollars than do their northern rivals.

Federalism has changed a great deal since its principles were first outlined at the Constitutional Convention. Our founding fathers might well see little resemblance between the federal model they created and its modern descendant. Today federalism has become a system not primarily for preserving the spheres of national and state authority but for implementing national policies on the local level.

Despite the encroachments of Washington, the federal system does continue to provide some benefits. The states continue to have the last word in deciding much of the private law. States and cities still draw building codes, sell hunting licenses, and share in the thankless job of running a welfare system.

The genius of federalism is that it tends to check tyranny—it permits no single institution to hold *all* the reins of authority. Though this characteristic has been weakened in recent years, it remains in the hands of responsible citizens to maintain the balance of the federal system—citizens that will assume responsibility for the course of their government, even as Madison in *Federalist No. 46* reminded critics:

> The Federal and State governments are in fact but different agents and trustees of the people, constituted with different powers, and designed for different purposes. The adversaries of the Constitution seem to have lost sight of the people altogether in their reasonings on this subject. . . . These gentlemen must here be reminded of their error. They must be told that the ultimate authority . . . resides in the people alone.

Section Review

1. What four obligations does the Constitution place on the national government in its relationship to the states?
2. What two political forces help preserve the division between the state and national levels of government?
3. How has the federal government used federal aid to gain control of state prerogatives?
4. Why is it difficult to reverse the policy of federal grants and to reduce federal costs?
5. Why do leaders in the Frostbelt say the current distribution of federal grants is unfair?

Chapter Review

Terms

federalism
delegated powers
enumerated powers
implied powers
necessary and proper clause
elastic clause
reserved powers

full faith and credit clause
privileges and immunities clause
extradition
states' rights
dual federalism
Sixteenth Amendment

New Deal
grants-in-aid
categorical grants
formula grants
project grants
block grants
revenue sharing

Content Questions

1. Why did the framers of the Constitution choose a federalist system of government?

2. What clause in the Constitution has been used by the federal government to extend its power at the expense of the states?

3. What constitutional amendment protects the reserved powers of the states and of the people?

4. What changes in American government and society in the early 1900s were key factors in the change of dual federalism to the interdependency we have today?

5. List and describe the three basic forms of federal grants-in-aid.

6. What constitutional and political forces still serve to maintain the separation between state and national governments?

7. What are some inherent problems with the current system of national grants-in-aid to the states?

Application Questions

1. What would the reaction of the founders likely be to the current state of federalism? Why would they respond this way?

2. Who is ultimately responsible for the rapid loss of powers once reserved for the people? Explain your answer.

3. Who is ultimately responsible for the recent loss of powers once reserved for the states? Explain your answer.

4. How does an understanding of man's sinful nature help explain the difficulty in reversing the changes in America's federalist system?

UNIT III

PARTY POLITICS

THE PARTY SYSTEM

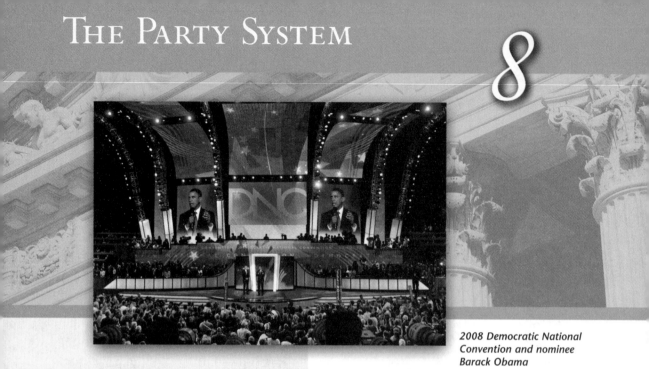

2008 Democratic National Convention and nominee Barack Obama

Politics describes the exercise of public power, the art and energy of governance. Over the past two units, the foundational principles and the constitutional provisions that make up our political system have been examined. Yet these ideas are only ideals unless put into action—political action.

This unit will explore the practice of politics that makes the United States government more than a paper model. This chapter will examine how political power is organized through the party sys-

1920 Republican National Convention

tem; the following chapter will look at how political power is achieved in the electoral process; and Chapter 10 will study how political power is shaped by interest groups.

In his first volume of *Democracy in America,* published in 1835, Alexis de Tocqueville described political parties by saying,

> But when the citizens entertain different opinions upon subjects which affect the whole country alike, such, for instance, as the principles upon which the government is to be conducted, then distinctions arise which may correctly be styled parties. Parties are a necessary evil in free governments; but they have not at all times the same character and the same propensities.

What is the character of America's political parties? What should the Christian's role be in the American political system? Christ describes believers as "the salt of the earth." Christians, through the power of the gospel, are to be a force for preservation in their neighborhood and nation. With a basic understanding of America's party system, one should determine to what degree God desires him or her to be involved in this avenue of service.

I. Parties and Their Function

Mugwump and Anti-Masonic, Greenback and Goldbug, Federalist and Free-Soil, Green and Grassroots, Democrat and Dixiecrat are just some of the parties and factions within factions that have entered America's colorful political glossary. Some of these groups are alive and well today; others are only historical curiosities. Yet, despite their diversity, all parties share a common definition as associations that promote certain political goals. This umbrella definition takes in all parties, both major parties and minor parties.

Party Defined

The simple definition of a political party as a group that advances certain political goals is one that could be applied to a multitude of organiza-

Dixiecrat presidential candidate Strom Thurmond on election day in Edgefield, S.C., in 1948

tions that are not parties, such as labor unions or civil rights groups. The key point that distinguishes political parties from groups that are simply politically oriented is that **political parties** are organized to gain power by winning elections. This distinction is especially true for the major parties in this country.

The two **major parties** that have been the dominant political competitors for well over a century are the Democratic and Republican parties. **Minor parties,** or **third parties,** are smaller parties that are usually organized around a particular issue. The positions minor parties promote may later be adopted by the major parties as public support builds for a particular cause.

The Constitution never mentions political parties, probably because many of its framers distrusted factions; yet many of these men would soon become the leaders of a very partisan struggle, the ratification process. The Constitution's chief architect, James Madison, observed in *The Federalist No. 10* that the causes of political division, or faction, are "sown in the nature of man." He noted that

> we see them everywhere brought into different degrees of activity, according to the different circumstances of civil society. A zeal for different opinions concerning religion, concerning government, and many other points, . . . an attachment to different leaders ambitiously contending for pre-eminence and power.

161

Madison was of course referring to the variety of divisions, the opinions and shades of opinion, that exist throughout any society on almost any subject. In a society that permits free speech and association, political parties are natural; and in a government that represents diversity, political parties are inevitable. Parties provide a bridge between the governed and their government. They are channels for expressing political opinion and for electing the men and women who will represent those positions.

Party Functions

Nominating Candidates—The political party's major purpose is to **nominate,** or name candidates for public office. A party's candidates are chosen either through a party's convention, a party's caucus, or a state primary. The nominated candidates are presented to all voters. Parties then work for their candidates, helping them win their elections by providing access to funds, professional staffers, volunteers, and endorsements. These nominating methods have proved effective as a democratic means of choosing a party's candidates as well as securing votes for them.

Governing—After candidates are nominated and elections won, parties continue to play an important role through the business of governing. Party ties provide a basis for legislative cooperation as well as obstruction. Congress is actually structured along party lines, with the majority party in the House and Senate empowered to control top committee posts and set the legislative agenda. The president may also use his party ties to help push legislation through Congress, uphold vetoes, and determine executive and judicial appointments. Much of the business conducted by Congress and state legislatures is based on **partisanship,** a strong devotion to a political party.

Watchdogs—Parties act as watchdogs over each other. This is especially true of the party out of power (the party that does not control the presidency). The behavior and policies of the party in power are watched carefully and reported on. The

result is to make that party more accountable to the people. However, the party out of power walks a fine line between giving the impression of mere opposition to the party in power and of greater loyalty to the nation.

Moderating Influence—At a more general level, political parties function as an important moderating influence over competing and even conflicting political forces. In the U.S. system the major parties tend to lessen extremism at both ends of the spectrum and bring diverse interests together in a consensus over broad principles.

The moderating influence of parties provides both benefit and danger. Its benefit is chiefly found in reducing the disruptive influence of political extremists while seeking to find common ground for opposing demands. This characteristic explains much about the tendency of our system of government to move to the middle through political compromise. The drawbacks of this influence can be its potential for quashing unpopular dissent, resisting needed change, compromising moral principle, and making centrist parties too much like each other. The Republican and Democratic parties have been compared to Lewis Carroll's nearly identical characters Tweedledee and Tweedledum.

Section Review

1. What are the differences between major and third political parties?

2. What does Madison say concerning the causes of political division?

3. What is the major purpose of a political party?

4. How do political parties play an important role in governing the nation?

5. Explain how political parties are a moderating influence.

II. The Two-Party System

Whenever political parties are under discussion, most Americans automatically think in terms of Republicans and Democrats. This fact simply reflects a dominant feature of American politics—the **two-party system.** This does not mean that there are only two parties in America but that there are only two major parties with which most of the electorate identifies.

Reasons for Formation

Tradition—The American two-party system has a history dating back to our earliest struggles as a nation. Partisan struggles and personality conflicts surrounding the ratification of the Constitution gave rise to two political camps, Federalists and Anti-Federalists. These camps formed the basis of the two-party system as a political fixture. This system also reflects a British influence, seen in the conflicts between Whigs and Tories in Parliament.

The donkey represents the Democrats, and the elephant represents the Republicans.

Competition—Though our two-party system has been well entrenched for nearly two centuries, it has not always been an equal contest. At times one of the major parties has dominated the other, either on a regional level or in one or more areas of the national government. The House of Representatives, for example, was controlled by the Democratic Party from 1955 until 1995. At the presidential level, the Democrats held the White House continuously from 1933 to 1953, while the

Republicans went on to win seven of the ten presidential elections between 1952 and 1988.

Competition between the two parties is also unequal in certain areas of the country. In fact, certain states could best be described as having a one-party system because of the total dominance of the Democratic or Republican Party over their politics. For instance, in the post–Civil War South, the Democratic Party dominated the politics of the region. The new Republican Party was the party of Lincoln and the party of radical Reconstruction—meaning it was not the party of many successful Southern politicians. The South, for all practical purposes, had a one-party system. Since the 1960s the Republicans, with their more conservative appeal, have made large inroads in the South; and Republican presidential candidates have generally found the old Confederacy to be an important power base.

This political shift in the South is indicative of the growing competitiveness between the major parties. Party strength may vary on the local level—as seen in Democratic control of major cities or Republican dominance in rural areas in the 2000 presidential election. However, the two-party rivalry remains strong on the whole.

The best indication of national competitiveness is the voting tally for the only office for which all eligible Americans from Maine to Maui cast ballots—the presidency. In 1960, for example, John Kennedy beat Richard Nixon's challenge for the presidency by a hair-breadth margin of fewer than 120,000 votes out of a total of over 68 million cast. Nixon came back in 1968 to edge out Democrat Hubert Humphrey by a close 43.4% to 42.7%

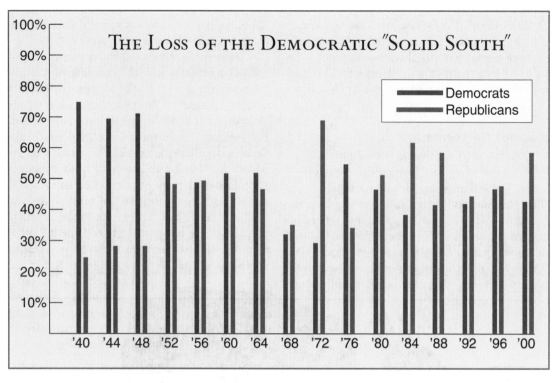

The Loss of the Democratic "Solid South"

Percent of votes cast by Democrats and Republicans in the 1940–2000 presidential elections in eleven southern states (Alabama, Arkansas, Georgia, Kentucky, Louisiana, Mississippi, North Carolina, South Carolina, Tennessee, Texas, and Virginia)

margin. The 1976 election was a close contest between Democrat Jimmy Carter's 50.1% of the electorate to Republican Gerald Ford's 48%. In the 2000 election Democrat Al Gore won the popular vote with about 537,000 more votes, but Republican George W. Bush won the presidency with a majority of electoral votes. In fact, since 1940 presidential races have been so close that few runners-up have received less than 40% of the total vote.

Electoral System—The American electoral system encourages a two-party system through single-member districts and election law. Most elections held in the United States, from the national level to the local level, are **single-member district** elections, legislative districts from which only one representative is chosen. It is a winner-take-all system based on the candidate receiving a **plurality,** or the largest number, of votes cast for the office. In

all states except Maine and Nebraska the presidential candidate who receives a plurality of the vote receives all of that state's electoral votes. Minor parties are discouraged since only one winner can come out of each election and since people usually perceive that there are only two electable candidates. The voter often does not want to "waste" a vote on a minor-party candidate.

In the United States, most election law is state rather than federal law. The majority of people who make these election laws happen to be Republicans and Democrats. The two major parties come together in a **bipartisan** manner, a spirit of two-party cooperation, to shape laws that make it difficult for a third-party candidate to be put on the ballot. Third-party candidates find it especially difficult to be listed on the ballots of every state. This was evidenced in the last seven presidential elections. In election 2000 even the two most prominent third parties failed to get on the ballot everywhere. Ralph Nader of the Green Party was on the ballot in only 44 states, and Pat Buchanan of the Reform Party was on 49 state ballots.

Characteristics

Diverse Support—America's diversity is mirrored in its two major parties. Supporters of both political camps come from many walks of life. People of different races, religions, incomes, and professions all come together in support of their particular party. The reasons for this diverse support, however, will likely differ. For example, Protestants concerned about abortion may support the Republican Party because of its pro-life platform. Some businessmen might support the Republican ticket because the Democratic candidate often identifies with big labor. Similarly, the Democratic Party draws support from a broad cross section of society because these groups like the emphasis of the party in areas such as urban programs, education, or foreign aid.

Broad Appeal—With diverse groups identifying with a major party for diverse reasons, the party must have broad appeal. Again, one of the prime purposes of political parties is to win elections. Therefore, both parties try to reach a majority of voters with a broad, moderate message. This is why opposing candidates may sound quite similar on a number of issues; they are attempting to reach the same voters—those in the middle. Proposals perceived as radical do not win elections, as Barry Goldwater learned in 1964 when he discussed abolishing Social Security. The closeness of the parties on some issues and the middle-of-the-road appeal that both parties make actually enhance the stability of our political system. If the two parties grew further and further apart, elections would become more bitter, leaving the country deeply divided.

Similar but Not the Same—The similarities between the parties apply to some issues but not all issues. Similarity is not sameness. Despite the assertion by Alabama governor George Wallace

that there is not a "dime's worth of difference" between the Democrats and Republicans, there are clear differences on a number of issues. The **party platform,** a formal statement of a party's position on current issues, is drafted at a party's national convention every four years and provides evidence of these distinctions. For example, the 2000 Democratic platform had this to say about abortion: "The Democratic Party stands behind the right of every woman to choose, consistent with *Roe* v. *Wade,* and regardless of ability to pay"—which translates as "the federal government should provide funding for abortions." The abortion plank in the 2000 Republican platform recognized that

> the unborn child has a fundamental individual right to life which cannot be infringed. We support a human life amendment to the Constitution, and we endorse legislation to make clear that the Fourteenth Amendment's protections apply to unborn children. Our purpose is to have legislative and judicial protection of that right against those who perform abortions. We oppose using public revenues for abortion and will not fund organizations which advocate it. We support the appointment of judges who respect traditional family values and the sanctity of innocent human life.

Different Ideologies—Differences also exist between the ideologies of the two parties. For example, a survey of the Democratic National Committee in 1980 revealed that 36% of its members described themselves as **liberal,** one whose political view seeks to change the political, economic, and social status quo to encourage the development and well-being of the individual. Only 1% of the Republican National Committee members described themselves as liberal. On the other hand, 63% of the Republican National Committee described themselves as conservative, compared to a slim 4% of conservatives on the Democratic side. A **conservative** is one whose political view defends the status quo against major changes in the political, economic, and social institutions of society. Since 1980 the philosophical rift has only deepened between the political camps. Nevertheless, the

165

Republican Party is not conservative enough for many conservatives, nor is the Democratic Party liberal enough for many liberals. This is simply another reflection of the middle-of-the-road focus that the major parties generally embrace.

CONSERVATIVE OR LIBERAL?

Conservative and *liberal* are terms used to describe the major political parties' ideologies and policies. What characterizes these different ideologies?

Conservatives tend to support:

- lower taxes
- less government regulation of business
- decreased spending for welfare programs
- increased spending for defense programs
- harsher penalties for crime
- traditional social values

President Reagan illustrated a conservative viewpoint during his first inaugural address on January 20, 1981, when he said, "It is not my intention to do away with government. It is rather to make it work—work with us, not over us; stand by our side, not ride on our back. Government can and must provide opportunity, not smother it; foster productivity, not stifle it."

Liberals tend to support:

- higher taxes
- more government regulation of business
- increased spending for welfare programs
- more protection for the environment
- greater protection for "diversity," including homosexuality and pornography

A liberal view may be seen by looking at Senator Ted Kennedy's voting record on certain issues. Senator Kennedy voted NO on cutting taxes, NO on banning partial birth abortions, and NO on prohibiting same-sex marriages.

Party Membership—Another important characteristic of the two major parties is the nature of party membership. A person can be a Democrat or a Republican simply by declaring himself one or the other; party membership is a matter of personal identification, not formal obligation. Political scientist William Keefe observed,

> In effect, anyone who considers himself a Democrat is a Democrat; anyone who considers himself a Republican is a Republican. A citizen may register one way and vote another or not vote at all. No obligations intrude on the party member. He can be a member without applying for admission, a beneficiary without paying dues or contributing to campaigns, a critic without attending meetings, an interpreter without knowing party vocabulary, an apostate without fearing discipline. To the citizen who takes politics casually, it may be the best of all worlds. The typical American is insensitive to the claims, problems, and doctrine of his party. His principal participation in party life is through the act of voting—sometimes for his party and sometimes not.

Many factors determine why a person may identify with one party over another. Of course, agreement on issues and ideology attracts many voters into a particular camp. Economic downturns and upturns can also affect allegiances. Yet the single most influential factor in most people's choice of a party or political philosophy is their family background. Political philosophy often bridges generations even though candidates and campaigns come and go. Though commitment among party members may be quite strong, the loose, nonbinding nature of party identification can result in shifts of allegiance. After the Civil War, for example, blacks supported the Republican Party, the party of emancipation. During the 1930s blacks began voting Democratic because of the help received through the New Deal. By the 1960s the shift was complete with the party's support of civil rights. Today, blacks constitute the Democratic Party's most loyal constituency, often delivering 90% of their voting strength to the Democrats. Similarly, white males, particularly Protestants, have turned out for the Republican Party in greater numbers in recent years as that party has become increasingly identified with conservative policies.

Stability—The two-party system provides more stability than a **multiparty system.** In multiparty politics, common among many European democracies, several parties compete for majority support. With so many factions dividing the electorate, it is very difficult for one party to win a majority. Some of these parties come together, forming a **coalition,** a temporary alliance of several groups, to gain a majority and thereby gain control of the government. These party coalitions do not always hold together, hence the instability of such systems.

Flexibility—The two-party system is more flexible than a one-party system. Having two parties provides an open forum for competing ideas and demonstrates the pliability necessary to meet the demands of democratic government. Thus, American politics is very stable. A one-party system, such as that in Cuba, simply provides a dictator with a rubber stamp for his actions. The act of voting in a one-party election is a peculiar charade. Individual dissent is not tolerated, and organized dissent exists only in underground form.

Development and Direction

Overview—The American party system has undergone three major periods of competition: the Federalist vs. Jeffersonian period, 1790s–1812; the Democratic vs. Whig period, 1824–1850s; and the Republican vs. Democratic era, 1850s to the present.

Democratic strength disintegrated along with the Union by 1860 when Republican Abraham Lincoln won the presidency in a four-way race. Union victory in the Civil War ensured Republican success until well into the twentieth century. During this period of Republican control, from 1860 to 1932, only two Democrats succeeded in winning the White House: Grover Cleveland and Woodrow Wilson.

This situation changed abruptly in 1932. The election of Democrat Franklin Roosevelt during the bleak depression years snapped the Republican hold on the presidency and Congress. Roosevelt's unprecedented and unrepeatable (Amendment XXII) string of four victories, along with Harry Truman's win in 1948, gave the Democrats control of the White House for twenty years. Since Eisenhower's 1952 election, however, the Republicans have dominated the highest office, even exceeding Franklin Roosevelt's impressive showing in the electoral college. Roosevelt's victories from 1932 to 1944 gained 88% of the electoral vote. Republican victories from 1972 to 1988 captured 91% of the electoral college. Change occurred again when the Democrats won the presidency in 1992 and 1996, but the Republicans recaptured it in 2000. The Republican Party made history in 2002 by winning control of the Senate and expanding its control of the House.

Section Review

1. How does the electoral system encourage a two-party system?

2. What are the characteristics of the two-party system?

3. Explain why a two-party system provides more stability than a multiparty system.

DONKEYS AND ELEPHANTS

The Democratic donkey first appeared in 1828 when Andrew Jackson's opponents tried to label him as a donkey for his populist views and his slogan, "Let the people rule." Jackson turned this to his advantage by using the donkey on his campaign posters. In 1870 cartoonist Thomas Nast first used the donkey in a *Harper's Weekly* cartoon to represent the Copperhead Press kicking a dead lion. Nast intended the donkey to represent an antiwar faction with whom he disagreed. However, the symbol became popular with the public, and Nast continued to use it.

The Republican elephant came into being in 1874. A newspaper editorial expressed alarm over the belief that Grant would seek a third presidential term. It was a false alarm, but the Democrats used the rumor to keep Republicans from participating in the congressional elections. At the same time, the *New York Herald* tried to increase circulation by falsifying a story about wild animals escaping from the Central Park Zoo. Cartoonist Nast drew a cartoon for *Harper's Weekly* that included a donkey (Democratic symbol) dressed in a lion's skin scaring other animals away. In the cartoon he labeled an elephant with "The Republican Vote." Nast said he selected the elephant because it was believed to be clever, steadfast, easily controlled, but unmanageable when frightened.

Other animals, such as the rooster and the moose, have represented various parties and campaigns, but only the donkey and the elephant have become permanent fixtures in the American political zoo.

"A LIVE JACKASS KICKING A DEAD LION."

THE THIRD-TERM PANIC.

Despite their commanding claim on the White House in the latter half of the twentieth century, Republicans rarely controlled Congress until the 1990s. (See the appendixes.) This dichotomy is illustrated by the five presidential elections between 1972 and 1988. Republican candidates won an overwhelming majority of electoral votes in states west of the Mississippi, yet many of these states regularly sent Democrats to Congress.

This overview of the ebb and flow of party control traces the historical shifts in our government but reveals little of the important changes that have taken place in the development of parties. The influences shaping the character of the parties behind the politics will be considered.

Founders' Fears—Political parties actually met with a chilly reception during the founding of the Republic. In his Farewell Address, George Washington warned his countrymen "against the baneful effects of the spirit of party," describing parties or "factions" as the worst enemy of popular government. John Adams was no less convinced of the party threat: "A division of the republic into two great parties . . . is to be dreaded as the greatest political evil under our Constitution." The prevailing sentiment of many of the founders could be summed up by Jonathan Swift's definition: "Party is the madness of many, for the gain of the few."

Because of the character of parties in Europe, the founders' fears were not unfounded. Parties there smacked of conspiracy and dangerous demagoguery. In addition, many feared that parties would threaten the effectiveness of Congress by stifling true debate, causing representatives merely to parrot the party line on an issue.

The founders, however, balanced their fears of conflict, conspiracy, and control with the recognition that citizens in a free society have a right to organize politically. Yet the founders hoped for a nonpartisan system in which the best men, like cream, would rise to the top. The original constitutional provision for electing the two highest officials reflected this hope. The candidate receiving the most electoral votes would be president, and the

second-place finisher would be vice president. Although such a scheme might have worked in a nonpartisan election, it would not work once candidates ran as representatives of parties. Political rivals would likely be elected as president and vice president. For instance, in 2000 Al Gore would have become vice president under George W. Bush.

This seemingly unlikely scenario was precisely what happened in 1796, when two bitter political enemies, John Adams and Thomas Jefferson, were elected president and vice president respectively. The problems caused by this nonpartisan arrangement were corrected in 1804 as a result of the Twelfth Amendment. Now electors vote for the office of president and vice president separately. This amendment gave tacit constitutional recognition to the existence of parties.

Jefferson and Jackson—The struggle over ratification during the Constitutional Convention was waged between two political camps: the Federalists, who favored the Constitution, and the Anti-Federalists, who opposed the proposed government in part or in whole. After the Constitution was approved, political differences persisted both in Congress and in President Washington's cabinet. The growing political rift was fueled in the 1790s by differences between Hamilton and Jefferson over the National Bank, tariffs, constitutional interpretation, and foreign policy. Alexander Hamilton headed the Federalist Party, while Thomas Jefferson led the opposition Anti-Federalist Party, which soon took the name Democratic-Republican. Curiously, this party, which carried the names of both of today's major parties, generally referred to itself as Republican, although it was the forerunner of today's Democratic Party.

The Jeffersonian victory in 1800 swept the Federalists out of power and began a long period of one-party domination. The Federalist Party slid steadily toward extinction when it opposed the War of 1812 and ceased to compete for national office after its presidential candidate carried only three states in the 1816 election. For the quarter-century that followed 1800, the Virginia dynasty of Jefferson,

Madison, and Monroe ruled the presidency while their followers controlled both houses of Congress. Because of the lack of effective party competition, the Jeffersonian era gradually became a nonpartisan one in which parties became as suspect as they had been in Washington's day. The problems with the nonpartisan system became quite apparent after the 1824 election, and the results transformed American politics.

In 1824 a four-man nonpartisan race for the presidency between William Crawford, Andrew Jackson, John Quincy Adams, and Henry Clay went to the House of Representatives to be settled. According to the Twelfth Amendment, if no candidate receives a majority of electoral votes, the House must elect the president from the top three contenders, in this case Jackson, Adams, and Crawford. Since Jackson had won the most popular and the most electoral votes, he was expected to be the House choice. Clay, however, who did not make it to the House ballot, became the "king maker." As Speaker of the House, he threw his support to Adams and later received an appointment as his secretary of state. Jackson and his supporters understandably cried foul and set about organizing to win the White House in 1828. Their efforts opened a new chapter in party development.

Martin Van Buren, a senator from New York and later Jackson's successor in the presidency, led in organizing Jackson's opposition party. In a break with old attitudes, Van Buren believed that the decline of two-party competition had hurt the democratic process by encouraging regional candidacies, which left the country divided and, as in the previous contest, forced the election to be decided by a few House members. In the 1828 election Van Buren put his ideas to work.

Old Hickory's triumph that year and the subsequent era that he dominated produced several notable results for political parties. First, organized competition broadened voter participation. The voting level in 1828 increased threefold over the turnout four years earlier, with that election

becoming the first in the young nation's history to exceed a million votes cast.

Second, the nomination process was expanded through the use of the **convention.** The convention, first used by the Anti-Mason Party in 1831 and then by the Democratic Party in 1832, is an assembly of party representatives, or **delegates,** elected from each state to nominate candidates for president and vice president. Prior to the advent of the convention, a party's nominees were chosen by a **caucus,** a small meeting of a party's top leaders and legislators in Congress. As democratic participation expanded, the closed-door nature of the caucus came under attack, and the nominating convention eventually became a political institution.

Possibly the single most influential factor in building party organization during the half-century following 1828 was **patronage,** the practice of giving jobs to friends and supporters. Also called the **spoils system,** patronage was begun by Andrew Jackson. With the arrival of a new administration, mass firings and hirings took place as party supporters were rewarded with government positions at all levels. Naturally, with this arrangement a man had greater incentive to get involved in a party and boost voter turnout for his candidate if he expected a payoff at the end of a victorious campaign.

Finally, the party system gave birth to the **political campaign,** an organized effort by a political party or candidate to attract voter support in an election. Jackson's strong personality and strong party led to the rise of an organized opposition party, which called itself the Whig Party. The Whigs were quick studies in the new art of campaigning. They observed the common-man appeal of General Jackson, and by 1840 the Whigs outgeneraled the general's party. That year the Whigs ran a war hero of their own, William Henry Harrison, against the incumbent Democrat, Martin Van Buren.

The raucous campaign to follow was run on slogans, personalities, and quantities of hard cider. The Whigs were the first to create a popular image greater than the candidate himself and "sell" it to the public. They recast the well-to-do Harrison as a common man of the frontier who was born in a log cabin, and they portrayed his hapless opponent as "Matty," a lightweight dandy (a man who focuses on his clothes and manners and gives little thought to life's important issues).

Harrison rode to the White House on his log cabin theme, and the Whigs introduced the country to one of its more colorful sideshows—the presidential campaign. The success of their venture is underscored by the fact that 80% of all eligible voters—the third highest total in our history—participated in the election.

The Powerful Few—Though party conventions allowed more individuals to participate in the nomination process, convention delegates were often chosen by party caucuses committed to a particular candidate or political boss. This meant that the outcome of the nomination remained in the hands of a few power brokers. And the candidates themselves were often those who survived the closet deals made in "smoke-filled rooms." Early in the twentieth century, demands for reform of the entire nominating process brought another important change in party development—the **primary,** a state election in which voters select the candidates who will run on each party's ticket in the general election.

There are two types of primaries—a nominating primary and a presidential primary. A **nominating primary** is a state-run election for the purpose of selecting the party nominee for most local, state, and national offices. For example, if two Republicans want to run for the congressional seat in their district, they must compete for their party's support in a primary election. The winner will go on to run as the Republican nominee in the general election. In a **presidential primary** voters elect the state party's delegates that will go to their political party's national convention to select the party's candidate. In 2000 the Republican Party in forty-two states and the Democratic Party in thirty-nine states used this method of delegate selection.

Primaries will be examined in greater detail in the next chapter, but one point is clear: primaries

As this Harrison poster reveals, the log cabin and "common man" image were popular themes for the Whigs' 1840 campaign.

have greatly weakened political parties by shifting the power focus from the party organization to the campaign organization. Primaries, among other things, have made the party the servant rather than the master of candidates and incumbents. The candidates themselves choose the issues, raise the money, and mobilize the voters.

Other Party Systems

Multiparty System—In this system, common in most European democracies, several major and many minor parties compete for and win public offices. Each party is based on a specific interest such as religious belief, political ideology, economic class, or section of the country. Those in support of the multiparty system maintain that this system gives broader, more diverse representation

Political Parties in the U.S. and Mexico

Even though the U.S. Constitution has no provision for political parties, a strong two-party system has dominated American political history. Debate over the ratification of the Constitution produced the Federalists and Anti-Federalists (later Democratic-Republicans or just Republicans) and a few decades later, opposition to Andrew Jackson's Democratic Party led to the rise of the Whigs. The Whigs' collapse was due to division over slavery, and just before the Civil War began, the Republicans built their party in opposition to slavery and in support of business. Democrats remained as the opposition to the Republicans.

Third parties routinely fail and pass from the scene, and Americans have become so accustomed to two-party politics that it is hard to imagine any other kind of political life. For much of the twentieth century, however, Mexico has had quite a different tradition—one-party rule. From 1929 to 2000, Mexico's Institutional Revolutionary Party (PRI) dominated the presidency. Having ruled over seventy years, the PRI was the longest-ruling party in the world at the time of its loss in 2000.

While the rest of the world was fighting World War I, Mexico had a bloody civil war over political succession that cost about a million lives. Out of that horrible experience in 1917 came a new constitution and, in the 1920s, the National Revolutionary Party, the forerunner of today's PRI. Mexico's leaders, revolutionary rivals, decided that all questions about political succession would be resolved within one political party instead of by bloody and destructive civil wars. One party dominated for over seventy years since leaders within the party chose candidates and everyone agreed to support them. Nomination by the party ensured election to office. The PRI, therefore, could control not only the presidency but also Congress, the governor, the state assembly, the mayor, and municipal councils.

The one-party domination thrived for another reason. Many national and local officials could not be reelected, according to the constitution; therefore, they were looking for appointments after completion of their terms. Loyalty to the president and the PRI helped them secure appointment to other positions in the government. Furthermore, this arrangement helped a Mexican president get his proposals through Congress, since members were generally eager to please him.

The PRI's power ended, at least for the moment, in 2000 with the election to the presidency of Vicente Fox, leader of the National Action Party. Years of corruption, economic woes, and political turmoil brought down the once invincible PRI.

President Bush and Mexican president Vicente Fox at Rancho San Cristobel

of the populace. However, this diversity proves to be a major weakness of the system because one party is usually unable to win a majority of the votes. It then becomes necessary for two or more parties to piece together their strength by forming a coalition in order to gain a majority and thus control the government. However, coalitions can produce some odd "marriages" that do not always hold together very well or very long. Italy, for example, averaged a new coalition government every nine months for over forty years until 1996.

One-Party System—Most of today's dictatorships have a **one-party system** of government in which only one political party is allowed. The party is controlled by a select few who rule the country using a centralized bureaucracy and an effective police force.

Section Review

1. What were four significant political results of Andrew Jackson's election to the presidency in 1832?
2. What was the single most influential factor in building political party organization after 1828, and why was it so influential?
3. When did political campaigning begin?
4. What are the differences between the nominating and presidential primaries?
5. How have primaries weakened political parties?

III. Third Parties

Republicans and Democrats are not the only ones in the political race. A number of minor parties also compete, although they usually run a distant third. These third parties have faced numerous obstacles within a system dominated by two parties. With many state election laws making it difficult for third parties even to make it onto the ballot, most voters do not take these political oddities seriously enough to desert one of the established parties. Despite these barriers, third parties, even

short-lived ones, have had an important impact on American politics.

Types

Issue Parties—Issue parties are third parties that spring up around a single burning issue—often one that the major parties find too hot to handle. For instance, the antebellum Free-Soil Party opposed the expansion of slavery into the West. In more recent times, the Right-to-Life Party has opposed legalized abortions. Both are examples of parties built around issues, and such parties gain a fiercely loyal political following. When an issue is resolved or public sentiment moves the major parties to adopt the cause, the corresponding third party declines and soon becomes a historical footnote.

Ideological Parties—Parties that rise from political and social ideas outside the mainstream are called ideological parties. Many of the ideological parties are the result of Marxist influence and, despite their small followings, they have demonstrated a knack for survival. The Socialist Labor

Eugene Debs campaigns for president on the Socialist ticket in 1912.

Party, for example, has run a presidential candidate since 1892, though averaging only 25,000 votes in each election. On an ideological spectrum that generally leans left, one major exception among the minors is the Libertarian Party, which advocates a minimalist government and broad-ranging personal freedom. In 2000, Libertarian presidential candidate Harry Browne received only 0.4% of the popular vote. Browne's name was on the ballot in forty-nine states and the District of Columbia.

American Independent candidate George Wallace

Depression Parties—Hard times also produce political undercurrents. A number of minor parties have sprung up during economic depressions. The fact that "misery loves company" has been a basic feature of these depression parties, which usually gather strength in rural pockets of the South and Midwest. These grassroots parties of discontent, such as the Populist Party of the 1890s, gradually lose strength as the economy improves. However, depression parties have left their stamp on American politics and government. For example, the direct election of senators (Amendment XVII), the federal income tax (Amendment XVI), and federal regulation of banks and railroads were all issues that originated in depression-party platforms.

Splinter Parties—As the name implies, splinter parties are minor parties that split from major parties, generally over policy but sometimes over personality conflicts. While depression parties have had an impact on legislation, splinter parties have had their greatest impact on elections. No splinter party has won a national election, but it often determines who will win by splitting the parent party's strength and throwing the election to the opposition.

This was precisely what happened in the 1912 election. Theodore Roosevelt's Progressive ("Bull Moose") Party, which splintered from the Republicans, divided that party's votes and delivered Democrat Woodrow Wilson an electoral landslide. If the popular votes for the Republicans and Pro-gressives could have been combined, Wilson would have been defeated.

Because of their election orientation, most splinter parties are identified with a man and an election year. For example, in addition to Theodore Roosevelt's Bull Moose Party in 1912, there were Robert LaFollette's Progressive Party in 1924, Strom Thurmond's Dixiecrats in 1948, and George Wallace's American Independent Party in 1968. When the election is over and the prodigal candidate returns to his old party, the splinter party, having lost its candidate and its cause, either disappears or takes a lower profile.

Importance

Despite the fact that most Americans have not supported third-party candidates, third parties have made an impact on the American political system. For instance, the Anti-Masons in 1831 were the first party to use a national convention to elect a presidential candidate. The following year the Democrats and Whigs did the same.

Even a relatively small third party can play an important role in a close contest. In 2000, Green Party candidate Ralph Nader received 3 percent of the popular vote and may have taken enough votes away from the Democratic candidate to allow a Republican victory.

174

Third parties draw attention to specific issues that major parties do not take a strong position on or simply ignore. Sometimes these single issues gain such popularity that the major parties will include them in their platform. Women's suffrage began as a third-party issue.

Third parties continue to be a visible, important part of the American political scene. Notable third parties with ballot status include the Constitution Party, Grassroots Party, Green Party, Libertarian Party, Natural Law Party, Prohibition Party, Reform Party, Right-to-Life Party, Socialist Party USA, Socialist Workers Party, and Workers World Party.

Section Review

1. List the four types of third parties.
2. Which amendments came into being because of specific third-party issues?
3. What type of third party is formed over a personality conflict or policy conflict within a major party?
4. List three ways third parties have influenced the American political system.

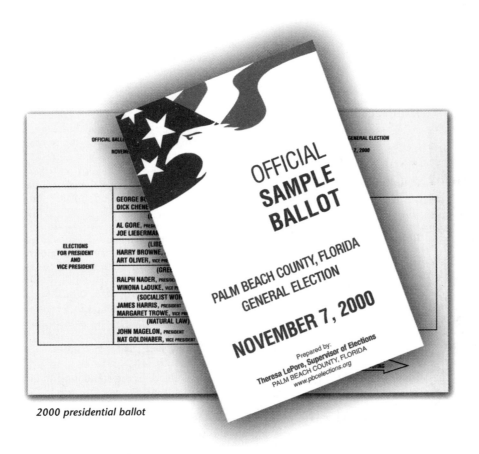

2000 presidential ballot

Ballot Status of Third Parties in 2000

Constitution Party	(Founded 1999) Opposes abortion and gun control; favors school prayer and reduced taxes. Ballot status in 41 states.
Grassroots Party	(Founded 1986) Favors legalized marijuana, hemp farming, universal health care, and reduced government intrusion into citizens' lives. Ballot status in 1 state.
Green Party	(Founded 1996) Committed to environmentalism, nonviolence, and social justice. Ballot status in 44 states.
Libertarian Party	(Founded 1971) Advocates total individual liberty (through drug legalization, abortion rights, legalized homosexual marriage, home school freedom, fewer gun-control laws) as well as total economic freedom (by reducing or limiting the welfare system, government regulation of business, and taxation). Ballot status in 49 states.
Natural Law Party	(Founded 1992) "New Age" and "scientific" remedies for national and international problems and transcendental meditation. Ballot status in 39 states.
Prohibition Party	(Founded 1869) Ultraconservative Christian social agenda, antidrug and anticommunist. Ballot status in 1 state.
Reform Party	(Founded 1995) Supports highest ethical principles for White House and Congress, campaign reform, balanced budget, and term limits. Ballot status in 49 states.
Socialist Party USA	(Founded 1901) Advocates limiting production to that which can be used (i.e., not for profit); also supports community-based cooperatives and ecological harmony. Ballot status in 7 states.
Socialist Workers Party	(Founded 1938) Advocates the authoritarian politics of Marx. Ballot status in 14 states.
Workers World Party	(Founded 1959) Supports worker revolutions, rioting, and street violence. Ballot status in 4 states.

V. Party Organization

Party organization more closely resembles a scattered army living off the land than a streamlined corporation. An organizational chart that diagrams the flow of power as a pyramid of national control over state levels and extending to a base of county and precinct organizations is far from reality. There are, in fact, widely differing amounts of organizational, financial, and political strength among a party's many components. There is also a remarkable degree of independence in the relationship between party levels. Keep in mind that each division of party organization, from the national level to the precinct, corresponds to an electoral division—a fact that underscores the purpose of each division. Before we examine the major organizational levels of a party, we must consider several important reasons for its fragmented nature.

Fragmented Nature

Membership Strength—The effectiveness of a party at any level often depends on the strength and motivation of its membership. The party sets a date for precinct members to meet—yet no law requires attendance at a precinct meeting. Despite the fact that every citizen in this country lives in a precinct, only a small fraction ever attend such meetings. The success of the party at even the most basic organizational level depends largely on individual initiative, a fact that should challenge and encourage Christians to get involved. Though it is true that man's fundamental need of redemption demands a divine rather than a political solution, there are many ways in which believers can be "salt" in society—and involvement in community politics is clearly one of those ways.

Any registered voter can attend precinct meetings, which are called every two years. Precinct officers are elected at this meeting. A percentage of each precinct's members can attend the party's county convention. At this convention, the county party chairman and committeemen are elected, as well as delegates and alternates to the state convention. When the state party convention is held, the party's state chairman and vice-chairmen are elected. During presidential election years, committeemen to the national party committee and delegates to the national convention are elected.

Federalism—The basic goal of the two major parties is to gain control of government by winning elective office. In the United States there are a half million positions at local, state, and national levels. This power dispersal encourages fragmentation by making parties operate at many different levels at the same time.

Nominating Process—Since candidates are nominated within the party, the selection process lends itself toward potential fighting. Although party members all hold allegiance to the same national party, they often become divided over a nomination. These intraparty conflicts are usually the result of two major factors. The first is the power of the position. Nominating candidates is, of course, the important party function essential to the electoral process. The candidate who wins the nomination wins leadership in the party and gains access to its resources. The second factor is party variety. America's two-party system brings a variety of factions and interests, along with their leaders and potential candidates, together under a single party label. Sometimes unity is difficult to achieve.

These two factors sometimes result in healthy competition and sometimes in bitter rivalry. Party nominees must often act quickly to heal party wounds in order to forge a united effort in the general campaign. Candidates who fail to reach out to their fellow party rivals may regret it on election day.

National Organization

There are four components of a national party. The national chairman and the national committee serve largely in an administrative capacity, while the national convention and the congressional campaign committees serve an electoral function.

National Convention—The national convention is the aspect of party organization with which most Americans are familiar. The convention, which meets in the summer of every presidential election year, is a gala gathering that usually attracts heavy media coverage. The primary purposes of the convention are to nominate the candidates for president and vice president and to approve the party's platform position on various issues. The hundreds of delegates in attendance at a national convention are elected at the state level. Chapter 13 will take a closer look at national conventions and national delegates.

National Committee—The national committee of each party carries on the administration of the party during the interim between national conventions. More importantly, it helps raise money and supply technical assistance in congressional races and important state races. The two national committees differ in both composition and approach. Both committees are composed of a committeeman and committeewoman elected by state conventions from each state and a number of territories. In addition, the **Republican National Committee (RNC)** includes several state party chairmen. However, the **Democratic National Committee (DNC)** has a much larger membership. The DNC also includes all state chairmen and vice-chairmen as well as a number of mayors, governors, and members of Congress. The RNC generally concentrates on strengthening national ties to the state organizations and thereby building a more unified party. The DNC has traditionally placed more emphasis on presidential politics and has been less effective at building strong state organizations.

National Chairman—In theory, the national chairman is the head of his party, a leader elected by members of the national committee. In reality the chairman is handpicked by the party's presidential nominee after the national convention and is given rubber-stamp approval by the national committee. Traditionally, the national chairman has had more prestige than power. The chairman of the party in power answers to the incumbent president, whereas the chairman of the party out of power has the rather thankless task of presiding over an array of factions and candidates jockeying for power and the next nomination. Two women have chaired the national committees; Mary Louise Smith of Iowa held the RNC chairmanship from 1974 to 1977, and Jean Westwood of Utah chaired the DNC from 1972 to 1973. The only African American to chair a national party was Ron Brown, who chaired the DNC from 1989 to 1993.

Congressional Campaign Committees—Another component of party organization at the national level is the congressional campaign committees. Both the Democrats and the Republicans have committees for both the House and the Senate. These organizations operate independently of their party's national committee, providing money and expertise to help reelect incumbents to Congress and to assist promising challengers in their bids for national office.

State and Local Levels

State—State party organization centers on a state committee headed by a state chairman in an arrangement similar to that at the national level. The chairman usually represents the governor, a U.S. senator, or other powerful leader or group in the politics of the state. The chairman and central committee work to further the party's interests in the state by building an effective organization, fostering

2008 Republican convention and nominees Sarah Palin and John McCain

2002 Michigan Republican Convention

party unity, and finding candidates and campaign funds. State committee members are generally elected from the county level in a convention or a primary. The influence of these state committees varies considerably, being tied to the political competitiveness within the state. For example, if the Democratic Party controlled virtually every state office from the governor to the local sheriffs, this lopsided situation would probably be reflected in the two parties' state machinery. The Republican state organization in this case would probably not be well organized or well funded, nor would it command as much media attention as the Democratic organization.

Local—Local party divisions across the country vary considerably in structure and strength. The structure usually follows an electoral map of the state. States are divided into congressional districts. In large cities the districts are divided into **wards** for the purpose of city council elections, then further divided into precincts. **Precincts** are the smallest units of election districts and party administration. These grassroots organizations provide the widest opportunity for political involvement as they carry out essential party efforts such as voter registration, candidate recruitment, campaign support, and poll management.

Section Review

1. List three factors contributing to the fragmented nature of political parties.
2. What are the two major purposes of a party's national convention?
3. What group manages national party activities during the time between national conventions?
4. Which person acts as the nominal party leader?
5. What is the smallest unit of election districts and party administrations?

Basic Party Structure

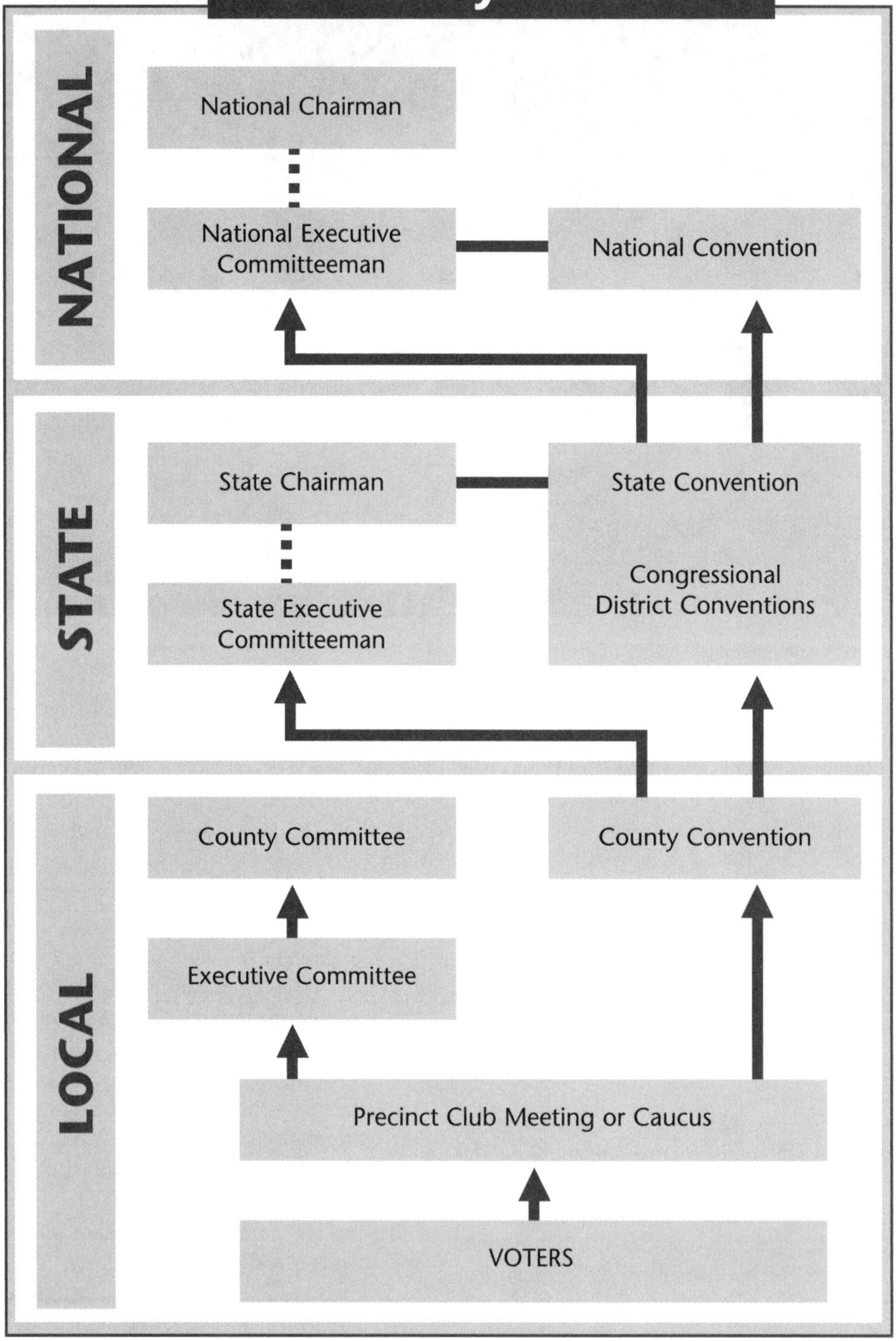

NATIONAL

National Chairman

National Executive Committeeman — National Convention

STATE

State Chairman — State Convention

State Executive Committeeman

Congressional District Conventions

LOCAL

County Committee — County Convention

Executive Committee

Precinct Club Meeting or Caucus

VOTERS

V. Party Decline

Like a mirror, political parties in America reflect the changes that have taken place in American society over the past two centuries. A number of trends have created dramatic changes in the purpose and effectiveness of party organizations. In the past, parties were a cohesive force in government. Strong parties provided control over factions, coordination in policymaking, and cooperation between the legislative and executive branches. New developments, however, have greatly weakened the traditional party, making it more a vehicle for nominating than a means of governing.

Changes

Primary Laws—Reformers at the turn of the century introduced the primary to open up the nominating process to broader participation. By placing the state parties under some degree of state regulation, primary laws lessened the power of party regulars and insiders to control delegates and nominations.

Despite the shift to state-regulated primaries, the majority of delegates to the parties' national conventions continued to be chosen in party-run caucuses. This meant that party bosses continued to

Lyndon Johnson's decision not to seek reelection in 1968 resulted in a volatile Democratic convention, which in turn spurred long-term reform.

dominate nominee selections. This undemocratic vestige came under severe attack in 1968 and was swept away, with mixed results.

Social Upheaval—The forces of social upheaval that characterized the 1960s all seemed to converge on the streets of Chicago outside the Democratic National Convention in 1968. Thousands of antiwar demonstrators, civil rights activists, and members of the radical Poor People's Campaign and the Youth International Party ("Yippies") clashed with police and national guardsmen before a nationwide television audience. Against this backdrop the Democrats nominated Vice President Hubert Humphrey, who had entered no primaries but was the choice of party leaders such as President Lyndon Johnson and Chicago mayor Richard Daley. The violence and charges of corruption surrounding Humphrey's nomination sparked widespread campaign reform.

Primary and Delegate Increase—Two important party changes of the post-1968 era were an increase in the number of presidential primaries and an increased number of national delegates drawn from those primaries. Today over 70% of the national delegates are chosen through the primary system. These changes have brought significant results. First, the changes have had a democratizing effect on the parties by opening up the nominating process to greater participation. Second, the reform movement has resulted in greater party involvement by **interest groups,** groups formed around a particular issue or agenda. Not only is the system more accessible for such groups to attempt to influence a nomination, but candidates for the nomination also solicit special interests in order to piece together an acceptable coalition of support. Of course, these groups expect to receive political dividends for their support if their candidate goes on to win the office.

Campaign Expense—Another result of the changes in the nomination process is that campaigns today are much longer and much more expensive than those in the past. Because today's primary marathon is of transcontinental proportions and is often crowded with contenders, many candidates begin organizing and actively campaigning two years before an election, particularly in the early primary states such as New Hampshire. Candidates must also amass considerable funds if they hope to sustain a strong campaign, and the money comes mostly from private, not party, sources.

Party Democratization—In general, party democratization resulting from primary and delegate-selection reforms has broken the parties down into component special interests and competing campaign organizations, thus contributing to a political process that is, ironically, less democratic. Rank-and-file participation in this century has declined as party reform has progressed. In the late nineteenth century, voter participation exceeded 80% in a number of presidential contests; today a bare majority casts ballots.

Independent Voters

Yellow-Dog Demise—"I'd rather vote for a yellow dog than a Republican," declared die-hard partisans of the Democrats' Solid South a generation ago.

These "Yellow-Dog Democrats," as they came to be known, and their counterparts in the Republican Party are a dwindling breed today. In the 1986 congressional elections, only 8.4% of the electorate said that the candidate's party was the first consideration in how they voted. This statistic is simply one reflection of the dramatic rise in the number of **independent voters,** voters who have no party affiliation, in the past forty years. The 2000 election also illustrated this independent trend.

Party Switching—The rise in the number of self-styled independent voters has not only weakened party control but has also made election trends and their aftermath less stable. For one, the number of independent voters has contributed to an increase in landslide elections (that is, the winner received at least 55%) in presidential contests. Between 1828 and 1900 only one landslide victory occurred; however, party-switching independents have contributed to eleven such lopsided victories during the twentieth century. For example, a number of Republicans supported Lyndon Johnson in 1964 to help drive up his electoral tally over Barry Goldwater. And in 1980 and 1984 a quarter of the Democrats, the so-called Reagan Democrats, defected from their party to support the top of the Republican ticket. In 1988 George Bush drew heavily from this same group to defeat the Democrat, Michael Dukakis. While there was no landslide in election 2000, the same block of independent voters created uncertainty. Republican George W. Bush and Democrat Al Gore were extremely close in their vote totals. As election day drew near, America was kept guessing as to how the independents would vote.

In addition, **ticket splitting,** voting for candidates of both parties for different offices, has become increasingly prevalent with the rise of independents. As was noted earlier, voters have shown a strong ticket-splitting tendency in recent years by sending a Republican to the White House and Democrats to Congress. Ticket splitting is even more predominant in state and local elections, a fact that sometimes hampers governing because of the awkward, highly charged, partisan atmosphere when the governor and lieutenant governor, for example, are from opposite parties. South Carolina illustrated this in the 1990 election with Republican Carroll Campbell elected as governor and Democrat Nick Theodore elected as lieutenant governor. In the 1998 election the reverse occurred, with Democrat Jim Hodges elected as governor and Republican Bob Peeler elected as lieutenant governor.

Media Impact

Television—Television has had a powerful influence on the effectiveness of our party system. Candidates with enough money can largely bypass the party apparatus and reach out directly to the voters by way of television. It is no longer necessary for a candidate to put in years of loyal service to a party in order to win its nomination. Because television reaches millions of homes instantaneously, the pursuit of office has become more of a personal matter than a party one. News organizations also affect campaign issues by picking the issues that will be addressed during their public broadcasts. Columnist George Will observed:

> Campaigning today is one of the purest forms of individual entrepreneurship available in an age of bureaucratized enterprises. A candidate

enlists a small staff, raises capital, invests it in marketing his product (himself), and the market decides.

The Internet—An even more recent form of media, the Internet, may bring great change in future campaigning methods. During the 2000 election the Internet increased in importance as a quick way for a candidate and voter to send and receive information. After John McCain won the New Hampshire primary, sixty thousand volunteers signed up online to help with his campaign. Through online donations, the McCain campaign raised one million dollars in forty-eight hours.

The next chapter will discuss further the changes in political campaigning resulting from past and present technology. Candidates on the trail these days are followed by a caravan of photographers, microphones, laptop computers, and dish

Nixon-Kennedy TV debates

antennas. And, of course, the sophistication of a campaign staff may be judged by whether or not it includes a makeup artist.

Despite the forces that have weakened the present party system, political parties show no signs of becoming extinct. Two-thirds of the electorate continue to identify with one of the major parties, and even many independents have a party preference. Parties, as a vehicle of self-government, will continue to adapt to social and technological changes and will continue to offer access to political participation and leadership.

Section Review

1. Widespread protests at what event sparked much campaign reform?
2. What two important changes resulted from these reforms?
3. What is ticket splitting?

Chapter Review

Terms

political parties
major parties
minor parties
third parties
nominate
partisanship
two-party system
single-member district
plurality
bipartisan
party platform

liberal
conservative
multiparty system
coalition
convention
delegates
caucus
patronage
spoils system
political campaign
primary

nominating primary
presidential primary
one-party system
Republican National
  Committee (RNC)
Democratic National
  Committee (DNC)
wards
precincts
interest groups
independent voters
ticket splitting

Content Questions

1. What sets political parties apart from other groups that are organized to promote political causes?

2. What are the present major political parties in America?

3. How does the existence of political parties affect the workings of Congress?

4. Why is a two-party system beneficial?

5. Why is a multiparty system unstable?

6. How did the rise of political parties necessitate the Twelfth Amendment?

7. What are the four components of national party leadership and organization?

8. How has the use of television and the Internet affected the strength of political parties?

Application Questions

1. How could the government have prevented the development of political parties, and what would have been the effects?

2. Should Christians become active in politics? Explain your answer.

3. Have political parties become too weak in recent decades? Explain your answer.

4. How loyal should a person be to his political party? Is voting a split ticket being disloyal?

CAMPAIGNS AND ELECTIONS

Senator Kay Bailey Hutchison of Texas

Politics in a free society involves a rich array of competing ideas, choices, personalities, and power. Add to this mix color, comedy, cameras, handshaking, speechmaking, and quantities of barbeque, and you have the American political campaign. John Quincy Adams said, "A stranger would think that the people of the United States had no other occupation than electioneering."

This chapter will examine this important American spectacle mostly from the congressional, state, and local perspectives. Presidential campaigns and elections will be highlighted in Chapter 13.

I. Candidate Nomination
Preliminaries

A primary function of United States political parties, as discussed in Chapter 8, is to nominate candidates for office. Candidate **nomination,** naming candidates for public office, is a key step in the election process. Prior to this key step, each candidate faces certain tasks. These include meeting the public office requirements, assembling a staff, establishing a campaign strategy, and campaigning for the party's nomination.

Senator Wayne Allard of Colorado

Office Requirements—Each public office has specific requirements that a person must meet in order to become a viable candidate. The United States House and Senate office requirements are established in the Constitution. Senate candidates are to be at least thirty years old and U.S. citizens for nine years. House candidates are to be at least twenty-five years of age and U.S. citizens for seven years. Office requirements for state elected positions vary from state to state. In Idaho, governor and lieutenant governor candidates are to be at least thirty years of age, U.S. citizens, and residents of Idaho for two years prior to the election. Pennsylvania has the same age requirements for governor and lieutenant governor candidates, but candidates have to be state residents for seven years prior to the election. Local office requirements vary within each state depending on the county. Requirements usually include filling out and submitting the appropriate forms, paying the filing fees, and setting up a campaign contribution account and headquarters. Candidates representing minor parties usually have different or additional requirements. It is important for potential candidates to understand what the requirements and commitments are before "throwing their hat into the ring."

Staff, Strategy, and Primary Campaigning— Campaign and staff workers are a temporary but important first step toward being elected to office. The **incumbent,** the current office holder, selects core staff from personal office staff. Challengers hire their own staff.

Additional campaign workers are divided into three groups. One group consists of unpaid, trusted senior advisors. These advisors have no personal political ambition but provide counsel for the candidate on important questions. A second group is made up of citizen volunteers who perform the routine jobs of the campaign. This group is composed of individuals seeking excitement, job seekers looking for appointments, or individuals drawn by the issues. Consultants represent the third group of campaign workers. They are paid professionals whose purpose is to help the candidate become more informed on subjects important to interest groups and issues focused on by the media. Consultants are a more recent campaign trend. Christians who fit into any of these groups would be of great value as "salt," helping those candidates who support biblical solutions to America's problems.

With the assembly of core staff and advisors, the candidate begins to develop a strategy for the campaign. The primary has to be won and strategic choices made. These choices include choosing a campaign theme, deciding on a campaign strategy (positive or negative), securing a finance chairperson who will raise campaign funds and properly use those funds, and gaining the support of local party members. Once the primary is won, the campaign is expanded, campaign strategy is refined, and more intense campaigning begins. Incumbent candidates and candidates not challenged for their

Campaign worker

party's nomination have most of their campaign funds available, giving them an advantage over other candidates. Those candidates who faced opponents for their party's nomination usually have to raise more campaign funds to mount an effective campaign.

Methods of Nomination

The United States has five methods of nomination: petition, self-announcement, caucus, convention, and direct primary.

Petition—This nominating method is widely used at the local level for municipal offices in small communities and nonpartisan school posts. A **petition** is a formal document signed by a specific number of qualified voters for a candidate in the election district. Petition is usually required by state law to nominate independent and minor-party candidates. Specifics of this process vary from city to city and state to state.

Independent Announcement—This oldest form of the nominating process in this country dates back to colonial times. **Independent announcement** occurs when one desirous of running for a particular office announces his intention of running or has someone else make the announcement. Independent announcement is also implemented when one does not win his or her party's nomination or cannot support the party's choice. This method is used when a write-in candidate enters an election. In 1954, U.S. senator Burnet Maybank of South Carolina died. Strom Thurmond, unable to support Edgar Brown, the Democratic Party nominee, ran as a write-in candidate. Thurmond won and became the first person in U.S. history to be elected to a major office by write-in ballot.

Caucus—Originally this private meeting was composed of a few like-minded, influential individuals who selected the candidates they would support in the upcoming elections. As political parties developed, the caucus was implemented and the membership expanded. With westward expansion and the spread of democracy, more Americans

disliked the closed, unrepresentative nature of the caucus. This dislike escalated with the four-way 1824 presidential race. It became a race between competing personalities and regions of the country with no candidate receiving a majority of the votes. The election was thrown into the House of Representatives because of the Twelfth Amendment requirement. When Henry Clay gave his support to John Quincy Adams (and subsequently received a position as Adams's secretary of state), Andrew Jackson's supporters claimed that Adams and Clay had made a "corrupt bargain." With these events, the caucus method of choosing presidential party candidates began to die. Today the caucus is used mainly in New England's local nominations. In the presidential primary, one or both of the major parties continue to use the caucus method to nominate candidates in some states. These states include Hawaii, Iowa, Michigan, Minnesota, North Dakota, South Carolina, and Wyoming.

Convention—During the Jacksonian period, the caucus was replaced by the convention, which seemed to be a more representative method. At the local level, party members met to select candidates for local offices and delegates to represent them at the county convention. At the county convention, county office candidates and delegates to the state convention were selected. At the state convention, delegates chose party nominees for governor and other statewide offices and national convention delegates. At the party's national convention, presidential and vice-presidential candidates were nominated. Unfortunately, party bosses began to control the system, and by the 1870s many sought to change the corrupted system. Today many independent parties use state conventions to nominate their party's candidates. In Connecticut and Utah the two major parties have nominating conventions prior to the primary. During presidential elections in some states, one or both major parties use the convention to nominate their candidate. These states are Alaska, Nevada, and Virginia.

Direct Primary—The **direct primary,** a preliminary election held to select candidates and/or delegates to party conventions, became state law in Wisconsin in 1903. In the 1910s the direct primary replaced the convention as the main nominating method in the American political process. Most states mandate that primaries are to be the method by which parties choose candidates for the U.S. Senate and House, for state governors and legislatures, and for most local offices. Some states select their candidates by a combination of the convention and primary systems. States set the primary dates; furnish election officials, polling places, ballots, and registration lists; and oversee the primary.

Major types of primaries are closed and open. In the **closed primary** participants must be registered as members of one party and may vote for the candidates from only the party to which they belong. On primary election day, registered voters go to their precinct polling place, where their name is on a list. The voter is given his party's ballot, and he votes. Twenty-six states and the District of Columbia use this method of candidate nomination.

The **open primary,** a primary in which voters do not have to declare their party membership, is found in twenty-four states. Any qualified voter on primary election day may tell a precinct official which party primary ballot he wants to vote on or, in some states, take both major party ballots and vote on only one. Three states—Washington, Cali-

State convention

fornia, and Alaska—had a different type of open primary. It was called the **blanket primary,** or "wide-open" primary. Voters received identical ballots that included the names of all the candidates. Voters could then choose to vote in the Republican primary election for one office and the Democratic primary for another. In 2000, however, the Supreme Court ruled this type of primary election unconstitutional.

Louisiana has yet another form of the open primary. The primary and election are combined to form "open-election law." All nominees are listed by office on a single primary ballot. Individuals who receive more than 50 percent of the primary vote win the office. Thus the primary ends up being the election. When there is no majority winner, the two who receive the most votes face each other in the **general election,** an election used to fill an elective office. This election is held on the first Tuesday after the first Monday in November.

The presidential primary developed out of the direct primary and will be discussed in Chapter 13.

Section Review

1. What preliminary requirements do candidates face when running for public office?
2. In what document were the requirements for U.S. Senate and House offices established?
3. Define *incumbent*.
4. What are the methods of candidate nomination?
5. What is the oldest form of the nominating process?
6. Define *direct primary*.
7. How does the blanket primary differ from a normal open primary?

II. The Campaign Trail

The intensity of a long campaign is an important way to test the physical and mental strength of the candidate. Weeks of travel, speechmaking, and scrutiny from the media enable voters to see how well the candidate withstands pressure and may bring out the true nature of the candidate's character. Rutherford B. Hayes said that nothing brought "out the lower traits of human nature like office-seeking. Men of good character and impulses are betrayed by it into all sorts of meanness."

Jeb Bush on 2002 campaign trail

Campaigns, Incumbents, Coattails

The Congressional Campaign—These campaigns are less competitive than presidential campaigns, with over 90 percent of incumbents reelected. Congressional candidates can distance themselves from the "problems" in Washington and hold the president responsible. Incumbents can take credit for improvements since they make the laws. However, local candidates are hurt when the economic policies of their party fail. Because congressional elections draw fewer voters, greater importance is placed on specific voter groups, such as pro-life voters or the growing Hispanic community. While seeking these votes, candidates must be careful. Missteps could result in defeat.

Incumbents—Candidates who challenge incumbents or vie for an open seat must begin campaigning at least a year and often longer before the general election. Incumbents are generally spared from all the preliminary rigors because they have many advantages—powers of their office, name recognition, financial backing, and the services of their **constituents,** residents of a district represented by an elected official. Unfortunately, because of well-entrenched incumbents, most congressional races are not very competitive. From 1960 to 2000, an average of 93 percent of U.S. House incumbents seeking reelection kept their seats, and 82 percent of U.S. Senate incumbents retained their seats.

Coattail Effect—The **coattail effect** is the ability of a strong candidate at the top of the ticket (usually the candidate for president) to attract votes for other members of his party running for lesser offices. For instance, in 1980, Republicans gained twelve Senate seats when Ronald Reagan was elected president. They won a majority in that house for the first time since the 1952 election, when many Republican members of Congress rode the coattails of Dwight Eisenhower. Since voters do not always vote a **straight ticket** (vote for all the candidates in one party), the coattails of the winning presidential candidate are not always long enough to pull in party members running for other offices. In 1976, for example, the victory of Jimmy

Carter brought an increase of only one Democratic senator and one representative. The same was true in 1988, when Republicans actually lost two seats in the House even though they easily won the White House. Generally speaking, the greater the popularity of the party's presidential candidate, the greater the opportunity for the coattail effect to operate. Therefore, congressional, state, and local candidates tie their fortunes to the top of the ticket if the presidential candidate is popular and a likely winner in the district. However, in the 1992, 1996, and 2000 elections there was little or no coattail effect.

Campaigning and the Media

Democrat William Jennings Bryan in 1896 traveled thousands of miles and gave hundreds of speeches with many newspaper reporters joining him on the campaign trail. National Republican Committee Chairman Mark Hanna countered by taking McKinley's "front-porch campaign" from the front porch to the voters. Hanna raised large sums of money, distributed millions of pamphlets, and sent information exalting McKinley to newspapers throughout the United States. Hanna also mounted a negative campaign and implied that if Bryan were elected many would lose their jobs. Thus the media began to be widely used in political campaigns. During that time period, newspapers and magazines were the major source of information for voters.

Radio—Harding's win over Cox was broadcast by radio in 1920. In a brief amount of time, radio could inform the nation of international and national events. Radio was first used during the presidential campaign of 1924, especially by Calvin Coolidge. Even after radio had been largely superseded by

television, the medium remained an important channel for political speech, as, for instance, in the conservative talk shows that went on the air during the 1990s.

McKinley campaigning on his front porch

Television—In the nineteenth century most Americans never saw their president during his administration, much less the various candidates vying for office during an election year. The 1952 presidential campaign saw the first significant use of television, and candidates had a medium that was both a blessing and a curse to their campaigns. The candidate could reach millions of homes with his message, outline his plans for the nation, and even target advertising to appeal to various groups. On the other hand, the television could become a "one-eyed monster" for some candidates when embarrassing incidents or ill-chosen words gained nationwide exposure. Little things could actually sidetrack a campaign, such as a candidate's attempts to recover from a gaffe. Senator Robert Dole's quest for the 1988 Republican presidential nomination was impaired by public exposure of a fit of frustration. Cameras captured an angry Dole telling George Bush to "stop lying about my record," and the negative image lingered to haunt him until he pulled out of the race.

Since television is primarily a visual medium, superficial factors become more noticeable. The fact that a candidate simply "looks good" on television can become a deciding factor in many voters' minds. This was evident during the Kennedy-Nixon debates in 1960. Those who listened to the debates over radio thought Nixon had won. Those watching said Kennedy was the winner. Kennedy's tanned, rested appearance was a huge contrast to Nixon's sweaty, unshaved look. Television also impacts congressional campaigns. During one of the televised New York Senate debates in 2000, Republican candidate Rick Lazio walked over to Democratic candidate Hillary Clinton, thrust out a written pledge for "soft money" restriction, and asked her to sign it. Lazio wanted his opponent to make a commitment on the soft-money issue, but viewers thought Lazio had "invaded" Clinton's personal space. The negative image of Lazio was burned into the minds of the voters.

In the 1984 campaign the incumbent, Ronald Reagan, made a weak showing in his first debate with the Democratic challenger, Walter Mondale. Although Reagan had enjoyed immense popularity, his scattered responses during a single televised hour raised questions about his age and competence. In fact, in the second debate Mondale himself

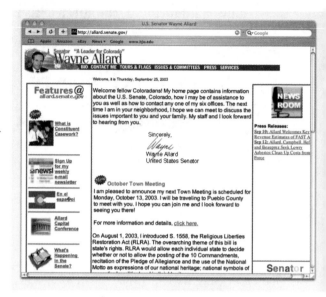

raised the age issue to the seventy-three-year-old president. With a surprising twist Reagan replied, "I am not going to exploit for political purposes my opponent's youth and inexperience." The quip was funny, and both candidates laughed (possibly for different reasons). Millions of television viewers laughed as well, and with that one-liner Reagan steadied the shaky image he had produced during the first debate. Such incidents involve no party platform, nor do they address key campaign issues; yet magnified by television, they can become a crucial factor in winning voters.

State and local candidates may best use the television medium by running **spots,** paid advertisements, or using **"free media,"** coverage of campaign activities on the nightly news. Free media does not cost the campaign any money and aids in name recognition for an unknown candidate.

Internet—The latest tool to aid the candidate's campaign is the Internet. Candidates may set up websites that enable voters to become more informed and also volunteer support. Voters can interact by sending and receiving information and can sign up to receive email updates. Candidates can also raise funds faster through the Internet. This media form, however, is still young, and its full potential has not been realized.

Rick Lazio

Section Review

1. Why are congressional campaigns less competitive than presidential campaigns?
2. Define *constituent*.
3. What is the coattail effect?
4. Which candidate first began making use of the media during his campaign, and when was this begun?
5. List the types of media that cover political campaigns.

III. Elections and Voting

The electors see their representative not only as a legislator for the state but also as the natural protector of local interests in the legislature; indeed, they almost seem to think that he has a power of attorney to represent each constituent, and they trust him to be as eager in their private interests as in those of the country. (Alexis de Tocqueville)

Federal and State Elections

Federal Elections—Election law in the United States is mainly state law because the majority of the elected offices are state and local offices. Election laws regarding the president, vice president, and both houses of Congress were established by the Constitution. Article I, Section 2, Clause 1 states that House of Representative members will be elected by the people every two years, and Clause 4 says that vacancies will be filled by special elections called by state governors. Article I, Section 3, Clause 1 says that two senators are to be chosen by each state legislature for a term of six years. In 1913 the Seventeenth Amendment was passed, allowing the senators to be directly elected by the people. Senate vacancies may be filled by special election or, in some states, may be appointed by a state governor. Article I, Section 4, Clause 1 also gave Congress the power to establish the date for congressional elections. Congress decided that the

general election was to be held on the first Tuesday after the first Monday in November of every even-numbered year. Election laws regarding the president and vice president will be discussed in a later chapter (see Chapter 13).

State Elections—The election date for state and local elections is usually the same as for federal elections. In odd-numbered years some states hold elections for governor, executive offices, or state legislators in November. Election dates for city, county, and other local elections vary from state to state and usually occur in the spring.

State elections are administered through each state's election offices. For example, in South Carolina, election offices consist of the State Election Commission, the State Board of Voting Machine Commissioners, and the Board of State Canvassers. Local offices include the County Board of Registration, Commissioners of Election, and the County Board of Canvassers. There are also election day officers—poll managers, clerks, and **poll watchers,** individuals appointed by political parties and candidates to observe the polls on election day. Their duties include questioning voters thought to be unqualified to vote and watching the ballot counting. Each group is to carry out its responsibilities to ensure a lawful, proper election.

Election Day

Whatever the outcome of the next day, the candidates can end their long campaigns on Monday night before the election. On election day they vote where they are registered and prepare for the election results by preparing two brief speeches, one for victory and another for defeat. The candidate's staff, however, continues working to get supporters out to vote at their **polling place,** a location in a specific precinct where residents of that area go to vote. Polling places include schools, churches, and fire stations. In the evening, after the polls close, supporters gather at their candidate's headquarters to watch the results and hopefully celebrate victory. In close races it is sometimes not until the next day that the results are known.

The Voter

The opportunity to vote in America is a responsibility, a privilege, and a constitutional guarantee. The Fifteenth Amendment gave voting rights to all citizens regardless of race. Women were given voting rights by the Nineteenth Amendment. The Twenty-fourth Amendment eliminated poll taxes, and the Twenty-sixth Amendment extended voting rights to eighteen-year-olds. Unfortunately, in recent elections only a little over half of registered voters exercised their constitutional right.

Many have expressed their thoughts about voting, including two former presidents. John Quincy Adams said, "Always vote for principle, though you may vote alone, and you may cherish the sweetest reflection that your vote is never lost." John F. Kennedy said, "The ignorance of one voter in a democracy impairs the security of all."

Registration—The basic requirements for a person who wishes to **register** to vote (to officially enroll for the purpose of voting) are the same in all states. A person must be a U.S. citizen, at least eighteen years old, and a resident (one who lives in a particular place for a specific period of time) of the state in which he or she will vote. Each state may impose additional requirements, and most do. Registration is not required in North Dakota, and Vermont lists only the basic requirements. In most states, if an individual has been convicted of a felony, imprisoned, or judged to be mentally incompetent, he cannot vote. A person can register by mail or in person at city hall or the county courthouse. Since the passage of the National Voter Registration Act, or "Motor Voter Law," in 1993, a person can also register when he or she applies for or renews a driver's license or at local state employment, welfare, or other social agency offices. In the weeks leading up to an election, registration tables are often set up in public places, such as fire stations, libraries, or shopping malls. To register, one must prove his age, usually accomplished with a birth certificate. Registering in the

Suffragettes marching in Washington, D.C.

future may be through the Internet. In some areas this is already a reality.

Profile—The profile of the American electorate has changed dramatically since the first presidential election. The voters at the time the Constitution was ratified were white, male property owners and taxpayers. Voting rights were eventually extended to former slaves, women, and eighteen-year-olds. In congressional, state, and local campaigns, candidates take into account the ethnic background, religion, education, income, age, occupation, and gender of the people in the voting area.

In presidential races geography has greater impact. For instance, in election 2000 Gore held a majority of votes in the heavily populated areas in and around cities. Bush carried the majority of counties, but they tended to be more rural. This illustrates the importance of the electoral college and will be discussed in Chapter 13. In congressional and state races, candidates take into account the state's geography. In the 2002 Republican primary for governor in South Carolina, well-known coastal candidates had to work harder in the upstate region making voters aware of their positions.

Gender and age are groups important to the major political parties. The under 30 and over 50 voters and women tend to vote for Democratic candidates. Reagan in 1984 and Bush in 1988 were able to swing younger voters to support their campaigns. In 1992 and 1996 Clinton regained these voters for the Democratic Party. In 2000 Bush and Gore received an equal percentage.

The voters' religious background can make a difference. Voters in the early years of American politics were mainly Protestant, but increased immigration brought Catholics, Jews, and other religions. The 1960 election of John F. Kennedy, first Catholic president, brought division between some Catholics and Protestants because many voters thought the Vatican would influence the president. Religion also influences the voters' positions on issues. Religious conservatives tend to support candidates who are anti-abortion and take conservative stands on other important issues.

Political parties focus on ethnic backgrounds also. Beginning in the late nineteenth century, immigrants settling in the cities were courted by the Democrats. In the 1930s African Americans shifted their support to the Democrats, and they have remained strong supporters of Democratic candidates since 1952. In 2000 the Hispanic vote was divided, with more Cuban Americans voting with Republicans and a large percentage of Mexican and Puerto Rican Americans voting with Democrats.

Registering to vote

What denomination are you?

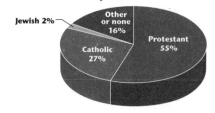

Is religion an important part of your life?

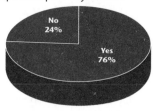

How often do you seek religious guidance?

How often do you attend church?

What is your attitude about biblical accuracy?

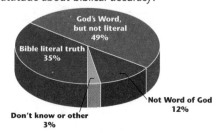

National Elections Studies, 2000 election; survey included all ages and races

195

Methods of Voting

Historical—America's early historical voting method was by voice. The voter voiced aloud his voting preference, and this method was looked upon as a "man's" way of voting. However, as the number of voters increased, corruption crept in. Candidates tried to buy votes and sometimes resorted to intimidation. By the middle of the 1800s, voters wrote their choice on pieces of paper and put their handmade ballots in the ballot box. Political parties and candidates began making their own ballots, but this soon proved not to be the most fair and honest method. Today, individual state election commissions, state boards of elections, or secretaries of state choose and certify the methods and equipment used for voting.

Paper Ballots—The system of paper ballots, or "Australian ballots," was first used in 1856 in the Australian State of Victoria. The official paper ballots had all candidates and issues listed. Also called the "secret ballot," paper ballots allowed voters to privately mark their choices and put their vote in a secured ballot box. The first American state to use this method was New York in its 1889 statewide elections. In many rural and small communities, this method continues to be used.

Mechanical Lever Machines—With the lever voting machine, each candidate or ballot issue is given a particular lever, and the voter pulls down the levers corresponding to the votes he wishes to cast. The first official lever machine was used in New York in 1892. By 1930 most major U.S. cities used this method, and by the 1960s over half of all U.S. voters were us-

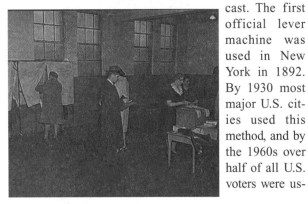

Old-fashioned voting booth with paper hand-marked ballot

Modern electronic voting booth

ing these machines. The machines are no longer being made and are usually replaced with computer-based or direct electronic systems.

Punch Cards—Using this system, the voter punches holes in the card opposite of the candidates or issues of choice. The voter then puts the card into a ballot box. After the polls close, the ballots are put into a tabulating device at the precinct where the punched holes are counted for each candidate or issue. One type of punch card, the butterfly ballot, puts the candidate names in two columns instead of one so that the text can be larger. The punch holes are located between the columns of names. In the 2000 presidential election, the use of butterfly ballots in Florida brought much controversy. Critics alleged that the ballots were confusing and that many voters had mistakenly voted for the wrong candidate. It was not until a month after the election that the final vote was made official.

Optical Scan—On an optical scan ballot card, voters fill in the empty ovals, circles, or rectangles next to the candidate they wish to vote for. The ballots are placed in a sealed box or into a tabulating machine where the darkened areas are counted.

Voting by Mail—This method is used mostly by absentee voters. **Absentee voters** are voters unable to vote at their polling place on election day. Individuals who fall into this category include those at college or on a business trip, the ill or disabled, and those serving in our military forces. These voters apply for an absentee ballot prior to the election during a specific time period. They mark their ballot, seal it, and return it to the appropriate election official prior to the election.

To encourage greater voter participation, some states have begun to allow practically anyone to cast absentee ballots before an election. Texas allots the greatest amount of time, giving up to seventeen days prior to an election for people to vote.

Internet—This potential voting method of the future has drawn mixed reactions. Many point to the potential problems—viruses, voter secrecy violations, inaccurate voter counts, blocked access, etc. Others view Internet voting as a way of increasing voter participation and reducing election costs. The 2000 election saw experimental, limited use. In the Arizona Democratic presidential primary, the Internet was an option for voters, and in the general election a few hundred military personnel stationed abroad were allowed to cast votes in their home states via the Internet.

Section Review

1. Where in the Constitution is provision made for the election of U.S. House and Senate members?
2. Define *polling place.*
3. Which amendment extended voting rights to eighteen-year-olds? to women? to all races?
4. What are the basic requirements for registering to vote?
5. How did the 1995 Motor Voter Law change voter registration?
6. What do candidates consider about voters when seeking their votes? Why?
7. What are "Australian Ballots," and when were they first used in U.S. elections?

IV. Campaign Finance

Will Rogers once said, "Politics has become so expensive that it takes a lot of money even to be defeated." Running for public office at federal and state levels has become a multi-million dollar pursuit. With money becoming a campaign necessity, the door opened for candidates to try to purchase their way into office or for interest groups to try to gain political favors with their campaign contributions. As a result, in the early 1900s campaign financing drew attention for reform. It was not until the 1970s that stricter laws were passed to govern campaign finance and the Federal Election Commission was established to see that these laws were obeyed. However, due to misuse and perceived misuse, the crusade for campaign finance reform continued throughout the 1990s and into the twenty-first century.

Laws

Federal Laws—Federal election campaign contributions to specific candidates were made illegal from corporations in 1907 and from labor unions in 1943. But with political campaigns receiving much of their funding through individuals, many thought additional reform was needed. After the expense of the 1972 presidential campaign and the scandal of Watergate in 1974, individual donations were limited to $1,000 per election per candidate and $20,000 to a political party.

Campaign money raised for a specific candidate in federal elections and spent according to federal laws and restrictions is called **hard money.** Because labor union contributions to federal candidates were made illegal in 1943, soft money came into being. **Soft money** is campaign money raised apart from federal regulations and given to local, state, and national party organizations to be used for "party-building" activities such as voter registration efforts and get-out-the-vote drives. Labor unions raise soft money using political action committees that receive voluntary donations from its members. **Political action committees,** or **PACs,** are committees formed by interest groups that raise money and make contributions to specific individuals' campaigns or causes. Only those PACs registered with the Federal Election Commission (FEC) can contribute to candidates seeking federal offices.

To better understand how soft money and PACs work, assume a family relative living in Bethlehem, Pennsylvania, is employed by Bethlehem Steel. He is a union member of the United Steelworkers of America (USWA), and its PAC is the United Steelworkers of America Political Action Fund. Your relative, along with other steelworkers, is concerned over the influx of cheaper steel from Europe, and it is also an election year. Your relative would contribute money to the USWA, which would in turn give those funds to the USWA Political Action Fund PAC. The PAC would contribute the funds to the political party of those candidates that want to slow the influx of cheaper European steel.

Presidential campaigns are also supported by the public through the Presidential Election Campaign Fund, which receives taxpayer donations. Beginning in 1971, taxpayers could check off a box on their income tax forms designating money for this fund. Through a 1974 amendment to the Federal Election Campaign Act (FECA), candidates proving that they have widespread support can get money from this fund. The candidates prove widespread support by collecting $100,000 from donations of $250 or less from at least twenty different states, with each state contributing at least $5,000 toward the goal. Candidates during presidential primaries can qualify for federal money matching the amount already raised. During the general election they can acquire a specific lump sum. However, to get these funds candidates agree not to go over specified spending limits.

Other 1974 amendments to the Federal Election Campaign Act established limits on money for federal candidates from individuals and PACs, candidate spending from personal and family resources, total campaign expenses, and independent expenditures. **Independent expenditures** are expenses by a person or group that communicates to the voters to help elect or defeat a candidate without the candidate's knowledge or support. For instance, during the 2000 primary elections, the Sierra Club ran a TV ad complaining about the environmental record of Texas governor George W. Bush. Because the Sierra Club did not use terms like "vote for," "defeat," or "elect," and because they did not coordinate directly with another candidate's campaign organization, federal election law allowed the environmental interest group to spend an unlimited (and unreported) amount on their "informational" campaign. (Another group calling itself Republicans for Clean Air spent $2.5 million on similar ads attacking the environmental voting record of Bush's primary rival, Sen. John McCain.)

Buckley v. *Valeo*—Soon after the amendments to the Federal Election Campaign Act were passed,

2002 Federal Campaign Contribution Limit				
	To a candidate or candidate committee per primary or general election	To a national party committee per year	To any other political committee per year	Per two-year election cycle
Individuals	$2,000	$25,000	$5,000	$95,000
PACs	$5,000	$15,000	$5,000	No limit

a suit was filed in federal court saying these provisions were unconstitutional. The plaintiffs said that limiting money used for political purposes restricted communication because important political communications involved spending money. Thus, the restrictions were a violation of the First Amendment. In 1976 the U.S. Supreme Court in *Buckley* v. *Valeo* said that the First Amendment was violated by the limitation of a candidate's spending of his own money, the restricting of the campaign's total expenses, and limiting independent expenditures. But the Court upheld the constitutionality of limiting donations by individuals and committees. The Court also ruled that if a candidate voluntarily accepted public financing, he would be subject to campaign spending limits.

State Laws—Local and state campaign finance laws govern the activity of state and local candidates

IN COMPARISON

Campaign Finance in the U.S. and Europe

In recent years Congress has wrestled with the issues of how political campaigns and elections should be financed. Some Americans complain that contributions by the wealthy and by special interests, such as business and labor unions, "buy" influence with elected officials. Furthermore, incumbents seeking another term have to spend a lot of time raising money rather than focusing completely on governing. Campaigns, especially those in populous areas that require television advertising, are expensive, and the high cost discourages good candidates from running.

U.S. law places limits on campaign contributions. Contributions directed to federal office candidates during elections are known as "hard money." "Soft money," money given directly to political parties and to Political Action Committees (PACs), is used to build the political party or aid PACs that may promote a single issue through television advertising. Obviously, soft money has an effect on campaigns even though it is not given directly to a candidate. The Supreme Court has ruled that soft money is part of free speech and is therefore protected by the Constitution. However, with unregulated soft money, the potential for corruption is great; during the 1996 presidential campaign, Bill Clinton had to return illegal foreign contributions.

President George W. Bush signed the Bipartisan Campaign Reform Act in 2002, which prompted opponents of the act to file another suit before the Supreme Court.

In Germany, Austria, and Sweden, there is generous public funding of political parties. Germany also provides a large tax deduction for contributions to political parties. The United States tried that on a smaller scale years ago, but after little success it was ended. European countries provide free radio and television time for parties as well as free billboard space, but individuals are not permitted to buy time for radio and television ads.

Europe's policies have little chance of success in the United States. While public funds go to parties in Europe, American politics is more candidate-oriented. Most European governments have a parliamentary system, whereby the leader of the majority party in the legislative body becomes the executive, or prime minister; in the U.S. the president is elected separately by the people. Furthermore, citizens in America tend to support less government and taxes than their European counterparts; therefore, more government involvement in financing of campaigns and elections is unlikely.

and PACs. State finance laws vary from state to state. Federal law takes precedence over state laws in two areas. The first of these areas includes restrictions on election financing activities by federally chartered corporations, national banks, and foreign nationals (foreign governments, political parties, corporations, associations, and partnerships). The second area includes those laws dealing with the organization and registration of political committees supporting federal candidates, disclosure of receipts and expenditures for federal candidates, and federal candidate contribution disclosure and limits.

Problems

Funding—One problem involving campaign finance reform is the way the Republican and Democratic parties acquire their funds. Each party has a different method. Reforms affecting one method of funding will hurt the party that utilizes that method and thereby give a distinct advantage to the other party.

Inflation—Since the passing of the 1974 laws that set the funding limits, there has been no adjustment for inflation. As costs have increased, candidates have come under pressure to raise more campaign money. This need for additional funding has encouraged candidates and their contributors to seek new ways around hard-money limits. Soft-money contributions and independent expenditures have been some of the ways used to get around the limits.

Federal Election Commission (FEC)—The FEC board is made up of six commissioners. They are appointed by the president and confirmed by the Senate. Each member serves a six-year term, with two seats subject to appointment every two years. No more than three members can be from the same political party, and four votes are required for any official action. This structure of the FEC board causes another problem. The six commissioners are usually divided into an equal number of

Democrats and Republicans, and the commissioners usually vote along party lines. Because decisions have to be approved by a majority vote, it takes a lot of time for a decision to be reached.

Incumbents—Campaign finance laws protect incumbents, making it difficult for a challenger to wage a successful campaign. Incumbents have name recognition and a staff already in place. Challengers have huge costs starting up their campaigns. Also, the proposed banning of political advertising sixty days before an election would further disadvantage the challenger since incumbents are already known.

Grassroots Politics— With the passage of the Federal Election Campaign Act, the ordinary citizen's options for supporting candidates were limited. Prior to this act, supporters could set up campaign headquarters, have rallies, print their own materials, collect money at local functions for their candidates, etc. But the Federal Election Campaign Act requires supporters to organize a committee, appoint a treasurer, and follow the established laws or run the risk of being fined by the Federal Election Commission. This has discouraged many constituents from becoming involved. When the FEC does fine a campaign, the campaign treasurer is responsible to pay the fine.

Elizabeth Dole campaigns in eastern North Carolina in 2002.

Reform Winners and Losers—Incumbents would benefit greatly from the proposed campaign finance reforms, but perhaps the greatest beneficiary would be the media. The media could endorse specific candidates, utilizing its First Amendment right without limitations. Conservative and Christian organizations would be the losers if reform continues in the direction it is headed. These groups could theoretically be banned from commenting on important moral and political issues during election campaigns. Thus, the First Amendment right to free speech would be allowed only to a select few.

Reform

After the reform efforts of the 1970s, it was not until the 1990s that reform was once again given attention. Senate Democrats, who held the majority in 1990, proposed reduced postage rates, reduced television time, and voluntary state-by-state spending limits. When the Republicans gained control of Congress in 1994, their reform focus was directed toward stopping labor unions from spending mandatory union dues on political activities, limiting PAC contributions, raising the amount that individuals can donate, and, on free speech grounds, opposing limitations on independent expenditures and the prohibition of soft money. The pressure for reform continued into the early twenty-first century. Specific proposals were given serious consideration.

McCain-Feingold—The most well known of the recently proposed campaign finance reform bills was introduced by Senators John McCain (R-Arizona) and Russell Feingold (D-Wisconsin). Its main provisions included bans on foreign national contributions, soft money, and postal franking (sending mail free of charge) for congressional members seeking reelection. The bill provided for closer scrutiny of independent expenditures and an end to bundling (combining a number of small contributions into one contribution for a campaign). The proposal also stated that contribution limits should be raised from $1,000 to $2,000 for a candidate whose opponent did not adhere to the spending limits. The majority of Republicans were opposed to this bill because of its failure to stop labor unions from using required union dues for political activities, its ban on soft money, and the restrictions on individual contribution limits.

In 2002 President George W. Bush listed the finance reform principles that he would like to see implemented. These principles included strong political parties, quick and complete disclosure of contributions, and an end to involuntary contributions and soft money contributions by unions and corporations. The president pledged support for rules that defend the individual's right to express his views by supporting specific issues, that raise the limits of candidate and party contributions, and that promote fair and equal constitutional methods of reform.

Reform Law—On March 27, 2002, President Bush signed the Bipartisan Campaign Reform Act of 2002. This new law stopped unions and corporations from making unregulated contributions, "soft money," to political parties. It increased the amount of money that individuals can give to candidates. It also strengthened the laws that oversee the disclosure of how much is contributed to political campaigns and by whom. At the signing of this reform law, the president stated that the act had flaws (limited contributions by political parties for federal elections, broad ban on issue advertising, and no further restrictions on corporate and labor union contributions). But despite the flaws the act would improve the present system. Almost immediately after the president signed the bill into law, Senator Mitch McConnell (R-Kentucky) filed a lawsuit to try to block it. Senator McConnell stated that he filed the suit to defend the First Amendment right of all Americans to fully take part in the political process.

Campaign finance reform debates continue. Government officials are seeking fair solutions through the legislative process and through the courts. Money has become a dominating force in the political arena. However, many forget that it is the grassroots effort of one-to-one campaigning by the candidate and his or her supporters that can make the biggest difference in the end.

Many Christians may not want to be involved in campaigns and elections or may desire only to participate through voting and prayer. I Timothy 2:1–2 says,

> I exhort therefore, that, first of all, supplications, prayers, intercessions, and giving of thanks, be made for all men; for kings, and for all that are in authority; that we may lead a quiet and peaceable life in all godliness and honesty.

Senator McConnell and Judge Starr holding a news conference

When Paul wrote this exhortation to Timothy and those Christians with him, he encouraged them to pray for kings and those ruling over them. The people at that time and place in history could not choose their civil authorities. Today, God has provided Americans the opportunity to help decide their leadership. This is indeed a special gift. Praying for one's country and voting for candidates who uphold Christian principles are extremely important. However, the Lord may desire you to do more, especially in the one-to-one grassroots efforts. Christians should seek what the Lord desires of them and possibly put their prayers into action.

Section Review

1. What is the difference between "hard" and "soft" money?
2. What prompted the raising of soft money through PACs?
3. Define *independent expenditures*.
4. List the problems surrounding campaign finance reform.
5. What is the most well known of the campaign finance reform proposals, and what did it propose?
6. What reform law was signed by President Bush in 2002? What did this law change?
7. What was the response to the 2002 reform law that President Bush signed?

Chapter Review

Terms

nomination
incumbent
petition
independent announcement
direct primary
closed primary
open primary
blanket primary

general election
constituents
coattail effect
straight ticket
spots
free media
poll watchers
polling place

register
absentee voters
hard money
soft money
political action committees
  (PACs)
independent expenditures

Content Questions

1. What are the office requirements for U.S. Senate and House of Representative candidates?

2. Describe the different types of workers candidates use to mount an effective campaign.

3. What do states contribute to primary elections?

4. Explain how Louisiana's nominating process differs from that of the other states.

5. How did television impact the 1960 presidential campaign?

6. How can state and local candidates effectively utilize television?

7. What determined the date for general elections, and when are these elections held?

8. What determines state election days, and when are these elections held?

9. In what state is voter registration not required?

10. Why was campaign finance reform initiated in the early 1900s?

11. What was *Buckley* v. *Valeo*?

12. Who would be perhaps the greatest beneficiary of campaign finance reform?

13. What specific reform principles did President Bush say were needed in 2002?

Application Questions

1. If the Supreme Court had not banned the blanket primary in 2000, how could political parties have used it to their advantage?

2. How might the Internet be used and misused in future campaigns? Should Congress propose legislation to prevent misuse? Support your answer.

3. With the growing Hispanic population in the U.S., could a candidate be hurt politically if he supported stricter immigration laws? if he supported a law making English the official language for business? Support your answers.

4. Which current voting method, in your opinion, is the most accurate, timely, and secure? What problems have accompanied particular voting methods?

5. What is the present status of campaign finance reform? Is reform continuing, and if so, what principles are being suggested?

PUBLIC POLICY AND POLITICS

10

Pro-life march on Washington, D.C.

The governor of Florida declares a state of emergency after a hurricane devastates four southeastern counties. Congress passes an education bill requiring greater accountability for student achievement in the nation's schools. The municipal government of Gypsum, Colorado, approves the installation of speed bumps near the high school in order to curtail speeding.

In each of the above cases, government has acted at either the federal, state, or local level. But why does government respond to these particular issues and not to others? This chapter will discuss the nature of public policy and will then examine non-governmental forces that help shape it.

I. Government and the Public

Every government interacts with the public at some level. Even the most autocratic and repressive governments involve themselves in the lives of their citizens, if only to repress their civil liberties. But in a democratic government, elected representatives compose a government that is "of the people, by the people, for the people." As such, government action in a republic should be both a reaction to and a reflection of public attitudes.

Definitions

Public policy is the sum of government's goals and actions made in response to public opinion. Most Americans have opinions about political issues. From increases in local property taxes to reductions in the national defense budget, from gun control to national health care, one's personal views may be collected by pollsters, revealed only to close friends, or just pondered by the individual himself. Collectively, ideas about political issues compose a public opinion.

Political scientist V. O. Key has defined **public opinion** as "those opinions held by private persons which governments find it prudent to heed." There are two noteworthy characteristics about public opinion. First, government does not gauge public opinion simply by determining the opinions of the average American. There are many "publics" with opinions. Members of a manufacturing association would likely favor trade restrictions, whereas dockworkers and import merchants would favor free trade. The elderly have strong opinions about Social Security benefits; farmers support agricultural subsidies. Government considers the opinions of these and many more segments of society, and then it responds to those issues it deems significant in the political arena.

Second, some issues, such as abortion, education reform, and capital punishment retain public interest for decades. Others, however, are as short-lived as fads or are important to only a limited group of people (for instance, the citizens of a small town in which a major factory is to be closed).

Liberalism and Conservatism

Frequently public opinion—and the public policy that it helps create—can be categorized as either liberal or conservative. During the early twentieth century, the terms *liberalism* and *conservatism* acquired their modern political meanings

(see Chapter 8). Franklin Roosevelt used the word *liberal* to describe policies that expanded the power and responsibilities of the federal government. Since then, **liberalism** has generally referred to policies that favor government action while **conservatism** has referred to a reluctance to expand government authority.

The meaning of the words *liberalism* and *conservatism* has changed considerably during the last two hundred years. Nineteenth-century liberalism combined biblical ideas about the dignity and worth of the individual—especially freedom of conscience in matters of religion—with unbiblical notions about the goodness of man and the belief that reason would eventually lead to human progress. Nineteenth-century liberals tended to oppose government restrictions of all sorts—political, economic, and religious—because they believed that government rules stifled individual freedom and equality of opportunity. For example, these liberals advocated *laissez faire* (the idea that government should not regulate the economy) because they believed that individual initiatives would provide greater material prosperity than government restrictions.

Nineteenth-century conservatism also had both biblical and nonbiblical roots. For instance, conservatives held the unbiblical belief that some men should have rights denied to others because of the circumstances of their birth. Still, nineteenth-century conservatives tended to emphasize the sinful nature of man, the frailty of human reason, and the necessity of governmental restraint to prevent man from slipping into chaos and then despotism.

During the early twentieth century, liberalism retained its belief in the basic goodness of man but abandoned faith in *laissez-faire* economics. Contemporary liberals argue that government should strive for economic equality by managing a "welfare state" in the public interest.

Meanwhile, conservatism retained its suspicion of man's goodness and continued to support government regulation of morality. But modern conservatives also tend to support individual conscience against "political correctness" and are likely to oppose governmental interference in the economy. The result of this shift in ideology is that contemporary political conservatives more often take positions closer to Scripture than do modern liberals.

Since the New Deal, public opinion and public policy have fluctuated between liberalism and conservatism. In the 1960s, liberalism seemed ascendant as the nation endorsed expansion of government entitlement programs. During the Reagan presidency in the 1980s, there was a shift toward conservatism, in part because of a frustration with earlier government failures. During the 1990s and 2000s, the nation accepted more liberal social policies, as for instance, an increased public acceptance of homosexuality. Economically, however, the nation remained quite conservative even during the Democratic Clinton administration.

Some citizens and politicians prefer to call themselves **moderates** rather than categorize themselves as liberals or conservatives. To some degree the term *moderate* means whatever its bearer wants it to mean. In general, moderates tend to have a pragmatic, "whatever works" approach to politics rather than any firm ideology.

Section Review

1. Define *public policy* and *public opinion*.
2. What are two noteworthy characteristics of public opinion?
3. What are the basic modern implications of the words *liberal* and *conservative?*
4. Describe the moderate ideological approach to politics.

II. Public Policy

Divisions

The Preamble of the Constitution outlines several basic goals of government—establishing justice, ensuring domestic tranquility, providing for the common defense, and promoting the general welfare. These goals generally define the arena of public policy.

A more basic way of examining public policy is to divide it between domestic and foreign policy. **Domestic policy** frequently involves economics, law, education, health, energy, environment, and civil liberties. **Foreign policy** includes diplomacy, trade relations, and war. Prior to the 2002 midterm elections, Republicans emphasized the war on terrorism (foreign policy), in which they believed they had support, while the Democrats stressed the weak economy (domestic policy) in which they believed they had support.

Development

The development of public policy is like a highway. Issues can enter or exit the process at various stages, travel at different speeds, and stay for different lengths of time. However, a simpler way to view the process is as a single trip from start to finish with clearly defined stages in between.

Issue Identification—Before public policy can be developed, government must identify an issue to deal with. Obviously, not every issue demands a response from government. You may have burnt your toast this morning, but you would hardly ask the government to do something about it. On the other hand, if your toaster was defective and caused a fire, you might seek government assistance through the Consumer Product Safety Commission.

Usually an issue does not become public policy unless it affects a sizable portion of the public (pervasive), it has a significant impact on the public (intensive), and the public sees the issue as a problem government should deal with (relative).

Measured against the governments of Europe and Canada, the United States government is comparatively uninvolved in the private lives of its citizens. Nevertheless, since the Great Depression of the 1930s, the national government has become involved with many more issues once handled on a state, local, or private level because Americans increasingly look to the national government to solve their problems.

Dust Bowl "Okies" on Route 66 to California

Christians should remember that although God has established government, a Christian's ultimate hope should rest in the Lord. Christ directs us to "take no thought, saying, What shall we eat? or, What shall we drink? or, Wherewithal shall we be clothed? (For after all these things do the Gentiles seek:) for your heavenly Father knoweth that ye have need of all these things" (Matt. 6:31-32).

Agenda Setting—Those issues government decides to address are said to be on the government's **agenda.** The agenda reflects the relative importance of the issues—some at the top, others at the bottom. Often the president outlines the government's agenda through the State of the Union address, although other government branches also help to establish the agenda. Depending on what issues the government targets, the agenda may be described as conservative or liberal.

Policy Formation—In the next phase, policy formation, government forms a response to the problem. In some cases this response may be nothing at all depending on the ideology of the party in power. Historically the legislative branch of government has been most influential in policy information. Much of the work is done in small committees within Congress, such as the Committee on Agriculture, the Committee on Government Reform, the Committee on Small Business, the Committee on Veteran Affairs, and the Select Committee on Homeland Security. These and other committees help to craft laws that become one of the most visible forms of public policy.

Within the last century, both the executive and judicial branches of government have become more involved in public policy. Executive orders, treaties, and diplomatic agreements are instruments of the executive branch. Likewise, court decisions shape public policy. During the 1950s the Warren Court interpreted the Constitution in a way that reflected its liberal agenda, and judicial activism has continued to the present at all court levels. Furthermore, unlike the legislative and executive branches of government, the judiciary does not answer to the people directly through elections. As a result, the courts can, to a considerable extent, ignore public opinion when they make public policy.

House Committee on Government Reform

Implementation and Evaluation—After it is formed, public policy must be implemented by the executive branch and its bureaucracy—or, in the case of foreign policy, by the military. Ideally the policy implemented will help solve the problem facing the public. However, many factors can limit the success of a public policy decision: a decision may be theoretically sound but be unworkable in fact; a court may rule a possible solution unconstitutional; or, despite the soundness of a public policy decision, the issue may be something that government has little power to deal with effectively.

Section Review

1. What are the two broad categories of public policy?
2. Identify the four stages of public policy development.
3. What three factors usually make an issue a matter of public policy?
4. How are the executive and judicial branches of government involved in public policy?

III. Public Opinion

Like the government's agenda, public opinion is linked to ideology. What people believe affects what they say and how they act; and how their opinions are formed is as varied as their life stories.

Origins of Opinion

Family—One of the most important influences on public opinion is the family. What people learn

from their parents and home environment often helps establish who they are as adults. God designed the family to teach truth and have a lasting impact: "Train up a child in the way he should go: and when he is old, he will not depart from it" (Prov. 22:6). Unfortunately, the family as an institution has been eroded by divorce and a redefinition by society to include homosexual unions. Furthermore, many families impart values to their children that are in opposition to the commands of God's Word.

Peers—Another influential factor in determining opinion is the influence of peers. Especially during the teen years, peers can be extremely influential. Scripture affirms the importance of choosing friends wisely: "He that walketh with wise men shall be wise: but a companion of fools shall be destroyed" (Prov. 13:20).

Events—Circumstances also contribute to how people think about public issues. An important national or international event can galvanize public opinion. For example, after the terrorist attacks of September 11, 2001, Americans were more willing to have their civil liberties curbed in order to ensure their safety.

Institutions—The school and the church can occupy large portions of time. Compulsory education makes the U.S. public school system a primary former of opinion in children. One reason for a conservative backlash against public schools is the left-leaning education students usually receive there. And at the college level, the liberal bias tends to be even greater.

Although once a center of civic life, churches have lost much of their influence in the modern world. Most "mainline" churches (those associated with the National Council of Churches) have declined in membership and influence as they have abandoned the gospel for social activism. However, non-Christian religions, especially Islam, have gained more adherents in the United States. In addition, non-institutional religions, such as agnosticism and secular humanism, have become more prevalent.

World Trade Center on 9/11

Christ—The power of Christ's presence transforms a person's ideas about public policy. "Therefore if any man be in Christ, he is a new creature: old things are passed away; behold, all things are become new" (II Cor. 5:17). Clearly, a person's mind is affected in salvation. Paul wrote, "And be not conformed to this world: but be ye transformed by the renewing of your mind, that ye may prove what is that good, and acceptable, and perfect, will of God" (Rom. 12:2).

Public opinion is more than a matter of taste or preference; what people think reflects their values. Public opinion can be a gauge of spirituality—or the absence of it.

Measuring Public Opinion

Elections—Because the people are the ultimate source of power in a democratic government, to seek reliable measures of public opinion is natural for government leaders. For two hundred years the primary expression of public opinion on political issues has been the ballot box. A winning candidate considers his victory an endorsement of his public record or his stand on the issues. But while election results indicate the public's general attitude, they are limited as a tool for measuring public opinion. A person might vote for a candidate for several reasons: he approves of the party platform; he dislikes the opposing party's platform; he prefers the candidate's personality; his family has always voted for that party, and so forth.

Perceptions—In the early twentieth century, political candidates and officeholders had to rely mainly on their own perceptions of public opinion. As they mingled with voters, they elicited opinions about matters of public interest. Officeholders might also have received letters and telegrams in support of, or in opposition to, certain government actions. Politicians would then assimilate their impressions into campaign strategies prior to elections and into decisions about public policy while in office. However, the development of reliable opinion polls during the middle decades of the twentieth century has given politicians a new and valuable (though still imperfect) tool for measuring public opinion.

Opinion Polls—**Opinion polls,** surveys of what the public thinks about particular subjects, were not unknown before the 1930s. Occasional polls had been taken even in the 1800s, but they were usually unreliable. Among the first practitioners of scientific polling was George Gallup, who introduced a more rigorous sampling technique during his mother-in-law's 1932 campaign to become secretary of state of Iowa. The success of Gallup's methods in predicting the outcome of the Iowa election was followed by a similar success in the 1936 presidential election.

Today the public is bombarded with statistics from political polls, particularly during election years. Political candidates conduct their own surveys, with presidential candidates now spending millions of dollars on polling alone. Why do candidates desire to know the voters' major concerns, the percentage of blue-collar workers and minorities supporting them, or the public's perception of their honesty and leadership skills? Besides the fact that selective use of polling information can be used

209

as political propaganda, polling data also alerts candidates to areas of vulnerability and indicates ways in which they might improve their campaigns.

Scientific Surveys—In 1936 the *Literary Digest* conducted a poll and used its findings to predict a victory for the Republican challenger, Alfred Landon, over Franklin Roosevelt in that year's presidential election. The magazine calculated that Landon would take 32 states with 370 electoral votes while FDR would win only 16 states and 161 electoral votes. The actual outcome was a landslide victory for FDR.

Why was the *Literary Digest* poll so inaccurate? The *Literary Digest* mailed ten million postcards to people asking that they indicate their presidential preference; two million people responded. The *Digest's* mistake was preparing the mailing list from telephone listings and automobile registrations. Although such a list would probably be representative of the population today, in 1936 the United States was in the depths of the depression. Large numbers of Americans did not have a telephone or car—and FDR received greater support from people who did not own telephones or cars. In the same election, George Gallup predicted the correct result by surveying only a few thousand people, yet his survey group was a **representative sample** of the voters who participated in the election.

Modern pollsters often take their samples from lists of registered voters. Others narrow their surveys further to those people who are both registered and likely to vote. Even so, scientific polls sample voters from all regions, all economic groups, all political parties, and all other major divisions in appropriate proportions so that the survey will be representative of the population that is expected to vote. Of course, no matter how carefully a survey sample is chosen, there will still be some margin of error.

Despite the *Literary Digest* fiasco, Americans are often given the results of nonrepresentative polls. Informal polls, often called **straw polls,** do not attempt to use valid sampling techniques, but

are conducted for a variety of purposes, especially to liven up boring news stories. For instance, a television reporter may poll a few passers-by on a street corner. The kinds of businesses and churches nearby may cause more than a representative number of people from certain economic, racial, religious, or age groups to be polled and thus distort the results of the survey.

Another kind of straw poll is one requiring participants to call in and register their opinion in response to a question posed on a television program or in a newspaper. In some cases, the viewer must pay a fee for the call, and thus only those willing to pay are surveyed. Many Internet news and opinion sites have included straw polls. Not only are the polls limited to people who use the Internet, but results often reflect the type of people who visit the site. A conservative site will tend to have conservative results, while a liberal site will tend to have liberal results. Furthermore, the "voters" are often able to vote as many times as they like. Therefore, straw polls cannot be regarded as an accurate reflection of public opinion.

Other Roadblocks to Reliability—Choosing a representative sample is necessary to obtain a reliable poll, but other factors can also reduce its accuracy. In 1948, after the lessons of the *Literary Digest* poll had been learned, pollsters suffered another humiliating blow. Virtually every major poll in the United States, including Gallup, predicted a victory for Thomas Dewey over Harry Truman in the presidential election. To the pollsters' dismay, the voters disagreed. The problem this time did not lie in a failure to poll representative samples. Instead, the polls failed to consider the possibility that public opinion changes over time. Most of the major pollsters had stopped surveying by September. The few polls taken during the weeks immediately before the November election indicated growing support for Truman. Later reports indicated that many voters had not made their decision until a few days before the election, and Truman apparently captured most of those votes. Pollsters learned that polls could be considered accurate only at the time the data was gathered. In 2000, Gallup Polls showed voter opinions flip-flopping at least five times between the first week of August and the November presidential election. Results ranged from 39% for Gore and 55% for Bush (Aug. 11–12) to 51% Gore, 40% Bush (Oct. 2–4).

Other conditions that may affect the reliability of a poll are the wording of the questions and the conditions under which the poll is taken. A question that leads the participant to choose a particular answer is an inappropriate method for discovering public opinion. For instance, if a pollster asked, "Do you want to clean up the nation's polluted waters?" the response of nearly everyone would be yes. Few Americans would say that they did not want to clean up polluted waters. However, the overwhelmingly positive reply to that question could not be used to imply that most Americans would support a particular piece of environmental legislation; nor would the reply indicate that they consider clean water a major public issue. Also, connotations of the words used in pollsters' questions may affect the outcome of the poll. For instance, in one survey 22% of those polled said that the nation was spending too little on "welfare," but 61% said that the nation was spending too little on "assistance to the poor."

Polling conditions may also affect poll results. Is the poll taken in person, by telephone, or in a written questionnaire? Often people are inclined to be more candid and truthful when they do not have to give their answers face to face. Also, the manner or appearance of the pollster may affect the participants' replies. For this reason, major polling operations use professional pollsters.

Although there are more than two hundred major polling organizations in the United States, polls are not a final authority on any public policy issue. Polls merely reflect some features of the complex mosaic that is public opinion.

The Danger of Public Opinion

Government leaders have many reasons to consider public opinion and allow it to guide their policymaking decisions. Foremost is the fact that the public voted them into office and can vote them out again. Even so, government leaders understand that public opinion is far from infallible. In fact, it can be very fickle and, at times, completely misguided. A single misleading piece of evidence may lead a public rush to judgment, or a demagogue may be able to stir popular emotions with charismatic appeals, as Hitler once did in Germany.

A FedEx plane crash on July 26, 2002, increased public demand for improved safety standards.

Evidences of the instability of public opinion are abundant. Airplane and factory accidents have resulted in public demands for greater security and improved safety standards. Yet when government's attempts to meet these demands result in delays, increased costs, and bureaucratic inconveniences, public opinion can shift from support to complaints. The public may praise a candidate's promises to increase aid for the poor, the elderly, and the handicapped, but if he is elected and keeps those promises, he is often criticized for raising the necessary taxes to support such programs. Obviously, politicians must follow public opinion cautiously, recognizing that making a wise but politically unpopular decision is better than making a bad decision dictated by a volatile public. No better example of the danger of following public opinion

Ecce Homo by Francesco de Mura, from the Bob Jones University Collection

can be found than in the choice made by the Roman governor Pontius Pilate, who, despite his own better judgment, was swayed by the roar of the crowds to crucify Jesus Christ.

can be found than in the choice made by the Roman governor Pontius Pilate, who, despite his own better judgment, was swayed by the roar of the crowds to crucify Jesus Christ.

Unfortunately, politicians are not the only ones who allow ill-informed opinions to influence their actions. Christians must constantly be wary of violating scriptural convictions in order to please others.

> Nevertheless among the chief rulers also many believed on [Christ]; but because of the Pharisees they did not confess him, lest they should be put out of the synagogue: For they loved the praise of men more than the praise of God. (John 12:42–43)

America's representative government was designed to allow government leaders to make decisions contrary to public opinion if in the interest of the public good. Thus while elected officials are supposed to be responsive to public opinion, they ought also to weigh the merits of their decision beforehand. Ideally this foresight will prompt them to act in the public interest regardless of pressure brought to bear by current public opinion.

Section Review

1. How does Romans 12:2 apply to the development of one's opinions?
2. What are opinion polls?
3. Why is it important to have a representative sample for an opinion poll?
4. Why is the wording of an opinion poll question significant?
5. Why must politicians be wary of public opinion?

IV. Interest Groups

Sharing their views with pollsters is not the only way that Americans can express their opinions to government leaders. Citizens also form **interest groups** (also called pressure groups) to influence government officials about some political issue or group of issues.

Purposes

Interest groups are not new. Even the Bible mentions factions that could be defined as interest groups. In Numbers 16, Korah and a group of his followers sought to influence Moses and Aaron and gain more power for themselves. As a result of their pride and ambition, the Lord caused the earth to swallow them up. In Acts 13, Paul and Barnabas were expelled from Antioch after a group of Jews stirred up "devout and honourable women, and the chief men of the city" against them.

However, not all interest groups are wicked. Christians may rightfully participate in interest groups that have proper goals and methods. Political participation is a freedom to be exercised. Even James Madison, who saw the danger of factions or interest groups, supported their existence. To abolish them completely, he recognized, would be to undermine liberty as expressed in the First Amendment: "the right of the people peaceably to assemble, and to petition the government for a redress of grievances."

1990 pro-life rally at the Washington Monument

Interest groups have long been a pervasive force in our own society. Farmers' organizations, merchants' groups, consumer protection lobbies, and the like have sprung up, often as grassroots movements, to eventually wield considerable political power.

Nevertheless, interest groups are not political parties. Their scope of activity is narrower because their concerns are focused on one major area—business or trade laws, gun control, agricultural policies, benefits for the aged—whereas political parties must be concerned with all aspects of public policy. Also, interest groups are generally more concerned with influencing governmental policies than with electing particular candidates.

During the twentieth century, interest groups increased in power and number. This change was partially a result of the decline in political parties (see Chapter 8), as well as several other factors. With the growth of governmental power, more groups organized to influence governmental policies. Improved communication and transportation have also allowed people to associate more easily and to reach the public, the media, and the politicians with their message. Then too, increased education and affluence have provided the time and resources needed for citizens to address their political concerns.

Kinds of Interest Groups

The nation's interest groups are countless, ranging from a small community parent-teacher organization interested in improving local schools to a nationwide organization with millions of members, such as the American Association of Retired Persons. Classifying these groups is difficult because of their variety. However, there are major headings under which many interest groups can be organized.

Economic—Since the late nineteenth century, business associations have dominated the interest group landscape. They first arose to check the growing power of labor unions and the increase of government regulation. Today, approximately seventy percent of interest groups represented in Washington are business associations. Among the most powerful are the National Federation of Independent Business, the Chamber of Commerce of the United States, and the National Beer Wholesalers Association. With the resources available to them, the pressure from business interest groups might seem overwhelming. Nevertheless, conflicts between these groups tend to reduce their influence.

Labor unions are also economic interest groups. Workers in various fields have created associations to seek economic benefits and better working conditions for their members. Democrats have traditionally enjoyed the support of labor unions and often rely on them for political support. The **AFL-CIO,** the largest labor union, has over thirteen million members in its affiliated unions; and despite declining membership, unions remain powerful voices in American politics.

Doctors, lawyers, accountants, and teachers have also formed professional organizations. The American Medical Association is one of the most powerful of these interest groups. Others include the Motion Picture Association of the United States, the Independent Insurance Agents of America, and the American Bar Association. People involved in agriculture also have organizations that speak to government in their behalf. Among them are the American Farm Bureau Federation, the American Cattlemen's Association, and the National Cotton Council.

Social—Other interest groups focus on social issues. Most of these organizations perform a variety of functions, including providing benefits for their members, but they also attempt to influence government. One of the largest of these groups is the American Association of Retired Persons (AARP). Among its chief concerns are health and welfare topics, such as low-cost medication and the defense of the Social Security system. Interest groups such as the National Council on Disability and the Council for Exceptional Children represent people with disabilities. The Sierra Club and Greenpeace concern themselves with environmental policy.

Several civil rights interest groups were formed during the 1960s and 1970s. One of the most visible is the National Organization for Women (NOW). (Interest groups often try to increase their influence by taking an inclusive title. For instance, NOW seems to speak for all women. However, its membership is about ninety thousand—fewer than one-tenth of one percent of American women.)

Single-Interest Groups—Although many interest groups have a wide range of concerns, others are **single-interest groups** concerned with a particular issue such as abortion or gun control. The National Right-to-Life Committee and the National Rifle Association are two of the many organizations in this category. One liberal interest group, EMILY's List, works specifically to elect pro-abortion Democratic women candidates to congressional seats and state governorships.

Religious and Ideological—As American culture has become increasingly fragmented, organizations have arisen to support varied religious and ideological beliefs. In the 1980s the Moral Majority, composed largely of religious conservatives (including Roman Catholics and Mormons), helped Ronald Reagan win the White House twice. Another conservative group, the Christian Coalition, helped Republicans gain control of the House and Senate during the 1990s. Not all such groups reflect Christian or conservative values. For instance, the Council for Secular Humanism and other anti-

Christian organizations have staged marches in Washington. Americans for Democratic Action has worked consistently for abortion rights, lesbian and gay rights, and the removal of Christian influence in public life.

Civic Groups—Other interest groups operate to further some civic cause or responsibility. For instance, the League of Women Voters promotes greater public participation in elections. Common Cause, an organization formed by consumer advocate Ralph Nader, attempts to prompt government action against hazardous products.

The National Rifle Association promotes the safe use of firearms.

Activities of Interest Groups

Interest groups use a variety of devices to influence public policy. Interest groups that support issues with widespread public acceptance may use highly visible tactics, while those with issues less favored by the public may be more discreet while working to change public opinion.

Lobbying—One important tactic is **lobbying,** the attempt to influence public officials in support of a special interest. Large interest groups often maintain a staff in Washington to compile information and chart strategies in order to win the support of members of Congress. The lobbyists who actually present the information to the lawmakers, either in personal interviews or in meetings with congressional committees, are usually experienced lawyers or former officeholders with the ability to gain the ear of policymakers. For instance, a lobbyist might invite a lawmaker to an expensive restaurant for lunch or ask him to speak (for a hefty honorarium) at a meeting of the organization. Even smaller interest groups without large professional staffs or the resources to entertain lavishly find ways to approach government leaders with their concerns.

Lobbying with the aid of gratuities (monetary gifts, goods, or services) is legal under current law, and such benefits increase the income of members of Congress. Although members of Congress cannot accept outright gifts of more than $250 per year, this prohibition does not apply to meals, trips, honorariums, and many other ingenious attention-getting tokens of appreciation. Some critics have declared these practices to be little better than bribery, even though members of Congress regularly insist that they remain unswayed by such blandishments. Undoubtedly, however, some members fall to these allurements. For example, in 1987 a truck manufacturer paid members of the House Armed Services Committee $2,000 each to attend a breakfast meeting. After the breakfast, the committee advised the army to buy five hundred more trucks than it needed.

Public Persuasion—In addition to lobbying public officials, interest groups may also try to attract public support for their causes and then utilize that support to influence the officials. Groups may use radio, television, newspaper, and magazine advertisements to sway public opinion, or they may send out newsletters or direct-mail advertising to citizens. Most interest groups now have websites. Some even include "report cards" that grade the voting records of individual politicians on issues important to the group. Interest groups also encourage citizens to contact their representatives personally in support of the organization's cause.

Protests and Rallies—Organizing picket lines, sit-ins, marches, and other forms of protest may also serve as an advantageous strategy for some interest groups. Environmentalists engage in sit-ins high up in trees to prevent loggers from cutting the trees down. A conglomeration of interest groups, some with violent agendas, has staged protests of the World Trade Organization. A prime example of this sort of political action was the 1963 March on Washington, D.C., by some two hundred thousand people seeking improved civil rights for blacks. The NAACP, CORE (Congress of Racial Equality), and other groups organized this peaceful protest, which gained the attention of the nation and the national government.

Political Action Committees—Another political activity of interest groups is involvement in political campaigns. The groups usually set up **political action committees** (**PACs**—see Chapter 9) to work in behalf of candidates deemed favorable to its goals. PACs not only enlist campaign workers to solicit votes but also make monetary contributions to the campaigns themselves. Most PAC money goes to incumbents for two reasons: the interest groups have greater access to politicians already in office, and the money may help win

1963 civil rights protest in Washington, D.C.

215

support on issues that arise before the election. In fact, incumbents in the House and Senate usually receive about three times as much PAC money as their opponents. Even incumbents who run unopposed (as over ninety members of Congress did in 1998) may receive hundreds of thousands of dollars in PAC money for their campaigns. Obviously, interest groups intend that these contributions will not only promote the reelection of the incumbent but will also keep him sympathetic to the group's political opinions.

Congressmen have been criticized for accepting gifts from lobbyists and PAC money, but Congress has been reluctant to halt these lucrative practices. Congress did pass a law that prevented future members from keeping surplus campaign money after they left Congress. (Members elected before 1980 were exempt and were able to take the campaign contributions with them.) Not only does taking PAC campaign money suggest impropriety, but large PAC contributions to incumbents also discourage possible challengers. Fewer than ten percent of congressional seats in each election cycle are taken by new members, and many of these seats are won only because the incumbent did not run for reelection.

Court Action—Some interest groups have focused their efforts on the judiciary by advocating positions in court cases important to the groups' cause. The most visible of these groups is the American Civil Liberties Union (ACLU), which has chapters in every state. In the name of civil liberty, the union has championed causes such as abortion rights, legalization of marijuana, abolition of the death penalty, the teaching of evolution, and bans on prayer in schools and the public display of the Ten Commandments. In 1990, Pat Robertson founded the American Center for Law and Justice (ACLJ) as a counter to the ACLU, and the ACLJ has attempted to protect the First Amendment rights of religious conservatives.

In some court cases, an interest group may act as an **amicus curiae,** or "friend of the court." While not a party in the case, the amicus curiae

The Boy Scouts—an ACLU target

may testify or file briefs in an attempt to influence the court's decision. Obviously some court cases have implications far beyond the matter at hand and might set a legal precedent affecting the interest group's position.

Although interest groups wield considerable power, there are countervailing factors. One is that voters can replace elected leaders when those officials blatantly ignore the interests of their constituents. Another is that for every interest group, there is probably another working just as hard to gain support for the opposite position. Diversity tends to dilute the influence of one particular organization. Thus elected officials often allow all sides to present their views before making a decision on a public issue.

Section Review

1. What is an interest group? Give another name for an interest group.
2. List the five major kinds of interest groups and give examples of each.
3. What interest group activities may be used to influence public policy?
4. What is an amicus curiae?

V. Mass Media

Politicians and interest groups have learned how to use **mass media** to their advantage as they seek to gain public support. Both can reach thousands—even millions—through radio, television, newspapers, magazines, and the Internet. But the media also exercise a power of their own in the creation of public policy.

Major Forms of Media

Newspapers—America's oldest form of mass media is the newspaper. John Campbell launched what could be called the first newspaper in 1704 with his *Boston News Letter,* but colonial papers had small circulations and narrow business interests. In the years prior to the Revolution, newspapers began to cover issues related to American dissatisfaction with the British government, but circulations remained low.

During the early national period, newspapers were usually mouthpieces of major parties. For instance, the *Gazette of the United States* promoted the Federalist position, while the *National Gazette* espoused Republican views. The era of the partisan paper reached its heyday during the Jackson presidency (1829–36). Several newspaper editors actually became part of Jackson's administration. By the 1830s newspapers began to target a mass audience. The *New York Sun* sold for a penny, giving rise to the name "penny press." These papers emphasized emotional and dramatic stories that might appeal to the less educated reader. In 1841 the *New York Tribune* became the first national paper when it started distribution in the Midwest and West. During the Civil War, readers eager for war news boosted circulation of the *New York Herald* to 100,000.

During the late nineteenth and early twentieth centuries, newspapers began to cover social issues, often with considerable sensationalism. At the same time, newspapers also attempted to increase circulation by giving the impression of objectivity—that they had no connection with any party or interest group. By and large, major media have tried to maintain this impression to the present.

During the twentieth century, many printing improvements were made, including the ability to print photographs in color. Satellite technology permitted large daily newspapers to distribute issues more quickly by printing them at regional distribution centers rather than at a central location. Today, the newspaper with the largest circulation is *USA Today,* followed by the *Wall Street Journal* and the *New York Times.*

The influence of newspapers eroded as new forms of media technology emerged. Newspapers cannot match the speed of radio and television in breaking the news. Neither can

newspapers compete with the visual appeal of television. But newspapers can provide news that is more in-depth than that provided by the broadcast media.

Radio—Within ten years of Guglielmo Marconi's 1898 invention of the radio, amateur radio operators had moved beyond transmitting Morse code signals to sending words and music. Commercial radio began in 1920 when KDKA Pittsburgh went on the air. The radio's usefulness in politics soon became apparent. One of the first uses of the radio was to relay the outcome of the 1920 presidential election in which Warren G. Harding triumphed over James Cox.

By 1933 two-thirds of American homes had radios, and radio broadcasts had become part of American life. People increasingly relied on the radio for news as well as entertainment. During the Depression and World War II, President Roosevelt reassured the nation with radio broadcasts known as "fireside chats." Presidents have continued to use radio ever since.

The Charlotte Observer, *September 11, 2003*

Radio's popularity declined as television became commercially feasible. Still, radio does offer advantages over other forms of media. First, it is easily accessible. Not only are radios portable, but people can listen while driving or engaged in another activity. Second, radio programs are much cheaper to broadcast than television programs are. Third, radio often offers a degree of interactivity. Listeners can call in and express their views while remaining relatively anonymous.

Today there are approximately thirteen thousand radio stations in operation in the United States. One major source of news programming is National Public Radio (NPR), which was formed in 1970 to provide noncommercial, public-interest programming. There are around seven hundred NPR member stations throughout the country, and the quality of their news coverage is superior to that of virtually all commercial stations. However, the Public Broadcasting Service (PBS) viewpoint leans toward the left of the political spectrum. To counteract liberal radio programs, conservatives launched commercial talk radio stations and programs during the 1990s, such as "The Rush Limbaugh Show," whose popularity frequently annoyed liberal opinion makers.

Television—When most Americans think "mass media," they think of television. According to the Television Advertising Bureau, the average American household watches seven-and-a-half hours of television each day; and around ninety-eight percent of all homes have at least one television set.

Although the television was introduced at New York City's World's Fair in 1939, not until after World War II did improvements in technology and a rise in household income make television commercially viable. In just a few years three major networks dominated the airwaves—CBS, NBC, and ABC. Besides entertainment, the networks brought the nightly news into homes. The nation witnessed on TV such events as the Cuban Missile Crisis, the Vietnam War, civil rights demonstrations, and the lunar landing. With so many Americans relying on only a few sources of information, television quickly gained an enormous power to shape opinions.

That power continues today although it has been somewhat diluted by the rise of cable television. Alternative networks such as Cable News Network (CNN) and FOX News now compete for ratings with the network giants. Another alternative to network coverage of politics is **C-SPAN,** a public service network created by the American cable television industry. The network's major goal is to provide the public with coverage of House and Senate proceedings "without editing, commentary or analysis and with a balanced presentation of points of view." Increased diversity has allowed more conservative news to reach audiences—although certainly not with a Christian worldview.

Television's advantage over other forms of media is its ability to deliver news quickly with images and action. Nevertheless, television's images tend to appeal to the emotions more than to the intellect. For instance, when Richard Nixon and John F. Kennedy held the first televised presidential debate in 1960, those listening by radio thought Nixon had won, while those watching the debates on TV chose Kennedy as the victor—not surprising considering Kennedy's tanned good looks in comparison to Nixon's washed-out appearance.

Television also tends to reduce news to sound bites—brief snippets of information. While the use of sound bites allows networks to cover more news between the commercials, the coverage has little substance and may provide more misinformation than anything else.

The Internet—A relatively new form of mass media is the Internet. The **Internet** is an interna-

ABC newscaster Peter Jennings

tional computer network originally developed by the U.S. Department of Defense as a means of decentralizing information. (In the event of a military attack on one location, information would not be destroyed because it could be passed on elsewhere.) Eventually the Internet was transformed into a commercial system for relaying information, sending messages, and conducting business. In the 1990s Internet usage grew rapidly, and websites of every conceivable nature appeared thanks to advancements in computer technology. Newspaper, radio, and television news outlets created online versions to tap this market. Government at all levels used the Internet to reach the public. For instance, the White House, the House of Representatives, and the Senate all have websites as do numerous governmental agencies and institutions, such as the Library of Congress, the National Archives, and the National Park Service.

Powers and Limits

The First Amendment guarantees freedom of the press and thereby gives the media the power to print or broadcast information without fear of government reprisal. This guarantee helps protect the media from government control or censorship that could allow elected officials to quash information about their wrongdoings. For instance, the *Washington Post* first uncovered the Watergate scandal, which eventually led to the resignation of President

Nixon. Without freedom of the press, Nixon's wrongdoing might never have been revealed.

However, freedom of the press also gives the media the ability to determine what is news and to present their version of it to the public in any manner they choose. The media is thus an independent influence on public opinion and the making of public policy. In fact, many newscasters, writers, editors, and producers admit that they enjoy their work in part because it allows them to influence public policy. Furthermore, surveys of media personnel indicate that the majority hold more liberal political views than those of the average American. The consequent liberal bias of the news should therefore not be surprising.

Legal Rights—In 2000 the government restricted Internet news sites from carrying any news except that obtained from state-controlled media outlets. Chat rooms were also banned from discussing topics the government deemed offensive or dangerous. Those guilty of these offenses faced fines and the shutdown of their sites. Thankfully, these were the actions of the *Chinese* government, not the *United States* government.

Our media enjoys freedoms almost unparalleled in the rest of the world, including the freedom from **prior restraint.** This term means that the government cannot review and censor information before it is presented to the public. The only exception to this media freedom is during wartime. During World War I, President Wilson created an agency called the Committee on Public Information (CPI). Antipatriotic and antiwar information was kept from the newspapers.

Nothing like the CPI exists in the United States today, but restrictions on wartime freedom of the press remain controversial. During the Vietnam War, reporters were allowed to accompany troops in action. The images they brought back were partially responsible for making the war unpopular at home. When the United States fought the Gulf War of 1991, only a few reporters were allowed to accompany the troops. Military officers also denied reporters access to certain areas of the war

zone. So unpopular were these nontraditional restrictions that the 2003 war in Iraq became the most openly covered war in history with reporters broadcasting live from the numerous military units in which they had been "embedded."

Outside wartime conditions the media enjoys additional freedom to scrutinize government actions. For instance, the **Freedom of Information Act (FOIA)** gives the media (as well as private individuals) broad powers to investigate files of the federal bureaucracy. The government may, however, exclude from disclosure information vital to national security.

Although not a legal freedom at the federal level, freedom of confidentiality is enjoyed by the media of some states. In order to gather the news, reporters sometimes rely on secret sources. Of course, secret sources do not usually wish their identities to be revealed in public or in court. In

World War I poster

over half of the states, the media enjoys some degree of legal protection of confidentiality through **shield laws.** In states with no shield law, reporters who refuse to divulge their source may be jailed for contempt of court. For instance, William Farr, a reporter for the *Los Angeles Herald Examiner,* spent forty-six days in prison for protecting a source related to the 1971 trial of Charles Manson.

Powers of Presentation—Besides legal freedoms, the media also enjoy the power to present the news in any manner they wish. Publishers and broadcasters do not always produce their reports with a conscious intention to influence public policy. Nevertheless, they do so naturally by selecting which items of news will be presented in the time or space available. A newspaper story can be given a front-page headline, buried near a back page, or ignored completely. A long lead story on the television news immediately conveys the idea that this subject is important.

Not only does the media have the power to determine how much coverage a piece of news should receive, but the media also can present information from the perspective it chooses. The media influence public opinion by the words and pictures used. A political candidate can be portrayed with a smile or a frown, and he can be labeled as "right-wing" or "moderate."

The media sometimes predict voting outcomes that could in themselves have significance for a political campaign. For instance, a reporter may say, "Candidate A needs to win 40% of the vote in this primary in order to establish himself as a major candidate." If the candidate fails to meet the media's expectations, his viability may be damaged. On the other hand, candidates who do better than the media's expectations might receive extra coverage, often with further gains in public recognition. Of course candidates realize the pitfall of high expectations and usually try to lower expectations so that if their modest prediction is exceeded, it will be viewed as a victory.

Exit Polls: 2000 Election and Florida

Election night November 7, 2000*

7:00 P.M. (EST): Polls close in Florida except for sections of the panhandle in Central Time.

7:40 P.M. (EST): Based on exit polling and statistical models, the Voter News Service informs networks that Gore is the likely winner.

7:50 P.M. (EST): Gore declared winner in Florida by major networks.

8:00 P.M. (EST): All polls closed in Florida.

9:40 P.M. (EST): VNS informs networks of Duval County vote tally error in Gore's favor. Information corrected.

10:20 P.M. (EST): Networks retract their call and place Florida back in the "too-close-to-call" column.

2:00 A.M. (EST): VNS now shows Bush ahead by 29,000 votes.

2:15 A.M. (EST): Bush declared the winner in Florida and next president of the United States. Gore calls Bush and concedes the race.

2:50 A.M. (EST): Volusia County mistake in Bush's favor corrected. Bush's lead narrows.

4:00 A.M. (EST): Florida moved back to the "too-close-to-call" column. Gore retracts concession to Bush. Networks end election night broadcast with winner of the election unknown.

*All times given are general estimates.

In the aftermath of the election, the TV networks were criticized for declaring a winner before sufficient results had come in. While several factors contributed to this fiasco, **exit polls**—surveys taken as voters leave polling places—may have contributed to an early prediction that Gore had won the election. Exit polls have usually been good indicators of election results, but as Florida demonstrated, even exit polls are no replacement for actual vote tallies.

An independent committee hired to study the media's failure in Florida discovered that all the major media outlets had relied on one source, VNS, for exit polling data. Mistakes made by VNS affected not one major news source, but six. Another problem was that refusal rates were higher in the 2000 election. That is, more people refused to take the exit poll, making the sample unrepresentative. Then too, there were more absentee votes in the 2000 election. Members of the armed services, who traditionally vote more conservatively, constituted a large block of absentee voters, and these votes could not be sampled by exit polls. Finally, the poll's margin of error (2.6) was too great to be reliable in such a close election. The independent committee recommended that the media stop using exit polls to call elections, and the networks complied during the 2002 mid-term elections.

Legal Limits—Two exemptions to the media's freedom under the First Amendment are laws against **libel** and **slander.** Libel is published false statements that injure one's reputation, while slander is oral communication that does the same. (The First Amendment also does not protect socially offensive communication, known as **obscenity.** This and other free speech limitations are discussed in Chapter 18.)

An important libel case was decided even before American independence. In 1735, John Zenger, a New York printer, was tried for seditious libel after his newspaper, the *New York Weekly-Journal,* attacked the administration of Governor William Cosby. Zenger's lawyer argued that Cosby had not been libeled because Zenger's statements about him were true. The jury then acquitted Zenger. The precedent of this acquittal established truth as a defense against libel, and the Zenger case is often cited as a landmark victory for freedom of the press. Nevertheless, politicians and other public figures are less protected from libel and slander than are private citizens. Following the precedent of *New York Times* v. *Sullivan* (1964), even falsehood is given constitutional protection unless a public figure can demonstrate that the source of the libel has acted in reckless disregard of the truth.

Government regulation is another form of legal limitation on the media. Again, American media enjoys much more freedom from government interference than those in other countries. In fact, to some degree, American media might be described as "self-regulating." Radio and television stations are licensed and regulated by the **Federal Communications Commission (FCC).** Although the FCC does not decide broadcast content, it can impose fines on stations for broadcasting obscene language or false advertising.

Currently the FCC does not regulate the Internet. Congress passed the Computer Decency Act (1996) in an attempt to control pornography on the Internet, but a year later the Supreme Court struck down the law as unconstitutional.

Press Pitfalls—With relatively few legal limits, mass media exercises great influence over the American public; two factors decrease the power of the press. According to a 2002 survey by the Pew Research Center, almost sixty percent of Americans view mass media as politically biased. Usually bias of most media outlets is tolerated, accepted, or adjusted for, but sometimes the media goes too far and alienates the public. Following the terrorist attacks of 2001, the public praised the media for its coverage. Within a year, however, the public criticized the media as unpatriotic for its repeated attacks on President Bush and his response to terrorism.

Another factor that limits media power is the vast information marketplace in the United States. Politicians are held accountable to the public on election day, but the media is held accountable every time viewers "vote" with their remote controls. If a media source alienates its audience, readers or viewers can read or view something more to their liking. Cable television, Internet news sites, and radio talk shows now provide a smorgasbord of political views from which to choose. The decentralization of political information seems to be a trend that will continue to shape American interaction with its media.

Pen-and-Ink Politics: Understanding Political Cartoons

Probably one of the most concise languages in the world is that of political cartooning. The best political cartoons combine art, humor, satire, and a pointed political message, all in a few square inches of space.

Political cartoons have been drawn in America for over two centuries; Benjamin Franklin's

Government Use of Media

Because politicians recognize the tremendous power wielded by the media, they make every effort to use its influence to their best advantage. The president and other politicians employ press secretaries or advisors who write flattering information about their activities or who help them prepare for press interviews.

Candidates for office try to keep their poise, their smiles, and (hopefully) their charm before the public by standing before the cameras and talking with reporters as much as possible. If polls reveal some particular weakness received by the voters, candidates will often try to modify public opinion during their next appearance on camera. A new line in a speech or a new setting for photographs may get the new point of view across. Of course, repeated image changes can backfire. During the 2000 campaign, presidential contender Al Gore tried several times to project different and more positive images of himself but ended by creating an image of superficiality.

Even the national nominating conventions of the political parties are now largely media events. Democrats and Republicans try to use the extensive coverage they receive to present a positive view of their platforms and their candidates. In fact, the media coverage of presidential campaigns now practically demands that parties choose candidates who are both politically *and* telegenically qualified. So much attention is focused on a candidate's image that an otherwise superb choice for president may be effectively disqualified because of his physical appearance or lackluster speaking ability.

Media Propaganda

In the popular mind, propaganda is false information distributed by dictators like Nazis or Communists. However, the actual meaning of the word is neither so narrow nor so sinister. **Propaganda** is

drawing of a snake (urging a stronger colonial union) was probably the earliest. However, political cartoons did not become part of the daily newspaper until the late nineteenth century, when print technology made cartoon reproduction fast and inexpensive. Today, political cartoons are a standard feature of the nation's newspapers. Some newspaper subscribers look at the editorial cartoon before reading the paper.

Interpreting political cartoons requires an understanding of a few of their basic characteristics. First, caricature, or exaggerating certain features of an individual, is often used to distinguish figures in a drawing and sometimes to make a statement about a person. Symbols too are an important part of political cartooning. Some of the more common ones include a star-spangled "Uncle Sam" representing the United States and the donkey and elephant symbolizing the Democratic and Republican parties. What the artist cannot convey through caricature or symbolism, he does through labels and captions.

Although political cartoons can be a powerful political force, cartoons by nature are limited. Even the best cartoons can usually express only one idea forcefully, and none can examine a complex issue in detail. And, of course, political cartoons reflect the political prejudices of their creators.

simply using various techniques to select and manipulate information so as to persuade or influence people effectively. Virtually everyone uses propaganda. A teenager who tells his parents that he wants something because all his friends have it is using a type of propaganda. Advertisers constantly use propaganda techniques as they bombard the public with reasons to buy their products.

The persuasive qualities of propaganda have not gone unnoticed by politicians and interest groups, and both use them constantly in their campaigns. The media not only help disseminate this propaganda but, through their reporting powers, also add propaganda of their own. The box below indicates the seven basic propaganda techniques used in politics.

Propaganda may be true and may influence people for good ends. However, propaganda tends to break down the listener's resistance, making him disregard contrary information. In other words, propaganda circumvents the rational by emphasizing the emotional. Therefore, propaganda has great potential to be used for evil purposes. Americans, particularly Christian Americans, need to be aware of the pervasive use of propaganda devices so that they may justly weigh the information about public policy rather than blindly follow some mass appeal. American democracy is endangered if the public allows itself to be manipulated into making unwise political decisions through the use of clever propaganda.

- **Bandwagon:** attempting to persuade people to follow a crowd by insisting that "everyone else is voting for this candidate," often implying that there is something wrong with those who do not "jump on the bandwagon"

- **Testimonial:** using the endorsements of celebrities to create the idea that important people are going to vote for a certain candidate

- **Card stacking:** using selective data from polls, government reports, and other sources to support one side of an issue while disregarding information to the contrary

- **Glittering generalities:** making broad statements that sound good but lack substance, such as "My party stands for peace and prosperity" or "We will fight poverty"

- **Transfer:** identifying with a symbol such as the Statue of Liberty or the American flag in an attempt to transfer the widespread admiration for such objects to the candidate

Propaganda Techniques

- **Name calling:** calling an opponent by a name with a negative connotation such as "ultraconservative," "leftwing," "radical," or "far right" without explanation

- **Plain folks:** creating the image of a common person (instead of an aloof politician), using slogans such as "friend of the common man" and "one of us," and appearing with factory workers, farmers, and other "average Americans"

Section Review

1. What are the major forms of media, and what is the term used to describe them all?
2. What is the FOIA, and what rights does it give the media?
3. In what ways can the media manipulate the information they relay to the public?
4. In what ways do political candidates use the media?
5. What is propaganda?

VI. Conclusion

Freedom of expression is necessary to maintain a republican government, but lawmakers cannot yield to every voice. Winston Churchill once remarked that although politicians should keep their "ear to the ground . . . they should also remember that this is not a very dignified attitude."

Christians should also strive to anchor their convictions in Scripture rather than allow themselves to be swayed by political propaganda—even propaganda circulated by conservative politicians and organizations. Christians will continue to differ with one another over nonessential issues, matters that can be compromised, but they should always remember that biblical truth should never be subject to the whims of popular opinion.

Chapter Review

Terms

public policy
public opinion
liberalism
conservatism
moderates
domestic policy
foreign policy
agenda
opinion polls
representative sample
straw polls

interest groups
AFL-CIO
single-interest groups
lobbying
political action committees
  (PACs)
amicus curiae
mass media
C-SPAN
Internet
prior restraint

Freedom of Information Act
  (FOIA)
shield laws
exit polls
libel
slander
obscenity
Federal Communications
  Commission (FCC)
propaganda

Content Questions

1. How is the development of public policy like a highway?

2. Should government leaders presume public opinion to be reliable? Explain your answer.

3. What conditions could make the results of an opinion poll invalid?

4. What is lobbying, and how do interest groups use this activity?

5. How has the emergence of PACs affected congressional elections?

6. How can the media affect the course of a political campaign?

7. How can propaganda be dangerous?

Application Questions

1. List several current public policy issues, and note a possible liberal response and a possible conservative response to each one.

2. In what ways might the growing influence of strong interest groups hurt the democratic nature of the American government?

3. Describe the media's powers of presentation as they apply to the coverage of a current event in the news.

A Trip to Washington, D.C.

For Americans, Washington, D.C., is more than just a city with thousands of people, large buildings, and traffic-filled streets. It is the "Federal City," the seat of the government of the United States, our capital. The activities of this city have shaped the nation's history for two hundred years, and today's leaders wield the powers of government within its bounds. The sights and sounds of Washington reflect the heritage of all Americans, and thus it is a special place for each of us.

The site of a federal district to serve as the capital was settled soon after the Constitution became operative. A political compromise balanced the acceptance of Alexander Hamilton's financial plans with the choice of a southern location for the capital. George Washington himself chose a spot along the Potomac River in 1790. Andrew Ellicott and Benjamin Banneker surveyed the ten-mile-square tract encompassing land from both Maryland and Virginia. (The Virginia land was later returned to the state.) Then Pierre L'Enfant drew up a plan for a city he wanted to call "Washingtonople." L'Enfant claimed that a high point in the tract, then known as Jenkins Hill, was a "pedestal awaiting a monument." Known as Capitol Hill today because it is the site of the Capitol building, this hill became the focal point from which the emerging city grew.

Most of the District of Columbia was still a wilderness of swamps and forests when in 1800 John Adams, Congress, and the rest of the government moved into their newly built city. At that time there were only about fifty houses in the central part of the district and one hundred thirty government workers. The fledgling capital grew slowly until the twentieth century, when it swelled into a modern metropolis of half a million people, with suburbs sprawling far into Virginia and Maryland.

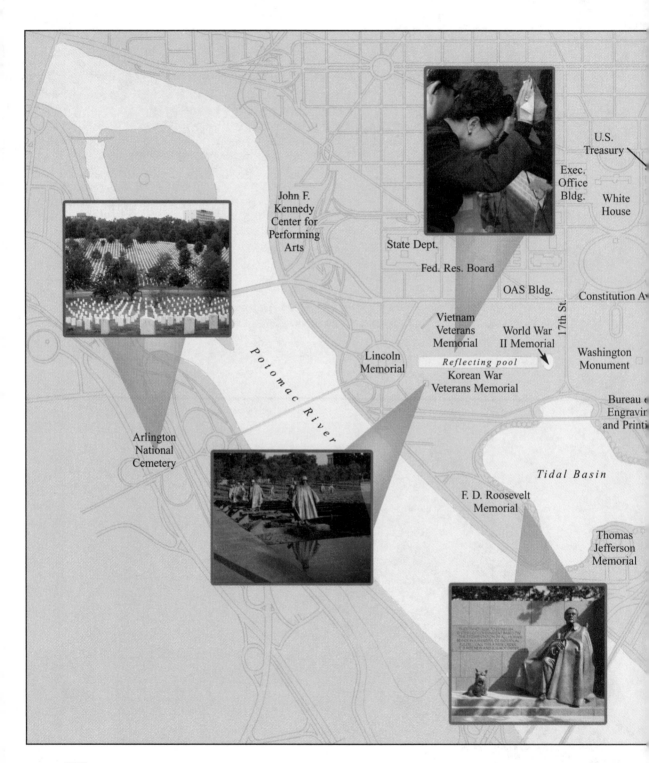

John F.
Kennedy
Center for
Performing
Arts

State Dept.

Fed. Res. Board

OAS Bldg.

U.S.
Treasury

Exec.
Office
Bldg.

White
House

Constitution A

17th St.

Vietnam
Veterans
Memorial

Lincoln
Memorial

Potomac River

Korean War
Veterans Memorial

World War
II Memorial

Reflecting pool

Washington
Monument

Bureau
Engravir
and Printi

Arlington
National
Cemetery

F. D. Roosevelt
Memorial

Tidal Basin

Thomas
Jefferson
Memorial

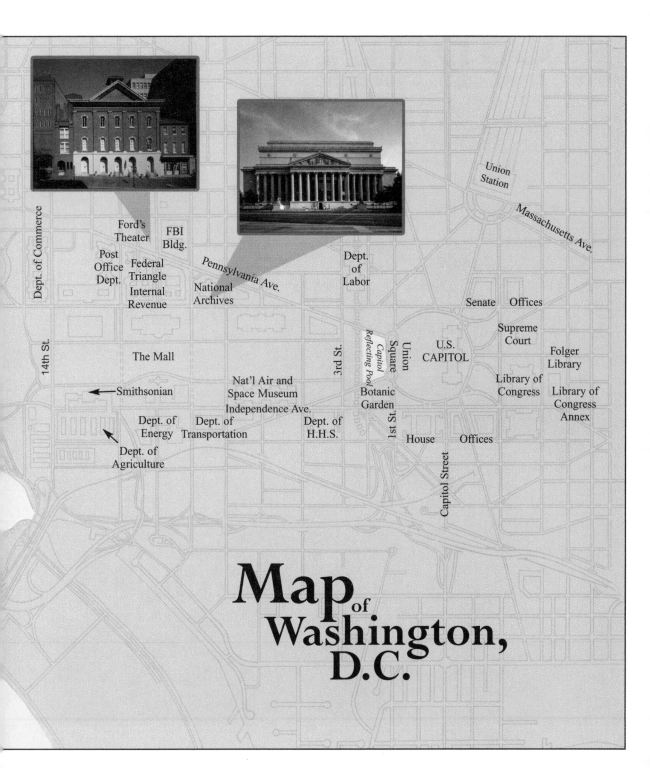

Dept. of Commerce

14th St.

Ford's Theater

FBI Bldg.

Post Office Dept.

Federal Triangle

Internal Revenue

National Archives

Pennsylvania Ave.

Dept. of Labor

Union Station

Massachusetts Ave.

Senate Offices

Supreme Court

Folger Library

The Mall

3rd St.

Capitol Reflecting Pool

Union Square

U.S. CAPITOL

Library of Congress

Library of Congress Annex

Smithsonian

Nat'l Air and Space Museum

Independence Ave.

Botanic Garden

Dept. of Energy

Dept. of Transportation

Dept. of H.H.S.

1st St.

House Offices

Capitol Street

Dept. of Agriculture

Map of Washington, D.C.

Look Back
at the
Capitol
and the
White House

These daguerreotypes, probably made in 1846 by John Plumbe Jr., are the earliest known photographs of these structures. The view of the Capitol shows the East Front with the old House wing on the left and the old Senate wing on the right. The photograph of the White House depicts the south side of that building as it appeared during James Polk's presidency.

In 1792, commissioners of the newly surveyed federal district authorized contests for architectural designs for both a building to house Congress and a home for the president. A young physician named William Thornton submitted a late entry in January 1793 that outshone the other designs offered for the Capitol. Washington and Jefferson praised Thornton's plan, and the cornerstone for it was laid in September of that year. Construction proceeded slowly. Only the Senate wing was ready for use when Congress occupied it in 1800. The House wing was finished in 1811, but the War of 1812 brought everything to a halt. The Capitol and the president's house were both burned by the British in August 1814.

Charles Bullfinch was responsible for rebuilding the Capitol building after the fire, and the dome visible in the 1846 photograph is of his design. The growing nation with its expanding number of senators and representatives, however, soon outgrew this refurbished building, and additional room was necessary. Thomas U. Walter designed the new Senate and House wings that were added in the 1850s. His new, larger dome was placed atop the rotunda during the Civil War to balance the design. The only major change in the building since that time has been the outward shift of the old East Front to give the Capitol additional office space in 1958–62.

Irish-born James Hoban submitted the winning design for the president's house. Thomas Jefferson had entered his design anonymously (signed A.Z.), but the Hoban drawings won greater admiration. The house began to take shape on the site L'Enfant had designated for it at one end of the rough path that would be Pennsylvania Avenue. The Capitol building arose at the other end. In 1800 John Adams and his family moved in to live the last few months of his administration in the still-unfinished house. The main staircase had not been built.

Walls lacked plaster, and the rooms were damp and cold. Nonetheless, Abigail Adams dismissed the discomforts, noting in a letter that "this House is built for the ages to come." Construction continued during the Jefferson administration, and then Dolley Madison was able to add her touch to the mansion before the British arrived.

The fire-darkened walls left by the British in 1814 required white paint thereafter, and eventually the painted house came to be called the "White House." It was not until the presidency of Theodore Roosevelt, however, that this term was used on official papers. The rebuilt mansion was provided with many new furnishings by James Monroe, and Andrew Jackson finally finished the decoration of the large East Room. As new presidential families moved in during the 1800s and early 1900s, they changed the decor to fit their needs and tastes. Most of the president's administrative offices remained in the original building until the addition of the West Wing in 1902, and the East Wing provided more office space in 1942.

Improvements and repairs to the White House were made constantly, but the ravages of time took their toll on the structure. By the time of the Truman administration, the mansion had become a safety hazard. Rather than demolish this symbol of American government to build a new mansion, however, a thorough renovation project was begun in 1948. The outside walls were left standing, but the interior was totally dismantled. New foundations were inserted, two levels of basement dug, and then the house interior was reassembled piece by piece. Since the completion of that project in 1952, the White House has become both a museum of America's presidential past and a comfortable home for the first family.

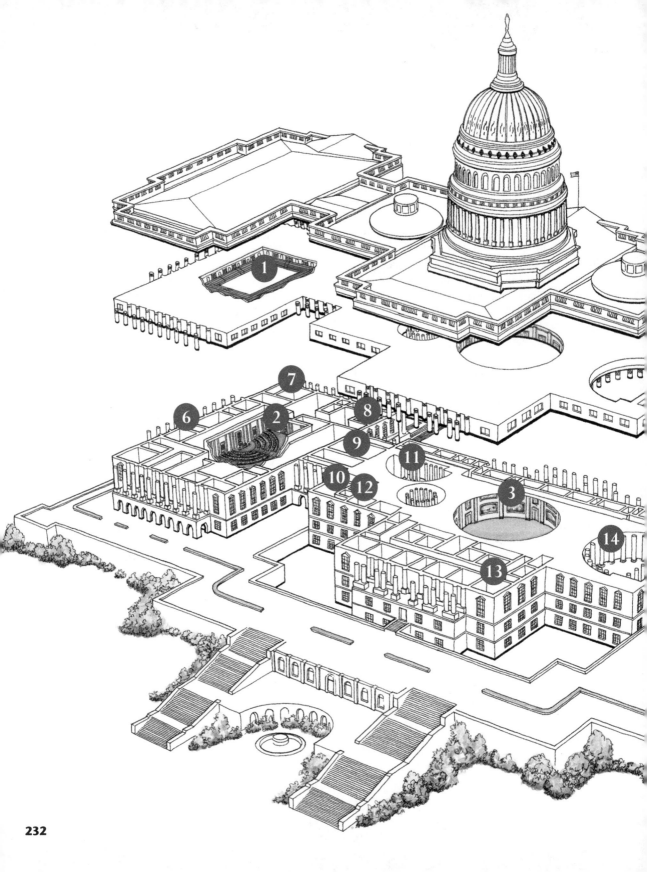

The Capitol Building

Artist's Rendering

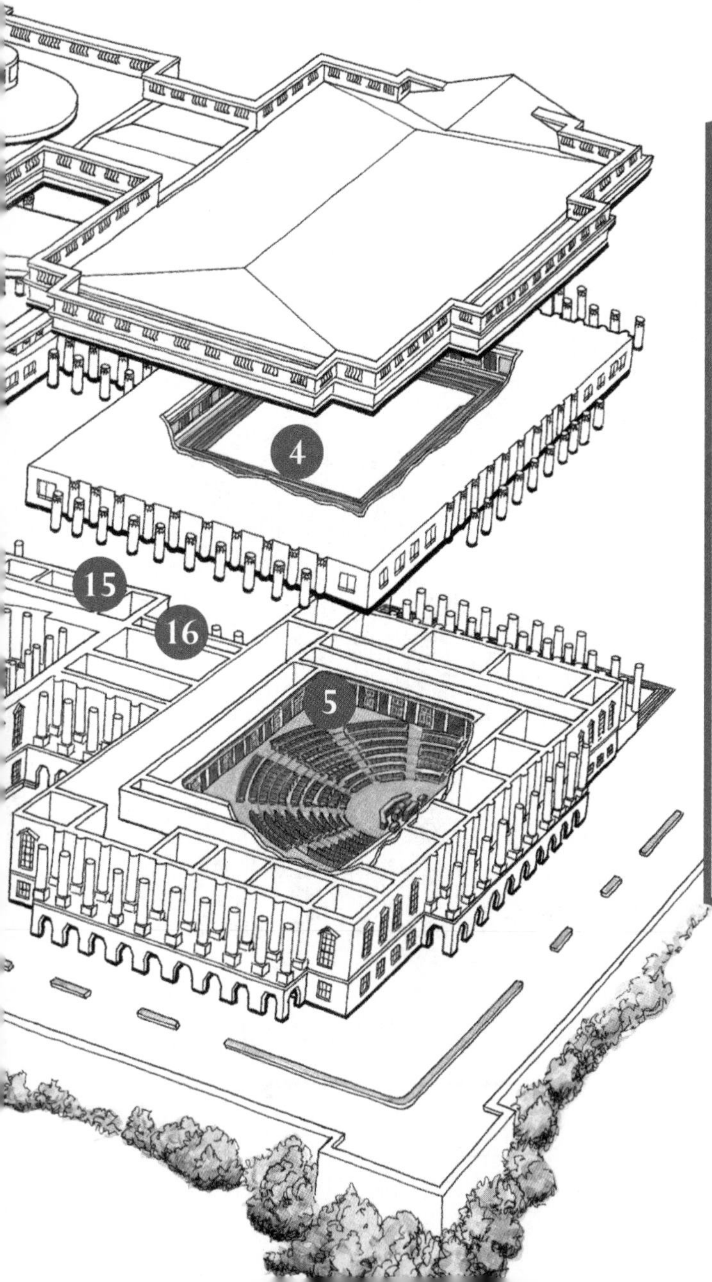

1. Senate Gallery
2. Senate Chamber
3. The Rotunda
4. House Gallery
5. House Chamber
6. President's Room
7. Vice President's Office
8. Senate Majority Leader's Office
9. Senate Conference Room
10. Senate Minority Leader's Office
11. Old Senate Chamber
12. Senate Rotunda
13. House Minority Leader's Office
14. Statuary Hall
15. Speaker's Office
16. House Reception Room

The
White
House

Artist's Rendering

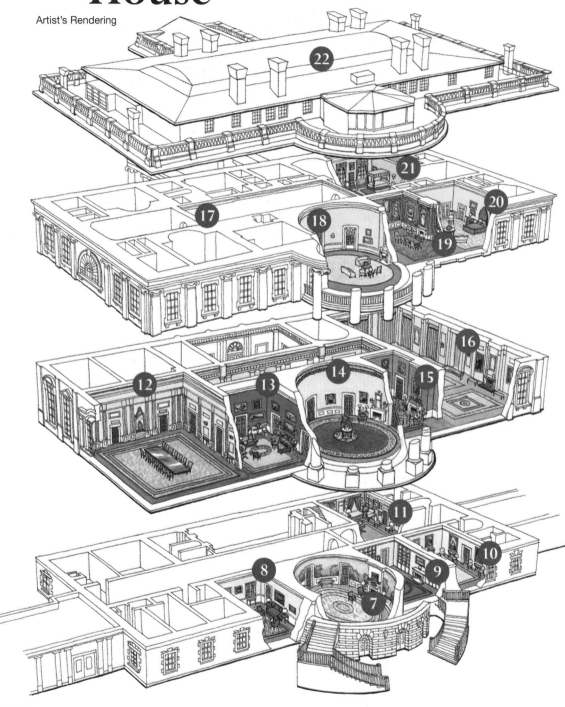

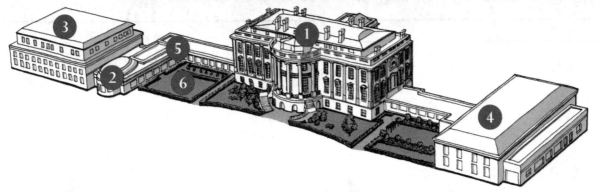

1. **The White House**

2. **Oval Office**—Since 1934 this important room has served as the president's formal office.

3. **West Wing**—Teddy Roosevelt tore down a massive greenhouse complex in 1902 and replaced it with an executive wing that now contains offices, a Cabinet Room, and press rooms.

4. **East Wing**—Franklin Roosevelt prompted the building of the East Wing in 1941 to provide more office and work space.

5. **James S. Brady Press Briefing Room**—The White House Press Secretary gives daily press releases to the media concerning the presidential schedule and answers questions concerning the president's policy or position on specific events.

6. **Rose Garden**—This area near the president's offices serves as a beautiful outdoor setting for official receptions. Richard Nixon's daughter Tricia was married in a Rose Garden wedding in 1971.

7. **Diplomatic Reception Room**—The president greets official guests at state functions in this drawing room. Franklin Roosevelt delivered his "Fireside Chats" while sitting before the fireplace in this room.

8. **Map Room**—President Franklin D. Roosevelt used this room as a situation room to follow the course of World War II. Today it serves as a private meeting room for the president or First Lady.

9. **China Room**—Almost every past president is represented in the China Room by either state or family china or glassware. The collection is arranged chronologically.

10. **Vermeil Room**—The White House Vermeil Room, sometimes called the Gold Room, serves as a display room and ladies' sitting room for formal occasions.

11. **Library**—This room served as a laundry area until Theodore Roosevelt's ground floor renovation in 1902 when it became a "Gentlemen's Ante-room." In 1935 the room was remodeled into a library for use by the president, his family, and his staff.

12. **State Dining Room**—This large, formal dining room can hold as many as 140 guests. All presidents have a portrait displayed in different areas of the White House. President Lincoln's is on display here. Carved in the fireplace mantle is an excerpt from a letter written by John Adams in 1800: "I Pray Heaven to Bestow the Best of Blessings on THIS HOUSE and on All that shall hereafter inhabit it. May none but honest and Wise Men ever rule under this Roof."

13. **Red Room**—Furnishings from the Empire period now grace this sitting room where Dolley Madison held receptions.

14. **Blue Room**—This room gained its color during Van Buren's presidency. Several pieces of French Empire furniture in this reception room date from the presidency of James Monroe.

15. **Green Room**—Thomas Jefferson placed a green cloth on the floor of this room, which he used as a dining room. The Monroes made it a sitting room and furnished it in green.

16. **East Room**—The East Room is the White House's largest formal meeting room and the site of many momentous occasions including concerts, weddings, and funerals. At times, White House occupants have found other uses for this room. First Lady Abigail Adams hung laundry to dry in this large and then unfinished room. A century later Teddy Roosevelt's children used it for roller-skating. His portrait is displayed in this room.

17. **Family Quarters**—This section contains bedrooms and other private rooms for the president and his family.

18. **Yellow Oval Room**—The president often uses this parlor for entertaining foreign leaders before state dinners.

19. **Treaty Room**—This room served as the Cabinet Room after the Civil War until the West Wing was built in 1902. The Kennedys redecorated it to resemble the Cabinet Room during the Grant presidency and renamed it because of the many treaties that have been and continue to be signed here. Presidents George Bush, Bill Clinton, and George W. Bush used this room for their private office.

20. **Lincoln's Bedroom**—President Lincoln used this as an office and cabinet meeting room, and it was the site of the signing of the Emancipation Proclamation. It now serves as a guest room furnished with the huge rosewood bed and other furnishings purchased by Mrs. Lincoln.

21. **Queen's Suite**—This bedroom and its neighboring sitting room earned its name in the 1960s after visits from Queen Elizabeth II of Britain, Queen Wilhelmina of the Netherlands, Queen Frederika of Greece, and several other royal ladies.

22. **Third Floor**—The roof of the White House was raised in 1927 to provide additional space for guest rooms, staff quarters, storage, a solarium, and living space for the first family.

Monuments, Memorials, and Museums

Daniel Chester French's imposing statue of Abraham Lincoln overlooks all that enter the Lincoln Memorial. The classic walls of the memorial, etched with Lincoln's memorable speeches, were completed in 1922. This famous landmark stands between the Potomac River and the giant Reflecting Pool.

The old House Chamber in the Capitol building became Statuary Hall in 1864. Each state was invited to send statues of two of its great statesmen for display. The statues now line Statuary Hall and occupy nearby corridors as well.

More than simply the home of the president, the White House is a virtual museum containing furniture, china, and other reminders of past presidencies. The White House is "the only residence of a head of state open to the public on a regular basis," and thus the nation's people may see its historic riches for themselves.

The Washington Monument rises 555 feet above the Capitol Mall and provides visitors with a panoramic view of the city. Construction of the marble obelisk began in 1848 but was halted for lack of funds at a height of 150 feet. Marble of a slightly different color marks this level where construction was finally resumed in 1876 and completed in 1884. The view across the Potomac includes Arlington National Cemetery, which is itself a memorial to the nation's fallen heroes. The famous Iwo Jima Statue stands just outside the cemetery.

The Rotunda of the Capitol building

The original Smithsonian Building, often called the "Red Castle on the Mall"

238

The Vietnam Veterans Memorial was dedicated in 1982. Standing before this long, introspective memorial is a statue of three soldiers facing the somber list of war casualties engraved on black granite.

The bronze statue of Thomas Jefferson stands nineteen feet tall above its large granite pedestal in the Jefferson Memorial. The memorial's portico faces the large Tidal Basin, which is surrounded by the city's famous cherry trees.

239

UNIT IV

THE LEGISLATIVE BRANCH

THE STRUCTURE OF CONGRESS

11

Capitol building grounds

The Constitutional framers deliberately made Congress the first branch of government, addressing it in Article I. History, ancient and modern, reveals why the framers placed the representative assemblies first. The American War of Independence was in large part a response to a tyrannical king, and a legislative body offered both a counterbalance to executive power and a voice in self-government.

Representative governments date back to the Greeks and Romans. Parliament in England developed in the late Middle Ages as wealthy barons insisted on advising monarchs. While part of the British Empire, American colonists enjoyed a measure of self-government through their colonial assemblies; British imperial policy even permitted some autonomy, as illustrated by the House of Burgesses in Virginia. During the Revolution the Continental Congress guided the Americans. Not surprisingly, when finally independent, the national government under the Articles of Confederation featured a dominant assembly.

In 1789 when the new central government began, Congress was expected to control America's affairs, due in part to what Madison called in *The*

Federalist No. 63 "the irresistible force possessed by that branch of a free government, which has the people on its side." The feisty Thaddeus Stevens once told his rival, President Andrew Johnson, "This is a Government of the people, and Congress *is* the people."

Congressional power peaked in the late nineteenth century. Congress wrestled control of Reconstruction away from the president, determined the procedure for the defeated southern states to return to the Union, and settled the disputed 1876 presidential election. In the era of big business, Congress cooperated with the titans of business and industry, and the presidents of that era (between Abraham Lincoln and Theodore Roosevelt) are barely remembered.

The twentieth century, however, is a different story. For several reasons the White House became more central to American political life. Theodore Roosevelt, through the force of his outgoing personality, his use of the office as a "bully pulpit," his understanding of how to use the media, his initiative in proposing legislation (for example, the Pure Food and Drug Act), and his aggressive "Big Stick" foreign policy, helped make him and later presidents the most important force in the national

Lyndon B. Johnson, promoter of the Great Society, in the Oval Office on January 17, 1968

government. The bureaucracy of the executive branch increased with the New Deal and Great Society of the 1930s and 1960s respectively, and the Cold War after World War II gave the White House even greater power in foreign policy to stop communist advances. However, despite the increase in executive authority, Congress still remains the main source of legislation, making it a force that the president cannot ignore. The following pages will introduce and discuss the structure and workings of the United States Congress.

I. Constitutional Framework

Bicameral Structure

Compromise at the Constitutional Convention led to the creation of a **bicameral,** or two-house, Congress. Big states such as Virginia pushed for representation based on population, and small states such as Maryland naturally feared the overwhelming power of the large ones. The Great Compromise resolved the matter. Creation of the House of Representatives, based on population, pleased large states; the Senate, composed of two Senators per state, satisfied the small ones. British Parliament was a bicameral legislature, as were many of the colonial governments; therefore, the idea of a divided legislature had broad support at the Constitutional Convention. The legislative branch was the only one of the three divisions of the national government to be divided.

A two-house legislature has other purposes than just satisfying big states and little states. It obviously provides for a more deliberate pace in passing laws. The benefits of carefulness outweigh the disadvantage of slowness in enacting laws. Also, the framers of the Constitution believed that the House would better represent "the people" more directly, particularly the large populations of the big states. Madison in *The Federalist No. 58* argued, "Notwithstanding the equal authority which will subsist between the two houses on all legislative subjects, except the originating of money bills, it cannot be doubted that the House, composed of the greater number of members, when supported by the more powerful States, and speaking the known and determined sense of a majority of the people, will have no small advantage in a question depending on the comparative firmness of the two houses."

On the other hand, Madison also pointed out in *Nos. 62* and *63* that the Senate serves as a check on the House, the more populous branch. He understood that in a republic, leaders elected by the people could violate the trust

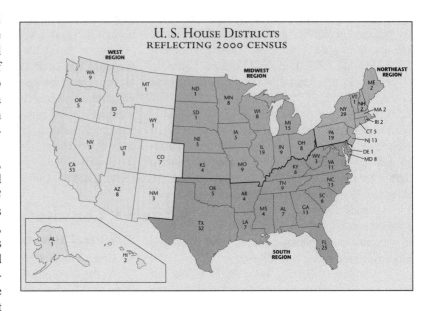

placed in them. Madison argued for the "necessity of some institution that will blend stability with liberty." His solution was the Senate, chosen by the state legislatures originally and more distant from the people. While not all of the founding fathers believed in man's sinfulness, they were influenced by the Enlightenment, which taught that government, by bringing man out of a "state of nature" where he was unruly, could restrain man. In Romans 13:4 Paul declares that government, created by God, restrains evildoers. Divided government helps ensure that one branch will not violate the freedoms of the people.

House of Representatives—The House of Representatives is the more democratic of the two houses in that the number of House members from each state is based on state population. For this reason California, the most populous state, has fifty-three House members while the seven least populous ones (Alaska, Delaware, Montana, North and South Dakota, Vermont, and Wyoming) have only one representative each. The growth and shifts in population in the nation, therefore, are an important factor in congressional elections. This problem was wisely anticipated by the Constitu-

tional framers, who instituted a ten-year **census** beginning in 1790. A census is an official count of a country's population. This kind of census, conducted primarily to ensure accurate representation, was unique in its time and reflects our founders' commitment to democratic government. Originally, House members had about forty thousand constituents. Today, with the number of representatives permanently fixed at 435, each member represents

Census form

about 646,000, based on the 2000 Census. After each census, state legislatures actually redraw the congressional district lines to reflect population shifts, and the procedure is called **reapportionment.** Redrawing these district boundaries to favor the political party that controls the state legislature is called **gerrymandering,** named for Elbridge Gerry, Republican governor of Massachusetts, who in 1812 persuaded the state legislature to create an unusually shaped district to favor the election of a fellow Republican.

Constitutional qualifications for representatives are certainly broad, merely requiring that a member be

1. at least twenty-five years old,
2. a U.S. citizen for no less than seven years, and
3. a citizen of the state he or she represents.

More specifically, a House member must reside in the **congressional district** he or she represents. A congressional district is a geographical area in a state represented by a House member. Although the Constitution does not discuss congressional districts, each state draws its congressional boundaries over roughly equal populations per representative. This means that each district is a **single-member district,** having one representative elected from a given region, thus increasing accountability for House members and improving accessibility for the constituents. Age, citizenship, and residence requirements, therefore, are the only constitutional restrictions placed upon congressmen, and these general restrictions differ little between the two houses.

The House of Representatives was to be, in the words of constitutional delegate George Mason, the "grand depository of the democratic principle of Government. . . . It ought to know and sympathize with every part of the community." This principle underlies the reason that terms for representatives are only two years long, with all congressional seats up for election at the same time. This helps make congressmen even more accountable and responsive

to those they represent. Accountability to one congressional district also tends to make a representative more localized in his viewpoint and voting. For example, because of its effect upon the local economy, a congressman would likely oppose a bill to cut military spending if its passage meant losing a profitable arms contract in his district.

Senate—While voters in a congressional district elect members of the House, voters on a statewide or **at large** basis elect United States senators, who, as a result, have a much larger constituency than their colleagues in the lower house. The framers of the Constitution designed the Senate to be less accessible to popular demands and control. In fact, the direct popular election of senators did not take place until 1913 with the passage of the **Seventeenth Amendment.** Prior to this amendment, members of state legislatures elected their senators. Within the legislative branch the Senate was to serve as a check and balance to the democratically elected and locally oriented House. Madison himself argued forcefully before his fellow delegates that such a Senate would meet *national* demands "with more coolness, with more system and with more wisdom, than the popular branch."

Senate requirements are only slightly more restrictive than those of the House of Representatives. A senator must be

1. at least thirty years old,
2. a United States citizen for at least nine years, and
3. a resident of the state he or she represents.

Delegates in Congress

There are, in addition to the 435 members of the House, 4 **delegates** and 1 Resident Commissioner who represent territories and the District of Columbia. All are nonvoting members, but they participate in the committee work, including standing, conference, and select committees. The Resident Commissioner from Puerto Rico can, in addition, participate in floor debate. The four delegates come from the District of Columbia, Guam, American Samoa, and the U.S. Virgin Islands. The Northern Mariana Islands, a U.S. possession, has no delegate.

Even though they cannot vote, these delegates are important for representing the interests of their constituents. These territories can also participate in the political process of the parties. They send delegates, for example, to the national conventions, but only the District of Columbia has electoral votes since the territories are not states and cannot vote in presidential elections.

Differences—There are several differences between the houses even though they make up one Congress. The differences mainly concern constitutional and operational aspects of the houses.

Politics in Congress—In addition to the constitutional divisions in Congress with the basic structure of the House and Senate, political parties also provide an important informal organization to both chambers. With rare exceptions, all members of Congress are either Republicans or Democrats. The majority party determines the leadership, rules, and much of the agenda of Congress, as well as the success of the president in pursuing his policies.

However, one political party controlling both houses does not ensure automatic success for a president of the same party. Jimmy Carter learned this on several frustrating occasions when enough of his fellow Democrats voted against him to stop some of his programs, including passage of the SALT II arms-control treaty. Bill Clinton's health-care reform failed to pass in Congress, despite the fact that his party, the Democrats, controlled both houses.

Differences Between House and Senate

Constitutional		Operational	
House	**Senate**	**House**	**Senate**
source of revenue bills	power to approve or reject treaties and major presidential appointments	more centralized leadership	less centralized leadership
power of impeachment	location of impeachment trials	more efficient procedures	slower-moving legislation; frequent filibusters (or threats of them)
two-year terms	six-year terms (one-third up for reelection every two years)	time and rules of debate controlled by Rules Committee and Speaker	flow of legislation controlled by majority leader—no Rules Committee
435 members (based on population	100 members (2 per state)	a more specialized legislative focus	broader legislative focus
must be 25 and a citizen for 7 years	must be 30 and a citizen for 9 years	high turnover	moderate turnover
		a focus on tax and revenue policies	a focus on foreign policy and judicial appointments, especially Supreme Court nominees
		limited debate	informal debate

Party members sometimes vote against each other and their president because of regional or ideological differences. When members of different parties join together in support of or in opposition to a bill because of some common interest, they form a **coalition.** For example, conservative Democrats and conservative Republicans may lay aside party labels and form a coalition to oppose some liberal legislation. Also, southern and midwestern congressmen of both parties may join in support of an agricultural program that would help the farmers from their regions. In short, the members of Congress sometimes have to do what the constituents want and also what will help them get reelected.

Leadership

Selection Process—The power structure within Congress is built largely along party lines. Within each party, leaders are chosen to help coordinate party action on proposals and to strengthen the party's position on a wide range of national issues.

The selection of party leadership is made in a **caucus.** A caucus (or *conference,* as Republicans call it) consists of all the members of a party within a house of Congress. The leadership positions open to a party depend upon its status as the majority or minority party within its branch of Congress. Three key positions are open to the majority party in the House: the Speaker, the majority leader, and the majority whip. The top posts open to the minority party in the House are the minority leader and the minority whip. In the upper chamber, the Senate majority leadership consists of the president *pro tempore* of the Senate, the majority leader, and the majority whip. Similarly, the minority party in the Senate is headed by the minority leader and the minority whip. The vice president of the United States serves as the President of the Senate, but this is mainly a figurehead role not related to the party structure of the upper house. He votes only to break a tie in the Senate.

Power Structures in Congress	
House of Representatives	**Senate**
Speaker	President *pro temp*
Majority leader	Majority leader
Majority whip	Majority whip
Minority leader	Minority leader
Minority whip	Minority whip

Leadership Power—The real power inherent in these offices lies in the overall strength of the party and in the skills of the individual leaders. In the House, the Speaker generally wields an enormous amount of power, though House rules permit him to vote only in the event of a tie. The Speaker makes decisions regarding which legislation will be considered, who will be recognized from the floor (allowed to speak), and who will be assigned to important committees. The majority and minority leaders serve as floor leaders and spokesmen for their respective parties. These leaders are assisted by party whips, who are primarily responsible for

A joint session of both houses of Congress

communicating with party members about their views on legislation and encouraging attendance at key voting sessions.

In the Senate a similar power structure exists, with one exception: the **president** *pro tempore,* unlike the Speaker of the House, is largely an honorary position given to the most senior member of the Senate's majority party. The most powerful position in the Senate is actually that of majority leader.

Congressional leaders cannot force party members to vote in a particular way, but through persuasion and political maneuvering these leaders help coordinate their party's response to legislation. In short, the main purposes of party leadership in Congress are to ensure communication between party members and their leaders and to help provide party cohesion in shaping laws.

Speaker of the House—The **Speaker of the House** is the only position in the House actually named in the Constitution. He presides over the House, manages House business, and serves as the official spokesperson for the body. His is the most powerful office in that chamber. The position is similar to one in the British House of Commons; a Speaker in Commons communicates the point of view of its members to the king or queen. A Speaker of the House of Representatives is formally elected by the whole House, but since the majority party's choice is going to prevail anyway, the one chosen earlier by the majority party in their caucus, or meeting, is going to win. Usually the one chosen to be Speaker has served several terms in Congress and has served in minor leadership roles in the House.

After the vice president, the Speaker is next in the line of presidential succession. He works with the White House on legislation, especially if he and the president are in the same party.

The power of the Speaker has waxed and waned over the decades. The first Speaker of the House was Frederick A. C. Muhlenberg, elected in 1789. Henry Clay was elected Speaker in 1810 during his first term in the House. With his own political skills and the powers of the office he became the

Newt Gingrich

first powerful Speaker. He appointed people who shared his views to important committees and used parliamentary procedure effectively. He holds the record for the longest service in the House in the nineteenth century: a total of six terms.

Joseph Cannon, who served from 1903 to 1910, was probably the most powerful Speaker in the history of the House of Representatives. Notoriously profane and perhaps a tool of the liquor interests, Cannon ruled the House with an iron hand, controlling committee assignments, deciding which legislation would come to the floor, and thwarting all attempts at reform. At one meeting he called himself the "Beelzebub of Congress." A rebellion by progressive Republicans eventually led to a reduction in the Speaker's power.

Newt Gingrich in 1994 became the first Republican Speaker in forty years, and during his tenure he became the most powerful Speaker since Cannon. Gingrich agreed to limit his time as Speaker to four consecutive terms in exchange for more institutional power for the Speaker. In addition, media attention gave Gingrich even greater power. Briefly, political observers thought he was more powerful than President Clinton, who had been weakened by the Republican takeover of Congress, the first since 1954, and the defeat of his health care plan. But Gingrich's glow faded quickly; Democrats and the media made him a symbol of the budget cuts and the supposed hardships that went with them. After a budget skirmish with President Clinton, Gingrich was blamed for the temporary shutdown of the government. Dozens of ethics charges were also filed against him, and for the first time in its history, the House voted to reprimand the Speaker. After the Republicans lost congressional seats in the 1998 election, Gingrich resigned both his office and his seat in Congress.

Behind the Scenes—Several officers do the routine work of Congress, and without them the place would not function and laws would never pass. These are nonmembers hired to do the work.

Senate

Secretary of the Senate—manages the legislative and administrative aspects of the chamber

Sergeant at Arms—maintains order in Senate

Journal Clerk—maintains the *Senate Journal*

Legislative Clerk—records votes and reports bills, messages, conference reports, and amendments to the Senate

Parliamentarian—advises presiding officer on official procedures

Official Reporters of Debates—prepare material for the *Congressional Record*

Chaplain—opens sessions with prayer and also provides counseling to any member of the Senate

Reverend Peter Marshall, pastor of the New York Avenue Presbyterian Church in Washington, D.C., preaching at Fort Lincoln Heights (Senate Chaplain 1947–48)

The Honorable Jeff Trandahl, Clerk of the U.S. House of Representatives

House

Clerk—performs the administrative duties of the chamber

Sergeant at Arms—maintains order in the House

Chief Administrative Officer—works with the Committee on House Administration to handle the finances and operation of the House

Chaplain—opens sessions with prayer and also provides counseling to any member of the House

Women in Congress

Jeannette Rankin was the first woman member of Congress, elected in 1916 and in 1940 from Montana. She won with a vigorous campaign and drew support from both parties even though she was a Republican. Her life focused on peace and women's rights. Rankin would later introduce the amendment in Congress that gave women the right to vote. She was in Congress at the time of American entry in both World Wars I and II, and she was the only person in Congress to vote against American entry into both wars. In 1968, when she was in her nineties, Rankin led about five thousand women in protest in Washington, D.C., against the Vietnam War.

The first woman to serve as senator was Rebecca Felton, a Democrat from Georgia. She was appointed to that position in 1922. The first woman elected to the Senate was Hattie Caraway, a Democrat from Arkansas, in 1932.

In 1992 voters sent a record number of women to Congress, and for the first time a state—California—elected two women to the U.S. Senate. By 2001 there were seventy-four women in Congress: fifty-nine in the House (as well as two nonvoting delegates) and thirteen in the Senate. In 2000 when Hillary Clinton was elected to the Senate from New York, she became the first former First Lady to hold elective office.

Even with more women, Congress still does not accurately reflect its constituency. Congress is more educated, more Caucasian, more male, and wealthier than the American population at large. In the 107th Congress (2001–2) the average age for House members was fifty-four; the average age for the Senate was fifty-nine.

Controversial Issues

Although members of Congress enjoy positions esteemed by most Americans, they often receive criticism from both supporters and opponents concerning a variety of issues. Two examples of these issues are term limits and congressional perks.

Term Limits—At the Constitutional Convention the delegates rejected the motion to limit House members to one term. But in the late 1980s Americans became increasingly frustrated with government and politicians. Congress and state legislatures seemed "gridlocked," and news of scandals was too frequent. For some voters the solution to the ineffectiveness and ethical problems was **term limits.** Citizens pushed for referenda that would limit the number of terms of state legislators and members of Congress. The movement was also fueled by those who dislike the notion of a "career" politician (one who serves for many years) in contrast to a "citizen" legislator (one who temporarily serves and then returns to a career).

Rep. Bob Inglis, who kept the term-limit pledge

Perks—Americans have been critical of Congress over the years for its perquisites (commonly called "perks"), which are additional benefits for senators and representatives. House salaries for the 108th Congress were $150,000 a year; the Speaker received $186,300 and other leaders, $161,200. In comparison, in 1789 members of the first Congress received $6 a day and the Speaker, $12 a day. Considering the high cost of living in Washington, D.C., and the incomes for lobbyists and attorneys, congressional pay seems modest. In addition, members of Congress have a **franking privilege** (free postage) as well as allowances for staff, offices, and travel. The average House member has seventeen full-time staff members and a senator forty-four. The aides and offices (in Washington and in the home district or state) help him do his job, which includes casework for the constituents. For example, if a constituent has a problem with Social Security, he or she may solicit help from congressional staff. However, some congressional aides are employed to work for their boss's re-election, and some home district offices operate as unofficial campaign headquarters at taxpayers' expense.

Conservative Republicans also pushed term limits because, before 1994, Democrats had controlled the House for forty years, and with the power of incumbency, term limits seemed the only viable option to open up more seats for Republicans to capture. In 1994, with their Contract with America, many Republicans running for Congress called for congressional action on term limits. Ten candidates for Congress made a term-limit pledge. In 1995 the U.S. Supreme Court declared that states could not limit the terms of U.S. Congress members. Therefore, the only option for congressional term limits was a difficult one—a constitutional amendment. A subsequent effort to propose such a constitutional amendment failed by sixty votes in the House, and a filibuster ended it in the Senate. In 2000 seven members of Congress remained true to their 1994 term-limit pledge; the three who broke their pledge were still reelected.

The major motivation for term limits, as previously mentioned, was for conservatives and Republicans to overcome the Democratic majority and take over the House. Since that happened in 1994 (and since that majority was maintained through the 2000 election), enthusiasm for term limits diminished.

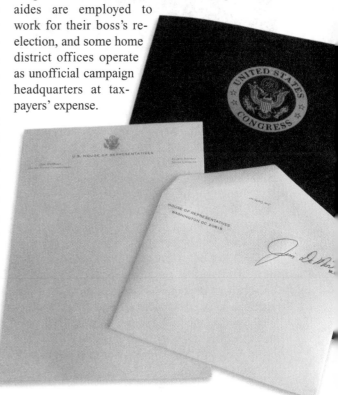

Chamber of the House of Representatives

Abuse of the congressional travel allowance often gets unfavorable attention. Members of Congress go on trips overseas to gather information useful for legislation. Many of these trips can be helpful, but too often they are not necessary, and critics dismiss them as **junkets,** seemingly unnecessary trips abroad. Sometimes taxpayers end up paying for "vacations" to the Caribbean, a favorite destination, and golf becomes more important than facts about legislation.

There are other important benefits for members of Congress. They get credit for federal funds—either grants or contracts—that are brought to the district, and as government officials they have regular access to the media, and that means free publicity. All of this helps them raise funds for their campaigns, and over 95 percent of incumbents who seek reelection win.

Congressional Sessions

Numbering—The first Congress met on March 4, 1789, in New York, and it remained in existence for two years until 1791—the length of the term of a House member and also one third of the Senate (which began with two-year terms). The second Congress, elected in 1790, replaced the first Congress. (Congresses are numbered each time a new House is elected. The House elected in 2002 is the 108th Congress, and the House elected in 2004 marks the beginning of the 109th Congress.) Each Congress, therefore, lasts for two years, while it physically convenes (called a session) once a year, as the Constitution requires.

Convening—The Congress of the Articles of Confederation provided that the new Congress under the Constitution would meet March 4, 1789. Thereafter, the Constitution provided that a Con-

252

gress elected in November would assemble the first Monday in December the following year, that is, thirteen months after being elected. Travel and communication obviously took a lot longer then, and newly elected members needed time to get their affairs in order. Often new presidents would call the old Congress into session in March, following an election the previous November. Since that Congress included members who had been defeated, it was called a "lame duck" Congress. The Twentieth Amendment, ratified in 1933, ended that problem by moving the presidential inauguration from March 4 to January 20 and the beginning of the newly-elected Congress to January 3. Travel and communication were no longer a problem. When the amendment was ratified, there was great urgency for Congress to convene because of the Great Depression. Unfortunately, the amendment was too late for the 1932–33 period. The new schedule did not begin until 1937.

Section Review

1. What is the primary advantage of a bicameral legislature?
2. What chamber of Congress is more democratic? Why?
3. How does the census affect the composition of Congress?
4. What are some major differences between the House of Representatives and the Senate?
5. How do political parties influence the leadership of Congress?
6. Why were the congressional elections of 1994 significant?
7. What are the roles of the majority leader in the Senate and the Speaker in the House of Representatives?
8. What are the responsibilities of the whips in Congress?

II. Legislative Workings

Committees

"Congress in committee is Congress at work." So said future president Woodrow Wilson when he was a graduate student studying this vital part of the national legislative process. Committees are basic to making laws, which is the main power given to Congress by the Constitution. Committees and subcommittees permit Congress to consider a vast number of proposals; some will be rejected, others will be accepted and refined with great care.

Types—There are four types of committees in Congress: standing, select, joint, and conference. **Standing committees** are permanent committees that are generally more powerful than other types of committees. The most important standing committees are those dealing with finances and legislative procedures. There are nineteen standing committees in the House and sixteen in the Senate. Subcommittees break down the work of a standing committee into manageable parts. Members of the subcommittee will work on a bill, hold hearings, listen to experts testify about the proposed bill, and, if a majority of the subcommittee agrees, report the bill to the full committee for further action. For example, the Senate Judiciary Committee in the 107th Congress had seven subcommittees, including ones on immigration and youth violence.

Select committees are those created for a specific purpose, generally to investigate a particular problem, and are therefore temporary. Congress created a select committee in May 2002 to investigate how much the FBI, CIA, and the executive branch knew about possible terrorist threats before September 11, 2001. **Joint committees** are permanent committees composed of members from both the House and Senate; they generally serve as an advisory board to other congressional committees, particularly on tax matters, but possess little real power beyond their recommendations. Finally, **conference committees** are ad hoc (temporary) committees drawn from both chambers that meet to work out a compromise agreement on a bill, or proposed law, that has emerged from both houses in

Standing Committees of 108th Congress
(2003–4)

House	Number of Members	Senate	Number of Members
Agriculture	51	Agriculture, Nutrition, and Forestry	21
Appropriations	65	Appropriations	29
Armed Services	60	Armed Services	25
Banking and Financial Services	70	Banking, Housing, and Urban Affairs	21
Budget	43	Budget	23
Education and the Workforce	49	Commerce, Science, and Transportation	23
Energy and Commerce	57	Energy and Natural Resources	23
Government Reform	44	Environment and Public Works	19
House Administration	9	Finance	21
International Relations	49	Foreign Relations	19
Judiciary	37	Governmental Affairs	17
Resources	52	Health, Education, Labor, and Pensions	21
Rules	13	Judiciary	19
Science	47	Rules and Administration	19
Small Business	36	Small Business	19
Standards of Official Conduct	10	Veterans Affairs	15
Transportation and Infrastructure	75		
Veterans Affairs	31		
Ways and Means	41		

different forms. Though short-lived, these committees are generally successful in getting their conference agreement passed by both houses.

Powers—Committees often have life-or-death power over a bill. Because this kind of legislative authority exists in a small group, the committee is designed to represent the Congress at large. For example, if the Republican Party holds a 55 percent majority in the House, then 55 percent of most House committees must be Republican. Although

better with matters in which they are interested or from which they expect a return. Members of Congress are no different. For this reason, many urban liberals seek committee posts concerned with housing and welfare services, and an unusual number of westerners can often be found on committees that deal with water projects and land management, since these are important issues with the constituents.

Advantages—Though committees cannot provide flawless representation, they do provide certain advantages to Congress at large. First, they permit Congress to increase its workload while at the same time giving more careful attention to proposals and their merits. Committees and subcommittees act as a kind of sieve through which proposals must pass on their way to becoming law. Each year thousands of measures are introduced, but many do not survive committee scrutiny. Approximately 5 percent of more than 9,000 bills proposed annually in Congress are enacted into law.

Second, the committee approach encourages expertise. Members of Congress in their first term are encouraged to do their "homework" in the committee field. Learning a great deal about a subject can make a member of Congress an asset in shaping laws.

Members—In each chamber, the party's selection committee determines who will make up the committees. Members of Congress typically seek committee assignments in line with their expertise (someone in business may want a seat on the Commerce or Small Business committee) or

A congressional committee room, the mace, the silver inkstand and glass inkwells from the House of Representatives

on the surface committees are to reflect the balance of Congress, in reality definite tendencies and interests can make the committee approach anything but representative or neutral. People usually work

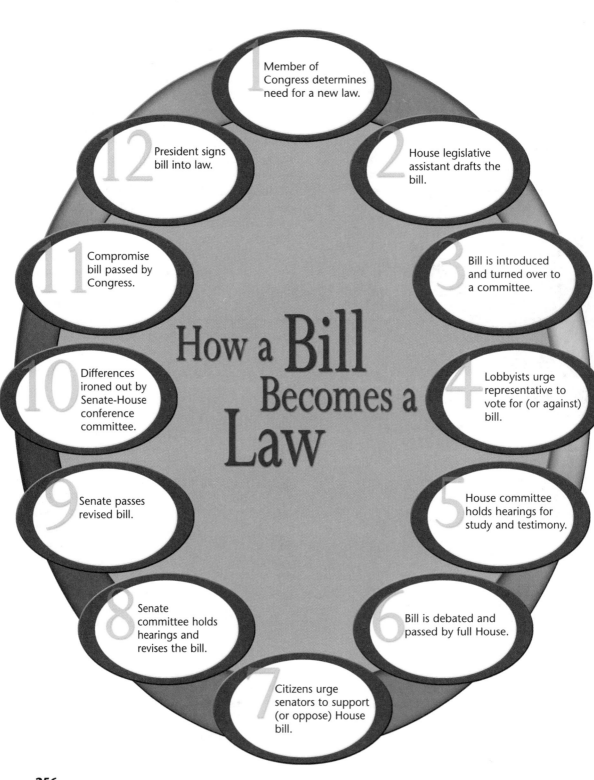

How a Bill Becomes a Law

1. Member of Congress determines need for a new law.

2. House legislative assistant drafts the bill.

3. Bill is introduced and turned over to a committee.

4. Lobbyists urge representative to vote for (or against) bill.

5. House committee holds hearings for study and testimony.

6. Bill is debated and passed by full House.

7. Citizens urge senators to support (or oppose) House bill.

8. Senate committee holds hearings and revises the bill.

9. Senate passes revised bill.

10. Differences ironed out by Senate-House conference committee.

11. Compromise bill passed by Congress.

12. President signs bill into law.

a committee that will allow them to help their constituents (if there is a military base in their district or state, they may want the Armed Services Committee). Each member is entitled to one committee assignment; however, House members average one to two standing committees and Senators three to four standing committees. Members with seniority generally get preferential treatment, and new members may have to take what they get.

Chairs of congressional committees have significant powers. In the 107th Congress, rules permitted a House committee chair, if he or she wished to kill a bill, to refrain from scheduling hearings on it. Chairs of committees could write legislation, control a committee staff budget of over a million dollars, and listen to lobbyists and people from the executive branch (including possibly the president himself) who want to influence legislation. Chairs could call meetings when opponents to the legislation were not there or could adjourn them if a bill was in trouble. Knowledge of the rules and the legislative field give a chair even greater influence.

Traditionally, chairs were members of the majority party with the greatest seniority, the longest continuous service. In 1995, however, when Republicans took over the House, important changes were made. Of course, chairs were still members of the majority party that ran the House and committees. No one, however, could serve as a committee chair for more than three consecutive terms, six years. Neither could they chair their subcommittees. Committee chairs have remained powerful since 1995: they can select all subcommittee chairs, convene the committee, and recommend majority party members for conference committees. In the House, chairs are no longer chosen based on seniority. In the 107th Congress, after the six-year limit from 1995 became effective, there were thirteen new House committee chairs. In the Senate those with greatest seniority in the majority party serve as chair. After the switch of Senator Jim Jeffords of Vermont from Republican to Independent in 2001, Democrats controlled the Senate by one vote. Their caucus, therefore, determined who would serve as committee chairs. In 2002, congressional power changed once again after election results gave Republicans a majority and the opportunity to determine committee chairs.

Making Laws

The chief constitutional function of Congress is to make laws that will affect the daily lives of Americans. A member of Congress gets proposals for laws from a variety of sources—the president, committees in Congress, bureaucracy, interest groups, or ordinary citizens. Only House or Senate members, however, can officially submit a bill in Congress. There are many hurdles for a bill, and about 95 percent of those introduced will not make it into law. It is easier to defeat a bill, since there are so many opportunities to do so, than it is to pass one.

Overall, a bill goes through three steps on its way to becoming law. (1) A standing committee in both the House and Senate must approve, (2) both chambers must vote for it on the floor, and (3) if there are differences between the two versions, a conference committee must resolve them, and its report must be accepted by both houses. The House and Senate have similar procedures, and usually the same bill is introduced simultaneously in both places.

Introducing the Bill—The first step begins when a member of Congress introduces a bill, although often several members will sponsor it to show broad support for it. Next, the clerk of the House or Senate gives it a number, preceded by HR for the House and S for the Senate (for example, HR 432 would mean it was the 432nd bill proposed in that session of the House). Congressional staff then print the bill, distribute it, and send it to the proper committee(s). Technically, the Speaker refers the bill to the committee in the House.

In the House when a person officially introduces a bill, he or she places it in the hopper, a container on the side of the clerk's desk. The clerk supplies the printed blank forms to use. Of course, the House has to be in session, but no permission is needed and no statement or speech has to be given on the House floor when a bill is presented. The bill then moves to the proper committee.

In the Senate, however, the bill to be introduced is given to clerks at the presiding officer's desk. This action can be done with or without comments from the floor of the Senate. If there is no objection, the bill goes to a committee; however, if one senator objects, the bill can be introduced the following day.

Strom Thurmond in his law office in Aiken, S.C., 1951

Committee Deliberation—Once at the committee, a bill is typically referred to a subcommittee, which researches it and possibly holds hearings on it. At those public hearings, witnesses will speak for and against the bill. Here is an opportunity for average citizens and lobbyists to give their opinions. After the hearings, the subcommittee makes changes in the bill if desired and then votes for or against it. If the bill passes, then it goes to the full committee, which in turn votes on it. If it is rejected, that is the end; but if it passes, it is reported to the House or Senate floor with the committee's recommendation.

Full House Vote—Action on the House or Senate floor, step two, varies in both chambers. In the House, the Rules Committee must approve the measure, provide the rules for debating it, decide if the bill may be amended, and schedule a time for considering the bill on the floor. The only exception is a budget bill, which does not go to the Rules Committee.

In the House there are four regular ways to vote: the voice vote (aye or no as groups), the division vote (members stand), the yea and nay vote (voice vote individually), or the record vote. This fourth option is done if forty-four members support

it. The procedure is electronic. Members go to one of the voting stations in the chamber, use a card that identifies them, and then press the button for the way they want to vote. In the Senate there are voice votes (aye or no) or, if eleven senators support it, roll call votes, in which the roll of the one hundred senators is called.

Congress has an elaborate system of lights, bells, and buzzers, which in various combinations communicate important messages to members: quorum calls (getting a minimum number of members present to conduct official business); calls for voting; indications that the session has adjourned or is in recess; indications that Congress is in session; and especially important since September 11, 2001, a civil defense warning.

To speed up floor debate on the bill, the House may organize itself into a Committee of the Whole, which means it may debate the bill with only one hundred members present. Debate is limited, given the size of the House. Members debate the bill on the floor, add amendments (if permitted by the

Rules Committee), and then vote on it. If it passes, it is then sent to the Senate, if it has not been introduced there already.

In the Senate the process moves more slowly than in the House. One senator may request a hold or a notification before a certain bill is taken to the Senate floor. This request means that Senate leadership and the bill's sponsor may face opposition from this individual, who may eventually filibuster the measure. Before 1999 these "holds" used to be secret, which made them even more powerful. In recent Congresses, holds were placed on two-thirds of bills approved in committees.

A **filibuster** is a more formal way of preventing or delaying the passage of a bill. Unlike the House, in the Senate there is unlimited debate, so opponents of a bill can try to "talk a bill to death" through long speeches. Filibusters became common during the years before the Civil War during Senate debates over slavery. All a senator has to do is keep talking; he or she may even read from a phone book or some other book. Typically, a team of senators will take turns to keep the filibuster going. Since 1900 the longest speech by an individual senator filibustering was given by South Carolina senator Strom Thurmond; in 1957 he spoke for 24 hours and 18 minutes to filibuster a civil rights bill. In 1964 a group of senators filibustered for 82 days. Currently in the Senate, the mere threat of a filibus-

ter will discourage senators from pursuing a particular piece of legislation. Filibusters can be broken only if sixteen senators sign a motion to invoke **cloture,** a motion to stop debate, and then sixty senators vote to end debate. If cloture is passed, there can be no more than thirty additional hours of debate on a bill. With the possibility of cloture, practically speaking, a senator really needs at least sixty senators supporting a bill in order for it to pass smoothly.

Conference Committee—After the bill clears the House and Senate, and there are differences, then the third stage for a bill becoming law is the conference committee. Composed of members from the original committees from both chambers, the conference committee works out an agreement on the content of the bill. If they cannot agree, the bill dies. If they do agree, the bill is sent back to both houses for a vote. The conference version cannot be amended in either the House or Senate. If both chambers pass it, the bill goes to the president; if the bill fails to pass in either house, it dies.

President Barack Obama signing a wage discrimination bill into law

Presidential Signature—The remaining hurdle for a bill becoming law is the president's action. He can do one of four things: (1) He can sign the bill, making it law. (2) He can veto the bill and kill it. Congress can override the veto if two-thirds of Congress vote for the measure. (3) He may ignore it, but if Congress is in session the bill becomes law within ten days. (4) If Congress is not in session during the ten days, and the president does not sign it, the bill dies. This is called a **pocket veto,** and it discourages Congress from "stuffing the pocket" of the president with bills hastily at the end of a session. If a pocket veto kills a bill, the bill may be reintroduced in the next session, but it would have to go through the whole process again.

Briefly presidents had a fifth option—the line-item veto, the ability to veto part of a bill without vetoing the entire bill. Congress passed a measure authorizing this option in 1996, and President Bill Clinton exercised the line-item veto eighty-two

times before the Supreme Court in 1998 declared it unconstitutional. Justices in a 6-3 decision said it violated the separation of powers since it gave the executive branch some lawmaking power; only Congress can make laws. A president has to respond to legislation from Congress in its entirety.

Section Review

1. What are the four types of congressional committees, and what function does each serve?
2. Why are committee chairmanships important?
3. What is the primary function of Congress?
4. How does the president affect the enactment of laws?
5. What are the stages a bill goes through to become a law?

President George W. Bush signing the National Defense Authorization Act (Nov. 2003)

Chapter Review

Terms

bicameral
census
reapportionment
gerrymandering
congressional district
single-member district
at large
Seventeenth Amendment
delegates
coalition

caucus
majority leader
minority leader
majority whip
minority whip
president *pro tempore*
Speaker of the House
term limits
franking privilege
junkets

standing committees
select committees
joint committees
conference committees
chairs
filibuster
cloture
pocket veto

Content Questions

1. Why did the Constitution begin with a discussion of Congress in Article I?

2. In American history which branch, Congress or the president, has been more powerful?

3. Why are some of the committees in Congress more powerful than others?

4. What financial benefits do members of Congress receive?

5. Why does the Senate often take longer to pass legislation than the House takes?

Application Questions

1. Why are *The Federalist Papers* so important?

2. Who is more powerful, a representative in the House or a senator in the Senate?

3. Are term limits for members of Congress a good idea? Defend your answer.

THE POWERS OF CONGRESS

12

House Speaker Nancy Pelosi

I. Enumerated Powers— Article I, Section 8

Chapter 11, "The Structure of Congress," describes the most important and obvious power of the legislative branch—the power to make laws. The House and Senate share this power. Specific powers given in Article I, Section 8 of the Constitution are **enumerated powers,** that is, listed powers. Through the years Congress has grown more powerful, largely at the expense of the state legislatures.

Financial Powers—Clauses 1, 2, 5, and 6

Article I, Section 8 of the Constitution gave to Congress one of the most significant powers of government, the power to tax. Because the American Revolution had been set in motion by British Parliament's attempts to tax the colonies, the founders were careful to require that all revenue bills originate in the House of Representatives, the branch of Congress closest to the people. In practice, the distinction has made little practical difference because the House and Senate frequently consider tax policy simultaneously, and both cham-

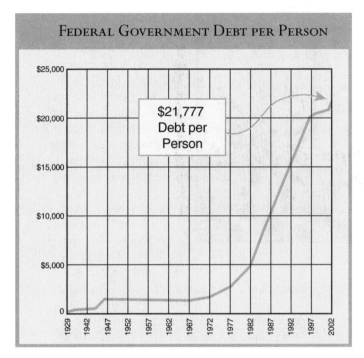

FEDERAL GOVERNMENT DEBT PER PERSON

$21,777 Debt per Person

A **duty** is a tax on an import—a good coming into the country from another nation. **Excises** are taxes on the production, sale, or use of items and taxes on certain business practices (for example, Congress has levied an excise tax on corporations in order for them to do business in the United States, and Social Security is funded by an excise tax on payrolls). "Impost" is an old-fashioned word that includes duties and excises.

The Constitution spells out how taxes are to be applied. Article I, Section 8, Clause 1 says that the taxes must be "uniform throughout the United States." All sections of the country have to be taxed the same. These taxes, mentioned in Article I, Section 2 and Section 9 as "direct" taxes, must be levied or administered based on population and evenly distributed throughout the country, with everyone paying the same amount. However,

bers must approve revenue bills before they can become law.

The first clause of Article I, Section 8 deals with taxes and gives the reasons for them: "to pay the debts and provide for the common defense and general welfare of the United States." The question of debts was a critical issue during the first few years of the new national government. During Washington's first term as president, his secretary of the treasury, Alexander Hamilton, proposed the controversial financial plan that the new national government assume the federal debt and state debts. This proposal passed and put the country on a sound financial footing. In the centuries that followed, national debt has often been controversial, especially when it rose dramatically in the 1980s and early 1990s.

Article I, Section 8 also describes some taxes as "duties, imposts and excises."

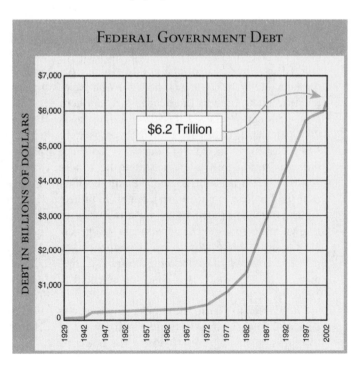

FEDERAL GOVERNMENT DEBT

$6.2 Trillion

DEBT IN BILLIONS OF DOLLARS

Boston Tea Party

the **Sixteenth Amendment** (income tax), ratified in 1913, allows Congress to tax without regard to population. If someone makes more money, he pays more taxes.

Another controversial power of Congress has been its ability to impose tariffs on goods imported into the United States. Before the passage of the Income Tax Amendment, tariffs not only generated most of the government's revenue but also increased the price of imported goods, which even played a role in the coming of the Civil War. Nineteenth-century farmers (and especially southern cotton farmers) believed that the foreign goods they purchased in exchange for their crops were being unfairly taxed to support northern industry. Although it is unlikely that the United States will ever again be threatened with disunion over tariff policy, congressional attempts to protect American-made products (and raise the price of foreign-made goods to consumers) can still generate considerable passion as was true during the debate over the North American Free Trade Agreement (NAFTA), which was first implemented in 1994.

In addition to Clause 1, Clauses 2, 5, and 6 also deal with financial matters or the fiscal powers of Congress. Clause 2 gives Congress the power to

borrow money. Given the national debt (over six trillion), that power has evidently been exercised. The United States may borrow from other countries, private banks, and individuals (bonds). Clause 5, the power to coin money and regulate its value, has been a controversial issue as well. During the Civil War millions of dollars of "greenbacks"—unsecured paper money—were printed by Congress to help pay for the conflict. Although paper money was once again tied to gold and silver during the late nineteenth century, Congress abandoned the gold standard for good during the Great Depression, initiating an era of "fiat" money—paper money whose value depends only on the trustworthiness of the government that issues it. In 1934 the Supreme Court ruled that Congress had the power to go off the gold standard, which had backed the paper currency. Clause 6 gives Congress the obvious authority to punish those who make counterfeit money.

If one looks at Clauses 1, 2, 5, 6, and 18 together (see pp. 110 and 112), Congress has enormous fiscal or financial powers: to create a national bank that states cannot tax, to create a Federal Reserve System, and to establish a currency, along with numerous other powers.

Finally, but significantly, Congress was authorized (in Clause 1) to provide for "the **general welfare** of the United States." James Madison maintained that this phrase simply allowed Congress to spend what was necessary to execute its other constitutional powers. Conversely, Alexander Hamilton argued that the clause gave Congress additional powers to tax and spend. Hamilton's view has prevailed.

Commerce Clause—Clause 3

Congressional regulation of commerce, the buying and selling of goods, has been a central issue throughout most of American history. British control of trade during the colonial period often led to conflict and was one of the issues that brought about the Revolution. The inability of the Articles of Confederation to regulate trade among the states set in motion events that created the Constitutional Convention in 1787 and the new national government. The framers, therefore, intended that the issue of commerce be dealt with by the Constitution. There was controversy over how much power to give Congress. Northerners, representing shipping and merchant interests, wanted broad powers for the new government; southerners feared that laws favoring the North would give northerners a competitive advantage over foreigners and that southerners would have more trouble getting their agricultural products to market. Southerners, as a result, wanted it to be more difficult for Congress to regulate commerce. Southerners were placated when export taxes were banned and the end of the slave trade was delayed for twenty years.

In a landmark case, *Gibbons* v. *Ogden,* in 1824, John Marshall, speaking for a unanimous Supreme Court, gave broad power to Congress to regulate **interstate commerce** (between or among the

states). The legal issue concerned which government, the state of New York or the United States government, could regulate trade between New York and New Jersey. Gibbons had a federal license for trade, and Ogden's authority came from the New York legislature. Although the Supreme Court left undefined the overlapping powers of the state and federal governments to regulate commerce, it ruled that the federal government had the right to regulate interstate commerce wherever it wished. The Court's decision was extremely popular because it destroyed state trade monopolies and allowed the United States to become one large free-trade zone. Of course, the decision also strengthened the federal government at the expense of the states.

By the mid-twentieth century, Supreme Court decisions had so expanded the power of Congress to regulate interstate commerce that virtually any economic activity, even intrastate (within the state) commerce, came under Congress's control. In 1942 in a famous case, *Wickard* v. *Filburn,* the Supreme Court ruled that even economic activity that wasn't "commerce" (a farmer keeping his wheat for personal consumption, not selling it) still affected commerce because its absence in the market affected prices and market conditions. Congress, therefore, could regulate the farmer's wheat crop.

Defense and Military—Clauses 10–16

Although Clause 1 mentions Congress's taxing power "to provide for the common defense," specific powers dealing with defense and military forces are found in Clauses 10–16. In ordaining human government, the Lord provides order and security for the people and also for the work of the church. National defense is one of the fundamental powers of government. Paul in Romans 13, speaking about a ruler punishing evil, declares, "He beareth not the sword in vain."

In Clause 10 Congress has the power "to define and punish piracies and felonies committed on the high seas and offenses against the law of nations." This clause authorizes Congress to legislate in the

M1 Abrams Tank

area of international law. Congress through legislation may prevent someone from breaking the law of another nation within the United States. For example, Congress has made the counterfeiting of a foreign currency in America illegal in the United States. This clause also empowers Congress to establish a military commission for prosecuting war crimes.

Clause 11, taken with Clauses 12–16 and 18 and Article II, Section 2, Clause 1, constitutes the **"war power"** of the national government. This war power is perhaps the single greatest authority given to our national government. Some constitutional scholars argue that the power would exist even if it had not been mentioned in the Constitution, because it is a basic right of government—to defend itself. On this question there are no competing states' rights. Historically, on America's home front during wartime, Supreme Courts have even allowed certain economic and personal freedoms to be curtailed because of the necessities of war; businesses may be heavily regulated, and freedom of speech may be curtailed. Probably the greatest violation of rights in American history occurred during World War II when Japanese-Americans were sent to "relocation centers" because of their alleged threat to national security. That action was defended under the war power of the national government and meekly upheld by the Supreme Court—until after the war was over.

In Clause 11, Congress is given the right to declare war. Nevertheless, because the American president serves as commander in chief, frequent disagreement has arisen over the role of Congress in wartime. More American wars have been undeclared than have been declared by Congress, beginning with an undeclared naval conflict with France (1798–1800). Even the most deadly of all American wars, the Civil War, was not declared; and no wars since World War II have been officially declared by Congress. In the aftermath of the Vietnam War, Congress attempted, somewhat ineffectively, to rein in presidential war making with the **War Powers Act** (1973). Of course, Congress can also show its displeasure with undeclared wars by limiting spending and conducting investigations of them.

Clause 11 mentions two technical matters related to military action. A **letter of marque** (not used for over a century and a half) is a license granted by a nation to a private citizen to capture a merchant ship of another nation. **Reprisal** is retaliation by one nation against another when provoked; it may involve seizing property or people. The final portion of this clause gives Congress power to deal with the issue of prisoners of war. Clauses 12–16 complete the description of Congress's power relating to war.

Other Powers

Naturalization and Bankruptcies, Clause 4— This paragraph contains two totally unrelated provisions—naturalization and bankruptcies; the only element that unites them is the adjective *uniform,* which applies to both.
The first section of

USS George Washington

the Fourteenth Amendment clarifies this clause: "All persons born or naturalized in the United States, and subject to the jurisdiction thereof, are citizens of the United States and of the State wherein they reside." This provision's main purpose was to cover African Americans after the Civil War who had just been freed from slavery.

Citizenship, belonging to and enjoying all the privileges, rights, and duties of a nation, is granted automatically to those born in the United States. This idea goes back to feudal law of the Middle Ages in Europe and, more specifically, British common law. The Supreme Court has even ruled that children born in the United States to temporary residents are citizens, unless the parents have diplomatic status. Congressional law has granted citizenship to children born outside the United States if one or both parents are citizens of the United States. In 1924 Congress conferred citizenship on Native Americans who were born in the United States.

Congress, through legislation, has regulated the process whereby foreigners, or aliens, become "naturalized" citizens. In 1798 the Federalists in Congress, fearing French and Irish immigrants who were becoming Republicans, placed restrictions on immigrants. After heavy immigration from southern and eastern Europe in the late nineteenth and early twentieth centuries, Congress significantly restricted immigration in the 1920s. In 1952 Congress prohibited discrimination based on race, sex, or marital status for those becoming naturalized citizens. During the Cold War, applicants for citizenship could not support or belong to a group that advocated the overthrow of the United States government. During the 1960s many restrictions were lifted, and during the late twentieth century, heavy immigration came from Asia and Latin America, not Europe, as had been true in the past.

Congress has also used this power to take away people's citizenship. One can lose his or her American citizenship, for example, by becoming a citizen of another country. Also, Congress can exclude aliens or foreigners from the country or control them if they live in the country. In 2002 Attorney

Immigrants becoming U.S. citizens

General John Ashcroft used strong measures to deport people who were believed to be terrorist threats. Of course, laws dealing with immigrants, legal and illegal, have to be weighed against America's long history of freedom and liberty.

Naturalization and immigration issues have fundamentally affected American government and politics. They have changed the racial and ethnic composition of the country. Support for or opposition to immigration has divided our nation at various times. Because of our heritage of immigration, America today is very diverse. In the Old Testament Israel was directed by God to be kind to the "strangers" in the land, because they, Israel, once were strangers in Egypt (Lev. 19:34). As Americans we want all laws enforced, but as Christians we should treat immigrants with kindness, seeking to share the gospel with them.

The **bankruptcy** provision of Clause 4 was another attempt by the founders to promote uniformity among the states. When a debtor declares bankruptcy, it is important to divide his remaining assets equally and honestly among his creditors.

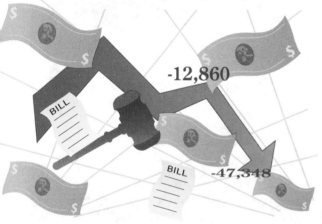

The founders understood that without federal supervision there would be a tendency for states to liberate resident debtors from their out-of-state debts. Despite the constitutional provision that specifically delegated the power to make bankruptcy laws to Congress, most bankruptcy laws in the nineteenth century were state laws, occasionally modified by state and federal court rulings to reduce obvious unfairness. Only in 1898 did Congress pass a national bankruptcy law that lasted longer than a few years.

Mail Service, Clause 7—Alexander Hamilton expected the U.S. Post Office to generate revenue for the Treasury. As it turned out, even when there was a surplus, Congress wisely used the money to expand the postal service to the frontiers. Although the postal system was called an "odious monopoly" as early as 1843, the government service has never been without some sort of private competition. Through the years these independent delivery companies have forced change on the government system, including a major reduction in postal rates in 1845 and the inauguration of Rural Free Delivery in 1896. Undoubtedly the advent of email and other electronic means of communication will eventually bring more change to a bureaucracy that now encompasses about one-third of all civilian employees of the federal government.

Stamp Designs

Who decides which designs go on stamps? Each year the post office produces stamps with designs ranging from flowers to famous personages. How are the designs for the stamps determined?

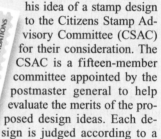

Ideas for stamp designs come from the public. Any person may send his idea of a stamp design to the Citizens Stamp Advisory Committee (CSAC) for their consideration. The CSAC is a fifteen-member committee appointed by the postmaster general to help evaluate the merits of the proposed design ideas. Each design is judged according to a list of twelve criteria. Stamp designs must be about America or American-related topics, no living person can be honored on the stamp, and no subject can be issued twice within ten years unless it is a general theme, such as Christmas or flags. These are just a few of the guidelines for choosing appropriate designs.

Once the CSAC has determined an idea is appropriate, it submits the idea to the postmaster general for consideration. About twenty-five or thirty ideas are recommended each year. Ideas must be submitted three years in advance to give enough time for design and production.

Patents and Copyrights, Clause 8—Patents and copyrights are critical powers for Congress in a democracy. In Clause 8 authors and inventors are given, for limited times, the exclusive right to their writings and discoveries. Congress cannot use this provision to create a monopoly; that is why there is a time limit. Today we know patents and copyrights as intellectual property rights. These rights have been expanded to protect photographs and movies as well as, more recently, computer programs and prescription drugs.

Federal Courts, Clause 9—With this provision, the separation of powers doctrine becomes blurred. Congress has the power to create federal courts below the Supreme Court and also to provide for other aspects of the national judiciary. This clause has to be examined in conjunction with Article III, Section 1, the part of the Constitution that deals with the courts. Congress has the authority to organize the Supreme Court and determine the number of judges. The **Judiciary Act of 1789** provided for a chief justice and five associate justices, three circuit courts where two Supreme Court justices served with one district court judge, and thirteen federal district courts with one judge each. This legislation also described the jurisdiction (what cases they could take and where they could operate) and organization and procedures for operation. At this time also, state courts were given the right to take some federal cases. During the Civil War there were ten members of the Supreme Court. During the late 1930s President Franklin Roosevelt tried, but failed, to expand the Supreme Court to fifteen. Today there are nine members of the Supreme Court, thirteen Circuit Courts of Appeals (which are now a separate entity), and ninety-four district courts. Congress has also created other specialized federal courts, including bankruptcy courts, the Court of International Trade, the U.S. Tax Court, and the Court of Federal Claims.

Congress also has the power to determine the jurisdiction of the federal courts, that is, the authority to hear and decide a case. The only exception is stated in Article III, Section 2, Clause 2: "In all cases affecting ambassadors, other public ministers and consuls, and those in which a State shall be party, the Supreme Court shall have original jurisdiction" (serve as the trial court). Congress can determine the appellate jurisdiction of the Supreme Court, deciding which cases the Supreme Court can take as an appeal from a lower court.

District of Columbia, Clause 17—Congress has power to govern the District of Columbia, the seat of the federal government since 1800. This clause also gives Congress the power to make laws governing all other federal properties, such as forts, military installations, and bases. Today this power also includes post offices, hospitals and hotels in federal parks, and locks and dams built to improve navigation. In 1790 Congress established the district with land ceded from Maryland and Virginia; however, in 1846 Virginia's land was returned to the state. Congress began more direct control of the district in 1871 when it abolished the charter of the city and ruled it as a territory. The Twenty-third Amendment, ratified in 1961, gave the district three electoral votes so that the citizens there could participate in presidential elections. The next major change occurred in 1967 when Congress instituted a mayor–city council form of government, which gave limited self-government. The District of Columbia also has a nonvoting delegate in the House.

Today partisan politics keep the district from having statehood, complete home rule. The district is heavily Democratic, and Republicans are not eager to add two more Democratic members to the United States Senate and one more Democratic representative to the House.

Necessary and Proper, Clause 18—This "necessary and proper" clause can be read to apply to all of the previous enumerated powers (Clauses

Federal District Courthouse, Haynsworth Building, Greenville, S.C.

1–17) and is the basis for the extraordinary powers of Congress and the federal government in general. In 1819 Chief Justice Marshall declared in the landmark *McCulloch* v. *Maryland* case: "Let the end be legitimate, let it be within the scope of the Constitution, and all means which are appropriate, which are plainly adapted to that end, which are not prohibited, but consist with the letter and spirit of the Constitution are constitutional." Little wonder this part of the Constitution has also been referred to as the "elastic" clause. Historical circumstances such as war, depression, and the personalities of presidents, members of Congress, and Supreme Court justices have built the power of the national government over the years based largely on this clause. The thinking behind such a broad interpretation of the "necessary and proper" clause is that the Constitution is based on "we the people" and not a union of the states and that the Constitution has to be adaptable to changing circumstances in our nation's development. Opponents of this view throughout American history have argued that the Constitution is describing a government that is a compact of sovereign states that retain ultimate power and that the Constitution should be interpreted more strictly. To those who have opposed more and more federal power, the "necessary and proper" clause means that Congress should do only what is "absolutely necessary."

Since the Civil War the power of the federal government has triumphed over the states, due in part to this provision. Clause 18 often has meant greater power for Congress over other branches of government. That power for Congress, it must be remembered, can be limited by the Supreme Court's power to declare acts of Congress unconstitutional. Clause 18, however, should be judged in connection with the "supremacy clause," Article VI, Clause 2: "This Constitution, and the laws of the United States which shall be made in pursuance thereof, and all treaties made, or which shall be made, under the authority of the United States, shall be the supreme law of the land; and the judges in every State shall be bound thereby, anything in

the Constitution or laws of any State to the contrary notwithstanding." So, for example, state governments are required to enforce federally set minimum wage requirements. Together, the "necessary and proper" clause and the "supremacy" clause have meant great power for the national government, not just Congress.

Section Review

1. Why is Article I, Section 8 of the Constitution so important for Congress?
2. From what sources does the federal government borrow money?
3. How did northerners and southerners disagree about trade before the Civil War?
4. What does Paul teach about government in Romans 13?
5. Where is the power of Congress to declare war found?
6. What is naturalization?
7. What does the Bible say about the treatment of immigrants?
8. Why is the "necessary and proper" clause so important?

II. Implied Powers

In addition to the enumerated powers, Congress also has inherent or **implied powers,** powers that a government has just by virtue of being a governmental body. Many of these implied powers come from the necessary and proper clause discussed above, and some of them date back to state legislatures, colonial assemblies, or even British Parliament. There are numerous examples. Congress used its constitutional power to establish roads for mail delivery as the legal basis for creating the interstate highway system. Congress can pass resolutions—declarations that do not have the authority of law, but rather express congressional opinion.

Congress has certain judicial powers or authority usually associated with a court. Those who violate the proceedings of Congress can be cited for contempt and punished, maybe even imprisoned. To force people to testify before a committee hearing, Congress can issue a **subpoena** ordering them to appear. To encourage them to give as much information as possible, authorities may grant witnesses immunity, which means that what they say cannot be used to indict them for a crime. Some famous congressional investigations include an inquiry into the bombing of Pearl Harbor, Senator Joseph McCarthy's notorious pursuit of communists in the government, and the Watergate investigation that led to the resignation of President Nixon.

Senator Joseph McCarthy

Also, members of Congress have another right that is usually associated with the courts—immunity from prosecution. Article I, Section 6 states, "They shall in all Cases, except Treason, Felony and Breach of the Peace, be privileged from Arrest during their Attendance at the Session of their respective Houses." The framers of the Constitution wanted members of Congress to have as much freedom as possible when legislating.

Since Congress has the power to wage war and the Senate to ratify treaties, the Supreme Court has ruled that Congress can acquire territory and govern it. That implied power obviously has been an important one for our nation's geographical expansion. Congress's war power has produced other significant implied powers. During Reconstruction, the Supreme Court ruled that the war power enabled Congress in peacetime to deal with the problems caused by the war. Legislation dealing with immigrants and naturalization, covered earlier, is based on implied powers. Any sovereign power has the authority to determine qualifications for citizenship.

Recently, Supreme Court decisions have expanded Congress's power under the commerce clause (covered above) by connecting it to the necessary and proper clause. Congress, as a result, has been allowed to regulate trains and planes (obviously not in use during the writing of the Constitution), set the minimum wage, and to require drug testing for some workers.

Section Review

1. Define *resolutions*.
2. According to Article 1, Section 6, what are the three things a member of Congress can be arrested for?
3. In what way did Congress expand its war powers during Reconstruction?

III. Nonlegislative Powers

Presidential Elections

A seldom used but significant House responsibility is the power to elect the president if no candidate receives a majority of the electoral votes. Under this arrangement, each state is permitted one vote. Though this power has been invoked on only two occasions—the 1800 election of Thomas Jefferson and the 1824 election of John Quincy Adams—it has figured in the strategies of third parties. A third-party candidate may not be able to win, but he may gain enough votes to throw the election into the House and thus obtain important concessions from the major parties in exchange for his support. In relation to this House power, the Senate is similarly charged with electing the vice president under the same circumstances—each senator gets one vote. Under the **Twenty-fifth Amendment,** if there is a vacancy in the vice-presidency, the president nominates and both houses of Congress elect a new vice president by a majority vote. Also, this amendment provides that if there is a dispute over a president's ability to serve, Congress ultimately resolves the issue.

Ratification and Confirmation

The United States Senate has sole responsibility in two important nonlegislative areas: treaty **ratification** and confirmation of executive and judicial appointments. Although the president directs foreign policy, his power is checked since all treaties must be approved by a two-thirds vote of the Senate. Perhaps the most graphic example of this was the Senate rejection of the Versailles Treaty after World War I.

Also, most top-level executive, diplomatic, and military positions and all federal judicial appointments are subject to Senate **confirmation** proceedings. Most proceedings are routine and confirmation is a formality, but some nominations involving top policymaking positions and appointees are subject to Senate scrutiny. Confirmation hearings often provide an opportunity for the Senate to present arguments against administration policy, even if the nominee is eventually confirmed.

Senate confirmation power is also influential in shaping the federal courts, including the Supreme Court, since senators have the last word on who is actually installed. To date, the Senate has rejected 27 of 148 Supreme Court appointments but only 9 of more than 700 cabinet appointees. In recent years Supreme Court nominations have become more contentious, particularly the 1987 Senate rejection of Robert Bork by a vote of 42 for and 58 against. Liberals charged that he was too conservative. Clarence Thomas was confirmed as a Supreme Court justice in 1991 by a slim margin of 52 to 48, again charged with being too conservative. George W. Bush also faced opposition concerning judicial nominations from a Democratic-controlled Senate in the first two years of his presidency. This op-

U.S. Supreme Court Justice Clarence Thomas

position focused on his nominees' conservative ideologies.

Impeachment

Among the constitutional duties shared by both houses is the power of **impeachment.** Impeachment, formally charging the president or other top government officials, including federal judges, with "treason, bribery, or other high crimes and misdemeanors," can be carried out only by the House of Representatives. Only the Senate conducts impeachment trials, and conviction is by a two-thirds vote. Only two presidents have ever been impeached by the House, Andrew Johnson in 1868 and Bill Clinton in 1998. The Senate acquitted both. In 1974 President Richard Nixon resigned from office; the House Judiciary Committee had voted to impeach him, and he wanted to avoid impeachment by the full House and conviction and removal from office by the Senate.

Determining Qualifications

Under Article I, Section 5, the Constitution gives Congress the power to determine "Qualifications of its own Members," and with that authority Congress has expelled members for criminal activity. In 2002 Congress expelled Representative Jim Traficant for bribery, racketeering, and tax evasion. Congress has also censured members for conduct that reflected badly on Congress, but that is a condemnation, not an expulsion. Past House members have been censured for using offensive language, insulting the Speaker, and physically attacking other members. Congress has censured four members since 1976; the last two to be censured were Daniel Crane and Gerry Studds, both for sexual misconduct.

Witnesses to the House Judiciary Committee's impeachment hearing are sworn in on Capitol Hill, Wednesday, December 9, 1998.

Amendments

Under Article V Congress has the power to propose amendments to the Constitution. Congress can propose them either by a two-thirds vote of both houses or by calling for a "Convention for proposing Amendments" when two-thirds of the states ask for it. This latter provision has never been used; the fear is that such a convention might seek broader and more dangerous changes. Congress also decides how a constitutional amendment is to be ratified: by three-fourths of state legislatures or three-fourths of state conventions.

IV. Powers Denied Congress

When discussing the broad powers given to the national government in general and Congress in particular by the Constitution, as interpreted by the courts and enlarged by tradition, one must remember that there are **reserved powers.** The Tenth Amendment states that "the powers not delegated to the United States by the Constitution, nor prohibited by it to the States, are reserved to the States respectively, or the people." These powers kept by the state enable the state to legislate for the public health and welfare of its citizens.

According to the First Amendment, Congress cannot restrict religious freedom, freedoms of speech and the press, or the rights to assemble and petition the government. Article I, Section 9 also denies certain powers to Congress. A few of those restrictions are that Congress may not suspend the writ of *habeas corpus,* pass a bill of attainder or *ex post facto* law, or tax exports from any state.

Section Review

1. In what way can a third-party candidate prosper even if he does not win a presidential election.
2. In what way can the Senate shape the federal judiciary?
3. In what two ways may Congress propose amendments to the Constitution?

Backdoor Spending

Congress seemingly has missed the point in the humorous barb attributed to Illinois Senator Everett Dirksen that "a million here and a million there and pretty soon you're talking real money." Actually, we are now talking about real debt as well, with a ten-digit debt figure on which interest payments alone require millions of tax dollars. How is it that with all the budget cuts in recent years the national debt continues to soar? The answer lies largely in "backdoor spending." The following are some of the ways Congress can annually spend billions that are basically off-limits from budget cuts or control and that continue to push the national debt to new heights.

Entitlements—**Entitlements** are government compensation programs that Congress has protected by law. Entitlements include such items as Social Security and Medicare, as well as many Great Society programs developed during Lyndon Johnson's administration. Entitlements today constitute well over half the annual budget and cost nearly a half trillion dollars.

Borrowing Power—Congress has granted billions in borrowing power to many federal agencies. Bureaucratic borrowing is neither subject to congressional approval nor part of the budget.

Guaranteed Loans—In order to encourage home ownership, Congress has authorized this means of backdoor spending by underwriting Federal Housing Administration (FHA) and Veteran's Administration (VA) home loans. If borrowers fail to pay their debts, the government is obligated to repay the loan.

Backdoor spending underscores Congress's poor record of stewardship. The Scriptures emphasize two important principles of stewardship: faithfulness and accountability. Congress has violated these principles with programs that are shielded from control. Such programs have encouraged irresponsible spending and unaccountable borrowing, thereby threatening our economic future.

Section Review

1. Which amendment reserves powers to the states?
2. List several ways that the Constitution restricts Congress's powers.

V. Congressional Criticism

In addition to complaints about money from interest groups and PACs (see Chapter 9) and perks (see previous chapter), there are other serious criticisms of Congress by the public. Consistently citizens give Congress low ratings in opinion polls. Congress is often viewed as self-serving, lazy, indifferent, and corrupt. A lot of blame is due to simple politics. Constituents of one party will attack members of Congress from another party. Some citizens will complain about how their representative votes on a particular bill or supports a certain interest group.

As Christians we have a higher standard by which to judge the actions of men—the Word of God. The Scriptures say, "Judge righteous judgment"; therefore, moving beyond party labels and personalities, our evaluations of our leaders must be based upon and tempered by biblical truth.

Plainly Congress is an arm of secular government, but in a republic it does represent all—including Christians. Citizens need to hold members of Congress accountable and demand the highest ethical standards. Is the member a good steward of his or her office? Does the member put the interests of the public above personal political ambition? Are his or her causes biblical ones or ones that advance an agenda contrary to the kingdom of Christ? The answers to these questions, rather than party membership, provide a superior gauge with which to measure the merits of a representative.

Pork-Barrel Politics

An ongoing criticism of Congress is its wasteful spending. In the nineteenth century, pork was salted and kept in barrels, and by the late nineteenth century the term "pork barrel" had become political slang for "goodies" for the local citizens paid for by taxpayers at large. **Pork-barrel** politics describes big spending projects that are designed to help a member of Congress be reelected. It is an example of Congress's abuse of its purse power, and it is a considerable part of its legislative program. Pork-barrel spending includes such things as funding for highway construction, irrigation projects, new post offices, harbor improvements, and military contracts. Citizens Against Government Waste defines pork-barrel spending as money requested by a single member of Congress, not requested by the president, not cleared through a congressional hearing, and serving only a local purpose. This kind of spending is viewed by congressional members as a kind of "gift" to a hopefully grateful and indebted constituency. However, a pork-barrel project is far from a gift, since its cost is paid by the taxpayers of both the host district and the nation at large.

Two factors contribute to the difficulty in defeating pork-barrel measures. First of all, there is the practice of **logrolling,** in which a member of Congress supports a colleague's spending project in return for support for his own pork-barrel legis-

lation. Secondly, pork-barrel projects are often combined with important spending legislation into one omnibus spending bill. This helps protect the wasteful spending from a presidential veto since it is in effect shielded by the parts of the bill that the president favors.

Recent outrageous examples include millions or billions for studies of cow flatulence and why more Americans don't ride bicycles to work, and in 2000 for an experiment for growing vegetables in outer space. Of course, not everyone sees pork-barrel spending as outlandish. To some in Congress, "one person's pork is another person's legitimate spending." Important projects funded by this spending could be viewed as representing their constituents and benefiting their districts, and if they don't get the money for them, the money will simply go elsewhere.

Seniority System

A tradition in Congress that has weakened some in recent years is the seniority system. The practice generally is that members who have served the longest and are in the majority party become chairs of committees and subcommittees. Critics charge that this system honors political longevity, getting reelected, and not ability or ideology. In the 1960s, for example, liberals trying to push Great Society (welfare state) legislation were frustrated because chairs of committees were often southern conservative Democrats who obstructed legislation. By the same token, conservatives in the late twentieth century were thwarted by liberals with seniority in Congress. Republicans in the 1990s introduced some reforms that altered the system: term limits and limiting the years members could serve as chairs of committee.

The abuse of power, money, and public trust certainly merits an outcry. Yet, the definition "Congress is the people" aptly points an accusing finger at American society at large. Members of Congress have no right to blame society for acts of dishonesty, for every man is responsible for his own sin (Ezek. 18:4). However, the Scripture teaches that at times God gives a nation the kind of government it deserves (I Sam. 8). Israel, in disobedience, demanded a king. The result was King Saul, who also became rebellious like many of his subjects. The weakness and self-concern of members of Congress in handling money and power reflects not simply their character flaws but also the moral weakness of the nation.

In Balance

Congressional criticism has always been a common pastime in America. Mark Twain, with his typical biting humor, declared, "It could probably be shown by facts and figures that there is no distinctly native American criminal class except Congress." However, it would be unjust to characterize the national legislature only by its most negative aspects. The important and difficult role that the popular branch has in national government often goes unappreciated. Congress has two fundamental tasks, nei-

ther of which is easy: representation and legislation. As representatives, members of Congress are to obey the voice of the people, but which people? How does a member determine whether he is listening to the voice of the majority or a small but well-organized interest group? As a legislator he must decide which laws are worth supporting and, in an atmosphere where political compromise determines a bill's future, decide how much he can give.

Another misunderstanding of Congress is the kind of leadership that it represents. Criticism often arises that Congress is a do-nothing branch that is slow to respond to national demands. Congress, with its bicameral structure and cumbersome legislative process, is not designed to act with decisiveness, but rather with deliberateness. Its approach is characterized by caution and compromise, which in its best sense provides essential balance to presidential leadership. In the congressional arena there is as much merit in killing a bad bill as in passing a good one. Many bills are so ill-conceived that if passed into law, they would be either dangerous or ineffective. The public is served by the legislative sifting. Congress is central to our representative form of government. Its members come from every corner of the nation, and they reflect a diversity of parties, personalities, and opinions. Their work in Washington is immense. As the first branch of government, Congress provides an important check and balance to the other branches. As the people's branch it helps "harmonize diversity." And as the legislative branch it passes laws that have shaped the nation's growth and direction in the world. In spite of its failures and the weight of its many responsibilities, Congress continues to have a strong voice in and for the Republic.

Section Review

1. What is the Christian's only standard for judging his political leaders' actions?
2. What two factors prevent the defeat of pork-barrel measures?
3. What are the benefits of a bicameral Congress?

Chapter Review

Terms

enumerated powers
duty
excises
Sixteenth Amendment
general welfare
interstate commerce
"war power"
War Powers Act

letter of marque
reprisal
citizenship
bankruptcy
Judiciary Act of 1789
implied powers
subpoena
Twenty-fifth Amendment

ratification
confirmation
impeachment
reserved powers
entitlements
pork-barrel
logrolling

Content Questions

1. Explain why it is important that Article I, Section 6 protect members of Congress from prosecution except for cases of treason, felony, and breaches of peace.

2. List the two times that Congress has invoked its power to elect the president in an election that did not give one candidate a majority of votes.

3. Which house of Congress has the sole responsibility to ratify treaties and confirm executive and judicial nominations? Discuss how this power allows Congress to check executive power.

4. Explain the role of both houses of Congress in impeachment.

5. How many United States presidents have been impeached? Who are they, and what years were they impeached?

6. What are the two ways Congress can propose an amendment to the Constitution?

Application Questions

1. Do you think the federal government's expansion based on the "necessary and proper" clause is legitimate? List and defend the reasons for your answer.

2. How does the Senate's power to confirm judicial and executive appointments affect the makeup of American government? Discuss the importance of a senator's beliefs and how they will impact his views of nominees.

3. Apply the scriptural principles of stewardship (faithfulness and accountability) to federal spending, law enforcement, and the environment; list your answers.

4. Evaluate how your Christian worldview would affect you as a member of Congress. How would the Bible affect the bills you would propose, the compromises you would be willing to make, the goals for your term of service, or the way you would handle yourself regarding ethics?

UNIT V

THE EXECUTIVE BRANCH

Presidents Ford, Reagan, Carter, and Nixon, whose terms extended from 1969 to 1989, share a light moment at a White House gathering in 1981.

The people . . . are not qualified to exercise themselves the Executive department; but they are qualified to name the person who shall exercise it. With us, therefore, they choose this officer every four years.

—*Thomas Jefferson to Abbe Arnoux, 1789*

The presidency—what political scientist James MacGregor Burns called the "seat of glory, the cockpit of raw conflict"—is one of the important power centers of our government. When Patrick Henry first read the Constitution, he grumbled, "It has an awful squinting—it squints toward monarchy. . . . Your President may easily become king." Henry came remarkably close to the truth. A modern president is, in some respects, an elected dictator with a personal staff that has swelled into the thousands. This chapter will examine presidential qualities, election to the office, and inauguration with its transfer of power.

I. Presidential Qualities

A study of the presidents of the United States is a study of United States history in miniature. Over the past two centuries their lives have contributed richly to the American experience, and their names have often characterized eras. Some presidents have shaped the nation and its future by the force of their personalities. Washington, for example, provided leadership and integrity that set a course for the young republic and provided a pattern for his successors. Theodore Roosevelt embodied a vibrant, burgeoning America awaking to its role as a world leader. In contrast, presidents such as Millard Fillmore or Franklin Pierce are noted more for their obscurity than for their accomplishments.

In the days of George Washington, America was little more than a band of states huddled along the eastern seaboard. Today the United States is a highly industrialized superpower stretching from Maine to California and encompassing Alaska,

IN COMPARISON

The American and French Presidencies

The nature of the American presidency has changed little since the beginning of the national government in 1789. He is elected by the electoral college to a four-year term. The Twelfth Amendment, ratified in 1804, required that presidential electors vote separately for president and vice president. Originally, the top vote receiver became president and the second-place winner was vice president. In 1800 this caused a problem when Jefferson and Burr tied in the electoral vote, throwing the election into the House of Representatives. Ratified in 1933 during the emergency of the Great Depression, the Twentieth Amendment moved inauguration from March to January. In 1951, in reaction to Franklin Roosevelt's election to four successive terms, the Twenty-second Amendment limited presidents to two terms. In 1967, in response to the Kennedy assassination, the Twenty-fifth Amendment dealt with presidential succession.

French political history has been more turbulent. In modern history the French have alternated between rule by a strong man, whether a monarch or military figure, and a republican form of government with a greater emphasis on democracy. The current constitution for the Fifth Republic dates back only to 1958 and was created after a crisis over France's colony of Algeria.

In response to the unstable Fourth Republic, which had been dominated by the legislative body, the constitution of the new republic created a strong president. He has a seven-year term, names the prime minister, may dissolve the National Assembly, and may declare a state of emergency and rule by decree. Originally, local officials (perhaps comparable to the American electoral college, chosen by the states) elected the French president, but since a 1962 referendum, a national vote determines the winner.

In 2000 French voters altered the presidency once more. The term was reduced to five years. The constitution for the Fifth Republic created an odd mix of presidential and parliamentary government. French presidents have paramount executive power, but the leader of the majority party in the National Assembly, the prime minister, conducts the day-to-day affairs of the government. In recent years it has not been uncommon for the president and prime minister to be from different parties. Shortening the term of the president, some argue, will improve coordination between the president and the National Assembly and make the executive branch more accountable to the will of the people. Time will show whether this line of reasoning will prove to be accurate.

Ulysses S. Grant

Hawaii, and even the far-flung territories in the South Pacific. The presidency, like the nation, has experienced change; yet at least one important feature has remained remarkably unchanged. Despite the growth in government and the demands of a new age, the president is still one person entrusted with the most important office in the land.

The founding fathers provided broad, fairly nonrestrictive qualifications for those seeking the presidency. Article II, Section 1 of the Constitution states,

> No person except a natural-born citizen . . . shall be eligible to the office of president; neither shall any person be eligible to that office who shall not have attained to the age of thirty-five years, and been fourteen years a resident within the United States.

These qualifications have basically made the office accessible to anyone who is mature, who is loyal, and who has an understanding of his American heritage. The qualification of "natural-born citizen" means anyone born in the United States or born outside the United States to U.S. citizens. To date, a person born out of the United States to American citizens has not run for the presidency.

Though these qualifications make the office accessible, there appear to be two main avenues to the White House: either a successful military career (Washington, Jackson, Grant, or Eisenhower, for example) or a course through lower-level politics. Of course, there have been notable exceptions to these approaches to the Oval Office. Herbert Hoover, for example, was an engineer, and Ronald Reagan's varied career included stints as an actor and a radio commentator. George W. Bush had been a businessman and a managing general partner of the Texas Rangers baseball team.

Many of the presidents surmounted great obstacles on their way to the White House. Lincoln was born in poverty and suffered many political losses before gaining the presidency. Andrew Johnson grew up in severe poverty. At fourteen he began work as a tailor's apprentice to support his widowed mother. Johnson did not learn to read or write until his wife taught him years later. The rough-hewn Andrew Jackson suffered a variety of physical ailments, including tuberculosis, malarial fever, chronic dysentery, and probably lead poisoning, the result of two bullets lodged in him from duels he survived. Theodore Roosevelt grew up in great wealth, but he was a sickly asthmatic. Roosevelt strove hard to build a strong body and was successful. However, the deaths of his wife and his mother, who in a tragic coincidence died on the same day in the same house, were events from which he never fully recovered. Bill Clinton was raised by a stepfather who was abusive to his (Clinton's) mother.

Whatever the road to the presidency, the forces that fashion a president are as varied as those who have held the office. These presidents, fashioned by wealth, health, and education, have played an important role in America's past and will continue to do so in its future.

Section Review

1. What are the three qualifications for a president?
2. In the past what have been the two main avenues leading to the presidency?

II. Nomination

Modern presidential campaigns are not for self-doubters or the faint of heart. The campaign trail is arduous and exhausting, and the candidate must raise millions of dollars just to stay in the race.

Step by Step to Presidential Election

Step One	Candidate announces his or her plan to run for the presidency.
Step Two	Candidate campaigns to win delegate and potential voter support. The delegates are party representatives who pledge to support the candidate's nomination at the national party convention.
Step Three	Caucuses and primary elections take place in the states. These are the methods that the general public uses to be part of nominating presidential candidates.
Step Four	The nominee for president is announced at the national party convention, and the election campaign begins. The candidate attends various events, makes speeches, and debates other presidential candidates.
Step Five	Citizens cast their votes on the Tuesday after the first Monday of November. The ballot the citizens cast is in reality selecting the group of electors in the electoral college.
Step Six	The electoral college casts its votes on the first Monday after the second Wednesday in December. In every state except Maine and Nebraska, all the electoral votes go to the candidate who leads the popular vote. At least 270 electoral votes are required to elect a president.
Step Seven	The president is inaugurated on January 20.

Campaign Rigors

Adlai Stevenson was no stranger to the campaign trail, giving Eisenhower consecutive challenges for the White House in 1952 and 1956. In the following account Stevenson gives the candidate's perspective on the tiresome task of modern campaigning.

At least for an inexperienced candidate, I suppose we have contrived few more exciting ordeals than a presidential campaign. You must emerge, bright and bubbling with wisdom and well-being, every morning at 8 o'clock, just in time for a charming and profound breakfast talk, shake hands with hundreds, often literally thousands, of people, make several inspiring, "newsworthy" speeches during the day, confer with political leaders along the

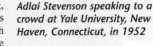

Adlai Stevenson speaking to a crowd at Yale University, New Haven, Connecticut, in 1952

way and with your staff all the time, write at every chance, think if possible, read mail and newspapers, talk on the telephone, talk to everybody, dictate, receive delegations, eat with decorum—and discretion!—and ride through city after city on the back of an open car, smiling until your mouth is dehydrated by the wind, waving until the blood runs out of your arm, and then bounce gaily, confidently, masterfully into great howling halls, shaved and all made up for television with the right color shirt and tie. . . . Then all you have to do is make a great, imperishable speech, get out through the pressing crowds with a few autographs, your clothes intact, your hands bruised, and back to the hotel—in time to see a few important people.

But the real work has just commenced—two or three, sometimes four hours of frenzied writing and editing of the next day's immortal mouthings so you can get something to the stenographers, so they can get something to the mimeograph machines, so they can get something to the reporters, so they can get something to their papers by deadline time. (And I quickly concluded that all deadlines were yesterday!) Finally, sleep, sweet sleep, steals you away, unless you worry—which I do.

The next day is the same.

Primary Hurdles

The Constitution offers no guidelines concerning the method of choosing presidential candidates. In the days before party labels existed, the framers of the Constitution hoped that the best men, like cream, would rise to the top—men of talent, intelligence, and experience, men whose only ambition was to serve their country. The one who received the most electoral votes, votes cast by electors in the electoral college, would become president, and the runner-up would become vice president. This ideal did not survive long in the rough-and-tumble world of politics. As we observed in Chapter 8, this nonpartisan selection process broke down into a system that was more party-oriented and democratic. Today that partisan process of choosing a nominee for the presidency begins with the primary.

The Rise of Presidential Primaries—The dawn of the twentieth century saw an outcry against the "undemocratic" conventions that had nominated presidential candidates during much of the nineteenth century. The method proposed in exchange was to give control of party nominations to the people in **direct primaries,** preliminary nominating elections held to select candidates and/or delegates to party conventions. In 1903 Wisconsin became the first state to allow direct primaries for state offices, and by 1912 fourteen states had adopted presidential primaries to select convention delegates. The platform of Teddy Roosevelt's Progressive (or "Bull Moose") Party in 1912 called for "nation-wide preferential primaries for candidates for the presidency."

The presidential primary became an attempt to circumvent the power of party bosses to control the national convention and thus the presidential nomination. However, over half a century passed before the method took hold. The slow adoption of these primaries was a result of several factors, including the cost of an extra election to the states and the reluctance of many candidates to campaign for votes in the primaries. In the 1940s and 1950s, some candidates began entering the existing primaries to demonstrate their ability to win votes. For example, John Kennedy's strong showing in the 1960 primaries helped convince Democratic leaders that a Roman Catholic could win support in Protestant America. The delegates to the national convention won for a candidate in the primaries were relatively few and of little consequence in those years, but that situation soon changed.

The political and social activism in the 1960s and 1970s helped spur an increase in the number and influence of presidential primaries. The Democrats, who had held primaries in fifteen states in 1968, doubled the number in eight years and had thirty-seven primaries in 1988. In the 2000 election thirty-nine Democratic primaries were held. Republican primaries increased in similar fashion. In the 2000 election Republicans held forty-two primaries. With this significant rise in the number of primaries has come a corresponding rise in the number of convention delegates won in the primaries. Thus serious candidates can no longer avoid participation

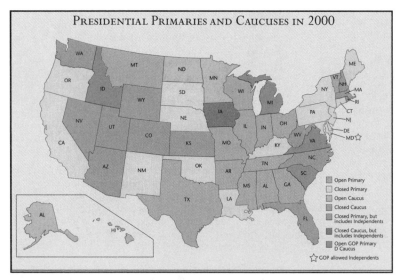

PRESIDENTIAL PRIMARIES AND CAUCUSES IN 2000

- Open Primary
- Closed Primary
- Open Caucus
- Closed Caucus
- Closed Primary, but includes Independents
- Closed Caucus, but includes Independents
- Open GOP Primary D Caucus
- ☆ GOP allowed Independents

in the majority of the primaries without risking the loss of too many committed delegates to other candidates.

The states that do not hold primaries use a form of district and state conventions generally known as a **caucus,** the Iowa caucus being the most prominent one. In these caucuses party members participate by the thousands in support of certain candidates, but their votes do not necessarily correspond to the state delegates' support for candidates in the national convention in the same way that primary votes usually do. In the course of the various caucus procedures, there is greater room for party leaders to influence the selection of delegates and their support for candidates. Despite the fact that

Loudspeaker equipment used on an automobile during the 1924 Coolidge campaign

President Truman in a parade in Seattle, Washington, in 1948

primaries have gained preeminence, presidential hopefuls cannot usually afford to ignore the caucus states. Candidates must campaign hard to win support, to influence the delegate selection, and, as always, to gain the media spotlight. Therefore, the results of both primaries and caucuses are watched carefully in light of their impact on party nominations.

The Purpose of Presidential Primaries—As we have seen, the party reform effort that resulted in presidential primaries sought to open up the nomination process to greater participation and to lessen the power of bosses to dictate the outcome. Primaries, therefore, have two basic purposes. First, the purpose of primaries is to open the field

up to more candidates, not just the ones that party insiders have approved. The primary season is long, expensive, and demanding, but it does permit a number of candidates the opportunity to demonstrate their vote-getting ability to the public. In addition, a central purpose of the presidential primary is to make national delegate selection more democratic. Since parties are regulated at the state rather that the national level, the primary process differs from state to state. We will take a general look, however, at primary voting and delegate-selection methods.

Ronald Reagan campaigning in 1980 with Nancy Reagan in Columbia, South Carolina

Iowa Caucus	Primaries in NH, DE, SC (R), AZ, MI, VA (R), WA Caucus in ND (R)	Primaries in CA, CT, GA, ME, MA, MO, NY, OH, RI, and VT Caucuses in HI (D), MN, ND Later Primaries in CO, UT, AZ (D), FL, LA, MS, OK, TN, TX, IL Later Caucuses in SC (D), WY, MI (D)	Primaries in PA, WI Caucus in KS (D)	Primaries in Washington, DC, IN, NC, NE, WV, OR, AR, ID, KY Conventions in AK, NV Caucuses in HI (R), KS (R)
JANUARY	FEBRUARY	MARCH	APRIL	MAY

In the presidential primary elections, held in the months before the national party conventions, the voters in each state usually choose the candidate they want their party to nominate for president. The delegates they send to the party national conventions must then support the candidates according to the dictates of the popular vote in the primaries. Rules vary from state to state. Either the winner receives the support of all of the state's delegates or else the leading candidates receive delegates according to a system based on the percentage of the vote they received. Thus, after every primary, the candidates can tally the delegate support they have won and compare their total with the number they need to win the nomination at the national convention (a simple majority of the total number of delegates). Because more than two-thirds of the delegates are selected in primary elections, choosing the nominee long before the convention is now typical.

George W. Bush campaigning in 2000 at Bob Jones University, Greenville, South Carolina

Primaries are conducted by the states, and they exist in several forms. **Closed primaries** are primaries in which the participants must be registered as members of one party and may vote for the candidates from only that one party in which they claim membership. In **open primaries,** the voters do not have to declare their party membership. They simply choose to support candidates from one party or the other.

The open primary certainly gives voters greater privacy and opportunity in their political participation, but party leaders have been particularly critical of this type of primary. Their major fear is **crossover voting.** When one party has a primary with a strong leading candidate who is certain of winning the nomination, its members could "cross over" to vote for a weak candidate in the opposing party's primary, and thereby cause confusion or greater difficulty in the opponent's nomination. Although the tactic has been attempted in some presidential primaries, the participants have been few and the results have proved inconsequential.

Although primary elections have increased popular participation in the selection of the presidential candidates, primaries have also created new problems for the parties. First, primary contests eliminate the ability of party leaders to help choose a moderate compromise candidate who would be the most acceptable with the party and most electable with the public. Vocal groups with specific interests can help push a candidate forward in the primaries without regard to his electability. If such a candidate without wide appeal among American voters is pushed toward nomination, the party is probably going to suffer a defeat in November. The Republican nomination of Barry Goldwater in 1964 and the Democratic nomination of George McGovern in 1972 are often-cited examples of this occurrence.

				Presidential Debates:	
				October 3 at J.F.K. Library	
				at U. Massachusetts, Boston	
				October 11 at Wake Forest U.	
Primaries in	**REPUBLICAN**	**DEMOCRATIC**		in North Carolina	
AL, MO, NJ, NM, SD	**NATIONAL**	**NATIONAL**		October 17 at Washington U.	
Convention in VA (D)	**CONVENTION**	**CONVENTION**	Campaigning	in St. Louis, Missouri	**ELECTION DAY**
JUNE	**JULY**	**AUGUST**	**SEPTEMBER**	**OCTOBER**	**NOVEMBER**

Another problem is that the primaries encourage each faction of the party to support its candidate for the primary election enthusiastically and devotedly. This can create wide divisions in the party that may be difficult to reconcile when the nomination falls to just one of the candidates. The result can be the creation of a splinter party, such as that initiated by John Anderson's break with the Republicans in 1980. Not only does that party risk some disunity, but additional factions also drain financial resources that could be best used in the general election.

The Course of Presidential Primaries—The early primaries and caucuses have become a key to party nominations. Media attention gained by candidates with good showings in the first few contests helps to propel those early leaders on to more primary victories. It also prompts more financial support for those candidates who quickly win a reputation for leading the race.

Although the Republican Party had some earlier caucuses in 1988, the stretch of primaries traditionally begins with the Iowa caucus and the New Hampshire primary. Beginning in 2004, the Iowa caucus and the New Hampshire primary were held in January, with other states' primaries and caucuses held after February 3. Prior to the caucuses and primary, an array of candidates crisscross these two states for months of campaigning in shopping malls, roadside diners, and high school gymnasiums. These initial tests, however, begin a rapid process of elimination. As the numbers come in from Iowa and New Hampshire, the media are quick to establish certain candidates as front-runners, others as impressive challengers, and still more as hopeless causes. Once this starting lineup is assessed, the reporters continue to interpret every step throughout the remaining four months of scheduled primaries and caucuses.

Some have criticized the Iowa caucus and New Hampshire primary because these states are not representative of most of the nation. They have relatively small populations without any large cities. These states are more rural, and there are fewer minorities. However, it must be added that no state is perfectly representative of the nation, and these states are in fact more representative than some, such as Nevada and Alaska. Possibly the biggest problem has been for the Democratic Party, whose activists tend to support more liberal candidates in these primaries. In fact, the Democratic Party has found itself with several candidates that are more liberal than its mainstream party members in recent years, at least in part because of the early support gained in these states. George McGovern was boosted to the Democratic nomination in 1972 by a win in the New Hampshire primary, and Michael Dukakis's New Hampshire win in 1988 helped set him in front of a crowded field of contenders.

However, it is not a foregone conclusion that early primaries will spell the success or the doom of a particular candidate. Bill Clinton lost the 1992 New Hampshire presidential primary but used the following primaries to rebound and capture the Democratic nomination. John McCain won the 2000 New Hampshire presidential primary but lost the Republican nomination.

The Democratic parties in the southern states tried to thwart the impact of Iowa and New Hampshire in the 1988 primaries by combining many of their primaries on one day. That "Super Tuesday" on March 8 offered primaries in fourteen southern states and held a large number of delegates for the winners. The southern states hoped that this prize would help swing a more conservative candidate

287

toward nomination despite any advantage gained by liberals in Iowa and New Hampshire. The South's hopes did not materialize, however, largely because of the tremendous African American vote captured by Jesse Jackson. That vote probably diverted strength from moderate candidates and allowed Michael Dukakis to continue as the front-runner. A similar strategy in the 2000 election prompted a number of big states to move their primaries up to March 7, and it was called "Titanic Tuesday." In 2002 the Democratic Party proposed a plan leading toward a national primary day on which as many as forty-eight states could hold Democratic primaries.

National Convention

National party conventions began in the 1830s and continue to be the means of formally nominating presidential candidates and regulating party organization. Until the rise of the primaries brought large numbers of committed delegates to the gatherings, the conventions were often scenes of political bargaining and backslapping as party bosses or campaign leaders sought more support for their candidates. In recent years, however, a leading candidate has usually entered each convention with enough support from delegates won in primaries to assure him the nomination and to remove the need for intense negotiation. Nevertheless, the national conventions remain colorful affairs that elicit a wave of support for the party nominee in the general election campaign.

Convention Preparations—Choosing the site of the party convention is an important step. In the past certain cities were often selected as a way of enticing the pivotal states in which they are located to swing their November votes to the party ticket. Now the committee members who make the choice for the party are usually most concerned with locating it in a place with an appropriately large convention center and ample hotels, restaurants, and entertainment for the delegates, reporters, campaign workers, and the curious who will flood the city for nearly a week.

The conventions have become expensive productions, and until the 1970s most of the money came from cities and businesses in efforts to convince the party to locate its meeting in their quarters. The ethical questions raised by this kind of fundraising prompted the federal government to begin allotting a large sum for each of the national party conventions.

Conventions for both parties normally meet in either July or August before the November election. Preparations begin well in

New York City: site of 2004 Republican National Convention

Boston: site of 2004 Democratic National Convention

advance, as does the work of the delegates assigned to a committee on resolutions. The committee draws up the initial party platform to be considered at the convention. The **party platform** is a formal statement of a party's position on current issues and is drafted at a party's national convention every four years.

Convention Participants—National conventions have become extremely large. In 2000 the Democratic convention in Los Angeles was attended by 4,339 delegates, and the Republican convention in Philadelphia had 2,066 delegates. The number each state is allowed to send varies in accordance with each party's equation for delegate representation. Republican National Convention delegates and alternates are elected by congressional district and state conventions. Democratic National Convention delegates and alternates are chosen by Democratic voters in each congressional district during the state primary election. Additional Democratic delegates include party leaders and elected officials.

The late 1960s and the 1970s saw some dramatic changes in the makeup of the convention delegates in both parties. Before that, most delegates were party leaders, politicians, businessmen, and other influential people in the state who could be in a position to use their influence for the party's good, monetarily or otherwise. Because most of these delegates were white males of middle age or older, women, young people, and minority groups began to protest their exclusion from party conventions. The Democrats were particularly troubled by the protests when they were fueled by the antiwar riots that broke out during their 1968 convention in Chicago. In reaction, the Democratic Party drew up guidelines for choosing more women, young people, and minorities to fill delegate slots. The efforts had to be modified, however, when the regulations brought in more than representative numbers of minorities and interest groups. Nevertheless, the changes opened the party conventions to people with less concern for party strength and unity and a greater desire to push for special concerns. The

Delegates at the 2008 Democratic convention cheer nominees Obama and Biden

Republican Party was able to gradually increase its number of women, young people, and minority delegates to adequate representative levels without imposing artificial guidelines for delegate selection. This process of democratization has weakened the traditional organizational mechanism of both major parties.

The Democratic Party instituted another change in its selection of delegates by including a specified percentage of **superdelegates,** party leaders and officeholders, to serve as uncommitted delegates. The superdelegate position was created out of a need to reform the reforms. The extreme segments of the Democratic Party had begun to send disproportionately large numbers of delegates to the conventions because of their ability to activate support in the primaries. The superdelegates are intended to provide a moderating influence on the outcome of the nomination by supporting the most electable candidate. The Democrats first introduced 568 superdelegates to the 1984 convention and by the 2000 convention had increased the number to 799. Republicans at their 2000 national convention began taking steps toward selecting superdelegates for their 2004 national convention.

Convention Procedures—The obvious purpose of the national conventions held by the major political parties has always been to nominate their party's candidates for president and vice president. The convention is also the place for adopting the

John McCain addresses the 2008 Republican convention

party platform and launching a unified campaign for the November elections.

The first day of the convention usually consists of routine organizational procedures. National party leaders and temporary officers lead in the session, giving welcomes to the delegates, making announcements about activities, and overseeing the election of the convention committees, which are made up of delegates attending the convention. The highlight of the first day is usually the **keynote address,** a speech made by a leading party member overflowing with enthusiasm for the party candidates in the election to come while criticizing the opposing party.

Further organizational tasks and the adoption of the party platform generally consume the following day or more of a convention. A committee on rules and order of business recommends the slate of procedural rules and the agenda for the convention. These guidelines are usually slight modifications of those from the previous convention and generally pass without difficulty, but certain changes or points can cause heated arguments on the convention floor before they gain approval. A credentials committee validates the claims of all the delegates to participate in the convention and prepares the official roll of delegates. Occasionally the authority of a delegate or even the entire delegation from a state is challenged and must be ruled on. Usually these are minor problems between rival party factions or personalities that can be settled easily with little consequence. Dwight Eisenhower, however, was able to take the Republican nomination from Robert Taft in 1952 when his forces contested the credentials of the Taft delegates from several southern states.

A committee on permanent organization recommends a list of permanent officers for the convention. One of these is the chairman, who will guide the remaining deliberations and activities. After those officers are approved and installed, the convention really gets down to business by adopting a party platform. The committee on platform and resolutions presents the draft it has prepared, and some debate usually follows. If much of the proposed platform provokes opposition, the proceedings may spill into the fourth day before compromises can be worked out and approved. Throughout these days of tending to party housekeeping chores, inspirational speeches are given to help keep enthusiasm alive.

Next comes the convention's premier event—the nomination of its presidential candidate. Both parties generally have the field narrowed down to one candidate before coming to the convention, but the proceedings remain colorful. Nomination speeches are generally made for several candidates. Many of these are simply attempts to honor popular party members with a speech rather than serious nominations. The speeches nominating the leading candidates or the chief contenders receive the most

Senator John F. Kennedy speaking at the 1960 Democratic convention in Los Angeles, California

Senator Lyndon B. Johnson at the Biltmore Hotel in Los Angeles, California, watching Speaker Sam Rayburn address the 1960 Democratic convention

attention. After hearing the glowing testimonials for these candidates, the convention delegates begin to vote state by state. In recent conventions the process has required only one ballot. Television reporters tally the votes as they are announced, and interested American viewers watch as the leading candidate reaches the number that puts him over the top. When this happens, the convention floor erupts into a melee of delegates romping, stomping, whooping, and whistling amid a downpour of confetti. Often the celebration continues for fifteen or twenty minutes until the hall can be quieted enough to allow the voting to conclude.

Even though first-ballot nominations have become normal, the failure to give one candidate a majority vote on the first roll call remains a possibility. The last time this happened was at the Democratic convention in 1952, when Adlai Stevenson was eventually nominated after three ballots. The fact that primaries now force many delegates to remain committed to certain candidates (at least for spe-

cific periods) precludes much of the bargaining for delegate votes that took place in the past. Therefore, if large blocks of committed delegates are split among three or more candidates, a convention could again reach an impasse, perhaps of the magnitude of the 1924 Democratic convention. In that year John W. Davis had to wait nine days for a total of 123 ballots before he finally won the nomination. Such a convention that requires lengthy balloting and an eventual settlement by bargaining and compromise is called a **brokered convention.** Any prolonged and heated situation like this usually impairs the party's unity and strength in the November election.

The final major item of business is nominating a vice-presidential candidate. In the past, party leaders made the choice, but now the decision is usually left to the presidential nominee. The choice generally centers on two considerations: geography and ideology. For example, an eastern liberal may team up with a western conservative to **balance the ticket,** which refers to a presidential candidate's choosing a running mate who can strengthen his chance of being elected due to specific ideology, geography, race, gender, or other characteristics. In 1960 John Kennedy, a Roman Catholic from Massachusetts, chose Lyndon Johnson, a Texas Protestant,

The Bidens and Obamas onstage at the 2008 Democratic convention

as his vice-presidential candidate to broaden his support within the party and throughout the country. In 2000 Vice President Al Gore, a Tennessee Protestant, chose Joe Lieberman, a Jewish senator from Connecticut, to balance his ticket.

Though balancing the ticket seems to make political sense in our diverse society, it can damage a candidate's credibility with his main supporters. This is particularly true when a candidate uses ideology to balance a ticket. In 1980 Ronald Reagan surprised his conservative supporters by choosing George Bush as his running mate. In his own campaign Bush had supported passage of the Equal Rights Amendment and had characterized Reagan's economic proposals as "voodoo economics." However, Reagan saw the choice of Bush for his running mate as a means of broadening his support within the Republican Party and of demonstrating his own strength by choosing his closest rival from the primaries.

Where is the party's primary candidate during the convention? The first and second days of the convention find the candidate on the campaign trail, working his way toward the convention. On the third day, the candidate arrives but does not come into the convention hall until his nomination is official. On the final convention day, the candidate gives an acceptance speech that encourages party unity and enthusiasm and then sends the delegates home to work vigorously for the success of the party ticket. With the party's nomination and full support in hand, the candidate begins increasing his campaign efforts as election day draws closer.

Debates

Debates between candidates have long been part of the American political process. The series of debates conducted in 1858 by Abraham Lincoln and Stephen A. Douglas, who were running for a U.S. Senate seat from Illinois, are the most famous. The Lincoln-Douglas debates over slavery and national expansion were pitched at a remarkably sophisticated level, considering the limited education of most of their audience.

Television changed everything. In 1960 John F. Kennedy and Richard Nixon were the first presidential candidates to broadcast their

Reagan-Mondale 1984 presidential debate

Bush-Gore 2000 presidential debate

292

debates on national television. Later studies revealed that four million voters decided whom to vote for while watching the debate. Three million of these voted for Kennedy. These decisions may have been based not on the intellectual content of the debate but on the appearance of the candidates—a well made-up Kennedy versus a haggard, washed-out Nixon who seemed to be in need of a shave. Kennedy himself said, "It was TV more than anything else that turned the tide."

In 2000 during the first debate between Al Gore and George W. Bush, Gore's mannerisms of sighing and rolling his eyes were thought to contribute to his slippage in the polls and ultimate defeat.

Section Review

1. What two forms of delegate selection are used in the presidential nominating process?
2. How do closed primaries differ from open primaries?
3. Which two states traditionally hold the earliest primary and caucus contests?
4. In recent years, what changes have taken place in the composition of national convention delegates?
5. What two basic considerations may influence how a ticket is "balanced"?

III. Election

After campaigning for as long as two years, the candidates who win their party nominations emerge from their conventions to run the final leg of their race—the **general election.** The election, held on the first Tuesday after the first Monday in November, determines not only which candidate will occupy the White House for the next four years but also which party will have preeminence in executive appointments and policymaking. At stake are history, leadership, and the most visible job in the world.

Campaign Strategy

A well-laid strategy is crucial to a successful campaign. Political strategists must shape the candidate's game plan, and much of that plan hinges on the fact that the electoral college is a winner-take-all system; if a candidate wins in a state by even a single popular vote, he receives all the electoral votes for that state. (Maine and Nebraska are exceptions.) Candidates therefore must campaign hardest in the states with the most electoral votes—New York, Texas, and California, for example. The goal is to capture at least 270 of the 538 electoral votes.

In 1960 Richard Nixon promised to visit all fifty states during his campaign. He kept his promise, but his strategy wasted valuable time in states that made only meager contributions to his electoral tally. Two basic considerations in any sound campaign strategy are the importance of targeting states with large numbers of electoral votes and campaigning hard in states where a close race could sweep the electoral votes either way. One factor in this strategy may be the selection of a running mate. As mentioned earlier, a vice-presidential candidate from a key state or region may help capture the vote there.

Addressing the issues that capture the public mind can be a great rallying point of support for a presidential contender. The candidate who is in touch with popular trends and attitudes and is able to shape them into a campaign issue will generally raise broad support for his program. On the other hand, a candidate whose ideas are out of touch with those of most voters faces an obvious difficulty. Walter Mondale's suggestion in 1984 that the government raise taxes to help reverse the growing deficit is an example of an idea that lacked popular support—and voters acted accordingly.

Campaign Slogans

It all began with "Tippecanoe and Tyler Too." Sure, there had been poems and songs in praise of presidential candidates before, but this one-line chant helped sweep William Henry Harrison, the hero of the Battle of Tippecanoe, into the White House in 1840. Harrison's victory at Tippecanoe represented flag-waving nationalism, and Tyler from Virginia represented southern sectionalism. Since then, campaign slogans have multiplied, adding their promises, accusations, insults, and idealism to the pandemonium of presidential races.

The word *slogan* comes from Gaelic words meaning "army call" or "battle cry," and campaigners have learned to use their slogans to rally voters to their cause or sound an attack against their opponent. "Fifty-four forty or fight" (Polk, 1844) and "Let us have peace" (Grant, 1868) both called men to the causes of their time. In 1924 the Democrats claimed that "A vote for Coolidge is a vote for chaos," and after three terms of FDR, Thomas Dewey declared that it was "Time for a change" in 1944.

Experts say that the best slogans usually have seven words or less, and many memorable campaign lines bear this out. Some are catchy phrases using rhyme or alliteration, "Keep Cool with Coolidge" (1924), "Win with Willkie"

(1940), and "All the way with LBJ" (Johnson, 1964). Others offer vague but attractive promises to the voters, such as prosperity: "A full dinner pail" (McKinley, 1896), "A chicken in every pot" (Hoover, 1928), "Happy days are here again" (Roosevelt, 1932); peace: "Return to Normalcy" (Harding, 1920), "Peace and freedom" (Nixon, 1960); and strength: "Let's make America great again" (Reagan, 1980). A few of these short sayings have been caustic. In 1884 the Republicans labeled the Democrats with "Rum, Romanism, and Rebellion"; and similarly, in 1952 the Democrats were tagged with "Communism, corruption, and Korea." In 1988 the Republicans poked fun at the diminutive Democratic candidate, Michael Dukakis, by twisting an old expression: "Beware of Greeks wearing lifts."

Probably the most venomous of all popular slogans was one used against Grover Cleveland in 1884. The ditty "Ma! Ma! Where's my pa? Gone to the White House. Ha! Ha! Ha!" accused him of fathering an illegitimate child. The Democrats did not take the jab lying down, however. They responded against Cleveland's opponent with a rousing "Blaine, Blaine, James G. Blaine, the continental liar from the state of Maine!"

Slogans have been clever: "We Polk'd you in 1844; we shall Pierce you in 1852"; some were ironic: "He kept us out of war" (Wilson, 1916); some were rude: "We don't want Eleanor either" (1940); and some were even comic: "Madly for Adlai" (Stevenson, 1952). Some have backfired, like the Goldwater line in 1964, "In your heart you know he's right." Responses ranged from "Far right!" to "In your guts you know he's nuts." A few have greatly extended the popularity of a candidate. "I like Ike" worked so well for Eisenhower in 1952 that he used it again with success in 1956.

More recent campaign slogans include "Kinder, gentler nation" (George Bush, 1988), "Don't stop thinking about tomorrow" (Clinton, 1992), "Ross for Boss" (Ross Perot, 1992), "Building a bridge to the 21st century" (Clinton, 1996), "Prosperity and progress" (Gore, 2000), and "Leave no child behind" and "Reformer with results" (George W. Bush, 2000).

"Another voice for Cleveland"

Although it illustrates how little things and even trivial things may shape the voters' thinking, a catchy slogan may actually have an important influence on the outcome of a presidential election. Old "Tippecanoe" surely started something, giving us one of the more colorful and effective weapons in our political arsenal.

Election Day

After all the hands have been shaken, stump speeches delivered, and television commercials aired, election day is the opportunity for the voters to get in the last word. The simple civic rite of voting is one of our most important privileges. While

many so-called free elections throughout the world are marked by violence and widespread corruption, Americans, by contrast, go to their polling places and vote unhindered and unthreatened. Collectively, some of the most powerful decisions of our day are made not in the Oval Office, or the halls of Congress, or even the Supreme Court chamber; they are made in voting booths in fire stations, school cafeterias, and church basements.

Exit Polls—Amid the excitement of voters casting their ballots on election day to elect America's next president or fill congressional, state, and local offices, the news media use exit polls to try to predict the outcome. **Exit polls** are polls taken of sample voters by various polling groups as voters leave their polling places. By late Tuesday evening, the news media begin to make their projections, tallying the expected number of electoral votes each presidential candidate has secured as well as keeping an eye on any close congressional races that might affect or change the majority party in either the U.S. House or Senate. These media projections are reasonably accurate. However, if it is a close race with several neck-and-neck contests in key states, it may be nearly dawn before a winner is announced. In the 2000 presidential election, it was a month before the elected winner was known.

In recent years these early media projections in presidential primaries and elections have brought criticism. With the time-zone differences, East Coast polls close earlier. TV news anchors have often called states for a specific candidate before the polls closed on the West Coast. Following the 1980 and 1984 elections, some thought West Coast voters had been influenced by these media predictions. The media's incorrect call of Florida twice on election night in the 2000 presidential election continued to bring criticism of the media and their use of exit polling. Also, the growing number of absentee voters increases the possibility that exit-poll results will be distorted.

Responsibility and a Civil Right—Though voting is one of the most important civil rights, it is also surely one of the most neglected. Throughout the 1990s and into 2000, less than half of the electorate bothered to vote. Christians who are able should make every effort not to be numbered with the apathetic. George Jean Nathan observed, "Bad officials are elected by good citizens who do not vote." As a matter of stewardship, Christians should use their ballots to make choices for the best government possible.

Presidential Election 2000

Tuesday, November 7, 2000

7:00 p.m. EST
TV networks begin to project winners of states across country.

8:00 p.m. EST
Gore is declared winner in Florida, Michigan, and Illinois.

8:47 p.m. EST
Gore is declared winner in Pennsylvania.

9:15 p.m. EST
Bush is declared winner in Ohio.

10:00 p.m. EST
Gore's Florida win is retracted; networks say too close to call.

11:00 p.m. EST
California, with 54 electoral votes, is called for Gore.

Wednesday, November 8, 2000

12:10 a.m. EST
Gore wins Washington. Bush wins Arkansas. Focus on Florida.

2:17 a.m. EST
Bush is declared winner of Florida.

2:30 a.m. EST
Gore calls Bush to congratulate him on his victory.

3:00 a.m. EST
Bush's lead in Florida drops.

3:30 a.m. EST
Gore calls Bush to retract his congratulations.

4:30 a.m. EST
Networks say Bush may not be the winner (246 electoral votes for Bush and 260 for Gore, with Oregon undeclared and Florida too close to call).

November 10, 2000, through January 20, 2001

Ballot hand-count in Florida counties is requested by Gore Democrats.

Nov. 10, 2000—Florida's unofficial results show Bush leading.

Nov. 12, 2000—Volusia County begins recount; Bush Republicans ask federal court to stop recount.

Nov. 13, 2000—U.S. district judge refuses to stop manual recount.

Nov. 15, 2000—Florida's secretary of state asks Florida Supreme Court to stop hand counts. Court denies request.

Nov. 17, 2000—Midnight deadline for receiving overseas absentee ballots. Florida Supreme Court stops secretary of state from vote certification.

Nov. 21, 2000—Florida Supreme Court rules recounts can continue, with Nov. 27 as new deadline.

Nov. 22, 2000—Bush lawyers file two appeals with U.S. Supreme Court to stop Florida manual recount. Florida secretary of state certifies count showing Bush ahead by 537 votes and declares Bush the winner. Bush gets transition team ready, but Clinton administration refuses office space and money for transition until election is settled.

Dec. 1, 2000—U.S. Supreme Court begins hearing arguments from both sides (first time high court has ever intervened in a presidential election).

Dec. 4, 2000—U.S. Supreme Court sends the Florida Supreme Court's ruling back to the state for clarification.

Dec. 7, 2000—One month since election. No decision by Florida Supreme Court on Gore's request for manual recount of disputed ballots.

Dec. 8, 2000—Bush team files appeals with U.S. Supreme Court to halt any recounts and overrule Florida court's ordered recount of Miami-Dade County.

Dec. 9, 2000—U.S. Supreme Court, in 5-4 vote, orders a halt to Florida hand counts.

Dec. 12, 2000—U.S. Supreme Court rules that Florida Supreme Court violated constitutional protections in its order for manual recount of thousands of disputed ballots. Ruling reverses Florida court decision.

Dec. 13, 2000—George W. Bush is officially the winner and Al Gore concedes defeat.

Dec. 18, 2000—Electoral college casts votes for the president.

Jan. 20, 2001—George W. Bush is inaugurated as 43rd president of the United States.

Judge Robert Rosenberg examining a disputed ballot at the Broward County Courthouse in Fort Lauderdale, Florida

U.S. Supreme Court

Texas governor George W. Bush with his parents in Austin, Texas, watching the election returns

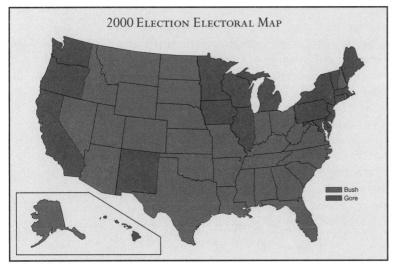

2000 ELECTION ELECTORAL MAP

Bush
Gore

Electoral College

Normally, within a day or two the election outcome is confirmed by the preliminary election counts, but the victorious candidate is not technically elected to office until the electoral college votes and its ballots are counted by the Senate.

Historically—During the Constitutional Convention of 1787, the founders established a structure for elections under which only the House of Representatives would be directly elected. Senators would be elected by state legislatures (changed by the Seventeenth Amendment in 1913), and the president would be elected by means of the **electoral college.** Article II, Section 1 of the Constitution details how the process is to work. The number of electoral votes that each state has is determined by its total number of House and Senate members. For example, Rhode Island has four electoral votes (two House, two Senate). Texas, on the other hand, has thirty-four electoral votes (thirty-two House, two Senate). The popular vote in each state determines which candidate will receive the state's electoral votes.

Why did the founding fathers believe the electoral college to be necessary? Their intention was to give smaller (less populous) states fair representation and to protect the rights of the few against the rights of the many. Without the safeguard of the electoral college, just a few populous states with large urban areas could determine the outcome of a presidential election.

Today—Article II, Section 1, Clause 2 of the Constitution states, "Each State shall appoint, in such manner as the legislature thereof may direct, a number of electors." The method of choosing electors varies from state to state. Most are chosen through a political party's state convention during an election year, by the party's executive committee, or in the primary. When a party's candidate wins the popular vote in a state, then the party's electors become the ones who will participate in the electoral college vote.

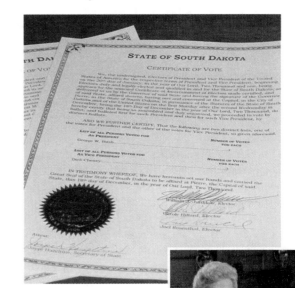

The Certificate of Vote

South Dakota Secretary of State Hazeltine displays a completed certificate.

In most states, the winner of the popular vote wins all of that state's electoral votes. Maine and Nebraska are exceptions. There, the electors are divided according to the winner in each congressional district. In twenty-seven states, the electors are legally bound to support the winner. New Mexico, North Carolina, South Carolina, Oklahoma, and Washington carry this a step further, adding a penalty for not supporting the winner. Even in states that do not legally require it, electors generally vote for the candidate who won in their state. However, occasionally an elector shows his independence by voting for someone else. In 1988, for example, one West Virginia elector voted for Lloyd Bentsen instead of Michael Dukakis.

The electoral college has 538 total votes (435 from the House of Representatives, 100 from the Senate, and 3 from Washington, D.C.). To win, a candidate must gain 270 of those votes. Currently, the states with the most electoral votes are California (55), New York (31), Texas (34), Florida (27), Pennsylvania (21), Illinois (21), and Ohio (20). A national census, taken every ten years, is the only thing that can change a state's number of votes. If a state's population changes, so does its number of representatives and thus its number of electoral votes.

Congress has ruled that the electors meet in their respective states to cast their ballots on the Monday after the second Wednesday in December. The ballots are sent to the Senate, where, in joint session with the House, the votes are counted after the new session of Congress convenes in January. The president of the Senate, the U.S. vice president, presides. Vice President George Bush was able to announce his own election to the presidency in this meeting in 1989, and he was the first sitting vice president to do so since Martin Van Buren in 1837. After the 2000 election Vice President Al Gore got to preside over his loss when he announced the election of his opponent, George W. Bush. If no candidate wins a majority, the House of Representatives chooses the president from among the three leading candidates, with each state casting one vote. By House rule, each state's vote is allotted to the candidate preferred by a majority of the state's House delegation. If there is a tie within a delegation, that state's vote is not counted. Twice presidential elections have been thrown into the House of Representatives. In 1800 Thomas Jefferson was chosen over Aaron Burr, and in 1824 John Quincy Adams was chosen over Andrew Jackson and William H. Crawford.

Section Review

1. By law, when are national elections held during an election year?
2. How does the electoral college arrangement influence campaign strategy?
3. What are exit polls?
4. What determines the number of electoral votes a state receives? Does this number change? If so, why?
5. How are electors chosen for the electoral college?

IV. Inauguration

"I do solemnly swear (or affirm) that I will faithfully execute the Office of President of the United States, and will to the best of my ability, preserve, protect and defend the Constitution of the United States."

—*Article II, Section 1, The United States Constitution*

Illustration of Washington taking his first oath of office

After a United States presidential election, it is the ordinary that is so extraordinary. Despite the political rivalry and vehement rhetoric, despite disagreements with friends or the disappointment of a hard-fought loss, life goes on. Republicans and Democrats, independents and indifferents, after the election are all Americans. There may be bitterness, but there is no bloodshed; there may be regret but no revenge. In Washington a transition team, not a military coup, discusses the transfer of power. The most visible symbol of this quiet, orderly, unifying transition is the president's inauguration.

Traditions

Many inaugural traditions were established with the first inauguration. Washington gave a special speech after his first swearing-in that established the **inaugural address.** For Washington's second oath of office, the tradition of Supreme Court justices administering the oath was begun. With later administrations came more traditions. Jefferson was the first to be sworn in as president in Washington, D.C. After Jefferson took the oath of office for his second term he mounted his horse and road back to the White House, followed by a large group of legislators, citizens, and others. Later presidents continued this custom of inaugural parades. Madison and his wife, Dolley, attended

the first official inaugural ball. In 1817 the inauguration ceremony was moved outdoors. It had been held in the House of Representatives, but Henry Clay, Speaker of the House, refused to allow senators to bring their cushioned chairs into the "people's" chamber. To Clay's thinking, such plush furnishings clashed terribly with the "décor" of republicanism. A compromise was reached so that the new executive now stands before the nation while taking the oath of office.

Transfer of Power

When Washington gave up the office of the presidency to John Adams in 1797, the first presidential transition of power occurred. Today, the transition of power begins shortly after the presidential election. After winning at the polls on election day, the president-elect has less than eleven weeks to develop his new administration. The transition process has three general parts: the use of executive orders and pardons by the outgoing administration; the allotment of funds to aid the transfer of power; and the changeover to the incoming administration's personnel.

***Orders and Pardons*—Executive orders** are presidential directives or actions that have the effect and force of law. Usually they are directed toward federal government agencies and officials, not citizens or the private sector. The Constitution is not specific regarding executive orders. Article II merely states that "the executive power shall be vested in the President of the United States." The President's reason for using executive orders is founded on personal, practical, or political reasons, and the orders are implemented without input or interference from Congress. This helps the president secure policymaking control by locking the next administration into specific policies and procedures. Some presidents use executive orders as a means of further establishing their presidential legacy.

President Clinton on his last day as president

The president also may issue pardons. Presidential **pardons** are issued by the president in order to release a convicted person from the remainder of his or her sentence. President Washington pardoned the Whiskey Rebellion rebels in 1795, and President Andrew Johnson pardoned Confederate rebels in 1868. More recent presidential pardons include Ford's pardon of Nixon in 1974, Carter's pardon of Vietnam draft dodgers in 1977, and Clinton's controversial last-minute pardons of 130 individuals, including some in prison for drug charges or tax evasion.

Presidential Transition Fund—Prior to 1963 presidential transition expenses were mainly funded by the political party organization of the incoming president and volunteer staff. After realizing the importance of presidential transitions and their effect upon government, Congress passed the Presidential Transition Act in 1963. Using some of the funds allocated by this act, the General Services Administration (GSA) coordinates the orientation of the president-elect's cabinet nominees and top executive branch personnel. Transition funds are available as soon as a presidential winner is declared and continue to be available until one month after the inauguration.

President George W. Bush sworn in as the 43rd president in January 2001

Changeover of Personnel—When a new administration transitions into power, over seven thousand civil service jobs in the executive and legislative branches of the federal government are opened up. These positions include heads of executive branch agencies; undersecretaries; assistant secretaries; directors of bureaus and services; and members and chairpersons of various boards, commissions, and committees.

Event

Official Date—The founding fathers designed the first presidential inauguration to take place on March 4, 1789, which was the same day the Constitution went into effect. March 4 continued to be Inauguration Day until 1933, when the crisis of the Great Depression led to a change. Americans wanted quick action from a new president and Congress, so Congress adopted the Twentieth Amendment, which changed the date to January 20. President Franklin D. Roosevelt was the first president to be inaugurated under the new amendment on January 20, 1937.

Location—Washington's first presidential inauguration took place on the balcony of Federal Hall in New York City. His second inauguration was in the Senate Chamber of Congress Hall in Philadelphia. Adams took the presidential oath in

President George Bush sworn in as the 41st president in January 1989

U.S. President Harry Truman, left, and his successor, president-elect Dwight D. Eisenhower, leave the White House in an open car for inauguration ceremonies in Washington, D.C., on January 20, 1953.

the House of Representatives Chamber of Philadelphia's Congress Hall. Once Washington, D.C., became the United States capital, most inaugurations took place in different locations within the Capitol Building. Depending on the circumstances, other places have been the site. James Monroe, the first president to take his oath of office outside, was inaugurated in front of the Old Brick Capitol, which is now the site of the U.S. Supreme Court Building. After President Lincoln was assassinated,

Andrew Johnson was sworn in at the Kirkwood Hotel in Washington, D.C. After Harding's death Coolidge took the oath of office at his family home in Vermont; his father, a notary public, administered the oath. After President Kennedy's assassination, Lyndon Johnson took the oath of office in the conference room aboard *Air Force One* at Love Field, Dallas, Texas. Most presidential inaugurations have taken place on the East Portico of the U.S. Capitol. But in 1981 President Reagan moved the ceremony to the terrace of the West Front of the Capitol, which looks up the Mall toward the Washington Monument. All presidents since then have used the West Front site.

The 1933 inauguration of Franklin D. Roosevelt

Inaugural Ceremony—Today the inaugural ceremony includes more than just the president's taking the oath of office. The ceremony may begin with a music prelude. The assembly is called to order, and welcoming remarks are given. A prayer and a musical selection may be included. The vice president-elect takes his oath of office. The president-elect takes his oath of office and gives the inaugural address. There is a closing prayer or benediction, and the national anthem may be played. Some elements of the ceremony vary according to the new president's wishes.

John F. Kennedy's inauguration on January 20, 1960

President and Mrs. Reagan in the inaugural parade in 1981

Inaugural Events—Inaugural activities span more than just one day. A few days prior to the swearing-in ceremony, the celebration of a newly elected president begins complete with balls, fire-works, and other special events. On the day of the inauguration, the president-elect may begin with a prayer service as President George W. Bush did in 2001 at St. John's Episcopal Church. Midmorning the president-elect and his wife come for coffee at the White House with the president and First Lady. Also in attendance are the vice president-elect, his wife, the vice president, his wife, the Congressional Inaugural Committee, and House and Senate members. The president-elect and president share a limousine to the Capitol for the official transfer of power. Following the ceremony, the new president, along with family, staff, members of Congress, and others, have a luncheon in the Capitol. During this time period, the former president's possessions are being moved out of the White House and the new first family is being moved in. Usually around 2:00 in the afternoon the inaugural parade begins. The president, First Lady, and others ride or walk part of the parade route to the reviewing stand, where

President George W. Bush and Commandant James M. Loy watching the inaugural parade in 2001

they watch the remainder of the parade. The evening includes multiple inaugural balls around the Washington, D.C., area. The president and First Lady visit each ball for a short period of time. The vice president and his wife also attend each ball. (The ball gown worn by the First Lady to the inaugural balls is exhibited at the Smithsonian.) The following day the president and First Lady open the White House, greet the public for a special tour, and begin a new chapter in America's history.

The Oval Office

At some point on Inauguration Day after being inaugurated President of the United States, the president enters his new office. The Oval Office is the place where he will consult with

heads of state, his staff, diplomats, and other dignitaries. At times he will address American citizens or the world by television or radio. On his first day the new president may also find a letter or note left for him from his predecessor in the Oval Office. President George W. Bush was left the same note his father, George Bush, had left President Clinton when President Clinton assumed the duties of the presidency.

The first Oval Office was constructed in 1909 in the center of the south side of the West Wing. In 1934 it was moved to its present location on the southeast corner overlooking the Rose Garden. With each new president, the Oval Office décor changes. The only office features that do not change are the original white marble mantel from the 1909 Oval Office, the two flags behind the president's desk (the U.S. flag and the presidential flag), and the presidential seal in the ceiling.

The desk the president chooses to use has traditionally been the Resolute desk, which was made from the wood of the HMS *Resolute,* an abandoned British ship found by an American vessel and returned to the Queen of England in 1856 as a sign of friendship and goodwill. After the ship was retired, Queen Victoria authorized the desk to be made and in 1880 had it presented to President Rutherford B. Hayes. Every president since Hayes has used it except for Johnson, Nixon, and Ford.

President John F. Kennedy's Oval Office

President Ronald Reagan's Oval Office

President Bill Clinton's Oval Office

The desk has been altered over the years by a few presidents. President Franklin Roosevelt had the kneehole fitted with a panel carved with the presidential coat-of-arms. President Ronald Reagan asked that the desk be put on a two-inch base to accommodate his six-foot, two-inch height. The desk was also made famous by a photo taken of President Kennedy's son, John Jr., peeking out from behind the kneehole panel.

Section Review

1. What is the most visible symbol of a presidential transition?
2. Whose administration began the tradition of Supreme Court justices administering the presidential oath of office?
3. What are the three parts of the presidential transfer of power?
4. What established the date for the presidential inauguration, and when is the inauguration to occur?

Chapter Review

Terms

direct primaries
caucus
closed primaries
open primaries
crossover voting
party platform

superdelegates
keynote address
brokered convention
balance the ticket
general election
exit polls

electoral college
inaugural address
executive orders
pardons

Content Questions

1. What disadvantages do presidential primaries pose for the parties?

2. How may a presidential nominee use his vice-presidential choice to unify his party?

3. Why is it important for a party's candidate to occupy the White House?

4. Why is the electoral college important?

5. How would executive orders and presidential pardons strengthen or weaken a president's legacy?

Application Questions

1. Which qualifications for the presidency have you already met, and which ones do you still lack?

2. What is the most likely route your career would take if you hoped one day to become president of the United States?

3. A number of critics have charged that election night news coverage and the use of exit polls should be restricted because of their adverse influence on voter turnout. Do you agree or disagree with these critics? Why?

4. Should Christians vote for candidates with whom they do not completely agree? Why or why not?

5. If the founding fathers had not included the electoral college in electing the president, how would presidential campaigns and elections be different in the state in which you live?

6. If you were to be inaugurated president of the United States, what would be your inaugural theme, what events would you want to include in your inaugural ceremony, where would you be sworn in, and what topics would your inaugural address include?

President Kennedy delivering the State of the Union address, January 14, 1963

I pray Heaven to bestow the best of Blessings on this House and all that shall hereafter inhabit it. May none but honest and wise Men ever rule under this roof.

> —*From a letter by John Adams on his second night in the White House*

The president occupies a position of tremendous prestige, power, and responsibility. To provide a better understanding of America's highest office, this chapter will examine the nature of the office and forces that have shaped it.

I. Presidential Powers

Chief Executive

"The executive power shall be vested in a President of the United States of America. . . . He shall take care that the laws be faithfully executed." Thus, Article II outlines an important task of the presidency, that of chief executive.

In seeing that laws are "faithfully executed," the president administers and enforces the law through the various departments under his

Theodore Roosevelt stumping in 1903; his forceful personality did much to shape the nation and the presidency.

control. For example, a bill passed by Congress raising the interstate speed limit to 75 miles per hour, if approved by the president, would be signed into law, and the implementation and enforcement of that change would be carried out through an executive agency—in this case the Department of Transportation.

As chief executive the president also administers a vast bureaucracy, which consists of the Executive Office of the President, fifteen cabinet departments, and a wide range of government agencies and corporations. All the cabinet secretaries and under-secretaries, and most of the other agencies' top officials (with the exception of the regulatory commissions), are under the direct responsibility of the chief executive. However, with over two million employees in the executive branch, sheer size makes controlling the bureaucracy difficult even for the president.

Since 1969 the chief executive's salary had been $200,000 per year. In September of 1999 President Clinton signed legislation increasing the president's salary to $400,000 per year. This salary is also taxable. In addition, the president receives free housing (White House), $50,000 for expenses, a $19,000 official entertainment account, $100,000 for travel costs, medical and dental services, an annual $150,000 lifetime pension, and $150,000 annually to maintain a staff after he retires from office. Although these figures certainly provide a comfortable living for the president, when compared with the salaries of corporate executives, the president's pay is reasonable. Being president means hard work, great responsibility, and incredible pressure. Harry Truman, for example, generally put in a seventy-hour week during his White House years. Given the demands of the office, the chief executive well earns his salary.

Presidential Air Travel

Over the years the necessity for rapid travel for the president has increased. Transportation vehicles for the president have included the *Ferdinand Magellan,* a custom-built Pullman railroad car; presidential yachts; specially equipped limousines; and air transportation by plane and helicopter. Today the president's main methods of air travel are via *Air Force One* and *Marine One.*

Air Force One: President Franklin D. Roosevelt in 1944 sought the creation of the Presidential Pilot Office (now called the Presidential Airlift Group) to provide air transportation for the president and his staff. For the next twenty years four-engine, propeller-driven aircraft were used. The first jet aircraft, a Boeing 707, was purchased in 1962 to be used as *Air Force One.* Today, the *Air Force One* fleet consists of two specifically outfitted 747-200B aircraft, and home base is at Andrews Air Force Base, Maryland. The aircraft provides the president and his staff with various services, including communications systems (eighty-seven different

Air Force One   **307**

Marine One

back of the plane, and VIPs sit up front. The more important the passenger, the closer he or she sits to the president. The plane is a military plane and is overseen by the air force, with every flight considered a military mission. It has highly classified defense capabilities, including antimissile devices. The designated *Air Force One* jet is the president's primary source of air travel, but when the president boards any air force aircraft, it is then called *Air Force One* for the duration of the flight.

Marine One: Since 1957 the pilots of marine squadron HMX-1 have been responsible for providing all helicopter transportation at home and overseas for the president, the vice president, the president's cabinet members, and foreign dignitaries when directed by the White House Military Office. When the president is onboard any rotary-wing aircraft, the call sign used is *Marine One*. Currently, the primary helicopter for presidential use is the Sikorsky VH-3D (Sea King). *Marine One* has a crew of four and can seat up to fifteen passengers. It has a cruising speed of 136 miles per hour, a range of 600 nautical miles, and a ceiling of 14,700 feet.

phone lines with twenty-eight that are secure and encrypted), an executive suite, the president's office, two galleys that can provide up to one hundred meals, and medical equipment. Many items onboard, including seat-belt buckles, pillows, blankets, napkins, and cups, display the Presidential Seal. To pilot *Air Force One,* one must have a spotless record, two thousand hours in the cockpit, and worldwide flight experience. The aircraft can fly halfway around the world without refueling and can provide for more than seventy passengers. Reporters are seated in the

AIR FORCE ONE
Artist's Rendering

WORK ROOM

CONFERENCE ROOM

COMMUNICATION CENTER

LOUNGE

COCKPIT

REAR SEATING

SEATING

GALLEY

PRESIDENTIAL SUITE

Commander in Chief

One of the most important and most influential roles of the president is his position as commander in chief of the military. His position underscores an important national principle that civilian power controls military power. This fact was well illustrated in 1951 during the Korean War, when President Truman dismissed Douglas MacArthur, the five-star general of the army, for insubordination. MacArthur had advocated bombing Communist China and expanding the war to bring a death blow to Asian communism. The president disagreed, and when the general made the dispute public, Truman dismissed him. This incident also illustrates the unpopularity that sometimes accompanies the actions of the commander in chief. MacArthur returned home to a hero's welcome, and while members of Congress lavished praise on the general, they also called for the impeachment of President Truman.

President Nixon greets his troops during a visit to South Vietnam.

The commander in chief uses his power to respond quickly during an emergency. The earliest example of this was President Washington's use of troops to subdue the Whiskey Rebellion in Pennsylvania. A more recent example of the exercise of this power occurred after the destruction of the World Trade Center in New York City on September 11, 2001. President George W. Bush responded with the formation of a seventeen-nation coalition of forces whose aim was to break up the Taliban terrorist network and stop any further terrorist activities. Operation Enduring Freedom began on October 17, 2001, with the bombing of Taliban centers in Afghanistan. President Bush's power to commit United States troops stemmed from the 1973 War Powers Resolution, which states under Purpose and Policy, Section 2(c):

> The Constitutional powers of the President as Commander-in-Chief to introduce United States Armed Forces into hostilities, or into situations where imminent involvement in hostilities is clearly indicated by the circumstances, are exercised only pursuant to (1) a declaration of war, (2) specific statutory authorization, or (3) a national emergency created by attack upon the United States, its territories or possessions, or its armed forces.

The president also has a vast national security and intelligence apparatus at his disposal with which he carries out **covert operations,** activities unknown to the public, and to a large extent, even Congress. Congress votes to give vast amounts of money to these agencies—of which the Central Intelligence Agency (CIA) is the best known—but provides almost no oversight of them. The Kennedy administration's support of an invasion at the Bay of Pigs; the Reagan administration's support of anticommunist forces in Nicaragua, Afghanistan, and Angola; George Bush's administration's involvement in Panama and the Persian Gulf; and the Clinton and George W. Bush administrations' war on terrorism have depended heavily on the CIA to carry out executive directives.

President Ford and Egyptian president Anwar Sadat discuss a Mideast peace proposal in Salzburg in 1975.

Diplomatic Leader

The constitutional basis for the president's role as diplomatic leader is also found in Article II, Section 2, Clause 2, where we read that the president "shall have power, by and with the advice and consent of the Senate, to make treaties, provided two thirds of the senators present concur; and he shall nominate, and by and with the advice and consent of the Senate, shall appoint ambassadors, other public ministers and consuls." Just as in his role as legislative leader the president shares power with Congress, so also as diplomatic leader the president must share foreign policy responsibilities; however, his authority and advantages in this sphere remain formidable.

President Eisenhower and French president Charles de Gaulle arrive at Camp David.

In initiating and implementing treaties or other foreign policy activities, the president has available important information and management resources—the State Department, the National Security Council, and the Central Intelligence Agency. Given these resources, along with a measure of political cooperation with the Senate, the president generally gains approval for treaties. There have been, however, notable exceptions to this rule. Woodrow Wilson, for example, failed to gain Senate ratification for the Treaty of Versailles in 1919, and President Carter was unable to persuade the Senate to approve SALT II in 1979.

In addition to treaty-making powers, the president also has the power of **executive agreement,** whereby he can have a written "understanding" with another head of state to carry out a particular action. Congress has little or no power over executive agreements as long as an agreement does not violate the law. Executive agreements underscore the independence that the president has in implementing foreign policy. Lyndon Johnson used executive agreements to escalate the war in Vietnam, and Richard Nixon ended American involvement in that country through an executive agreement with the North Vietnamese.

Camp David

During World War II President Franklin D. Roosevelt sought an area near Washington, D.C., to be used for a presidential retreat. Officials from the National Park Service looked for a location that would be close to Washington, at an elevation to provide coolness because of FDR's health, and where presidential security would be ensured. Three sites were suggested, and on April 24, 1942, President Roosevelt inspected two sites in Maryland. Two days later a site in the Catoctin Mountains had been selected, and FDR's ideas for construction of the retreat were submitted. On May 11 construction began. Roosevelt named the retreat "Shangri-La," in reference to the mountain kingdom in James Hilton's book *Lost Horizon*. President Eisenhower renamed the facility Camp David (in honor of his grandson) because he thought Shangri-La too unusual and different.

Over the years many presidents have taken advantage of Camp David to discuss war plans, negotiate peace, and entertain foreign leaders. There FDR discussed war strategy with British Prime Minister Churchill, and President Nixon met with Soviet Premier Brezhnev. President Carter held meetings that led to the signing of the Camp David Accords, and President Clinton hosted a Mid-East Summit. After September 11, 2001, President George W. Bush met with his National Security Advisors at Camp David.

President Nixon with Soviet Premier Brezhnev

Many presidents have enjoyed more recreational activities with family and friends. FDR worked on his stamp collection. Truman walked, watched films, and drove the camp jeep. Eisenhower shot skeet and golfed. The Kennedys rode horses and enjoyed family outings. The Johnsons bowled at the camp's bowling lanes. Nixon wrote speeches and enjoyed the swimming pool. In winter Ford rode around the camp on a snowmobile. The Carters bicycled. The Reagans rode horses. George Bush pitched horseshoes, had large family gatherings, and celebrated the only

Evergreen Chapel, June 1991

wedding to be held at Camp David. The Clintons partook of Thanksgiving dinners. George W. Bush continued the Bush family tradition of holiday family gatherings.

Camp David has also changed over the years as different administrations improved the facility. While FDR used it only during the summers, Truman had heat installed to allow year-round use. Eisenhower added air conditioning, a three-hole golf course, a skeet range, and a bowling alley. Kennedy added the stables. Nixon enlarged the facility, adding more buildings and a swimming pool. The Reagans redecorated and

President and Mrs. Reagan with their dog, Rex, in January 1988

beautified the area with flower additions. George Bush added horseshoe pits and a chapel built with private donations.

Camp David provides a place away from the rest of the world for the president's family and friends to gather as well as a place to entertain heads of state or discuss many of the nation's most pressing matters. No one, not even the press, is allowed in except by invitation. Navy personnel operate Camp David. Troops from the marine barracks in Washington, D.C., provide permanent security.

Legislative Leader

During the twentieth century, as the president became nearly sovereign in the area of foreign relations, his domestic influence in relation to Congress grew as well. The Great Depression, the two world wars, the Cold War, and the increase of technological change made the president the chief beneficiary of increasing federal power.

As late as 1885, political scientist (and future president) Woodrow Wilson argued that the president exerted virtually no legislative influence. Presidents might suggest legislation in their annual message, but policy belonged to Congress. Yet only a decade later the presidency began its rise to dominance in the constitutional system. Both William McKinley and Theodore Roosevelt skillfully advanced their own bills through Congress. Woodrow Wilson, who had earlier criticized congressional leadership, presented his reform program in person and with all the force he could muster, even going over the heads of recalcitrant congressmen to make his case to the people. During the crisis of the Great Depression, Franklin Roosevelt, with large Democratic majorities behind him, made the laws himself. Congress set aside its traditional procedures in order to pass Roosevelt's bills quickly and also reduced congressional powers by delegating them to the executive branch and the federal bureaucracy.

State of the Union Address

Article II, Section 3 states that the president "shall from time to time give to the Congress information of the state of the union, and recommend to their consideration such measures as he shall judge necessary and expedient." This authorization to recommend legislation to Congress has made the president a kind of chief lobbyist and agenda-setter. The president uses his annual **State of the Union** speech to establish a legislative agenda, rally his party members, reach out to opponents, and influence public opinion. The address is given before a joint session of the House and Senate in the House chamber in the Capitol.

The first State of the Union address was filled with pomp, reminiscent of the ceremony surrounding the British monarchy. The Annual Message, as it was then called, was delivered by Washington to both the House and Senate in the Senate chamber. Thomas Jefferson disliked this practice and instead sent a written message to be presented to Congress. The written address continued until 1913, when Woodrow Wilson brought back the practice of delivering the address in person. The title "Annual Message" was changed to "State of the Union" in 1945. With the advent of television, President Johnson in 1965 changed the time of the address to the evening (rather than midday) in order to reach a greater audience. In 1986 the address was postponed for the first time because of the explosion of the space shuttle *Challenger* on the day of the scheduled address. President Clinton in 1999 was the first president to give a State of the Union address to a Congress that was considering his removal from office and was also the first to have his speech on the Internet.

In addition to the State of the Union address, the president also delivers an annual budget message and an economic message to Congress.

Along with his ability to set a legislative agenda, the president can also exercise **veto** power over Congress. If the president opposes a bill passed by Congress, he may veto it, or refuse to

The president as a ceremonial figure is illustrated by Ronald Reagan warming up in the Oval Office before meeting the Super Bowl champions in 1985.

sign it into law. Vetoes may be overridden by a two-thirds vote in both houses of Congress. However, historically this has been difficult to accomplish: 96% of all presidential vetoes have been successful. An additional veto power of the president, which cannot be overridden, is the **pocket veto.** If the president leaves a bill unsigned for ten days during a congressional adjournment, that bill is automatically vetoed. If the president ignores a bill while Congress is in session, then the bill becomes law without the president's signature.

In the 1990s many conservatives wanted to give the president the line-item veto so that he could more easily cut "pork" from legislative bills. This would give him more legislative power. The **line-item veto** allows the president to veto part of a bill without vetoing the entire bill. In 1996 Congress approved the practice, but in 1998 the Supreme Court struck it down as unconstitutional, stating that Congress did not have the authority to give the president legislative power. The Court further stated that if Congress wanted to give the

president that power it would have to pass a constitutional amendment.

Chief of State

The president of the United States is both the national leader and a national symbol. As chief of

Calvin Coolidge opens the 1925 baseball season.

state, the president represents America at home and abroad, by hosting or visiting foreign dignitaries and by leading important ceremonial events. Though the glitter of ceremony may seem far removed from the president's business of politics and governing, his presence on such occasions is an important part of our national experience.

State Dinners

A state dinner is a special dinner held by the president and First Lady to honor a visiting leader from another country. It provides an opportunity to renew ties and strengthen the relationship between the United States and the country of the visiting head of state. However, a nation may be invited for a state dinner only once during a president's time in office.

Representatives of the two nations begin preparations for the dinner months ahead of time. The guest list includes specific officials from the country being honored, U.S. elected officials, cabinet members, business and community leaders, educators, and entertainers. Once the list is decided upon, the White House calligraphers prepare the invitations.

The dinner may take place in the White House State Dining Room. State dinners have also taken place in the East Room and the Rose Garden. After the menu is approved, its preparation is carried out by the White House chef, pastry chef, and kitchen staff. The White House florist creates the floral arrangements. Other decisions include table settings, entertainment, and seating arrangements. Traditionally, couples are not seated side-by-side, and guests receive envelopes containing seating assignments when they arrive at the White House.

State dinners vary according to the wishes of each president. When President George W. Bush hosted a state dinner for Mexican President Fox, the events of the evening began with the president and First Lady greeting their guests of honor at the White House north entrance, which is reserved for formal occasions. In the Yellow

Oval Room, the president, First Lady, and President and Mrs. Fox had a private meeting before descending the residential stairs to the East Room. There the other guests had gathered for a reception, with the Marine Band presenting the music. The guests moved to the State Dining Room for the president's official welcome, President Fox's response, and dinner. During dessert, brass and string instruments provided music. After dinner everyone returned to the East Room for special musical entertainment. The evening officially ended with a fireworks display viewed by the guests from the balcony off the Blue Room.

The identification that Americans make with their president has been most evident during times of national tragedy. Millions mourned the death of Franklin Roosevelt, who had led the country through the Great Depression and a global war. Few Americans old enough to remember 1963 can forget the assassination of President Kennedy and the resulting national grief. More recently, the wounding of President Reagan during a 1981 assassination attempt brought a nationwide outpouring of concern and prayer for his recovery.

Presidential Protection

The Secret Service, the major source for presidential protection, was established in 1865 for the purpose of stopping counterfeit money and was placed within the Treasury Department in 1883. (In 2002 it became part of the Department of Homeland Security.) After President William McKinley was assassinated, Congress asked that the Service protect the president. In 1902 the Secret Service acquired full responsibility for protecting the president while also continuing its mission of criminal investigations. A White House Police Force was requested by President Harding in 1922 and was subsequently placed under the control of the Secret Service in 1930. After an assassination attempt on President Truman in 1951, Congress passed legislation to permanently provide Secret Service protection for the president, his immediate family, the president-elect, and the vice president if he desired it. In 1962 Congress extended protection to include the vice president or the next officer to succeed the president and the vice president-elect. In 1965 Congress extended the protection of former presidents and spouses throughout their lifetimes as well as for their minor children until the age of 16. Protection by the Secret Service was expanded to visiting heads of a foreign state in 1971. Congress passed legislation in 1997 to restrict protection of former presidents to ten years after their leaving office. President Clinton was the last president to receive lifetime protection.

Former president Bush and Mrs. Bush, with secret service personnel, watch the keel-laying ceremony of the USS George H. W. Bush (CVN-77) in August 2003.

First
Ladies

Though their names do not appear on the ballot, though their "position" is not subject to Senate confirmation, and though they have no duties prescribed by law, the wives of presidents have positions of great responsibility and often of great power.

The First Lady's primary responsibility since the time of Martha Washington has been to receive and entertain the president's guests. This job usually includes not only greeting and socializing with visitors such as foreign rulers and dignitaries and Americans from all walks of life, but also supervising the staff who will serve during the visits, approving menus, and overseeing

Dolley MADISON

Dolley Madison enlivened the capital with her flair for entertaining, and she remained a prominent social influence until her death in 1849. When she became First Lady, the women of Washington lacked a title with which to address Dolley. They finally settled on "Madame Presidentess." (portrait of Dolley Payne Todd Madison by Gilbert Stuart)

Angelica VAN BUREN

When Angelica Singleton visited Washington in the 1830s to call on her relative Dolley Madison, Dolley took her to the White House to meet Martin Van Buren and his sons. The eldest son, Abraham, was charmed by the young lady, and they soon married. Thereafter, Angelica served as the White House hostess for her widower father-in-law. (portrait of Angelica Singleton Van Buren by Henry Inman)

Mary LINCOLN

Undeniably capricious, excitable, and extravagant, Mary Lincoln received excessive criticism and little sympathy during her husband's war-torn administration.

Frances CLEVELAND

Grover Cleveland became the first president to be married in a White House ceremony when he took a twenty-two-year-old bride. It was said that Grover Cleveland was the most popular person in the United States—with the exception of Mrs. Cleveland.

Grace COOLIDGE

Howard Chandler Christy painted this portrait of the charming and elegant Mrs. Coolidge with her collie, Rob Roy. As both a teacher and trustee for the Clarke School for the Deaf, Grace Coolidge was a lifelong supporter of deaf education.

details such as seating arrangements, tableware, and entertainment. In this capacity none have excelled Dolley Madison, who not only served during her husband's administration but also filled in as hostess at times for Thomas Jefferson, a widower, and aided later administrations as well. Her reputation for graciousness, warmth, and wit made her as famous as her husband. When the British burned the White House during the War of 1812, Dolley Madison's winsome personality helped both her husband and the people of Washington get through those difficult years.

Beyond the traditional role as hostess, the duties of the First Lady have increased through the years. She accompanies the president on many trips at home and abroad where she must act as a representative for her husband or the nation, and most modern First Ladies also make some of these trips on their own. A president's wife usually lends her support to certain charities or political causes, and she often undertakes special projects for the White House or other public

Eleanor ROOSEVELT

Mrs. Roosevelt served as eyes, ears, and legs for her handicapped husband. She traveled, spoke, and wrote on behalf of her own public concerns as well as for the administration's, and she became a notable influence in America politics.

Bess TRUMAN

The 150-year-old White House was renovated during the Truman administration, and Bess Truman spent part of her years as First Lady living across the street in Blair House.

concerns. In addition to these taxing responsibilities, a First Lady must answer the tons of mail she receives from the public and, of course, offer the continual support that her husband needs during his presidency. This position of personal confidante has allowed many First Ladies to exert important influence on their husbands' careers and decisions. Edith Wilson, for example, carried on the routine administrative chores at the White House while her husband was recovering from a stroke, Although the president's enemies referred to her as "Mrs.

Jacqueline KENNEDY

The care of two small children and an extensive project of restoring the historic furnishings of the White House occupied much of Jackie Kennedy's time as First Lady.

Laura BUSH

A former teacher and librarian, Mrs. Bush initially drew attention to education and her national initiative called Ready to Read, Ready to Learn. After the September 11 attacks on the United States, Mrs. Bush channeled her energy toward helping our nation, especially children, through the difficult recovery process. Mrs. Bush became the first First Lady to record a full presidential radio address.

the severity of Woodrow Wilson's condition. Harry Truman depended on his wife, Bess, for her political insight and her advice, and with a good-natured alteration often referred to Bess as "Boss."

With the tremendous responsibilities and the scrutinizing spotlight placed on the president's wife today, it is little wonder that First Lady Betty Ford observed that the task is "much more of a 24-hour job than anyone would guess."

Michelle OBAMA ▼

Mrs. Obama, a Harvard Law School graduate, worked in the Chicago law firm in which her future husband was also an intern. She was assistant dean of student services at the University of Chicago and served on the boards of several organizations. As First Lady, she installed bee hives at the White House and planted a family garden of organic foods. Although she has frequently visited homeless shelters and soup kitchens and advocated public service, it remains to be seen what her major focus as the first African American First Lady will be.

Barbara BUSH ▼

As First Lady she continued to support causes that she had promoted during her many years in public life: literacy, cancer research, and helping the homeless. Mrs. Bush did more than simply speak out on these issues; she also set an example of volunteerism by working with homeless children and even by helping out in a Washington soup kitchen.

Nancy REAGAN ▼

Nancy Davis gave up a successful acting career of her own to marry the then-actor Ronald Reagan. She adapted gracefully to political life as he became governor of California and later president. As First Lady she lent her support to several public service programs, including an anti-drug campaign.

Party Leader

The founding fathers did not envision the president as leader of his political party because political parties did not exist at the time. Nevertheless, the president's role as political leader is an important aspect of presidential power.

Generally a presidential candidate controls his party through personnel and through his position. At the national convention the presidential nominee appoints a party chairman from his ranks of supporters and thereby exercises control over the personnel receiving policymaking positions within the party. When elected, the president continues to be the spokesman for his party through his position and the high visibility of the office.

As party leader the president returns to the campaign trail to help elect congressional or gubernatorial candidates of his party. Though the president must be the leader of all Americans, his partisan leadership and loyalty is expected and understandable, given the importance of the two-party system in this country and the fact that every president depends on his political party to get elected.

Restrictions and Interpretations

Our founding fathers at the Constitutional Convention had just endured six years of bloodshed to gain their independence from a hostile monarchy. With this in mind, they set about forging an executive branch in which presidential power was limited by the Constitution, checked by the legislative and judicial branches, and yet given powers broad enough to lead the nation effectively.

Tenure—Article II of the Constitution deals with the restrictions and responsibilities of the executive branch. Though some of these restrictions and responsibilities are clearly outlined, many are vague and have thus been defined by interpretation or precedent. For example, the Constitution plainly states (Article II, Section 1, Clause 1) that a president's **tenure** or term of office will be four years. However, presidents since Washington have interpreted this restriction as simply applying to the length of a single term, but not restricting the number of terms. In light of this, Washington served two terms, establishing an important precedent for his successors, one that survived for nearly a century and a half until Franklin Roosevelt's unprecedented third- and fourth-term elections in 1940 and 1944.

With the passage of the **Twenty-second Amendment,** the president was restricted to two terms. A vice president who succeeds to the presidency in order to finish an uncompleted term may not exceed a total of ten years in the highest office. If a successor serves more than two years of a predecessor's term, he can be elected for only one more term. When President Kennedy was assassinated, Vice President Lyndon Johnson became president and finished President Kennedy's remaining term of fourteen months. Johnson ran for reelection and won. If President Johnson had decided to run again he could have, because another four-year term would not have exceeded the ten-year limit. This would not have been the case for President Ford. He could run only once for reelection since he finished President Nixon's remaining term of three years and five months.

The Twenty-second Amendment provided an additional limitation on presidential power in that the two-term restriction can result in a kind of lame duck period for the president. A president is considered a **lame duck** when he has lost an election or cannot stand for reelection and yet must serve out the remainder of his term. This position tends to decrease his effectiveness with Congress, since members of Congress no longer have to be concerned about his ability to muster widespread support at the polls. In effect, the president becomes an easier figure to attack or ignore.

Chief executives have usually had a more difficult time during a second term, but much depends on the popularity of the president and the political make-up of Congress. For example, Ronald Reagan won a landslide reelection in 1984 and maintained a slim Republican majority in the Senate, thus continuing his successful legislative record. How-

Andrew Johnson

ever, in 1986 the Republicans lost their Senate majority, a fact that hampered Reagan's legislative ability, especially since he could no longer take his cause to the electorate in a national election.

Impeachment—Another constitutional restriction on the presidency is impeachment. Article II, Section 4 states:

> The President, Vice-President, and all civil officers of the United States shall be removed from office on impeachment for, and conviction of, treason, bribery, or other high crimes and misdemeanors.

This restriction is the ultimate check on the power of the office. It underscores a fundamental principle of democratic government—that no one, including the president, is above the law. **Impeachment,** or bringing charges against the president or major federal officials, can be carried out only by a majority vote in the House of Representatives. Conviction on those same charges requires a two-thirds majority vote in the Senate. A vote of conviction in the Senate can result only in the official's removal from office. If laws have been broken, it is the responsibility of the courts to prosecute after the dismissal.

Richard Nixon resigned in 1974 because of the threat of impeachment. Andrew Johnson and Bill Clinton hold the distinction of being the only presidents to be impeached. Neither impeachment trial resulted in removal, however. Johnson's case provides a good example of the vagueness of the impeachment clause and its use for political ends.

Andrew Johnson sought a speedy and lenient reconstruction process for the South following the Civil War. His program was in keeping with Abraham Lincoln's desire "to bind up the nation's wounds." Because of his lenient dealings with the former Confederate States, Johnson faced intense opposition from the Radical Republicans, who sought a harsh, vindictive reconstruction program. In 1868 the House impeached Johnson because of political tensions with the Radicals. The case then went to the Senate for a vote of conviction, where Johnson was acquitted by just one vote. The Senate's action not only demonstrated the legislature's check over the executive branch but also helped to remove impeachment as a tool of partisan politics, reserving it for matters of serious misconduct.

Bill Clinton was impeached in 1998 by the House for the criminal conduct of perjury and obstruction of justice. However, the issue went deeper, as it was to decide whether anyone, even a king or president, was above the law. The prosecution argued that President Clinton, in an attempt to conceal his adulterous affair with White House intern Monica Lewinsky, committed perjury when he lied under oath to a grand jury and obstructed justice by tampering with evidence and witnesses. The prosecution concluded that the president should be removed from office. The defense argued that President Clinton had not done

Bill Clinton

321

Impeachment Procedures

The Constitution does not give a specific plan for the impeachment process, but the House and Senate have historically followed a basic pattern.

House of Representatives' Role

- The House of Representatives is granted "sole power of impeachment" in Article I, Section 2, Clause 5 of the Constitution.
- House custom is to begin with a resolution giving the Judiciary Committee the authority to investigate the charges.
- Investigations and hearings of the charges are held by the House Judiciary Committee.
- If the charges are supported by the Judiciary Committee's findings, an impeachment resolution including Articles of Impeachment is issued to the full House. If the committee's findings prove impeachment is not justified, a resolution to that effect is issued to the full House.
- The House considers the resolution. If any one of the Articles of Impeachment is adopted by the House, the official is considered impeached, and the matter goes to the Senate for trial.

Senate's Role

- The Constitution in Article I, Section 3, Clause 6 says that "the Senate shall have the sole power to try all impeachments."
- A certain number of House members (traditionally five to eleven) function as "managers" or prosecutors at the Senate trial. They are chosen by the House Speaker or by ballot.
- Lawyers representing the impeached official present the defense. The impeached official can cross-examine witnesses and has the right to testify as in any criminal trial.
- The jury is the full Senate.
- The Constitution states that the chief justice of the Supreme Court will preside over the trial if the president of the United States is being tried.
- At the trial's end, the Senate meets in closed session to discuss the verdict. Each senator is allowed fifteen minutes of debate.
- Each Article of Impeachment is voted on by the Senate in open session. A two-thirds vote decides a conviction. If a conviction is determined, the Senate could have a separate vote to remove the impeached official from office. However, the Constitution says that federal officials will be removed from office when impeached and convicted. If no article is approved by a two-thirds vote, the official is cleared of the accusations.
- A vote to disqualify the convicted official from holding future federal office could be held by the Senate and would be decided by a majority.

anything legally wrong—it was just an attempt by a married man to hide an extramarital affair from the press. Thus, the circumstances did not justify the president's removal from office. The Senate, after hearing the prosecution and defense arguments, acquitted Clinton on both charges—with a

President Truman with his cabinet in 1949

fifty-five to forty-five vote on the perjury charge and a fifty-fifty vote on obstruction of justice. Despite the outcome, the Clinton impeachment illustrated to the world that even the president of the United States might be brought to account if accused of violating the law.

Executive Order—The Constitution and acts of Congress give the president ordinance power to issue **executive orders,** presidential directives having the force of law. In 1947 President Truman issued an executive order creating the National Security Council. President Johnson, concerned over a famine in India, issued an order in 1965 to the Secretary of Agriculture about the Indian food situation. With an executive order in 1983, President Reagan initiated a study to determine whether or not NASA should develop a manned, permanently based space station. With increased national and world concerns, ordinance power has allowed

the president greater opportunity to provide help where needed.

Appointment Power—Good leaders surround themselves with good people and delegate authority to these people. The Bible illustrates this principle in Acts 6:1–4. When the disciples became overwhelmed trying to meet both the spiritual and physical needs of the church, they chose "seven men of honest report" to take care of the people's physical needs. The founding fathers understood the principle of delegating responsibility and granted the power of appointment to the president through Article II, Section 2, Clause 2, which states:

> He shall have power, by and with the advice and consent of the Senate, to make treaties, provided two-thirds of the senators present concur; and he shall nominate, and by and with the advice and consent of the Senate, shall appoint ambassadors, other public ministers and consuls, judges of the Supreme Court, and all other officers of the United States, whose appointments are not herein otherwise provided for, and which shall be established by law. But the Congress may by law vest the appointment of such inferior officers, as they think proper in the President alone, in the courts of law, or in the heads of departments.

With this constitutional provision, the president may appoint cabinet members and their top aides, ambassadors and other diplomats, heads of independent agencies, all federal judges, U.S. marshals and attorneys, and the heads of the armed forces.

The Constitution both restricts and outlines presidential power; however, the exercise of that power has varied considerably, depending upon the occupants of the White House. Some presidents, such as Calvin Coolidge, have had a rather passive view of presidential power. Coolidge said that his first rule of action was "never doing anything that someone else can do for you." William Howard Taft also took a narrow view of executive power, saying,

> The president can exercise no power which cannot be fairly and reasonably traced to some

specific grant of power. . . . Such specific grants must be either in the federal constitution or in the pursuance thereof. There is no undefined residuum of power which can be exercised which seems to him to be in the public interest.

Taft's predecessor could not have been more different. Theodore Roosevelt found the presidency to be, in his words, a "bully pulpit"; from that "pulpit" Roosevelt took a broad view of his power:

My belief was that it was not only his [the president's] right but his duty to do anything that the needs of the nation demanded, unless such action was forbidden by the Constitution or by the laws. Under this interpretation of executive power I did and caused to be done many things not previously done by the president and the heads of departments. I did not usurp the power, but I did greatly broaden the use of executive power.

Regardless of a president's personal definition of power, certain general responsibilities are clearly outlined: chief executive, commander-in-chief, legislative leader, diplomatic leader, chief of state, and party boss. The president wears many "hats," and the complexity of his job description often requires that he act in more than one role at a time—as when he travels overseas to negotiate as a diplomatic leader while also representing the United States as the chief of state.

II. Executive Organization

The president's immense task of governing is carried out through three major levels of the executive bureaucracy: the Executive Office of the President, the cabinet departments, and the service agencies. The civilian and military employees of the vast executive bureaucracy number over two million. Though the bureaucracy is large and complex, it has become indispensable to modern American government.

Vice President

Constitutional Direction—One important office that is not part of the president's bureaucratic pyramid is the office of vice president. The Constitution lists two vice-presidential responsibilities. According to Article I, Section 3, Clause 4, "the Vice President of the United States shall be President of the Senate, but shall have no vote, unless they be equally divided." Thus, the Vice President votes only to break a tie. The second vice-presidential duty given is considered the office's main purpose for existence. Article II, Section 1, Clause 5 states,

In case of the removal of the President from office, or of his death, resignation, or inability to discharge the powers and duties of the said office, the same shall devolve on the Vice President, and the Congress may by law provide for

---

Section Review

1. What are the five chief functions of the presidency as outlined in the Constitution, and what does each one entail?

2. What influential function of the president was not included in the Constitution and was never envisioned by its framers?

3. What are the two most significant restrictions on the power of the president?

4. Who were the only presidents ever to be impeached?

Richard Nixon was the first vice president to assume a highly visible role. Here he confronts a Uruguayan Communist during a tour of South America in 1958.

the case of removal, death, resignation, or inability, both of the President and Vice President, declaring what officer shall then act as President, and such officer shall act accordingly, until the disability be removed, or a President shall be elected.

Thus the powers and duties "devolve" or pass on to the vice president if the president is unable to fulfill his duties. Many men have found the second spot a dull, dead-end job. Having political ambitions while being overshadowed by a powerful chief executive can be a frustrating experience. However, fourteen vice presidents have become president because of the death or resignation of the chief executive or by later election.

Expanding Role—As noted earlier in Chapter 13, the vice-presidential candidate is generally chosen during the presidential campaign for the political "balance" that he can bring to the ticket. In the past this was generally the most important contribution that the vice president made to his chief's administration. In recent years, though, the vice president has assumed greater responsibility and more visible leadership roles, such as serving on the National Security Council, leading presidential commissions, and representing the president at official state ceremonies.

Twenty-fifth Amendment—By far the most important role of the vice president is to succeed the president on his death or disability. This constitutional function was first tested in 1841, when William Henry Harrison caught a cold while delivering his inaugural speech (the speech lasted for about two hours) and died of pneumonia a month later. Vice President John Tyler then succeeded Harrison, leaving a vacancy in the vice-presidency, a problem not dealt with in the Constitution at that time. For a combined total of over thirty-seven years in our nation's history, presidents have served without a vice president. The Constitution did not require the president to choose a vice president if the vice-presidency became vacant. President Lyndon Johnson was the last president not to have a vice president for part of his presidency (from

Line of Presidential Succession

The line of presidential succession is as follows, from the vice president to the latest cabinet office. During the State of the Union address one person in the line of succession "hides" in case of an attack on the Capitol Building. This practice is especially important since the 9/11 terrorists attacks.

Vice President

Speaker of the House

President *Pro Tempore* of the Senate

Secretary of State

Secretary of the Treasury

Secretary of Defense

Attorney General

Secretary of the Interior

Secretary of Agriculture

Secretary of Commerce

Secretary of Labor

Secretary of Health and Human Services

Secretary of Housing and Urban Development

Secretary of Transportation

Secretary of Energy

Secretary of Education

Secretary of Veterans Affairs

Secretary of Homeland Security

325

November of 1963 until January of 1965). This situation was remedied in 1967 with the passage of the **Twenty-fifth Amendment,** whereby any vice presidential vacancy is to be filled through a nomination by the president and confirmation by a majority vote in both houses of Congress. The passage of this amendment was timely, considering that it was used in 1973 on the resignation of Vice President Spiro Agnew, when President Nixon appointed Gerald Ford to fill the vacancy. The following year Ford succeeded to the presidency on Nixon's resignation. Nelson Rockefeller was then nominated and confirmed as the vice president, creating an unprecedented situation in which both the president and the vice president served without being elected.

Vice President Cheney joins President George W. Bush with General Henry Shelton (Chairman, Joint Chiefs of Staff) and Defense Secretary William Cohen in January 2001.

President Reagan and Vice President Bush in 1988

Presidential Disability—If the president knows he will be incapacitated for a brief period of time, he may decide to transfer his duties to the vice president for that time period. The president does this by giving a written declaration to the president *pro tempore* of the Senate and the Speaker of the House of Representatives. In 1985 while President Reagan had surgery, Vice President George Bush became "acting president" for a few hours. In 2002 with the nation at war with terrorists, President George W. Bush was sedated while undergoing a medical procedure. Vice President Cheney served as president for over two hours.

The Executive Office of the President

As America grew, so grew its problems and its demands on the president. Franklin Roosevelt decided to confront the complexities of these national demands that were gradually paralyzing presidential power by their sheer weight. In 1936 he appointed Louis Brownlow to head a committee of scholars to study the problem. The Brownlow Report opened with a sentence that put the problem in capsule form: "The President needs help." The eventual result of this report was the 1939 formation of the **Executive Office of the President (EOP).** The EOP is made up of White House offices and agencies that help develop and implement the president's programs and policies.

The Executive Office probably exerts more influence on the president's policies and his legislative program than any other segment of the executive branch. Top aides serving in the **White House Office** include the president's press secretary, counsel or legal advisor, and physician. The First Lady's chief of staff and press secretary are also assistants to the president. At least four hundred members make up the White House Office, and their offices are located in the East and West Wings. The president's top aides often have daily access to him and even travel with him on weekends and vacations. It is not unusual for presidents to place longtime friends into the position of aide and confidant. President Carter gave Hamilton Jordan and Jody Powell, friends from his early days in Georgia politics, top advisory posts. A similar relationship existed between President Reagan and his longtime California supporters Edwin Meese and Caspar Weinberger.

A variety of agencies within the Executive Office serve the president in management, intelligence, and economic matters. Primary among these are the **National Security Council (NSC)** and the **Office of Management and Budget (OMB).** With its close ties to the Central Intelligence Agency and the Defense and State Departments, the NSC serves an important role in intelligence gathering, policy formulation, and crisis management. The OMB has the important task of preparing the nation's annual budget for Congress as well as coordinating policy among departments. The OMB director exercises such control over the budget and how it reflects the president's policies that his selection by the president is subject to Senate approval. Chapter 15 will give greater insight into the Executive Office of the President and its agencies.

The Cabinet

The **cabinet** offices of the executive branch were developed to assist the president in his constitutional duties and to meet the demands of America's growth. The term *cabinet* comes from the French word for a closed or private room where a king would meet with his advisors.

In Britain, where cabinet government first developed, cabinet members are generally drawn from the majority party in Parliament and serve both an executive and a legislative function. In the United States, by contrast, cabinet members or secretaries are not members of Congress. **Cabinet secretaries** are individuals responsible to the president for the departments that they head.

The framers of the Constitution made no attempt to outline and limit the number of cabinet offices. Article II, Section 2 simply states that the president "may require the opinion, in writing, of the principal officer in each of the executive departments." In 1789 President Washington's cabinet consisted of four departments. Over the years new departments were added and some were consolidated. Today there are fifteen cabinet offices: State, Treasury, Interior, Justice, Agriculture, Commerce, Labor, Defense, Health and Human Services, Housing and Urban Development, Transportation, Energy, Education, Veterans Affairs, and Homeland Security. Other cabinet-rank members include the vice president, the president's chief of staff, the administrator of the Environmental Protection Agency, the director of the Office of Management and Budget, the director of the National Drug Control Policy, and the U.S. trade representative. Chapter 15 will discuss the president's cabinet in greater depth.

Administrative Agencies

Beneath the cabinet departments are a variety of administrative agencies. This executive level consists of more than fifty agencies and service commissions that manage a variety of concerns, ranging from environmental protection to postal service and space exploration. The directors of these administrative agencies are nominated by the president and confirmed by the Senate. The operation and importance of these bureaucratic agencies will be examined more closely in the next chapter.

Section Review

1. What two responsibilities does the Constitution place on the vice president?
2. What is the Executive Office of the President? Why was it formed? What are its main offices?
3. What is the function of the president's cabinet? How many departments does it have?

Presidential
Greatness

Throughout history the leadership qualities of individual presidents have been compared and scrutinized. In 2000 C-SPAN, which was established in 1979 by the cable industry as a public service to the nation, surveyed fifty-eight historians and presidential observers who had worked on C-SPAN's forty-one-week presidential biography series and asked them to rate each president's abilities and performance. Viewers were also given the opportunity to be a part of the survey, with 1,145 people participating. The categories included public persuasion, moral authority, relations with Congress, crisis leadership, international relations, vision/setting an agenda, performance within context of the times, economic management, administrative skills, and pursuit of equal justice for all. The overall results for both the historian survey and the viewer survey are as follows, from the highest ranking score to the lowest.

Historian Survey

1. Abraham Lincoln 900
2. Franklin D. Roosevelt 876
3. George Washington 842
4. Theodore Roosevelt 810
5. Harry S. Truman 753
6. Woodrow Wilson 723
7. Thomas Jefferson 711
8. John F. Kennedy 704
9. Dwight D. Eisenhower 699
10. Lyndon B. Johnson 655
11. Ronald Reagan 634
12. James K. Polk 632
13. Andrew Jackson 632
14. James Monroe 602
15. William McKinley 601
16. John Adams 598
17. Grover Cleveland 576
18. James Madison 567
19. John Q. Adams 564
20. George Bush 548
21. Bill Clinton 539
22. Jimmy Carter 518
23. Gerald Ford 495
24. William H. Taft 491
25. Richard Nixon 477
26. Rutherford B. Hayes 477
27. Calvin Coolidge 451
28. Zachary Taylor 447
29. James A. Garfield 444
30. Martin Van Buren 429
31. Benjamin Harrison 426
32. Chester Arthur 423
33. Ulysses S. Grant 403
34. Herbert Hoover 400
35. Millard Fillmore 395
36. John Tyler 369
37. William H. Harrison 329
38. Warren G. Harding 326
39. Franklin Pierce 286
40. Andrew Johnson 280
41. James Buchanan 259

Viewer Survey

1. Abraham Lincoln 856
2. George Washington 840
3. Theodore Roosevelt 826
4. Franklin D. Roosevelt 798
5. Thomas Jefferson 793
6. Ronald Reagan 771
7. Harry S. Truman 760
8. Dwight D. Eisenhower 720
9. James Monroe 707
10. James Madison 691
11. John Adams 676
12. John F. Kennedy 675
13. Woodrow Wilson 672
14. Andrew Jackson 663
15. John Q. Adams 649
16. George Bush 648
17. James K. Polk 640
18. William McKinley 597
19. Lyndon B. Johnson 589
20. Richard Nixon 571
21. Grover Cleveland 567
22. Calvin Coolidge 562
23. Gerald Ford 556
24. William H. Taft 542
25. Zachary Taylor 518
26. Rutherford B. Hayes 517
27. Jimmy Carter 511
28. James A. Garfield 503
29. Ulysses S. Grant 503
30. Martin Van Buren 500
31. Benjamin Harrison 491
32. John Tyler 481
33. Herbert Hoover 476
34. Chester Arthur 472
35. William H. Harrison 461
36. Bill Clinton 455
37. Millard Fillmore 437
38. Andrew Johnson 428
39. Franklin Pierce 410
40. Warren G. Harding 385
41. James Buchanan 366

III. Pitfalls and Greatness

Presidential Pitfalls

Because of his exceptional authority and responsibility, a president may be tempted to use his extraordinary powers illegally and immorally. The fawning attention a president attracts by occupying the most powerful human office may be enough to divert him from the just use of his authority. King Saul was raised to leadership when he was "little" in his own eyes (I Sam. 15:17), but he permitted the kingship to change his perception of himself. In the end, he made choices that destroyed him and injured the nation of Israel. Presidents ensnared by the arrogance of power have likewise damaged their country and destroyed their reputations and political power—as Richard Nixon and Bill Clinton notoriously demonstrated.

As Christians, we should obey the command of I Timothy 2:1–2 to make "supplications, prayers, intercessions, and giving of thanks . . . for kings, and for all that are in authority" so that "we may lead a quiet and peaceable life." We should also

The pressures of the office are great: President Lyndon Johnson in 1968 at the height of the Vietnam War.

submit to the authority of the president so long as that submission is not a clear violation of Scripture. Nevertheless, any president who wishes to rule well must, like Solomon, acknowledge his need of a wisdom beyond himself, a wisdom that can come only from God.

A soldier tends his wounded comrade during the Vietnam War.

Presidential Greatness

All presidents make it into the history books, but it is more difficult to determine which were great and which were not. Former presidents have moved up and down in the lists of respective greatness depending on who was passing judgment and when they were being judged. Still, we can be certain that Pierce, Buchanan, and Harding will never surpass Washington, Lincoln, and FDR on any rational scale of greatness.

Great presidents have been clear about their goals and have retained a self-confidence about their objectives that was unshaken by popular opinion. More importantly, great presidents have successfully met the challenge of national crises, as, for instance, the establishment of the new constitutional system under Washington and the maintenance of the Union under Lincoln. Refusing to face a crisis, as did the vacillating Buchanan before the Civil War (he said secession was wrong but promised not to stop it), is almost a sure ticket to the bottom rungs of presidential greatness. Likewise, choosing especially poor or corrupt advisors, as did Grant, Harding, and Nixon, often results in lower rankings. On the other hand, some presidents, such as McKinley, might have been judged more highly had they been tested in the crucible of a national emergency.

Though even great presidents have had significant moral flaws, most have had a strong desire to serve their country and its people. As the historian and essayist Russell Kirk wrote, "Nearly all the presidents of the United States, whatever their antecedents, have been gentlemen."

Christ defined the qualification for true greatness that is unaltered by time, circumstances, or polls. It is service. He explained to His disciples that "whosoever will be great among you, let him be your minister; and whosoever will be chief among you, let him be your servant" (Matt. 20:26–27). Often the world's definition of greatness is not greatness at all; it is mere popularity. There is an important difference between popularity and greatness. Popularity means having the favor of many people, but this favor does not survive well over time. Take the most popular politicians, writers, and musicians of a generation ago, and often the only things more difficult to recall about them than their names are their accomplishments. In contrast, greatness transcends the glitter and noise of popular acclaim; focus on living for immortal things. Greatness comes through giving, serving, and following Christ's example.

Section Review

1. What are some of the many pitfalls faced by the president?
2. What is the difference between popularity and greatness?

Chapter Review

Terms

covert operations
executive agreement
State of the Union
veto
pocket veto
line-item veto
tenure

Twenty-second Amendment
lame duck
impeachment
executive orders
Twenty-fifth Amendment
Executive Office of the
   President (EOP)

White House Office
National Security Council
   (NSC)
Office of Management and
   Budget (OMB)
cabinet
cabinet secretaries

Content Questions

1. What are the six main presidential powers and the two main restrictions on these powers?

2. What two responsibilities does the Constitution assign to the vice president?

3. What problem did the Brownlow Report address, and what was the result?

Application Questions

1. Is it wrong for the president to campaign for his party? Defend your answer.

2. What are the advantages and disadvantages of limiting the presidential tenure to two terms?

3. Why is it difficult to be an effective leader? What qualities does a good leader require?

THE FEDERAL BUREAUCRACY

15

FBI building

For forms of government let fools contest;
Whate'er is best administer'd is best.

—Alexander Pope

In almost every United States election, campaigning office-seekers make promises about harnessing our government's bureaucratic giant made up of appointed officials and civil servants. These office-seekers usually receive a hearty round of applause from their constituents. However, politicians, even those with the best intentions, find it difficult to halt the growth of the bureaucracy and nearly impossible to reduce its size.

I. Bureaucratic Development

Overview

***Bureaucracy Defined*—Bureaucracy** refers to an administrative system in which agencies staffed largely by nonelected officials perform specific tasks in accordance with standard procedures. Much of the work of the bureaucracy involves the implementation and administration of laws or programs. For this reason most of the federal bureaucracy is within the executive branch. In contrast to

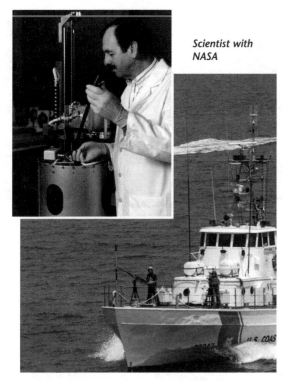

Scientist with NASA

Coast Guard Missions Day at Yorktown, Virginia

the popular image of a **bureaucrat** (a civil servant dedicated to the details of administrative procedure) as a white-collar functionary laboring through stacks of paperwork, employees of the federal bureaucracy actually perform a variety of tasks. In addition to administrative and clerical duties, members of the bureaucracy also deliver mail, work as computer technicians and plumbers, and serve as nurses.

When defining bureaucracy it is also important to remember the principle of **delegation,** committing or entrusting a task or power to another. Modern society contains a complex interaction of social, economic, and technological forces combined with an attitude that often favors government intervention in a broad range of issues. Responding to people's problems and managing the resources of government is a tremendous responsibility—a responsibility much too great for the president and his advisors alone.

Moses took a similar view of his responsibilities in leading the nation of Israel. Exodus 18 points out that Moses sat all day listening to the problems that the people brought to him and deciding how to solve them. His father-in-law, Jethro, rightly pointed out that Moses' administrative approach was inefficient and exhausting: "For this thing is too heavy for thee; thou art not able to perform it thyself alone." Jethro then encouraged Moses to get some help by delegating the authority to judge lesser matters to others and thus getting capable men to "bear the burden with thee." Moses acknowledged the practical wisdom of the suggestion by organizing a bureaucracy to meet the needs of the people. At the same time he retained final authority, as God's chosen leader and spokesman, over all decisions.

Bureaucracy Features—America's bureaucracy has three key features. The first is its hierarchical authority. The organization is constructed like a pyramid, with the chain of command going from top to bottom. Another key feature is job specialization, a specific division of labor within the organization. Each worker has specified responsibilities. Formalized rules are the third feature. These rules enable the bureaucracy to work according to an established set of regulations and procedures.

Bureaucracy Benefits—America's bureaucratic features produce benefits that allow people to work together on large and complex tasks in a more efficient manner. Hierarchical authority can increase agency speed by limiting conflicts over who has the authority to make the decisions. Efficiency and productivity are promoted by job specialization because workers can center on a specific task using their specialized skills and knowledge. With decisions based on defined standards, not someone's preferences, work can continue in spite of workers leaving the organization and new workers replacing them.

History and Growth

[The President] shall nominate, and by and with the advice and consent of the Senate, shall appoint ambassadors, other public ministers and consuls, judges of the Supreme Court, and other officers of the United States, whose appointments are not herein otherwise provided for, and which shall be established by law. But the Congress may by law vest the appointment of such inferior officers, as they think proper, in the President alone, in the courts of law, or in the heads of departments.

—*Article II, Section 2, Clause 2*

Federal Hall, New York City

The First Congress—In 1789 the First Congress, meeting at New York City's Federal Hall, considered a bill that would create the State Department. Both houses discussed whether appointed officials could be removed by the president alone. Opponents wanted officials to be removed only with the Senate's consent. James Madison, speaking for the Washington administration, argued that if the president were restricted in his ability to remove subordinates then he would not be able to control them. Madison also pointed out that the president would be unable to perform

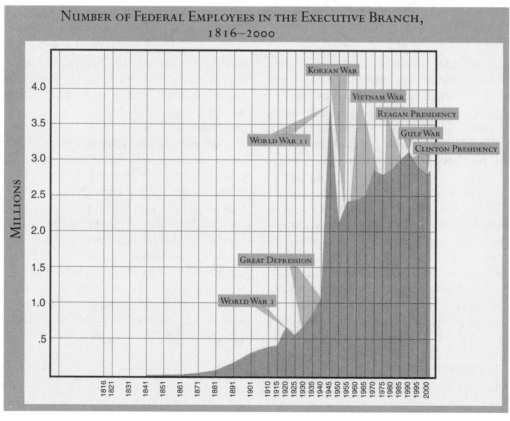

NUMBER OF FEDERAL EMPLOYEES IN THE EXECUTIVE BRANCH, 1816–2000

his constitutional obligation to "take care that the laws be faithfully executed." Madison's view won by a narrow margin. The result was that the Department of State and all other created cabinet departments would be administered by people whom the president could remove. Congress did keep the right to appropriate money, investigate the administration, and shape the laws that would be carried out by the administration.

Civil Service—Since the Constitution has little to say concerning civilian employees, Washington along with Jefferson set the early standards for the **civil service,** the civilian employees who carry out the administrative tasks of government. Washington recognized that the new government's success would depend on whom he appointed to office. He wanted the most qualified individuals and made selections accordingly. Adams continued Washington's method of choice. Jefferson agreed with Washington's fitness standard for office but combined it with political acceptability. Jefferson replaced Federalists with members of his own Democratic-Republican Party.

Spoils System—Andrew Jackson initiated the spoils system when he gave government posts as a reward for campaign support. He reasoned that since public office duties were simple, any intelligent person could fill the office. Jackson also thought that many should have the privilege of serving in government and that serving too long in office would lead to tyranny and inefficiency. He felt that people were entitled to have the party they placed in power in control of government offices from the top to the bottom. The spoils system grew as many saw this as a method of building and holding on to power.

Civil War Effects—A great turning point in bureaucratic development was the Civil War, which led to the hiring of many new officials. The war illuminated the federal government's administrative weaknesses. Reformers' demands for a better civil service were heard when the rapid postwar industrialization and emerging national economy showed that state governments could not manage alone.

Post–Civil War—The political motivation behind the job assignments did not always put the most qualified people into office. President Grant acknowledged the inadequacy of the spoils system when he said, "There is no duty which so much embarrasses the Executive and heads of Departments as that of appointments. . . . The present system does not secure the best men, and often not even fit men, for public place." Since the president could hire or fire these employees at will, the bureaucracy was highly responsive to the president's wishes.

As the system increased, many positions were filled with ill-equipped people. Inefficiency and corruption occurred, with many calling for reform. It was not until President Garfield was shot and killed by a disappointed office-seeker that a horrified nation and President Arthur, former vice president under Garfield, demanded reform. Reform came in the form of the Pendleton Act of 1883.

Pendleton Act—The new standard for hiring and promotion of civil employees was the quality of one's work, or **merit.** The **Pendleton Act** of 1883 established the Civil Service Commission (the predecessor of the Office of Personnel Management) and abolished the old patronage or spoils system.

Between 1861 and 1901 federal employees increased by more than 200,000 with the creation of new agencies to handle the growing economy. These agencies were created to serve (do research, gather statistics, pass out benefits), not regulate. Not until 1887 and the Interstate Commerce Commission, the first regulatory agency, did the federal government begin to regulate the economy.

Wars and the New Deal—A huge expansion of government-regulated economy came about as a result of United States involvement in World War I. During wartime, restrictions on what administrators could do were set aside in order to meet the increased needs and demands brought about by war. After the war there was a reduction of personnel, but war almost always leaves a larger number of federal employees behind.

The implementation of the New Deal plus World War II produced our present-day bureaucracy. The New Deal established government agencies to help Americans who had lost homes, jobs, and savings during the Great Depression. The Federal Emergency Relief Administration (FERA) provided funds directly to the needy. The Civilian Conservation Corps (CCC) and Tennessee Valley Authority (TVA) put millions to work on public projects. The Social Security Act established a pension program and a state and federal system to provide for unemployment insurance. World War II brought further bureaucratic changes, with some government agencies (such as the CCC) shutting down and their employees changing to defense jobs. The war also expanded the number of business personnel to administer an increased economy and war production.

Following the New Deal, the average American, whatever his political persuasion, expected the federal government to solve economic and social problems. The United States Supreme Court also began to uphold laws permitting Congress to authorize agencies to make whatever decisions seemed necessary to solve a problem or serve the public interest. During World War II the government for the first time relied heavily on income taxes on individuals and corporations to fund its activities. The result was great financial gain for the government. The government used the increased funds to increase many programs and support more administrators.

Pay and Benefits—Congress sets the pay and other job conditions for federal workers. Civil service pay at the lower and middle levels compares fairly with salaries in the private sector. However,

As this political cartoon from the Grant administration indicates, the spoils system often created a scramble for government favors.

upper-level positions cannot compete with private sector salaries. Holiday, vacation, sick leave, disability, and life insurance benefits are better in the private sector. However, civil service employees have better benefits in the areas of retirement, health insurance, and retiree health insurance.

Political Activities—Federal employees were first limited in their political activities by the Hatch Act of 1939. The law allowed federal workers to vote in elections, but they could not take part in partisan political activities. Critics of the Hatch Act said unnecessary, unjustifiable limits had been placed on federal workers' political and civil rights. The Supreme Court rejected several First Amendment challenges to the law. It was not until 1993 with the passage of the Federal Employees Political Activities Act that federal employees were allowed greater political opportunities. Today, federal employees can vote, help register new voters, contribute money to candidates and parties, participate in campaigns, and hold office in a political party. They cannot run in partisan elections, participate in party work on government property or while on the job, collect political contributions for workers in lower positions or the general public, or use a government position to influence an election.

Today—Most of the rank and file of the federal bureaucracy are hired through the merit system, and generally they may hold lifelong tenure if they so choose. They are paid and promoted on the basis of written evaluations by their superiors and are also protected from disciplinary actions or dismissal for partisan reasons. However, the president still maintains appointive power over about one thousand positions. Many of these are top policymaking posts, such as secretaries (cabinet offices), undersecretaries, directors, and commissioners. Thus the president has a measure of control over the bureaucratic pyramid. Since most civil servants, if they so choose, enjoy lifelong tenure regardless of who occupies the White House, the president's appointive power is an important tool in seeing that his policies are implemented.

Section Review

1. What is a bureaucracy?
2. What important principle should be remembered when defining bureaucracy?
3. What are the benefits produced by America's bureaucracy?
4. What were Madison's arguments for allowing the president unrestricted power to remove subordinates?
5. What historical event highlighted the federal government's administrative weaknesses?
6. Which event led to civil service reform?
7. How does war expand bureaucracy?
8. Contrast the spoils system and the merit system.

II. Bureaucratic Structure

The true test of a good government is its aptitude and tendency to produce a good administration.

—*Alexander Hamilton,* The Federalist No. 76

The vast bureaucratic machine of the executive branch is organized like a pyramid, though one with a very broad base. At the pinnacle is the chief executive; beneath him stretches an array of agencies that are both impressive in their number and bewildering in their organization. The federal bureaucracy is so vast that one of President Carter's aides responsible for reorganizing the bureaucracy could not even determine how many agencies existed.

Executive Office of the President

The first level of the bureaucracy beneath the president is the Executive Office of the President. This powerful segment of the executive branch is largely a policymaking and managing level that has the greatest access to the president and is most responsive to his ideas. The Executive Office was

GOVERNMENT AND AGENCIES

Legislative Branch

THE CONGRESS
Senate   House

Legislative Offices & Departments
Architect of the Capitol
United States Botanic Gardens
General Accounting Office
Government Printing Office
Library of Congress
Congressional Budget Office
Office of Technology Assessment
Copyright Royalty Tribunal
United States Tax Court

Executive Branch

Executive Office of the President
The White House Office
Office of the Vice President
    of the U.S.
Council of Economic Advisors
Council on Environmental Quality
National Security Council
Office of Administration
Office of Management and Budget
Office of National Drug Control Policy
Office of Science and Technology
    Policy
Office of United States Trade
    Representative

Judicial Branch

THE U.S. SUPREME COURT
Other Courts
Administrative Office of the U.S.
Federal Judicial System
Courts of Appeals
District Courts
Federal Claims Court
Court of Appeals for the Federal
    Circuit
Court of International Trade
Territorial Courts
Court of Appeals for Armed Forces
Court of Appeals for Veterans

Executive Departments

AGRICULTURE	COMMERCE	DEFENSE	EDUCATION	ENERGY	HEALTH AND HUMAN SERVICES	HOUSING AND URBAN DEVELOPMENT
HOMELAND SECURITY	THE INTERIOR	JUSTICE	LABOR	STATE	TRANS-PORTATION	THE TREASURY	VETERANS AFFAIRS

*Independent Agencies

Central Intelligence Agency
Federal Mediation and Conciliation Service
Commission on Civil Rights
Federal Reserve System
Commodity Futures Trading Commission
Federal Trade Commission
Consumer Product Safety Commission
General Services Administration
Corporation for National and Community Service
National Aeronautics and Space Administration
Defense Nuclear Facilities Safety Board
National Labor Relations Board
Environmental Protection Agency
National Transportation Safety Board
Equal Employment Opportunity Commission
Nuclear Regulatory Commission

Export-Import Bank of the United States
Office of Personnel Management
Farm Credit Administration
Securities and Exchange Commission
Federal Communications Commission
Selective Service System
Federal Deposit Insurance Corporation
Small Business Administration
Federal Election Commission
Social Security Administration
Federal Emergency Management Agency
Tennessee Valley Authority
Federal Housing Finance Board
United States Arms Control and Disarmament Agency
Federal Maritime Commission
United States Postal Service

* More than 150 independent agencies are in the executive branch

formed during the administration of Franklin Roosevelt to help the president manage the burdens of modern government, illustrating the importance of the New Deal and World War II. The size and responsibilities of the Executive Office have greatly expanded in the half-century since its inception, so that it numbers some five thousand employees today. The principal agencies within the Executive Office include the White House Office, the Office of Management and Budget, and the National Security Council.

The West Wing

The center of activity in the White House is the West Wing. The president's Oval Office, the offices of the executive staff (including the vice president), the Cabinet Room, the Roosevelt Room, and the Brady Press Briefing Room are located in this section of the White House.

As the country and the Office of the President grew, the residence of the White House proved to be too small. The administrations of Harrison, Cleveland, and McKinley sought to improve the crowded conditions, but it was not until 1902 under Theodore Roosevelt that the president's offices were removed from the residence to the addition named the West Wing. The East Wing was added in 1942.

The White House Office—The president's front-line staff is the White House Office. Its members serve him by communicating his policies to the appropriate agencies as well as to the American public. Top aides within the White House exercise an enormous amount of influence as they operate behind the scenes. Typically presidents appoint close friends or long-time supporters to these top posts because of the trust and confidentiality required. Such closeness between a president and his aides is understandable, but it can be inherently dangerous. Advisors who try to shield the president from damaging information or who simply tell him

what he wants to hear can do great, even irreparable, harm to a president's credibility.

The integrity of an advisor obviously has a great deal to do with the integrity of his advice. Christ underscored this fact when he denounced the Pharisees: "How can ye, being evil, speak good things? for out of the abundance of the heart the mouth speaketh" (Matt. 12:34). The dishonesty of President Nixon's advisors, H. R. Haldeman and John Ehrlichman, and their involvement in the Watergate affair led to cover-ups, criminality, and eventually the downfall of the president.

The White House Office includes the chief of staff, staff secretary, Office of Management and Administration, presidential personnel director, counsel to the president, Press Office, and Office of Communications. The president's **chief of staff** advises the president on issues of politics, policy, and management; selects key people on the White House staff; controls and manages people, information, and paperwork into the Oval Office; and is expected to be a regular presence on the Sunday morning television talk shows.

The staff secretary controls the paper flow to the president and follows up on the paper flow out of the Oval Office. He or she also oversees the offices of the executive clerk, Records Management, and Correspondence.

The Office of Management and Administration is the backbone of the White House staff. This office administers staff salaries; allots staff positions, mess privileges, parking places, and passes; manages the White House and Executive Office budgets; is a liaison with and works in association with the Secret Service; and manages the White House computer systems.

The presidential personnel director is usually chosen as soon as a presidential candidate is nominated at the party's national convention. The director begins to fill the critical White House positions. Over six thousand appointed positions must be filled, twelve hundred of these Senate-confirmed.

The counsel for the president, described as the "presidency's lawyer," monitors ethics matters,

President George W. Bush with the National Security Council in the cabinet room on September 12, 2001

coordinates the president's message and agenda within the executive branch, negotiates with Congress on the president's behalf, recommends actions to the president, and interprets the law throughout the executive branch. The counsel for the president is the legal protector of the office and a "mirror" held up to the highest office in the land.

The Press Office serves the president, the White House staff, and reporters. The **press secretary** channels information, represents constituents, and aids in administration and communication planning. The press secretary is the official spokesperson for an administration. The Press Office has offices in the West Wing and the Eisenhower Executive Office Building, located next door to the West Wing.

President Nixon created the Office of Communications in 1969 for the purpose of sending information to out-of-town news organizations. The White House communications director is said to be the presidential "fire-walker" and reflects the strength and styles of the President. The director works with the president, chief of staff, press secretary, and others in the White House.

The Office of Management and Budget (OMB)—This office wields great influence for an administration. In addition to preparing the president's annual budget for Congress, the OMB serves as a clearing-house by coordinating programs among various agencies and by evaluating budgetary requests from executive departments. The OMB also exercises important control over the president's legislative program. A proposal that originates from a bureaucratic agency must generally get OMB approval before it ever reaches the president.

The National Security Council (NSC)—The NSC is the president's policymaking group over security and intelligence matters. The NSC was formed in 1947, in the early years of the Cold War, to advise the president on military policy and covert operations and to serve as a crisis-management team. Today the NSC also serves as the president's principal arm for coordinating these policies among various government agencies. The president receives national security briefings daily. The president chairs the council; and regular attendees include the vice president, the national security advisor, and the secretaries of state, defense, and treasury. The chairman of the Joint Chiefs of Staff is the military advisor to the council, and the director of the Central Intelligence Agency is the intelligence advisor. The chief of staff to the president, counsel to the president, and the assistant to the president for economic policy are invited to attend any meeting. The attorney general and the director of the Office of Management and Budget are invited to attend meetings pertaining to their responsibilities. When appropriate, the heads of other executive departments and agencies are invited to attend the NSC meetings.

During the Truman and Eisenhower years, the NSC was largely an information-gathering agency. During the Vietnam War, however, the NSC took an increasing role in formulating and implementing foreign policy and advising on military activity. For example, Henry Kissinger, an NSC staff member during the Nixon years, personally negotiated an end to American involvement in Vietnam and prepared the way for summits with both China and the Soviet Union.

Other EOP Agencies—The Executive Office of the President includes other agencies that advise and assist the president. In 1989 the Office of National Drug Control Policy was established, with the director labeled by the media as the nation's "drug czar." This agency acts as an advisory and planning agency. The Office of the United States Trade Representative advises the president in all matters of foreign trade. The representative is appointed by the president and confirmed by the Senate, carries the rank of ambassador, and represents the president in foreign trade negotiations. The Office of the Vice President aids the vice president in performing his duties. The Office of Faith-Based and Community Initiatives was created by President George W. Bush in January 2001. Its purpose is to seek ways to involve religious and other private groups more directly in many of the government's social welfare programs. The most recent agency to be added to the EOP is the Office of Global Communications, established in 2003. The agency's purpose is to coordinate important communications with people throughout the world, incorporating the president's ideas into new and existing programs. Other EOP offices include the Council of Economic Advisors, the Office of Policy Development, the Council on Environmental Quality, the Office of Science and Technology Policy, and the Office of Administration.

Eisenhower Executive Office Building

On May 7, 2002, President George W. Bush dedicated the Old Executive Office Building to President Dwight David Eisenhower. President Bush at the dedication said he was proud to dedicate this historic building to the lasting memory

of a great man. The building is located next to the West Wing on the White House premises.

Many national figures have participated in historical events that have taken place in this building. Presidents and secretaries of state, war, and the navy have had offices there. Winston Churchill walked its corridors. After the bombing of Pearl Harbor, Secretary of State Cordell Hull met there with Japanese emissaries and confronted them with evidence of the bombing. President Hoover used the secretary of the navy's office for a few months after a fire in the Oval Office on Christmas Eve, 1929. Richard Nixon had a private office there during his presidency. Since 1960 all vice presidents, beginning with Lyndon B. Johnson, have had offices in this building. Today, the former office of the secretary of the navy is used by the vice president for meetings and press interviews. It is considered a "ceremonial" office since its restoration.

Cabinet

History and Purpose—The cabinet constitutes the next level of the bureaucracy. The **cabinet,** an informal advisory body brought together by the president to serve his needs, is not specifically mentioned in the Constitution nor established by Congress but is a result of custom and habit. The Constitution's only possible reference to a cabinet is under Article II, Section 2, Clause 1, where the president is given the power to "require the opinion, in writing, of the principal officer in each of the executive departments, upon any subject relating to the duties of the respective offices." It was not until

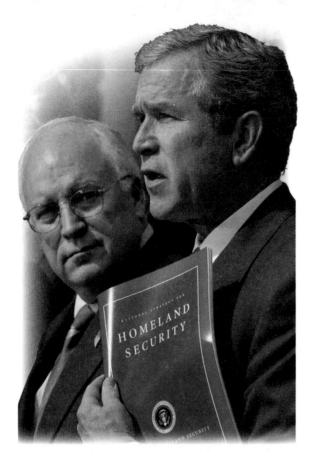

President Bush with Vice President Cheney on July 12, 2002

the country and of government involvement in social issues. Thousands of bureaucrats work together within the cabinet departments. Fifteen cabinet departments serve the president today: the departments of State, Treasury, Interior, Justice, Agriculture, Commerce, Labor, Defense, Housing and Urban Development, Transportation, Health and Human Services, Energy, Education, Veterans Affairs, and Homeland Security. Most of these departments are headed by a secretary, an undersecretary, and various assistant secretaries. These positions are filled by presidential appointment with a vote of approval by a majority of the Senate. Each department enables the president to make more informed decisions when carrying out the executive branch's administrative duties. Each cabinet department has its own building complex located in Washington, D.C., or Virginia. (For some of the cabinet department locations, see the Washington, D.C., map on pages 228–29.) The following summary lists the cabinet departments in the order that they were created and reflecting the order of presidential succession.

Department of State—One of the original four cabinet departments, the State Department is

1907 in an act of Congress that the cabinet was officially mentioned.

William Howard Taft said, "The Constitution . . . contains no suggestion of a meeting of all the department heads in consultation over general governmental matters. The Cabinet is a mere creation of the President's will. It exists only by custom. If the President desired to dispense with it, he could do so." John F. Kennedy viewed his cabinet as a waste of time. Other presidents had other unofficial advisory groups. Andrew Jackson had his "Kitchen Cabinet" in 1829, Franklin Roosevelt his "Brain Trust" in the 1930s, and Harry Truman his "Cronies" in the late 1940s. Today's cabinet members advise the president and serve as administrative heads of the executive departments.

The growth in the number and responsibilities of the cabinet departments reflects the growth of

Treasury building

Pentagon

responsible for issuing U.S. citizens' passports, visas, and travel warnings and giving information when emergencies occur outside of the United States. The secretary of state, who heads this department, is also the permanent United States representative to the United Nations. The secretary advises the president on foreign policy and represents the U.S. in foreign policy negotiations. State Department agencies include the Foreign Service and the Bureau of Consular Affairs.

Department of the Treasury—The Treasury, also an original cabinet department, is responsible for collecting taxes, borrowing money for the government, minting coins, printing bills, and enforcing alcohol, tobacco, and firearms laws. The Treasury building is the third oldest building in Washington, D.C., and is the only federal building to occupy its original site; its design influenced other federal buildings. Treasury agencies include the U.S. Mint; Internal Revenue Service (IRS);

Bureau of Alcohol, Tobacco and Firearms (ATF); Secret Service when dealing with counterfeiting; and Customs Service.

Department of Defense—Another original cabinet department, first called the Department of War, is now known as the Defense Department. Its primary function is national security. Most Defense personnel work in the Pentagon, and Defense agencies include the Joint Chiefs of Staff, the army, the navy, the air force, the marines, and the Inspector General. The Inspector General is the principal advisor to the secretary of defense concerning fraud, abuses, and deficiencies, and he helps avoid duplication among the military departments while helping to ensure effective coordination.

Department of Justice—The last of the original four cabinet departments, the Justice Department was titled the Attorney General's Office until 1872. The head of the Justice Department is addressed as the attorney general rather than

343

"secretary." The department enforces federal law, gives legal advice to the president, represents the U.S. court system, and runs federal prisons. Agencies included in this department are the FBI, U.S. Drug Enforcement Administration (DEA), Civil Rights Division, and Criminal Division.

Department of the Interior—In 1849 the Department of the Interior became part of the cabinet. The department manages public lands, national parks, wildlife refuges, hydroelectric power plants, Native American affairs, mining, and the nation's water, energy, and mineral resources. Some of the agencies included in the Department of the Interior are the National Park Service, the U.S. Fish and Wildlife Service, the Bureau of Indian Affairs, and the U.S. Geological Survey.

Department of Agriculture (USDA)—Raised to cabinet status in 1889, the Department of Agriculture is the United States' largest conservation agency. Some of the USDA functions are inspecting food, managing school lunch and food stamp programs, helping farmers and ranchers, managing national forests, and helping promote U.S. agricultural products overseas. Some agencies within the USDA are the Food and Nutrition Service and the Food Safety and Inspection Service.

Department of Commerce—In 1903 the Department of Commerce was added to the cabinet. Its functions include international trade, economic growth, the census, protection of ocean and coastal resources while assisting in their economic development, and patents and trademarks. Some agencies within the department are the National Oceanic and Atmosphere Administration, the Bureau of Census, and the Patent and Trademark Office.

Department of Labor—Part of the Commerce Department until 1913, the Department of Labor enforces work laws such as the minimum wage and safe working conditions, promotes job training programs, and addresses childcare issues. The Bureau of Labor Statistics and the Occupational Safety and Health Administration are two of Labor's agencies.

Department of Health and Human Services—The roots of Health and Human Services go back to 1789 and the establishment of a marine hospital to care for seafarers. In 1953 the Department of Health, Education, and Welfare was created. Education became a separate department in 1979, and in 1980 Health and Welfare became the Department of Health and Human Services. In 2001 this department responded to the nation's first bioterrorist attack when anthrax bacteria were delivered through the mail. This department's functions include health care programs, prevention and control of diseases, administration of Medicare and Medicaid, and enforcement of food and drug laws. Two of the agencies within Health and Human Services are the Centers for Disease Control and Prevention and the Food and Drug Administration (FDA). The Department of Health and Human Services has the distinction of having the largest budget among the cabinet departments.

Department of Housing and Urban Development (HUD)—The origins of Housing and Urban Development began with the U.S. Housing Act of 1937. The act's purpose was to provide low-income families with safe, sanitary shelter and economic opportunity. In 1965 the Department of Housing and Urban Development obtained cabinet status. HUD oversees public housing, home financing, and fair housing and helps the homeless. The Office of Fair Housing and Equal Opportunity is a HUD agency.

Department of Transportation—In 1966 Transportation was established, and it oversees highways, mass transit, air travel, railroads, pipelines, and maritime laws. Agencies under the Transportation administration include the Federal Aviation Administration (FAA) and the Federal Highway Administration. The U.S. Coast Guard and the Transportation Security Administration were previously included in this department. However, after the September 11, 2001, terrorist attacks, President George W. Bush requested that those agencies be transferred to the Department of Homeland Security.

Department of Energy—The Manhattan Project (the race to develop the atomic bomb during World War II) was the forerunner of the Department of Energy. The 1970s energy crisis led to the establishment of this department in 1977. Energy oversees energy technology, nuclear weapons research, and hydroelectric power and operates facilities in thirty-five states. Today's Energy Department focus includes ensuring our energy security, maintaining the safety and reliability of our nuclear stockpiles, and cleaning up the environment from the Cold War era. The Energy Department administrates the Office of Nuclear Energy, Science, and Technology.

Department of Education—President Andrew Johnson created the first Department of Education in 1867. Its purpose was to collect information and statistics about the nation's schools. Many thought the department would have too much control over local schools, so it was demoted to the Office of Education in 1868. From 1953 to 1979 the agency was part of Health, Education, and Welfare. With the expansion of education programs in the 1970s, the Department of Education gained cabinet status in 1979. The Education Department gives federal aid to public schools and oversees educational research. Agencies within the department include the Office of Elementary and Secondary Education and the Office of Educational Research and Improvement.

Department of Veterans Affairs—The roots of Veterans Affairs go back to 1636 when the Pilgrims of Plymouth Colony were at war with the Pequot Indians. The Pilgrims passed a law stating that disabled soldiers would be supported by the colony. The Continental Congress of 1776 encouraged enlistments during the Revolutionary War by providing disabled soldiers with pensions. The Department of Veterans Affairs became a cabinet-level department in 1989. The department oversees benefits, pensions, and medical programs for veterans and maintains military cemeteries. Agencies within the department include the Veterans Health Administration and the National Cemetery System. When Veterans Affairs became a cabinet-level department, President George Bush said, "There is only one place for the veterans of America: in the Cabinet Room, at the table with the President of the United States of America."

Department of Homeland Security—The Department of Homeland Security was created after the September 11, 2001, terrorist attacks on the World Trade Center and the Pentagon. The department's mission is to prevent terrorist attacks within the United States, reduce America's vulnerability to terrorism, and minimize the damage from and speed the recovery following attacks that do occur. Homeland Security was originally a part of the Executive Office of the President, but it was elevated to cabinet status in 2002. A few of the agencies and organizations that became part of the Department of Homeland Security include the U.S. Customs Service (Treasury), Immigration and Naturalization (the service and benefit functions; Justice), the Federal Law Enforcement Training Center (Treasury), the Nuclear Incident Response Team (Energy), the Secret Service, and the Coast Guard.

Independent Agencies

The final level of the bureaucratic pyramid is made up of independent agencies. These agencies

World War II North Africa American Cemetery and Memorial in Carthage, Tunisia

345

are independent only because they are not located within the fifteen cabinet departments. Some are given independent status because they do not fit within any department, or to protect them from partisan political pressures, or because of their particular, sensitive functions, especially the regulatory commissions. These agencies are divided into three groups: independent executive agencies, government corporations, and regulatory commissions. Remember that all of these agencies are part of the executive branch and are accountable to the president.

Independent Executive Agencies—Most independent agencies fit into this category. Some of these agencies have thousands of employees with multimillion dollar budgets, are organized like cabinet departments, but do not have cabinet status. An example is NASA. Most independent executive agencies, however, have few employees and small budgets and draw very little attention. The American Battle Monuments Commission is an example.

Government Corporations—Congress established government corporations to carry out certain business-like activities. The first government corporation was the Bank of the United States, established in 1791. However, it was not until World War I and the Great De-

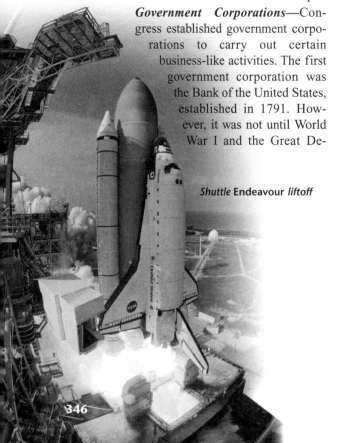

Shuttle **Endeavour** *liftoff*

Norris Dam, Tennessee Valley Authority

pression of the 1930s that Congress set up many corporations to carry out emergency programs. Today, there are more than fifty corporations. Examples are the United States Postal Service and the Tennessee Valley Authority, which generates, sells, and distributes electric power.

Regulatory Commissions—Though the president has appointive power over the commissioners and directors on this level, they are not accountable to him for how they run their agencies. These agencies, such as the Federal Communications Commission (FCC) and the Securities and Exchange Commission (SEC), reflect the increasing pace of government intervention and control in citizens' lives. As the table on page 348 shows, the regulatory agencies affect everything from highways and airways to food and water.

The scope and power of these regulatory commissions have generated a chorus of complaints from industry and individuals alike. Though bureaucratic tyranny can result from the strictness and independence with which some regulatory commissions operate, the principal purpose of regulation remains necessary.

Regulation is essential because man as a sinner cannot always be trusted to do right. Man's selfish nature causes him to cut corners. For example, some employers might well be tempted to save thousands of dollars rather than to create a safe working place for their employees if government regulations did not outline and enforce safety measures. Bureaucratic edicts, as we shall see, may be burdensome, insensitive, and dictatorial (for bureaucrats have selfish natures too), but man continues to prove that when left to himself, he does what is "right in his own eyes" (Judg. 21:25). If an employer concerns himself with the welfare of his workers, then the regulations do not seem so burdensome. As Paul observes, "Rulers are not a terror to good works, but to the evil" (Rom. 13:3).

Operation

The federal bureaucracy has been described as a quasi-legislative, quasi-executive, quasi-judicial system. This observation is valid because of the broad powers with which the bureaucracy operates. These powers have accumulated over time to give the bureaucracy an imposing role in the connection between government and the people.

The bureaucracy serves a legislative role by recommending bills to Congress and to the president, generally by way of the Office of Management and Budget. Of course, the Constitution empowers Congress to pass bills that become **statutory law,** law passed by the legislature. However, such laws are often written in vague terms out of either a lack of information or fear of offending constituents. The bureaucracy has the responsibility of drawing up specific regulations that implement congressional statutes. These regulations have the force of law and are known as **administrative law.** The creation of laws by nonelected officials is a formidable power. It is a power acquired by congressional default and a power expanded by firmly entrenched bureaucrats. In its judicial role the bureaucracy provides due process for individuals or groups involved in disputes with an agency. Due process provides all parties involved the right to a fair hearing and the right to appeal bureaucratic decisions.

In addition to implementing administrative law, each bureaucratic unit exercises its responsibility in specific areas. At times there may be some overlapping of responsibilities in law enforcement; for example, both the Federal Bureau of Investigation and the Drug Enforcement Agency may investigate a case involving the importation of illegal narcotics. However, most agencies serve a specific need of a particular group. The members of such groups are known as **clients.** An individual may be the client of more than one agency at a time; for example, a retired veteran may seek help from both the Social Security Administration and Veterans Affairs. Clients are not always provided a service in the sense of benefits, though. Certain agencies function as regulators and controllers: the Environmental Protection Agency (EPA) regulates the development and use of pesticides, and the Internal Revenue Service regulates all taxpayers.

Bureaucracies operate according to clearly defined procedures. These methods, known as **standard operating procedures** (SOPs), have both a positive and negative side. Positively, they help ensure that everyone is treated alike and that decisions are less subjective. Negatively, SOPs are rigid, making it difficult for individuals having exceptional situations to receive prompt help. SOPs may seem to make the relationship between agency and client an impersonal one; however, when adhered to, these rules help control bureaucratic authority by lessening the discretionary power of the bureaucrats. For example, when housing assistance is provided to low-income families, clearly defined procedures and conditions help prevent bureaucrats from exercising their own judgment to exclude a particular client who might otherwise qualify for help.

Major Federal Regulators

	Agency	Basic Statistics	Major Functions
TRADE	Antitrust Division (Justice Department)	8 offices	Mission is to promote and protect the competitive process and the American economy through the enforcement of antitrust laws
	Federal Trade Commission (FTC)	Created in 1914; 7 regional offices	Has broad discretion to curb unfair trade practices, to protect consumers, and to maintain competition
	Food and Drug Administration (FDA)	Founded in 1906 as the Bureau of Chemistry; employs 9,100	Is responsible for the safety and efficacy of drugs and medical devices and the safety and purity of food; regulates labeling; oversees about $1 trillion worth of industrial output
FINANCE AND COMPETITION	Federal Deposit Insurance Corporation (FDIC)	Created in 1933; 8 regional and 90 field offices	Created during New Deal in response to bank failures; promotes safe, sound banking practices; shares regulatory power with the states over state-chartered banks not in the Federal Reserve System
	Federal Communications Commission (FCC)	Created in 1934; directly responsible to Congress; 5 commissioners; 6 bureaus; 10 staff offices	Regulates interstate and international communications by radio, television, wire, satellite, and cable; jurisdiction covers 50 states, District of Columbia, and U.S. possessions
	Securities and Exchange Commission (SEC)	Created in 1934; 2,900 employees; 5 commissioners; 4 divisions; 11 regional and district offices	Protects investors and maintains the integrity of the securities market; enforces public-disclosure and securities-fraud laws
	Civil Aeronautics Board	Created in 1938	Regulates airline fares and routes
CONSUMER PROTECTION	Federal Aviation Administration (FAA)	Created in 1958; 15 regional and office centers	Regulates civil aviation to promote safety and fulfill national defense requirements; operates common system of air traffic control for civil and military aircraft; regulates U.S. commercial space transportation
	National Highway Traffic Safety Administration	Created in 1970; 10 regional offices	Sets and enforces safety standards for motor vehicles and equipment; investigates safety defects; promotes use of safety belts, child safety seats, air bags, etc.; conducts research on driver behavior and traffic safety
	Environmental Protection Agency (EPA)	Created in 1970; employs 18,000; 10 offices; 17 laboratories	Develops and enforces standards for clean air and water; controls pollution from pesticides and toxic substances; approves state pollution abatement plans; rules on environmental-impact statements
	Occupational Safety and Health Administration (OSHA)	Created in 1971; employs 2,100 inspectors plus support personnel; 200 offices	Federal and state governments work in partnership to save lives, prevent injuries, and protect the health of the American worker
	Consumer Product Safety Commission	Established in 1972; 6 offices; employs 480	Designed to reduce product-related injuries to consumers by mandating better design, labeling, and instruction sheets

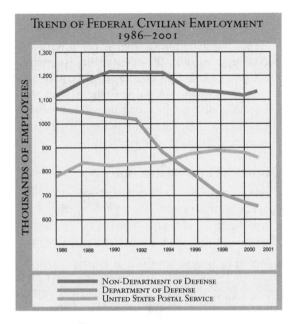

TREND OF FEDERAL CIVILIAN EMPLOYMENT
1986–2001

THOUSANDS OF EMPLOYEES

NON-DEPARTMENT OF DEFENSE
DEPARTMENT OF DEFENSE
UNITED STATES POSTAL SERVICE

Section Review

1. Why is the EOP the most powerful segment of the executive branch?

2. Why is the Office of Management and Budget so influential?

3. What is the purpose of the National Security Council? Describe how it came into being.

4. Define *cabinet* and explain what the Constitution says concerning it.

5. What does the cabinet's growth reflect? How are cabinet positions filled?

6. Why are independent agencies independent? How are they grouped?

7. How is the American bureaucracy quasi-legislative? quasi-executive? quasi-judicial?

III. Bureaucratic Realities

In framing a government which is to be administrated by men over men, the great difficulty lies in this: you must first enable the government to control the governed; and in the next place oblige it to control itself.

—*James Madison,* The Federalist No. 51

The Fourth Branch

The Congress, the president, and the courts all exercise constitutionally derived power as three separate but interdependent branches of the national government. Given its power and pervasiveness, the federal bureaucracy is sometimes referred to as the **fourth branch** of government. There are four major causes for this reference: separation of powers, size, skills, and desire for security.

Separation of Powers—The bureaucracy often increases its independence by taking advantage of the separation of powers of the three major branches of government. For example, an agency having strong ties with a congressional committee may seek help on a proposal that has met with executive resistance. This may result in legislation that will force the president to consider the program. For years the FBI has maintained considerable independence from both the president and the attorney general because of the bureau's strong congressional ties.

Size—Another factor supporting the idea that the bureaucracy is a "fourth branch" of government is size. The growth in the number and size of federal agencies has made the bureaucracy the largest segment of the national government, with millions of civilian employees in the executive branch alone. Size creates problems of supervision. The president cannot supervise all the federal departments. In fact, the Executive Office of the President, originally created to help the president supervise the bureaucracy, has become so large that it too now requires supervision. However, there has been an increased effort to reduce bureaucratic size. For a short period of time, the Clinton administration did trim the bureaucracy below three million by cutting jobs within the Department of Defense. The George W. Bush administration encouraged more privatization of government services.

Skills—The skills that many agency officials provide also strengthen the independence of the bureaucracy. Expertise in a variety of technical fields such as pollution control, aircraft design,

USS Seawolf *(SSN-21)*

laser weaponry, and census statistics means that bureaucrats are sought out for their advice on legislative matters. These agency officials can easily control the information Congress receives and thereby influence legislation and shape policy.

Desire for Security—The independence of the federal bureaucracy is further illustrated by the intense struggle for security that agencies exercise over their internal affairs. Bureaucrats who break the code of silence by disclosing evidence of waste and mismanagement often do so at the risk of their own jobs. These "whistle-blowers," as they are called, may be fired, retired, or relocated for making public complaints about costly bureaucratic bungling.

M1A1 Abrams tanks with the 1ˢᵗ Armored Division in Glamor, Bosnia and Herzegovina, April 2, 1998

The so-called "fourth branch" is powerful and pervasive. Its capacity for independence is certainly great given its size, its role in implementing law, and the complexity of its responsibilities. The president and Congress, however, both maintain powerful checks to help curb the power of the giant bureaucratic machine.

Oversight and Restriction

Oversight—Bureaucrats cannot operate without congressional **oversight,** the process of examining a department's compliance with the law and scrutinizing its budget requests. Members of Congress

F-22 Raptors

have constitutional powers over agencies and policy interests in how agencies function. No agency may exist without congressional approval except for a few presidential offices and commissions. Before the 1960s Congress passed statutes giving broad discretion to regulatory agencies such as the Federal Communications Commission. Since the 1960s, however, Congress has tended to restrict agency discretion. Agencies also may not spend **appropriations,** legislative grants of money to finance a government program, unless the money is first authorized and set aside by Congress. There has been a trend toward requiring annual authorizations to strengthen congressional control over certain executive agencies. Examples include NASA and those agencies that administer foreign aid or procure military equipment for the Defense Department. Appropriating funds may have a budget-cutting effect since appropriations can be less than authorized.

Restrictions—The Congress, the president, and the public restrict bureaucratic power through various means. Congress can exercise checks over the bureaucracy by authorizing the **General Accounting Office** (GAO) to audit an agency's finances and monitor its activities. Since the GAO may request public hearings about an agency's programs, officials are generally highly responsive to a GAO investigation.

The president helps restrict bureaucratic power by reorganizing parts of the bureaucracy or appointing an investigative task force. The president cannot directly fire civil servants, but by agency reorganization he can do away with their jobs. For example, President Nixon established the Office of Management and Budget to replace the old Bureau of the Budget, gaining greater control over the budget and policy decisions. President Reagan's action of appointing a task force to investigate government regulations resulted in substantial reductions in federal regulations as well as savings in agency operating costs. The *Federal Register,* a multi-thousand-page document that lists the regulations proposed and approved for a single year, was reduced by 42% during Reagan's first four years.

The bureaucracy poses a threat to democratic government when it fails to be responsive to the voice of the people and their elected representatives or when it attempts to rule instead of serve. Citizen involvement can help restrict this potential threat. Through legislation during the 1970s and 1980s, the bureaucratic process was opened up to greater citizen input. In 1974 the amended **Freedom of Information Act** (FOIA) provided citizens access to information previously withheld. Information about bureaucratic activities permits more effective challenge and greater control by concerned citizens. Dangers are inherent in this law, though, from those who attempt to acquire and exploit sensitive information about national security. However, if used properly, the FOIA can be a helpful tool for restricting the bureaucracy. The **Sunshine Act** has also provided greater citizen participation in bureaucratic decision-making. This law cast some light on previously closed-door meetings by requiring federal agencies to hold well-announced public hearings. The Sunshine Act allows citizens access to agency officials and a stronger voice in bureaucratic proceedings.

Problems

Criticizing the bureaucracy is one of America's favorite pastimes. Criticism against bureaucrats comes from every level of society: from rich and poor; from Democrats and Republicans; from Wisconsin dairy farmers and Detroit autoworkers. All criticize the bureaucracy in general and some agencies in particular. Even some bureaucrats, at the risk of losing their own jobs, criticize bureaucrats. There are six major bureaucratic problems at which these criticisms are leveled—red tape, conflict, duplication, vague goals, waste, and bureaucratic language.

Red Tape—Bureaucratic paperwork, **red tape,** can be one of the more frustrating problems that individuals and businesses alike confront when dealing with government agencies. Businesses in particular are hardest hit by government red tape as they attempt to comply with confusing and at times conflicting demands from a variety of agencies covering everything from employment practices and health and safety standards to pollution control. A large amount of governmental red tape results from the need to satisfy political and legal requirements for accountability, citizen access, and fairness. The government, for example, must often buy from American rather than foreign suppliers even if the latter charges a lower price. It must use contractors that employ minorities and hire only union laborers and pay them a high wage. The government must allow the public to inspect its records

USDA meat inspector

and is often required to select contractors favored by influential members of Congress. The requirements go on and on. Private groups do not have to adhere to all these rules and can therefore save money.

Conflict—Some agencies, misunderstanding each other's purposes, seem to be working against each other, resulting in conflict. For example, the State Department may want to make concessions on arms testing to help a diplomatic venture, whereas the Defense Department may think the tests are necessary for long-term national security.

Duplication—Duplication, two government agencies doing the same thing, results in inefficiency. This was evidenced in the late 1990s when President Clinton wanted to expand the federal government by $1 trillion. Before granting the president's request, the Senate asked for a report from the Inspectors General. When the report was presented, case after case of government duplication was noted. It was found that if a plant produced pizzas with meat toppings, the USDA was responsible for inspecting the plant. But if the same plant put cheese on those meat pizzas, the FDA was also responsible to inspect. Other examples include baked beans with bacon being inspected by the USDA while pork and beans inspections were by the FDA; hot dogs in a roll were inspected by the FDA while hot dogs in a pastry were inspected by the USDA. After this information was presented,

the Senate naturally had misgivings about approving the president's request.

Vague Goals—When Congress has not set clear goals for an agency, the agency will sometimes take the greatest view of its power, or interest groups and judges will rush in to take advantage of the vague goals. For instance, in 1973 the Department of Transportation, when pressured by organized groups of handicapped people, changed a vague antidiscrimination provision in the Rehabilitation Act into a requirement: every big-city bus must have a device installed to lift wheelchairs onboard. This requirement was an unrealistic, expensive solution to the problem, and the rule was later repealed.

Waste—Possibly the biggest criticism leveled at the federal bureaucracy is with regard to **waste,** mismanagement of money, time, and personnel. Government waste is staggering. President Reagan tried to tackle the problem of wasteful spending by appointing the Grace Commission to investigate federal agencies. The commission report, released in 1984, found that the federal bureaucracy was the worst-run "business" in America. However, unlike a business concerned about maximizing profits, government agencies have weak incentives to keep costs down. If a business employee cuts costs, the firm gets to add the savings to its profits and the employee may even receive a raise or a bonus. If a government employee cuts costs, he or she receives no reward, and the agency cannot keep the savings because the money goes back to the Treasury.

Bureaucratic Language—Another problem with the bureaucratic system is the use of "gobbledygook"—vague, sprawling language to describe something simple. This wordy jargon, often called **bureaucratese** or doublespeak, is the language of bureaucratic regulations, documents, and forms. Doublespeak hides meaning in imprecision and can make bad things seem positive. For example, the State Department described the killing of political prisoners under certain Latin American regimes as the "unlawful or arbitrary deprivation of life."

Bureaucratic language does not simply represent an alternate writing style; it represents a contempt for the truth. Solomon was a wise and learned ruler whose words, even centuries later, ring with simplicity and truth. The book of Proverbs does not refer to a man who disobeys God's Word and way as an "individual exhibiting inordinacy"; Solomon calls him a "fool." He also refuses to label "subjectively interpreted intrapersonal rehearsal" as anything less than gossip, or "tale-bearing." In Proverbs 10:19 Solomon notes that sin can often be found in a "multitude of words." Our words must be true, clear, and honest because they come from a heart that loves Him who is the Truth.

Change

The federal bureaucracy is big, powerful, and expensive. Politicians annually promise to curb bureaucratic power, and ironically many of the offices that have been established to control federal agencies and implement presidential policies eventually blend in with their surroundings and become just another cog in the bureaucratic machine. In short, the bureaucracy resists change. President Carter learned this fact, much to his chagrin, when his attempts to reorganize and trim the bureaucracy met with stubborn resistance. In fact, the bureaucracy actually grew during the Carter years.

Federal agencies resist not only the president but each other as well. Agencies engage in power struggles with other agencies over bigger budgets, larger staffs, and greater jurisdiction. At times departments are at odds with each other over basic goals.

Presidents have long bemoaned the unresponsiveness of the federal bureaucracy. The distance between presidential policy and bureaucratic implementation may be great indeed. Foot dragging, quiet opposition, or just the long paper trail down the bureaucratic pyramid can produce significant delays in acting on a White House request. President Truman underscored the problem well in his remarks about his successor, Eisenhower: "Poor Ike; he'll sit here and he'll say, 'Do this.' 'Do that.' And nothing will happen. It won't be a bit like the Army. He'll find it very frustrating."

Part of the difficulty between presidents and their bureaucratic subordinates is the basic issue of time. Presidents serve for a few years, but many bureaucrats can expect to keep their jobs until retirement. (Cabinet officials and most of the EOP change with each administration.) If a department particularly resents a White House policy, bureaucrats may slow down action or even stop it. President Nixon sought to correct this problem by placing some of his appointees in lower-level positions to increase the likelihood of action on his policies.

During the 1990s the Clinton administration tried to make government more streamlined through its National Performance Review, more popularly called "reinventing government" (REGO). This program's focus was not like previous efforts that sought to strengthen presidential power or incorporate independent agencies into a few big departments. REGO sought to "cut red tape," "empower employees," and "put customers first." The goal of REGO was to create a government that "works better and costs less." Some positive changes did occur. The Office of Personnel Management simplified the way bureaucrats are hired and fired. Many agencies created customer-service standards. For example, the Postal Service promised to deliver local first-class mail within one day.

Distinctiveness and Achievements

Distinctiveness—All modern societies, whether democratic or nondemocratic, possess a bureaucracy. However, there are four aspects of the United States' constitutional system and political traditions that give its bureaucracy a distinctive character. The first aspect is that the presidency and Congress share political authority over the bureaucracy. Senior appointed officials have at least two masters: congressional committees and executive committees. Divided authority enables bureaucrats to play one branch of government against another

Tom Moreland Interchange, Atlanta, Georgia

Achievements—It would be an injustice to outline the previously noted problems and needed changes of the federal bureaucracy without mentioning its impressive accomplishments.

Technological advances such as the development of the atomic bomb, which brought a swift end to World War II, and landing Americans on the moon were both the work of federal agencies. Numerous consumer services are provided by

Nebraska soybean bus

and also make great use of the media. In nations with parliamentary governments, such as Great Britain, where the prime minister and cabinet control the bureaucracy, this division of authority is unknown.

The second aspect of American government distinctiveness is that most federal agencies share their functions with related agencies in state and local governments. Some federal agencies, such as the Postal Service, deal directly with the people, but federal agencies associated with education or housing work with state agencies. In France these types of programs are run by the central government with no local government control.

Americans' interest in preserving and even demanding their rights, fueled by political and social movements of the 1960s, is a third distinction. Lawsuits and various political actions have given personal rights a central focus. American government agencies receive greater public scrutiny, with more potential court challenges, than almost any other nation.

The fourth distinctive of America's bureaucracy is its differing range and style. Most governments in Western Europe own and operate large parts of their economies. In parts of Europe 12 percent of all employment is through publicly-owned enterprises. In the United States it is less than 3 percent. However, the United States government regulates privately-owned enterprises to a greater degree than many other countries do.

groups within the bureaucracy. Each year the United States Postal Service handles millions of letters and packages efficiently. The interstate highway system, a bureaucratic effort, is the largest, best-built road system in the world. Millions of Americans over the age of sixty-five enjoy retirement benefits provided through the Social Security Administration. The efforts of federal agencies in consumer protection have doubtless saved thousands of lives. The safety standards imposed by the Consumer Product Safety Commission led to a 40 percent drop in infant deaths from poisons and crib strangulation. Measures taken by the National Highway Traffic Safety Administration have saved countless lives on America's highways.

The bureaucracy is a necessary part of modern American government. Though many negatives are often associated with the bureaucracy, the valuable services that it provides should not be minimized.

Section Review

1. List the reasons the federal bureaucracy is sometimes called the "fourth branch" of government.

2. What body has oversight over most American bureaucratic agencies?

3. How does Congress use the General Accounting Office to check the federal bureaucracy?

4. How can the president restrict bureaucratic power?

5. What acts enable citizens to keep the bureaucracy more accountable?

6. What are six problems with America's bureaucracy?

7. How did Clinton's "reinventing government" differ from past attempts to modify or change government?

8. How does America's bureaucracy differ from Great Britain's?

Chapter Review

Terms

bureaucracy
bureaucrat
delegation
civil service
merit
Pendleton Act
chief of staff
press secretary

cabinet
statutory law
administrative law
clients
standard operating procedures
fourth branch
oversight
appropriations

General Accounting Office (GAO)
Freedom of Information Act (FOIA)
Sunshine Act
red tape
waste
bureaucratese

Content Questions

1. Why is bureaucracy necessary? Give a biblical precedent for bureaucracy.

2. Contrast the spoils system and the modern merit system of selecting civil servants.

3. What are the different levels of the bureaucratic pyramid beneath the president? What are the primary duties at each level?

4. How do Congress, the president, and private citizens "check" the bureaucracy?

5. How is America's bureaucracy distinct from other governments' bureaucracies?

Application Questions

1. Can a large business or institution be run efficiently without the help of a bureaucratic pyramid?

2. What legitimate complaints can you make about the federal bureaucracy, and what can you do about them?

3. Why does bureaucratese conflict with Scripture and biblical principles?

4. How does the existence of a bureaucracy threaten to undermine the separation of powers in the federal government?

5. How would personal responsibility and individual initiative be better options than federal control of some of the services now provided by the government? Give specific examples.

Secretary of Defense Donald Rumsfeld with Portuguese Minister of State and Defense Paulo Portas

Red carpet, crisp uniforms, and a brass band provide an impressive backdrop as the president of the United States welcomes a visiting head of state to the White House. In Riyadh, Saudi Arabia, an Arab businessman checks the Coca-Cola dispenser at his Kentucky Fried Chicken franchise. Over a dry California lakebed, an air force test pilot soars upward as he pulls back on the throttle of an experimental aircraft. From his Washington office, a federal agent works feverishly to track an Internet virus originating somewhere in the Far East. All these events reflect some aspect of American foreign policy.

I. Foreign Policy Goals

Foreign policy is the policy of the United States designed to achieve American objectives in its interaction with other nations. Despite changes in political leadership, advances in military technology, and shifts in the geopolitical balance, certain basic goals remain central to American foreign policy: national security, alliance security, international stability, and economic development.

Although the goals remain largely the same, the means of achieving them change. For example, during the Cold War the United States successfully countered an attempt by the Soviet Union to spread communism throughout the world. But after the collapse of the Soviet empire and the rise of global terrorism, the United States tried to make an ally of Russia, the Soviet Union's largest successor state. Likewise, before the Great Depression, the United States believed that its economic interests were best served by maintaining high tariffs. Then after World War II, the United States helped form the General Agreement on Tariffs and Trade (GATT) and the World Trade Organization (WTO), which attempted to lower tariffs. In each case the United States government pursued a foreign policy that was perceived to be in the best interest of the nation at that time.

Security watch on the USS Theodore Roosevelt during Suez Canal transit

National Security

A primary goal of foreign policy is national security, protecting the nation and its citizens and property abroad. In fact, providing protection for a nation's citizens is a biblical justification for government. Throughout American history, national defense has been a constant theme—a theme voiced as early as 1798 in the anti-French slogan "Millions for defense, but not one cent for tribute!"

Nevertheless, American security was rarely threatened in the nineteenth century. After winning its independence, the United States never experienced a foreign invasion except during the War of 1812. Sheltered by two oceans, flanked by weak neighbors, and guided by a policy of isolation from turbulent Europe, America faced few challenges to its safety.

But beginning with World War II, a shrinking world meant increased threats to American security. Following the Japanese attack on Pearl Harbor in 1941, the United States shifted decisively from isolationism to international involvement. Concern about national security only deepened during the Cold War. In response to a Soviet nuclear threat, the United States maintained a large peacetime military force, sought to ease tensions diplomatically, and fought limited wars against communism in Korea, Vietnam, and Central America. Even after the fall of the Soviet Union in 1991, maintaining national security continued to be a costly necessity because of the growth of international terrorism. In the words of Thomas Jefferson, "Eternal vigilance is the price of liberty."

Alliance Security

One way for the government to protect America is to support its allies abroad. Such support may involve diplomatic cooperation, economic assistance, and even military intervention. For instance, twice in the twentieth century the United States fought beside its beleaguered friends in Europe.

Sometimes support for allied nations is ratified by a formal **alliance,** a treaty that unites its participants in a common cause. Military alliances often

A meeting of NATO's North Atlantic Council in 2004

include a **collective security,** or mutual defense, pact promising that an attack on one member will be treated as an attack on all. Following World War II, the United States organized the North Atlantic Treaty Organization (NATO) to present a united front against the Soviet Union and its satellite states. Even today, NATO remains a significant part of U.S. foreign policy.

International Stability

Another method of protecting American security is to encourage international stability. The United States has often taken the lead in trying to end war or threats of war with diplomacy. Given the modern interdependence of nations, cooling global hot spots in order to retard the spread of violence to other areas of the world has become a foreign policy objective. The United States promotes international stability through direct diplomacy by acting as a diplomatic intermediary between hostile nations and by working through international organizations such as the United Nations.

For instance, the United States has long attempted to promote international stability in the oil-rich Middle East, where the United States has important economic interests. The United States

has close ties with Israel, a westernized nation surrounded by hostile and less economically developed Arab states. At the same time, the United States has also recognized the legitimate rights of the Arab people. During the 1973 Yom Kippur War, Arab nations cut off oil shipments to the United States and other nations that supported Israel in its war with Egypt and Syria. Through skillful diplomacy, Secretary of State Henry Kissinger forged a shaky peace between Israel, Egypt, and Syria that resulted in the lifting of the oil embargo. In 1978 President Carter brought the leaders of Israel and Egypt together in an attempt to build a "framework for peace" in the Middle East. The result was the Camp David Accords, in which the Israelis made territorial concessions while the Egyptians officially recognized Israel as a nation.

Nevertheless, all attempts at making peace in the Middle East have been limited at best. Every president since Carter has faced his own Middle East crisis, and each has had to nurture—or attempt to resuscitate—the peace process.

Attempts at peacemaking are commendable, and there is no shortage of work to be done, but

President Carter celebrating the Camp David Accords with Anwar Sadat and Menachem Begin

Distributing humanitarian rations in Iraq

resolutions of international conflicts are often temporary. The search for lasting peace is elusive because man's sinful nature produces injustice, hatred, greed, and cruelty. The sinfulness of man ensures that world peace can never be permanent until the return of Jesus Christ, the Prince of Peace.

Economic Development

Economic development is another important part of American foreign policy. Participation in economic development moves third-world countries toward the free world and gains necessary markets for capitalist economies. Although private trade and investment abroad have stimulated most economic development, the United States government has also given direct aid to countries stricken by war, famine, and natural disasters. Relief (usually given in the form of American goods) has been provided to millions abroad. For instance, after World War II, the United States responded to European devastation with the **Marshall Plan,** which supplied billions of dollars to Western Europe to

rebuild shattered economies and thereby bolster democracy.

The Marshall Plan well illustrated an important goal of American economic aid—building self-sustaining economies rather than encouraging dependence on American dollars. Following the rebuilding of Europe, America sent assistance to underdeveloped nations in Asia, Africa, and Latin America, though usually with less than satisfying results.

Section Review

1. What are the four basic goals of American foreign policy?
2. What threats have changed U.S. foreign policy toward national security since World War II?
3. What is the most significant modern military alliance to which the United States now belongs?
4. How has the growing interdependence of nations affected foreign policy?
5. What positive effects can economic development have for both the receiving nation as well as the United States?

II. The Progress of Policy
Isolation, 1790–1890

The dominant theme of foreign policy during America's first century was **isolationism,** a policy first formulated during the Washington administration. Alexander Hamilton, the first secretary of the treasury, urged strong ties with Great Britain, while Thomas Jefferson advocated a pro-French policy. George Washington, however, believed that America's fortunes should not be tied to Europe. In his influential Farewell Address, the aging president wrote:

> Europe has a set of primary interests which to us have none; or a very remote relation. Hence she must be engaged in frequent controversies, the causes of which are essentially foreign to

Thomas Jefferson

our concerns. . . . Our detached and distant situation invites and enables us to pursue a different course. . . . It is our true policy to steer clear of permanent alliances with any portion of the reign world; . . . [but] we may safely trust to temporary alliances for extraordinary emergencies.

Some years later, President Jefferson echoed Washington's words when he declared, "Peace, commerce, and honest friendship with all nations, *entangling alliances with none.*"

Though *isolationism* is the term generally used to characterize nineteenth-century American foreign policy, the expression is somewhat misleading. The United States did not cut itself off from foreign contacts. The fledgling nation fought one undeclared naval war with France over freedom of the seas and another against pirates in the Mediterranean. Throughout the nineteenth century the United States established strong commercial ties in Europe, Africa, and Asia. In 1853, Commodore Matthew Perry negotiated the first treaty between Japan and a Western nation. American missionaries helped bring the gospel to China, and Adoniram Judson was the first to preach salvation through Christ in Burma.

America's nineteenth-century policy of isolation can best be described as an attempt to preserve its independence while it busied itself with continental expansion. One of the clearest assertions of this policy was the **Monroe Doctrine** issued in 1823. Fearing that Europeans might threaten the United States by reasserting control over weak Latin American states that had recently thrown off the yoke of Spain, Monroe declared,

> We owe it, therefore, to candor and to the amicable relations existing between the United States and those powers to declare that we should consider any attempt on their part to extend their system to any portion of this hemisphere as dangerous to our peace and safety.

The Monroe Doctrine restated a long-standing opposition to a European presence in the Western Hemisphere, even though at the time, the policy was mostly brash talk from a nation whose capital had been burned by British troops only nine years earlier. Fortunately, the British themselves had a trading interest in a free Latin America and effectively defended the Monroe Doctrine with their own navy.

As the United States grew stronger, so did the Monroe Doctrine. Several nineteenth-century presidents threatened Europe with military force because of their violations of the doctrine. President Kennedy invoked the Monroe Doctrine in 1962 when he blocked the Soviet attempt to install missiles in Cuba. The policy was also used to justify arming an anticommunist army fighting Nicaragua's Soviet- and Cuban-backed regime.

Expansion, 1890–1910

By the last decade of the nineteenth century, the United States was an emerging force in the world community and had an important manufacturing sector. With the continental frontier now nearly a memory, the United States abandoned isolationism for both an increased participation in international commerce and a contemporary craving for colonies. One excuse for the latter was that its new steam-powered navy seemed to demand coaling stations in the Pacific and the Caribbean. In 1898 the United States annexed the Hawaiian Islands and took from Spain its Pacific and Caribbean holdings—the Philippines, Guam, Puerto Rico, and

Cuba. The following year the U.S. acquired the Samoan Islands and announced the Open Door Policy in an attempt to preserve its markets in China.

These new imperialist policies were opposed at home and abroad, but powerful voices defended an expanded American role in world affairs. Against the charge that distance made overseas possessions impractical and improper, Senator Albert Beveridge, a leading expansionist, replied that steam, electricity, and the United States Navy would shortly "make them contiguous."

U.S. troops in World War I

Vacillation, 1910–1940

America's empire-building period was heady but short-lived. Expansionism declined as domestic concerns reasserted themselves. Yet because it was now a world power, the United States had unwittingly embarked on a course of global involvement from which there could be no turning back. Although Woodrow Wilson won reelection in 1916 because "he kept our boys out of war," they were eventually sent anyway to support American allies in World War I.

At the end of the war, Wilson the isolationist became Wilson the architect of the League of Nations, an organization he believed would inaugurate an era of world peace. Yet for all his dreams of the League's potential and his own dogged efforts to see the United States join the organization, isolationist feeling remained strong enough for the U.S. Senate to reject American participation.

While Adolf Hitler was rebuilding the German war machine during the 1930s, the United States was passing neutrality legislation in a naïve attempt to stay out of another European conflict. By 1940 Hitler had conquered most of Europe, and only Britain remained in the fight against him. During the presidential campaign of that year, both the incumbent Franklin Roosevelt and the challenger Wendell Willkie promised that, if elected, they would keep America out of war. In October Roosevelt declared, "I have said this before, but I shall say it again and again and again: your boys are not going to be sent into any foreign war."

Obligation, 1940–1991

Pearl Harbor helped transform the United States into a superpower. The United States poured men and materiel (the equipment, apparatus, or supplies of a military force) into the effort to liberate the Pacific from the Japanese while, at the same time, subsidizing battered Allies—Britain, France, and the Soviet Union—in a successful effort to destroy the German war machine in Europe.

Unfortunately, along with the German defeat came Soviet conquest of Eastern Europe. By 1949 the Chinese mainland had also fallen to communist tyranny. Against the threat of expanding communism, isolation was not only dangerous but impossible.

During the **Cold War** between the United States and the Soviet Union, the United States practiced **nuclear deterrence,** discouraging Soviet aggression by building a nuclear arsenal so large that the Soviets faced massive retaliation if they attacked the United States or its allies. A second foreign policy theme was **containment,** confronting the Russians with counterforce whenever they tried to expand the communist empire. At times the policy of containment turned the Cold War into hot wars, as in Korea and Vietnam.

The losing war in Vietnam dealt a blow to the theory of containment. The Soviet-backed North

Satellite photo of Cuban missile site in 1962

Vietnamese forced the American military into a long and costly struggle, a struggle in which fifty-eight thousand Americans died in a futile effort to protect the region from communist domination. The last American troops withdrew in 1973, and South Vietnam fell to the communists two years later. American defeat in Southeast Asia led to a new "psychological isolationism" best expressed by the slogan "No more Vietnams!"

Nevertheless, the election of Ronald Reagan to the presidency in 1980 proved a turning point in the American struggle against the Russians and their allies. Reagan openly dubbed the Soviet Union an "evil empire" and doubled the national debt in order to rebuild the American military in such a way that the Soviets could not match it. Furthermore, Reagan promised to roll back communism by supporting anticommunist insurgencies abroad. Weakened by its pathetic economy and by its own "Vietnam" in Afghanistan, the Russian empire suddenly collapsed after the fall of the Berlin Wall in 1989. In 1991, the Soviet Union itself disintegrated into its component parts.

Transition, 1991 to the Present

The relative peace of the 1990s strengthened economic growth around the world. The United States joined a free-trade agreement (NAFTA) with Mexico and Canada and also sought to integrate developing countries and former communist states into a world economy.

The United States now stood alone as the world's only superpower. Instead of facing a single threat from the Russians, The U.S. encountered smaller, more unpredictable dangers from nearly every part of the globe. The United States moved cautiously in assessing its new role, struggling to maintain the peace while also trying to avoid becoming the world's policeman.

After Iraqi dictator Saddam Hussein invaded Kuwait and threatened to manipulate a sizable percentage of the world's known oil reserves, a coalition of forces led by the United States defeated the Iraqis in 1991. Nevertheless, because the United States feared offending its allies and suffering more casualties, Saddam Hussein was allowed to remain in power.

In the 1990s American forces performed peacekeeping operations in the Balkans, Somalia, and Haiti, while more risky trouble spots were ignored or treated with superficiality. As with everything else, President Bill Clinton took a pragmatic approach to foreign policy. He intervened abroad when the stakes seemed low and the probability of success high.

On September 11, 2001, American optimism about national security in the post–Cold War world evaporated when Muslim terrorists seized four planes and killed more than three thousand people in attacks on the World Trade Center and the Pentagon. President George W. Bush sent troops to Afghanistan to eliminate the terrorist leaders (some trained by Americans to fight the Russians two decades before) and the Taliban regime that harbored them. In 2003, Bush continued a policy of preemptive action against supporters of terrorism by making war on Iraq and removing Saddam Hussein from power.

A marine sights his target during Operation Desert Storm in Saudi Arabia, 1991.

At the dawn of the twenty-first century, protecting the United States from foreign threats remained as complicated as ever. Attempts to counter terrorism on a grand scale prompted questions about the balance between national security and individual liberty at home and the limits to which the United States could unilaterally exercise its superpower status abroad.

Section Review

1. What was the Monroe Doctrine, and how did it demonstrate isolationism?
2. Give an example of American attempts at expansion.
3. What two themes shaped U.S. foreign policy during the Cold War?
4. How have the terrorist attacks of September 11, 2001, shaped American foreign policy?

III. Policymakers

The President

The president occupies the center stage in the making of American foreign policy both because of the powers granted to him by the Constitution and because of those he has acquired by tradition. In his role as commander in chief, the president heads the military forces of the United States. As head of state, he represents the United States abroad and initiates treaties and agreements with foreign leaders. As chief executive, the president appoints the secretaries of state and defense (the top foreign policy making departments) as well as the diplomatic corps.

Given the extent of the president's power, it is hardly surprising that a president's personality and interests have shaped foreign policy. For instance, Theodore Roosevelt enjoyed the power of the presidency as few other chief executives have, and his foreign policy reflected his pugnacious exuberance. Roosevelt ordered American troops to the

Dominican Republic just to collect that country's debts to European investors. After the Colombian government attempted to hike the price of a right-of-way for an isthmian canal, Roosevelt sponsored a revolution that led to the creation of the new state of Panama—which proved much more amenable to American demands. When Roosevelt sent the American navy—the Great White Fleet—around the world, a group of congressmen threatened to cut off its funding. "Very well," replied Roosevelt. "The existing appropriation will carry the Navy halfway around the world, and if Congress chooses to leave it on the other side, all right."

Roosevelt's initiatives stimulated national pride and deterred potential enemies of the United States, at least temporarily. But Roosevelt's "big stick" policies resulted in some unintended consequences, including growing resentment of Yankee power on the part of Latin American nations.

Executive Office

As noted earlier, advisors within the Executive Office of the President help the president shape and implement foreign policy.

National Security Council—The **National Security Council (NSC),** which supplies informa-

NSC meeting

tion and guidance for the president, includes the vice president; the secretaries of state, defense, and the treasury; the chairman of the Joint Chiefs of Staff; and the director of the Central Intelligence Agency. The **national security advisor** serves as NSC director. Some advisors have been relatively faceless; Ronald Reagan had five. Others, such as Henry Kissinger in Richard Nixon's administration, have played important roles in the making of administration policy. Likewise, Condoleezza Rice, the first female national security advisor, emerged as an influential foreign policy player in the George W. Bush administration.

The president receives national security briefings daily. During periods of international tension, such as the aftermath of the September 11 attack, the national security advisor and other close advisors, such as the chief of staff, form a crisis management team.

The **State Department** and the **Defense Department** administer the two arms of American foreign policy, international relations and national security. The department secretaries are usually influential members of the president's cabinet.

State Department—The Department of State is the oldest and the most prestigious cabinet office. Many

Roosevelt with his "big stick"

United States Department of State

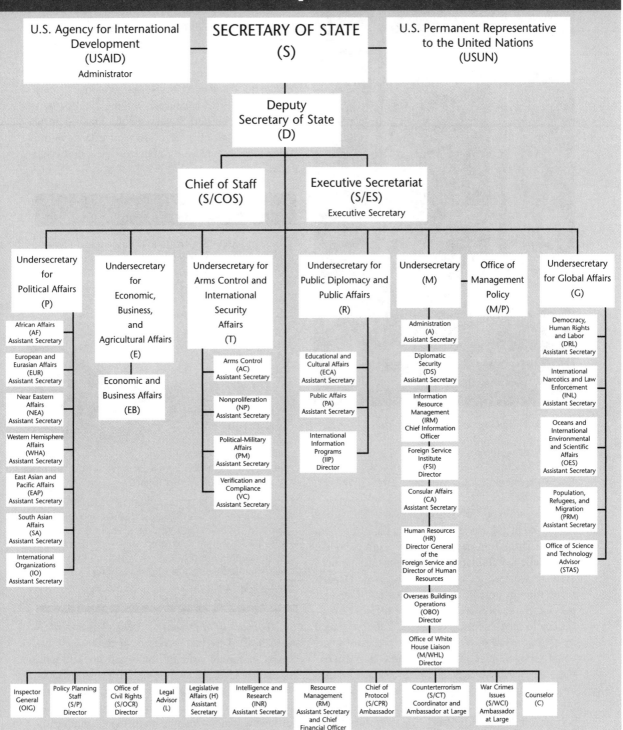

U.S. Agency for International Development (USAID)
Administrator

SECRETARY OF STATE (S)

U.S. Permanent Representative to the United Nations (USUN)

Deputy Secretary of State (D)

Chief of Staff (S/COS)

Executive Secretariat (S/ES)
Executive Secretary

Undersecretary for Political Affairs (P)
- African Affairs (AF) Assistant Secretary
- European and Eurasian Affairs (EUR) Assistant Secretary
- Near Eastern Affairs (NEA) Assistant Secretary
- Western Hemisphere Affairs (WHA) Assistant Secretary
- East Asian and Pacific Affairs (EAP) Assistant Secretary
- South Asian Affairs (SA) Assistant Secretary
- International Organizations (IO) Assistant Secretary

Undersecretary for Economic, Business, and Agricultural Affairs (E)
- Economic and Business Affairs (EB)

Undersecretary for Arms Control and International Security Affairs (T)
- Arms Control (AC) Assistant Secretary
- Nonproliferation (NP) Assistant Secretary
- Political-Military Affairs (PM) Assistant Secretary
- Verification and Compliance (VC) Assistant Secretary

Undersecretary for Public Diplomacy and Public Affairs (R)
- Educational and Cultural Affairs (ECA) Assistant Secretary
- Public Affairs (PA) Assistant Secretary
- International Information Programs (IIP) Director

Undersecretary (M)
- Administration (A) Assistant Secretary
- Diplomatic Security (DS) Assistant Secretary
- Information Resource Management (IRM) Chief Information Officer
- Foreign Service Institute (FSI) Director
- Consular Affairs (CA) Assistant Secretary
- Human Resources (HR) Director General of the Foreign Service and Director of Human Resources
- Overseas Buildings Operations (OBO) Director
- Office of White House Liaison (M/WHL) Director

Office of Management Policy (M/P)

Undersecretary for Global Affairs (G)
- Democracy, Human Rights and Labor (DRL) Assistant Secretary
- International Narcotics and Law Enforcement (INL) Assistant Secretary
- Oceans and International Environmental and Scientific Affairs (OES) Assistant Secretary
- Population, Refugees, and Migration (PRM) Assistant Secretary
- Office of Science and Technology Advisor (STAS)

Inspector General (OIG)

Policy Planning Staff (S/P) Director

Office of Civil Rights (S/OCR) Director

Legal Advisor (L)

Legislative Affairs (H) Assistant Secretary

Intelligence and Research (INR) Assistant Secretary

Resource Management (RM) Assistant Secretary and Chief Financial Officer

Chief of Protocol (S/CPR) Ambassador

Counterterrorism (S/CT) Coordinator and Ambassador at Large

War Crimes Issues (S/WCI) Ambassador at Large

Counselor (C)

United States Embassy in Kabul, Afghanistan

distinguished individuals have headed the department, including Thomas Jefferson (and five other future presidents), John Marshall, Daniel Webster, and Henry Clay.

The **secretary of state** oversees more than twenty-eight thousand employees, many of them serving abroad as part of the **Foreign Service,** maintaining diplomatic relations in one hundred eighty countries. On the front line of State Department foreign policy are embassies and consular offices. **Embassies** are government offices or residences located in foreign capitals. Each is headed by an **ambassador,** who acts as the president's personal representative. The ambassador, a presidential appointee with Senate approval, generally has Foreign Service experience, although some posts are awarded as political favors. An ambassador's responsibility is to keep the administration informed about affairs in his country and to protect Americans and American interests within his area of responsibility.

Consular offices, or **consulates,** are located in foreign ports and other overseas trade centers. They exist primarily to encourage commercial contacts between the United States and the host country. Consulates also offer legal assistance to traveling Americans, provide immigration advice, and issue passports.

Passports

A **passport** is an official document that identifies and confirms the citizenship of a traveler. Canada, Mexico, and many Caribbean countries do not require Americans to carry passports while on short visits, but almost all other nations do. In addition, many countries require a **visa,** especially if the visitor plans an extended stay. A visa is an official endorsement of the passport by the government of the country to be visited. Visas are usually obtained from a consulate of the foreign nation in the United States.

The State Department issues passports to U.S. citizens. The prospective traveler applies by completing a form, submitting proofs of citizenship and identity, and supplying two identical passport photographs. Passports are valid for ten years in the case of adults, five years for children under eighteen.

Department of Defense—The Defense Department, headed by the **secretary of defense,** is the largest segment of the national government. Formed in 1947 by combining the Department of War and the Department of the Navy, the Defense Department comprises almost one and a half million men and women in uniform and another six

Pentagon

hundred thousand civilian employees. These personnel provide the force necessary to maintain American security.

There are three major levels in the Defense Department's organization. The secretary of defense chairs the department. The congressional act that created the department ordered that the secretary be a civilian who had not served in active military duty for at least ten years. This provision was intended to reflect the constitutional principle that military power should be subordinate to civilian power.

The founding fathers were well aware of military tyranny in both history and their contemporary world, and they were determined not to allow the military to play a dominant role in the United States government. Some extremists even advocated limiting the entire army to three thousand soldiers. Nevertheless, liberty had to be defended from aggressors without as well as from subversives within. As James Madison wrote in *Federalist No. 41,* the realities of greed and aggression made security against foreign danger a necessity. Therefore, the demands of both a free society and national security were balanced by establishing a military force that could be checked at several points by civilian authority.

The principle of civilian control extends to the next level of the defense organization as well.

Assisting the secretary of defense are civilian officials who work at the **Pentagon,** the huge Defense Department headquarters in Arlington, Virginia. These civilian officials—including the secretaries of the army, navy, and air force—are joined by top military officers—the **Joint Chiefs of Staff (JCS)**—in helping the secretary of defense shape defense policy. The Joint Chiefs are the highest-ranking officers of the army, navy, air force, and marines. Membership in this elite group is not based on seniority; rather, the Joint Chiefs are presidential appointees subject to Senate confirmation. During World War II, JCS members had command authority over their military branches, but today they serve only as military advisors. The civilian and military officials at this level make up the Armed Forces Policy Council, the major policy-making and coordinating group of the defense establishment.

A third level of the Defense Department is composed of the military branches: the army, navy, and air force. The army is the largest branch, operating primarily on land with infantry, artillery, tank, engineering, and chemical warfare units. The navy, with its fleet of approximately three hundred ships, maintains sea-lanes and, if necessary, delivers troops and firepower to hostile areas. The Marine

Iwo Jima Marine Corps War Memorial

367

Corps is a part of the navy but functions as a separate military branch. The primary mission of the marines is to secure beachheads for sea, air, and land operations. The air force, originally part of the army, was reorganized as a separate branch in 1947. The air force maintains both tactical (short-range) and strategic (long-range) aircraft as well as advanced missile systems.

Department of Homeland Security—Following the attacks of September 11, 2001, President George W. Bush responded with the largest reorganization of government since 1947. The new **Department of Homeland Security** treats a relatively new aspect of foreign relations—terrorist attacks on American soil. The department's responsibilities include four major categories: Border and Transportation Security; Emergency Preparedness and Response; Chemical, Biological, Radiological, and Nuclear Countermeasures; and Information Analysis and Infrastructure Protection. Several older government agencies were subordinated to this massive new department, including the Secret Service, the Coast Guard, the Federal Emergency Management Agency (FEMA), and part of the Immigration and Naturalization Service (INS). While the department is designed to guard against external dangers, some Americans have become concerned about the possible internal threat that the new department may pose to civil liberties.

Central Intelligence Agency—The **Central Intelligence Agency (CIA)** is another important element in the making and implementation of American foreign policy. The director of the CIA is a member of the NSC and generally enjoys regular access to the president. The CIA serves as the chief gatherer of intelligence, or information activities in foreign countries.

Intelligence gathering is as old as ancient warfare. Numbers 13 records how Moses sent twelve spies on a fact-finding mission to Canaan. Later Joshua, himself a former spy, sent two spies to Jericho in preparation for its conquest. George Washington made effective use of espionage during the American Revolution. During the Civil War, the Confederate victory at First Manassas was aided by an attractive brunette named Rose Greenhow who gleaned military information from the Washington social circuit. Nevertheless, intelligence gathering is not all cloak-and-dagger operations. The CIA gathers information from such obvious sources as foreign newspapers, radio broadcasts, and websites as well as from covert operations and satellite reconnaissance.

Congress

The president's superior position in making foreign policy is unquestioned; however, his power is at least nominally shared with Congress. As previously noted, the Senate is constitutionally empowered to approve treaties by a two-thirds vote. Senators may also append reservations and conditions to a treaty that were not part of the original agreement.

Ratified treaties generally require wide, bipartisan support, since the two-thirds requirement means that one-third plus one may veto a treaty. Treaties have sometimes been handled roughly by the Senate, as, for instance, the Treaty of Versailles during the Wilson administration and the SALT II agreement during the Carter administration.

The first Homeland Security secretary, Tom Ridge

The Senate's power to approve nominees for State and Defense Department positions provides it with a forum for discussing foreign policy. Similarly, the power of the purse gives the House of Representatives influence in such areas as defense spending and foreign aid.

Congress also has the constitutional power to declare war, but presidents have frequently authorized military action without congressional approval. Congress, on the other hand, has never declared war without presidential approval.

Media

No discussion of foreign policy making would be complete without considering the media—particularly television. Today satellites can beam live images from distant corners of the world to American living rooms. The ability of the media to provide world news nearly instantaneously is a powerful force in shaping public opinion and thus in influencing foreign policy.

This ability of shaping public opinion may make government more responsible. Nevertheless, the media can also mislead the public with distorted analyses of foreign events. In extreme cases, the media even creates the events. Newspaper mogul William Randolph Hearst told his illustrator Frederic Remington to remain in Cuba in 1897 despite the lack of news: "You furnish the pictures; I'll furnish the war." Although Hearst exaggerated, sensational stories in the yellow press (sensational journalism) were at least partially responsible for the outbreak of the Spanish-American War the following year. In 1967, CBS News showed pictures of a U.S. Army soldier severing the ear from the body of a dead Vietnamese—without mentioning that the reporter's cameraman had persuaded the soldier to perform the deed and had furnished the knife.

The Vietnam War was the first "television war." Americans were daily supplied with graphic images and a tally of American casualties. Not surprisingly, polls indicated a gradual disenchantment with the war, which in turn fueled opposition in Congress. Access to the South Vietnamese army allowed the media to disparage America's allies more than the North Vietnamese enemy. For instance, whereas reporters were able to film South Vietnamese mistreatment of its prisoners of war, North Vietnamese atrocities remained largely invisible because they were out of American camera range.

During World War I, British, French, and German newspapers did not publish a single photograph of a corpse even though more than four million men were killed in battle. Perhaps less government censorship would have shortened that war. Nevertheless, the emotional impact of modern media can be used to destroy the will of a free society to defend itself.

Section Review

1. What constitutional roles of the president give him primary control over foreign policy?

2. What is the purpose of the National Security Council?

3. What two basic aspects of foreign policy do the State Department and the Defense Department administer?

4. What are the three major levels of the Defense Department?

5. What steps has Congress taken to ensure that military power in the United States is subordinate to civilian power?

6. What four broad categories outline the Department of Homeland Security's responsibilities?

7. What are the three main opportunities for Congress to influence foreign policy?

IV. Policy Methods

Foreign policy is shaped through methods as subtle as a diplomat's smile and as forceful as a smart bomb striking foreign soil. Through its history, the United States has used a variety of methods to achieve its foreign policy goals.

Diplomacy

The first diplomatic mission for the United States began during its fight for independence

Benjamin Franklin's reception in France

when Benjamin Franklin sailed to France in 1779. Today the United States has diplomatic relations with 180 of the 193 countries of the world.

Diplomacy is not used only to preserve good relations with American allies; the United States maintains diplomatic relations with most hostile nations as well and usually engages in diplomatic discussions before resorting to force. Of course, force, even when unused, can powerfully influence diplomacy. President Theodore Roosevelt popularized the phrase "Speak softly and carry a big stick."

Indirect diplomacy may also be used to encourage negotiations between foreign nations that are hostile to one another. For instance, the United States has long attempted to act as a peace broker between Israel, its Arab neighbors, and the Palestinians.

Although a host of Foreign Service workers carry out diplomacy on a day-to-day basis, the secretary of state or the president may perform high-level diplomatic missions. In 2002, Secretary of State Colin Powell made sixteen trips abroad, visited forty-one countries, and traveled more than 160,000 miles.

Treaties and Multinational Organizations

Two additional tools used in achieving foreign policy are treaties and multinational organizations. **Treaties** are formal agreements made between nations or groups of nations. Treaties are popularly associated with the ending of wars, but treaties can also settle boundary disputes, establish commercial relations, and decide legal issues.

Treaties can be called by various names, including "agreement," "convention," "charter," "accord," and "protocol." Formal treaties require ratification by two-thirds of the Senate as described in Article II, Section 2 of the Constitution, but presidents have the ability to sign **executive agreements** with foreign heads of state. Executive agreements do not require Senate ratification. Although they have the same effect in international law as treaties, they are not valid in the United States to the extent that they conflict with federal statutes.

Often themselves the outgrowth of a treaty, **multinational organizations** are bodies established to allow nations to work collectively on certain issues. **Globalization,** the increasing integration of world markets, politics, and culture, has made an isolationist foreign policy impossible. Nevertheless, the United States must determine whether it has a sufficient common interest with other nations or multinational organizations before committing itself to a treaty relationship. Amos asks the rhetorical question, "Can two walk together, except they be agreed?" (Amos 3:3)

Today the United States is party to many treaties and multinational organizations. Perhaps the most prominent of the latter is the United Nations.

United Nations—The **United Nations** was created in 1945, at the end of World War II, with the stated purpose of maintaining world peace and upholding human rights. It offered hope as an instrument for peace by providing a forum for nations to negotiate their differences rather than go to war. Although the organization has grown to include 191 countries, it has had a mixed record as a peacemaker, with more failures than successes.

Six major divisions of the United Nations act as decision-making and policy-implementing bodies:

The **Secretariat**
- headed by the **secretary-general**
- acts as the main administrative body of the UN

The **General Assembly**
- primary representative body of the UN
- made up of delegates from each member nation

The **Security Council**
- deals with peace and security issues
- made up of five permanent members (China, France, Russia, the United Kingdom, and the United States) and fifteen other member nations who have two-year terms

The **Economic and Social Council**
- promotes fundamental human rights as defined by the UN
- composed of representatives from fifty-four member nations (three-year terms) within five broad geographic regions

The **Trusteeship Council**
- oversaw the independence of several small territories until it suspended operation in 1994
- composed of the five permanent members of the Security Council

The **International Court of Justice**
- located at the Hague in the Netherlands
- main judicial body of the UN dealing with international law
- consists of fifteen judges of different nationalities who are elected for nine-year terms by the General Assembly and the Security Council

Although the United States hosts the UN headquarters in New York City and pays 25 percent of the UN budget, the United Nations has spent extravagantly on its bureaucracy while disparaging American interests. In 2001 the UN voted the United States off the Commission on Human Rights, although Sudan, China, and Libya—major violators of human rights—were retained as members. (In retaliation, Congress withheld part of its back dues.) Not only does the United Nations Charter promise the impossible—"to save succeeding generations from the scourge of war"—it has also promoted abortion as a means of population control and has created an International Criminal Court that threatens to undermine American sovereignty.

Military Relations—To meet the threat of an expansionist Soviet Union after World War II, the United States and its allies formed several regional military alliances. The first and most important of these was the **North Atlantic Treaty Organization (NATO)** established in 1949 by the United States and twelve other nations. NATO was intended to protect Western Europe

and North America from Soviet aggression and served this purpose until the breakup of the Soviet Union in 1991.

Since that time NATO has focused on peace-keeping missions, such as those in the Balkans during the 1990s. During the same period, NATO accepted many former communist-bloc countries as members in order to promote cooperation between these nations and the West. NATO has also addressed the issues of weapons of mass destruction, human rights violations, and global terrorism. Following the September 11, 2001, terrorist attacks on the United States, NATO invoked Article V of its constitution, which states that an attack on one member of the alliance is considered an attack on all.

Another military agreement involving the United States is the Inter-American Treaty of Reciprocal Assistance, usually known as the **Rio Treaty.** The United States and a number of Latin American countries signed this treaty in 1947 with the intent of providing collective security in the Western Hemisphere. Like NATO, the Rio Treaty states that an attack on one treaty member is to be regarded as an attack on all; however, the Rio Treaty recognizes the UN Security Council as a higher authority. For the most part, the treaty has been ineffective, as, for instance, when Castro overtook Cuba despite Cuba's membership in the treaty, and in 1982 during the Falklands War when Argentina's request for assistance was ignored.

Economic Relations—Although there has been a general trend toward open markets world-wide, close economic ties between nations have been largely the product of regional agreements. Many European nations have joined the **European Union (EU).** This confederation does have political implications, but it is foremost an economic alliance. In 2002 the EU introduced the euro—a common currency for most states of the European Union.

While the United States has shied away from a union as binding as the EU, it has engaged in its own regional economic agreement. In 1992, the U.S., Canada, and Mexico signed the **North American Free Trade Agreement (NAFTA).** The agreement calls for free trade to be gradually implemented between these neighboring nations. NAFTA has opened new markets for American products while also allowing the importation of low-priced goods with which some American-made products cannot compete.

The United States is also involved in broader attempts to lower world tariff barriers. Once a part of the UN, the **General Agreement on Tariffs and Trade (GATT)** acted as an international body in the interest of breaking down trade barriers between nations until the **World Trade Organization (WTO)** replaced it in 1995. In recent years the WTO has been opposed by a loose coalition of leftists, including labor organizers, consumer advocates, and environmentalists who mistrust corporations and globalization. Some meetings of the WTO, notably its 1999 meeting in Seattle, have been marked by violent protests.

The United States also takes part in the **International Monetary Fund (IMF),** a UN agency. The IMF helps to maintain world economic stability by providing funds to nations that are in financial crisis or that are rebuilding their economies. Member nations also receive technical assistance with monetary transactions.

As the United States strives to build foreign relations through treaties and multinational agreements, it must consider potential dangers. The United States risks compromising its own sovereignty the more it relies on collective agreements to achieve its foreign policy goals.

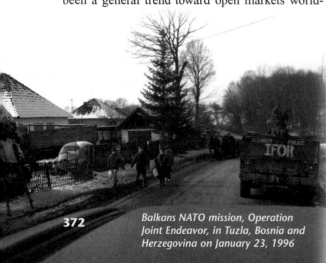

Balkans NATO mission, Operation Joint Endeavor, in Tuzla, Bosnia and Herzegovina on January 23, 1996

Foreign Aid

American prosperity has been shared with the world. The United States has given over $350 billion to more than a hundred nations since the end of World War II in the belief that foreign aid, if properly directed, can promote economic and political stability in the world.

The United States Agency for International Development (USAID) is chiefly responsible for delivering foreign aid. Organized during the Kennedy administration, this agency provides food as well as health and education services to needy countries while attempting to promote a free market economy within recipient nations.

Having countries "graduate" from American aid as they create their own economic prosperity has been a difficult goal to accomplish. There have been notable successes, such as Taiwan and South Korea, but there have also been many failures. Some recipient governments have discouraged land reform and private enterprise, and USAID has failed to promote development over distribution as the prime goal of its third-world assistance. As one critic noted, "AID continues to distribute over 90 percent of its funds as 'government-to-government transfers,' thereby directly fueling the growth of huge, bureaucratic state sectors in the Third World."

The result is that funds are often wasted and the people who most need the aid receive only trickles through quagmires of corruption and mismanagement. For example, in 1984 hundreds of thousands of Ethiopians starved to death during a severe drought. Americans were stirred to assist them after seeing the grim pictures on their television screens. Millions of dollars and tons of food and medical supplies were rushed to Ethiopia only to be bottled up by a cruel Marxist regime that deliberately restricted distribution of food to its own suffering people.

D-day invasion

Sanctions

In some ways, **sanctions** are the reverse of foreign aid. In international affairs, sanctions refer to coercive acts taken against a nation in an attempt to influence its actions. Sanctions are usually economic in nature, which means that the nation imposing the sanction usually restricts the flow of certain goods to or from the sanctioned country.

Both the president and Congress have power to impose sanctions. The president's power is detailed in the **International Emergency Economic Powers Act (IEEPA)** of 1977. He can establish sanctions in the event that a nation poses an "unusual and extraordinary threat" to the "national security, foreign policy or economy of the United States." Every year the president must renew any sanctions declared under the act by resubmitting them to Congress. In Congress the Senate Banking Committee and the House International Relations Committee create most bills that impose sanctions against foreign nations.

Because of the economic strength of the United States, sanctions are an important tool against rogue nations and evil regimes. In the past the United States has imposed sanctions on Iraq, North Korea, Libya, Sudan, and Cuba.

Battle of Midway, June 1942

Military Action and Espionage

Military Action—As noted earlier, military action is usually used only when diplomacy has failed, although there have been instances (such as the Mexican American War of 1846–48) in which the United States did little to discourage war. In some cases, military action was taken in response to a threat to American security. For instance, the United States undertook military action against al-Qaeda, the Taliban regime in Afghanistan, and Iraq after the devastating terrorist attacks of September 2001.

God's Word does not forbid war. In fact, one purpose of government is to provide necessary security for a nation. However, man is also directed to seek peace and avoid violence whenever that is possible (Ps. 11:5; 34:14).

Espionage—To maintain national security, the government must sometimes gather information and take action without revealing those activities to either the American public or to other nations. The FBI carries out such operations within the United States, the CIA and the National Security Agency (NSA) in foreign countries.

The history of U.S. intelligence has included such notable successes as cracking the Japanese code during World War II. With the ability to read Japanese military communications, the U.S. discovered enemy plans to invade Midway Island. The result was a decisive U.S. victory in the Pacific, widely regarded as the turning point of the war. Today American intelligence has the important responsibility of investigating terrorist activities both at home and abroad.

Section Review

1. How does Roosevelt's phrase "Speak softly and carry a big stick" apply to diplomacy?
2. What is the difference between a treaty and an executive agreement?
3. What are the six major divisions of the United Nations?
4. How has NATO changed since the fall of the Soviet Union?
5. Why is foreign aid often unsuccessful?
6. What two agencies carry out espionage in foreign affairs?

V. Challenges Abroad

As we have seen, national security has always been the primary goal of American foreign policy. Nevertheless, the position of the United States as the world's only superpower now poses additional challenges in maintaining that security.

Wars and Weapons

World War I was once called "the war to end all wars," but the world has continued to be consumed by conflict. Even powerful efforts to conclude wars have been thwarted by man's sinful nature. The reason for wars has not changed. "From whence come wars and fightings among you? come they not hence, even of your lusts that war in your members?" (James 4:1). But methods of warfare certainly differ from those of even the recent past.

Terrorism—**Terrorism** is the use of unlawful means of war to achieve one's goals. Usually it involves an attempt to intimidate government or the practice of psychological warfare against civilians. Terrorism is frequently used by small groups who stand no chance of winning a traditional war. The Palestinian Liberation Organization (PLO) and the Irish Republican Army (IRA) have used terrorism to advance political goals. Others, such as the Muslim al-Qaeda and the Japanese doomsday cult Aum Shinrikyo, have practiced terrorism for broad religious purposes.

While terrorism is not new—World War I began with an assassination in the Balkans—it has become more popular and more effective for several reasons. First, because of improved communications, a terrorist attack can quickly maximize its psychological impact. Few Americans did not see pictures of planes hitting the World Trade Center or the subsequent collapse of the buildings. Second, terrorism is a low-budget affair. One man with one bomb or vial can attack thousands, perhaps millions. Anthrax attacks in 2001 paralyzed the nation with fear even though only four tainted letters were found. Third, because of technological advances, terrorists can now build weapons of mass destruction far more easily and cheaply than ever before.

Simply securing America's borders is a difficult responsibility. The United States has more than 7,000 miles of land border and 12,000 miles of coastline. Furthermore, terrorists can now enter the United States electronically. The potential for cyber-terrorism threatens disruption of government and commerce as well as aspects of personal life.

Fourth-Generation Warfare

The September 11 attacks and the subsequent "war on terror" against al-Qaeda may indicate a new trend in warfare, first given the name "fourth-generation warfare" in 1989. **Fourth-generation warfare** is low-intensity (no big, decisive battles) guerilla warfare waged by non-state religious, political, or ideological groups such as al-Qaeda. Fourth-generation warfare has also been more simply defined as any form of

Marines on their way to the Persian Gulf

conflict "where the other side refuses to stand up and fight fair."

The rise of fourth-generation warfare has been attributed to the decline of strong central governments and their subsequent inability to control cultural, religious, or ideological groups within their own borders. Incapable of funding large armies, these groups fight superior powers by harassing them with ambushes, attacking civilians and symbolic structures, and using the media to instill fear. Meanwhile, they may also cultivate sympathy among ideological sympathizers throughout the world. These groups are often funded through a global network of supporters and sustained by fanatically loyal members willing to die, even to commit suicide, for their cause.

Preventing attacks from such groups is more difficult than thwarting conventional enemies, in part because large population centers most susceptible to terror attacks are hard to protect. Retaliating against terrorists is also challenging because they are not necessarily associated with a single nation. Finally, democratic states find it difficult to maintain morale in a war with few victories or to avoid sinking to the immoral level of their enemies.

In response to the terrorist attacks on the World Trade Center and the Pentagon, the United States initiated several changes in its foreign policy. The U.S. established coalitions with nations not normally her allies in order to pursue al-Qaeda and other terrorist groups throughout the world. The president created a new cabinet position and department to handle homeland security issues and declared that he was willing to use preemptive strikes against potential aggressors. Finally, new legislation enhanced federal and state law enforcement powers to pursue and arrest individuals suspected of terrorist activities.

Rogue Nations—Although there is no clear definition of a **"rogue nation,"** the term usually refers to nations that seek to develop weapons of mass destruction; those that supply, support, or provide safe havens for terrorist organizations; those that disregard international law and violate human rights; and those that threaten regional or world security.

Many nations fall under this broad definition, but only the most serious international threats are labeled "rogue nations" or "pariah (outcast) states." In his 2002 State of the Union address, President Bush called three such nations an "Axis of Evil"—Iraq, Iran, and North Korea.

Regional Conflicts—Several chronic conflicts threaten regional and world security, and the United States has become involved in attempts to settle them peacefully.

Since gaining independence in 1947, India and Pakistan have intermittently wrestled for control of Kashmir, a mountainous region on their northern borders. In the first year of the conflict, fifteen million refugees fled and more than a half million people were killed. The conflict has since taken an even more perilous turn because both nations have developed nuclear weapons.

To the east another equally long-standing conflict is that between China and Taiwan. Communist China considers Taiwan part of its empire, while capitalist Taiwan has acted as an independent state since 1949. China regularly threatens to conquer the small island and has lobbed missiles and carried out military exercises nearby. From an economic standpoint, the United States is interested in peace between these nations because both are major (and equally valuable) trading partners. Economic ties between China and Taiwan have grown recently and may help to smooth relations.

Russia has long been involved in a regional conflict with Muslim Chechnya, a breakaway republic near the Caucasus Mountains. The combination of Russia's heavy-handed military tactics and the Chechens' terrorist attacks has fully sustained a bitter conflict that originated several centuries ago.

Likewise, the decades-old dispute between Israelis and Palestinians has proved nearly incurable. A number of U.S. presidents have attempted to broker a peace agreement, seeing it as a crucial first step to Middle East peace. However, the mixture of distrust, bitterness, and extreme religious and ethnic hatred makes any peace agreement little more than transitory at best.

Weapons of Mass Destruction—Despite the fall of the Soviet Union, the threat of nuclear war has continued. Unstable regimes now control old Soviet stockpiles of **nuclear weapons**—those that use the release of nuclear energy as the force of their explosion. Although only a few nations are known to possess them, many more are actively seeking material through the black market. Terrorist organizations also seek to acquire such weapons. A cheaper, though no less deadly, alternative is a **radiological weapon,** or "dirty bomb." These weapons use conventional explosives surrounded by radioactive material. The explosion and the casualties caused by it might not be greater than those from a conventional bomb, but public panic about radioactivity and the cost of cleanup measures—especially in large cities—could paralyze a local economy for years.

Another threat is that of chemical and biological weapons. **Chemical weapons** use substances such as mustard gas, sarin, and VX to poison the enemy. Most of the weapons developed by terrorists and rogue regimes include nerve agents that may cause death within a few minutes. **Biological weapons** use fatal diseases or organic toxins as weapons. Examples include ricin, smallpox, and botulinum toxin. Anthrax, a particularly deadly disease, was mailed to House and Senate leaders and members of the media in 2001. No government officials were infected, but

seven other people died. Although biological and chemical weapons are easier to create than to use, the fear of such potent agents of death makes them powerful psychological weapons.

The use of both biological and chemical weapons has been banned by international treaty, and the United States has been active in talks to reduce nuclear arms. Nevertheless, it is important that the United States develop defenses against these **weapons of mass destruction.** Since the Reagan administration there has been an interest in creating a national missile defense system. And although the United States does not use chemical and biological weapons, scientists are actively seeking to develop antidotes.

Globalization

Globalization is a term often used by politicians and economists. From an economic standpoint it is the integration of world markets through increased communications, foreign investment, and free trade. Globalization allows businesses and (to a lesser extent) journalists, social activists, and academics to operate as if national borders did not exist. Globalization also results in some degree of integration of politics, society, and culture.

Globalization has been a natural outgrowth of the communications revolution, which has helped connect our world. The fall of the Soviet Union also aided its development. The Soviet Union's failed socialist experiment prompted many other governments to turn their economic policies toward open market capitalism.

The United States faces several foreign policy challenges in a "globalized" world. First, not only do businesses have more influence on government in a global environment, but terrorists can also use global integration to their advantage. For instance, al-Qaeda used mobile phones, satellite connections, and global markets to plan their attacks—and to fund them as well.

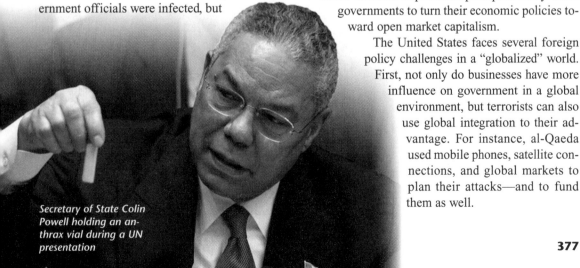

Secretary of State Colin Powell holding an anthrax vial during a UN presentation

Second, globalization has heightened the debate between free trade and protectionism. Free trade stimulates most businesses and raises the standard of living. But industries endangered by this expanded free trade lobby the government for more protection. During George W. Bush's presidency, Congress passed laws to protect the agriculture and the steel industry from increased competition abroad.

Third, globalization has rapidly disseminated many different ideas and cultures. Obviously, there are benefits to the spread of ideas. For instance, oppressive regimes have found it increasingly difficult to keep democratic notions from their people. Nevertheless, globalization threatens to further erode the Christian heritage of the United States.

Finally, foreign countries are concerned that globalization will increase American political and economic power. Therefore, globalization has created another foreign policy challenge to the United States—anti-Americanism.

Anti-Americanism

Since the fall of the Soviet Union, the United States has been the only superpower. Although the United States has never built a political empire as have other powerful nations of the past, some people contend that the U.S. has engaged in **"cultural imperialism"**—the promotion of its culture at the expense of others. American culture *is* perhaps the greatest export of the United States. Through television, movies, popular music, and the Internet, the world has been inundated with American culture. Coca-Cola and Big Macs can be purchased in Oman and Malaysia. In the Third World, American culture is both embraced and resented as it challenges local cultures—especially when those cultures have long been predicated on traditional religion.

Fear of American political power has also encouraged anti-Americanism. Though the United

States has rarely used its power capriciously, the simple existence of its military troubles many non-Americans. As a result, even when the United States attacked the rogue state of Iraq, traditional allies of the United States opposed the use of force. There have also been attempts to form coalitions of power to balance that of the United States. Although the European Union is largely an economic alliance, the member states would like to become a political coalition sometime in the future. Then, too, an alliance between Russia and China might someday counter the political strength of the United States.

Cultural Relativity

Many countries resent the "cultural imperialism" of the United States, charging that America does not respect other cultures. Often these nations reject the idea of a standard by which to judge cultural morality and argue that cultures should be judged by their own set of values. This belief is called cultural relativism.

A logical conclusion of cultural relativism is that no one ought to criticize or attempt to change cultures that oppress women, enslave children, threaten another's peace, burn widows on funeral pyres, or deny certain classes of people the right

Child labor in India

to participate in government. Each culture should decide for itself what is just.

Although many recognize that cultural relativism is ethically unsatisfying, they differ as to what standard might be used to judge the morality of a culture. Some resort to the UN's Universal Declaration of Human Rights as the standard; but adopting this pronouncement merely shifts the source of the standard from an individual culture to a consensus of human cultures. Man remains the standard by which man is judged.

A Christian understands that the Bible is the only unchangeable, absolute standard for judging culture because Scripture is the revelation of an unchanging God. When God promised in Malachi 3:5 to judge Judah for its sorcery, lying, adultery,

oppression, and maltreatment of immigrants, He made clear the nature of an immoral culture. Likewise, God's judgment on Sodom and Gomorrah revealed that a sexually perverse culture is unacceptable in His sight.

Conversely, the Ten Commandments reveal that cultures that forbid murder, theft, covetousness, disrespect for parents, and the worship of false gods please the Creator. Those cultures that act justly, protect life, help the poor and weak, use God's creation productively, and keep His commandments are good cultures (Mic. 6:8). Christians must reject those aspects of their culture that are condemned in Scripture and promote those that are praised.

Udari range in northwestern Kuwait

Fear and Uncertainty

Fear is characteristic of our age. Agents of destruction armed with chemical, biological, and nuclear weapons threaten our country, our cities, and our homes. Destruction like that of the September 11 attacks may be minutes away. Our perilous world foreshadows the Great Tribulation, when, as Christ foretold, men's hearts will fail them for fear (Luke 21:26).

Nevertheless, this present age is not the first to fear swift destruction. Even ancient history provides examples of sudden calamity, such as those included in the historical books of the Old Testament.

Fear of destruction is *natural* but not *spiritual*. Christians have not been given "the spirit of fear; but of power, and of love, and of a sound mind" (II Tim. 1:7). No matter who sits in the White House or how many terrorists exist, God is still on the throne, and our confidence is in Him. We learn this truth even from the lips of Nebuchadnezzar, an earthly king whom God humbled as a beast of the earth:

> I blessed the most High, and I praised and honoured him that liveth for ever, whose dominion is an everlasting dominion, and his kingdom is from generation to generation: and all the inhabitants of the earth are reputed as nothing: and he doeth according to his will in the army of heaven, and among the inhabitants of the earth: and none can stay his hand, or say unto him, What doest thou? (Dan. 4:34–35)

God remains in control, and His timetable for the world will not have to be hastily rewritten.

The assurance that believers maintain in an uncertain world does not remove their responsibility to defend their country or to oppose tyranny. What assurance in God does provide is a sense that, in spite of fearful world conditions, the Christian may enjoy a settled peace, a steady confidence, and a sure destiny.

Section Review

1. What is terrorism, and why have more groups turned to terrorism tactics?
2. What regional conflicts continue to influence foreign policy?
3. List the different kinds of weapons of mass destruction.
4. Describe some of the challenges facing U.S. foreign policy as a result of globalization.
5. What should the Christian's attitude be toward the threats of this age?

Chapter Review

Terms

foreign policy
alliance
collective security
Marshall Plan
isolationism
Monroe Doctrine
Cold War
nuclear deterrence
containment
National Security Council (NSC)
national security advisor
State Department
Defense Department
secretary of state
Foreign Service
embassies
ambassador
consulates
passport
visa
secretary of defense

Pentagon
Joint Chiefs of Staff (JCS)
Department of Homeland Security
Central Intelligence Agency (CIA)
treaties
executive agreements
multinational organizations
globalization
United Nations
Secretariat
secretary-general
General Assembly
Security Council
Economic and Social Council
Trusteeship Council
International Court of Justice
North Atlantic Treaty Organization (NATO)
Rio Treaty
European Union (EU)
North American Free Trade Agreement (NAFTA)

General Agreement on Tariffs and Trade (GATT)
World Trade Organization (WTO)
International Monetary Fund (IMF)
United States Agency for International Development (USAID)
sanctions
International Emergency Economic Powers Act (IEEPA)
National Security Agency (NSA)
terrorism
fourth-generation warfare
rogue nation
nuclear weapons
radiological weapon
chemical weapons
biological weapons
weapons of mass destruction
cultural imperialism

Content Questions

1. What four basic American goals guide the president as he formulates foreign policy?

2. Summarize the significant foreign policies associated with each of these presidents: Washington, Monroe, Theodore Roosevelt, Wilson, Franklin Roosevelt, Reagan, Clinton, and George W. Bush.

3. Identify the three main cabinet departments involved in foreign policy and summarize their responsibilities.

4. Why has the United Nations failed to bring world peace?

5. What are the main foreign policy methods used by the United States? Identify the government officials, departments, or agencies associated with each.

6. What are rogue nations, and which nations have been identified as such?

7. Why has the United States sometimes been accused of cultural imperialism?

Application Questions

1. Why does foreign policy change?

2. Give an example of each foreign policy method from current events.

3. Why does the Constitution give the president the greatest control over foreign policy?

4. What aspects of the media should you keep in mind when trying to determine the facts about world events?

5. What changes in the world would make an isolationist policy difficult to uphold today?

UNIT VI

THE JUDICIAL BRANCH

THE JUDICIARY

General Court of colonial Williamsburg

". . . a government of laws and not of men."
—John Adams, *Declaration of Rights, Massachusetts Constitution, 1780*

"The historic phrase 'a government of laws and not of men' epitomizes the distinguishing character of our political society. . . . [L]aw alone saves a society from being . . . ruled by mere brute power however disguised."

—*Justice Felix Frankfurter, concurring in* U.S. v. Mine Workers, *330 U.S. 258 (1947)*

In *The Roots of American Order* (1974) Russell Kirk tells the story of a Menshevik, a moderate socialist, who at the time of the Russian Revolution had fled to the Black Sea city of Odessa. The Menshevik found the city in anarchy. "Bands of young men commandeered street-cars and clattered wildly through the heart of Odessa, firing with rifles at any pedestrian, as though they were hunting pigeons. At any moment, one's apartment might be invaded by a casual criminal or fanatic, murdering for the sake of a loaf of bread. In this anarchy, justice and freedom were only words. 'Then I learned that before we can know justice and freedom, we must have order,' my friend said. 'Much though I hated the Communists, I saw then that even the grim order of Communism is better than no order at all. Many might survive under Communism; no one could survive in general disorder.'"

Despotic laws that produce order are more desirable than unrestrained freedom, but such laws are not just. Law in its truest sense originates from God and stands above all human government. Judges, the human interpreters of law, can impose order even when they reject the law of God, but society is just only in proportion to the extent that human judges permit scriptural morality to restrain human wickedness. Only then can any legal system truly be "a government of laws and not of men."

I. Sources of American Law

Scriptural Foundation

"Evil men understand not judgment: but they that seek the Lord understand all things."

—Proverbs 28:5

Law and justice are almost transparently obvious themes of Scripture. The first five books of the Bible are called "the Law." When Abraham pleads for the lives of the righteous in Sodom, he asks God rhetorically, "Shall not the Judge of all the earth do right?" (Gen. 18:25). The psalmist praises the Lord with the words, "Thou dost establish equity, thou executest judgment and righteousness in Jacob" (Ps. 99:4), and he warns that the Lord will "judge the poor of the people, he shall save the children of the needy, and shall break in pieces the oppressor" (Ps. 72:4).

Furthermore, God also calls men to do justice, especially for those unable to defend themselves. Micah 6:8 commands Christians to "do justly, . . . love mercy, and . . . walk humbly with thy God"; and in Amos 5, the Lord reveals that He prefers justice even to His own formal worship.

The justice that God requires is not simply fairness in everyday life but the justice of the courtroom as well. Moses chose "men of truth" to assist him in settling legal disputes—disputes in which

Moses himself acted as a kind of Supreme Court (Exod. 18:17–26). When the Bible illustrates the wisdom of Solomon, it does so by portraying him in his role as a judge (I Kings 3:16–28). After Jehoshaphat instituted reforms in Judah following the death of the wicked king Ahab, he warned his newly appointed judges: "Take heed what ye do: for ye judge not for man, but for the Lord, who is with you in the judgment" (II Chron. 19:6).

God's standard of justice is His own character. Moses said of God that "all his ways are judgment [justice]: a God of truth and without iniquity, just and right is he" (Deut. 32:4). **Justice** is, therefore, conformity to God's character. God has revealed His divine character in the Bible, and to the extent that any human law does not conform to His character, that law is unjust.

Historical Foundation

It is hardly surprising that pagan rulers of the ancient Near East credited their gods with having created law. Not only did a divine origin make the law easier to enforce, but rulers could also count on the belief among ordinary people that the true law stands above all transitory legal systems.

Although the first known law code was produced by one Ur-Nammu of Ur about 2050 B.C. (roughly the time of Abraham), undoubtedly the most famous ancient law materials are those of Hammurabi, king of Babylon and emperor of Mesopotamia (c. eighteenth century B.C.). Hammurabi's document is called a law code, although it is really a collection of legal decisions rather than an attempt to treat every possible legal contingency.

In Greece the best minds gave themselves to philosophy, but in Rome, men of leisure and intelligence more often considered law. At the beginning of the Roman Republic, legal knowledge was handed down in certain upper-class families before popular agitation led to its codification in the Law of the Twelve Tables (fifth century B.C.). Nevertheless, the Twelve Tables was a relatively unimportant contribution to the ultimate greatness of Roman

Written Law Codes Throughout History

2050 B.C.	Ur-Nammu's Code
1750 B.C.	Hammurabi's Code
1440 B.C.	Ten Commandments
1200 B.C.	Laws of Manu (India)
621 B.C.	Draco's Law (Athens)
550 B.C.	Solon's Law
450 B.C.	Twelve Tables (Rome)
A.D. 533	*Corpus Juris Civilis*
A.D. 653	T'ang Code
A.D. 1215	Magna Carta
A.D. 1689	English Bill of Rights
A.D. 1787	United States Constitution
A.D. 1791	United States Bill of Rights
A.D. 1804	Napoleonic Code
A.D. 1864	Geneva Convention

law. The inventiveness of the Romans lay in their finding commonsense solutions to everyday legal problems. A respected class of private experts combined the reasoning of legal decisions made over centuries in an attempt to generalize about how future cases should be decided. Even during the grimmest periods of imperial autocracy, Romans never abandoned the belief that law remained above the dictates of any particular ruler and that it could not be arbitrarily altered. Eventually, in A.D. 533, the Roman emperor Justinian collected many Roman legal materials from previous centuries and published an organized compilation called the ***Corpus Juris Civilis.***

Following the fall of the Roman Empire, knowledge of Roman law never entirely disappeared in the West, but a sophisticated legal system was hardly needed during the Dark Ages in any case. By the tenth or eleventh century, though, interest in Justinian's code revived as legal problems once solved by the Romans reappeared on the streets of European cities. After centuries of examination, students of Justinian managed to blend the best elements of the *Corpus Juris* into local legal materials and write their own law codes. Perhaps the most famous of these is the *Code Napoléon* (1804).

Code Napoléon

Before the French Revolution, France was governed by a mixture of Roman law derived from Justinian's code and a Germanic customary law that had developed gradually through the centuries like English common law. Unlike the situation in England, however, French law was not one thing or another but a confusing mixture of both in different proportions depending on the location. Customary law dominated in the north of France, Roman law in the south; and three hundred or more towns and villages had their own local systems. In a famous quip that was hardly an exaggeration, Voltaire charged that the French traveler changed laws as often as he changed horses. The law was so diffuse and confusing that even judges were suspected of not understanding it. Common people were said to have prayed, "God protect us from the fairness of the courts."

There had been attempts to organize French law as early as the fifteenth century, but the Revolution made codification easier because it abolished feudal privileges and local customary law. The revolutionaries were also interested in producing a law code because it would help to unify France and because constructing a logically organized legal code reflected the contemporary faith in reason. Nevertheless, the revolutionaries had other pressing problems, including fighting the rest of Europe and guillotining one another.

Shortly after Napoleon's coup d'etat of 1799, the new ruler appointed a four-man commission of distinguished jurists to draft a uniform civil code for France. The commission sensibly decided that its business was to conserve and organize what had come down from the past rather than try to create new laws out of thin air. The commission sounded decidedly unrevolutionary (and almost English) when it declared that "codes of people develop in time; properly speaking, one does not make them."

Eventually a draft of the Code was debated in Napoleon's Council of State. Though only thirty-two years old and unlearned in the law, Napoleon himself made important personal contributions to the final document, his force of character also ensuring that the project stayed on track. At first the French legislature hindered passage of the Code, but after Napoleon further consolidated his power in 1802, he made over that body into something more to his liking.

The completed Code Napoléon (or Code Civil, as it is known today) was declared the law of France in 1804. It is about one hundred twenty thousand words long (about the length of a substantial book) and is written in clear, precise French. The novelist Stendhal said that the Code served him as a model of literary clarity and simplicity.

Modern commentators often criticize the patriarchal aspects of the Code and even suggest that Napoleon and his codifiers were attempting to suppress the feminism of the revolutionary era. Certainly, the Code did not treat husbands and wives as equals. For instance, a woman found guilty of adultery could be imprisoned for a term of up to two years, depending on the inclination of the husband. A husband could not be convicted of adultery at all unless he brought his mistress home to live with his family; then he might be fined. Nevertheless, the family law enshrined in the Code was typical of its era, and it has probably attracted so much negative attention from scholars in part because, unlike the English common law, its provisions had to be laid out in unequivocating starkness. Actually, the Code provided protections for married women that were advanced in comparison with pre-Revolutionary France and some other European countries.

The importance of the Napoleonic Code was magnified when French armies exported it to northern Italy, the Low Countries, parts of Germany, and even Poland. After Napoleon made his brother Louis king of Holland, he told him to adopt the French civil code. "The Romans gave their laws to their allies," said Napoleon. "Why should not France have hers adopted in Holland?" In 1808 the Code was modified to become the law of Louisiana, and even after the fall of Napoleon, his Code became the basis for others in Quebec, Egypt, Greece, and many Latin American countries.

During the Middle Ages and Renaissance only England managed to hold out against the "reception" of the *Corpus Juris* and develop its own system, the **common law**—common because it was not local feudal law but common to the whole realm of England. Unlike legal systems of continental Europe that were based on the codified Roman law, the common law was grounded in case law, a body of opinions written by royal judges who, at least in theory, followed the **precedents** (prior, authoritative rulings) of those who came before them. (This practice of rendering judicial decisions on the basis of precedents is called *stare decisis* [STAH-ree duh-SIGH-sus].) Therefore, even though common law was not codified, in a sense it more closely resembled the legal system of Rome, in which legal experts had generalized about commonsense solutions to practical problems on the basis of past experience.

English common law also encouraged the development of jury trials. Prior to the thirteenth century, guilt or innocence in English courts could be determined by ordeal, battle, or compurgation (wager of law)—all superstitious methods of attempting to make God reveal guilt or innocence. Juries had the advantage of being more rational than the older methods, and because juries made their decisions secretly, they were also mysterious enough to be regarded as revealing the mind of God.

Ancient Modes of Trial

Prior to the introduction of jury trials in the twelfth century, English courts used three basic methods to determine guilt or innocence: battle, ordeals, and wager of law. In battle, the accused and the accuser—or (if not a criminal case) more usually the accuser's hired champion—fought each other. Some very litigious landowners retained full-time champions to fight on their behalf.

Ordeals included carrying a hot iron nine feet or plucking a stone out of a pot of boiling water. The burnt hand would then be bound up. If after three days the hand was not infected, the accused was considered innocent. But if "unhealthy matter" were found, he would "be deemed guilty and unclean."

The ordeal of cold water was usually reserved for the lowest classes. After the hands of the accused were tied together under his bent knees and his body was bound with a rope around his waist, he was gently lowered into a pool of water "so as not to make a splash. If he sinks down to the knot [around his waist] he shall be drawn up saved; otherwise let him be adjudged a guilty man by the spectators."

Wager of law was a bizarre character test. The court would call on the accused to present a number of people to testify that his oath was trustworthy. The witnesses would then swear in a set of ritualistic words that the accused had told the truth. If a witness made a mistake in the formula, his testimony was disregarded. A perfect recitation was counted as true—even if it were a perfect lie.

Like other western European countries, England took its legal system to its colonies, and the common law now roughly holds sway wherever English is the native tongue. Although it is likely that the common-law system would have been adopted in the United States, that result was not absolutely certain. The common law had been developed by and for the royal courts, and even in England there were rival systems of law (such as *equity,* mentioned in Article III, Section 1 of the Constitution). Finally, because it was not codified, the common law had developed over many centuries into a crazy quilt of complicated legal fictions with no explanatory guide for either laymen or lawyers.

Ten years before the American Revolution, William Blackstone (1723–80), Oxford's first professor of English law, produced a handy key to the system in his ***Commentaries on the Laws of England*** (1765). The *Commentaries* were a bestseller in America and strongly influenced the American founders.

Although Blackstone was a Tory who opposed the American Revolution, his book probably restrained whatever urge American lawyers may have had to abandon the wisdom of the common law and strike out on their own to compile a legal code. Furthermore, Blackstone, like most men of his generation, believed that the common law was derived from the law of God. To Blackstone, God had expressed His law through both creation, a **natural law** that is given to all men (what the apostle Paul referred to in Romans 2:15), and God's **revealed law** contained in the Bible. "Upon these two foundations," said Blackstone, "the law of nature and the law of revelation, depend all human laws; that is to say, no human laws should be suffered to contradict these."

There are several reasons why the adoption of the common law was advantageous for the new republic. First, the common law was a product of human experience, not the pronouncement of some ruler or a committee of experts. Second, the common law had not been created by the ruler but was rather the source of his power. Finally, the common law, with its emphasis on a law that was in existence from time immemorial, was reflective of Christian truth. When Cain killed his brother, he did not argue that there was no law against it. The law forbidding murder was already in his heart.

Common Legal Terms

Affirm To approve the decision of a lower court

Appeal To petition a higher court to review a lower court decision

Appellate jurisdiction A court's power to decide appeals

Brief A legal document that presents arguments supporting a client's position in a case

Civil law 1. The division of law dealing with the legal rights of private citizens in disputes with other citizens; 2. A system of law based on codified Roman law; distinguished from common law

Common law The system of law developed in England and based on tradition and the decisions of courts rather than on legal codes; distinguished from civil law

Constitutional law The division of law dealing with the constitutional interpretation of laws and government actions

Criminal law The division of law that treats crimes that will be prosecuted by the government

Original jurisdiction A court's power to hear a case before it is considered by any other court

Precedent A court decision that serves to guide subsequent decisions in related cases

Reverse To rule against a lower court decision by virtue of a higher court's authority.

Stare decisis Literally "let the decision stand," a principle of law that bases decisions on judicial precedent

Writ of certiorari Latin for "to be made more certain"; an order from a superior court (especially the United States Supreme Court) to a lower court to send the entire record of a case for review

Section Review

1. What is the standard for judging a society's judicial system?

2. Who compiled the *Corpus Juris Civilis?* What is the *Corpus Juris Civilis?*

3. Define *common law.*

4. How did William Blackstone's *Commentaries on the Laws of England* affect the American colonies?

5. Why was adopting English common law advantageous for the colonies?

II. Structure of the Courts

Judicial Federalism

Each of the new American states already had common-law courts in place when the Constitution was written. The relationship these preexisting state courts would have with the new national courts that would be created by the Constitution was a delicate issue the founders wisely chose not to answer during the summer of 1787.

The founders almost certainly understood that national courts would have to exercise judicial review over state courts, but they could not have imagined the modern power of the Supreme Court to make public policy. At the end of the eighteenth century, judges were expected to find law, not make it. And the law they were expected to find was generally private law, the law governing disputes between individuals, not the rules regulating the relationship between individuals and their government. In *Federalist No. 78,* Alexander Hamilton

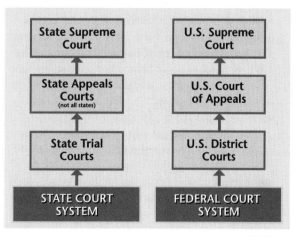

called the proposed federal judiciary the "least dangerous branch" of the new government.

Article III, Section 1 of the Constitution was written as concisely and vaguely as possible. It vested the nation's judicial power "in one Supreme Court, and in such lower inferior Courts as the Congress may from time to time ordain and establish." In theory, the national government might have made do with only a Supreme Court.

According to Article III of the Constitution, federal courts are empowered to hear the following cases:

- Constitutional violations
- Congressional violations
- Treaty violations
- Lawsuits between foreign countries and the United States or an American citizen
- Cases involving U.S. ambassadors or consuls
- Cases involving crimes committed at sea aboard American vessels
- Cases involving crimes committed on federal lands or federal property
- Lawsuits between states or citizens of different states

Although the Constitution establishes the general bounds of federal jurisdiction, Congress establishes the jurisdiction of a particular court within these constitutional boundaries.

Even though Congress quickly established a more elaborate federal judicial system, the United States also became the testing ground for a unique system of coexisting federal and state courts—**judicial federalism**—an organizational scheme that had never been tried before. Even through the Civil War, questions of federal law were sometimes heard in state courts, and gifted state judges made as great a contribution to the development of American law as did the U.S. Supreme Court.

Even today, despite a vast expansion of federal power, state courts are still important. More than 95 percent of the nation's legal actions—tens of millions of cases—are heard in state courts each year. Once a case has been decided in the highest court of a state, it will not be admitted into the fed-

eral system unless there is a federal question involved.

Nevertheless, some cases can be heard in either state or federal courts, as for example in a civil suit where the amount at issue is more than fifty thousand dollars and the parties reside in different states. Likewise, the kidnapping of a federal marshal might be prosecuted in either a state or federal court. Furthermore, criminal suspects can sometimes be tried for the same activity in *both* state and federal courts. For instance, a suspect charged with a racially motivated beating might be tried in state court for the beating itself and then be tried in federal court for violating the victim's civil rights. The Supreme Court has ruled that such prosecutions do not violate the Fifth Amendment's prohibition against double jeopardy, being tried twice for the same offense.

Haynesworth Building, Greenville, S.C.

District Courts

Passing the Judiciary Act of 1789, the first Congress created a system of inferior courts and launched the United States Supreme Court as well. The act created thirteen **district courts,** the trial courts of the federal judicial system. Today the United States has ninety-four district courts in the fifty states, the District of Columbia, Puerto Rico, and three territories. Each state has from one to four districts, depending on its population. District courts exercise **original jurisdiction,** meaning that they are the first to hear a case before any other court considers it.

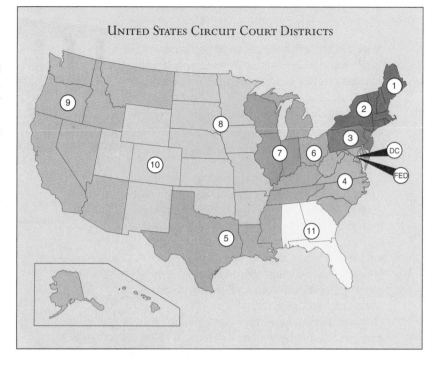

UNITED STATES CIRCUIT COURT DISTRICTS

As in most state courts, district courts use a **grand jury** to indict or charge accused criminals, and a **petit** or **trial jury** to hear the case and decide its outcome. Each year approximately three hundred thousand cases are heard in federal district courts, about 85 percent of the federal judicial workload.

The president, with the consent of the Senate, appoints a United States attorney and a U.S. marshal for each district. The U.S. attorney and his assistants prosecute criminal cases and represent the federal government in all civil cases. The U.S. marshal and the deputy marshals provide protection for the federal judiciary, transport federal prisoners, protect endangered federal witnesses, and manage assets seized from criminal enterprises. In addition, the men and women of the Marshals Service pursue and arrest federal fugitives.

Circuit Courts of Appeals

The Circuit Courts of Appeals are the second tier of the federal judicial system. The Judiciary Act of 1789 established three circuits. Today there are twelve Circuit Courts of Appeals, eleven circuits plus one for the District of Columbia. (A thirteenth, the oddly named United States Court of Appeals for the Federal Circuit, has a national jurisdiction but reviews only specialized appeals, such as tax, patent, and trademark cases and claims against the federal government.)

Originally two Supreme Court judges and a district judge were assigned to each circuit. That meant that justices of the Supreme Court regularly

U.S. marshal

"rode circuit," often thousands of miles annually in public conveyances. Although some people argued that this practice brought national justice closer to the people, it also required that judges have a good deal of physical stamina. Further, as Gouverneur Morris wryly noted, "riding rapidly from one end of this country to another" was not the best method of becoming learned in the law.

As the name implies, Circuit Courts of Appeals have **appellate jurisdiction** only—that is, they do not hold trials but only hear appeals from the district courts in their circuit, examining the actions and rulings of district judges for possible errors in procedure or legal interpretation. Circuit court judges usually sit in rotating panels of three and decide most cases on the basis of written briefs, although occasionally they may sit *en banc,* as a group. Only about 4 percent of decisions from the circuit courts are successfully appealed to the Supreme Court.

Today there are 179 circuit court judges, and the number of judges assigned to each circuit is roughly determined by its population. Some circuit courts have so many members that they operate like small legislatures. The ninth circuit, based in San Francisco, is by far the largest, serving 45 million people with 28 judges.

The Supreme Court

The United States Supreme Court is the third tier of the federal judicial system and the most powerful court in the world. But at the beginning of the republic, it was so feeble that the government had difficulty attracting able men to sit on it. Alexander Hamilton preferred private law practice to joining the Court. John Jay, the first chief justice, had so little responsibility that he was sent off to England as an ambassador while still holding office. When he returned, he resigned to become governor of New York. Later, when asked to rejoin the Court, Jay refused on the ground that the U.S. Supreme Court lacked not only "energy, weight, and dignity" but also "public confidence and respect."

SUPREME COURT

4. U.S. Supreme Court may consider if constitutional issue is involved

3. State supreme court rules

2. Loser goes to state appellate court.

1. Defendant loses trial in state court

3. Appeals—court ruling submitted to U.S. Supreme Court

2. Loser goes to U.S. Circuit Court of Appeals

1. Case tried in federal district court

The period of Supreme Court weakness gradually ended after John Marshall became chief justice in 1802. Marshall had a brilliant mind and an amiable, unassuming personality that easily won others to his views. In 1804, all the Court's opinions were unanimous. Marshall's leadership attracted able associates, and the early nineteenth-century Court was also blessed with a number of long tenures and an unblemished record of honesty and high legal craftsmanship. Certainly by 1900, the Supreme Court had become equal in power and prestige to Congress and the president.

Justices and Their Jurisdiction—Supreme Court judges are known as **justices.** The Constitution does not stipulate a specific number, and the first Congress appointed six. Between 1807 and 1869, the number ranged from seven to ten. Since 1869, nine justices—one chief justice and eight associate justices—have composed the Supreme Court. There have been nine justices for so long that another number would be considered revolutionary, even though more or less would be absolutely constitutional.

The Supreme Court is empowered to exercise both original and appellate jurisdiction. Nevertheless, original jurisdiction cases (usually one state suing another or cases involving U.S. ambassadors and consuls) compose only a tiny fraction of the Court's caseload. The vast majority of cases come to the Supreme Court on **writ of certiorari** [suhr-shee-uh-RAR-ee] (Latin for "to be made more certain") from the federal circuit courts and state supreme courts.

Caseload—During the first half of the nineteenth century the caseload of the Supreme Court was so light that arguments often rambled on for days. In the famous case of *Dartmouth College* v. *Woodward* (1819), Daniel Webster spoke for four hours straight.

With the rapid growth of American industry and the expansion of federal power following the Civil War, the Court's caseload escalated. Congress appointed full-time circuit court judges in 1869 and gave them their modern powers in 1891. Even with these reforms, the Supreme Court was still hearing over five hundred cases a year. Many of these cases were mundane, having arrived at the Supreme Court only because they involved citizens of different states or because they had originated in the territories.

In 1925, Congress reduced the Court's caseload dramatically by granting the Court nearly unlimited discretion to choose which cases and what issues it wanted to decide. Although litigation has continued to swell state and lower federal dockets, the Supreme Court has been virtually untouched by the flood below. Of the thousands of cases entered each year on the Supreme Court docket, the Court decides only about 2 percent, fewer than a hundred cases per year. During the 1990s the number of cases decided actually fell. All remaining cases on the docket are denied review, thus allowing the lower court rulings to stand.

Petitions for writ of certiorari or "cert" are delegated to the justices' law clerks—some of the best and brightest of the nation's recent law school graduates. The clerks write short memos about the cases, and the justices vote in conference about which of them to hear. Review of a case will be granted if four justices agree to hear it. As a rule, the Court only takes cases on which lower courts have disagreed or those that involve significant matters of public policy.

Homes of the U.S. Supreme Court

Even though it is the highest court of the United States, the Supreme Court did not have its own home for the first 146 years of its existence. During those years the Court sat in many different buildings in three different cities, even meeting in private homes and taverns after the British burned Washington, D.C., during the War of 1812.

The Court spent its first two sessions, February 1–10 and August 2–3, 1790, at the Royal Exchange building in New York City. When the United States capital moved to

City Hall, Philadelphia

Old Supreme Court Chamber

Philadelphia, the Supreme Court met in Independence Hall for two days in 1791. The session was short because the Court had no cases to hear.

For the next decade, the Court met in the east wing of Philadelphia's City Hall while Congress met in the west wing.

When the government moved to Washington, D.C., the Supreme Court convened in a number of different rooms in the unfinished Capitol until it was given a specially designed courtroom, now restored as the Old Supreme Court Chamber. The Court occupied this space from 1819 to 1860.

From 1860 to 1935, the Supreme Court met in the Old Senate Chamber after the Senate left for larger quarters.

Finally, Chief Justice William Howard Taft persuaded Congress to appropriate funds for a permanent Supreme Court building in 1929. Built in the style of a Greco-Roman temple, the current home of the Supreme Court is 304 feet wide by 385 feet long. Construction cost $9,646,000—$94,000 under budget! Neither Taft nor the architect, Cass Gilbert, lived to see the building completed in 1935.

Decision Making—Supreme Court sessions begin on the first Monday in October and continue through the following June. The nine-month term has alternating two-week sessions, with court days running Monday through Wednesday. Justices meet on Wednesday afternoons and Fridays to discuss that week's cases and to take tentative votes on the outcomes.

When the Supreme Court accepts a case, lawyers for each side present written briefs detailing their positions. ("Brief" is a figure of speech; in major cases the combined briefs can be book-length.) The case is then argued for exactly one hour, thirty minutes per side. But justices may interrupt with questions—and take the lawyers' time—whenever they choose. Following each two-week session there is a two-week recess in which the justices and their clerks write draft opinions and study those written by other justices.

A case is won by a simple majority vote of the justices. If the chief justice votes with the majority, he or someone he assigns writes the **majority opinion.** If the chief justice is in the minority, the senior justice on the winning side assigns the writing of the opinion. Justices on the losing side frequently issue a **dissenting opinion,** sometimes in the hope that a future court will vindicate their position. Justices who agree with the majority or the minority but who disagree with the reasons for the decision or dissent may issue **concurring opinions.** Majority opinions are sometimes modified to win more majority votes or to blunt well-reasoned

Supreme Court justices, 2003: (standing left to right) Ruth Bader Ginsburg, David Souter, Clarence Thomas, Stephen Breyer; (seated left to right) Antonin Scalia, John Paul Stevens, Chief Justice William Rehnquist, Sandra Day O'Connor, and Anthony Kennedy

dissents. Occasionally a justice may change his view of a case, but rarely will a dissenting opinion become the majority opinion.

Some decisions (known as *per curiam,* "by the court") are issued without a written opinion. But recently, written opinions of the justices have tended to grow longer and more legalistic, and dissents and concurrences have become more numerous. Each justice now has four law clerks to "draft" (a polite way of saying "write") his decisions, and so it has become easier for each justice to put his individual stamp on each decided case. Unfortunately the Court is sometimes so splintered by concurring decisions that a majority decision is more of a plurality decision. Deciphering what the Court has actually decided becomes an exercise in logic splitting. Although under unusual circumstances, such as the disputed 2000 presidential election, the decision-making process may be hurried along, the Court generally does not announce its decision for several months after oral arguments—usually on a Monday.

Bush v. Gore, 2000

The controversies surrounding the 2000 presidential election produced a flurry of lawsuits that illustrate the American judicial process. After an extremely close race in Florida marred by flaws in the voting process, both Republicans and Democrats filed lawsuits in a final attempt to win the general election.

Federal Judiciary—The Bush campaign challenged a manual recount of the Florida ballots in the federal court system.

November 11—The Bush campaign files a federal lawsuit in a U.S. District Court to stop manual recount.

November 13—The U.S. District Court denies the request to end the manual recount.

November 15—The Bush campaign appeals the district court's ruling to the Eleventh Circuit Court of Appeals in Atlanta.

November 17—The Eleventh Circuit Court of Appeals rejects the Bush petition.

November 24—The U.S. Supreme Court refuses to hear an appeal of the circuit court decision.

State Judiciary—On November 26, Kathleen Harris, Florida's secretary of state, certified Bush the winner of the Florida election. Vice President Gore contested her certification in the Florida state courts.

November 27—Gore contests Secretary of State Harris's certification of Bush's victory in the Leon County Circuit Court.

December 4—The Florida circuit court judge dismisses Gore's challenge. Gore appeals the decision to the Florida Supreme Court.

December 7—The Florida Supreme Court hears Gore's argument.

December 8—The Florida Supreme Court rules in Gore's favor. Bush appeals the decision to the U.S. Supreme Court.

December 9—The U.S. Supreme Court stays the Florida Supreme Court's ruling.

December 11—The U.S. Supreme Court hears oral arguments.

December 12—The U.S. Supreme Court overturns the Florida Supreme Court's ruling.

Section Review

1. What is judicial federalism?
2. When was the federal court system first established?
3. What are the three basic levels of federal courts, and what jurisdiction does each court have?
4. Why do few cases reach the Supreme Court?
5. Describe the three kinds of opinions that a Supreme Court justice may write about a decided case.

III. Selection of Judges

State Judges—Unlike many European legal systems, a person does not need specific training to become a judge in the United States. Nevertheless, virtually all American judges have a legal background, and involvement in partisan politics is at least helpful, if not mandatory.

State judges are chosen in five basic ways (with a number of complex variations): partisan election, nonpartisan election, gubernatorial appointment, legislative selection, and the Missouri Plan. In partisan elections, candidates are listed on the ballot with their party designation (that is, whether they are a Democrat or Republican). In nonpartisan elections candidates are listed without party designations, often because the state hopes to limit the power of political parties in the selection process. States that allow the governor to choose state judges often restrict his power by requiring that he pick from a list approved by a committee or by requiring that his choice be approved by the state senate. Only four states allow the legislature to choose state judges, and legislative selection has been criticized for resulting in the election of judges who have a great deal of political clout—especially past and present members of the legislature.

In the Missouri Plan, a more formal attempt to reduce the influence of partisan politics on the selection of judges, the governor appoints one candidate from a short list nominated by a judicial commission. The new judge assumes office but then must be approved by voters in a retention election. No opposition candidate is allowed; the voters can only approve or disapprove of the new judge. Proponents of this method of judicial selection argue that it produces more qualified judges who are less dependent on their political connections. Of course, since voters rarely refuse to seat a judge who has no opponent, selection by a commission of lawyers becomes nearly tantamount to election.

Unlike the federal system, in which judges serve for life, the vast majority of state judges serve for stated terms, often six years for lower courts and six to twelve years for appellate courts. Again unlike the federal system, most states have mandatory retirement ages, usually seventy.

Federal Judges—According to Article II, Section 2 of the Constitution, the president appoints all federal judges with the approval of the Senate. Like state judges, federal judges are largely selected for political reasons. For instance, a candidate for a federal judgeship may have managed a successful senatorial campaign or a state primary for the president. At the district court level, a prospective judge is, in fact, often chosen by his state's senator through **senatorial courtesy.** This practice gives a senator from the president's party power to effectively veto appointments of people from his state of which he does not approve. Sometimes the senator and president engage in political horse trading, exchanging the senator's vote on a piece of legislation that the president wants for the nomination of a judicial candidate whom the senator prefers.

The president will usually have more control over circuit court nominations because the circuits cover several states. Nevertheless, his choices will still be limited by the political need to balance the courts by sex, race, ethnicity, and geographical region.

Federal judges hold office "during good behavior," that is, practically speaking, for life unless impeached by Congress. (Only seven federal judges have ever been impeached and removed from office.) Life terms tend to insulate judges from political pressure, which is undemocratic but may encourage a more thoughtful approach to the judicial process. Likewise, very old judges are able to use their years of experience to better unravel complex legal questions. Sometimes, however, such judges are also tempted to continue in office even after they have clearly become impaired.

Justices of the Supreme Court—Supreme Court nominations are so important and so rare that it is difficult to formulate any general rule about whom the president might nominate when the opportunity arises. Although the president would prefer to choose someone with similar ideological

Stephen G. Breyer's swearing in

nents to embarrass the president and torpedo the nomination.

Likewise, at the hearings themselves, hostile senators will try to draw out the nominee and encourage him to make a political blunder. The nominee, for his part, will attempt to distance himself from earlier decisions or writings that may be seen as "politically incorrect." He will also protest that he cannot give his opinion about issues that might some day arise before the Supreme Court. As in the cases of Robert Bork and Clarence Thomas, confirmation hearings can be especially bitter if different parties control the presidency and the Senate.

views, the president will try not to nominate a candidate whom he knows the Senate will reject. Then too, as with lower court nominations, the president will consider sex, race, and religion. When Thurgood Marshall, the first African American justice, retired in 1991, President George Bush nominated another African American, Clarence Thomas, to take his seat. As of this writing, there has never been a Hispanic or Asian justice, and the president is well aware of that fact.

Judicial Confirmation—Until the past few decades, it was uncommon for nominees of district and circuit court positions to meet more than token resistance in the Senate. But today the increased politicization of the confirmation process and the importance (and sometimes near finality) of decisions made at the circuit court level have led to Senate challenges, filibusters, and simple foot-dragging on presidential nominations to lower federal courts.

Supreme Court nominees are appropriately subjected to even more scrutiny. The nominee's professional qualifications are examined, and the American Bar Association will pronounce on his suitability for office. Nevertheless, the technical investigation is often little more than an attempt to discover information that will allow political oppo-

Supreme Court Appointments

The present Court consists of appointees spanning several presidential administrations. The following chart lists the present Court members, the presidents who appointed them, and the day the justices took the Judicial Oath.

Justice	President	Date
William H. Rehnquist	Nixon	January 7, 1972
Rehnquist as Chief Justice	Reagan	September 26, 1986
John Paul Stevens	Ford	December 19, 1975
Sandra Day O'Connor	Reagan	September 25, 1981
Antonin Scalia	Reagan	September 26, 1986
Anthony M. Kennedy	Reagan	February 18, 1988
David H. Souter	Bush	October 9, 1990
Clarence Thomas	Bush	October 23, 1991
Ruth Bader Ginsburg	Clinton	August 10, 1993
Stephen G. Breyer	Clinton	August 3, 1994

The Bork Nomination

Political opposition to Supreme Court nominees began in 1795 when the Senate rejected John Rutledge, a professionally well-qualified nominee, because he had vigorously denounced the Jay Treaty, which the majority of senators supported. (Slandering nominees began at the same moment. Rutledge's opponents spread the lie that the judge was mentally incompetent.)

Political opposition to Supreme Court nominees grew more intense after the turn of the twentieth century when it became clear that the Supreme Court was able to make public policy in ways that were virtually irreversible. Nevertheless, President Ronald Reagan's unsuccessful nomination of Robert Bork, a distinguished law professor and judge, to the U.S. Supreme Court in 1987 proved something of a milestone in the evolution of the confirmation process. Liberals were candid in their determination not to relinquish a swing vote in the Supreme Court to an articulate conservative, and Bork became the last Supreme Court nominee to fully discuss his legal views during Senate hearings.

Reagan may have underestimated the liberal opposition. Democrats had regained control of the Senate in 1986, and Bork had frequently and comprehensively expressed his views on a variety of constitutional subjects. The Bork nomination was denounced by such liberal stalwarts as the American Civil Liberties Union and the AFL-CIO. People for the American Way raised two million dollars to initiate a media campaign against the nomination.

At least no one claimed that Bork was unqualified for the position. Bork had served as solicitor general in the Nixon administration and had won confirmation as a federal appeals judge without objection. Former president Gerald Ford introduced him to the Senate and retired chief justice Warren Burger testified on Bork's behalf.

The Senate hearings dragged on for eighty-seven hours, and Bork himself testified for thirty of those in a vain attempt to explain and amend his well-publicized views about legal issues. Ironically, Bork's candid discussion of his judicial philosophy probably ended whatever chance he may have had to win confirmation. The Senate rejected his nomination 42-58.

Since the Bork fiasco, presidents have sometimes nominated "stealth nominees" for federal court positions (one of whom, David Souter, was confirmed as a Supreme Court justice in 1990). Such nominees have a meager paper trail, and their views about controversial issues are, at least officially, shrouded in mystery. Likewise, since 1987, most Supreme Court nominees have been as tightlipped as possible about their political ideology, often testifying (improbably) at confirmation hearings that they have no considered opinion about such topics as abortion and affirmative action.

Even after the Senate confirms a presidential nominee, there is no guarantee that the new justice will nudge the Court in the direction the president would like to see it go, especially over the twenty or thirty years of his tenure. As the late constitutional scholar Alexander Bickel once reflected, "You shoot an arrow into a far-distant future when you appoint a justice, and not even the man himself can tell you what he will think about some of the problems he will face." Presidential disappointment in Supreme Court nominees has been a recurring lament in American history. Jeffersonian Republicans nominated a series of justices whom they thought would challenge John Marshall; but once seated on the Court, most consistently voted with the chief justice. When Dwight Eisenhower was asked if he had made any mistakes during his term of office, he replied, "Yes, two, and they are both sitting on the Supreme Court."

Chief Justice John Marshall

IV. Constitutional and Legal Change

From the perspective of the twenty-first century, it is difficult to imagine the frailty of the Supreme Court two hundred years ago. As has been mentioned earlier, Chief Justice John Marshall crafted the Court's rise in prestige and power.

A fundamental question that had to be resolved was whether each branch of the federal government or the individual states, rather than the Supreme Court, might determine when the Constitution had been violated. In *Marbury* v. *Madison* (1803), Marshall cautiously declared the doctrine of **judicial review**—the right of courts to declare executive and congressional acts unconstitutional. In Marshall's view, it was "emphatically the province and the duty of the judicial department to say what the law is."

Marbury v. Madison (1803)

After John Adams lost the 1800 presidential election to Thomas Jefferson, Adams attempted to pack the judiciary with Federalists before Jefferson could be inaugurated in March 1801. As Adams's secretary of state, John Marshall was given charge of certifying and delivering the new judicial commissions. Marshall managed to deliver most of them before he left office.

The Republicans were furious at the appointment of these "midnight judges," and Jefferson ordered the new Secretary of State, James Madison, to withhold the undelivered commissions. Four Federalists who had been promised positions, including one William Marbury, sued Madison for their commissions and asked the Supreme Court to issue a writ of mandamus (Latin for "we command") ordering Madison to hand them over.

John Marshall, now the chief justice of the Supreme Court, faced a dilemma. If the Court ruled for Madison, it would admit its inability to enforce the law. If, on the other hand, the Court ruled for Marbury, Madison might refuse to deliver the commissions anyway, and the refusal would likewise reveal the inability of the Court to enforce the law. Worse, the Jeffersonians, now in a testy mood, might impeach Marshall. (In passing, it should be noted that a modern judge would disqualify himself from deciding such a case. After all, it was Marshall himself who was responsible for not delivering the four commissions.)

Marshall found an ingenious solution to the problem. The Supreme Court ruled that Marbury had a legitimate grievance and that the government should grant him his commission. Nevertheless, Marshall also ruled that the Court had no power to issue a writ of mandamus because the provision in the Judiciary Act of 1789 giving the Court that power was unconstitutional. Thus Marshall cleverly managed to lecture Jefferson on the injustice of withholding the commissions while avoiding a showdown with the Republicans.

Thus *Marbury* v. *Madison* marks the first important (though guarded) claim of the Supreme Court to exercise the power of judicial review. But it should also be noted that the Supreme Court did not rule another act of Congress unconstitutional for fifty-four more years—and that was in the disastrous Dred Scott decision.

Likewise, as a strong nationalist, Marshall also took seriously the **supremacy clause** of the Constitution that declared the Constitution and the laws of the United States "the supreme law of the land . . . anything in the constitution or laws of any state to the contrary notwithstanding." In the case of *McCulloch* v. *Maryland* (1819), the Marshall Court ruled that state taxation of the second Bank of the United States was unconstitutional, even though chartering banks was not a power specifically granted to Congress in the Constitution. Such a power could be implied from the "necessary and proper" clause, said Marshall, and Maryland law must therefore be unconstitutional because "the power to tax involves the power to destroy."

The Marshall Court also increased the power of the federal government in other ways, for instance, making federal commerce laws supreme over state laws and guaranteeing the sanctity of contracts that would have otherwise been violated by state action. Jefferson called the judiciary a "corps of sappers and miners" chipping away at state power, but there is no doubt that private property and economic prosperity benefited from the Court's decisions.

Ironically, federal power over the states was also indirectly enhanced by one of the most misguided Supreme Court decisions in its history, the Dred Scott case (1857), in which Chief Justice

Roger Taney attempted to settle the question of slavery by judicial fiat. Taney's declaration that Negroes could not be citizens of the United States unleashed a storm of northern protest that indirectly led to the Civil War as well as the nationalization of the federal system.

Following the Civil War, the Supreme Court made further encroachments on state power by reinterpreting the Fourteenth Amendment. Intending to undo the Dred Scott decision and prevent civil discrimination against blacks, the Court instead interpreted the amendment's "due process" clause so as to apply to corporations seeking relief from state regulatory legislation. The Court's caseload expanded rapidly, and so did its rulings on the unconstitutionality of various pieces of state legislation. For instance, in the Minnesota Freight Rate case (1890), the Court ruled that a railroad was deprived of due process by a state law that reduced its fees. Between 1896 and 1905, the Supreme Court viewed 297 cases under the microscope of the Fourteenth Amendment. Meanwhile, the intended beneficiaries of the amendment, southern blacks, were virtually ignored.

Activism vs. Restraint

Whether federal judges interpret the Constitution with concern for its literal meaning or whether, in the words of Woodrow Wilson, they act like "a constitutional convention in continuous session" depends on their judicial philosophy. There are two major schools of constitutional interpretation: strict constructionism, also called **judicial restraint;** and broad constructionism, also called **judicial activism.** Strict constructionists argue that judges should apply only the clear statements of the Constitution to make their decisions and not use idiosyncratic interpretations to make social policy. Proponents of broad constructionism view the Court's role as that of policymaker, interpreting the Constitution to meet present needs. Of course, the line between the two positions is often less clear than frequently believed. That the "Vice President of the United States shall be President of the Senate" is a statement obvious on its face; but it is more difficult to strictly interpret phrases such as "due process," "unreasonable searches and seizures," or "make no law respecting the establishment of religion."

Further, strict constructionism is usually equated with conservatism and broad constructionism with liberalism. This has not always been the case, nor is it always even the case today. Prior to the New Deal, conservatives usually took a broader view of the Constitution in order to rule against state regulation of business. Even today it is possible to reach a conservative end via an activist judicial position. For instance, in *Bush* v. *Gore* (2000), the Supreme Court reached a conservative end—assuring the election of George W. Bush—by overruling the Florida State Supreme Court on the meaning of state election law, an activist means.

The activism of the Supreme Court met its match in the crisis of the Great Depression and the popularity of the New Deal. When the Supreme Court ruled much of the dubious legislation of Franklin Roosevelt unconstitutional, Roosevelt struck back with a plan to "pack" the Court with additional justices of his own choosing. The Court shortly changed its mind about the constitutionality of New Deal legislation—"a switch in time saves nine"—and several justices retired, allowing Roosevelt to make his own nominations. But many Americans were genuinely shocked by the president's attack on the institution of the Supreme Court, so revered had it become.

Many justices named by Roosevelt were still sitting on the Court when Dwight Eisenhower selected Earl Warren to be chief justice in 1953. The Warren Court became the most influential in American history after that of John Marshall. It wrote the unanimous decision in *Brown* v. *Board of Education of Topeka* (1953), which forbade segregation in schools—largely on sociological rather than legal grounds. The Warren Court ruled that police could not use evidence seized without a warrant, that suspected criminals must be informed of

their rights in *Miranda* v. *Arizona* (1966), and that states must redraw their congressional districts on the basis of "one man, one vote."

Despite complaints from liberals that post-Warren Courts have been too conservative, succeeding decades have witnessed increased attacks against biblical morality by Supreme Court decisions. As the late nineteenth-century Court had created a "freedom of contract" not mentioned by the Constitution, so the late twentieth-century Court created a likewise unmentioned (and more dangerous) "right of privacy." Right of privacy provided legal props for *Roe* v. *Wade* (1973), the infamous decision that legalized abortion, and *Lawrence and Garner* v. *Texas* (2003), a decision that invalidated state laws against sodomy. The Court also redefined free speech to include pornography and adult entertainment.

This decline in constitutional jurisprudence was part of a broader, long-term decay in the understanding of the common law. As late as 1868, Joel Bishop, a respected legal treatise writer, could say,

> When there is a concurrence of all the circumstances essential to a sound administration of justice, . . . "Almighty God" appears in the midst of the tribunal where it sits, and reveals the right way to the understandings of the judges, as surely as he appears in the tempest.

Such language has not been heard again from a legal scholar of first rank. Bishop's contemporary Christopher Columbus Langdell, the father of modern legal education, wrote just three years later that law was "a science" with doctrines that had come into being "by slow degrees." In other words, law was the product of an evolutionary process. To Langdell, the way to study law was through past cases—at least those selected by Langdell.

Bishop and Langdell

Joel Prentiss Bishop (1814–1901) and Christopher Columbus Langdell (1826–1906) were contemporaries who, at the height of their careers, lived in Cambridge, Massachusetts, within walking distance of each other. Both were poor boys who acquired education through their own efforts, and both lived the life of bachelor scholars, devoting themselves to study and writing. (Langdell did marry late in life but had no children.) Almost no information about their private lives has survived.

Both Bishop and Langdell viewed law as "scientific," but that word meant something different to each of them. Bishop believed that law was scientific in the sense that God had established a few legal principles, and men could comprehend those principles by sound reason. To Bishop, all men possessed a "moral sense," and therefore, judges who were properly trained and morally upright would be led to a proper judicial decision almost as if God Himself were sitting with them on the bench.

Langdell, the first dean of Harvard Law School, also believed that there were only a few "scientific" principles of law. But their source was not God, nor was discovering them a matter of moral uprightness. To Langdell, one came to a proper judgment about a legal problem from the study of past cases. The result was a logical system of technical rules, applicable in the courts, but which had no necessary connection with moral truth. In one notorious case, Langdell prefaced his discussion of a common-law rule with the statement that concern for promoting justice was irrelevant.

Both Bishop and Langdell were honored in their own lifetimes. More than one legal periodical regarded Bishop as the most important legal writer of his day, and he received an honorary degree from the University of Berne, Switzerland. Langdell proved an effective administrator at Harvard, and he lived to see his method of teaching law through selected cases embraced by the most prestigious law schools in the country. Today Langdell remains a familiar name to legal professionals. A Harvard building is named for him. But Bishop is virtually unknown even by specialists. A recent multivolume legal encyclopedia for laymen devotes two pages to a biography of Langdell, but nothing to Bishop.

Although dependence on *stare decisis* probably seemed a safe route to many religious men of the late nineteenth century, Bishop knew better. *Stare decisis* could provide order, but it ignored the higher law and the God who made it. Finding truth in the old cases hardly lasted a generation before legal thinkers asked why they should be bound by decisions made hundreds of years before and why they could not find a sounder basis for law in anthropology, sociology, or psychology. To them, man guided by the scientific method could discover any legal rules that there might be.

It is said that Learned Hand, a federal judge, once drove Oliver Wendell Holmes Jr. to the Supreme Court and bid him goodbye with the words "Do justice." Holmes is supposed to have replied, "That is not my job—my job is to play the game according to the rules." A tremendous amount of spiritual capital has been built into our country by previous generations. Many judges still rule biblically even though they do not know the God who made the law. But the more judges play by rules of their own making, the more antibiblical American law will become. Our nation will then truly be a government of men and not of laws.

Section Review

1. What two declarations did Justice John Marshall make with the following two cases: *Marbury* v. *Madison; McCulloch* v. *Maryland?*

2. Contrast the philosophies of judicial restraint and judicial activism.

Chapter Review

Terms

justice
Corpus Juris Civilis
common law
precedents
stare decisis
Commentaries on the Laws of England
natural law
revealed law
judicial federalism

district courts
original jurisdiction
grand jury
petit or trial jury
appellate jurisdiction
en banc
justices
writ of certiorari
majority opinion
dissenting opinion

concurring opinions
senatorial courtesy
Marbury v. *Madison*
judicial review
supremacy clause
McCulloch v. *Maryland*
judicial restraint
judicial activism
Roe v. *Wade*

Content Questions

1. What verse of Scripture commands men to do justice?
2. Who was Oxford's first professor of English law? What contribution did he make to American law?
3. What percentage of the nation's legal actions do states hear? What does this percentage indicate about the importance of state judiciaries in American jurisprudence?
4. What are the major differences among the district courts, the circuit courts, and the Supreme Court?
5. What is the significance of *Marbury* v. *Madison?*
6. Why is the prerogative of judicial review such a potent power of the Supreme Court?

Application Questions

1. Define *justice.* How do society's prevalent ideas about justice compare to the standards of justice in the Bible?
2. What are the advantages of the relatively modern legal concepts of common law, *stare decisis,* and trial by jury?
3. Why is the Supreme Court, which hears only about one hundred fifty cases a year, more powerful than the district courts, which hear three hundred thousand cases per year?
4. How is the third branch of the government, the federal courts, subject to the will of the president and Congress? How are the courts independent?

CIVIL RIGHTS AND CIVIL RESPONSIBILITIES

FREEDOM OF SPEECH
FREEDOM OF WORSHIP
FREEDOM FROM WANT
FREEDOM FROM FEAR

The Declaration of Independence asserts it to be "self-evident" that "all men are endowed by their Creator with certain unalienable Rights." Although the American founders may not have recognized the God of the Bible in this statement of universal rights, this statement is true in any case because man was created in God's image. Today citizens of the United States enjoy greater civil rights and civil liberties than most of the world's people, in part because Americans have long, if imperfectly, recognized God as the ultimate source of liberty. This chapter examines American civil liberties and civil rights and concludes with a brief discussion of the responsibilities that our privileged citizenship requires.

I. Civil Liberties

The terms *civil liberties* and *civil rights* are often used interchangeably, but there is an important distinction between them. **Civil rights** are governmental actions that attempt to ensure that liberty is extended to everyone. For instance, the Civil Rights Act of 1964 prohibited discrimination due to race, sex, religion, or national origin. The right to a fair trial and the right to vote are also rights protected by potential government intervention.

Civil liberties, on the other hand, protect individual freedoms *from* government. For instance, Americans are promised that their freedoms of worship and speech will not be arbitrarily limited by government intrusion.

Rights	Liberties
Freedom from discrimination	Free speech
Right to vote	Free worship
Right of association	Fair trial

Freedom of Religion

Many of our most cherished civil liberties are outlined in the First Amendment to the Constitution, and the Supreme Court has continued to delineate these rights. It is noteworthy that the first declaration of the Bill of Rights defends freedom of religious conscience: "Congress shall make no law respecting an establishment of religion, or prohibiting the free exercise thereof." The two parts of this provision, the **establishment clause** and the **free exercise clause,** create a natural division in which to examine the First Amendment.

Madison's *Memorial and Remonstrance* of 1785

In 1784 the Virginia Assembly proposed to tax property owners to support a Christian denomination of the taxpayer's choice. The proposition pitted James Madison and Thomas Jefferson against Patrick Henry and George Mason before either the Constitution (1789) or the Bill of Rights (1791) had been written. Henry and Mason supported the tax as a means of upholding morality while Jefferson and Madison opposed it as an encroachment on religious freedom. Because Jefferson was serving as U.S.

minister to France, Madison led the opposition with his *Memorial and Remonstrance.* Madison's basic points were (1) that one's duty to God could only be directed "by reason and conviction, not by force or violence;" (2) that a government that had the power to tax on behalf of religion generally might eventually force citizens to conform to a particular specific religious establishment; and (3) that past attempts to support religion by taxation, "instead of maintaining the purity and efficacy of Religion, . . . had a contrary operation."

Petitions and memorials signed by over eleven thousand Virginians deluged the Virginia state legislature, and nine out of ten signers condemned the tax. To a considerable extent, rationalists and Christian evangelicals agreed in their opposition but on different grounds. Rationalists tended to emphasize the harmful effects of establishment on the government while evangelicals stressed its negative effects on the spread of the gospel.

The legislature allowed the bill to die and voted instead to adopt Jefferson's Virginia Statute for Religious Freedom, which asserted that "no man shall be compelled to frequent or support any religious worship, place, or ministry whatsoever."

Establishment Clause—It is not accidental that the First Amendment was worded in such a way as to prevent Congress, but not the states, from establishing a religion. When the First Amendment was adopted, several New England states still maintained established churches. The establishment clause of the First Amendment was therefore intended to protect the religious diversity of the states from the power of the national government, not to make the government a rival or enemy of religion.

The founders understood that the success of republican government depended on the morality of its citizens. To support that morality, Congress appointed chaplains to the armed forces (and to Congress itself) and granted tax exemptions to religious organizations. There was no suggestion that Congress was thereby violating the First Amendment.

By the time the Supreme Court "incorporated" the First Amendment into the Fourteenth at the end of the nineteenth century, state religious establishments had been dismantled. Yet the Supreme Court continued to allow Bible reading in schools, released-time programs for religious instruction, and even state funding for transportation to parochial schools. In 1952 William O. Douglas, one of the most liberal of all New Deal Supreme Court justices wrote, "We are a religious people whose institutions presuppose a Supreme Being."

Nevertheless, in the 1960s the Supreme Court began to imply that there was a complete "wall of separation" between church and state. (The phrase "wall of separation" originated in a brief commentary on the First Amendment by Thomas Jefferson and does not appear in the Constitution.) In **Engel v. Vitale** (1962), the Supreme Court forbade teacher-led prayers in public schools, even if they were nonsectarian and noncompulsory. A year later the Court struck down a Pennsylvania statute that required ten verses from the Bible be read daily in its public schools. When some states then required a voluntary moment of silence in schools, the Supreme Court ruled this action too a violation of the Constitution. More recently the Supreme Court has ruled student-led prayers at football games unconstitutional and even upheld a school district's right to restrict religious content in a valedictorian's speech.

In **Lemon v. Kurtzman** (1971), the Supreme Court ruled that state statutes affecting religion must meet a three-fold test to be sustained: (1) the state law would need a "secular legislative purpose"; (2) it could not either "advance or inhibit religion"; and (3) it could not foster an "excessive government entanglement with religion." Aptly named the "*Lemon* test," these rules have mired the Court in hopeless contradiction and have led to rulings on such trivia as whether a Santa Claus and some elves added

to a manger scene make a Christmas scene secular enough to be displayed in a public space.

Free Exercise—The free exercise clause of the First Amendment protects religious practices within broad boundaries. Generally speaking, freedom of conscience means that a person may not only believe what he chooses but may also act on those beliefs.

Nevertheless, government must also protect public safety and morality, so free exercise of religion cannot be absolute. For example, in the celebrated case of *Reynolds* v. *United States* (1879), laws forbidding the Mormon practice of polygamy were sustained, even though polygamy was said to

Civic rituals such as reciting the Pledge of Allegiance have been challenged by some religious groups as a violation of their First Amendment rights.

be a matter of religious duty for late nineteenth-century Mormons. Chief Justice Morrison Waite noted that the government would certainly have to prohibit human sacrifice even if it were a sincerely held religious belief (as it was, for instance, in the Hinduism of his day). Whether the refusal of Jehovah's Witnesses to salute the American flag is as heinous as human sacrifice or polygamy was answered twice by the Supreme Court: yes in 1940 and no in 1943.

Section Review

1. What is the difference between civil liberties and civil rights?
2. What two clauses describe freedom of religion in the First Amendment?
3. What was the original purpose of each of these clauses? How have these clauses come to be interpreted?
4. What is the name of the threefold test used by the courts to determine the constitutionality of state laws affecting religious institutions, and what are the three parts of that test?

Freedoms of Speech and Press

Freedom of expression through speech and print is fundamental to personal liberty and to the success of a free society. Freedom of conscience is of little value without freedom of communication, and a democracy requires an informed public that arises from the free exchange of ideas. Freedom of expression restrains arbitrary government and allows unpopular views to be heard and even prevail if those ideas have merit. For this reason, totalitarian states suppress free speech.

Defending the principle of free expression involves defending the right of others to say obnoxious things. Even so, reasonable men acknowledge that there are limits to what a person may lawfully say or write. In Justice Oliver Wendell Holmes's classic instance, "The most stringent protection of free speech would not protect a man in falsely shouting 'fire' in a theater and causing a panic."

Limitations on Speech—The government may legitimately restrict four types of speech: speech threatening public safety; speech intended to overthrow the government or endanger national security (**sedition**); speech attempting to damage an individual's reputation or property; and obscene speech.

The government may restrict *disruptive speech,* speech that threatens public safety and public order, but speech may not be limited simply because it is disagreeable. In the landmark case *Schenk* v. *United States* (1919), the Supreme Court established the **clear and present danger test,** which requires that the danger be genuine and that the speech actually incite violence rather than simply endorse it. The courts have also upheld local laws prohibiting speech that disturbs the peace, as, for instance, by the use of amplifiers.

Although treason, sabotage, and spying are all actions that have fairly clear legal definitions, *sedition* has been more difficult for the courts to define. The government certainly has a right to

Ethel and Julius Rosenberg during their trial for espionage in New York City in 1951

defend itself against **subversion**—attempts to undermine its authority and existence. In 1940 Congress passed the **Smith Act,** making it illegal to advocate the violent overthrow of the government, to teach others to take such actions, or to be a member of an organization that conspires to overthrow the government. In 1948 Eugene Dennis, General Secretary of the American Communist Party, and eleven other party members were prosecuted under the Smith Act for teaching and promoting the overthrow of the United States government. The Supreme Court upheld the Smith Act in *Dennis* v. *United States* (1951).

Nevertheless, with the decline of American communism and the growth of libertarianism, the Supreme Court began to interpret the Smith Act in a way that made the act virtually unenforceable and sedition a crime nearly impossible to prove in court.

Defamation is malicious words, whether spoken (**slander**) or written (**libel**). Private individuals still can, and do, sue for defamation; but in *New York Times Co. v. Sullivan* (1969), the Supreme Court ruled that attacks on public officials, even if inaccurate, were constitutionally protected unless made in "reckless disregard" of the truth. Eventually celebrities also lost much of their ability to sue for defamation, and this inability lowered the barrier to gossip-mongering about the famous.

Generally the government may not suppress a story prior to its publication. In *New York Times v. United States* (1971)—the Pentagon Papers Case—Daniel Ellsberg, a former Defense Department analyst, stole classified documents that outlined the progress of American involvement in the Vietnam War. Ellsberg then made the documents available to the *New York Times* and other newspapers. Richard Nixon's Justice Department sought to ban publication of the papers, citing a threat to national security; but the Supreme Court ruled for the *Times* on the grounds that the government was attempting to exert **prior restraint** on the publisher. The Court did not exclude the possibility that the

Times could be prosecuted *after* the Pentagon Papers had been published.

The courts have long agreed that *obscenity* does not have the protection of the First Amendment, but they no longer agree on its definition. In any case, all definitions have degenerated with the culture. In *Miller* v. *California* (1973), the Supreme Court gave communities greater ability to set their own obscenity standards. Sexually explicit material was supposed to have some "serious literary, artistic, political, or scientific value" if it were not to be judged obscene. Standards of decency continued to fall. Censorship of movies was abandoned in 1967 and replaced with a voluntary rating system. Pornographic films are virtually never banned today, just rated.

Free Speech and Business—Commercial speech has never enjoyed the same protection as other forms of speech. For instance, local laws may limit the distribution of commercial advertising and the posting of "for sale" signs on private property, and the Federal Trade Commission can prohibit advertising that is obviously false or makes claims that cannot be proved.

Perhaps the best-known example of restricted business speech is government regulation of tobacco advertising. In 1965 Congress required tobacco manufacturers to put Surgeon General's warnings on cigarette packages. Later restrictions banned tobacco companies from advertising on television and radio. Since 1998 tobacco companies have not been able to use cartoons to advertise tobacco products, nor have they been able to

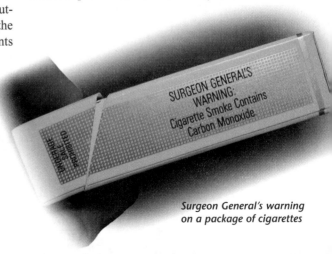

Surgeon General's warning on a package of cigarettes

advertise on billboards or on buses. Nevertheless, in 2001 the Supreme Court ruled that a Massachusetts law further restricting tobacco advertisements was an unconstitutional breach of commercial free speech. The Court has also given greater protection to commercial speech in such cases as advertising for an abortion clinic and publicizing the prices of prescription drugs.

Symbolic Speech—The Supreme Court has also protected **symbolic speech,** the expression of ideas through actions instead of words. For instance, the Court has protected such "expressive activity" as wearing the American flag on the seat of one's pants or displaying a peace symbol superimposed on the American flag.

In 1984 Gregory Lee Johnson burned an American flag outside the Republican National Convention. He was arrested and convicted under a Texas law that prohibited desecration of the flag. In *Texas v. Johnson* (1989), the Supreme Court reversed the conviction in a 5-4 decision, ruling that flag burning was a form of symbolic speech and thus protected by the Constitution. The ruling precipitated a nationwide uproar. Congress immediately passed the Flag Protection Act, which the Supreme Court struck down the following year. There was talk of a constitutional amendment to reverse the decision, but both public interest and flag burning waned simultaneously.

Flag Etiquette

Because the American flag symbolizes the nation and its freedoms, the flag should be treated with respect. The following guidelines are taken from the U.S. Flag Code (4 US Code 1).

1. When reciting the Pledge of Allegiance to the flag, one should stand at attention facing the flag with the right hand over the heart. When not in uniform, men should remove head coverings.
2. Flags should be flown only from sunrise to sunset unless properly illuminated.
3. Flags should not be flown in bad weather unless they are all-weather flags.

Boys displaying proper flag-folding technique

4. No other flag or pennant should be placed above or, if on the same level, to the right of the American flag.
5. The flag should not be dipped to any person or thing.
6. The flag should not be displayed with the union (the blue section) down except to signal an emergency.
7. The flag should never touch anything beneath it—ground, floor, water, or merchandise.
8. The flag should never be used as wearing apparel, bedding, or drapery.
9. The flag should not have words or pictures placed on it.
10. The flag should never be used for advertising purposes.
11. No part of the flag should be used as a costume or athletic uniform. It may be attached to military or civilian uniforms.
12. When no longer fit for display, the flag should be destroyed in a dignified way, preferably (and ironically) by burning.

Freedoms of Assembly and Petition

"Congress shall make no law . . . abridging . . . the right of the people peaceably to assemble and to petition the government for a redress of grievances."

The freedom to carry out peaceful demonstrations, to circulate petitions, or to write letters in support of (or opposition to) a particular cause is a natural extension of the free speech clause. The freedom to organize into groups to influence public opinion, public officials, and legislation is also basic to our political system.

Nevertheless, the freedoms of assembly and petition protect only peaceful activity, not riots, property destruction, nor the obstruction of streets and businesses. Courts have consistently upheld the right of local governments to enforce **time-place-manner laws** that may, for instance, restrict demonstrations to particular streets, sidewalks, or public parks during specified periods of time. Local governments may also require that demonstrators acquire a permit in advance.

Further, assembly and petition rights do not supersede property rights. Citizens outraged over a city council ruling may legitimately demonstrate in front of city hall, but they may not trample the mayor's lawn. Use of a shopping mall for public petitioning and demonstrations is a much thornier issue. Most courts have considered shopping malls to be private property; others have ruled malls diversified enough to be considered "public forums" for First Amendment purposes.

The right of peaceful demonstration may be subject to time-place-manner laws.

Civil Disobedience and the Bible

Civil disobedience has become a favored device of antiwar protesters, pro-life advocates, animal rights activists, and radical environmentalists to protest laws or policies. Is civil disobedience a legitimate tool for Christians?

The Bible teaches that Christians must disobey the laws of men if those laws require them to disobey God's laws (Acts 5:29). This principle is illustrated in the Bible by the midwives who disobeyed Pharaoh (Exod. 1), the Hebrew youths who refused to bow to an idol (Dan. 3), Daniel's refusal to cease praying (Dan. 6), and Peter's refusal to stop preaching the gospel (Acts 5). These examples teach that Christians should not obey laws that force them to disobey the laws of God, but the biblical examples do not permit Christians to disobey laws that only allow disobedience to God's laws. A general principle in the Bible is that Christians must obey their rulers because rulers are God's servants (Rom. 13:1–4). When it becomes necessary for Christians to disobey a government command, they should expect to be punished just as Peter and the other disciples were punished during the first century.

Boy Scouts in front of the USS **Yorktown**

Freedom of association is not mentioned in the Constitution, but the Supreme Court has inferred it from the rights of free speech and petition. When the state of Alabama ordered the National Association for the Advancement of Colored People (NAACP) to surrender its membership lists, the Supreme Court ruled in 1957 that members of the organization ought to be able to "pursue their lawful private interests privately and . . . associate freely with others in doing so." Likewise, in *Boy Scouts of America* v. *Dale* (2000), the Supreme Court ruled that the Boy Scouts could revoke the membership of an assistant scout leader and avowed homosexual, despite a New Jersey antidiscrimination law. Otherwise, said the Court, the government would be forcing a private organization to admit a member it did not want.

Section Review

1. What are two important reasons for the guarantees of free speech and free press?
2. What are four kinds of speech that the government may legitimately restrict?
3. Explain the difference between slander and libel.
4. What is symbolic speech?
5. What are the limitations of America's freedoms of assembly and petition?
6. From what is the freedom of association inferred?

II. Civil Rights

Ever since Jefferson asserted man's inalienable rights of "life, liberty, and the pursuit of happiness," the nature of civil rights has been debated in America. From the late nineteenth century through the present, the struggle of minorities and women for full political rights has resulted in constitutional guarantees being interpreted, expanded, and sometimes created by the U.S. Supreme Court.

Right of Privacy

The right of privacy is another right that has been implied by the Supreme Court, even though it is not explicitly stated in the Constitution. The right to privacy mirrors an important contemporary (and anti-Christian) belief that "It's my life, and I can do what I want with it" without interference from others.

The Supreme Court created the right of privacy in *Griswold* v. *Connecticut* (1965), which ruled unconstitutional a Connecticut statute prohibiting the use of contraceptives even by married couples. Justice William O. Douglas, who wrote the decision, asserted that although a right of privacy was not mentioned in the Constitution, the Bill of Rights had "penumbras, formed by emanations from those guarantees." (This phrase means that the Bill of Rights has a gray area formed by the implications of its guarantees.) Eight years later, *Griswold* became a legal prop for *Roe* v. *Wade* (1973), which asserted that women have the right to have an abortion—at least reasonably early in the pregnancy. (The "emanations" from the Bill of Rights were apparently getting more specific.) Since 1973, both Congress and the states have attempted to restrict abortions in various minor ways. Sometimes the Court has accepted the restrictions and sometimes not. Of course, a Christian cannot recognize as legitimate a right declared by the Supreme Court that God has declared to be immoral.

Substantive due process means that the substance of laws must protect a person's basic freedoms. Furthermore, these laws must be justly

Due Process	
Substantive	**Procedural**
Free speech	Right to a fair trial
Free press	Presence at trial
Freedom of association	Taxes only for public use
Right of privacy	Miranda rights

administered and enforced through **procedural due process.** The police, for example, may not make arbitrary arrests.

Prior to the ratification of the Fourteenth Amendment, the Bill of Rights applied largely to the national government rather than to the states. During the nineteenth century, the Supreme Court began to incorporate the Bill of Rights into the Fourteenth Amendment (**incorporation**), largely in order to rule state regulation of corporations unconstitutional. In *Gitlow* v. *New York* (1925), the Court first applied the Fourteenth Amendment to a state law restricting free speech. During the New Deal era, the nationalization of the Bill of Rights became a central issue in constitutional law.

Incorporation was greatly accelerated under the activist court of Chief Justice Earl Warren (1953–69), so that today most (but not all) of the Bill of Rights has been brought under the umbrella of the Fourteenth Amendment. This expansion of the Bill of Rights means that most state laws must conform to requirements established by the Supreme Court.

The Fourteenth Amendment reads in part:

> No state shall make or enforce any law which shall abridge the privileges or immunities of citizens of the United States; nor shall any state deprive any person of life, liberty, or property, without due process of law; nor deny to any person within its jurisdiction the equal protection of the laws.

The incorporation of the Bill of Rights into the Fourteenth Amendment has enhanced the power of the judiciary, altered the nature of federation, and enlarged the scope of constitutional rights. These expanded rights will be examined in three categories: security rights, procedural rights, and voting rights.

Security Rights

The security of the individual and his property is protected by the Second, Third, and Fourth Amendments.

The Right to Bear Arms—The Second Amendment states:

> A well-regulated militia being necessary to the security of a free state, the right of the people to keep and bear arms shall not be infringed.

The right to bear arms is protected by the Second Amendment; however, this right is subject to regulation by the states.

Although the Second Amendment was written with citizen-soldiers in mind, it also reflects an underlying right of self-defense. The Supreme Court has not incorporated the Second Amendment into the Fourteenth, so state legislatures may freely regulate the sale and possession of firearms. The Supreme Court has also upheld a federal law that banned the interstate transport of unregistered sawed-off shotguns and silencers, since such items were hardly "necessary to the security of a free state."

No Forced Quartering of Troops—The Third Amendment prohibits the forced quartering of troops in private homes during peacetime. Forced quartering of British troops was a major irritant before the American Revolution and a bitter memory thereafter. The Third Amendment was probably violated during the War of 1812 and the Civil War, but these violations were never litigated through the courts.

No Unreasonable Searches—The Fourth Amendment protects citizens from unreasonable searches and seizures:

> The right of the people to be secure in their persons, houses, papers, and effects, against unreasonable searches and seizures, shall not be violated; and no warrants shall issue, but upon probable cause, supported by oath or affirmation, and particularly describing the place to be searched, and the persons or things to be seized.

A legal search takes place when there exists **probable cause** that a crime has been committed or is about to be committed. Generally a legal search also requires a search warrant. The Supreme Court has determined that a search necessitates a warrant if the person searched has an expectation of privacy regarded as reasonable by society.

Nevertheless, when a proper arrest is made, it is unnecessary to obtain a warrant in order to search the person or the area under his immediate control. Search warrants are also not required to search vehicles if there is probable cause to suspect contraband, in cases of "hot pursuit," or when evidence is in danger of being destroyed. Search warrants are also unnecessary when the owner of a building gives his consent to a search (although the police are not supposed to obtain the consent by force or intimidation). Abandoned property may also be searched without a warrant—that is, trash left on curbs or thrown in dumpsters. Mandatory drug testing has been contested as an illegitimate search, but the courts have upheld the constitutionality of such tests for athletes and prospective employees. Finally, the Supreme Court has also ruled that "reasonable" administrative searches in schools or workplaces do not require search warrants.

Advances in technology have added an additional dimension to rules about search and seizure. The Supreme Court has ruled that electronic eavesdropping violates privacy and is therefore illegal without a warrant, but the Court has allowed wiretaps and "bugs" in investigations related to national security.

During the heyday of the Warren Court's activism, it created the **exclusionary rule** in *Mapp v. Ohio* (1961). The rule holds that evidence obtained illegally is inadmissible in court (as, for example, evidence obtained without a proper search warrant). The purpose of the exclusionary rule was to restrain the police from making illegal searches and seizures, but the new rule also allowed some criminals to escape punishment, especially before the police could adjust to the new circumstances. More recently the Supreme Court has relaxed the exclusionary rule somewhat. For instance, in 1984 the Court ruled that evidence obtained by an officer acting reasonably and in good faith could not be excluded from testimony simply because the warrant was defective.

Procedural Rights

The Fifth, Sixth, Seventh, and Eighth Amendments outline the rights of those accused of crimes and guarantee fair judicial procedures. These rights support a fundamental assumption of our court system: that a person is innocent until proven guilty.

The Fifth Amendment: Rights of the Accused—The Fifth Amendment provides important protections for the accused. A citizen accused of criminal activity cannot be forced to answer for federal crimes unless indicted by a grand jury. (The requirement of a grand jury has not been incorporated into the due process clause of the Fourteenth Amendment and so is not obligatory for state court systems.) More importantly, the amendment protects citizens from **double jeopardy,** being tried twice for the same crime in the same court. (If a crime violates both a federal and state law, however, the accused may be tried at both the federal and state levels.) In addition, the Fifth Amendment protects citizens from **self-incrimination.** No one is required to make admissions in a criminal case that could be used against him in court. The burden of proving guilt rests on the prosecution.

To protect citizens from self-incrimination while being held in police custody, the Supreme Court ruled in *Miranda v. Arizona* (1966) that it would throw out any conviction in which a suspect was not informed of his constitutional rights against self-incrimination. The case established a nearly legislative **Miranda warning,** a list that the police must recite to the accused prior to questioning:

1. He has the right to remain silent in order to avoid self-incrimination.

2. If he chooses to speak, what he says can be used against him in court.

3. He has the right to an attorney. If he cannot afford counsel, an attorney will be provided by the state.

4. He has the right to end police questioning whenever he chooses.

The Miranda rule is one of the most familiar features of the American criminal justice system because it is so often repeated on TV police shows. (Canadian criminals have complained about not being read their Miranda rights.) Although there have been complaints that the Miranda rule has hindered criminal justice, the evidence has been inconclusive—at least since the police have adjusted to the new rule. Most accused criminals do talk to the police before a lawyer arrives (and tells them to be quiet), and many continue to confess their crimes to the police.

The Fifth Amendment also ensures that no citizen may "be deprived of life, liberty, or property, without due process of law," that is, only after a fair and proper trial. However, if the government condemns land necessary for a public purpose, such as a new road, it must pay the owner "just compensation" for the property.

The Sixth Amendment: Rights of the Accused in Criminal Court—Additional procedural rights protecting the accused include the Sixth Amendment right to a "speedy and public trial" in criminal cases. The Sixth Amendment also ensures the right of a jury trial (unless waived by the accused,

Criminal Justice Process

1. Arrest

2. Booking—The suspect is photographed and fingerprinted, and his personal information is recorded.

3. Initial appearance—The accused meets with a magistrate within hours of arrest to hear the charges, be reminded of his rights, and be considered for bail.

4. Preliminary hearing—A judge determines if there is enough evidence to continue the judicial process

5. Grand jury review—The grand jury hears evidence and decides whether to issue an indictment (applicable in federal courts and in twenty states).

6. Arraignment—The accused first appears in trial court; the judge reads the indictment; and the accused enters a plea—"guilty," "not guilty," or "no contest."

7. Trial

8. Sentencing—The judge decides what punishment the convicted will receive.

Officer reading an individual the Miranda rights

or in cases where the penalty is less than six months in prison). In a criminal case, a unanimous jury must be convinced beyond reasonable doubt that the accused is guilty.

Furthermore, the Sixth Amendment ensures that the accused is informed of the "nature and cause of accusation," that he is able to face his accusers, that he has the opportunity to gather witnesses for his innocence, and that he has the right to an adequate defense. Courts will appoint a lawyer to defend those who cannot afford one.

The Seventh Amendment: Rights of Citizens in Civil Trials—The Seventh Amendment guarantees the right to jury trials for civil cases involving disputes between citizens if the disputed amount exceeds twenty dollars. Civil trials decide issues between individuals or groups of people, and they encompass such things as disputes over land ownership, breaches of contract, and negligence in automobile accidents. (In criminal trials the state prosecutes the accused violator of criminal law.)

The Eighth Amendment: Cruel, Unusual, and Unjust Punishment—The Eighth Amendment protects the accused from being assigned bail higher than necessary to assure that he will appear in court and submit to punishment if convicted. The Eighth Amendment also protects those convicted of crimes from being subjected to "cruel and unusual punishment."

Most cases that have come before the Court over this provision involve **capital punishment,** the death penalty. Opponents of capital punishment contend that the death penalty is itself cruel and unusual, regardless of the reason or the manner in which it is carried out. In *Furman* v. *Georgia* (1972) the Supreme Court threw out all state death penalty statutes on the ground that they were too vague and too inconsistently applied. In the words of the majority, the randomness of executions was "cruel and unusual in the same way that being struck by lightning is cruel and unusual." Although two justices believed the death penalty was unconstitutional in all circumstances, the majority could only agree that the *existing* death penalty statutes were unacceptable. Perhaps the Court thought that its decision might end capital punishment anyway.

Instead, many states passed *mandatory* death penalty statutes, which would almost certainly have increased the number of American executions. However, the Court struck the laws down. Other states passed laws that made capital punishment possible under "special circumstances," as, for instance, torturing a victim, killing a police officer, or killing more than one person. These laws have generally survived Supreme Court scrutiny. In any case, few murderers are executed, and those who are executed usually spend many years on death row appealing their sentences.

Constitutional Protection—In Article I, Section 9, the Constitution offers additional protection from oppressive and capricious laws by ensuring that the defendant may apply for a writ of *habeas* *corpus* and by prohibiting bills of attainder and *ex post facto* laws.

If the authorities do not bring charges against and try an arrested person, the courts will grant a **writ of *habeas corpus*** requiring that the defendant be released from custody. **Bills of attainder** permit punishment without a trial. ***Ex post facto* laws** criminalize activities that were not crimes when they were committed or require harsher punishments than were mandated at the time of the act.

What Does the Bible Say About Capital Punishment?

God pronounced the first death penalty in the Garden of Eden after man rebelled against Him (Gen. 2:17; 3:19). Later, when God saw that the earth was filled with violence, He passed a death penalty upon all mankind except for Noah and his family (Gen. 6:13). After the Flood, the Lord conferred on human government the duty of carrying out the death penalty: "Whoso sheddeth man's blood, by man shall his blood be shed: for in the image of God made he man" (Gen. 9:6).

This command preceded the Mosaic law, and the sixth commandment did not alter it. "Thou shalt not kill" applies to individuals rather than the state. Furthermore, the Hebrew word translated *kill* in the sixth commandment refers to murder, not to the execution of criminals. The state has the responsibility to execute criminals in order to render justice. For instance, God prescribes the death penalty for kidnapping (Exod. 21:16).

The Mosaic law provided specific instructions about how the death penalty was to be applied. It differentiated between premeditated murder, murder without prior malice, involuntary manslaughter, and death by negligence (Exod. 21:12–36). First-degree murder and death by willful negligence were punishable by death (v. 14). Israel was not consistent in applying these penalties, but its inconsistency did not invalidate the law.

Even though the Mosaic law is not binding on Christians, Scripture makes it clear that God still intends government to inflict the death penalty.

Paul said, "Rulers are not a terror to good works, but to the evil. . . . But if thou do that which is evil, be afraid; for he beareth not the sword in vain: for he is the minister of God, a revenger to execute wrath upon him that doeth evil" (Rom. 13:3–4). The sword here symbolizes punishment, which God requires the state to wield in the cause of justice. For men who deliberately take life, the death penalty is a just reward.

Voting Rights

The right to vote is a constitutional guarantee that has been expanded over the course of our nation's history. The franchise was extended to all adult white men as property requirements were gradually abolished during the early nineteenth century; to all adult black men (at least in theory) as a result of the **Fifteenth Amendment** in 1870; to all women as a result of the **Nineteenth Amendment** in 1920; and to those between eighteen and twenty-one years of age as a result of the **Twenty-sixth Amendment** in 1971.

Voting Requirements—Voters must be citizens of the United States and at least eighteen years old. In addition, citizens must satisfy the **residence requirements** of their state. Residence requirements attempt to ensure that voters have some knowledge of the issues and candidates in their locality—and that they have not suddenly appeared in the district simply to manipulate an election. Although residency requirements vary from state to state, the maximum requirement is thirty days residence in the voter's **precinct,** or voting district.

Registration is another requirement for voting. Every state except North Dakota requires that voters be properly enrolled with local election officials. Typically a registered voter goes to the polling place in his precinct and presents his voter registration card or driver's license to an election official. The official then checks for that voter's name on the list of registered voters. If everything is in order, the voter may cast his ballot.

Registration is a simple process but usually must be accomplished at least a few weeks before

an election. Online registration is available in most states and makes the registration process even easier. Unless a voter changes his residence or fails to vote for several years, he remains registered on his precinct rolls.

Registration not only identifies qualified voters but also prevents voting fraud. Without registration requirements, dishonest voters could vote for their candidate in more than one precinct. Registration prevents people from taking literally the old joke about voting "early and often."

Litigation and Legislation—Despite the constitutional guarantees incorporated in the Fifteenth, Nineteenth, and Twenty-sixth Amendments, black citizens were effectively denied the right to vote in many southern states. During the nineteenth century, jurisdictions throughout the country had required prospective voters to pass literacy tests on the sensible grounds that responsible voting required at least a basic understanding of political issues. But literacy tests in the South were not applied evenhandedly and, in fact, were specifically designed to disenfranchise blacks. (Interestingly, southern white voting declined as well even though voting officials were notoriously more lenient about certifying illiterate whites.) In addition, poor blacks were often barred from voting because of their inability to pay a **poll tax,** money paid in order to vote.

In the 1940s and 1950s, American racism became an embarrassment. The United States had just defeated the archracist Hitler and hoped to minimize communist propaganda about racial inequality in the United States. While northern blacks were now able to exercise considerable economic and political clout, southern blacks still had few political opportunities in states where they were denied the vote. The federal courts became somewhat reluctant champions of black civil rights during the 1940s and 1950s.

The courts began to enforce the Fifteenth Amendment (ratified in 1870) by overturning state laws that restricted the voting rights of blacks. In 1948 the Supreme Court prevented states from

enforcing housing covenants (neighborhood contracts) that were racially discriminatory. Even more importantly, in a series of cases, the Court struck down segregation in education, culminating in ***Brown v. Board of Education of Topeka*** (1954), which declared all segregated school facilities to be in violation of the Fourteenth Amendment.

By the mid-1950s, the American civil rights movement had passed from courtroom arguments to mass protests. Civil rights activists, led by Martin Luther King Jr., challenged discrimination against African Americans in the South with boycotts and demonstrations. Even after King's own house in Montgomery, Alabama, was bombed, King continued to advocate nonviolent disobedience of southern laws that sustained racial segregation. This strategy proved shrewd and highly effective, especially when southern law enforcement officers were captured on film brutalizing nonviolent demonstrators. King's assassination in 1968 almost immediately elevated him to the status of martyr and national hero.

Martin Luther King and other protesters during the March on Washington for Jobs and Freedom, 1963

In 1964 Congress, spurred by President Lyndon Johnson, passed the landmark **Civil Rights Act of 1964.** Virtually no business—hotel, cafeteria, gas station, or theater—could any longer discriminate on the basis of race. The act created the Equal Employment Opportunity Commission (EEOC) to root out discrimination in hiring. Under its provisions the Justice Department was authorized to enforce voting rights and to promote racial integration in public schools, in keeping with the *Brown* decision.

President Lyndon Johnson signs the Voting Rights Act of 1965 into law.

Even more important was the Voting Rights Act of 1965, which swept aside state poll taxes, literacy tests, and other southern dodges to prevent black voting. (The **Twenty-fourth Amendment** [1964] ended poll taxes in federal elections.) The Voting Rights Act also authorized the attorney general and the Justice Department to supervise local elections in areas where voter discrimination was suspected and gave the Justice Department power to review any changes in state election laws. Southern politics were turned upside down as white officeholders were suddenly made responsible to black voters.

Section Review

1. Which amendment enabled the courts to begin applying the Bill of Rights to state and local governments?
2. Which amendments guarantee security rights? procedural rights? What specific rights are covered in each of these amendments?
3. When may authorities search without a warrant?
4. What is the fundamental assumption of the U.S. court system?
5. Which rights does the Sixth Amendment ensure for accused criminals?
6. What are the minimum requirements of voters in most states?
7. What requirements have some states used to restrict the right to vote?

III. Civil Responsibilities
The Limits of Liberty

As we have seen throughout this chapter, civil rights and liberties are privileges with limits. Civil rights must be constrained by law. Both individuals and the state are responsible to protect citizens' rights. The Constitution is mere parchment when government officials exceed their constitutional powers. For example, in 1942 President Franklin

Roosevelt ordered approximately 150,000 American citizens of Japanese descent to be confined in war relocation camps as a precaution against Japanese espionage. Although this action of the United States government must be judged in its wartime context, constitutional liberties were clearly trampled, and that with the blessing of the Supreme Court. More recently, heightened security measures taken in reaction to the September 11 terrorist attacks have again raised fears that similar encroachments might take place.

Further, civil rights also require personal responsibility. The eighteenth-century British statesman Edmund Burke observed,

> Men are qualified for civil liberty in exact proportion to their disposition to put moral chains upon their own appetites. . . . It is ordained in the eternal constitution of things that men of intemperate minds cannot be free. Their passions forge their fetters.

Thousands of Japanese-Americans, such as this young girl, were placed in detention camps during the early part of World War II.

Christians have a responsibility to participate in a government that is "of the people, by the people, and for the people." They must not forfeit their God-given opportunity to work for the freest atmosphere in which to exercise their faith and spread the gospel.

Rights Redefined

Today the term *civil rights* has been given a different meaning from the historic examples treated in this chapter. Traditionally, civil rights referred to legal rights that provided equal protection and equal opportunity for all citizens. But the goal of many new rights groups is not equality of opportunity but the impossible goal of equality of condition.

For instance, the District of Columbia Human Rights Act prohibits discrimination

> including, but not limited to, discrimination by reason of race, color, religion, national origin, sex, age, marital status, personal appearance, sexual orientation, familial status, family responsibilities, matriculation, political affiliation, disability, source of income, and place of residence or business.

If taken seriously, such an attempt at achieving equality of condition would require an impossible amount of government supervision and would intrude into private lives and institutions to such an extent that it would ultimately destroy American freedom.

Rights groups also tend to undermine the democratic process by relying on courts rather than legislatures to obtain their demands. Because courts are more arbitrary and less responsive to the people, personal liberty is further endangered.

Finally, the modern emphasis on rights often stresses acceptance of perversion. For example, the American Civil Liberties Union (ACLU) has defended the legalization of narcotics and the right of child pornographers to produce and distribute obscene materials. The ACLU argued that "the introduction of substances into one's own body" is a civil liberty that should be protected by law regardless of its effect on the individual or ordered society.

The attempt to make evil appear good by giving it an agreeable name is nothing new. God warned in Isaiah 5:20, "Woe unto them that call evil good, and good evil." When homosexuals call sin a "sexual preference" or abortionists describe destroying unborn life as a "choice," they call evil good.

Constitutional guarantees are among the most prized birthrights of American citizens. But Christians enjoy freedom that excels even that provided by the Constitution. Paul underscored this fact in Romans 6:22: "But now being made free from sin, and become servants to God, ye have your fruit unto holiness, and the end everlasting life." Note that the believer is not born free, as a person born in America would be. Rather, he is "made free" in a spiritual sense when he places saving faith in Christ. The believer then possesses a freedom from sin and for service that is not dependent upon the power of the courts or Congress to maintain. Such is the freedom that rests in the power of God, for "if the Son therefore shall make you free, ye shall be free indeed" (John 8:36).

Section Review

1. Whose responsibility is it to protect the rights of citizens?

2. How has the expression *civil rights* been redefined in recent years?

3. What trends have resulted from the recent change in the use of the term *civil rights?*

Chapter Review

Terms

civil rights
civil liberties
establishment clause
free exercise clause
Engel v. *Vitale*
Lemon v. *Kurtzman*
sedition
clear and present danger test
subversion
Smith Act
slander
libel
New York Times Co. v.
    Sullivan

New York Times v.
    United States
prior restraint
symbolic speech
time-place-manner laws
freedom of association
substantive due process
procedural due process
incorporation
probable cause
exclusionary rule
Mapp v. *Ohio*
double jeopardy
self-incrimination
Miranda v. *Arizona*

Miranda warning
capital punishment
writ of *habeas corpus*
bills of attainder
ex post facto laws
Fifteenth Amendment
Nineteenth Amendment
Twenty-sixth Amendment
residence requirements
precinct
registration
poll tax
Brown v. *Board of Education
    of Topeka*
Civil Rights Act of 1964
Twenty-fourth Amendment

Content Questions

1. What is the difference between civil liberties and civil rights?

2. What five civil liberties are guaranteed by the Constitution? Why is each of them important in a democracy?

3. What change in the interpretation of the Constitution led to the court ban on teacher-led prayers and Bible reading in the public schools?

4. How did the Bill of Rights come to be applied to state governments as well as the federal government?

5. What three major categories of civil rights are guaranteed by the Constitution?

6. How are the terms *gay rights* and *abortion rights* based on a false understanding of civil rights? What dangerous trends have resulted from this false interpretation?

Application Questions

1. Why is it important that some restrictions be placed on civil liberties and civil rights?

2. What right, if any, does the government have to regulate religious practice in America?

3. Does the government have a right to enforce time-place-manner laws on the public preaching of the gospel? Explain your answer.

4. How are the guarantees of the First Amendment all related?

5. In what ways would a biblical worldview affect Americans' current fixation on "my rights"? Construct and defend a biblically based list of rights that could be used for a country.

Epilogue:
A Call for
Christian
Leaders

"Let every soul be subject unto the higher powers. For there is no power but of God: the powers that be are ordained of God" (Rom. 13:1). Government is not the result of social evolution or man's ingenuity, nor is it something inherently evil. Government is the direct result of God's will. God instituted government to rule over His creation by rewarding good and punishing evil. When a government submits to its God-ordained purposes, it brings glory to God. When it does not submit, it withholds glory from God.

Over the past few decades, Christians have withdrawn from government involvement because of disillusionment, because of the suspicion that politics is inherently corrupt, or because they think Christians should not involve themselves in so earthly a pursuit. There are probably many more reasons, but the end result of each is the same—government is left to those who do not fear God. But the shameful result of this abandonment is not simply the expulsion of prayer and Bible-reading from public schools, the legalization of abortion, or the decline of society's morality. The shame of leaving government to non-Christians is that the glories of our God are not proclaimed in an institution He created for His glory. By withdrawing from government, Christians have unwittingly reinforced the humanistic idea that government should be godless.

According to Revelation 4:11, God is worthy to receive glory, honor, and power from all of creation since all things exist because of His will. Romans 11:36 says that all things (government included) are "of him, and through him, and to him . . . to whom be glory forever." One of the United States' greatest needs is for her government to glorify God, but that can happen only when Christians involve themselves directly in the governing of this nation for the purpose of ruling according to His Word. God's glory demands that His people participate in government so that He receives the honor due to His name.

The need for God to be glorified in American government also demands that Christians pray. Paul writes that it pleases God for us to make "supplications, prayers, intercessions, and giving of thanks for . . . kings, and for all that are in authority" (I Tim. 2:1–2). The result of these prayers is a quiet and peaceful life, but what are we to pray for that will secure this lifestyle? This prayer is not for government noninterference; it is a prayer for government authorities to be saved and to know the truth. We should not think it strange or beyond belief that our presidents, congressmen, and justices would be saved. "For there is one God, and one mediator between God and men, the man Christ Jesus; who gave himself a ransom for all, to be testified in due time" (I Tim. 2:5–6). A country led by saved authorities will create an environment that engenders quiet and peaceful lives for believers. This type of government glorifies God. Christians, let us pray for Christian rulers who will rule in a manner that declares the glories of our great God.

Appendixes

The Articles of Confederation

To all to whom these presents shall come, we the undersigned delegates of the states affixed to our names send greeting. Whereas the delegates of the United States of America in congress assembled did on the fifteenth day of November in the year of our Lord one thousand seven hundred and seventy seven, and in the second year of the independence of America, agree to certain articles of Confederation and Perpetual Union between the states of New Hampshire, Massachusetts Bay, Rhode Island and Providence plantations, Connecticut, New York, New Jersey, Pennsylvania, Delaware, Maryland, Virginia, North Carolina, South Carolina, and Georgia in the words following, viz.: Articles of Confederation and Perpetual Union between the states [as aforesaid].

Article I

The style of this confederacy shall be "The United States of America."

Article II

Each state retains its sovereignty, freedom, and independence, and every power, jurisdiction, and right which is not by this confederation expressly delegated to the United States in congress assembled.

Article III

The said states hereby severally enter into a firm league of friendship with each other, for their common defense, the security of their liberties, and their mutual and general welfare, binding themselves to assist each other against all force offered to or attacks made upon them, or any of them, on account of religion, sovereignty, trade, or any other pretense whatever.

Article IV

The better to secure and perpetuate mutual friendship and intercourse among the people of the different states in this union, the free inhabitants of each of these states–paupers, vagabonds, and fugitives from justice excepted–shall be entitled to all privileges and immunities of free citizens in the several states; and the people of each state shall have free ingress and regress to and from any other state, and shall enjoy therein all the privileges of trade and commerce, subject to the same duties, impositions, and restrictions as the inhabitants thereof respectively, provided that such restrictions shall not extend so far as to prevent the removal of property imported into any state, to any other state of which the owner is an inhabitant; provided also that no imposition, duties, or restriction shall be laid by any state on the property of the United States or either of them.

If any person guilty of or charged with treason, felony, or other high misdemeanor in any state shall flee from justice and be found in any of the United States, he shall, upon demand of the governor or executive power of the state from which he fled, be delivered to the state having jurisdiction of his offense.

Full faith-and-credit shall be given in each of these states to the records, acts, and judicial proceedings of the courts and magistrates of every other state.

Article V

For the more convenient management of the general interests of the United States, delegates shall be annually appointed in such a manner as the legislature of each state shall direct, to meet in congress on the first Monday in November in every year, with power reserved to each state to recall its delegates, or any of them, at any time within the year and to send others in their stead, for the remainder of the year.

No state shall be represented in congress by less than two nor by more than seven members; and no person shall be capable of being a delegate for more than three years in any term of six years; nor shall any person, being a delegate, be capable of holding any office under the United States, for which he or another for his benefit receives any salary, fees, or emolument of any kind.

Each state shall maintain its own delegates in a meeting of the states and while they act as members of the committee in the states.

In determining questions in the United States in congress assembled, each state shall have one vote.

Freedom of speech and debate in congress shall not be impeached or questioned in any court or place out of congress, and the members of congress shall be protected in their persons from arrest and imprisonments during the time of their going to and from, and attendance on congress, except for treason, felony, or breach of the peace.

Article VI

No state, without the consent of the United States in congress assembled, shall send any embassy to, or receive any embassy from, or enter into any conference, agreement, alliance or treaty with any king, prince, or state; nor shall any person holding any office or profit or trust under the United States, or any of them, accept of any present, emolument, office, or title of any kind whatever from any king, prince, or foreign state; nor shall the United States in congress assembled, or any of them, grant any title of nobility.

No two or more states shall enter into any treaty, confederation, or alliance whatever between them, without the consent of the United States in congress assembled, specifying accurately the purposes for which the same is to be entered into, and how long it shall continue.

No state shall lay imposts or duties which may interfere with any stipulations in treaties entered into by the United States in congress assembled, with any king, prince, or state, in pursuance of any treaties already proposed by congress to the courts of France and Spain.

No vessels of war shall be kept up in time of peace by any state, except such number only as shall be deemed necessary by the United States in congress assembled, for the defense of such state or its trade; nor shall any body of forces be kept up by any state in time of peace, except such number only as in the judgment of the United States in congress assembled shall be deemed requisite to garrison the forts necessary for the defense of such state; but every state shall always keep up a well-regulated and disciplined militia, sufficiently armed and accoutered, and shall provide and constantly have ready for use, in public stores, a due number of field pieces and tents and a proper quantity of arms, ammunition, and camp equipage.

No state shall engage in any war without the consent of the United States in congress assembled, unless such state be actually invaded by enemies, or shall have received certain advice of a resolution being formed by some nation of Indians to invade such state, and the danger is so imminent as not to admit of a delay till the United States in congress assembled can be consulted: nor shall any state grant commissions to any ships or vessels of war, nor letters of marque or reprisal, except it be after a declaration of war by the United States in congress assembled, and then only against the kingdom or state and the subjects thereof, against which war has been so declared, and under such regulations as shall be established by the United States in congress assembled, unless such state be infested by pirates, in which case vessels of war may be fitted out for that occasion and kept so long as the danger shall continue, or until the United States in congress assembled shall determine otherwise.

Article VII

When land forces are raised by any state for the common defense, all officers of or under the rank of colonel shall be appointed by the legislature of each state respectively by whom such forces shall be raised, or in such manner as such state shall direct, and all vacancies shall be filled up by the state which first made the appointment.

Article VIII

All charges of war, and all other expenses that shall be incurred for the common defense or general welfare, and allowed by the United States in congress assembled, shall be defrayed out of a common treasury, which shall be supplied by the several states, in proportion to the value of all land within each state, granted to or surveyed for any person, as such land and the buildings and improvements thereon shall be estimated according to such mode as the United States in congress assembled shall from time to time direct and appoint.

The taxes for paying that proportion shall be laid and levied by the authority and direction of the legislatures of the several states within the time agreed upon by the United States in congress assembled.

Article IX

The United States in congress assembled shall have the sole and exclusive right and power of determining on peace and war, except in the cases mentioned in the sixth article; of sending and receiving ambassadors; entering into treaties and alliances, provided that no treaty of commerce shall be made whereby the legislative power of the respective states shall be restrained from imposing such imposts and duties on foreigners as their own people are subjected to, or from prohibiting the exportation or importation of any species of goods or commodities whatsoever; of establishing rules for deciding in all cases what captures on land or water shall be legal, and in what manner prizes taken by land or naval forces in the service of the United States shall be divided or appropriated; of granting letters of marque and reprisal in times of peace; appointing courts for the trial of piracies and felonies committed on the high seas and establishing courts for receiving and determining finally appeals in all cases of captures, provided that no member of congress shall be appointed a judge of any of the said courts.

The United States in congress assembled shall also be the last resort on appeal in all disputes and differences now subsisting or that hereafter may arise between two or more states concerning boundary, jurisdiction, or any other cause whatever; which authority shall always be exercised in the manner following. Whenever the legislative or executive authority or lawful agent of any state in controversy with another shall present a petition to congress, stating the matter in question and praying for a hearing, notice thereof shall be given by order of congress to the legislative or executive authority of the other state in controversy, and a day assigned for the appearance of the parties by their lawful agents, who shall then be directed to appoint by joint consent commissioners or judges to constitute a court for hearing and determining the matter in question: but if they cannot agree, congress shall name three persons out of each of the United States, and from the list of such persons each party shall alternately strike out one, the petitioners beginning, until the number shall be reduced to thirteen; and from that number not less than seven nor more than nine names, as congress shall direct, shall in the presence of congress be drawn out by lot, and the persons whose names shall be so drawn, or any five of them, shall be commissioners or judges, to hear and finally determine the controversy, so always as a major part of the judges who shall hear the cause shall agree in the determination: and if either party shall neglect to attend at the day appointed, without showing reasons which congress shall judge sufficient, or being present shall refuse to strike, the congress shall proceed to nominate three persons out of each state, and the secretary of congress shall strike in behalf of such party absent or refusing; and the judgment and sentence of court to be appointed, in the manner before prescribed, shall be final and conclusive; and if any of the parties shall refuse to submit to the authority of such court, or to appear or defend their claim or cause, the court shall nevertheless proceed to pronounce sentence, or judgment, which shall in like manner be final and decisive, the judgment or sentence and other proceedings being in either case provided that every commissioner, before he sits in judgment, shall take an oath to be administered by one of the judges of the supreme or superior court of the state where the cause shall be tried, "well and truly to hear and determine the matter in question, according to the best of his judgment, without favor, affection, or hope of reward": provided, also, that no state shall be deprived of territory for the benefit of the United States.

All controversies concerning the private right of soil claimed under different grants of two or more states, whose jurisdictions as they may respect such lands, and the states which passed such grants, are adjusted, the said grants or either of them being at the same time claimed to have originated antecedent to such settlement of jurisdiction, shall, on the petition of either party to the congress of the United States, be finally determined as near as may be in the same manner as is before prescribed for deciding disputes respecting territorial jurisdiction between different states.

The United States in congress assembled shall also have the sole and exclusive right and power of regulating the alloy and value of coin struck by their own authority, or by that of the respective states; fixing the standard of weights and measures throughout the United States; regulating the trade and managing all affairs with the Indians, not members of any of the states, provided that the legislative right of any state within its own limits be not infringed or violated; establishing and regulating post offices from one state to another, throughout all the United States, and exacting such postage on the papers passing through the same as may be requisite to defray the expenses of the said office; appointing all officers of the land forces in the service of the United States, excepting regimental officers; appointing all the officers of the naval forces, and commissioning all officers whatever in the service of the United States; making rules for the government and regulation of the said land and naval forces, and directing their operations.

The United States in congress assembled shall have authority to appoint a committee to sit in the recess of congress, to be denominated "a committee of the states," and to consist of one delegate from each state; and to appoint such other committees and civil officers as may be necessary for managing the general affairs of the United States under their direction; to appoint one of their number to preside, provided that no person be allowed to serve in the office of president more than one year in any term of three years; to ascertain the necessary sums of money to be raised for the service of the United States, and to appropriate and apply the same for defraying the public expenses; to borrow money, or emit bills on the credit of the United States, transmitting every half year to the respective states an account of the sums of money so borrowed or emitted; to build and equip a navy; to agree upon the number of land forces, and to make requisitions from each state for its quota, in proportion to the number of white inhabitants in such state; which requisitions shall be binding, and thereupon the legislature of each state shall appoint the regimental officers, raise the men, and clothe, arm, and equip them in a soldier-like manner, at the expense of the United States; and the officers and men so clothed, armed, and equipped shall march to the place appointed, and within the time agreed on by the United States in congress assembled: but if the United States in congress assembled shall, on consideration of circumstances, judge proper that any state should not raise men, or should raise men, or should raise a smaller number of men than its quota, and that any other state should raise a greater number of men than the quota thereof, such extra number shall be raised, officered, clothed, armed, and equipped in the same manner as the quota of such state, unless the legislature of such state shall judge that such extra number cannot be safely spared out of the same, in which case they shall raise, officer, clothe, arm, and equip as many of such extra number as they judge can be safely spared. And the officers and men so clothed, armed, and equipped shall march to the place appointed, and within the time agreed on by the United States in congress assembled.

The United States in congress assembled shall never engage in war, nor grant letter of marque and reprisal in time of peace, nor enter into any treaties or alliances, nor coin money, nor regulate the value thereof, nor ascertain the sums and expenses necessary for the defense and welfare of the United States, or any of them, nor emit bills, nor borrow money on the credit of the United States, nor appropriate money, nor agree upon the number of vessels of war to be built or purchased, or the number of land or sea forces to be raised, nor appoint a commander in chief of the army or navy, unless nine states assent to the same: nor shall a question on any other point, except for adjourning from day to day, be determined, unless by the votes of a majority of the United States in congress assembled.

The congress of the United States shall have power to adjourn to any time within the year, and to any place within the United States, so that no period of adjournment be for a longer duration than the space of six months, and shall publish the journal of their proceedings monthly, except such parts thereof relating to treaties, alliances or military operations, as in their judgment require secrecy; and the yeas and nays of the delegates of each state on any question shall be entered on the journal, when it is desired by any delegate; and the delegates of a state, or any of them, at his or their request shall be furnished with a transcript of the said journal, except such parts as are above excepted, to lay before the legislatures of the several states.

Article X

The committee of the states, or any nine of them, shall be authorized to execute, in the recess of congress, such of the powers of congress as the United States in congress assembled, by the consent of nine states, shall from time to time think expedient to vest them with; provided that no power be delegated to the said committee, for the exercise of which, by the Articles of Confederation, the voice of nine states in the congress of the United States assembled is requisite.

Article XI

Canada acceding to this confederation, and joining in the measures of the United States, shall be admitted into and entitled to all the advantages of this Union: but no other colony shall be admitted into the same, unless such admission be agreed to by nine states.

Article XII

All bills of credit emitted, monies borrowed, and debts contracted by or under the authority of congress, before the assembling of the United States, in pursuance of the present confederation, shall be deemed and considered as a charge against the United States, for payment and satisfaction whereof the said United States and the public faith are hereby solemnly pledged.

Article XIII

Every state shall abide by the determinations of the United States in congress assembled on all questions which by this confederation are submitted to them. And the articles of this confederation shall be inviolably observed by every state, and the union shall be perpetual; nor shall any alteration at any time hereafter be made in any of them; unless such alteration be agreed to in a congress of the United States, and be afterwards confirmed by the legislatures of every state.

And whereas it has pleased the great Governor of the world to incline the hearts of the legislatures we respectively represent in congress, to approve of, and to authorize us to ratify the said Articles of Confederation and Perpetual Union, know ye that we the undersigned delegates, by virtue of the power and authority to us given for that purpose, do by these present, in the name and in behalf of our respective constituents, fully and entirely ratify and confirm each and every of the said Articles of Confederation and Perpetual Union, and all and singular the matters and things therein contained: and we do further solemnly plight and engage the faith of our respective constituents, that they shall abide by the determinations of the United States in congress assembled, on all questions, which by the said confederation are submitted to them; and that the articles thereof shall be inviolably observed by the states we respectively represent, and that the union shall be perpetual. In witness whereof we have hereunto set our hands in Congress. Done at Philadelphia in the state of Pennsylvania the ninth day of July, in the year of our Lord one thousand seven hundred and seventy-eight, and in the third year of the independence of America.

PRESIDENTIAL ELECTIONS

Year	Number of States	Major Candidates	Parties	Popular Vote	% of Popular Vote	Electoral Vote	% Voter participation
1789	11	**George Washington** John Adams Other candidates	No party designations			69 34 35	
1792	15	**George Washington** John Adams George Clinton Other candidates	No party designations			132 77 50 5	
1796	16	**John Adams** Thomas Jefferson Thomas Pinckney Aaron Burr Other candidates	Federalist Democratic-Republican Federalist Democratic-Republican			71 68 59 30 48	
1800	16	**Thomas Jefferson** Aaron Burr John Adams Charles C. Pinckney John Jay	Democratic-Republican Democratic-Republican Federalist Federalist Federalist			73 73 65 64 1	
1804	17	**Thomas Jefferson** Charles C. Pinckney	Democratic-Republican Federalist			162 14	
1808	17	**James Madison** Charles C. Pinckney George Clinton	Democratic-Republican Federalist Democratic-Republican			122 47 6	
1812	18	**James Madison** DeWitt Clinton	Democratic-Republican Federalist			128 89	
1816	19	**James Monroe** Rufus King	Democratic-Republican Federalist			183 34	
1820	24	**James Monroe** John Quincy Adams	Democratic-Republican Independent Republican			231 1	
1824	24	**John Quincy Adams** Andrew Jackson Henry Clay William H. Crawford	Democratic-Republican Democratic-Republican Democratic-Republican Democratic-Republican	108,740 153,544 47,136 46,618	30.5 43.1 13.2 13.1	84 99 37 41	26.9
1828	24	**Andrew Jackson** John Quincy Adams	Democratic National Republican	647,286 508,064	56.0 44.0	178 83	57.6
1832	24	**Andrew Jackson** Henry Clay William Wirt John Floyd	Democratic National Republican Anti-Masonic Democratic	687,502 530,189 101,051	54.5 37.5 8.0	219 49 7 11	55.4

Candidates receiving less than 1 percent of the popular vote have been omitted. Thus the percentage of popular vote given for any election year may not total 100 percent. Before 1824, most presidential electors were chosen by state legislatures, not by popular vote.

Year	Number of States	Major Candidates	Parties	Popular Vote	% of Popular Vote	Electoral Vote	% Voter participation
1836	26	**Martin Van Buren**	Democratic	762,678	50.9	170	57.8
		William H. Harrison	Whig	735,651	49.1	73	
		Hugh L. White	Whig			26	
		Daniel Webster	Whig			14	
		W. P. Mangum	Whig			11	
1840	26	**William H. Harrison**	Whig	1,275,016	53.1	234	80.2
		Martin Van Buren	Democratic	1,129,102	46.9	60	
1844	26	**James K. Polk**	Democratic	1,337,243	49.6	170	78.9
		Henry Clay	Whig	1,299,062	48.1	105	
		James G. Birney	Liberty	62,300	2.3		
1848	30	**Zachary Taylor**	Whig	1,360,099	47.4	163	72.7
		Lewis Cass	Democratic	1,220,544	42.5	127	
		Martin Van Buren	Free-Soil	291,263	10.1		
1852	31	**Franklin Pierce**	Democratic	1,601,274	50.9	254	69.6
		Winfield Scott	Whig	1,386,580	44.1	42	
		John P. Hale	Free-Soil	155,825	5.0		
1856	31	**James Buchanan**	Democratic	1,838,169	45.3	174	78.9
		John C. Fremont	Republican	1,341,264	33.1	114	
		Millard Fillmore	American	871,731	21.6	8	
1860	33	**Abraham Lincoln**	Republican	1,866,452	39.8	180	81.2
		Stephen A. Douglas	Democratic	1,382,713	29.5	12	
		John C. Breckinridge	Democratic	847,953	18.1	72	
		John Bell	Constitutional Union	592,906	12.6	39	
1864	36	**Abraham Lincoln**	Republican	2,213,665	55.0	212	73.8
		George B. McClellan	Democratic	1,805,237	45.0	21	
1868	37	**Ulysses S. Grant**	Republican	3,012,833	52.7	214	78.1
		Horatio Seymour	Democratic	2,703,249	47.3	80	
1872	37	**Ulysses S. Grant**	Republican	3,597,132	55.6	286	71.3
		Horace Greeley	Democratic	2,834,125	43.9	*	
1876	38	**Rutherford B. Hayes**	Republican	4,036,298	48.0	185	81.8
		Samuel J. Tilden	Democratic	4,300,590	51.0	184	
1880	38	**James A. Garfield**	Republican	4,454,416	48.5	214	79.4
		Winfield S. Hancock	Democratic	4,444,952	48.1	155	
		James B. Weaver	Greenback-Labor	308,578	3.4		
1884	38	**Grover Cleveland**	Democratic	4,874,986	48.5	219	77.5
		James G. Blaine	Republican	4,851,981	48.2	182	
		Benjamin F. Butler	Greenback-Labor	175,370	1.8		
		John P. St. John	Prohibition	150,369	1.5		
1888	38	**Benjamin Harrison**	Republican	5,439,853	47.9	233	79.3
		Grover Cleveland	Democratic	5,540,309	48.6	168	
		Clinton B. Fisk	Prohibition	249,506	2.2		
		Anson J. Streeter	Union Labor	146,935	1.3		

Greeley died shortly after the election; the electors supporting him then divided their votes among minor candidates.

Year	Number of States	Major Candidates	Parties	Popular Vote	% of Popular Vote	Electoral Vote	% Voter partici-pation
1892	44	**Grover Cleveland**	Democratic	5,556,918	46.1	277	74.7
		Benjamin Harrison	Republican	5,176,108	43.0	145	
		James B. Weaver	People's	1,029,846	8.5	22	
		John Bidwell	Prohibition	264,133	2.2		
1896	45	**William McKinley**	Republican	7,104,779	51.1	271	79.3
		William J. Bryan	Democratic; Populist	6,502,925	47.7	176	
1900	45	**William McKinley**	Republican	7,207,923	51.7	292	73.2
		William J. Bryan	Democratic	6,358,133	45.5	155	
		John G. Woolley	Prohibition	208,914	1.5		
1904	45	**Theodore Roosevelt**	Republican	7,623,486	57.4	336	65.2
		Alton B. Parker	Democratic	5,077,911	37.6	140	
		Eugene V. Debs	Socialist	402,283	3.0		
		Silas C. Swallow	Prohibition	258,536	1.9		
1908	46	**William H. Taft**	Republican	7,678,908	51.6	321	65.4
		William J. Bryan	Democratic	6,409,104	43.1	162	
		Eugene V. Debs	Socialist	420,793	2.8		
		Eugene W. Chafin	Prohibition	253,840	1.7		
1912	48	**Woodrow Wilson**	Democratic	6,293,454	41.9	435	58.8
		Theodore Roosevelt	Progressive	4,119,207	27.4	88	
		William H. Taft	Republican	3,486,720	23.2	8	
		Eugene V. Debs	Socialist	900,672	6.0		
		Eugene W. Chafin	Prohibition	206,275	1.4		
1916	48	**Woodrow Wilson**	Democratic	9,129,606	49.4	277	61.6
		Charles E. Hughes	Republican	8,538,221	46.2	254	
		A.L. Benson	Socialist	585,113	3.2		
		J. Frank Hanly	Prohibition	220,506	1.2		
1920	48	**Warren G. Harding**	Republican	16,152,200	60.4	404	49.2
		James M. Cox	Democratic	9,147,353	34.2	127	
		Eugene V. Debs	Socialist	919,799	3.4		
		P. P. Christensen	Farmer-Labor	265,411	1.0		
1924	48	**Calvin Coolidge**	Republican	15,725,016	54.0	382	48.9
		John W. Davis	Democratic	8,386,503	28.8	136	
		Robert M. La Follette	Progressive	4,822,856	16.6	13	
1928	48	**Herbert C. Hoover**	Republican	21,391,381	58.2	444	56.9
		Alfred E. Smith	Democratic	15,016,443	40.9	87	
1932	48	**Franklin D. Roosevelt**	Democratic	22,821,857	57.4	472	56.9
		Herbert C. Hoover	Republican	15,761,841	39.7	59	
		Norman Thomas	Socialist	884,781	2.2		
1936	48	**Franklin D. Roosevelt**	Democratic	27,751,597	60.8	523	61.0
		Alfred M. Landon	Republican	16,679,583	36.5	8	
		William Lemke	Union	882,479	1.9		
1940	48	**Franklin D. Roosevelt**	Democratic	27,244,160	54.8	449	62.5
		Wendell L. Willkie	Republican	22,305,198	44.8	82	

Year	Number of States	Major Candidates	Parties	Popular Vote	% of Popular Vote	Electoral Vote	% Voter partici-pation
1944	48	**Franklin D. Roosevelt** Thomas E. Dewey	Democratic Republican	25,602,504 22,006,285	53.5 46.0	432 99	55.9
1948	48	**Harry S. Truman** Thomas E. Dewey J. Strom Thurmond	Democratic Republican States' Rights	24,105,695 21,969,170 1,169,021	49.6 45.1 2.4	303 189 39	53.0
1952	48	**Dwight D. Eisenhower** Adlai E. Stevenson	Republican Democratic	33,778,963 27,314,992	55.1 44.4	442 89	63.3
1956	48	**Dwight D. Eisenhower** Adlai E. Stevenson	Republican Democratic	35,581,003 25,738,765	57.6 42.1	457 73	60.6
1960	50	**John F. Kennedy** Richard M. Nixon	Democratic Republican	34,227,096 34,107,646	49.7 49.5	303 219	64.0
1964	50	**Lyndon B. Johnson** Barry M. Goldwater	Democratic Republican	42,825,463 27,146,969	61.1 38.5	486 52	61.7
1968	50	**Richard M. Nixon** Hubert H. Humphrey George C. Wallace	Republican Democratic American Independent	31,710,470 30,898,055 9,906,473	43.4 42.7 13.5	301 191 46	60.6
1972	50	**Richard M. Nixon** George S. McGovern	Republican Democratic	46,740,323 28,901,598	60.7 37.5	520 17	55.5
1976	50	**Jimmy Carter** Gerald R. Ford	Democratic Republican	40,825,839 39,147,770	50.1 48.0	297 240	54.3
1980	50	**Ronald Reagan** Jimmy Carter John B. Anderson	Republican Democratic Independent	43,901,812 35,483,820 5,719,437	50.7 41.0 6.6	489 49	53.0
1984	50	**Ronald Reagan** Walter Mondale	Republican Democratic	54,455,000 37,577,000	58.8 40.6	525 13	53.2
1988	50	**George Bush** Michael Dukakis	Republican Democratic	47,946,000 41,016,000	53.4 45.6	426 111	50.1
1992	50	**William J. Clinton** George Bush H. Ross Perot	Democratic Republican Independent	44,908,254 39,102,343 19,741,065	43.3 37.7 19.0	370 168	61.3
1996	50	**William J. Clinton** Robert Dole H. Ross Perot	Democratic Republican Reform	45,590,703 37,816,307 7,866,284	50.0 42.0 8.0	379 159	54.2
2000	50	**George W. Bush** Al Gore	Republican Democratic	50,456,062 50,996,582	47.87 48.38	271 266	51.3
2004	50	**George W. Bush** John Kerry	Republican Democratic	62,039,073 59,027,478	50.7 48.3	286 251	55.3
2008	50	**Barack Obama** John McCain	Democratic Republican	66,882,230 58,343,671	53.0 46.0	364 174	61.6

Information from the Federal Register

PARTY CONTROL OF CONGRESS

Congressional Session		House Parties			Senate Parties			President	Party in Power
		Majority	Minority	Others	Majority	Minority	Others		
1st	1789–91	Ad—38	Op —26		Ad—17	Op—9		Washington	Ad
2nd	1791–93	F—37	DR —33		F—16	DR—13		Washington	F
3rd	1793–95	DR—57	F —48		F —17	DR—13		Washington	F
4th	1795–97	F—54	DR —52		F —19	DR—13		Washington	F
5th	1797–99	F—58	DR —48		F —20	DR—12		J. Adams	F
6th	1799–1801	F—64	DR —42		F —19	DR—13		J. Adams	F
7th	1801–03	DR—69	F —36		DR —18	F—13		Jefferson	DR
8th	1803–05	DR—102	F —39		DR —25	F—9		Jefferson	DR
9th	1805–07	DR—116	F —25		DR —27	F—7		Jefferson	DR
10th	1807–09	DR—118	F —24		DR —28	F—6		Jefferson	DR
11th	1809–11	DR—94	F —48		DR —28	F—6		Madison	DR
12th	1811–13	DR—108	F —36		DR —30	F—6		Madison	DR
13th	1813–15	DR—112	F —68		DR —27	F—9		Madison	DR
14th	1815–17	DR—117	F —65		DR —25	F—11		Madison	DR
15th	1817–19	DR—141	F —42		DR —34	F—10		Monroe	DR
16th	1819–21	DR—156	F —27		DR —35	F—7		Monroe	DR
17th	1821–23	DR—158	F —25		DR —44	F—4		Monroe	DR
18th	1823–25	DR—187	F —26		DR —44	F—4		Monroe	DR
19th	1825–27	Ad—105	J —97		Ad —26	J—20		J. Q. Adams	C
20th	1827–29	J—119	Ad —94		J —28	Ad—20		J. Q. Adams	C
21st	1829–31	D—139	NR —74		D —26	NR—22		Jackson	D
22nd	1831–33	D—141	NR —58	14	D —25	NR—21	2	Jackson	D

*Ad = Administration; AM = Anti-Masonic; C = Coalition; D = Democratic; DR = Democratic-Republican;
F = Federalist; J = Jacksonian; NR = National Republican; Op = Opposition; R = Republican;
U = Unionist; W = Whig.*

Congressional Session		House Parties			Senate Parties			President	Party in Power
		Majority	Minority	Others	Majority	Minority	Others		
23rd	1833–35	D—147	AM—53	60	D—20	NR—20	8	Jackson	D
24th	1835–37	D—145	W—98		D—27	W—25		Jackson	D
25th	1837–39	D—108	W—107	24	D—30	W—18	4	Van Buren	D
26th	1839–41	D—124	W—118		D—28	W—22		Van Buren	W
27th	1841–43	W—133	D—102	6	W—28	D—22	2	W. Harrison; Tyler	W
28th	1843–45	D—142	W—79	1	W—28	D—25	1	Tyler	W
29th	1845–47	D—143	W—77	6	D—31	W—25		Polk	D
30th	1847–49	W—115	D—108	4	D—36	W—21	1	Polk	D
31st	1849–51	D—112	W—109	9	D—35	W—25	2	Taylor; Fillmore	W
32nd	1851–53	D—140	W—88	5	D—35	W—24	3	Fillmore	W
33rd	1853–55	D—159	W—71	4	D—38	W—22	2	Pierce	W
34th	1855–57	R—108	D—83	43	D—40	R—15	5	Pierce	D
35th	1857–59	D—118	R—92	26	D—36	R—20	8	Buchanan	D
36th	1859–61	R—114	D—92	31	D—36	R—26	4	Buchanan	D
37th	1861–63	R—105	D—43	30	R—31	D—10	8	Lincoln	R
38th	1863–65	R—102	D—75	9	R—36	D—9	5	Lincoln	R
39th	1865–67	U—149	D—42		U—42	D—10		Lincoln; Johnson	R
40th	1867–69	R—143	D—49		R—42	D—11		Johnson	R
41st	1869–71	R—149	D—63		R—56	D—11		Grant	R
42nd	1871–73	R—134	D—104	5	R—52	D—17	5	Grant	R
43rd	1873–75	R—194	D—92	14	R—49	D—19	5	Grant	R
44th	1875–77	D—169	R—109	14	R—45	D—29	2	Grant	R
45th	1877–79	D—153	R—140		R—39	D—36	1	Hayes	R

Congressional Session		House Parties			Senate Parties			President	Party in Power
		Majority	Minority	Others	Majority	Minority	Others		
46th	1879–81	D—149	R—130	14	D—42	R—33	1	Hayes	R
47th	1881–83	D—147	R—135	11	R—37	D—37	1	Garfield; Arthur	R
48th	1883–85	D—197	R—118	10	R—38	D—36	2	Arthur	R
49th	1885–87	D—183	R—140	2	R—43	D—34	2	Cleveland	D
50th	1887–89	D—169	R—152	4	R—39	D—37	3	Cleveland	D
51st	1889–91	R—166	D—159		R—39	D—37	6	B. Harrison	R
52nd	1891–93	D—235	R—88	9	R—47	D—39	7	B. Harrison	R
53rd	1893–95	D—218	R—127	11	D—44	R—38	8	Cleveland	D
54th	1895–97	R—244	D—105	7	R—43	D—39	4	Cleveland	D
55th	1897–99	R—204	D—113	40	R—47	D—34		McKinley	R
56th	1899–1901	R—185	D—163	9	R—53	D—26		McKinley	R
57th	1901–03	R—197	D—151	9	R—55	D—31		McKinley; T. Roosevelt	R
58th	1903–05	R—208	D—178	1	R—57	D—33		T. Roosevelt	R
59th	1905–07	R—250	D—136	17	R—57	D—33		T. Roosevelt	R
60th	1907–09	R—222	D—164	9	R—61	D—31		T. Roosevelt	R
61st	1909–11	R—219	D—172	6	R—61	D—32		Taft	R
62nd	1911–13	D—228	R—161	3	R—51	D—41		Taft	R
63rd	1913–15	D—291	R—127	1	D—51	R—44	1	Wilson	D
64th	1915–17	D—230	R—196	5	D—56	R—40		Wilson	D
65th	1917–19	D—216	R—210	4	D—53	R—42		Wilson	D
66th	1919–21	R—240	D—190	3	R—49	D—47		Wilson	D
67th	1921–23	R—301	D—131	1	R—59	D—37		Harding	R
68th	1923–25	R—225	RD—140	1	R—51	D—43	1	Coolidge	R

Congressional Session		House Parties			Senate Parties			President	Party in Power
		Majority	Minority	Others	Majority	Minority	Others		
69th	1925–27	R—247	D—183	4	R—56	D—39	1	Coolidge	R
70th	1927–29	R—237	D—195	3	R—49	D—46	1	Coolidge	R
71st	1929–31	R—267	D—167	1	R—56	D—39	1	Hoover	R
72nd	1931–33	D—220	R—214	1	R—48	D—47	1	Hoover	R
73rd	1933–35	D—310	R—117	5	D—60	R—35	1	F. Roosevelt	D
74th	1935–37	D—319	R—103	10	D—69	R—25	2	F. Roosevelt	D
75th	1937–39	D—331	R—89	13	D—76	R—16	4	F. Roosevelt	D
76th	1939–41	D—261	R—164	4	D—69	R—23	4	F. Roosevelt	D
77th	1941–43	D—268	R—162	5	D—66	R—28	2	F. Roosevelt	D
78th	1943–45	D—218	R—208	4	D—58	R—37	1	F. Roosevelt	D
79th	1945–47	D—242	R—190	2	D—56	R—38	1	Truman	D
80th	1947–49	R—245	D—188	1	R—51	D—45		Truman	D
81st	1949–51	D—263	R—171	1	D—54	R—42		Truman	D
82nd	1951–53	D—234	R—199	1	D—49	R—47		Truman	D
83rd	1953–55	R—221	D—211		R—48	D—47	1	Eisenhower	R
84th	1955–57	D—232	R—203		D—48	R—47	1	Eisenhower	R
85th	1957–59	D—233	R—200		D—49	R—47		Eisenhower	R
86th	1959–61	D—284	R—153		D—65	R—35		Eisenhower	R
87th	1961–63	D—263	R—174		D—65	R—35		Kennedy	D
88th	1963–65	D—258	R—177		D—67	R—33		Kennedy; Johnson	D
89th	1965–67	D—295	R—140		D—68	R—32		Johnson	D
90th	1967–69	D—247	R—187		D—64	R—36		Johnson	D
91st	1969–71	D—243	R—192		D—57	R—43		Nixon	R

Congressional Session		House Parties			Senate Parties			President	Party in Power
		Majority	Minority	Others	Majority	Minority	Others		
92nd	1971–73	D—254	R—180		D—54	R—44	2	Nixon	R
93rd	1973–75	D—239	R—192		D—56	R—42	2	Nixon	R
94th	1975–77	D—291	R—144		D—60	R—37	3	Ford	R
95th	1977–79	D—292	R—143		D—61	R—38	1	Carter	D
96th	1979–81	D—276	R—157		D—58	R—41		Carter	D
97th	1981–83	D—243	R—192		R—53	D—46		Reagan	R
98th	1983–85	D—264	R—165		R—54	D—46		Reagan	R
99th	1985–87	D—252	R—182		R—53	D—47		Reagan	R
100th	1987–89	D—258	R—177		D—55	R—45		Reagan	R
101st	1989–91	D—260	R—175		D—55	R—45		G. Bush	R
102nd	1991–93	D—267	R—167	1	D—56	R—44		G. Bush	R
103rd	1993–95	D—258	R—176	1	D—57	R—43		Clinton	D
104th	1995–97	R—230	D—204	1	R—52	D—48		Clinton	D
105th	1997–99	R—228	D—206	1	R—55	D—45		Clinton	D
106th	1999–01	R—223	D—211	1	R—55	D—45		Clinton	D
*107th	2001–03	R—221	D—212	2	D—50 R—50 D—50 R—50	R—50[1] D—50[2] R—40[3] D—48[4]	1 2	G W. Bush	R
108th	2003–05	R—229	D—205	1	R—51	D—48	1	G. W. Bush	R
109th	2005–07	R—232	D—202	1	R—55	D—44	1	G. W. Bush	R
110th	2007–09	D—233	R—202		D—49	R—49	2	G. W. Bush	D
111th	2009–11	D—257	R—178		D—55	R—41	2	Barack Obama	D

*[1] January 3–30, 2001, [2] January 20–June 6, 2001, [3] June 6, 2001–November 12, 2002, [4] November 12, 2002–January 3, 2003

Because the Democrats had the deciding vote of Vice President Gore, they were the majority January 3–20. Vice President Cheney (R) took office on January 20, 2001, shifting power to the Republicans. On May 24, 2001, Vermont senator Jeffords switched from Republican to Independent but caucused with the Democrats, shifting control back to the Democrats. On October 25, 2001, Paul Wellstone (D-MN) died, and his seat was filled by Dean Barkley (I). On November 5, 2002, James Talent (R-MO) replaced Democrat Jean Carnahan, again shifting power to the Republicans.

PRESIDENTS OF THE UNITED STATES

President	Term	Political Party	Home State	Vice President
George Washington	1789–1797	None	Virginia	John Adams
John Adams	1797–1801	Federalist	Massachusetts	Thomas Jefferson
Thomas Jefferson	1801–1809	Democratic–Republican	Virginia	Aaron Burr George Clinton
James Madison	1809–1817	Democratic–Republican	Virginia	George Clinton Elbridge Gerry
James Monroe	1817–1825	Democratic–Republican	Virginia	Daniel D. Tompkins
John Quincy Adams	1825–1829	Democratic–Republican	Massachusetts	John C. Calhoun
Andrew Jackson	1829–1837	Democratic	Tennessee	John C. Calhoun Martin Van Buren
Martin Van Buren	1837–1841	Democratic	New York	Richard M. Johnson
William H. Harrison	1841	Whig	Ohio	John Tyler
John Tyler	1841–1845	Whig	Virginia	
James K. Polk	1845–1849	Democratic	Tennessee	George M. Dallas
Zachary Taylor	1849–1850	Whig	Louisiana	Millard Fillmore
Millard Fillmore	1850–1853	Whig	New York	
Franklin Pierce	1853–1857	Democratic	New Hampshire	William R. King
James Buchanan	1857–1861	Democratic	Pennsylvania	John C. Breckinridge
Abraham Lincoln	1861–1865	Republican	Illinois	Hannibal Hamlin Andrew Johnson
Andrew Johnson	1865–1869	Republican	Tennessee	
Ulysses S. Grant	1869–1877	Republican	Illinois	Schuyler Colfax Henry Wilson
Rutherford B. Hayes	1877–1881	Republican	Ohio	William A. Wheeler
James A. Garfield	1881	Republican	Ohio	Chester A. Arthur
Chester A. Arthur	1881–1885	Republican	New York	
Grover Cleveland	1885–1889	Democratic	New York	Thomas A. Hendricks
Benjamin Harrison	1889–1893	Republican	Indiana	Levi P. Morton

President	Term	Political Party	Home State	Vice President
Grover Cleveland	1893–1897	Democratic	New York	Adlai E. Stevenson
William McKinley	1897–1901	Republican	Ohio	Garret A. Hobart Theodore Roosevelt
Theodore Roosevelt	1901–1909	Republican	New York	Charles W. Fairbanks
William H. Taft	1909–1913	Republican	Ohio	James S. Sherman
Woodrow Wilson	1913–1921	Democratic	New Jersey	Thomas R. Marshall
Warren G. Harding	1921–1923	Republican	Ohio	Calvin Coolidge
Calvin Coolidge	1923–1929	Republican	Massachusetts	Charles G. Dawes
Herbert Hoover	1929–1933	Republican	California	Charles Curtis
Franklin D. Roosevelt	1933–1945	Democratic	New York	John Nance Garner Henry A. Wallace Harry S. Truman
Harry S. Truman	1945–1953	Democratic	Missouri	Alben W. Barkley
Dwight D. Eisenhower	1953–1961	Republican	Pennsylvania	Richard M. Nixon
John F. Kennedy	1961–1963	Democratic	Massachusetts	Lyndon B. Johnson
Lyndon B. Johnson	1963–1969	Democratic	Texas	Hubert H. Humphrey
Richard M. Nixon	1969–1974	Republican	California	Spiro T. Agnew Gerald R. Ford
Gerald R. Ford	1974–1977	Republican	Michigan	Nelson A. Rockefeller
Jimmy Carter	1977–1981	Democratic	Georgia	Walter F. Mondale
Ronald Reagan	1981–1989	Republican	California	George Bush
George Bush	1989–1993	Republican	Texas	Dan Quayle
Bill Clinton	1993–2001	Democratic	Arkansas	Al Gore
George W. Bush	2001–2009	Republican	Texas	Richard Cheney
Barack Obama	2009–	Democratic	Illinois	Joe Biden

SUPREME COURT JUSTICES

Justice	Tenure in Office	Years of Service	Life Span	Justice	Tenure in Office	Years of Service	Life Span
John Jay	1789–1795	5	1745–1829	Henry Baldwin	1830–1844	14	1780–1844
John Rutledge	1789–1791	1	1739–1800	James M. Wayne	1835–1867	32	1790–1867
William Cushing	1789–1810	20	1732–1810	**Roger B. Taney**	1836–1864	28	1777–1864
James Wilson	1789–1798	8	1742–1798	Philip P. Barbour	1836–1841	4	1783–1841
John Blair	1789–1796	6	1732–1800	John Catron	1837–1865	28	1786–1865
Robert H. Harrison	1789–1790	–	1745–1790	John McKinley	1837–1852	15	1780–1852
James Iredell	1790–1799	9	1751–1799	Peter V. Daniel	1841–1860	19	1784–1860
Thomas Johnson	1791–1793	1	1732–1819	Samuel Nelson	1845–1872	27	1792–1873
William Paterson	1793–1806	13	1745–1806	Levi Woodbury	1845–1851	5	1789–1851
John Rutledge*	1795	–	1739–1800	Robert C. Grier	1846–1870	23	1794–1870
Samuel Chase	1796–1811	15	1741–1811	Benjamin R. Curtis	1851–1857	6	1809–1874
Oliver Ellsworth	1796–1800	4	1745–1807	John A. Campbell	1853–1861	8	1811–1889
Bushrod Washington	1798–1829	31	1762–1829	Nathan Clifford	1858–1881	23	1803–1881
Alfred Moore	1799–1804	4	1755–1810	Noah H. Swayne	1862–1881	18	1804–1884
John Marshall	1801–1835	34	1755–1835	Samuel F. Miller	1862–1890	28	1816–1890
William Johnson	1804–1834	30	1771–1834	David Davis	1862–1877	14	1815–1886
H. Brockholst Livingston	1806–1823	16	1757–1823	Stephen J. Field	1863–1897	34	1816–1899
Thomas Todd	1807–1826	18	1765–1826	**Salmon P. Chase**	1864–1873	8	1808–1873
Joseph Story	1811–1845	33	1779–1845	William Strong	1870–1880	10	1808–1895
Gabriel Duval	1811–1835	24	1752–1844	Joseph P. Bradley	1870–1892	22	1813–1892
Smith Thompson	1823–1843	20	1768–1843	Ward Hunt	1873–1882	9	1810–1886
Robert Trimble	1826–1828	2	1777–1828	**Morrison R. Waite**	1874–1888	14	1816–1888
John McLean	1829–1861	32	1785–1861	John M. Harlan	1877–1911	34	1833–1911

*Appointed and served one term, but not confirmed by the Senate.
NOTE: Chief justices are in boldface.

Justice	Tenure in Office	Years of Service	Life Span	Justice	Tenure in Office	Years of Service	Life Span
William B. Woods	1880–1887	7	1824–1887	John H. Clarke	1916–1922	6	1857–1945
Stanley Matthews	1881–1889	7	1824–1889	**William H. Taft**	1921–1930	8	1857–1930
Horace Gray	1882–1902	20	1828–1902	George Sutherland	1922–1938	15	1862–1942
Samuel Blatchford	1882–1893	11	1820–1893	Pierce Butler	1922–1939	16	1866–1939
Lucius Q. C. Lamar	1888–1893	5	1825–1893	Edward T. Sanford	1923–1930	7	1865–1930
Melville W. Fuller	1888–1910	21	1833–1910	Harlan F. Stone	1925–1941	16	1872–1946
David J. Brewer	1890–1910	20	1837–1910	**Charles E. Hughes**	1930–1941	11	1862–1948
Henry B. Brown	1890–1906	16	1836–1913	Owen J. Roberts	1930–1945	15	1875–1955
George Shiras, Jr.	1892–1903	10	1832–1924	Benjamin N. Cardozo	1932–1938	6	1870–1938
Howell E. Jackson	1893–1895	2	1832–1895	Hugo L. Black	1937–1971	34	1886–1971
Edward D. White	1894–1910	16	1845–1921	Stanley F. Reed	1938–1957	19	1884–1980
Rufus W. Peckham	1895–1909	14	1838–1909	Felix Frankfurter	1939–1962	23	1882–1965
Joseph McKenna	1898–1925	26	1843–1926	William O. Douglas	1939–1975	36	1898–1980
Oliver W. Holmes	1902–1932	30	1841–1935	Frank Murphy	1940–1949	9	1890–1949
William R. Day	1903–1922	19	1849–1923	**Harlan F. Stone**	1941–1946	5	1872–1946
William H. Moody	1906–1910	3	1853–1917	James F. Byrnes	1941–1942	1	1879–1972
Horace H. Lurton	1910–1914	4	1844–1914	Robert H. Jackson	1941–1954	13	1892–1954
Charles E. Hughes	1910–1916	5	1862–1948	Wiley B. Rutledge	1943–1949	6	1894–1949
Willis Van Devanter	1911–1937	26	1859–1941	Harold H. Burton	1945–1958	13	1888–1964
Joseph R. Lamar	1911–1916	5	1857–1916	**Fred M. Vinson**	1946–1953	7	1890–1953
Edward D. White	1910–1921	11	1845–1921	Tom C. Clark	1949–1967	18	1899–1977
Mahlon Pitney	1912–1922	10	1858–1924	Sherman Minton	1949–1956	7	1890–1965
James C. McReynolds	1914–1941	26	1862–1946	**Earl Warren**	1953–1969	16	1891–1974
Louis D. Brandeis	1916–1939	22	1856–1941	John Marshall Harlan	1955–1971	16	1899–1971

Justice	Tenure in Office	Years of Service	Life Span	Justice	Tenure in Office	Years of Service	Life Span
William J. Brennan Jr.	1956–1990	33	1906–1997	John P. Stevens III	1975–	–	1920–
Charles E. Whittaker	1957–1962	5	1901–1973	Sandra Day O'Connor	1981–2006	25	1930–
Potter Stewart	1958–1981	23	1915–1985	**William H. Rehnquist**	1986–2005	19	1924–2005
Byron R. White	1962–1993	31	1917–2002	Antonin Scalia	1986–	–	1936–
Arthur J. Goldberg	1962–1965	3	1908–1990	Anthony Kennedy	1988–	–	1936–
Abe Fortas	1965–1969	4	1910–1982	David H. Souter	1990–	–	1939–
Thurgood Marshall	1967–1991	24	1908–1993	Clarence Thomas	1991–	–	1948
Warren E. Burger	1969–1986	17	1907–1995	Ruth Bader Ginsburg	1993–	–	1933–
Harry A. Blackmun	1970–1994	24	1908–1999	Stephen G. Breyer	1994–	–	1938–
Lewis F. Powell Jr.	1972–1987	15	1907–1998	**John Roberts**	2005–	–	1955–
William H. Rehnquist	1972–1986	14	1924–2005	Samuel Alito	2006–	–	1950–

How to Email or Write to Public Officials

I. Tips for Emailing or Writing to Your Congressman

The following hints on how to email or write a member of Congress were suggested by congressional sources and the League of Women Voters.

- Write to your own senators or representative. Emails or letters sent to other members will end up on the desk of members from your state.

- Write at the proper time, when a bill is being discussed in committee or on the floor.

- Use your own words and your own stationery when emailing or writing. Avoid signing and sending a form letter.

- Don't be a pen pal. Don't try to instruct the representative or senator on every issue that comes up.

- Whenever possible, identify all bills by their number.

- If possible, include pertinent editorials from local papers.

- Be constructive. If a bill deals with a problem you admit exists but you believe the bill is the wrong approach, tell what you think the right approach is.

- If you have expert knowledge or wide experience in particular areas, share it with the member. But don't pretend to wield vast political influence.

- Write to the member when he does something you approve of. A note of appreciation will make him remember you more favorably the next time.

- Feel free to email or write when you have a question or problem dealing with procedures of government departments.

- Be brief and try to keep the message under 400 words (about one page length). When writing a letter, write legibly. Be sure to use the proper form of address. Feminine forms of address should be substituted as appropriate.

II. Correct Email and Letter Forms

Email subject line: Identify your message bill number or topic. Example: H.R. _____ (House bill); S._____ (Senate bill)

Format for the body of the message:
> Your name
> Address
> City, State ZIP
>
> Dear Mr. President: or Dear Mr. Vice President:
> or
> Dear Senator_____ (last name): or
> Dear Representative _____ (last name):

When writing to the chair of a committee, the Speaker of the House, or a cabinet secretary, address him or her as:

> Dear Mr. Chairman: or Dear Madam Chairwoman: or Dear Mr. Speaker: or Dear Mr. or Madam Secretary:
> Body of your message.

Closing your message:
> To the president: Very respectfully yours,
> To other officials: Sincerely yours,

III. Letters Addresses

President
The President
The White House
1600 Pennsylvania Avenue NW
Washington, D.C. 20500

Vice President
The Vice President
1600 Pennsylvania Avenue NW
Washington, D.C. 20501

Senator
Honorable _____
United States Senate
Washington, D.C. 20510

Representative
Honorable _____
House of Representatives
Washington, D.C. 20515

Member of the Cabinet
Honorable _____
The Secretary of _____
    (Each cabinet department has an
    individual street address)
Washington, D.C. 20520

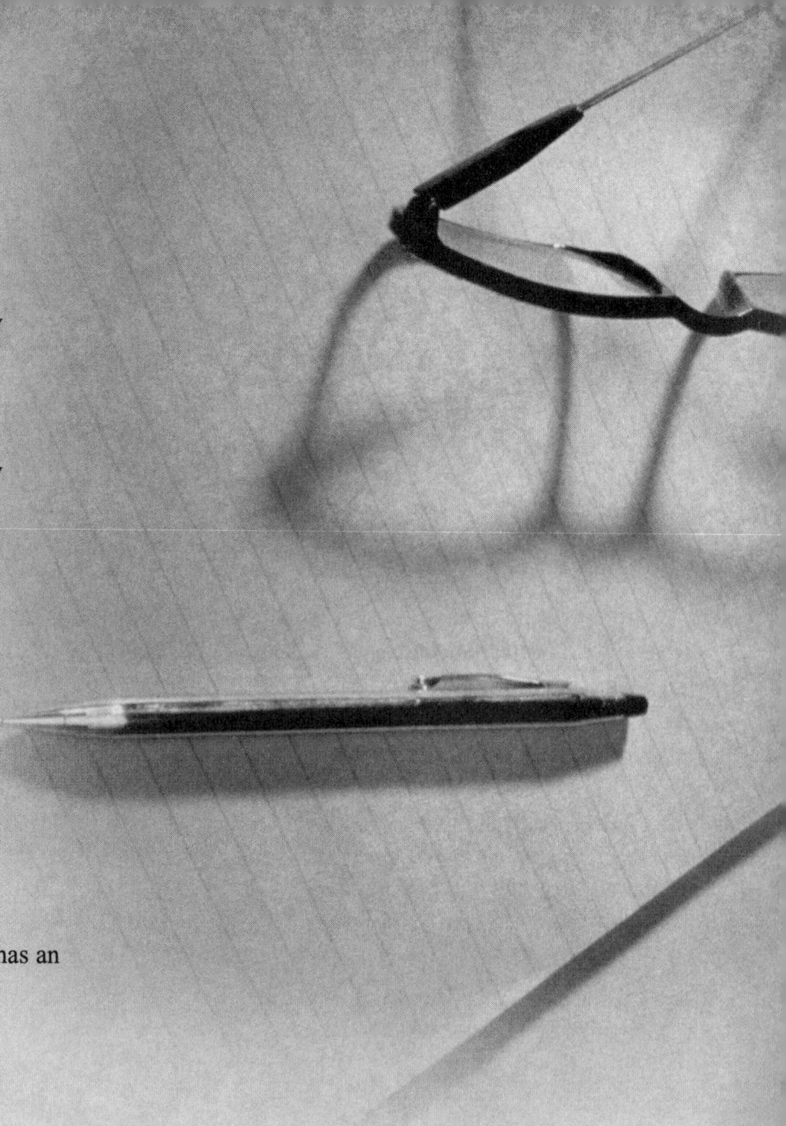

A

absentee voters Voters unable to vote at their polling place on election day who use absentee ballots prior to the election to cast their votes (Ch. 9)

act of admission A congressional act organizing a petitioning area into a state. Once the act is signed by the president, the area becomes a state (Ch. 4)

administrative law Regulations drawn up by government bureaucracy that have the force of law. *See also* statutory law (Ch. 15)

affirm The approval by a higher court of a lower court decision (Ch. 17)

agenda Those issues the government decides to deal with (Ch. 10)

alliance Treaty that unites the participant nations behind common causes; usually military in nature (Ch. 16)

ambassador The head of an embassy and the president's personal representative to the host country. *See also* embassy (Ch. 16)

amicus curiae In court, an individual or group not involved in the litigation but who is allowed to supply testimony or file a brief that may influence the court's decision; often used by interest groups (Ch. 10)

anarchy The absence of government or law (Ch. 1, 3)

appeal To petition a higher court to review a lower court decision (Ch. 17)

appellate jurisdiction A court's power to decide appeals. *See also* original jurisdiction (Ch. 17)

appropriations Grants of money allocated by Congress to finance government programs (Ch. 15)

at large An elected official who represents an entire state rather than a particular district (Ch. 11)

autocracy A government ruled by one person who holds supreme power (Ch. 4)

B

bail Money deposited to guarantee a court appearance; allows the accused freedom while awaiting trial (Ch. 18)

balance the ticket The practice of choosing a running mate based on specific ideology, geography, race, gender, or other characteristics in order to strengthen one's own chance of being elected (Ch. 13)

bankruptcy A financial status declared when a debtor is unable to meet his financial obligations; allows a judge to supervise his finances (Ch. 12)

bicameral A legislative branch divided into two separate houses. *See also* unicameral (Ch. 3, 6)

bill A legislative proposal that becomes a law if it passes both the House and the Senate and receives the president's approval (Ch. 11)

bill of attainder A bill permitting punishment without trial (Ch. 18)

Bill of Rights (1789) The first ten amendments of the Constitution, which protect citizens' democratic rights by placing restrictions on the state and national governments (Ch. 4, 6)

bipartisan Two major parties working together to support an issue (Ch. 8)

blanket primary "Wide open" primary in which every voter receives a ballot listing all party candidates for nomination and selects one candidate for each office. *See also* open primary (Ch. 9)

block grants Federal grants-in-aid that combine several categorical grants under a general umbrella to simplify use in the local governments. *See also* categorical grants *and* revenue sharing (Ch. 7)

boycott An act of protest in which individuals withhold their business or support (Ch. 5)

brief A legal document that presents arguments supporting a client's position in a case (Ch. 17)

broad constructionists Those who take a broader and sometimes more creative approach to consti-

tutional interpretation. *See also* strict constructionists (Ch. 6, 17)

brokered convention A convention requiring
lengthy balloting and an eventual settlement by
means of bargaining and compromise (Ch. 13)

bureaucracy An administrative system staffed
largely by non-elected officials who implement
and oversee government departments and programs; includes the Executive Office of the
President, fifteen cabinet departments, and
numerous government agencies and corporations
(Ch. 15)

bureaucrat *See* civil servant (Ch. 15)

bureaucratese Language of bureaucratic regulations, documents, and forms; wordy jargon (Ch. 15)

C

cabinet Offices of the executive branch developed to assist the president in his constitutional
duties and to meet the demands of America's
growth; currently consists of fifteen departments
(Ch. 14, 15)

cabinet secretary Individual responsible to the
president for the department that he or she heads
(Ch. 14)

capital punishment The death penalty (Ch. 18)

categorical grants Federal programs granting
monies for specific purposes within state and
local governments. *See also* block grants *and* revenue sharing (Ch. 7)

caucus (1) Historically, a small meeting of a
political party's top leaders and legislators in
Congress in order to select party nominees (Ch. 8)

(2) A form of district and state conventions used
to nominate candidates in areas that do not hold
primaries (Ch. 9, 13)

(3) A meeting of all members of a party in the
House or Senate (Ch. 11)

census Official government count of United
States citizens taken every ten years and used to
determine the number of representatives for each
state (Ch. 11)

chair The head of a congressional committee
(Ch. 11)

charter A document that establishes a city's
name and serves as its constitution. *See also* incorporation (Ch. 3, 4)

checks and balances The principle of keeping
each branch of government in check through the
power of another branch of government with the
goal of hindering the concentration of power and
thus protecting personal liberty (Ch. 6)

citizenship Belonging to and enjoying all the
privileges, rights, and responsibilities provided by
a nation (Ch. 12)

civil law The division of law dealing with the
legal rights of private citizens in disputes with
other citizens (Ch. 17)

civil liberties Protection from arbitrary government intrusion upon individual freedoms and
rights (Ch. 18)

civil rights Governmental actions ensuring that
liberties protected in the Constitution, the Bill of
Rights, and Amendments XI–XXVII are extended
to all citizens (Ch. 18)

civil servant One who works for the civil service
and deals with the details of administrative procedure (Ch. 15)

civil service The civilian branch of the bureaucracy that carries out the administrative tasks of
government (Ch. 15)

clear and present danger test A test for justifying limitations on free speech based on the requirement that the danger be genuine and that the
speech actually incites violent action rather than
just endorses it (Ch. 18)

clients Members of groups whose needs are
served by government agencies (Ch. 15)

closed primary A primary in which participants
must be registered as members of one party and
may vote only for the candidates from that party.
See also open primary (Ch. 9, 13)

cloture A motion made by sixteen or more senators to stop debate on a piece of legislation. If
sixty or more senators support the motion, cloture

is passed; often used to end a filibuster. *See also* filibuster (Ch. 11)

coalition A temporary alliance of several groups (Ch. 8, 11)

coattail effect Occurs when a strong candidate on the ballot helps attract voters to other candidates from the same party (Ch. 9)

collective security Also called mutual defense; an attack on one ally is viewed as an attack on all, resulting in a unified response (Ch. 16)

concurring opinion An opinion written by a Supreme Court justice who sided with the majority or minority vote but for differing reasons than those expressed in the majority or dissenting opinion. *See also* majority opinion *and* dissenting opinion (Ch. 17)

confederate government System in which regional governments retain supremacy while delegating limited power to the national government (Ch. 3, 4)

conference committees Temporary committees drawn from both chambers of Congress formed to work out a compromise between differing Senate and House versions of a bill or proposed law (Ch. 11)

confirmation Senate proceedings some government appointees have to go through to be approved for their position (Ch. 12)

congregationalism Church government in which church members elect their leaders (Ch. 2)

Congress At the federal level, the legislative branch of American government; a bicameral legislature composed of a lower house called the House of Representatives and a higher house called the Senate (Ch. 3)

congressional district Geographical area in a state represented by a House member (Ch. 11)

conservative, conservatism A political philosophy that defends against major changes by the government to the political, economic, and social institutions of society, but rather seeks nonbureaucratic solutions to political issues (Ch. 8, 10)

constituents Residents of a district represented by an elected official (Ch. 9)

constitutional law The division of law dealing with the constitutional interpretation of laws and government actions (Ch. 17)

consular office *See* consulate (Ch. 16)

consulate Also called consular office; government offices established abroad to encourage commercial contact between the represented country and the host nation (Ch. 16)

convention An assembly of political party representatives at the national, state, or county level for the purpose of establishing a platform, electing party leadership, and nominating candidates (Ch. 8)

covert operations Government activities not made known to the public (Ch. 14)

criminal law The division of law concerned with criminal actions and punishments—citizens versus government. *See also* civil law (Ch. 17)

crossover voting To vote for a weak candidate in the opposing party's primary, causing confusion or greater difficulty in the opponent's nomination (Ch. 13)

cultural imperialism The advance of one nation's culture at the expense of others (Ch. 16)

D

Declaration of Independence (1776) The formal document, written by Thomas Jefferson, which established the principles of government that justified the colonies' break with England (Ch. 5)

defamation Malicious words damaging reputation or character. *See also* libel *and* slander (Ch. 18)

delegated powers Powers given to the national government by the Constitution that define the limits of its authority (Ch. 3, 4)

delegates (1) Historically, the representatives at the Constitutional Convention (Ch. 5)

(2) Political party representatives to the party convention (Ch. 8)

(3) Nonvoting members of Congress who represent various U.S. territories and the District of Columbia (Ch. 11)

delegation The act of committing or entrusting a task or power to another (Ch. 15)

democracy Government by the people (Ch. 4)

dictatorship An authoritative form of government in which the ruler or rulers have unshared power over the making and enforcing of laws. *See also* autocracy *and* oligarchy (Ch. 4)

direct democracy Also called pure democracy; a form of government in which the people directly affect a government's policies and actions (Ch. 4)

direct primary Preliminary election held to select candidates and/or delegates to the party's convention (Ch. 9, 13)

dissenting opinion The written opinion of those Supreme Court justices voting in the minority; gives reasons for their opposition to the majority vote. *See also* majority opinion (Ch. 17)

district courts Ninety-four federal judiciary trial courts, which comprise the base of the federal judicial pyramid (Ch. 17)

divine right of kings A theory that kings received their authority directly from God and that no matter how tyrannical or contrary to God's laws they acted, they were accountable only to God and could not be removed from authority by the people (Ch. 2)

domestic policy The principles and activities that constitute a government's public policy regarding issues within the nation. *See also* public policy *and* foreign policy (Ch. 10)

double jeopardy Trying a person twice for the same crime in the same court (Ch. 18)

dual federalism A system in which the national and state levels are sovereign within their own spheres (Ch. 7)

due process Certain legal procedures by which the government must abide in order to protect the rights of the accused (Ch. 4, 18)

- **Substantive due process** Regulations ensuring that the substance of laws, their purposes and provisions, must protect fundamental rights (Ch. 18)
- **Procedural due process** Regulations that ensure the just administration and enforcement of laws (Ch. 18)

duty Also called a tariff; a tax on an import (Ch. 12)

E

elastic clause *See* necessary and proper clause (Ch. 6, 7)

electoral college The system used to elect the U.S. president; each state has a number of electors equal to the state's representation; at least 270 electoral votes are needed to win the presidency (Ch. 4, 6, 13)

electoral votes Votes cast by electors in the electoral college (Ch. 13)

electors Representatives to the electoral college; currently there are 538 electors (Ch. 13)

embassy A government office or residence headed by an ambassador and located in a foreign capital. *See also* ambassador (Ch. 16)

enabling act An order given by Congress directing a group to write a constitution for a proposed state (Ch. 4)

entitlements Government compensation programs that Congress has protected by law (Ch. 12)

enumerated powers Also called expressed powers; government powers specifically listed in the Constitution. *See also* implied powers (Ch. 12)

establishment clause Prevents the government from establishing any religion as the official national religion; in subsequent court cases it has been interpreted as justification for a wall of separation between church and state (Ch. 18)

excise An internal tax on the production, sale, or use of items as well as on certain business practices (Ch. 12)

exclusionary rule Excludes illegally obtained evidence from use in court (Ch. 18)

executive agreement A nonbinding presidential agreement made with another head of state in which both sides agree to carry out a particular action. *See also* treaty (Ch. 14, 16)

executive orders Presidential directives or actions that have the effect and force of law (Ch. 13, 14)

exit polls Public opinion polls taken by various polling agencies as voters leave their polling place; used to predict election outcomes (Ch. 13)

***ex post facto* laws** Laws passed and applied to actions that were not criminal when they were committed; laws that impose harsher punishments than the law allowed at the time of the criminal act (Ch. 18)

expressed powers *See* enumerated powers (Ch. 12)

extradition Legal process of returning a fugitive to the state in which he has been charged with a crime (Ch. 7)

F

federalism (1) System in which governmental power is divided into two or more levels, usually a central government and component local governments (Ch. 3, 4, 6, 7)

(2) Different governments simultaneously asserting authority on the people (Ch. 3)

filibuster Tactic used in the Senate to prevent or delay a bill's passage; usually consists of one or more senators giving extended speeches (Ch. 11)

foreign policy The principles and activities that constitute a nation's public policy regarding issues abroad. *See also* public policy *and* domestic policy (Ch. 10, 16)

formula grant A grant that is governed by a demographic formula, such as unemployment figures. *See also* Project grant (Ch. 7)

fourth branch Term sometimes applied to the federal bureaucracy (Ch. 15)

franchise Also called suffrage; the right to vote (Ch. 6)

franking privilege The privilege enabling members of Congress to send official mail free of charge (Ch. 6, 11)

free exercise clause Protects religious practices from government restriction within broad, reasonable boundaries (Ch. 18)

free media Campaign activities covered on the nightly news or by other media outlets; does not cost the campaign any money and aids in the name recognition of the candidate (Ch. 9)

full faith and credit clause Constitutional clause requiring states to respect each other's public acts, records, and judicial rulings (Ch. 7)

G

general election The election used to fill elective offices; at the national level it is held on the first Tuesday after the first Monday in November (Ch. 9, 13)

gerrymandering The redrawing of district boundaries to favor a particular party or group of people (Ch. 6, 11)

globalization The increased integration of world markets, politics, and culture (Ch. 16)

"good faith" rule Supreme Court ruling that evidence obtained by an officer acting reasonably and in good faith cannot be excluded from testimony even if the warrant was defective (Ch. 18)

government Any system of public rule or authority (Ch. 1)

grand jury A jury consisting of a panel of citizens who consider the prosecution's case against the accused and decide whether to issue an indictment (Ch. 6, 18)

grants-in-aid Federal programs that dispense monies to states, cities, counties, or other local governments; used to enforce national policies on the local level (Ch. 7)

gridlock Occurs when one branch of government purposely brings the political process to a halt (Ch. 6)

H

hard money Campaign money raised for a specific candidate in federal elections and spent according to federal laws and restrictions. *See also* soft money (Ch. 9)

House of Representatives The lower house in Congress; representation is based on state population. *See also* Senate (Ch. 3, 11)

I

impeachment The House's power to file criminal charges against the president or any other government officials; the Senate acts as a trial court for impeachment cases (Ch. 14)

implied powers National government powers derived from powers expressly given by the Constitution. *See also* enumerated powers (Ch. 7)

inaugural address Special speech given by the president after he is sworn into office (Ch. 13)

incorporation (1) Process by which a state establishes a city as a legal government body by giving it a charter establishing the parameters in which it can operate (Ch. 3)

(2) Process by which the Bill of Rights was incorporated into the due process clause of the Fourteenth Amendment and thereby applied to all state and local governments (Ch. 18)

incumbent A candidate who is the current officeholder (Ch. 9)

independent announcement Occurs when one desirous of running for a particular office announces his intention of running or has someone else make the announcement (Ch. 9)

independent expenditures Expenses by a person or group that desires to help elect or defeat a candidate; made without the candidate's knowledge or support (Ch. 9)

independent voters Voters who have no party affiliation (Ch. 8)

indirect democracy Also called representative democracy; form of government in which the people elect representatives to operate the government on their behalf (Ch. 4)

interest groups Also called pressure groups; a group of individuals that share like opinions on a political issue or group of issues and that unite in some organization to influence government officials and further their views (Ch. 8, 10)

interstate commerce Business transactions between states (Ch. 12)

J

jingoism Unquestioning support for the state (Ch. 1)

joint committees Permanent committees composed of House and Senate members acting as an advisory board for other committees, especially on tax issues (Ch. 11)

judicial activism Ideology that constitutional interpretation should be flexible to address the current demands of society and to correct its deficiencies (Ch. 17)

judicial restraint Ideology that considers the Constitution as the supreme law of the land to be taken at word value, not used as a tool for social change (Ch. 17)

judicial review The power of the judicial branch of government to examine any government action and to nullify it if it is not in agreement with the court's constitutional interpretation (Ch. 6, 17)

junkets Unnecessary trips made by members of Congress at the taxpayers' expense (Ch. 11)

jurisdiction The authority of a court to hear a case. General jurisdiction empowers a court to hear all cases involving the federal government; courts with limited jurisdiction are limited by such factors as geographical boundaries or subject matter (Ch. 17)

justice *See* righteousness

justices Judges of the Supreme Court (Ch. 17)

K

keynote address Speech made at the national convention by a leading party member (Ch. 13)

L

lame duck An elected official who is still in office but has not been reelected; often refers to a president who has lost an election or cannot stand for reelection and must serve out the remainder of his term (Ch. 6, 14)

legislative government Government by elected, representative assembly (Ch. 5)

Lemon test A three-pronged test used to guide court decisions regarding the establishment clause; laws must have a secular legislative purpose, neither advance or inhibit religion, and produce no excessive entanglement between government and a religious institution. *See also* establishment clause (Ch. 18)

letter of marque A license granted by a nation to a private citizen to capture a merchant ship of another nation (Ch. 11)

libel Published false statements that damage reputation or character (Ch. 6, 18)

liberal, liberalism A political philosophy that seeks through government action to change the political, economic, and social status quo and to encourage the development and well-being of the individual. *See also* conservative, conservatism (Ch. 8, 10)

limited government A principle that limits government to only those powers granted by law (Ch. 1, 5, 6)

line-item veto Allows the president to veto part of a bill without vetoing the entire bill (Ch. 14)

litigation Legal proceedings, such as lawsuits (Ch. 18)

lobbying Tactics used by interest groups to influence public officials (Ch. 10)

local government Organized government that provides order and leadership in localized communities such as counties, municipalities, towns, and cities (Ch. 3, 5)

logrolling The practice in Congress of one member supporting a colleague's spending project in return for support of his or her own pork-barrel project. *See also* pork-barrel (Ch. 12)

M

majority leader The leader chosen by the party with the most members in the House or Senate; in the House, next to the Speaker in authority, but in the Senate, the most powerful member (Ch. 11)

majority opinion The written opinion justifying and clarifying a Supreme Court decision; written by one of the justices voting with the majority. *See also* dissenting opinion (Ch. 17)

majority rule A principle of government that asserts that a numerical majority of the electorate can make decisions binding upon the entire electorate (Ch. 4)

majority whip In the House and Senate, the assistant majority leader chosen by the party with the most seats in that body of Congress; responsibilities include overseeing communication, tracking votes, and summarizing bills (Ch. 11)

major parties The dominant parties in the political landscape; in American politics, the Republican and Democratic parties (Ch. 8)

mass media The major forms of media (radio, television, newspapers, magazines, Internet) and the news organizations associated with them (Ch. 10)

merit The quality of one's work; in the civil service, the standard for employment (Ch. 15)

minority leader The leader chosen by the party with the second most members in the House or Senate (Ch. 11)

minority whip In the House and Senate, the assistant minority leader chosen by the party with the second most seats in that body of Congress; responsibilities include overseeing communication, tracking votes, and summarizing bills (Ch. 11)

minor parties Also called third parties; smaller political parties usually organized around a particular issue (Ch. 8)

Miranda rule A list of rights and warnings of which the police must inform the accused prior to questioning (Ch. 18)

moderate A middle-of-the-road political philosophy that tends to use a pragmatic approach to political issues rather than principles of a firm ideology (Ch. 10)

moral dissent A protest against government concentration and abuse of power in both the church and the state (Ch. 2)

multiparty system Political system in which several parties compete for public office and majority support (Ch. 8)

municipality Urban, local systems of government including cities, villages, and towns (Ch. 3)

mutual defense *See* Collective security (Ch. 16)

N

naturalization The process by which a foreign-born person gains citizenship (Ch. 6)

natural law The revelation of God's law through creation. *See also* revealed law (Ch. 17)

necessary and proper clause Also called the elastic clause; constitutional clause giving law-makers great leeway in making laws "necessary and proper" for the execution of enumerated and implied powers (Ch. 6, 7)

nominate, Nomination To name candidates for public office (Ch. 8, 9)

nominating primary A state-run or state-regulated election for the purpose of selecting the party nominee for most local, state, and national offices. *See also* primary *and* presidential primary (Ch. 8)

O

obscenity Socially offensive communication not protected by the First Amendment (Ch. 10)

oligarchy A form of dictatorship government ruled by an elite group with supreme power. *See also* autocracy (Ch. 4)

one-party system Government system in which only one political party is allowed and a select few from that party rule the country using a centralized bureaucracy and an effective police force (Ch. 8)

original jurisdiction A court's power to hear a case before it is considered by any other court. *See also* appellate jurisdiction (Ch. 6, 17)

open primary Primary in which voters do not have to declare their party membership. *See also* closed primary *and* blanket primary (Ch. 9)

opinion polls Surveys of public thought on particular subjects (Ch. 10)

oversight The process of examining a government department's compliance with the law and scrutinizing its budget requests (Ch. 15)

P

pardon The president's power to give complete forgiveness of a crime and its consequent punishment, thereby releasing someone from the remainder of his or her sentence. *See also* reprieve (Ch. 6, 13)

parliamentary system A system in which the people elect legislative representatives from different parties; the winning party's leader becomes the head of the executive branch, the Prime Minister, and establishes a cabinet (Ch. 3, 4)

partisanship Strong devotion to a political party (Ch. 8)

party platform Formal statement of a party's position on current issues; drafted at a party's national convention (Ch. 8, 13)

passport An official document that identifies and confirms the citizenship of a traveler; in the United States, issued by the State Department. *See also* visa (Ch. 16)

patriotism Love and devotion to one's country and a concern for its social, political, and overriding spiritual welfare (Ch. 1)

patronage Also called spoils system; the practice of giving government jobs to friends and supporters (Ch. 8)

petition A form of nomination in which a formal document is signed by a specific number of qualified voters in favor of a candidate in the election district (Ch. 9)

petty offences Those offences warranting a sentence of six months or less and consequently not requiring a jury trial (Ch. 18)

pluralistic society A society in which differing opinions and parties exist freely (Ch. 4)

plurality The largest number of votes cast for a candidate or a bill (Ch. 8)

pocket veto The automatic veto of a bill if the president leaves it unsigned for ten days during a congressional adjournment (Ch. 6, 11, 14)

political action committees (pacs) Committees formed by special-interest groups that raise money and make contributions to specific individuals' campaigns or causes (Ch. 9, 10)

political campaigns Organized effort by a political party or candidate to attract voter support in an election (Ch. 8)

political party A group that advances certain political goals and gains power by winning elections (Ch. 8)

polling place Location in a specific precinct where those who live in that area go to vote (Ch. 9)

poll watchers Individuals appointed by political parties and candidates to observe the polls on election day (Ch. 9)

popular government Form of government in which citizens participate in the making and enforcement of laws and policies. *See also* democracy *and* republic (Ch. 3)

popular majority A majority consisting of a majority of all voting citizens. *See also* Representative majority (Ch. 4)

popular sovereignty Philosophy of government that asserts that the people are the ultimate source of their government's authority (Ch. 6)

pork-barrel Big spending projects that are designed to help a member of Congress be reelected. *See also* logrolling (Ch. 12)

precedent A court decision that serves to guide subsequent decisions in related cases (Ch. 17)

precincts Smallest units of election districts and party administration (Ch. 9, 18)

president The chief executive officer and head of the executive branch in the U.S. system of government. (Ch. 3)

presidential primary A primary election in which voters indicate their preference for their party's presidential candidate and elect state party delegates to represent their choice at the national convention. *See also* primary *and* nominating primary (Ch. 8)

presidential system A system in which the people directly elect the head of the executive branch independently of the legislative branch; the two branches are separate and equal (Ch. 3, 4)

president of the Senate The position held by the vice president while in the Senate; largely a figurehead role (Ch. 11)

president *pro tempore* Honorary position given to the most senior member of the Senate's majority party; he presides over the Senate when the vice president is absent (Ch. 6, 11)

pressure groups *See* Interest groups (Ch. 8, 10)

primary An election prior to the general election in which voters select the candidates who will run on each party's ticket (Ch. 8)

prior restraint Principle that the government may not suppress a story prior to its publication (Ch. 10, 18)

privileges and immunities clause A constitutional clause guaranteeing the "privileges and immunities of citizens in the several states" (Ch. 7)

probable cause Reasonable evidence that a crime has been committed or is about to be committed (Ch. 18)

project grant A grant that permits Washington or the governing body greater discretion over how much aid is given to a project. *See also* formula grant (Ch. 7)

propaganda Techniques used to select and manipulate information so that it may persuade or influence people effectively (Ch. 10)

proposal The formal introduction of a constitutional amendment. *See also* ratification (Ch. 6)

public opinion Opinions held by the public that the government responds to through the development of public policy. *See also* public policy (Ch. 10)

public policy The sum of government's goals and actions made in response to public issues. *See also* public opinion (Ch. 10)

Q

quorum The minimum number of members needed to transact business in the House or Senate (Ch. 6)

R

ratification The formal approval process of a constitution, constitutional amendment, or treaty. *See also* proposal (Ch. 5, 6, 12)

reapportionment The process of redrawing congressional district lines to reflect population shifts (Ch. 11)

red tape Bureaucratic paperwork (Ch. 15)

registration Official enrollment with local election officials for the purpose of voting (Ch. 9, 18)

representative democracy *See* Indirect democracy (Ch. 4)

representative majority A majority of elected officials. *See also* Popular majority (Ch. 4)

representative sample An accurate representation of the population involved in an opinion poll. *See also* opinion poll (Ch. 10)

reprieve The presidential power to grant a person temporary postponement of punishment. *See also* pardon (Ch. 6)

reprisal Retaliation by one nation against another when provoked (Ch. 11)

republic State in which the supreme power rests in the people and their elected representatives or officers. *See also* popular government *and* democracy (Ch. 3, 4)

reserved powers Powers the Constitution withholds from the national government but does not withhold from state governments (Ch. 3, 7, 12)

revealed law The revelation of God's law through the Scriptures. *See also* natural law (Ch. 17)

revenue sharing Federal program returning portions of the federal tax income to state and local governments for basically unrestricted use. *See also* categorical grants *and* block grants (Ch. 7)

reverse To rule against a lower court decision by virtue of a higher court's authority (Ch. 17)

righteousness Conformity to a standard; in law and morality it is conformity to the character of the God of the Bible. (Ch. 1, 17)

rogue nation A nation that does one or more of the following—seeks to develop nuclear or other weapons of mass destruction; supplies, supports, or provides safe haven for terrorist organizations; disregards international law and violates human rights; and threatens regional or world security (Ch. 16)

S

sanctions Coercive actions taken against a nation to influence its policies (Ch. 16)

search warrant A warrant giving legal authorization for a search (Ch. 18)

sedition Speech aimed at overthrowing the government and endangering national security (Ch. 18)

select committees Temporary congressional committees created for a specific purpose, usually to investigate particular problems (Ch. 11)

self-incrimination Testimony in a criminal case that would incriminate the witness giving the testimony (Ch. 18)

Senate Higher house in Congress; representation is equal for each state with each state having two senators. *See also* House of Representatives (Ch. 3, 11)

separation of powers The principle of separating powers among different branches of government in order to prevent any group or individual from gaining too much control (Ch. 6)

shield laws Laws protecting the journalist's right to refuse to divulge the identity of a secret source (Ch. 10, 18)

single-member district Legislative districts from which only one representative is chosen (Ch. 8, 11)

slander False verbally communicated statements which damage one's reputation or character (Ch. 6, 10, 18)

social contract Theory of government that states that government is formed by the consent of the governed (Ch. 2, 5)

sociological law A system that permits society to shape law rather than the law to shape society; consequently, a society's laws in this system are relative to its changing circumstances (Ch. 17)

soft money Campaign money raised apart from federal regulations and given to local, state, and national party organizations or PACs to be used for voting-related activities. *See also* hard money (Ch. 9)

Speaker of the House Head of the House of Representatives who presides over the House, manages House business, and serves as the official spokesman for the House; elected by the House members and usually from the majority party (Ch. 11)

special districts Districts, independent of the city and county, especially established to provide government functions on the local level (Ch. 3, 4)

spoils system *See* patronage (Ch. 8)

spots Paid advertisements used by state and local candidates (Ch. 9)

standard operating procedures (sops) Clearly defined procedures upon which bureaucracies operate (Ch. 15)

standing committees Permanent committees in Congress (Ch. 11)

Stare decisis Literally "let the decision stand," a principle of law that bases decisions on judicial precedent (Ch. 17)

State of the Union address Annual speech, given by the president before a joint session of the House and Senate, which establishes the president's legislative agenda (Ch. 14)

statutory law Law passed by the legislature (Ch. 15)

straight ticket To vote for all the candidates in one party (Ch. 9)

strict constructionists Those who believe that the text of the Constitution is important and that any interpretation should be kept to a minimum. *See also* Loose constructionists (Ch. 6)

subpoena A document requiring a person to appear as a witness before a court or congressional hearing (Ch. 6, 12, 17)

subversion Attempts to undermine and overthrow government authority (Ch. 18)

suffrage *See* Franchise (Ch. 6)

superdelegates Party leaders and officeholders who serve as uncommitted delegates at the party convention (Ch. 13)

supremacy clause Constitutional clause that upholds the United States Constitution as the supreme law of the nation (Ch. 6, 17)

Supreme court The highest court in the land (Ch. 3, 17)

symbolic speech The expression of ideas through actions or symbols instead of words (Ch. 18)

T

tariff *See* duty (Ch. 12)

tenure Term of office (Ch. 14)

term limits Limits on the number of terms an elected official can serve (Ch. 11)

terrorism The use of unlawful means of war to achieve one's goals (Ch. 16)

theocracy A government ruled directly by God or religious leadership (Ch. 1)

third parties *See* minor parties (Ch. 8)

ticket splitting Voting for candidates of both parties for different offices (Ch. 8)

time-place-manner laws Local government ordinances restricting public demonstrations to particular streets, sidewalks, or public parks during specified periods of time (Ch. 18)

totalitarianism System of government in which the state has complete control over all aspects of its citizens' lives (Ch. 3)

township A political subdivision of a county (Ch. 3)

treaty A formal agreement made between nations or groups of nations. *See also* executive agreement (Ch. 16)

two-party system A political system dominated by two major parties (Ch. 8)

U

unalienable right A right that cannot be given by government because it is not government's to give; it is a gift of God (Ch. 2)

unicameral A legislature made up of only one house (Ch. 3, 5)

unitary government A system in which the people give authority to one centralized level of government which then creates other levels of government to help administer the law (Ch. 3)

V

veto The president's power to refuse to sign a bill into law (Ch. 6, 14)

visa An official endorsement of a passport by the government of the country to be visited. *See also* passport (Ch. 16)

W

wards units into which cities are often divided for city council elections and then further divided into precincts (Ch. 8)

waste Bureaucratic mismanagement of money, time, and personnel (Ch. 15)

writ of *certiorari* Literally "to make certain," a request that the Supreme Court consider a lower court decision; the high court may refuse the writ, in which case the lower court decision stands (Ch. 17)

writ of *habeas corpus* A court order that forces authorities to quickly charge and try an arrested person or else release him (Ch. 6, 18)

Index

Italic type indicates that an illustration of the entry appears on that page.

Photograph Credits

The following agencies and individuals have furnished materials to meet the photographic needs of this textbook. We wish to express our gratitude to them for their important contribution.

Senator Wayne Allard
Suzanne Altizer
American Battle Monuments Commission
American Tract Society
Arttoday
AP/Wide World (Associated Press)
Architect of the Capitol
Archiving Early America
Art Resource
Alan Bailey
Bob Jones University Museum and Gallery
Jim Brennan
Carol Highsmith Photography
Charlotte Observer
Christ Church Philadelphia
CIA Museum
City of Greenville
Clemson University Libraries, Special Collections
George Collins
John R. Collins
Colonial Williamsburg Foundation
Comstock
Corbis
COREL Corporation
DC Public Library
Jim DeMint
Department of Defense
Department of Natural Resources
Elizabeth Dole
Eastman Chemicals Division
Dwight D. Eisenhower Library
Federal Election Commission
Dave Fisher
Florida Division of Emergency Management
Florida Supreme Court
Franklin D. Roosevelt Presidential Library
George H.W. Bush Presidential Library
Georgia Department of Transportation
Gerald R. Ford Presidential Library
Getty Images
Good News Ministries
Jay R. Hackleman
Dr. Grace Hargis
Harper's Weekly
Harry S. Truman Presidential Museum and Library
Hemera Technologies, Inc.
House Committee on Government Reform
Independence National Historical Park

Franz Jantzen
Jimmy Carter Presidential Library
John Fitzgerald Kennedy Presidential Library
Brian Johnson
Jupiter Images
Justice Department
Office of Edward M. Kennedy
Tim Kessee
Joyce Landis
Office of Rick Lazio
Library of Congress
Lyndon B. Johnson Presidential Library
Massachusetts Board of Tourism
Senator Mitch McConnell
The McKinley Museum
Naples News
NASA
NATO
National Archives
National Park Service
National Right to Life
National Law Enforcement Officers Memorial Fund
Nebraska Soybean Board
Nebraska Unicameral Information Office
New England Primer
New York Daily News
Office of Election Administration
Palm Beach County, Florida
Susan Perry
PhotoDisc/Getty Images
The Philadelphia Inquirer
Philadelphia Visitors and Convention Bureau
Robin Romano
Ronald Regan Presidential Library
South Carolina Dept. of Transportation
South Dakota Governor's Office
Speaker.gov
Strom Thurmond Institute at Clemson University
The Supreme Court Historical Society
Supreme Court of the United States
Tennessee Valley Authority
Tiger Eye Design
Unusual Films
US Air Force
US Capitol Office of the Clerk
US Census Bureau
USDA
US Army
US Coast Guard
US Department of the Interior

US Marine Corp
US Marshall Service
US Mint
US Navy
Wake Forest University
The White House
White House Historical Association
Wikimedia Commons
Dick Wright

All maps and globes: Cartesia Software

Front Cover
The White House

Front Matter
The White House i (background); PhotoDisc/Getty Images ii (both); Corbis iii, v–iv; Unusual Films vii (background)

Unit I
Architect of the Capitol viii–ix

Chapter 1
Corbis x (background); Architect of the Capitol x (top); from the Bob Jones University Collection x (bottom), 1, 5; Colonial Williamsburg Foundation 3; ©2009 JupiterImages Corporation 4; photograph by Franz Jantzen, collection of the Supreme Court of the United States 6; ©2003 Hemera Technologies, Inc., All Rights Reserved 7; George Collins 8; Justice Department 12; American Battle Monuments Commission, Arlington, VA 14

Chapter 2
Corbis 16 (background), 19 (background); Massachusetts Board of Tourism 16 (inset); Bob Jones University Museum and Gallery 17, 26; Unusual Films 19 (top), 30 (both); Architect of the Capitol 19 (bottom); from the *New England Primer* 20; George Whitefield, by John Russell (died 1806), given to the National Portrait Gallery, London in 1917/Wikimedia Commons 22 (top); American Tract Society 22 (bottom); Library of Congress 23; James Caldwell at the Battle of Springfield, waterpainting by Henry Alexander Ogden/Wikimedia Commons 24; National Portrait Gallery/ Smithsonian Institution/ Art Resource, NY 25; photo by Will Brown, courtesy of Christ Church Philadelphia 29

Chapter 3

Corbis 32 (background); PhotoDisc/Getty Images 32 (inset), 42; AP/Wide World Photo 34; © 2003 Hemera Technologies, Inc, All Rights Reserved 36; Library of Congress 38; Unusual Films 39; Nebraska Unicameral Information Office 40; Florida Supreme Court 41

Chapter 4

Corbis 44 (background), 47 (flag), 48 (flag); PhotoDisc/Getty Images 44 (inset), 45 (both), 46 (top left, top right), 56, 60; US Department of the Interior, NPS photo by Cecil Stauton 46 (bottom left); Unusual Films 47 (Constitution), 48 (Constitution); Architect of the Capitol 51; AP/Wide World Photo 55; Dan Evans/Good New Ministries 59

Unit II

Carol Highsmith Photography 64-65

Chapter 5

Corbis 66 (background), 73 (background); Architect of the Capitol 66 (inset), 83, 92; Joyce Landis 67; Library of Congress 68, 69, 80; Unusual Films 70 (top), 73 (Constitution); Independence National Historical Park 70 (bottom), 79, 91; George Collins 71; Rembrandt Peale - "Porthole" portrait of George Washington, 1825-1860, Cincinnati Art Museum/Wikimedia Commons 77; United States Mint 88, 89

Chapter 6

Corbis 94 (background), 101 (right); PhotoDisc/Getty Images 94 (inset), 96, 98 101 (left); Franklin D. Roosevelt Presidential Library 97; Dave Fisher 101 (top); Unusual Films 106-139 (background); Susan Biddle/ The White House 116; Getty Images/Photos.com/Thinkstock 117; Architect of the Capitol 123, 124, 130; Library of Congress 132, 133

Chapter 7

Corbis 140 (background), 154; Clemson University Libraries, Special Collections 140 (inset); Library of Congress 141; Rob Thompson/SCDOT 143; White House 144; PhotoDisc/Getty Images 146; Susan Perry 148; Franklin D. Roosevelt Library 149; photo courtesy of City of Greenville Parks and Recreation 151; AP/Wide World Photo 153

Unit III

Associated Press 158-159

Chapter 8

Corbis 160 (background), 176 (flag); AFP/Getty Images 160 (top); Library of Congress 160 (bottom); Strom Thurmond Institute at Clemson University 161; PhotoDisc/Getty Images 163 (both); Courtesy of Ronald Regan Presidential Library 166 (top); Courtesy of the Office of Edward M. Kennedy 166 (bottom); Thomas Nast/Wikimedia Commons/public domain 168 (top); Harper's Weekly 168 (bottom); Public Domain 171; White House Photo Office 172; National Archives 173; Lyndon B. Johnson Presidential Library, Photo by Yoichi Okamoto 174; Courtesy of Palm Beach County, Florida 175; Getty Images 178; Jay R. Hackleman 179; Lyndon B. Johnson Presidential Library 181; Tiger Eye Design, Versailles, www.tigereyedesign.com 182; National Park Service 183; Alan Bailey/www.abailey.org 184

Chapter 9

Corbis 186 (background); Department of Defense 186 (inset); Senator Wayne Allard's Office 187 (top); Dr. Grace Hargis 187 (bottom); Strom Thurmond Institute/Clemson University 188; Jay R. Hackleman 189; *Naples Daily News*/Gary Coronado 190; Used with permission of Philadelphia Inquirer Copyright© 2010. All rights reserved. 191 (left); Used by permission of the McKinley Presidential Library & Museum 191 (right); Office of Senator Wayne Allard 192 (top); Office of Rick Lazio 192 (bottom); Library of Congress 194, 196 (bottom); Susan Perry 195; Getty Images 196 (top); Federal Election Commission 200 (top); Courtesy Elizabeth Dole 200 (bottom); Courtesy of Senator Mitch McConnell (R-KY) 202

Chapter 10

Corbis 204 (background), 216 (flag); Associated Press 204 (inset), 209, 219; Franklin D. Roosevelt Presidential Library 207 (top); Courtesy of the House Committee on Government Reform 207 (bottom); ©2009 JupiterImages Corporation 208; Florida Division of Emergency Management 211; From the Bob Jones University Collection 212; National Right to Life 213; Unusual Films 214, 216, 218 (right); Library of Congress 215, 220; Courtesy Archiving Early America 217; reprinted with permission of *The Charlotte Observer*;

copyright owned by *The Charlotte Observer* 218 (left); Reprinted with permission of Dick Wright 223; US Navy/PH 2 Charles A Edwards 224

A Trip to Washington, DC

PhotoDisc/Getty Images 226 (columns), 228-229 (background), 236 (top), 237 (top), 238 (bottom), 239 (bottom right); Corbis 226-227 (background), 230-231 (background); Carol Highsmith Photography 227, 228 (bottom left, bottom right), 229 (both); US Department of the Army 228 (top left); Associated Press 228 (top right); Library of Congress 230 (both); Architect of the Capitol 236 (bottom), 238 (top); NPS/ Cecil Stauton 237 (bottom right); COREL Corporation 237 (bottom left); NPS/ Jonathan Scott Arms 239 (top); Dave Fisher 239 (bottom left)

Unit IV

PhotoDisc/Getty Images 240-241

Chapter 11

Corbis 242 (background); Architect of the Capitol 242, 247, 252, 255 (all); Lyndon B. Johnson Presidential Library 243; US Census Bureau 244 (bottom); Courtesy of Jim DeMint 245; AP/Wide World Photos 248; Library of Congress 249; US Capitol Office of Clerk 250; Unusual Films 251 (top); Joyce Landis 251 (bottom); The Strom Thurmond Institute at Clemson University 258; AFP/Getty Images 259; Department of Defense photo by Helene C. Stikkel 260

Chapter 12

Corbis 262 (background); Source: www.Speaker.gov 262 (inset); Library of Congress 264; © 2003 Hemera Technologies, Inc. All Rights Reserved 265; US Army photo by Sgt. Derek Gaines 266 (top); US Navy photo by Photographer's Mate 3rd Class Summer M. Anderson 266 (bottom); PhotoDisc/Getty Images 267; ©2009 JupiterImages Corporation 268 (both); Suzanne Altizer 269; Courtesy DC Public Library, Star Collection, © Washington Post 271; US government/Wikimedia Commons/public domain 272; AP/Wide World Photos 273; Department of Natural Resources 275

Unit V

PhotoDisc/Getty Images 278-279

Chapter 13

Corbis 280 (background); White House Photo 280 (inset); Library of Congress 282, 283, 285 (top), 294, 298; Harry S. Truman Presidential Museum and

Library 285 (middle); Courtesy Ronald Reagan Presidential Library 285 (bottom), 302 (top); Unusual Films 286; John R. Collins 288 (left); PhotoDisc/Getty Images 288 (right); Getty Images 289, 290 (top), 291 (bottom); AP/Wide World Photos 290 (bottom), 296 (middle, right), 301 (top); Lyndon B. Johnson Presidential Library 291 (top); White House/Michael Evans 292 (left); Wake Forest University/Scott K. Brown 292 (right); Suzanne Altizer 295; ©2004 www.arttoday.com 296 (left); South Dakota Governor's Office 297 (both); Harry Hamburg/*New York Daily News* 299; White House/Susan Biddle 300 (top); White House/John Ficaro 300 (bottom); Franklin D. Roosevelt Presidential Library 301 (bottom right); John F. Kennedy Presidential Library 301 (bottom left); US Coast Guard photo by PA2 Jacquelyn Zettles 302 (bottom); John F. Kennedy Presidential Library/Robert Knudsen, White House 303 (left); Official White House Photograph 303 (right); White House Historical Association 304

Chapter 14

Corbis 306 (background); John Fitzgerald Kennedy Presidential Library/Cecil Stauton, White House 306 (inset); Library of Congress 307 (top), 313 (bottom), 317 (top, bottom right), 321 (top); US Air Force 307 (bottom); Department of Defense/Tech. Sgt. Gary R. Coppage 308; National Archives 309, 311 (bottom left), 324, 329 (bottom); courtesy Gerald R. Ford Presidential Library 310 (top); Dwight D. Eisenhower Presidential Library/US Navy 310 (bottom right and left); Courtesy of Ronald Reagan Presidential Library 311 (bottom right); George H.W. Bush Presidential Library 311 (top); White House Official photograph/Bill Fitzpatrick 313 (top); White House Photo Office 314, 319 (all), 321 (bottom), 326 (bottom); US Navy 315; White House Historical Association/White House Collection 316 (both), 317 (bottom); PhotoDisc/Getty Images 316-319 (background), 322, 325; Franklin D. Roosevelt Library 318 (top); Greta Kampton Courtesy Harry S. Truman Library 318 (middle); John F. Kennedy Presidential Library 318 (bottom); Harry

S. Truman Presidential Museum and Library 323; Department of Defense 326 (top); National Park Service/Richard Frear 328; Lyndon B. Johnson Presidential Library 329 (top)

Chapter 15

Corbis 332 (background), 338 (background); John R. Collins 332 (inset), 341, 342 (bottom); NASA 333 (top), 346 (bottom); US Coast Guard 333 (bottom); National Park Service/Richard Frear 334; Library of Congress 336; White House Photo Office 340; Associated Press 342 (top); PhotoDisc/Getty Images 343, 348 (all); American Battle Monuments Commission, Arlington, VA 345; Tennessee Valley Authority 346 (top); US Navy/Jim Brennan 350 (top); US Air Force Photo 350 (middle); Department of Defense photo by Pfc. R. Alan Mitchell, US Army 350 (bottom); USDA 352; Georgia Department of Transportation 354 (left); Nebraska Soybean Board 354 (right)

Chapter 16

Corbis 356 (background); Department of Defense/R.D. Ward 356 (inset), 364 (top); US Navy/Photographers Mate Chief Johnny Bivera 357; NATO 358 (top); Jimmy Carter Presidential Library/National Archives 358 (bottom); US Army/Sgt. Kyran V. Adams 359; National Park Service/J. Strider Moler 360; courtesy of Tim Kessee 361; John F. Kennedy Presidential Library 362; US Army/Sgt. Derek Gaines 363, 366 (right), 372; Library of Congress 364 (bottom), 370; Staff Sgt. Gregory K. Funk, USMC 366 (left); Department of Defense/Master Sgt. Ken Hammond, US Air Force 367 (top); National Park Service/ W.E. Dutton 367 (bottom); National Law Enforcement Officers Memorial 368; Carol Highsmith Photography 371; Franklin D. Roosevelt Presidential Library 373; courtesy CIA Museum 374 (top); National Archives 374 (bottom); Department of Defense 375; Associated Press 377; © 2000 Romano/Stolen Childhoods 378; Sgt. 1st Class David K. Dismukes, CFLCC/US Army 379; PhotoDisc/Getty Images 380

Unit V

www.comstock.com 382-383

Chapter 17

Corbis 384 (background); Colonial Williamsburg Foundation 384 (inset); Suzanne Altizer 390; David Sacks, US Marshall Service 391; Philadelphia Visitors and Convention Bureau/Jim McWilliams 393; Architect of the Capitol 394 (top); Steve Petteway, Collection of the Supreme Court of the United States 394 (bottom); photograph by Ken Heinen, collection of the Supreme Court of the United States 397; AP/Wide World Photos 398; Library of Congress 399

Chapter 18

Corbis 404 (background, flag); Carol Highsmith Photography 404 (inset); Eastman Chemicals Division 406 (top); PhotoDisc/Getty Images 406 (bottom); AP/Wide World Photos 407; Joyce Landis 408; Unusual Films 409; Library of Congress 410; Brian Johnson 411; PhotoDisc/Getty Images 412; Suzanne Altizer 415; Office of Election Administration 417; National Archives 418 (top), 419; Lyndon B. Johnson Presidential Library 418 (bottom)

Epilogue

Corbis 422-423 (both)

Appendixes

Unusual Films 425 (left), 425-448 (background); PhotoDisc/Getty Images 425 (top and right), 437-441 (background), 444-446 (background), 447, 448; Courtesy of Tim Keesee 433-436 (background); John F. Kennedy Presidential Library 442-443 (background)